Neuere Aspekte in der Philosophie:
Aktuelle Projekte von Philosophinnen am Forschungsstandort Österreich

Women Philosophers at work
A Series of SWIP-Austria

BAND I

NEUERE ASPEKTE IN DER PHILOSOPHIE: AKTUELLE PROJEKTE VON PHILOSOPHINNEN AM FORSCHUNGSSTANDORT ÖSTERREICH

BRIGITTE BUCHHAMMER (HG.)

Axia Academic Publishers

◆ Wien ◆

Bibliographische Information der Deutschen Nationalbibliothek
Die Deutsche Nationalbibliothek verzeichnet diese Publikation in der
Deutschen Nationalbibliographie, detaillierte bibliographische Daten sind
im Internet unter http://dnb.dnb.de aufrufbar.

ISSN 2413-9416
ISBN 978-3-903068-17-9

www.axiapublishers.com

Inhalt

Einleitung

Brigitte Buchhammer 9

Neuere Aspekte in der Philosophie: aktuelle Projekte von Philosophinnen am Forschungsstandort Österreich

Gertrude Postl
Feminist Philosophy – A Question of Style? 19

Esther Hutfless & Elisabeth Schäfer
Don't put up a brave front! Fragmente Queerer Anarchien am Rand,
an der Grenze, im Zwischen 32

Waltraud Ernst
Intime Begegnungen: Narrative des Erotischen in naturwissenschaft-
licher Forschung 38

Alice Pechriggl
Eros zwischen Platon und Freud: Wie sinnvoll ist die anachronistische Annahme einer platonischen Sublimierungstheorie 58

Edit Anna Lukács
Das Wissen Gottes in der theologischen Lehre an der Universität Wien
(1385c. – 1420): Skizze eines Forschungsprojekts begleitet von der
Edition eines Disputation-Fragmentes 73

Rodica Pop
From the "Egotism of Suffering" to the "Insatiable Compassion".
A Philosophical and Theological Perspective on Dostoevsky's
Female Characters 92

Esther Redolfi Widmann
Die Frau *als* Spannungsverhältnis von Situationsgebundenheit und
Freiheit in Simone de Beauvoirs *Eine gebrochene Frau* 114

CORNELIA EŞIANU
Kunst und Offenbarung bei Friedrich Schlegel 129

BRIGITTA KEINTZEL
Liebe als Versöhnung oder Liebe als Gerechtigkeit?
Hegel und Levinas im Dialog 147

BRIGITTE BUCHHAMMER
Religion und Geschlechtergerechtigkeit. Feministisch-
philosophische Reflexionen im Anschluss an Hegel 168

ANNE SIEGETSLEITNER
Susan Stebbing and the Vienna Circle on Moral Philosophy 206

SUSANNE MOSER
Werte und Gefühle:
Max Scheler und Ronald de Sousa im Vergleich 213

ANKE GRANESS
Die Geschichte der Philosophie und Afrika.
Zur Marginalisierung von Traditionen 247

ELISABETH LIST
Care, Care work and life 274

BIRGE KRONDORFER
Feministische Einwürfe zu Anarchie und Autonomie.
Aktuelle Paradoxien von ‚Selbst'-Bestimmung 280

UTTA ISOP
Institutionelle Gewalt: Die Lust am Hierarchisieren –
Einschließen – Ausschließen 298

HEIDE HAMMER
Taking a back seat: Lässliche Klassenfragen 327

DORIS LEIBETSEDER
Prekärer Sex: eine queer-feministische dis/ability Ethik 335

Susanne Klapper
Intersexualität in einer zweigeschlechtlichen Gesellschaft 359

Bettina Zehetner
Emanzipation als Dienstleistung?
Feministische Philosophie in der psychosozialen Praxis 379

Esther Hutfless
q:p Queering Psychoanalysis –
Research Group on Bodies and Sexualities 389

Autorinnen 398

EINLEITUNG

Wie sehr freue ich mich, diesen ersten Band der neu konzipierten Reihe *Women Philosophers at work. A Series of SWIP-Austria* mit dem Titel: *Neuere Aspekte in der Philosophie – aktuelle Projekte von Philosoph_innen am Forschungsstandort Österreich* nun der Leser_innenschaft präsentieren zu können!

Im Spätherbst 2013 trat ich an einige engagierte Philosophinnen Österreichs mit dem Gedanken heran, eine *Society for Women in Philosophy* (SWIP) in Österreich zu gründen, als Einrichtung zur Vernetzung, Sichtbarmachung und Unterstützung von Frauen in der Philosophie: SWIP Austria als eine weitere SWIP, wie es sie in vielen Ländern schon gibt: SWIP UK, Ireland, Australasian, Canada, Netherlands, USA, Germany. SWIP Austria ist aber nicht gedacht als Konkurrenz zur *International Association for Women Philosophers* (IAPh) oder zum *Wiener Philosophinnen Club*, sondern als Ergänzung auf gesamtösterreichischer Ebene.

Der Zweck von SWIP Austria liegt in der Förderung der Gleichstellung von wissenschaftlich arbeitenden Frauen im Bereich der Philosophie im universitären und außeruniversitären Bereich. Ein organisatorischer Zusammenschluss der Philosoph_innen und feministisch arbeitenden Philosoph_innen ist im Kontext der aktuellen institutionellen Situation auch in Österreich von großer Bedeutung. Hervorheben möchte ich, dass es um die *Sichtbarmachung und Unterstützung von Philosoph_innen* geht, also um *Forscher_innen aus allen philosophischen Teildisziplinen und den verschiedenen Richtungen der Philosophie*, nicht allein um Feminist_innen und Gender-Forscher_innen. Der Verein ist gedacht als Denk- und Diskussionsort für Doktorand_innen, Forscher_innen, Lehrende, Professor_innen und außeruniversitär arbeitende Philosoph_innen *in allen Bereichen des Faches Philosophie*, das heißt für Philosoph_innen, auch für jene, die sich selber nicht als Feminist_innen oder Gender-Forscher_innen verstehen, einerseits, und Feminist_innen andererseits.

Die Ziele des Vereins lassen sich folgendermaßen gliedern: Ermöglichung und Förderung der Kooperation von Frauen in der Philosophie; Unterstützung und Förderung philosophischer Arbeiten von

Frauen und von feministischen Projekten; Förderung feministischer Perspektiven in der Philosophie; Bereitstellung wichtiger Informationen für Frauen in der Philosophie; Sensibilisierung für gegenwärtige sowie zurückliegende Diskriminierung von Frauen in der Philosophie; Beendigung von geschlechtsspezifischer Diskriminierung.

Im Interview „Wie können Frauen in der Philosophie gefördert werden?" in der Zeitschrift *Information Philosophie* sagt *Rebecca Gutwald* über die Bedeutung von Frauennetzwerken in der Philosophie: „Zudem gibt es trotz der zunehmenden Entstehung von Frauengruppen in der Philosophie ein Netzwerkproblem, das sich weiter perpetuiert, je weniger Frauen in die Wissenschaft gehen. Die Welt der ‚Academia' ist doch sehr stark von ungeschriebenen Regeln und networking geprägt. Über diese Kanäle werden aber eine ganze Reihe von Wissen, Kontakte (...) weitergereicht. Für Frauen scheint es, so meine Beobachtung, schwieriger, ein Netzwerk zu finden, das ähnlich eng geknüpft ist wie die bereits bestehenden Netzwerke zwischen Männern in den verschiedenen Positionen, (...)." (Gutwald 2015, 40) Mit der Gründung von SWIP Austria, so meine Intention, könnte ein Raum entstehen für Vernetzung, Austausch, Diskussion und Unterstützung.

Dass die Förderung von Frauen immer Thema feministischer Bemühungen war, liegt auf der Hand. Wie sieht die Situation der Feministischen Philosophie an österreichischen philosophischen Instituten aus? Ich beziehe mich auf *Charlotte Annerl* in dem bereits erwähnten Interview in der *Information Philosophie*: „Der Terminus Feministische Philosophie signalisiert zweifellos stärker als die Bezeichnung Gender Studies einen moralisch-politischen Anspruch. So waren beispielsweise am Institut für Philosophie in Wien eine feministische Professur und eine institutionelle Verankerung der feministischen Forschung unverzichtbare Wegbereiter für eine universitäre Öffnung, dank der heute acht männliche sieben weiblichen Professoren, die ein breites Forschungsfeld abdecken, gegenüberstehen. Indem im Augenblick für die Fortführung der derzeit nicht nachbesetzten feministischen Professur(en) in der Philosophie (...) gekämpft wird, taucht dieser Begriff wieder verstärkt in den Diskussionen auf, nachdem er zuvor in internen Kritiken bereits als ‚historisch' überholt, ja als ‚Opferfeminismus' abgeschrieben wurde." (ebd., 46) Feministische Philosophie soll kein separater Bereich sein, sondern das

Desiderat besteht darin, dass Feministische Philosophie einen Frage- und Forschungsaspekt in allen Teildisziplinen der Philosophie darstellt. An dieser Stelle möchte ich an die Intention der feministisch-philosophischen Forschung von *Herta Nagl-Docekal* erinnern. So schreibt sie: „Welchen Beitrag kann Philosophie zur Beseitigung von Strukturen der Benachteiligung und Unterdrückung leisten? Diese Frage war und ist für meine Forschungen im Bereich feministischer Theorie ausschlaggebend. Insbesondere in meinem Buch *Feministische Philosophie. Ergebnisse, Probleme, Perspektiven* suchte ich das kritische Potential herauszuarbeiten, über das zentrale philosophische Teildisziplinen – von der philosophischen Anthropologie über die Ästhetik, die Vernunft- und Wissenschaftstheorie bis zur Rechtsphilosophie – verfügen. Mit Methoden philosophischer Analyse können die verbreiteten, tief sitzenden geschlechterhierarchischen Vorstellungen präzise aufgezeigt und argumentativ zurück gewiesen werden, zB. in Form des Nachweises, dass sie auf einem naturalistischen Fehlschluss beruhen. Dieses kritische Potential kann freilich erst dann zur vollen Entfaltung gelangen, wenn thematisiert wird, dass und in welcher Weise diskriminierende Auffassungen auch im bisherigen ‚mainstream' philosophischen Denkens vielfältigen Ausdruck gefunden haben. Im Gegenzug geht es mir darum, einsichtig zu machen, dass der Blickwinkel der Geschlechtergerechtigkeit zu einem selbstverständlichen Element der heutigen Philosophie werden sollte. Unterbleibt dies, sind für eine angemessene philosophische Auseinandersetzung mit den globalen Problemstellungen der Gegenwart die nötigen Voraussetzungen nicht gegeben. Es ist sehr zu bedauern, dass sich unter den jüngsten Publikationen auch der deutschsprachigen Philosophie noch immer viele finden, in denen dieser Gesichtspunkt nicht beachtet wird." (Nagl-Docekal 2010, 113) Um auf der Höhe der Zeit Philosophie zu betreiben, darf der feministisch-philosophische Gesichtspunkt nicht ignoriert werden. Nagl-Docekal erläutert: „Wer heute zu philosophischer Anthropologie arbeitet und dabei den Diskurs zur Konstruktion von Geschlecht unberücksichtigt lassen wollte, könnte nicht beanspruchen, dem letzten Stand der Forschung gerecht zu werden. Wer heute eine umfassende Rechtsphilosophie entwickeln möchte, ohne das Problem der Geschlechtergerechtigkeit zu erörtern, könnte seinen komprehensiven Anspruch ebenfalls nicht einlösen. Dasselbe gilt für den Bereich der Philoso-

12

phiegeschichte. Wer heute Ausführungen der ‚Klassiker' zu Themen wie ‚Familie', ‚Erziehung', ‚Privatheit', ‚Arbeit' oder ‚Staatsbürgerschaft' interpretiert, ohne die Ergebnisse der feministischen Lektüren aufzugreifen, kann nicht geltend machen, alle verfügbaren Analysemethoden rezipiert zu haben." (Nagl-Docekal 2004, 53) Feministisch motivierte Forschung betrifft das gesamte Fach Philosophie.

Mein Wunsch für SWIP Austria liegt auch darin, die so differenten, pluralen und manchmal kontroversiellen Strömungen innerhalb der Philosophie, aber auch der Kunst und Performance, miteinander in einen respektvollen streitbaren Dialog zu bringen, um über all die Themen, die Menschen heute brennend bewegen, zu diskutieren. Es ist viel spannender, zusammen zu kommen, um „eine offene und akzeptierende Streitkultur" (Ruth Großmaß – Christine Schmerl 1989, 280) zu entwickeln, als den Dialog mit jenen, die andere philosophische Standpunkte vertreten, zu verweigern. Ich greife einen Terminus von Cornelia Eşianu auf, den sie von Schlegel übernommen hat, nämlich den des *Symphilosophierens*. Was für ein schöner Gedanke! Ein Projekt, bei dem es darum geht, in amikaler Atmosphäre über all die spannenden philosophischen Themen zu diskutieren, ohne Abwertung und Kampfrhetorik, einander zuzuhören, und gerade im achtsamen Zuhören Raum zu eröffnen für Kreativität.

Im Dezember 2014 fand das erste zweitätige Symposium von SWIP Austria statt unter dem Titel: *„Neuere Aspekte in der Philosophie – aktuelle Projekte von Philosophinnen am Forschungsstandort Österreich"*. Der Konferenztitel war bewusst sehr offen formuliert, um die Vielfältigkeit der Forschungsprojekte von Frauen in den Blick zu rücken. Die Tagung war nicht in Sektionen gegliedert (daher gibt es im Sammelband keine Kapitel-Einteilung), um zu gewährleisten, dass alle Teilnehmerinnen miteinander unmittelbar in Diskussionen und Gespräche eintreten und erste Vernetzungen bilden konnten. Die Philosophinnen präsentierten ihre aktuellen Arbeiten und konnten somit in Sicht bringen, wie facettenreich die Projekte am Forschungsstandort Österreich sind. Der Band soll die Breite und Pluralität der Themen und die Themenoffenheit widerspiegeln. Er enthält 21 Beiträge aus den verschiedensten Teildisziplinen der Philosophie, wie zB. feministische Sprachphilosophie (Gertrude Postl), Performance/Philosophie (Esther Hutfless und Elisabeth Schäfer), Erkenntnis- und Wissenschaftstheorie (Waltraud Ernst,

Alice Pechriggl), Wissenschaftsgeschichte (Edit Anna Lukács), philosophische Bezugnahme auf Literatur (Rodica Pop), feministisch-philosophische Literaturbetrachtung (Esther Redolfi Widmann), praktische Philosophie, Religion und Ethik (Cornelia Eşianu, Brigitte Buchhammer, Brigitta Keintzel, Anna Siegetsleitner, Susanne Moser, Elisabeth List), interkulturelle Philosophie (Anke Graness), feministisch-politische Theorie, feministische Sozialphilosophie, queere Perspektiven (Birge Krondorfer, Heide Hammer, Utta Isop, Doris Leibetseder, Susanne Klapper, Bettina Zehetner, Esther Hutfless).

Gertrude Postl folgt mit ihrer feministischen Sprachkritik der Spur der Frage nach neuen sprachlichen Formen, die die traditionelle akademische, „die Anderen" (Frauen, Körper, Gefühle, people of color, ...) ausgrenzende Sprache stören, unterbrechen, zerreißen (disrupt) können. Dabei schlägt sie ein re-reading von Irigaray und Cixous vor, öffnet aber den Horizont für neue Akzente und rückt eine Gruppe junger Wiener Philosoph_innen in den Blick („Aktionskollektiv Philosophieren von unten": AKPhu), die mit ihrem *Liquid Manifesto* ermutigen, mit Sprache zu experimentieren. Dieses Stören, Aufbrechen (disrupting) der gewohnten akademischen Sprache impliziert auch politische Befreiungsintentionen. Philosophieren von unten sei emotional, körperlich, prekär, rhizomatisch, zynisch, wild, lustvoll, poetisch, ... Der daran anschließende Text von *Esther Hutfless und Elisabeth Schäfer* nimmt die Leser_innen mit auf eine Reise in jene fragile, verletzliche, powervolle, emotional-rationale, lebendige, lustvoll pulsierende Welt neuer philosophischer Ausdrucksmöglichkeiten.

Waltraud Ernst erforscht in ihrem Essay die Narrative des Erotischen in der Sprache naturwissenschaftlicher Theorien. Sie erforscht die Funktion des Erotischen in den Naturwissenschaften Chemie und Biologie in deren Entstehungszeit, wobei sie die These vertritt, dass das Erotische als erklärendes und zu erklärendes Moment hinsichtlich der Entwicklung der genannten Wissenschaften eine zentrale Rolle, die aber bisher marginalisiert worden sei, einnahm. Sie richtet ihren Blick auf die Verschränkung von „natürlichen" Erklärungen für kulturelle Prozesse und von kulturellen Deutungen von „Entdeckungen" im Bereich der Natur. Die Frage nach der Bedeutung des Erotischen hinsichtlich der Entwicklung der Kategorie „Geschlecht" und der Dichotomisierung der Geschlechter steht im Zentrum von Ernsts

14

Analysen. Sie folgt der forschungsleitenden Hypothese, die besagt, dass Veränderungen der Bedeutung von Wissenschaft eng mit dem Wandel des Erotischen zu dieser Zeit verflochten sind. Entgegen der gängigen Annahme in der historischen Forschung und in der Philosophiegeschichte, dass Anachronismen vermieden werden sollen, geht *Alice Pechriggl* in ihrem Aufsatz der Frage nach, ob die These der Vorwegnahme der platonischen Sublimierungstheorie durch Freud einen Anachronismus darstellt und wenn ja, ob dieser nicht eine sinnvolle Ressource darstellen könnte. Der kontrollierte Gebrauch von Anachronismen ermöglicht, wie Pechriggl luzide darzulegen vermag, aus der Perspektive aktueller Problemstellungen einen überraschenden und erkenntnisbereichernden Blick auf Vergangenes. Stellt der Anachronismus als erkenntnistheoretisches tool, als Interpretament sui generis, eine Möglichkeit der Erhellung sowohl des Vergangenen als auch des Zeitraums, aus dem heraus die Forschungsfragen gestellt werden, dar?, so ihre Frage. Mit welcher Methodologie kommt die theologische Forschung im Mittelalter an der Universität Wien zum Wissen über das Wissen Gottes? Welche Relevanz und Reichweite kann die rezente Beschäftigung mit der Mittelalterphilosophie haben? Diese philosophischen Fragen entwickelt *Edit Anna Lukács* in ihrem Aufsatz.

Rodica Pop untersucht in ihrem Beitrag zwei ausgewählte Romane Dostojewskis unter dem Aspekt der Frage nach der Rolle der Frau in diesen Werken und der Standhaftigkeit der Frauen im Leiden, der Spannung zwischen dem Egoismus des Leidens und ihrer Fähigkeit zu echtem Mitgefühl in „Der Idiot" und „Schuld und Sühne". In einem knappen Aufriss skizziert *Esther Redolfi Widmann* Beauvoirs intellektuelle Entwicklung und geht der Entfaltung des Begriffs der situierten Freiheit der Frau im Werk von Beauvoir nach: Freiheit ist auch bei der Frau eine Transzendenz, die über die eigene Situation hinaus ein autonom erstrebtes Ziel fokussiert. Die Frau *als* Spannungsfeld von Situationsgebundenheit und Freiheit, damit meint Beauvoir, dass die Frau ein Geschöpf ist, das sich mit dem Zwang konfrontiert sieht, einer gesellschaftlich konstruierten Rolle gerecht zu werden. Diesem Zwang kann sie nur durch Verwirklichung ihrer Freiheit entkommen. An Hand Simone de Beauvoirs Roman *Eine gebrochene Frau* zeigt Redolfi diese Freiheitstheorie auf.

Cornelia Eşianu widmet sich in ihrer Studie dem Verhältnis von Kunst und Offenbarung bei Friedrich Schlegel vor dem Hintergrund der generellen Frage nach der Relevanz des Geistigen für die heutige praktische Philosophie. Sie greift ein Schlegel'sches Motiv auf, das Kunst in der Spannung zwischen Moral und Religion in den Blick nimmt. *Brigitta Keintzel* untersucht die Bedeutung des Phänomens Liebe im philosophischen Werk von Hegel und Levinas: dabei bringt sie Hegel (Zusammenhang von Liebe und Versöhnung) und Levinas (Liebe und Gerechtigkeit) in einen spannenden, für die Gegenwart bedeutsamen Dialog. In der präreflexiven Einstellung der Liebe, wie Levinas sie fasst, war der Andere immer schon vor dem Selbst da, er ist vorzeitig *und* ethisch primär. Dies kennzeichnet auch die Konzeption von Freiheit, die verwirklicht wird in asymmetrischer Verantwortung und Stellvertretung. Keintzel betont die Frage, die Hegel und Levinas beschäftigt, wie eine subjektphilosophische Entfaltung des Phänomens der Liebe gelebter praktizierter Verantwortung entsprechen kann. Erhellend zeigt sie auf, inwiefern Levinas einen Perspektivenwechsel zu Hegels mehrschichtigem Liebeskonzept, dessen Kern in der Versöhnung liegt, vollzogen hat. Für Hegel und Levinas sind Eros und ethische Liebe auf vielfältige Weise miteinander verschränkt, Einsicht in sittliches Handeln ist nicht bloß Ergebnis rationaler Prozesse, sondern ein Liebesakt: „Handle so, dass die Maximen deiner Handlung verallgemeinerbar sind, indem du Liebe nicht nur als Bereicherung deines Selbstgefühls begreifst, sondern auch als Einschränkung deiner Selbstliebe und als Infragestellung des Absolutheitsanspruchs einer ich-zentrierten Ausrichtung", wie Brigitta Keintzel in ihrem Beitrag schreibt. *Brigitte Buchhammer* skizziert in ihrer religionsphilosophischen Arbeit eine feministisch-philosophische Anknüpfung an zentrale Thesen Hegels unter der Frageperspektive, welche Potentiale im Kontext von Religion vorhanden sind hinsichtlich des Engagements für mehr Geschlechtergerechtigkeit in Kirchen und Gesellschaft. Über eine wenig rezipierte Philosophin, Susanne Stebbing und deren Beziehung zum Wiener Kreis im Horizont der Moralphilosophie schreibt *Anne Siegetsleitner* in ihrem Essay. Der erste Eindruck einer großen Differenz zwischen Stebbing und dem Wiener Kreis bestätigt sich bei genauerer Lektüre nicht, denn Stebbing, Neurath, Carnap und Schlick vertreten den Standpunkt eines wissenschaftlichen Humanismus, demgemäß es

16

genuine Aufgabe der Menschheit ist, zu einem Fortschritt hinsichtlich der Bedingungen des menschlichen Lebens beizutragen und die *Sciences* sind ein brauchbares und wertvolles Mittel, um dieses Ziel zu erreichen. *Susanne Moser* schlägt in ihrem Beitrag eine Relektüre der Wertphilosophie Max Schelers im Hinblick auf die Neuaufnahme axiologischer Fragestellungen im Kontext zeitgenössischer Gefühlsforschung vor. Ihr gelingt ein Dialog zwischen Max Scheler und Ronald de Sousa, die sich beide darum bemühen, einen Zusammenhang zwischen Gefühlen und Werten aufzuzeigen. *Elisabeth List* analysiert die Begriffe des Lebens, des Carings, der curativen Arbeit aus feministisch-philosophischer Perspektive. In ihren Reflexionen über den Begriff der Natur liefert sie auch eine kritisch-feministische Auseinandersetzung mit zentralen marxistischen Theorien und den dort herrschenden Hierarchisierungen.

Anke Graness richtet in ihrem Essay den Blick auf die Philosophiegeschichte und ihre Methodik vor dem Hintergrund interkultureller Fragestellungen. Philosophiegeschichte als Teildisziplin der Philosophie ist selber eine philosophische Tätigkeit, die im Schreiben der Geschichte der Philosophie einen neuen Diskurs generiert, der vorausliegende Debatten umfasst *und* verändert. Graness nimmt kritisch den ausschließenden Prozess des Schreibens von Philosophiegeschichte ins Visier: Entscheidend ist, welche Autor_innen in den Kanon aufgenommen und welche ausgeschlossen werden. Sie zeigt die verheerende Wirkung des Ausschlusses aus dem Kanon am Beispiel von Afrika. Diese Ausschlüsse sind „bis heute mitverantwortlich für die Geringschätzung Afrikas als Quelle von Wissen, Wissenschaft und kulturellen Errungenschaften – wie eben auch der Philosophie", wie Graneß in ihrem Artikel argumentiert. Sie moniert diese „epistemische oder kognitive Ungerechtigkeit" und schließt mit der Frage, wie diese korrigiert werden könnte.

Birge Krondorfer untersucht eine der feministischen Kernthesen, die der Selbstbestimmung, in den Konzeptionen von Anarchie und Autonomie. Ihre Frage: Ist die Kategorie Autonomie „im verschwindenden Politischen" heute noch brauchbar für etwas Unvorhergesehenes, für einen „kleinen Spalt der Öffnung"? *Heide Hammer* beschreibt anarchistisch-feministische Kerntopoi als Basis für ihre Kritik an kapitalistischen, sexistischen, rassistischen, hierarchischen und anderen diskriminierenden Strukturen. *Utta Isop* fokussiert Prozesse des Einschließens, Ausschließens und Hierarchisierens in Institutionen, erforscht philosophisch die Lust an diesen Prozessen, wobei ihre Hierarchiekritik auch politische Praktiken umfasst und sogar Ausblicke gibt in postfundamentalistische Optionen des Regierens. *Doris Leibetseder* rückt in ihrem Vorhaben, eine nicht-normative queer-feministische Ethik zu entwickeln, die prekäre Lebenssituation queerer, transgender, intersexueller Personen, Menschen mit Dis/Ability und die Fragilität des biologischen Geschlechts in den Blick. Dabei geht sie auch der Frage nach, welche Rolle die *Neuen Reproduktiven und Genetischen Technologien* für die Entwicklung einer nicht-normativen queeren Ethik spielen. *Susanne Klapper* problematisiert in ihrem Essay den gesellschaftlichen Umgang mit dem Phänomen Intersexualität. Wichtige Anforderungen an eine vorwiegend zweigeschlechtlich orientierte Gesellschaft sind Respekt und menschenwürdiger Umgang mit intersexuellen Menschen als moralische Basis auch für Gesetzesnovellierungen. *Bettina Zehetner* geht es in ihrem Beitrag „um die Erschließung des kreativen Potentials von Philosophie als explorativer Praxis, um Reflexionsräume im Alltagsleben zu eröffnen. So kann feministische Philosophie in der psychosozialen Beratung als emanzipatorische gesellschaftliche Praxis wirksam werden", wie sie selber ihr Projekt erläutert. *Esther Hutfless* skizziert in ihrem Beitrag die von ihr und ihren Kolleginnen Barbara Zach und Anke Müller Morocutti gegründete Gruppe *q : p Queering Psychoanalysis – Research Group on Bodies and Sexualities*. „Mit dem Begriff ‚queering Psychoanalysis' möchten wir die Logik und Idee des ‚Normalen' in der Psychoanalyse kritisch hinterfragen und, ganz im Sinne Freuds die Hierarchisierung, die sich durch die Entgegensetzung von ‚normal' und ‚pathologisch' ergibt, in Frage stellen. Wir möchten durch und mit der Psychoanalyse produktive theoretische und praktische Zugänge zu Körpern, Sexualität, Geschlecht, Identität, Identifizierung, etc. entwickeln bzw. weiterdenken.", wie sie sagt.

* * *

Ich danke allen, die durch Engagement, Mitwirkung und Kritik zum Gelingen des Symposiums und der Publikation beigetragen haben: den Referentinnen und Moderatorinnen, den Autorinnen der

18

Beiträge, den Mitgliedern des Vereins SWIP Austria für ihr Interesse an den Vereinszielen, den Frauen im Vorstand für ihre tatkräftige Unterstützung, Elisabeth Menschl für die Zurverfügungstellung der Ressourcen der Johannes Kepler-Universität; Monika Rohrauer für die Bereitschaft, ganz spontan immer wieder zu helfen, Cornelia Esianu für kritische Vorschläge, Gertrude Postl für hilfreiche Anregungen und Yvanka B. Raynova, Programmleiterin des Verlags Axia Academic Publishers, für die engagierte Hilfe. Mein besonderer Dank gilt Herta Nagl-Docekal für die Unterstützung meines Vorhabens von Anfang an.

Brigitte Buchhammer, Obfrau von SWIP Austria

Wien, im November 2015

Bibliographie

Ruth Großmaß – Christine Schmerl, „Nur im Streit wird die Wahrheit geboren ... Gedanken zu einer prozeßbezogenen feministischen Methodologie". In: Dies. (Hg.), Feministischer Kompaß, patriarchales Gepäck. Kritik konservativer Anteile in neueren feministischen Theorien, Frankfurt-New York: Campus, 1989

Gutwald, Rebecca und Charlotte Annerl im Interview „Wie können Frauen in der Philosophie gefördert werden?" In: Information Philosophie, Juni 2015, 2, 36 - 47.

Nagl-Docekal, Herta. „Zur Aktualität dieses Buches". In: Maria Isabel Pena Aguado, Bettina Schmitz (Hg.), Klassikerinnen des modernen Feminismus. Aachen: einFach, 2010, 112-117.

Nagl-Docekal, Herta. „Feministische Philosophie – aktuelle Perspektiven". In: Brigitte Doetsch (Hg.), Philosophinnen im dritten Jahrtausend. Ein Einblick in aktuelle Forschungsfelder. Bielefeld: Kleine, 2004, 53-68.

GERTRUDE POSTL

FEMINIST PHILOSOPHY – A QUESTION OF STYLE?

Disrupting the Philosophical Discourse

In *This Sex Which Is Not One* Luce Irigaray states that "it is indeed precisely the philosophical discourse that we have to challenge, and *disrupt*, inasmuch as this discourse sets forth the law for all others, inasmuch as it constitutes the discourse on discourse" (Irigaray 1985b, 74). The project of feminist philosophy has been a critical project from the start but what exactly does it mean to "disrupt" the philosophical discourse? And – given that feminist philosophical scholarship also wants to be part of this discourse – how far can we go in this disruption? It cannot possibly be the goal of feminist philosophy to undermine the very subject matter that it aims to investigate. Irigaray's statement points at a central dilemma of feminist philosophy: how to do philosophy without submitting to the standards and falling into the traps of a discipline that had always excluded the feminine and that contributed – due to its central position with respect to other discourses – to women's oppression at large?

I will in the following take the demand for a "disruption of the philosophical discourse" as a programmatic blueprint for a critical feminist response to the discipline of philosophy that differs significantly from arguing a point of critique within the confinements of this very discipline. And, I will furthermore claim that this "disruption of the philosophical discourse" can only be achieved if we turn to questions of language and style. In short, critically analyzing the misogynist premises of some key notions of philosophy is one thing, disrupting the entire discourse is quite another.

Already in the early '70s, during the beginning period of feminist philosophy, the radicalism expressed in the phrase "disrupting the philosophical discourse" found its most far-reaching manifestations in the linguistic experimentations of authors such as Irigaray, Hélène Cixous, and Julia Kristeva (but also, in a very different sense Mary Daly in the US). The shared assumption of those authors was a radical sexual difference that allegedly never was allowed to appear within the history of Western thought. In that the male power over women had been exercised also on the level of language, the general agreement was that linguistic systems of representation have always been masculine with woman/the feminine never having had any representation on its own terms. Going far beyond any attempts to reform sexist language or to correct gender-marked speech behavior (pursued predominantly in feminist sociolinguistics and communications theory), difference feminists – working within a psychoanalytic theoretical framework – conceived of the feminine as culturally repressed never being allowed to have a voice of its own. "…with a few rare exceptions, there has not yet been any writing that inscribes femininity" (Cixous 2000, 260). This exclusion of the feminine from language, thus also from writing, was perceived within the context of a critique of metaphysical dualisms, such as body/mind, emotion/reason, irrational/rational, unconscious/conscious, nature/culture, etc. Again, in the words of Hélène Cixous: "Nearly the entire history of writing is confounded with the history of reason (Cixous 2000, 261).

Accordingly, any attempt to enter the masculine realm of speech and writing – and thus respond to the history of reason being a male prerogative – required a "new style" or a woman's language/writing (famously labelled *parler femme* and *écriture féminine*). The promise associated with these newly to be created modes of speech and writing was a vision of liberation that went far beyond the dominant political themes of the time (women's sexual exploitation, inequality in the workplace, the double burden of household and career or underrepresentation in political office) and that positioned difference feminism at the radical forefront of feminist philosophical criticism. This liberation through language was supposed to free women's bodies, their sexuality, their imagination, their unconscious – areas that a traditional male philosophy either devalued or ignored. By insisting that language is always already bodily and that therefore the body "speaks," the metaphysical dualism of body vs. mind as well as the devaluation of the body and the senses, typical for the history of Western philosophy since Plato, was supposed to be overcome. If women want to enter the philosophical scene, they first have to change that scene by changing the very language that constitutes it. The critique of dichotomous thinking, of the universalization of the male experience, of grounding humanity exclusively in a certain notion of reason, or of the exclusion of the body, cannot possibly be conducted in the same language which was used to establish these rigid intellectual systems in the first place. If the philosophical discourse is to be *disrupted*, a new language is called for. Or, as Audre Lorde famously put it: "The master's tools will never dismantle the master's house" (*Sister Outsider*, 110).

A Politics of Writing

But it so happened that this search for new linguistic tools did not seem to convince the feminist philosophical community. Attempts towards experimentation with language and the search for a new style soon became discredited and, by now, have fallen out of fashion. In the best case they are considered a cute historical oddity, a remembrance of things past; in the worst case, they are viewed as a dangerous misapprehension of the feminist project – an unpolitical reaffirmation of those aspects of the feminine that contributed to women's downfall: the irrational, the body, the sensuous, the unknown zones of the unconscious. What better "proof" for this trend *away* from linguistic experimentation than Luce Irigaray's attempts to be stylistically more accessible and more explicitly political in her later texts?[1]

The debate over the (political) usefulness of a feminist work on language was loaded from the beginning with misconceptions. Although the term *écriture feminine* refers to the feminine and was never intended to be a language exclusively for women,[2] it was immediately interpreted as a writing style for women and soon dismissed on essentialist grounds. This criticism conveniently overlooked that attempts towards a new style of writing were predominantly concerned with exclusion, and thus, with issues of liberation exercised through language. *Écriture féminine* was supposed to set free what was not permitted to be expressed within the established systems of representation – the body, the unconscious, the feminine, but also other oppressed social groups or excluded modes of expression, e.g. more literary or

---

[1] From *Democracy Begins Between Two* [2000, ital. 1994] on.

[2] Hélène Cixous tirelessly reiterated that *écriture féminine* is not to be understood in a biological sense, mentioning Genet, Kleist, or Joyce as examples for an alternative writing style by men; the same can be claimed for Kristeva's account of the semiotic which was to be understood as a different mode of expression, not per se affiliated with any gender.

poetic renderings of language. Cixous' programmatic call that "(w)oman must write her self: must write about women and bring women to writing, from which they have been driven away… Woman must put herself into the text – as into the world and into history… (Cixous 2000, 257) is not necessarily limited to women but can be extended to any group that has been driven away from writing, from putting themselves into the world and into history through language.

Contrary to a strictly argumentative order of thought, the writing of the feminine was to follow a different representational economy (in Cixous' terminology), an economy of giving, of an unequal exchange, of openness, of a different order, of a multiplicity of styles or voices. This other representational economy was by no means limited to women. And, as Irigaray as well as Cixous made very clear, this style of writing cannot be defined. Talking about the writing of women, Irigaray states "Its 'style' resists and explodes every firmly established form, figure, idea, or concept… (it) cannot be upheld as a thesis, cannot be the object of a position" (Irigaray1985b, 79). Even more straightforward, Cixous states: "It is impossible to *define* a feminine practice of writing, and this is an impossibility that will remain, for this practice can never be theorized, enclosed, coded…" (Cixous 2000, 264).

Misunderstood by the critics was furthermore the conception of the body in *écriture féminine*. This body, which has to be freed and which is supposedly able to express itself, is not a natural, mere biological, untreated entity but something always already shaped and molded by cultural processes. Rather than being in opposition to the mind or language, the expressivity of the body promoted by difference feminists undermines this very opposition itself. There is no body without language and no language without a bodily materiality. In the words of Abigail Bray, talking about Cixous: "For Cixous the material texture of writing is produced through and with the body… writing demonstrates the impossibility of sustaining the mind/body dichotomy" (Bray 2004, 96).

In addition, given the affinity of authors such as Irigaray, Cixous, or Kristeva with deconstruction and post-structuralism, the feminist debate soon became a replay of the continental-analytic divide in philosophy. Feminist philosophers were basically accused of similar "wrongdoings" as some of their male colleagues (most prominently Jacques Derrida). Critics pointed out that this type of philosophy –

allegedly non-political and just a fancy "play with words" – would be turning everything into a text, thereby minimizing or ignoring the problems of the so-called "real world" of politics, social affairs, or legal inequalities.

The onset of queer theory, gender studies, and the debate over transgender identity further contributed to the growing (political) irrelevance of a concept of a writing style that allegedly rests on the assumption of a radical sexual difference in terms of Two. Talking about a distinct language or style of the feminine seems outdated and no longer politically correct within a practical and theoretical context that went far beyond the claim of a radical sexual difference.

In spite of these developments and even at the risk of appearing hopelessly retro and stuck in the past, I would like to revive the old debate about a language or writing style of the feminine, if for no other reason than the suspicion that its inherently political force has not yet been (fully) explored. The need to "disrupt" the philosophical discourse is as relevant and urgent today as it was in 1977 (when Irigaray wrote *Ce Sexe qui n'en est pas un*). While Irigray's demand was mostly directed at the history of philosophy, the rules and regulations that currently dominate the academic day-to-day practice of philosophy could also use some disruption and irritation. The discipline of philosophy in its institutionalized manifestation at university departments, academic societies, conferences, publishing houses, etc. might actually benefit from a more liberal attitude to the question as to what constitutes a philosophical text. Linguistic interventions and rhetorical strategies are indispensable for philosophy to stay alive; and they are indispensable in particular for feminist philosophy if it wants to maintain its status as a critical project with a utopian potential. There is a difference between *arguing* a point of critique and *writing* a point of critique, between *explaining* an issue and *expressing* it, between *describing* something and *"showing"* it through words. In short, the concern for language that marked the beginnings of feminist philosophy has to be revived. Linguistic experimentation, the use of rhetorical figures, playfulness, irony, ambiguity, multiple layers of meaning, sensuality and musicality of language, the literary qualities of a text, can all serve as forceful, critical tools for the goal of *disrupting* the philosophical discourse rather than just critically participating in it.

One way of disrupting the philosophical discourse is to dissolve traditional categorizations of disciplines or genres. Again, Hélène Cixous' "The Laugh of the Medusa" is a case in point, drawing on a variety of areas – literature, philosophy, psychoanalysis, mythology, autobiography, accounts of women's experience, etc. – to accomplish its exuberant, energetic call for women to start writing (and laughing). It has been called a feminist manifesto, a critique of metaphysics, a new type of philosophy, a poetic translation of women's experience, an imitation of Derrida's explorations on writing, a political utopia... What this text is exactly cannot be decided – it is all of the above and neither. With stylistic means, Cixous undermines not only the distinction between philosophy and literature but also the metaphysical opposition between the body and writing. There is a materiality to writing and a signifying dimension to the body. In this text resonates voice, music, song; it has a certain rhythmic sensuality that moves easily between abstract arguments, references to mythology, descriptions of personal experience, and the upbeat tone of a political pamphlet. For Cixous, there is no mind without body, no culture without nature, no philosophy without poetry, and most importantly, no body without language and no language without a body – desire is a form of signification. But none of this is explicitly "stated" or cast in an argument. It is "expressed" through the entire corpus of Cixous' words. It is difficult to pinpoint her position by picking out one sentence that would summarize her "argument" – there is no argument! There is a text that, preferably, should be read in its entirety in order to actually hear it, to get all the interwoven layers of textual genres, to fully grasp that every sentence of this text has more than one meaning.

Linguistic interventions of this kind are political in a radical sense. Rather than affirming existing systems of representation (e.g. the philosophical discourse) which necessarily always contribute to and reproduce oppressive structures (see Foucault 1972), they introduce new modes of representation, opening spaces for previously excluded voices to appear – feminine or otherwise. This applies as much to the history of philosophy as it does to the linguistic limitations and confinements of an institutionalized academic philosophy. In the words of Hélène Cixous: "... writing is precisely *the very possibility of change*, the space that can serve as a springboard for subversive thought, the precursory movement of a transformation of social and cultural structures" (Cixous 2000, 261)

However, if writing is to serve as springboard for "subversive thought" or for the disruption of the philosophical discourse, the concept of writing and the very structure of language itself has to be rethought. Irigaray talks about a "feminine syntax" where "there would no longer be either subject or object... there would no longer be proper meanings, proper names, 'proper' attributes... Instead, that 'syntax' would involve nearness, proximity... it would preclude... any form of appropriation" (Irigaray 1985b, 134). This would be a language or writing style that allows for several meanings at once, that shifts between genres and established stylistic figures, that transgresses the proper rules of grammar, a language that does not distinguish between the forces of the unconscious and conscious thought, between body and concept, sound and word. This language or style would necessarily allow for a multiplicity of voices and a greater diversity of texts. And it would escape any preconceived determination as to what is worth being put into words and what is not. Cixous talks about "the language of 1,000 tongues which knows neither enclosure nor death" (Cixous 2000, 270). Or, as Irigaray asks: "Why only one song, one speech, one text at a time?" (Irigaray 1985b, 209).

This feminine concept of writing also entails a radical rethinking of the relationship between author and reader and of the relation between texts. Cixous' demand that "(w)oman... must bring women to writing" emphasizes the connection between a woman-author and a woman-reader, thus the connection between texts. In her account, texts are not the manifestation of a self-centered movement of an author, not the extension of a writing self into words, but rather the initiation of more texts to come, of a self-generating network of texts. Women have to start writing and they can do so in continuous interaction with each other, thereby producing a corpus of textuality that renders the question of textual origin and authorship secondary and that eliminates the distinction between author and reader – authors are also readers, readers become authors. And again, there is nothing essential or biological about this concept of writing; anybody who has been driven away from language can join in and write the next text, thereby opening spaces for stylistic innovation and experimentation not accessible within a system of writing based on authorship, on hierarchy and categorization (e.g. of disciplines, genres, styles, or preconceived rhetorical figures), on "mine" and "yours," on footnotes and bibliography lists. Cixous' concept of writing can best be imagined in terms of a horizontally growing network of texts – some responding to the past (Irigaray's reading of the philosophical canon), others envisioning a future to come (Cixous' laughing Medusa as the new woman). And, these multiple voices of the previously excluded will necessarily be disruptive, not only in their stylistic innovation and creative daring but in the challenge they pose to traditional notions of writing. The liberating potential of this process – far from being a politically irrelevant "play with words" – constitutes a form of intervention and disruption that can be considered politics with different means and on a different level. "When the 'repressed' of their culture and their society returns, it's an explosive, *utterly* destructive, staggering return, with a force never yet unleashed…" (Cixous 2000, 267).

Many Ways to Talk about Plato

Critically examining famous texts from the history of philosophy is one of the main goals of feminist philosophy. This critical examination can be conducted in many different ways – by either employing "the master's tools" (thus leaving the philosophical discourse intact) or by destroying them in the very process and thereby establishing a new type of discourse. Two examples shall serve to demonstrate the point.

Luce Irigaray's strategy with respect to the history of philosophy (in response to the self-imposed task of disrupting the philosophical discourse) was a mimetic reading and writing practice that undermined the canonical texts she was reading by linguistically experimenting with the very words of these texts. Making use of a variety of rhetorical figures – metaphors, metonymy, substitutions, paraphrasing, alliterations, repetitions, etc. – she managed to re-read key texts of the history of philosophy by changing the meaning of these very texts so as to reveal the repression of sexual difference (one of the main points of her theory) by using the original philosopher's own words.

Her famous reading of Plato's Cave Allegory in *Speculum* – a "classic" of feminist criticism by now – basically rests on her interpretation of the cave in terms of women's sexual organs: the cave is read as hystera or womb, the passageway as vagina, the small wall separating the prisoners from the people/objects carried by as hymen, etc. The overall point being that Plato's text can serve as an example for the elimination of sexual difference (through forgetting/repression of the female mother body, the hystera) in favor of an order of the One – thus making this particular text representative for the history of philosophy in general. All this could have been said in a few sentences. The argumentative claim could have been made that Plato's denigration of the sensual world corresponded to his denigration of women or the feminine and that his celebration of a world of pure forms was actually a representation of the superiority of the masculine One. Contrary to a straight forward argument, Irigaray takes over a hundred pages (in the English translation) to develop her reading of Plato's cave. Rather than arguing her point, she is demonstrating it; rather than talking about Plato's text, she is "doing" something with it, using Plato's words and "story line" as raw material to construct her own text:

"So, let us make reading the myth of the cave our point of departure… As the story goes, then, men – with no specification of sex – are living in one, same, place. A place shaped like a cave or a womb… And the only thing they can still do is to look at whatever presents itself before their eyes… Heads forward, eyes front, genitals aligned, fixed in a straight direction and always straining forward, in a straight line. A phallic direction, a phallic line, a phallic time, backs turned on origin… The *hystera*, faceless, unseen, will never be presented, represented as such…But there is also *a path*, no doubt made in the image of the conduit, neck, passage, corridor which goes up… out of the cave toward the light of day, toward the sight of day… A conduit which is taken up and reproduced *inside* the cave. A repetition, representation, figuration reenacted within the cave of that passage which we are told leads in and out of it. Of the path *in between*… Between the "world outside" and the "world inside," between the "world above" and the "world below." Between the light of the sky and the fire of the earth. Between the gaze of the man who has left the cave and that of the prisoner. Between truth and shadow, between truth and fantasy, between "truth" and whatever "veils" the truth. Between reality and dream. Between… Between the intelligible and the sensible. Between good and evil. The One and the many. Between anything you like… But what has been forgotten in all these oppositions, and with good reason, is how to pass through the passage, how to negotiate it – the forgotten transition... *Forgotten vagina*" (Irigaray1985a, 243-247).

The stylistic effort that went into the creation of this text is obvious. Descriptive in some parts, analytic in others, Irigaray blends literary devices and rhetorical figures with philosophical insights – e.g. the use of alliterations, the metaphors used to describe the passageway, the repetition of the term "between." As a result, the line between literature and philosophy can no longer be clearly drawn. The effect of reading this type of text is very different from reading a feminist analysis which states that Plato's negative judgment about the senses and his plea for an inner world of ideas can be understood in terms of an unequal gender arrangement that disadvantaged women.

To demonstrate the contrast, here a quote from Elizabeth Spelman's famous text "Woman as Body: Ancient and Contemporary Views," originally published in 1982 in *Feminist Studies*:

"Plato was both a dualist and a misogynist, and his negative views about women were connected to his negative views about the body, insofar as he depicted women's lives as quintessentially body-directed... Plato does not merely embrace a distinction between soul and body... There is a highly polished moral gloss to the soul/body distinction in Plato. One of his favorite devices for bringing this moral gloss to a high luster is holding up for our contempt and ridicule, the lives of women" (Spelman 1999, 40).

Without diminishing the value of Spelman's quite influential text, her reading follows the (often unspoken) guidelines for a conventional form of criticism. Its argument is clearly laid out step by step; it uses well established classifications such as "dualist" and "misogynist" to categorize Plato; it explicitly explains Plato by pointing out that, according to his view, the "lives of women" serve as representation for that which goes wrong. While aiming at the same target – Plato's conception of the relationship between body and soul and the role women play within this relationship – the way Irigaray and Spelman develop their criticism of Plato differs significantly from each other. Irigaray's text is subversive, it disrupts the philosophical discourse (to the extent that it isn't even clear any longer whether a text is philosophy or not). Spelman adds a novel perspective, but remains within the traditional parameters of a proper academic philosophical text. The latter does not question the traditional philosophical "tools;" authors, such as Irigaray or Cixous, use those "tools" but take them apart by demonstrating their limitations.

New Beginnings

Fortunately, questions of *how* to write rather than just *what* to write have not totally disappeared from the philosophical scene. A recently formed group of young philosophers at the University of Vienna, mixed gender, mixed sexual orientation, calling themselves the "Aktionskollektiv Philosophieren von unten" (AKPhu) made it their goal to publish a new journal, entitled *Sublin/mes* (online and in print format), that very explicitly addresses issues of style. Contrary to the examples from the beginning period of feminist philosophy, this current publication does not claim to be in the tradition of *écriture féminine* and its main target is not the (male) history of philosophy. What it has in common with *écriture féminine*, though, is a demand for a multiplicity of voices, for Cixous' "1000 tongues." In doing so it aims to respond to the established narrow standards of academic writing and the institutionalization of philosophy. The gender issue – totally in accordance with more recent developments away from dual gender arrangements and a notion of sexual difference in terms of Two – is addressed within the context of queer theory, but even that with a twist. As the authors explain, *Sublin/mes* aims to offer a "queere Philosophie" (obviously a cross between German "quer" and English "queer," whereby "queer" also resonates "peer" as in "peer-reviewed").

The so-called "Liquid Manifesto," included in each issue, explains philosophizing from below: "Philosophizing from below is affective, bodily, precarious, rhizomatic, cynic, wild, feminine, full of pleasure, poetic, prosaic, horizontal, performative, fierce, tender, abyssal, underlying, sublime, dangerous, erotizing, sexy, magnetic, repellent, sensitive, brute and rough, rhythmic, expanded, disadvantageous, powerful. And still much more" (http://sublinesblog.wordpress.com/).[3]

This programmatic call should encourage philosophers to write what most likely would be rejected by departmental committees, peer-

---

[3] Eeach Issue of *Sublin/mes* includes the so called "Liquid Manifesto" in addition to an issue-specific "Manifestation" for each Volume. The online version of the "Liquid Manifesto" of *Sublin/mes* provides an English, French, and Italian translation.

reviews, or publishing houses, a form of writing that takes place outside, beyond, underneath the institutional confinements of academic philosophy. And like in Cixous' Medusa-text, writing is viewed in terms of a liberation – in this case a liberation from academic standards, from self-imposed linguistic impoverishment, from a willingness to subordinate to alienating modes of expression, but most importantly, a liberation of thinking: "Philosophizing from below shall not colonize the territories of thinking but rediscover and free them, take them seriously, pour them, let them grow and prosper, expose the force-fields of thinking, in which something arises – unplanned, turbulent and subtle. To let it come to expression, to let it become writing" (http://sublinesblog.wordpress.com/). Philosophy, expressed in writing, is about thinking and this should be allowed to develop freely, only then can it have an impact outside the purely academic structures – "writing is precisely *the very possibility of change*" (Cixous 2000, 261).

Whether the *Sublin/mes* project will manage to subvert and disrupt the philosophical discourse remains to be seen – its strategy seems to be to work from the outside or "from below." But still, subversive waves from the outside could reach into the inside of the philosophical discourse, into the inside of philosophy departments and selection committees, could even manage to shake up the so-called objective criteria of the peer-review process, thereby disclosing the restrictions and norms that keep perpetuating the institutionalized degenerations of philosophy that limit thinking rather than expanding and exploring it. Like Irigaray who wanted to make visible the repressed sexual difference of the history of Western culture, *Sublin/mes* wants to make visible the restrictions, exclusions, and hierarchies that dictate what is considered a proper philosophical text and what is not. "Freed from the rampant terror of peer-review-proceedings which level academic legitimate writing to a globally unified standard, *Sublin/mes* will awake again the pleasure with and of the text" (http://sublinesblog.wordpress.com/).

The styles of a text, the intricacies of its written configuration, are not just a decorative addition to some essential, deep philosophical thoughts. Rather, they are the very means through which those thoughts come to life. Already Hegel pointed out that form and content cannot be separated from each other. There is no thought beyond or outside of how this thought is put into words. And this applies to feminist philosophy as much as any other philosophy. "Philosophizing from below wants to release – finally but unendingly – the lust in writing and thinking!" (http://sublinesblog.wordpress.com/). Feminist philosophy has to recover this "lust in writing and thinking," typical for its beginnings, if it wants to survive and continue its critical agenda.

Literature:

Aktionskollektiv Philosophieren von unten (eds.), *Sublin/mes. A Queer Reviewed Journal.* Issues #1 – #4. Online: http://sublinesblog.wordpress.com/ (last download: September 01.st 2015)

Bray, Abigail, *Hélène Cixous. Writing and Sexual Difference*, New York: Palgrave Macmillan, 2004.

Cixous, Hélène, "The Laugh of the Medusa," in Kelly Oliver (ed.), *French Feminism Reader*, Lanham, Bolder, New York, Oxford: Rowman and Littlefield, 2000, S. 257-275. Originally publ. in: *Signs* 1, no.4, 1975, S. 875-899.

Foucault, Michel, "The Discourse on Language," trans. Robert Swyer. In: *The Archaeology of Knowledge*, New York: Pantheon Books, 1972.

Irigaray, Luce, *Speculum of the Other Woman*, trans. Gillian Gill, Ithaca, N.Y.: Cornell University Press, 1985a.

- , *This Sex Which is Not One*, trans. Catherine Porter and Carolyn Burke, Ithaca, N.Y.: Cornell University Press, 1985b.

Lorde, Audre, *Sister Outsider. Essays and Speeches*. New York: Crossing Press, 1984, 1977.

Spelman, Elizabeth, "Woman as Body: Ancient and Contemporary Views." In: Janet Price, Margrit Shildrick (eds.), *Feminist Theory and the Body: A Reader*, New York: Routledge, 1999, S. 32-41.

ESTHER HUTFLESS & ELISABETH SCHÄFER

DON'T PUT UP A BRAVE FRONT!
FRAGMENTE QUEERER ANARCHIEN AM RAND, AN DER GRENZE, IM ZWISCHEN

Es ist eine schlaflos wachende Welt. Wir sagen, sie pulsiert. Isn't this fishy?!

Die Städte leuchten, alle – Horizonte verlieren ihre Bedeutungen vor gigantisch strahlenden Skylines; dort stehen die großen Werte, Marktwerte, Und-noch-mehr-Werte; aufgeladen mit ausschweifenden Phantasien; wir verspekulieren uns mit der Unmöglichkeit des Kapitals, weil wir sie für seine Möglichkeit halten.

Wir finden schwer ein Ende, vom Anfang wollen wir gar nicht sprechen; wir arbeiten, wir investieren und kapitalisieren, wir beantragen, erfinden und speichern, wir prosperieren und privatisieren, wir verlinken und vernetzen; wir posten, networken und keuchen, wir sind online, wir prokrastinieren, bilden Rettungsgassen und -schirme. Wir arbeiten, auch wenn es keine Arbeit (mehr) gibt. Wir verausgaben uns permanent. Die Ausgaben sind immens.

Wir erschöpfen und verzehren uns. Es ist eine schlaflos wachende Welt. Wir sagen, sie pulsiert. Wie ein lebendiger Körper?! Isn't this fishy?!

Es ist eine schlaflos wachende Welt. Aber pulsiert sie?! Atmet?! Wie ein Hase?! Der Brustkorb hebt und senkt sich. Im Zeitraffer sieht der Prozess der Verwesung dem des Lebens zum Verwechseln ähnlich.[1]

Der Fisch fängt vom Kopf zu stinken an ...

... oder stinkt er doch vom Schwanz?! Die Tranchier-Werkzeuge zur Hand. Ein Hieb. Ein Stich. Ein Schnitt. Stück für Stück trennen

---

[1] In einem Film von Christoph Schlingensief, der im Rahmen seiner Parzifal-Inszenierung in Bayreuth projiziert wurde, sieht es zunächst so aus, als ob ein Hase atme, aber es ist die Verwesung, der Prozess, die Bewegung der Zersetzung – im Zeitraffer – die den Körper hebt und senkt... „Der Hasenverwesungsfilm im Bayreuth war natürlich auch so ein Transformationsvorgang. Das, was man im Zeitraffer sieht, dieses vermeintliche Atmen des toten Hasen ist eigentlich ein Verwesungsprozess: [...]." (Schlingensief 2012, 130)

wir das Genießbare vom Fauligen. Es besteht Ansteckungsgefahr. Einsperren oder Aussperren. Keine Durchlässigkeit.

Amputiert wird gerne. Mit der Säge oder den Grenzzäunen. Mit Asylkarten und Stacheldraht. Wer setzt wo seinen oder ihren Fuß auf den Boden – *dry foot or wet foot policies*[2], wer darf mit welchen Füßen wo bleiben, weitergehen und ist am neuen Ort mit wem in Kontakt, in welcher Gemeinschaft – wie lauten hier die Richtungen: back to blood[3]?!

Eine Welt in Tranchen, in mundgerechten Happen. Schwanz und Kopf gesteuert. Phallisch und zephal. Steiff und fest. Bleib wo Du bist! Oder: Werde wie wir! Wenn Du gehst, wenn Du kommst, wenn Du aus- ein- und durchwanderst, wenn Du vor Italien ertrinkst ... Meere, Seen und Flüsse, Wüsten und Wälder, Berge – elementare Umgebung – Luftraum: Betreten auf eigene Gefahr! Border-Management sagt der Fachjargon, geordnete Migration.

Schuhe aus! Denken findet ab jetzt barfuß statt! *Barefoot policies!* Waten wir durchs Wasser, gehen wir über den scharfen, spitzen und steinigen Sand, fliegen wir, und schlängeln wir uns durchs Dickicht; und denken, schaffen wir neue Grenzen; denken, schaffen wir eine Zone, die wir auch berühren können, ohne dabei zu sterben: Grenzen, die nicht mehr das Ende sind und bringen sondern die Möglichkeit eines Anfangs! *Don't put up a brave front!*

Denken wir die Dinge ohne Kopf und ohne Schwanz. Den Corpus und die Anarchie. Diese Schwärmereien und wilden Phantasien. Eine Anarchie, deren Vitalität sich nicht aus dem Ideologisch-Geistigen

---

[2] Die Unterscheidung zwischen sogenannten „dry foots" und „wet foots" ist eine Ausnahmeregelung der Einwanderung für Kubaner_innen in Amerika. Siehe: http://immigration.about.com/od/immigrationlawandpolicy/a/U-S-Allows-Cuban-Migrants-Different-Treatment.htm

[3] Siehe dazu Wolfe 2013: Eine aktuelle bissige, grelle und satirische Gesellschaftsstudie zur Frage von Gelingen oder Scheitern von Integration und pluralen Gesellschaftsmodellen, exemplarisch vorgeführt und platziert in einer der verrücktesten Städte Amerikas: Miami. Tom Wolfe konturiert das Scheitern der Pluralität in dieser Stadt, die Spanisch sprechenden Kubaner_innen inzwischen die Mehrheit, aber die Weißen immer noch das Geld haben. Mehr ein Comic eines Romans, als ein Roman – aber durch und durch von journalistischer Genauigkeit zeichnet Tom Wolfe dieses grelle Bild einer Welt, in der alle einander radikal andere sind, niemand weiß, was die anderen wohl essen, sprechen, denken. Der Titel des Romans „Back to Blood" ist zugleich die beunruhigende Diagnose in welche Richtung das Scheitern von Pluralität führt: zurück zu den Blutsbanden.

speist oder aus der Allmacht des sich selbst transzendierenden Subjekts. Denken wir polymorph perverse Kräfte, die sich nicht im Haupt- Phallus- und Grenzprimat verdichten, die nichts errichten, die nichts normieren und kontrollieren.

Denken wir offene Körper und offene Räume. Eine andere Vernetzung. Einen anderen Kontakt, der nicht Verdrängung bedeutet. Eine andere Kastration. Azephallisch. Ohne Zentrum. Ohne Wachturm. Ohne Oben und Unten. Ohne Außen und Innen. Ohne Ohne.

In sekreten Höhlungen könnte man sich verlieren. Aber vielleicht würden uns auch Flügel wachsen oder Schwimmhäute zwischen den Zehen ...

Reißen wir die Grenzen nieder, die wir in konzentrischen Kreisen um uns aufgerichtet haben! Staats-, Unions-, Kontinentalgrenzen. Sogar Körpergrenzen; gesetzt durch Markierungen, Vermessungen und Dispositive.

Hören wir auf zu gehorchen! Riskieren wir die Entitäten des immer selben, dekonstruieren wir die Identitäten, die immer Identitäten gegen ... sind.

Grenzüberschreitungen dürfen nicht mehr verboten sein!

Geben wir der Anarchie eine ontologische Möglichkeit! Machen wir die Anarchie nicht zur Sache des Seinen, Einen, Meinen und Einzigen! Lassen wir sie dem Sein die Stirn bieten, machen wir sie zur Sache des Seins, zur Sache von allen oder keinen, zur Sache radikaler Adressierungen, vielfältiger und ungezähmter, ungezügelter Ansprüche. Denken wir die Abwesenheit von Herrschaft – aber keineswegs die einer Kraft, vielleicht sogar Macht.

Arché ohne Archonten – oder arché neben, mit, rund um, zwischen, durch, außer- oder unterhalb der Wohnsitze - durchquerend die Wohnsitze jener Archonten, die die herrschenden Beamten sind, die Bureaukraten, die Verwalter der Ordnungen, denen man – wie Derrida uns erinnert – zugleich „das Recht und die Kompetenz der Auslegung" zuerkannte und immer noch zuerkennt, „die Macht, die Archive zu interpretieren". Alle Archive, auch die, in denen die Impressionen zur Frage verzeichnet sind: Wie zusammen leben? Diese „Überkreuzung des Topologischen und Nomologischen" ist charakteristisch für die archontische Aufgabe. Zudem vereint die archontische Macht „auch die Funktionen der Vereinheitlichung, der Identifikation und der Einordnung" und übt „im Versammeln der

Zeichen" „Konsignationsmacht" aus – mit einer schwerwiegenden Folge: „Die Konsignation strebt an, ein einziges Korpus zu einem System oder zu einer Synchronie zusammenzufügen, in dem alle Elemente die Einheit einer idealen Konfiguration bilden" (Derrida 1997, 11f.). „Kein Archiv ohne die eingerichtete Verräumlichung eines Ortes des Eindrucks" (ebd.: Waschzettel s. p.).

Ort des Eindrucks: Da sind wir, das ist auch Staat, Nationalstaat, genauer: Territorium, eingegrenzt, umgrenzt, umzäunt, verschlossen, zu kartographierender Landstrich, auch einzelner Organismus – mit Kopf, der organisiert, und Schwanz, der wedelt, also Gefühle zeigt, oder ähnliches, dazwischen Rumpf, oder der Rest, Behälter für Organe, genauer: die gehorchenden, ausführenden Abteilungen, et cetera.

Der Fisch fängt, so sagen wir, vom Kopf zu stinken an. Denken wir also keine arché der Archonten. Arché, das heißt, Kraft, die ins Werden ruft – Anfang –, aber auch Herrschaft. Denken wir eine wilde, queere arché; eine Kraft der Überschreitung, des Ausuferns, des Werdens, eine unerhört unbändige Kraft, die nicht konserviert und organisiert, die nichts verwaltet, eine Kraft, die nicht allein aus dem schöpft, was es schon gibt. Queere arché, das meint Schöpfung ohne Verleugnung, die Kraft der Geschichte eine neue Zukunft zu geben, im Sinne von an-arché, das heißt: Kraft, die sich nicht restlos instrumentalisieren, kontrollieren, bündeln und ordnen lässt: Unverfügbarkeit: Die Anerkennung des Lebendigen als sich entziehende Kraft: *Anarchy of becoming.*

Die radikale Unverfügbarkeit dieser Kraft lässt sie kontinuierlich frei vagabundieren, die Institutionen und Organe durchqueren, verunsichern, durchwandern – queeren – und an allem rütteln, was sie in Bewegung setzen kann. Kein Staat ist mit dieser Kraft zu machen und kein Bureau für Anarchie zu eröffnen. Weniger Substantivum, weniger das, was für sich allein stehen kann, was Grundfesten legt, sondern das, was gründet in Bezug und Bewegung.

So müssen wir auch – not-wendigerweise – andere Körper denken, andere Räume, anarchische und chaosmische Sphären des Zusammen, des Zwischen und so weiter.

„Ist es nicht die Lust, die vom Elementarsten zum Sublimsten führt?" (Irigaray 1991, 67) Raum, das bedeutet Ausdehnung bis in die Unendlichkeit. Unendlichkeit ist dem Raum immanent. Der

Raum ist nicht der exklusive geometrische Ort, an dem das Gesetz des Einen regiert, der nur Platz für je einen und einzelne hat. An dessen Grenze Krieg, Vertreibung und Verdrängung herrschen. Die Verdrängung ist dem Raum fremd. Der Raum wächst, wuchert, dehnt sich aus, wie das Lebendige selbst, von dem er nicht zu trennen ist. Der Raum, wenn er etwas tut, räumt. Er räumt ein, das heißt, der Raum ist gastlich und lässt zu. Er räumt aus, das heißt, der Raum öffnet sich, öffnet sich allem, was kommt, was ankommen will und wird; der Raum öffnet sich auch der Leere; dem, was ausbleibt. Der Raum ist mit den Körpern im Werden, die je schon offen sind. Durch jede Pore atmen und trinken, fühlen und sprechen. Der Raum ist nicht begrenzt und nicht unbegrenzt. Kein Raum ohne Grenzen und keine Grenzen ohne Räume. Sie sind in- und aneinander gefaltet. Raum, das ist selbst das Geschehen einer Grenze, an der Räume sich auslassen – die Ausgelassenheit der Grenzen, das ist der Raum. Ausgelassen ist der Raum der Körper auch zwischen den Körpern, den Dingen, den Staaten, den Gemeinschaften, den Worten, den Büchern, den Werken und Bruchstücken, den Kulturen, den Zellen und den Ländern, Landstrichen, Regionen, den Nationen und den Wohnstätten, den Lokalitäten, et cetera.

Der Zwischenraum zwischen den Körpern – den sexuellen, den lebendigen, den menschlichen, den tierischen, den symbolischen, den konstruierten und dekonstruierten, den öffentlichen und privaten, den parlamentarischen und juristischen, den territorialen, et cetera Körpern –, die Lücke zwischen den Körpern ermöglicht erst Bewegung, Veränderung; im Zwischen ereignet sich Bewegung. Dadurch wird das Zwischen, der Raum des Zwischen zum Raum des Begehrens. Nur scheinbar, nur aus dem Augenwinkel bleiben die Orte, Punkte, die Positionen, die Wohnsitze im Raum beständig, nur scheinbar bleiben sie in sich und an sich gleich; Luce Irigaray entlarvt diesen spitzen Winkel des fixierenden Blicks; erst in Bewegung, *im Zuge* beständiger Wechsel, Ortswechsel, in Verschiebungen, in Auseinander, Zueinander, Umeinander, Voneinander, Wanderschaften – *migrating bodies* – findet statt, was wir Raum nennen: als Verräumlichung des Zwischen. So wird dem Ort, der Position im Raum, dem Wo-einer-steht, Wo-eine-steht die Beständigkeit, die Behäbigkeit, Beharrlichkeit, die *Restance* genommen. Auch das Wo-eine und Wo-einer-zu-sein-hat. Weder Form noch Körper, sondern eher die Bedingung von Form und Körper, die mit beiden einhergeht, in einem Zug mit ihnen sich realisiert, ist der Ort, das Wo-genau-wir-uns-befinden. Zwischenraum, das ist vor allem: Die radikale *Verräumlichung des Zusammen.* Zusammen ist kompliziert; es ist das Zusammen radikal Anderer, beständig in Gefahr gespalten, hierarchisiert, normiert und organisiert zu werden. Vereinnahmt durch fatale Allianzen mit der Macht. Daher ist es notwendig die Anarchie als andere Grenzpolitik zu begreifen. *Résistance.* Ein queeres Zusammen zu denken, das Identitäten nicht instrumentalisiert, nicht als Identitäten *gegen* andere in Stellung bringt, sondern lebendig, offen, beweglich, porös und im Werden hält. Hier könnten, wüchsen sie sich nur ungebremst über den Kopf in die Körper hinaus, queere Grenzpolitiken Stätte finden.[4]

Literaturangaben

Derrida, Jacques. *Dem Archiv verschrieben. Eine Freudsche Impression.* Berlin: Brinkmann&Bose, 1997.
Irigaray, Luce. „Der Ort der Zwischenraum." In: Dies. *Ethik der sexuellen Differenz.* Frankfurt am Main: Suhrkamp, 1991.
Schlingensief, Christoph. *Ich weiß, ich war's.* Köln: Kiepenheuer & Witsch, 2012.
Wolfe, Tom. *Back to Blood.* München: Karl Blessing Verlag, 2013.

---

[4] Der vorliegende Text wurde zuerst in einer leicht veränderten Fassung veröffentlicht in: *Sublin/mes. philosophieren von unten. A queer reviewed Journal,* Heft #2, Wien 2013. Online unter: http://sublinesblog.wordpress.com/ausgaben-2/

WALTRAUD ERNST

INTIME BEGEGNUNGEN: NARRATIVE DES EROTISCHEN IN NATURWISSENSCHAFTLICHER FORSCHUNG[1]

> „Letztlich wäre es möglich, daß die Archäologie nichts anderes macht, als die Rolle eines Instruments zu spielen, das auf weniger ungenaue Weise als in der Vergangenheit die Analyse der gesellschaftlichen Formationen und die epistemologischen Beschreibungen zu artikulieren gestattet, oder das erlaubt, eine Analyse der Positionen des Subjekts mit einer Theorie der Geschichte der Wissenschaften zu verbinden, oder das die Feststellung des Kreuzungspunktes zwischen einer allgemeinen Theorie der Produktion und einer generativen Analyse der Aussagen erlaubt.“
>
> *Michel Foucault* (Archäologie des Wissens, 1981, 296)

> „Wird die Liebesbeziehung vor allem durch wechselseitige Erwartungen charakterisiert, so erhebt sich die Frage, was geschieht, wenn diese Erwartungen nicht erfüllt werden. Kann eine liebende Verbundenheit überhaupt glücken, wenn die Beteiligten reziprok mit einem bestimmten Verhalten des jeweils anderen ‚rechnen‘?“
>
> *Herta Nagl-Docekal* (Innere Freiheit, 2014, 57)

In diesem Beitrag wird das Auftauchen und die Wirkungsweise des Erotischen in den entstehenden Naturwissenschaften Chemie im 18. Jahrhundert und Biologie im 19. Jahrhundert untersucht. Ausgangsthese ist, dass das Erotische in der Funktion von Explanans und Explanandum, als erklärendes und zu erklärendes Moment, eine bisher übersehene, zentrale Rolle bei der Entwicklung dieser Wissenschaften einnahm. Dabei ist die Wechselseitigkeit von „natürlichen“ Erklärungen für kulturelle Prozesse und kulturellen oder philosophischen Deutungen von „Entdeckungen“ in der Natur von besonderem Interesse. Die Bedeutung des Erotischen für die Entwicklung der Kategorie „Geschlecht“ und die Dichotomisierung der Geschlechter steht dabei im Zentrum der

---

[1] Forschung zu diesem Aufsatz wurde großteils im Rahmen der Hertha-Firnberg-Stelle "Erotische Ökonomien der Wissenschaft" am Institut für Philosophie der Universität Wien durchgeführt und vom FWF gefördert. Für hilfreiche Anmerkungen zu einer Vorfassung des Manuskripts danke ich Elisabeth Greif und Sylvia Sadinski.

Analyse. Die diese Studie leitende Hypothese ist, dass die Veränderungen, Spezifizierungen und Regulierungen der Bedeutung von Wissenschaft auf das engste mit den Veränderungen, Spezifizierungen und Regulierungen des Erotischen während dieser Zeit verwoben sind. Ziel der Untersuchung ist herauszufinden, auf welche Weise genau diese beiden wichtigen sozialen Felder miteinander verwoben waren, welche normativen Einstellungen und kulturellen Annahmen daraus resultierten und welche ethischen, erkenntnistheoretischen und wissenschaftsphilosophischen Auseinandersetzungen sie bis heute provozieren.

Einleitend wird zunächst in die historische Deutung der sich verändernden Körper- und Geschlechtergrenzen eingeführt, soweit dies den Untersuchungszeitraum betrifft. Anschließend wird der Begriff des Erotischen vorläufig entwickelt und der methodologische Zugang der Erforschung von „Narrativen des Erotischen" erläutert. Ebenso wird die These näher spezifiziert. In den folgenden Abschnitten werden chemische Affinitätstheorien und biologische Evolutionstheorien auf ihre Verhandlungen des Erotischen hin befragt. In einer abschließenden Zusammenführung werden Konsequenzen für ein Wissenschaftsverständnis und menschliches Zusammenleben erörtert. Ausblickend wird eine alternative onto-epistemologische Betrachtungsweise des Zusammenhangs ins Spiel gebracht.

Körpergrenzen - Geschlechtergrenzen

Die (Selbst-)Wahrnehmung des Erotischen unterliegt ebenso wie Gefühl oder Leidenschaft einer historischen und kulturellen Variabilität, die in Auseinandersetzung des als persönlich Erlebten mit dem jeweils autorisierten (z.B. wissenschaftlichen) Wissen entsteht (vgl. Frevert 2011). Diese Auseinandersetzung findet mittels Narrativen statt, Erzählstrategien und Deutungsmuster, die auch (natur-)wissenschaftliche Forschungen nutzen und die mit Methoden der historischen Epistemologie erforscht werden können (Barberi 2000; Lécourt 1969). Barbara Dudens Arbeit „Geschichte unter der Haut. Ein Eisenacher Arzt und seine Patientinnen um 1730" gilt in diesem Zusammenhang als bahnbrechendes Werk. Ihre von Michel Foucault (1973) methodisch inspirierte Analyse erweckt die „Klagen der Frauen" in den veröffentlichten Berichten des Arztes zu einer lebendigen Geschichte, die „Vorstellungen vom Leibesinneren", wie sie für diese bzw. ihren Arzt „handlungsleitend und sinngebend waren", nachvollziehbar machen. Das narrative Ziel der Historikerin scheint darin zu liegen, eine mehr oder weniger historische Alternative zur modernen „anatomisch-medizinischen Beschreibung" aufzuzeigen. Damit kann sie auf die historische Kontingenz der letzteren, als eine von mehreren möglichen Darstellungen des Darzustellenden, hinweisen. Im Fokus scheinen dabei die vom medizinischen Diskurs am Ende des 20. Jahrhunderts postulierten starren Körpergrenzen zu stehen, denen Duden mit ihrem (wissenschafts- und kulturhistorischen) Rückgriff eine Vorstellung des z.B. durch Körperflüssigkeiten mit der Umgebung beständig interagierenden Inneren eines erlebten Leibes gegenüberstellt (Duden 1987). Die Kritik Donna Haraways an der Darstellung des Körpers in der Immunbiologie des ausgehenden 20. Jahrhunderts als klar umgrenzter Raum, der gegen invasive Elemente abzuschotten ist, zielt in eine ähnliche Richtung. Nach Haraway ist die Grenzziehung zwischen Körpern und ihrer Umgebung ebenso wie zwischen verschiedenen einzelnen Körpern etwas, das in einem vielschichtigen Diskurs von unterschiedlich situierten Akteur_innen innerhalb und außerhalb akademischer Räume immer wieder neu verhandelt wird (Haraway 1995).

Die Ergebnisse solcher epistemischen Verhandlungsprozesse über „körperliche" (Haraway) oder "eigenleibliche" (Duden) Erfahrungen und Prozesse allgemein zeugen von unterschiedlich gelagerten Interessen in Macht- und Herrschaftsverhältnissen. Dies verdeutlicht Claudia Honeggers Geschichte der Entstehung der sog. weiblichen Sonderanthropologie als Vorläuferin der Gynäkologie (Honegger 1991). Honegger legt dar, wie im Zuge der Entstehung der Wissenschaften vom Menschen um 1800 in komplexen diskursiven Interaktionsprozessen auf dem Weg einer immer stärkeren Fokussierung des Uterus als zentrales, spezifisch weibliches Organ für eine Differenzierung der Geschlechter argumentiert wurde, die weitreichende philosophische Deutungen über das unterschiedliche Wesen von Frauen und Männern enthielt: "Das moderne Deutungsmuster ,Geschlechterdifferenz' hat sich im Zusammenwirken von mannigfaltigen Handlungsproblemen, alltagsweltlichen Interpretationen, tradierten und erodierenden Wissensbeständen und wissenschaftlicher Systematisierungen entwickelt und stabilisiert" (Honegger 1991, 213). Mit diesem verbunden wurde bis zum Ende des 19. Jahrhunderts ein Deutungsmuster ,(Fortpflanzungs-)Sexualität', das den vielfältigen Manifestationen von erotischem Begehren und Vergnügen,

Praktiken und Beziehungen nicht gerecht werden konnte und bis heute in zahlreichen (natur-)wissenschaftlichen Disziplinen aufzufinden ist.

Narrative des Erotischen

Wie solche Deutungsmuster und Verschiebungen in dem was als wissenswertes Wissen gilt, sich auf das Verständnis des erotischen Potenzials geschlechtlich bestimmter Personen auswirken, macht Nancy Tuana in ihrer Untersuchung zum verfügbaren Wissen über die Klitoris als zentrales Organ des Lustempfindens deutlich. Sie fragt, warum es in biologischen Lehrbüchern keine Bilder und Diskussionen der beachtlichen Schwämme, Texturen und Strukturen unter der Haut um die Klitoris herum gibt, oder wenigstens in aktuellen anatomischen oder medizinischen Abhandlungen zur weiblichen Sexualität, die in irgendeiner Weise mit der ausführlichen Bebilderung des Penis oder gar der erotischen Praktiken, die Erregung erzeugen, vergleichbar wären. Die von ihr untersuchten Lehrbücher zwischen 1940 und 1970 verzichteten sogar gänzlich auf bildliche Darstellungen der Klitoris. Tuana kann zeigen, wie das Wissen über die Bedeutung der Klitoris für die Lust von Frauen, die 1559 von Renaldus Columbus "entdeckt" worden war, für mehrere Jahrhunderte aus dem (akademischen) biologischen Wissen über menschliche Körper ausgeklammert wurde, als die These über den Zusammenhang von weiblichem Orgasmus und Befruchtung fallen gelassen worden war (Tuana 2004). Daher hält sie es für notwendig, die Praktiken zu erforschen, die zu einem kollektiven Verlernen in Bereichen führen, die früher Bereiche des Wissens waren. Sie spricht in diesem Zusammenhang in methodischer Anlehnung an Charles Mills (Mills 1997) von *epistemologies of ignorance*, worunter die Erforschung von Fragen des Nichtwissens, Unwissens oder Nicht-mehr-Wissens zu verstehen ist (vgl. auch Sullivan/Tuana 2007). Sullivan und Tuana legen dar, wie Wissen über natürliche Fakten und historische Zusammenhänge nicht nur nach besten Kräften akkumuliert und verbessert wird, sondern bereits bestehendes Wissen in komplexen epistemisch-politischen Prozessen aus dem Bereich des verfügbaren Wissens entfernt und sogar gezielt unterdrückt werden kann.

In diesem Sinne verstehe ich naturwissenschaftliche Texte als Erzählungen über die Natur und Bedeutung sozialer Beziehungen. Donna Haraways Analysen der Primatenforschung (1989) und der Gentechnologie (1997) zeigen, dass gerade die narrativen Elemente (techno-) wissenschaftlichen Wissens wesentliche Faktoren der Überzeugungskraft von Theorien darstellen. Im Anschluss an Haraway möchte ich hier fragen: Was erzählen die sogenannten exakten Wissenschaften über das Erotische? Das Erotische verstehe ich hier als erotisches Begehren und Vergnügen, erotische Praktiken und Verhältnisse, die in ihrer Vielfalt und Ambivalenz ganz offensichtlich wissenschaftliche Berechnungen und staatliche Kontrollen übersteigen. Gleichzeitig scheinen erotisches Begehren und Vergnügen, erotische Praktiken und Verhältnisse immer wieder wissenschaftliche Berechnungen und staatliche Kontrollen herauszufordern. Linda Singer begründet dies im Anschluss an Michel Foucault mit der ökonomischen Relevanz des Erotischen. In ihrem Buch „Erotic Welfare. Sexual Theory and Politics in the Age of Epidemic" teilt Singer Sexualität in der Profitlogik des Spätkapitalismus in zwei Zentren des Profits, das Reproduktive und das Erotische. Sie stellen keine Opposition dar. Das reproduktive Zentrum stellt die Reproduktion von Arbeiter_innen und Konsument_innen in möglichst großer, jedoch staatlich kontrollierter Anzahl dar. Das erotische Zentrum bezieht sich auf die nicht nützliche Dimension der Sexualität, die Lust, den erotischen Exzess. Sie führt aus, wie die auf den ersten Blick im kapitalistischen Sinn nicht nützliche Erotik als eine der kontinuierlichsten Wachstumsbereiche im Spätkapitalismus nutzbar wird (Singer 1993, 34-61). Die ökonomische Relevanz des Erotischen scheint daher für die heterosexuelle Ehe und vergleichbare homosexuelle Institutionen ebenso zu gelten wie für Prostitution, Pornographie, Filmindustrie und Sextourismus (vgl. hierzu auch Hunt 1993; Engel 2009; Hofer 2012; Weichselbaumer 2012).

Ich möchte hier Linda Singers Begriff des Erotischen als Vorstellung des Begehrens und Erfüllens sinnlicher, körperlicher, sexueller Lust und Vergnügens aufgreifen, das seinen Zweck zunächst nur in sich selbst hat und darüber hinaus funktionslos ist. Dies geschieht in Abgrenzung zu Platons Begriff des Eros, insofern Platon dem „Eros" als Begehren des Schönen und Guten eine metaphysische Funktion des Erkenntnisgewinns zurechnet (vgl. Pechriggl 2009). Auf der anderen Seite stellt der hier entwickelte Begriff des Erotischen eine Abgrenzung zur evolutionstheoretischen Funktionalisierung dar. Wie später ausgeführt wird, verknüpfen Charles Darwin und andere evolutionstheoretisch orientierte Naturforscher_innen und Humanwissenschaftler_innen dieses Begehren des Schönen mit der Reproduktion der Spezies und ordnen ihm eine zentrale Funktion im Evolutionsprozess zu, nämlich die Vervollkommnung der Art als Ziel evolutionärer Prozesse. Im Folgenden wird daher argumentiert, dass die Naturalisierung des Erotischen per se nicht die eigentliche Problematik (natur-)wissenschaftlicher Narrative darstellt, sondern deren Verknüpfung mit einer Funktionalisierung. Funktionalisierung meine ich hier nicht nur in einem ökonomischen und politischen Sinn, sondern auch in einem epistemologischen Sinn. Genauer gesagt, wird problematisiert, dass erotische Anziehung in der Evolutionstheorie Darwins funktional erklärt wird. Es scheint sogar, als diene erotische Anziehung unter dem Stichwort „sexual selection" bis heute als Paradebeispiel funktionaler Erklärungen in einer evolutionstheoretisch orientierten Biologie (vgl. West-Eberhard 2003, 2005). Dadurch erhält die Erforschung der Narrative des Erotischen in der Wissenschafts- und Philosophiegeschichte gerade ihre Brisanz.

Im Folgenden werden zwei verschiedene naturwissenschaftliche Erzählungen des Erotischen analysiert und miteinander in Bezug gesetzt: die Affinitätstheorien in der Chemie des 18. Jahrhunderts und die Evolutionstheorie Charles Darwins in der Biologie des 19. Jahrhunderts. Die Affinitätstheorien in der Chemie des 18. Jahrhunderts erweisen sich als ein Ort, an dem die Anziehungskräfte zwischen Körpern als Affinität und Zuneigung diskutiert wurden, deren Resultat und Dauer als letztendlich nicht berechenbar galt. Ungefähr ein Jahrhundert später, in Darwins Evolutionstheorie in der Biologie des 19. Jahrhunderts, vollzieht sich erotische Anziehung nach natürlichen Mechanismen der Selektion, die in Begriffen von Naturgesetzen beschrieben und vorausberechnet werden können. Das Erotische wurde so als Fortpflanzungssexualität zum Steuerungsmechanismus der Entwicklung von Populationen.

Der Beitrag geht der Frage nach, welche Art von Wissen produziert wird und wie die angesprochenen Fragen mit den jeweiligen Anliegen einzelner, ganzer Gruppen oder kultureller Epochen verwoben sind bzw. waren. Dabei dienen die Prinzipien der Affinität und der Evolution als signifikante wissenschaftshistorische und -philosophische Fallstudien, da mit der Konstitution dieser beiden Begriffsfelder sich in beiden Fällen die jeweilige Disziplin auf wegweisend neue, moderne, Weise konstituierte. Das Erotische wird dabei in kultur- und wissenschaftshistorisch folgenschwerer Weise als Narrativ konstituiert: einerseits als

44

Explanandum, als etwas, das der Erklärung bedarf, und gleichzeitig als Explanans, als etwas, das (z.B. Vorgänge) erklärt. Affinität wird wie Evolution als Prinzip verstanden, das natürliche Entitäten in Bewegung bringt. Die jeweiligen Entitäten sind ganz verschieden. Affinität wird zwischen (chemisch definierten) Stoffen, bzw. Körpern diskutiert, während Evolution die Veränderung von Organismen thematisiert. Das, was beide Prinzipien verbindet, ist die Vorstellung, dass sie nicht-intentionale natürliche „Mechanismen" sind, die nicht von einer göttlichen oder menschlichen Macht gesteuert werden. Sie werden als Naturgesetze verstanden bzw. „entdeckt". Was bedeutet das? Worin unterscheiden sich diese beiden Prinzipien? Worin unterscheiden sich die beteiligten Entitäten? Ich behaupte, in beiden Theorien, der Affinitätstheorie in der Chemie ebenso wie in der Evolutionstheorie in der Biologie, geht es um die Faszination an Verbindungen von einzelnen oder individuellen Entitäten, in einem Fall materielle Substanzen, die körperhaft vorgestellt werden, im anderen Fall zweigeschlechtlich definierte Organismen. Die Narrative, die entwickelt werden, müssen als Beitrag zur jeweiligen zeitgenössischen Debatte um erotisches Begehren und Vergnügen, erotische Praktiken und Beziehungen von Personen verstanden werden.

Affinität

Der Affinitätsbegriff war in der Chemie im 18. Jahrhundert in mehreren europäischen Ländern gebräuchlich und zeigt eine interessante Auseinandersetzung zwischen Homogenität und Heterogenität des Forschungsgegenstands. Die Chemie galt im Frankreich des 18. Jahrhunderts als Wissenschaft des Heterogenen - Heterogenität sowohl hinsichtlich des zu erforschenden Materials als auch hinsichtlich der Methoden. Gabriel-François Venel definiert in seinem Artikel „*Chymie*" von 1753 in Diderots *Encyclopédie* „Affinität" durch ihren Gegensatz zur Physik, die aggregative Einheiten untersuche, während die Chemie mixtive Einheiten untersuche, wo Homogenes aus Heterogenem entstehe. Dabei konnte Venel auf dem allgemeinen Verständnis der Chemiker seiner Zeit aufbauen, wonach eine chemische Reaktion immer in Richtung der stärksten Affinität ablief, auch wenn Faktoren wie der Aggregatzustand sie hemmen könnten oder Wärme das Hindernis beseitigen könnte. So lief nach Torbern Bergman eine chemische Reaktion dann vollständig ab, wenn „ein Körper zu einem anderen eine stärkere Affinität unterhält als jene, die der zweite Körper zu einem dritten unterhält, mit dem er verbunden ist." (Stengers 1994, 554) Insofern der erste den dritten vollständig vertreibe, handele es sich um eine Wahlverwandtschaft. Da keineswegs alle chemischen Reaktionen dieser Gesetzmäßigkeit der Affinität folgten, gab es zu Bergmans Affinitätsgesetzen immer wieder Fälle von „Anomalien", die er nur bedingt erklären konnte. Trotzdem hielt sich die Theorie lange, dass chemische Affinität, also eine Ähnlichkeit zwischen Substanzen, dasselbe sei wie physikalische Attraktion, also die durch Gravitation oder Schwerkraft bedingte Bewegung von Körpern. Nur Venel, so führt Stengers aus, habe als erklärter Gegner der newtonschen Chemie darauf bestanden, dass „die Massenanziehung nicht erklären könne, wie zwei heterogene Körper einen homogenen dritten bildeten"; dies werde jedoch im Begriff der vollständigen Reaktion vorausgesetzt (Stengers 1994, 554).

Im Zusammenhang mit der rationelleren Produktion des Salpeters für die Herstellung von Schießpulver stellte zur Zeit der französischen Revolution Louis Berthollet 1795 die allgemeine Theorie auf, dass sich die Neigung eines Körpers, sich mit einem anderen zu verbinden, proportional mit dem Grad der bereits hergestellten Verbindung abnimmt. Damit bestimmte er die Affinität nicht mehr als etwas, was einen Körper in seiner Beziehung zu einem anderen charakterisiert, sondern zu einer Funktion des physikalisch-chemischen Zustands der Umgebung und der Konzentration der anwesenden Reagenzien. In seiner 1803 veröffentlichten „Statique chimique" stellte Berthollet sogar die allgemeine Unvollständigkeit der chemischen Reaktionen und ihre innere Abhängigkeit von „Umständen" als normale Folgerungen aus der Deutung der Affinität als newtonsche Anziehungskraft dar. Damit ist die sogenannte vollständige Reaktion, die Torbern Bergman zur Basis seiner Affinitätslehre machte, zum Sonderfall bestimmt worden und die Umgebung, in der sich die Reagenzien befinden, ist nicht mehr als zu vermeidende Störung, sondern zum Ausgangspunkt des Experiments geworden. Die Begriffe sind dieselben geblieben, ihre Deutung, das was sie beschrieben, etwas ganz anderes (vgl. hierzu auch Klein 1994).

Weiters hebt Berthollet die Vorstellung einer „natürlichen Richtung" der Reaktion auf, in der ein_e Chemiker_in die Umstände so manipulieren muss, dass sich die „wahren" chemischen Affinitäten äußerten. Die Richtung einer chemischen Reaktion wurde vielmehr zur Funktion einer

46

rein chemischen Affinität, die im Experiment in Form der „Umstände" (Konzentration, Temperatur) hergestellt wird. So wurde die Affinität zu einem Element der Umstände. Damit bestätigte Berthollet Venel in einem wesentlichen Punkt: „Die Anziehungskraft vermag nur das *Gemisch* und seine Proportionen zu erklären, nicht jedoch die chemische *Verbindung*, die heterogene Körper in neue homogene Körper verwandelt" (Stengers 1994, 557-558). Venels Begriff der „mixtiven Einheit" verlor damit an Bedeutung, denn bei Berthollet war das Produkt einer chemischen Reaktion nichts anderes als ein Gleichgewichtszustand, in dem verschiedene Arten von Zusammensetzungen als Gemisch existierten. Jeder Körper wurde also als Gemisch verstanden, es gab in dieser Konzeption weder „reine Produkte" noch „wohldefinierte Identitäten". Ein Körper konnte demnach auch nicht durch eine größere Anziehungskraft einen anderen Körper aus der Nachbarschaft eines dritten vollständig vertreiben. Dieser komme vielmehr dann höchstens in einer bedeutenderen Quantität in der Nachbarschaft des dritten vor als der zweite. Stengers sieht in Berthollets Theorie ein kontextualisiertes, prozessuales und interrelationales Körperverständnis: „Die Zusammensetzung eines Körpers hängt von seiner Geschichte und von verschiedenen Faktoren ab, welche die Umgebung der Reaktion charakterisieren, in der er entstanden ist" (Stengers 1994, 558).

Die Analogisierung zwischen chemischen Affinitäten und menschlichen Beziehungen ist in der Wissenschaftsphilosophie nicht unumstritten, insbesondere Gaston Bachelard warnte davor. Stengers wendet sich jedoch gegen Bachelards Warnung und folgt einer auf Bachelard selbst zurückgehenden Methode der historischen Epistemologie. Sie verweist auf einen breiten zeitgenössischen philosophischen und literarischen Diskurs, der den chemischen Begriff der Affinität auf erotisches Begehren überträgt und dessen Schicksalhaftigkeit diskutiert. Dabei standen der Autorin zufolge sinnliche, unwillkürliche Anziehungskräfte und Leidenschaften einer gesellschaftlich sinnvollen sittlichen Ordnung bzw. transzendentaler moralischer Tugend gegenüber.[2] Stengers interessiert an der Analogie zwischen Chemie und erotischer Anziehung in der Diskussion zwischen Charlotte, Eduard und dem Hauptmann über die „Verwandtschaften" von Mineralien in Goethes Roman „Die Wahlverwandtschaften" besonders die verbindende Unabsehbarkeit: „So wenig wie die chemischen Verbindungen und Trennungen sind die menschli-

---

[2] Stengers verweist auf Schelling, Hegel, Nietzsche und Goethe.

chen Leidenschaften rationaler Voraussicht zugänglich" (Stengers 1994, 546-547).

Tatsächlich schlägt Goethes Text die Analogie nur bezüglich des Verhältnisses von „Mensch und Natur" vor. Der „reiche Baron" Eduard versucht die Verwirrung seiner Gattin Charlotte über seinen Vortrag zu erklären: „Hier wird freilich nur von Erden und Mineralien gehandelt, aber der Mensch ist ein wahrer Narziß; er bespiegelt sich überall gern selbst; er legt sich als Folie der ganzen Welt unter" (Goethe 1956 [1809], 33). Der Begriff der „Wahlverwandtschaft" wird im Text vom Hauptmann als Deutung der Verbindung von Kalkerde mit Schwefelsäure zu Gips eingeführt. Charlotte widerspricht dieser Deutung. Eine solche Verbindung sei weder eine Wahl noch eine Naturnotwendigkeit, vielmehr schaffe die Gelegenheit Verhältnisse und chemische Reaktionen fänden durch die Anordnung des Chemikers statt (vgl. Goethe 1956 [1809], 34-39).

Gibt nun Isabelle Stengers Geschichte des Affinitätsbegriffs in der Chemie des 18. Jahrhunderts Hinweise auf eine Diskussion erotischen Begehrens zwischen Personen? Affinität als energetische (unwillkürliche) Anziehung zwischen - menschlichen - Körpern scheint zunächst bedeutenden personalen Konzeptionen in der Philosophie um 1800 entgegenzustehen: Nach Kant sind Personen vernunftbegabt und sollen daher moralischen Pflichten folgen, nach Fichtes Ehegesetzen sollen sie sich einer klaren hierarchischen Geschlechterordnung beugen und nach dem Vorschlag des preußischen Staatsphilosophen Hegel wird die Sittlichkeit der bürgerlichen Ehe jegliche Sinnlichkeit transzendieren (vgl. auch Hunt 1992; Nagl-Docekal 2014; Heinz 1998). − Meine Frage ist daher: Ging es im Streit um die Rolle von Affinität zwischen chemischen Körpern auch um die Frage der Etablierung einer verbindlichen Ordnung erotischer Verhältnisse zwischen Personen? Meines Erachtens vollzieht Stengers in ihrem Text selbst eine Analogisierung sozialer Beziehungen zwischen Personen mit einer materialistischen Theorie der Chemie und damit eine nachträgliche Bestätigung der Goetheschen Naturalisierung bürgerlicher Eheprobleme als quasi unvermeidliches Drama der Natur. Die Frage, welche Geschichte die Autorin Stengers damit erzählt, stellt sich umso dringlicher, als dass sich Goethes "Wahlverwandtschaften" im Laufe der Erzählung immer mehr von einem Aufklärungsroman zu einem bürgerlichen Trauerspiel entwickelt, an dessen Ende die jüngste und statusärmste Teilnehmerin am ungleichen

Spiel mit den Leidenschaften, Ottilie, nach einem missglückten Flucht-versuch sich buchstäblich zu Tode hungert.

Hier deutet sich schon an, dass naturwissenschaftliche Theorien im 18. und 19. Jahrhundert auf komplexe Fragen des menschlichen Zu-sammenlebens, insbesondere des erotischen, Antworten an einem Ort außerhalb des Sozialen suchen, in der Natur. Das Erotische wird dabei entweder als Natürliches dem Kulturellen gegenüber gestellt, oder als etwas beschrieben, das sich in fragilen Entwicklungsprozessen befindet, zwischen einem „noch nicht" und einem „zuviel" an Zivilisiertheit und dadurch ständiger Berechnung und Kontrolle bedarf (Ernst 2009). In der Gegenüberstellung mit Darwins Evolutionstheorie wird das Bestreben, Veränderungen berechenbar zu machen, noch klarer.

Evolution

Einen wesentlichen Baustein in der Naturalisierung der menschli-chen Zweigeschlechtlichkeit, der Etablierung des Mannes als treibende Kraft des Evolutionsprozesses und der heteronormativen Deutung der Sexualität bildeten die Veröffentlichungen Charles Darwins (1809-1882) „Über die Entstehung der Arten" von 1859 und „Die Abstam-mung des Menschen und die geschlechtliche Zuchtwahl" von 1871. Darwins Ausgangsfrage ist, was der Grund für die Vielfalt und die Ver-änderung der Tier- und Pflanzenarten ist und in welchem Verhältnis Menschen dazu stehen. Schon auf der ersten Seite des Kapitels „Natür-liche Zuchtwahl" klärt er die Frage menschlicher Intentionalität und schließt Menschen als direkt verursachendes Prinzip hinsichtlich der Artenvielfalt selbst bei domestizierten Arten aus. Die Praxis der Züch-tung, von der Darwin seinen gesamten Ansatz ableitet, besteht nicht darin, „Varietäten entstehen [zu] machen, noch ihr Entstehen [zu] hin-dern; er [der Mensch] kann nur die vorkommenden erhalten und häu-fen" (Darwin 1876, 100). Demgegenüber postuliert er sowohl bei do-mestizierten Arten, als auch „in der Natur" die sich verändernden Le-bensbedingungen als temporale und kausale Voraussetzung für „Varia-bilität".

Dieses abstrakte Prinzip der Veränderung spezifiziert Darwin als "natural selection" oder „natürliche Zuchtwahl" in vier Gedankenschrit-ten: Basis ist die Festlegung, dass alle organischen Wesen in wechselsei-tigen Beziehungen zueinander stehen. Die Überlegung, dass vielfältige

Abänderungen jedem Wesen unter wechselnden Lebensbedingungen nützlich sein können, bildet die wesentliche Prämisse. Die Feststellung, dass für Menschen nützliche Abänderungen vorgekommen sind, macht es für ihn wahrscheinlich, dass vorteilhafte Abänderungen im „Kampfe um's Leben" für jedes Wesen im Laufe vieler Generationen aufgetreten sind. Aus der Existenz dieser vorteilhaften Abänderungen schließt Darwin wiederum, dass diese „überdauern" und sich reproduzieren, wogegen nachteilige Abänderungen zur Zerstörung der Lebensform führen. Nicht mehr und nicht weniger heißt für Darwin „natürliche Zuchtwahl" oder „Überleben des Passendsten" (Darwin 1876, 101).

Dabei changiert die Beschreibung in Darwins Narration der „natürlichen Zuchtwahl" zwischen einem voluntaristischen Prinzip, das nur positives hervorbringt und an das Modell eines guten Schöpfergottes erinnert und einem Zufallsprinzip, das quasi unendliche Variation hervorbringt. Bei letzterem entscheidet erst ein alltäglicher „Kampf um's Überleben", welche Variation Beständigkeit erhält. Darwin leitet zwar die „natürliche Zuchtwahl" von der Züchtung domestizierter Tier- und Pflanzenarten ab, prognostiziert „für die Natur" jedoch aufgrund längerer zur Verfügung stehender Zeiträume weitaus präzisere Zuchtwahl. Demnach setzen sich individuelle Verschiedenheiten über einen langen Zeitraum hinweg als Modifikation der gesamten „Species" durch.

Die Länge der Zeiträume wird jedoch zum heuristischen Problem. Darwin gesteht ein, dass diese Veränderungsprozesse empirisch nicht nachvollziehbar sind: „Wir sehen nichts von diesen langsam fortschreitenden Veränderungen" (Darwin 1876, 105). Wenn seine Hypothese aber nicht empirisch überprüft werden kann, bedeutet dies ein epistemologisches Problem der Verifizierung seiner Theorie (vgl. hierzu auch Hull 1995). Daher schlägt Darwin vor, das Überprüfungskriterium dahingehend zu verändern, dass untersucht wird, „wie weit die Hypothese mit den allgemeinen Erscheinungen der Natur übereinstimmt und sie erklärt" (Darwin 1876, 105). Was aber sind diese allgemeinen Erscheinungen der Natur, wer kennt sie, wer legt sie fest? Das, was Darwin im Anschluss als allgemeine Erscheinungen der Natur beschreibt, sind abgesehen von Beispielen über Tarnfarben von Insekten und Waldhühnern allerdings wieder die „zivilisierte" Natur der Schaf- und Schweinezucht sowie der Obstbaumveredlung.

Seine Beobachtungen der lokalen Tier- und Pflanzenzucht um seinen Landsitz, wo er in der Zeit nach seiner Rückkehr von der Reise nach

50

Feuerland und den Galapagosinseln auf dem Schiff „Beagle" (1831-1836) ab den 1840er Jahren lebt, dient Darwin also - trotz seines vielen Tier- und Pflanzenmaterials aus seiner Weltreise – nicht nur als Ausgangspunkt, sondern letztlich auch als „Beweis" seiner Hypothesen über die Vielfalt und Veränderung der Fauna und Flora der gesamten Welt. Auf dieses Verhältnis zwischen Lokalität und Globalität wissenschaftlicher Wissensproduktion möchte ich hier aufmerksam machen, denn es scheint mir paradigmatisch für die Hybris der großen europäischen Klassifizierungssysteme im 19. Jahrhundert: Nicht nur ihr theoretischer, sondern auch ihr empirischer Bezugspunkt war von sehr spezifischer Lokalität und Temporalität. Ihr Gültigkeitsanspruch war demgegenüber global und zeitlich ungebunden.

Auch bei seiner Konzeption der „sexuellen Zuchtwahl" (*sexual selection*) schließt Darwin von der domestizierten Tierzucht auf den sogenannten Naturzustand. Bei der „sexuellen Zuchtwahl", so unterscheidet Darwin, handelt es sich nicht um den „Kampf um's Überleben" mit anderen Organismen, sondern um den Kampf unter Artgenoss_innen desselben Geschlechts, „meistens der Männchen um den Besitz des anderen Geschlechts". Das Ziel ist auch nicht die Vernichtung der Artgenoss_innen. Der Sieg besteht vielmehr darin, dass „die kräftigsten, die ihre Stelle in der Natur am besten ausfüllenden Männchen die meiste Nachkommenschaft hinterlassen" (Darwin 1876, 109). Zentrale Elemente hierbei sind die sogenannten sekundären Geschlechtscharaktere oder psychischen Geschlechtsunterschiede, wie zum Beispiel stärkere Kampfbereitschaft und größere Leidenschaft bei den Männchen.[3] Die sekundären Geschlechtscharaktere werden vererbt und zwar entlang der geschlechtlichen Trennung von den Weibchen auf weibliche Nachkommen und den Männchen auf männliche Nachkommen.

Die „sexuelle Zuchtwahl" besteht nun Darwin zufolge darin, dass das leidenschaftlichere und kampflustigere Männchen immer gewinnt, und sich so öfter fortpflanzt. Das gewählte Weibchen wiederum wird umso öfter gewählt, je passiver es ist.[4] Daraus ergibt sich die dichotome

---

[3] Die Unterscheidung ‚primär' und ‚sekundär' übernimmt Darwin von dem britischen Chirurgen John Hunter, laut Katrin Schmersahl, Medizin und Geschlecht, 1998, S. 76. Sie erinnert meines Erachtens nicht zufällig an die Unterscheidung von ‚sex' und ‚gender' im feministischen Diskurs des späten 20. Jahrhunderts.

[4] Vgl. hierzu und für die Auswirkungen dieser Darstellung auf die aktuelle Soziobiologie Ruth Hubbard 1989.

Ausdifferenzierung der sekundären Geschlechtscharaktere bei Tieren. Darwin nennt allerdings auch „einige wenige anomale Fälle" in fast allen Klassen, „bei welchen sich eine fast völlige Umkehrung der Charactere, welche den beiden Geschlechtern eigen sind, findet, so dass die Weibchen Charactere annehmen, welche eigentlich den Männchen gehören" (Darwin 1875, 374). Etwas weiter unten unterscheidet er sogar zwei Arten des „geschlechtlichen Kampfes", wobei der wesentliche Unterschied darin besteht, dass bei der ersten Art die männlichen Rivalen einander vertreiben oder töten und „die Weibchen passiv bleiben", in der zweiten Art die Individuen des einen Geschlechts kämpfen, „um die des andern Geschlechts zu reizen oder zu bezaubern, und zwar meist die Weibchen, wobei aber die letzteren nicht mehr passiv bleiben, sondern die angenehmeren Genossen sich wählen" (ebenda, 375). An dieser Stelle wird deutlich, dass die Kategorien des Normalen und Abnormalen bei Darwin wesentliche Elemente sowohl der Klassifizierung seiner „Geschlechtercharactere" als auch derjenigen des Verhaltens im „geschlechtlichen Kampf" bilden. Eine Ausdehnung seines allgemeinen Prinzips der „sexuellen Zuchtwahl" auf Menschen schlug Darwin selbst am Ende seiner Abhandlung vor (vgl. Darwin 1875, 378). Er appellierte dabei allerdings an die moralische Verantwortung der einzelnen, sich bei mangelnder Vollkommenheit oder bei Armut nicht fortzupflanzen.

Darwins Evolutionstheorie enthält also im Wesentlichen zwei Prinzipien, „natürliche Zuchtwahl" und „sexuelle" oder „geschlechtliche Zuchtwahl", wie er es später nennt. Die beiden Prinzipien wirken dabei sich gegenseitig verstärkend hin zu einer Vervollkommnung der Arten. Erotische Anziehung bzw. stattdessen „sexuelle Zuchtwahl" wird mit Darwin also zum Gegenstand eines Naturgesetzes zur Dichotomisierung geschlechtlicher Differenz. Diese Anziehung bzw. Wahl wird nur gegengeschlechtlich gedacht und zur natürlichen Grundlage der Geschlechterdifferenz, insofern die wesentliche Differenz nicht zwischen Tieren und Menschen, sondern zwischen den männlichen und weiblichen Lebewesen hergestellt wird (im Gegensatz zum „moralischen Empfinden", das zur Unterscheidung zwischen Menschen und Tieren dient). Bezogen auf erotische Anziehung wird also das Geschlecht zum signifikanteren Faktor der Differenz als das Menschsein oder Tiersein. Diese Idee eines Naturgesetzes des Erotischen im Sinne einer immer größeren Verschärfung von Differenzen zwischen Organismen bezüglich Geschlecht und Ethnie bildet meines Erachtens bis heute eine der mächtigsten sozialen Herrschaftsinstrumente, welche die Biowissenschaften hervorgebracht haben.

David Hull zeigt in seiner Arbeit über „Die Rezeption von Darwins Evolutionstheorie bei britischen Wissenschaftsphilosophen des 19. Jahrhunderts", dass Darwins Veröffentlichung von *Origin of Species* (1859) einerseits mitten in eine wissenschaftsphilosophische Debatte fällt, um den Wert von Hypothesen und der Legitimität deduktiver Schlüsse gegenüber empirischer Datensammlung und dem induktiven Schließen daraus auf generelle Zusammenhänge in der Natur. An dieser Debatte waren laut Hull John Frederick Herschel, William Whewell und John Stuart Mill beteiligt. Alle drei beurteilten Darwins Theorie nach ihren jeweiligen Maßstäben eher skeptisch (Hull 1995). Andererseits, und das ist für meine Frage hier wichtiger, fällt beim Lesen des Textes von *Origin of Species* auf, wie Darwin sich mit dieser wissenschaftsphilosophischen Kontroverse im Text auseinandersetzt – oder, anders ausgedrückt, wie diese Debatte im Text eingeschrieben ist. Die vorangehende Analyse zeigt, dass Darwin – und mit, vor und nach ihm andere Theoretiker_innen der Evolution – diese wissenschaftsphilosophische Debatte dadurch lösen, dass sie eine neue Art der wissenschaftlichen Erklärung einführen, ohne diese theoretisch zu hinterfragen: die funktionalen Erklärungen. Das heißt, etwas wird nicht dadurch wissenschaftlich erklärt, dass es von einer überzeugenden Hypothese abgeleitet wird (deduktiv), oder dass ein Zusammenhang durch ausreichende Datensammlungen als bewiesen gilt (induktiv), sondern dadurch, dass seine Funktion in einem größeren Zusammenhang überzeugend gemacht werden kann.

Zusammenführung und Ausblick

Es wurden hier wissenschaftliche Theorien von chemischen Elementen, Pflanzen und Tieren, die zwischen der Mitte des 18. und der Mitte des 19. Jahrhundert entwickelt wurden, als Narrative des Erotischen untersucht. Es wurden ihre Erzählungen und Deutungsmuster von erotischem Begehren und Vergnügen, erotischen Verhältnissen und Praktiken als natürliche Phänomene analysiert. Anhand von Affinitätstheorien in der Chemie und Evolutionstheorien in der Biologie konnte gezeigt werden, dass Fragen danach, welche Kräfte erotischem Begehren und Vergnügen, erotischen Verhältnissen und Praktiken zugrunde lagen, eine zentrale Rolle in diesen Theorien spielten. Diese Kräfte des Begehrens wurden in früheren Ansätzen als organische Anziehungskräfte zwischen Körpern beschrieben, deren Resultat und Dauer als letztendlich nicht berechenbar galten. So erwiesen sich die Affinitätstheorien in der Chemie des 18. Jahrhunderts als ein Ort, an dem die Anziehungskräfte zwischen Körpern als Affinitäten und Zuneigungen diskutiert wurden. Andererseits inspirierten Affinitätstheorien wiederum kulturelle Diskurse über erotische Verhältnisse zwischen Personen, wie zum Beispiel das viel diskutierte Werk Johann Wolfgang von Goethes, „Die Wahlverwandtschaften".

Das heißt, im Laufe der Entwicklung der modernen europäischen Naturwissenschaften war und ist die Differenzierung von Körpern ebenso wie die Berechenbarkeit von Verbindungen zwischen Körpern eine zentrale Frage. Diese Frage wurde auf verschiedenen Ebenen gestellt und beantwortet. Auf der Ebene der chemischen Verbindungen einigten sich die Protagonist_innen im späteren Verlauf des 19. Jahrhunderts sowohl auf eine Quantifizierung als auch auf eine Vorausbestimmbarkeit der einzelnen Komponenten der Verbindungen chemisch isolierter Substanzen. Die Anziehung zwischen Körpern wurde einer Gesetzmäßigkeit unterstellt, einem Gesetz, das in der Natur „entdeckt" wurde. Dabei wurden andere Aspekte der Untersuchung und Beschreibung, wie die der Affinitäten, als unbedeutend erklärt. Auf komplexen argumentativen und rhetorischen Wegen wurden richtungsweisende Erzählungen über die Natur und die Bedeutung des Erotischen entwickelt. In späteren biologischen Ansätzen, insbesondere in Charles Darwins Evolutionstheorie, vollzog sich erotische Anziehung nach natürlichen Mechanismen der Selektion, die in Begriffen von Naturgesetzen beschrieben und vorausberechnet werden konnten. Das Erotische wurde in der Verknüpfung von „natural selection" und „sexual selection" zum Steuerungsmechanismus der Entwicklung von Populationen.

Auf diese Weise lieferten Theorien der Natur Argumente, die in weiteren Diskursen dazu genutzt werden konnten, legitime erotische Verhältnisse von illegitimen Verhältnissen zu unterscheiden und natürliche von unnatürlichen. So wurden in der Folge manche erotischen Praktiken mit dem Argument legitimiert, dass sie hinsichtlich der Entstehung neuen Lebens oder der Reproduktion der Art einen übergeordneten Zweck erfüllten (vgl. Russett 1989). Mit der Fokussierung der Reproduktion als eigentlicher Funktion erotischer Anziehung erschienen dann im Anschluss an diese Narrative nicht-reproduktive Praktiken und Verhältnisse, wie z.B. Masturbation und gleichgeschlechtliche Verbindungen, als Abweichung oder Anomalie „der Natur" bzw. erhielten den Status des „Unnatürlichen", dessen körperliche Manifestation erforscht werden sollte (vgl. Laqueur 2003; Terry 1995). Fortpflanzungsorientierte Heterosexualität wurde so als quasi einzig „natürliche" Sexualität etabliert und als soziale Norm durch naturwissenschaftliche Forschung legitimiert. Die Vielfalt erotischer Anziehung und Lust als selbstverständlicher Bestandteil „der Natur" geriet für lange Zeit in den Hintergrund (vgl. Ebeling 2002; Haraway 1986).

Die Naturalisierung und Funktionalisierung des Erotischen muss daher als Teil einer groß angelegten ökonomischen und politischen Neuordnung von Natur und Gesellschaft in dieser Zeit verstanden werden, einer „politischen Ökonomie der Bevölkerung" (Foucault 1983, 39) und einer patriarchalen Geschlechterordnung (vgl. Klinger 1990). Einen wesentlichen Beitrag hierfür lieferten, so zeigte sich, die mechanistisch und funktionalistisch formulierten Naturgesetze der aufblühenden "empirischen" Naturforschung und ihrer Etablierung als wissenschaftliche Disziplinen im 19. Jahrhundert. Die interrelationalen Bewegungen, Begegnungen und Verbindungen zwischen Körpern, Stoffen und Organismen wurden als naturgesetzliche Prinzipien ob als Affinität (im Sinne einer unwillkürlichen Anziehung) oder als Evolution (im Sinne einer Entwicklung hin zu einer immer stärkeren Dichotomisierung von Geschlechterdifferenzen, aufgrund einer nicht näher begründeten Präferenz, Auswahl oder Vorliebe, die für alle Organismen als gültig betrachtet wurde) beschrieben. Komplexes menschliches erotisches Begehren und Vergnügen, Praktiken und Beziehungen konnten auf diese Weise nicht erfasst werden.

Abschließend soll noch die Frage aufgeworfen werden, ob im Zuge einer onto-epistemologischen Neudiskussion materiell-semiotischer Akteur_innen und deren „intra-active entanglements" zwischen menschlichen und nicht-menschlichen Organismen sowie nicht-organischer Materie (vgl. Barad 2007) das Erotische in seiner dynamischen Vielfalt in queer-feministischer Hinsicht neu diskutiert werden kann.

Literatur:

Barad, Karen. *Meeting the Universe Halfway. Quantum Physics and the Entanglement of Matter and Meaning.* Durham/London: Duke University Press, 2007.

Barberi, Alessandro. "Editorial: Historische Epistemologie & Diskursanalyse". In: *Österreichische Zeitschrift für Geschichtswissenschaften* 11, 4, 2000 , S. 5-9.

Darwin, Charles. *Die Abstammung des Menschen und die geschlechtliche Zuchtwahl.* 2. Bd.. In: Ders. *Gesammelte Werke* Bd. 6, aus dem Englischen von J. Victor Carus, Stuttgart, 1875 [Orig. 1871].

Darwin, Charles. *Über die Entstehung der Arten durch natürliche Zuchtwahl oder die Erhaltung der begünstigten Rassen im Kampfe um's Dasein,* aus dem Englischen von H. G. Bronn, überarbeitet von J. Victor Carus, Stuttgart, 1876 [Orig. 1859].

Duden, Barbara. *Geschichte unter der Haut. Ein Eisenacher Arzt und seine Patientinnen um 1730.* Stuttgart, 1987.

Engel, Antke. *Bilder von Sexualität und Ökonomie. Queere kulturelle Politik im Neoliberalismus.* Bielefeld, 2009.

Ernst, Waltraud. "Metapher und Materie? Zur Wissenschaftsgeschichte des erotischen Körpers". In: Bidwell-Steiner, Marlene/Zangl, Veronika (Hrsg.): *Körperkonstruktionen und Geschlechtermetaphern. Zum Zusammenhang von Rhetorik und Embodiment.* Innsbruck, 2009, S. 45-56.

Foucault, Michel. *Die Geburt der Klinik. Eine Archäologie des ärztlichen Blicks.* München, 1973.

Foucault, Michel. *Archäologie des Wissens.* Frankfurt a. M., 1981.

Foucault, Michel. *Der Wille zum Wissen. Sexualität und Wahrheit 1.* Frankfurt a.M., 1983.

Frevert, Ute/Scheer, Monique/Schmidt, Anne/ u.a.. *Gefühlswissen: Eine lexikalische Spurensuche in der Moderne.* Frankfurt a. M., 2011.

Goethe, Johann Wolfgang von. *Die Wahlverwandtschaften.* Stuttgart, 1956 [Orig. 1809].

Haraway, Donna. "Primatology is politics by other means". In: Ruth Bleier (Hrsg.): *Feminist approaches to science.* New York, 1986, S. 77–118.

Haraway, Donna. *Primate Visions. Gender, Race, and Nature in the World of Modern Science.* New York, 1989.

Haraway, Donna. "Die Biopolitik postmoderner Körper. Konstitutionen des Selbst im Diskurs des Immunsystems". In: Dies. *Die Neuerfindung der Natur.*

Primaten, Cyborgs und Frauen. Carmen Hammer (Hrsg.). Frankfurt a.M., 1995, S. 160-199.

Haraway, Donna. *Modest_Witness@Second_Millenium. FemaleMan©_Meets_OncoMouse™. Feminism and Technoscience*. New York/London, 1997.

Heinz, Marion. "Liebe und Ehe. Untersuchungen zu Fichtes Eherecht". In: Marion Heinz / Friederike Kuster (Hrsg.). *Geschlechtertheorie, Geschlechterforschung. Ein interdisziplinäres Kolloquium*. Bielefeld: Kleine Verlag 1998, S. 11-26.

Hofer, Kristina Pia. "Frühes Kino und Pornografie im Internet: Eine "parallax historiography" in der Diskussion zweier 'neuer' Medien?" In: *Österreichische Zeitschrift für Geschichtswissenschaften* 23, 2, 2012, S. 82-109.

Hubbard, Ruth. "Hat die Evolution die Frauen übersehen?" In: List, Elisabeth/Studer, Herlinde (Hrsg.): *Denkverhältnisse. Feminismus und Kritik*, Frankfurt a. M., 1989, S. 301-332.

Hull, David. "Die Rezeption von Darwins Evolutionstheorie bei britischen Wissenschaftsphilosophen des 19. Jahrhunderts". In: Engels, Eve-Marie (Hrsg.): *Die Rezeption von Evolutionstheorien im 19. Jahrhundert*, Frankfurt a. M., 1995, S. 67-104.

Hunt, Lynn. "The Family Romance of the French Revolution". London, 1992.

Hunt, Lynn (Hrsg.). *The Invention of Pornography*. New York, 1993.

Klein, Ursula. *Verbindung und Affinität. Die Grundlegung der neuzeitlichen Chemie an der Wende vom 17.zum 18. Jahrhundert*. Basel/Boston/Berlin, 1994.

Klinger, Cornelia. "Frau – Landschaft – Kunstwerk. Gegenwelten oder Reservoire des Patriarchats?" In: Herta Nagl-Docekal (Hrsg.). *Feministische Philosophie*. Wien: Oldenbourg, 1990, S. 63-94.

Laqueur, Thomas. *Solitary Sex. A Cultural History of Masturbation*. New York, 2003.

Lecourt, Dominique. *L'èpistemologie historique de Gaston Bachelard*. Paris, 1969.

Mills, Charles. The Racial Contract. Ithaca, NY, 1997.

Nagl-Docekal, Herta. *Innere Freiheit. Grenzen der nachmetaphysischen Moralkonzeptionen*, Berlin/Boston: De Gruyter, 2014.

Pechriggl, Alice. *Eros*. Wien, 2009.

Russett, Cynthia Eagle. *Sexual Science. The Victorian Construction of Womanhood*. Cambridge, MA/London, UK, 1989.

Schmersahl, Katrin. *Medizin und Geschlecht. Zur Konstruktion der Kategorie Geschlecht im medizinischen Diskurs des 19. Jahrhunderts*. Opladen, 1998.

Singer, Linda. *Erotic Welfare. Sexual Theory and Politics in the Age of Epidemic*. New York/London, 1993.

Stengers, Isabelle. "Die doppelsinnige Affinität: Der newtonsche Traum der Chemie im achtzehnten Jahrhundert". In: Serres,Michel (Hrsg.): *Elemente einer Geschichte der Wissenschaften*. Frankfurt a. M., 1994, S. 527-567.

Sullivan, Shannon/Tuana, Nancy (Hrsg.). *Race and Epistemologies of Ignorance*. Albany, 2007.

Terry, Jennifer. "Anxious Slippages between "Us" and "Them". A Brief History of the Scientific Search for Homosexual Bodies". In: Terry, Jennifer/Urla, Jacqueline (Hrsg.). *Deviant Bodies. Critical Perspectives on Difference in Science and Popular Culture*. Bloomington and Indianapolis, 1995, S. 129-169.

Tuana, Nancy. "Coming to understand: Orgasm and the Epistemology of Ignorance". In: *Hypatia* 19,1, 2004, S. 194-232.

Weichselbaumer, Doris. "Sex, romance and the carnivalesque between female tourists and Caribbean men". In: *Tourism Management* 33, 5, 2012, S. 1220-1229.

West-Eberhard, Mary Jane. *Developmental Plasticity and Evolution*. Oxford: Oxford University Press, 2003.

West-Eberhard, Mary Jane. "The Maintenance of Sex as a Developmental Trap Due to Sexual Selection". In: *The Quarterly Review of Biology* 80 (1), 2005, S. 47–53.

ALICE PECHRIGGL

EROS ZWISCHEN PLATON UND FREUD: WIE SINNVOLL IST DIE ANACHRONISTISCHE ANNAHME EINER PLATONISCHEN SUBLIMIERUNGSTHEORIE?[1]

Es scheint für die historische Forschung – auch in der Philosophiegeschichte – eine Selbstverständlichkeit, dass Anachronismen zu vermeiden sind. Ich möchte im Folgenden der Frage nachgehen, ob es sich bei der Sichtweise, dass Platon Freuds Sublimierungstheorie vorweggenommen hat, um einen Anachronismus handelt und wenn ja, ob dieser Anachronismus nicht mehr Sinnvolles erschließt als die „chronologisch korrekte" Behauptung, dass Freud seine Theorie von der erotischen Sublimierung unter anderem in Anlehnung an Platon entwickelt hat, dass bei diesem selbst aber keine Sublimierungstheorie zu finden ist, auch keine implizite. Ich werde dabei von der These ausgehen, dass, um es mit Nicole Loraux zu formulieren, die vom „kontrollierten Gebrauch des Anachronismus" sprach, oder in Weiterführung von Benjamins „dialektischem Bild" (Benjamin 1983), die nach Verwechslung oder Projektion der „eigenen Zeit" in die (längst und unwiederbringlich) „vergangene Zeit" aussehende Ungleichzeitigkeit eine spezifische Form der *epochê* (Innehalten, Aussetzen eines Urteils...) erlaubt; diese *epochê* ermöglicht uns durch das Zeitfenster eines aktuellen, meist konflikthaften Erkenntnisinteresses, einen neuen, vielleicht nie da gewesenen Blick auf Vergangenes. Im Falle des platonischen Eros betrifft das die Verbindung zwischen Geschlechtlichkeit und Sexualität, zwischen Hetero-, Bi- und Homosexualität, zwischen Eros und Thanatos. Alle drei sind in ihrer Verwobenheit sowohl für Platons als auch für Freuds Sublimierungstheorie konstitutiv. Diese begriffliche Verknüpfung, die mehr ist als bloßer „Einfluss",

---

[1] Dieser Text ist die Weiterführung meiner Auseinandersetzung mit Platons Erostheorie aus einer methodologischen Perspektive, die ich mit einer kritischen Lektüre von Kelsens Platon-Buch eröffnete (siehe FN 2) und mit einem Beitrag zum gezielten Einsatz des Anachronismus im Werk von Nicole Loraux weiterführte: „Linking psychoanalysis and historiography in the «controlled use of anachronism»" (*classics@: An online journal, Volume 7*, 2011). Der vorliegende Text ist das überarbeitete Manuskript für einen Gastvortrag am Institut für Philosophie der Ertös Lorand Universität Budapest am 26. April 2013.

wird aber nur verständlich, wenn wir gezielt anachronistisch vorgehen; konkreter war sie mir nur möglich, weil ich zuerst etwas ungezielt und dann expliziter und systematischer anachronistisch vorgegangen bin.

Wenn wir den Anachronismus als ein erkenntnistheoretisches Werkzeug sehen, sozusagen als ein Interpretament *sui generis*, dann könnte die Analyse des Anachronismus in seinem je spezifischen Anwendungsfeld Erhellung bringen, und zwar sowohl für den Zeitraum, aus dem heraus wir forschen, als auch für jenen zurückliegenden, den wir philosophiehistorisch und -systematisch, nicht nur philologisch, zu erforschen trachten. Der Text selbst wird niemals als „Text an sich" in Erscheinung treten, aber an der Schnittstelle möglichst exakter räumlicher und zeitlicher Verortungen des Textes in seinen historisch-gesellschaftlichen Kontexten und über die Differenzen in der Rezeptionsgeschichte können wir, gleichsam wie mit der Triangulierung beim Peilen in der Navigation oder über die Parallaxe, eine genauere Kenntnis der Texte erlangen.

Vorausgeschickt sei damit, dass Platon bzw. Sokrates sowie der Platonische Korpus nicht nur als zentrale Projektionsflächen zu fast allen Zeiten[2] der europäischen Philosophiegeschichte fungieren, sondern dass die Texte auch hinter dieser gesellschaftlich-geschichtlich sich verändernden Projektionsfläche auf andere Art und Weise existieren. Man könnte das den, der Lokalisierung und zeitlichen Bestimmung zumindest implizit zugrundeliegenden „Textrealismus" der Philosophiehistorie nennen. Dieser methodologische „Textrealismus" ist ebenso wichtig für akkurate philosophiehistorische Arbeit wie die Grundannahme, dass die Worte und Sätze in einem Text nicht zufällig dort so stehen, wo bzw. wie sie dort stehen, sondern, weil der Autor/die Autorin sie so und nicht anders dahin gesetzt hat. Diese – abgeschwächt positivistische[3] –Annahme ist selbstverständlich keine posi-

---

[2] Ich hatte statt „Zeiten" zuerst, aus Gewohnheit, „Epochen" geschrieben, doch ich halte es in Sachen „Epoche", wie auch in Sachen „Mittelalter" mit Kurt Flasch: „ (...) sonst würde ich vorschlagen, die nächsten 30 Jahre die Ausdrücke „Epoche", „Mittelalter" und „Neuzeit" nicht mehr zu gebrauchen." (Flasch 2003, 134)

[3] Es kann sich hier selbstverständlich nicht um eine – notwendig naive – Neuauflage des Positivismus handeln, sondern um eine Haltung, in der wir uns der Setzungs- bzw. Instituierungsproblematik gerade auch im Anschluss an Kelsen und Castoriadis bewusst sind. Das hilft uns zugleich einen für Philosphiehistoriker_innen unwürdigen und jedenfalls ideologisch geführten Schulenstreit außen vor zu lassen. (Wir haben alle unsere Vorlieben und Sozialisierungen, aber daraus eine Glaubenssache

tive, assertorische Aussage über diese Setzung und schon gar nicht über die Intention der Autorin/des Autors, sie ist vielmehr eine Eingrenzung unserer interpretatorischen Freiheit, ein Anker für die Positivität des Textes als Text eines anderen, den wir nicht nach Belieben unserem hermeneutischen Zirkel einverleiben können.

Kurze Erläuterung des Anachronismus
im Zeichen des dialektischen Bildes

Wenn ich nun über Anachronismus im Umgang mit Platons Erostheorie spreche, dann werde ich keine Exegese der landläufig bekannten Topoi ins Feld führen, auch werde ich mich nicht mit den eher oberflächlich gehaltenen Zusammenführungen von Freud und Platon befassen, wie sie etwa Santas (*Plato and Freud: Two Theories of Love*, 1988) oder Yvon Brès (*La Psychologie de Platon*, 1968) vorgelegt haben; schon eher könnte man für die Erhellung der Sublimierungsfrage bei Platon und Freud auf den bereits 1933 erschienenen Text von Hans Kelsen „Die platonische Liebe" Bezug nehmen, die in der von Freud herausgegebenen Zeitschrift *Imago* erschien.[4] (Imago, 1933)

Ich möchte im Folgenden aber mehr diejenigen Aspekte der Platonischen Erostheorie hervorheben, für die bzw. für deren Entdeckung und systematische Herausarbeitung mir ein gezielt eingesetzter Anachronismus hilfreich war, und die meines Erachtens auch Kelsen in ihrer Vielschichtigkeit bei Platon verkannt hat.[5] Diese Aspekte betreffen nicht nur die allgemeinere Frage nach der – je unterschiedlich gewichteten – Sublimierung, sondern auch die spezifischere Frage nach den drei Arten des Eros, wie sie in der Aristophanes-Rede des

---

und Identifikationsgrundlage zu machen ist, was ich als unwürdig bezeichne; das trifft übrigens auch für bestimmte feministische Positionen in den Geistes-, Kultur- und Sozialwissenschaften, nicht nur in der Philosophie zu.)

[4] „Günter Hefler schrieb in seiner Arbeit über Kelsen: ‚Der Heroisierung Platons als Politiker, die nach 1933 zu einer Parallelisierung der Biographien Platons und Hitlers führte, setzt Kelsen seine psychoanalytisch orientierte Charakterisierung Platons als eines seine Homosexualität sublimierenden Neurotikers entgegen; Platons Idealstaat wird zur Zwangsvorstellung, deren affirmative Rezeption einzig Aufschluß über den Sozialcharakter moderner Interpreten geben könnte.'"[4] (Pechriggl, 2006)

[5] Für eine übersichtlichere Darstellung meiner Interpretation von Platons Erostheorien siehe Pechriggl 2009 (a) Kap. 1.

Symposion über den Mythos von den Kugelmenschen dargelegt werden: Die dreifältige Erostheorie des Aristophanes versucht sowohl dem weiblich und männlich homosexuellen als auch dem heterosexuellen Eros Rechnung zu tragen, der bisexuelle wird nicht gesondert ausgeführt, obwohl nach heutigem – von Foucault geprägtem – Dafürhalten die Bisexualität als „normalere" Praxis denn die Homosexualität in der – pauschalisierten – „griechischen Antike" gewesen sei (in Wirklichkeit geht es hier um die Zeit und den Ort der Athenischen Demokratie). Es geht mir in diesem Text Platons vor allem um die Verknüpfung von Ausblendung bzw. Tabuisierung und – im Hegelschen Sinn gefasste – Aufhebung der Homosexualität im sublimierten Eros. Diese lange Zeit durch bigotte Tabus, Abspaltungen und Ausblendungen gekappte Verknüpfung ist, so meine These, nur im Anschluss an Freud und an die Befreiungsbewegungen der Lesben und Schwulen in Europa und den USA begrifflich wieder herzustellen gewesen, also durch einen zuerst naiven, dann immer systematischer eingesetzten Anachronismus.

Obwohl ihre Anfänge genau um die vorvorige Jahrhundertwende in Europa und den USA anzusiedeln sind, setzten die Lesbian- and Gay-Rights-Bewegungen so richtig erst Jahrzehnte nach dem erwähnten Aufsatz von Kelsen ein, was aus heutiger Sicht die scheinbare „Beschränktheit" seiner durchaus revolutionären Einsichten erhellt. Nicht unbedeutend ist in diesem Zusammenhang die Bedeutung von „Sappho", die Platon explizit erwähnt und deren Verse er im *Phaidros* (252 a-b) gleichsam aus dem Gedächtnis oder wie einen Topos „zitiert".

Es ist vielleicht trivial aber nicht unwichtig zu bemerken, dass mich methodologisch die Rezeptionsgeschichte aus einem spezifischen Erkenntnisinteresse in Bezug auf Platon beschäftigt. Im Zuge einer seit 1990 währenden, manchmal mehr, manchmal weniger intensiven Auseinandersetzung mit dem Werk Platons, erschien es mir immer dringlicher, die Frage nach dem Anachronismus aufzuwerfen und so systematisch wie möglich zu behandeln, und zwar stets in Verbindung mit der Begriffsfigur des Chiasma, χ, das die Überkreuzlegung zweier begrifflicher Gegensatzpaare bezeichnet (z.B. aktiv-passiv / weiblich-männlich). Einen Ausgangspunkt dafür stellte der Aufsatz von Gregory Vlastos „Was Platon a feminist?" dar. Dieser Aufsatz erschien 1989 im TLS[6] (siehe TSL 1989, 276) und ist seither mehrmals wieder veröf-

---

[6] Wiederabgedruckt unter anderen in: G. Vlastos 1995.

fentlicht worden, zuletzt in der von Nancy Tuana 1994 herausgegebenen Anthologie *Feminist Interpretations of Plato*.

Ich erwähne dies, weil mich dieser Aufsatz nicht nur tief beeindruckt hat, sondern auch, weil er mir inmitten der Vorherrschaft deutscher hermeneutisch-idealistischer Platonrezeption, der ich während meines Studiums an der Universität Wien in der zweiten Hälfte der 80er Jahre begegnete (ich möchte sagen ausgeliefert war, denn es gab keine Alternativen), wie eine erfrischende Lichtung erschien. Unter diesem explizit anachronistischen Titel befasst sich Vlastos mit der Frage nach der Rolle der *archousai*, der philosophischen Herrscherinnen, also mit der Frage nach den Geschlechterherrschaftsverhältnissen. Platon / Sokrates spricht in der *Politeia* gegen die gängige Meinung im Sinne einer gewissen Gleichberechtigung der Frauen und Männer in der Ausübung der politischen Macht bzw. der gesellschaftlichen Herrschaft. (siehe Platon, Politeia 540b ff) Er weist dabei auf den Mut hin, dessen es bedarf, derart ungewöhnliche – im Sinne von „wunderliche" aber auch von „revolutionäre" – Dinge vorzuschlagen. Uns fallen dazu nicht nur andere platonische Topoi der Gefährlichkeit der Rede ein, sondern auch jene Gefährlichkeit der *parrhesia*[7] ganz allgemein, und im besonderen jene, die in der Athenischen Ekklesia mit dem Einbringen von gesetzlichen Neuerungen, d.h. mit der *graphê paranomon*[8] verbunden war.

Die Frage nach der Beteiligung der Frauen an den politischen Ämtern, die Sokrates / Platon vorschlug (nicht ohne sich zugleich über eine Gesellschaft lustig zu machen, in der Frauen zu viele Rechte haben, ebenso Hunde), setzt in der klassischen Antike mit der Thematisierung des Ausschlusses der Frauen aus den politischen Ämtern ein. Sie mag, nicht zuletzt dank Vlastos und feministischer Bewegung, aus

---

[7] Zur Parrhesia haben vor allem Hannah Arendt und Michel Foucault gearbeitet, auf die ich aber hier nicht eingehen kann. Für einen Vergangenheit und Gegenwart verbindenden Überblick zu beiden siehe Maria Tamboukou 2012.

[8] http://www.stoa.org/projects/demos/article_law_glossary?section=paranomon (Juni 2015). Ganz nebenbei zeigt diese Bestimmung die (demokratisch) verfassungsbezogene, politische und philosophische Bedeutung von *nomos / nomoi*, d.h. Grundgesetz / Gesetze in Bezug zu *psephismata*, d.h. (abgestimmte) „Bestimmungen", was bereits, gezielt anachronistisch gesprochen, in Richtung Kelsens „systematischen Aufbau des Rechts" verweist und keineswegs in Richtung Schmitts autoritäre Mystifizierung des „Nomos".

heutiger Sicht auf die Antike nicht mehr so ungewöhnlich erscheinen wie noch vor 30 Jahren. Anders verhält es sich mit der an die „Geschlechterfrage" unmittelbar geknüpfte Frage nach Homo-, Bi- und Heterosexualität. Obschon von Dover über Foucault, Halperin, Brisson, Calame zu uns vieles zum Thema veröffentlicht wurde, bleibt sie in philosophiehistorischen Kreisen, deutschen allemal, tabuisiert. Nun sind beide – sowohl die soziopolitische und sexuelle Hierarchie der Geschlechter(rollen) als auch das Verhältnis zwischen Hetero-, Homo- und Bisexualität – mit der Frage nach der Sublimierung und jener nach dem „Platonischen Eros" bzw. nach der „Platonische Liebe" aufs Engste verbunden.

Aktiv-passiv, männlich-weiblich, erastes-eromenos stehen im Zentrum der Diskussion der hetero- und homosexuellen Praktiken in der antiken (klassischen) athenischen Polis. Im Anschluss an Foucaults Buch *Sexualität und Wahrheit* scheint sich die Behauptung, es hätte keine Homosexualität gegeben, sondern nur Bisexualität oder geschlechtsspezifische Rollenverteilung, gleichsam dogmatisch verselbstständigt zu haben. (Es lohnte sich daher für eine skeptische, ja gegensätzliche Beurteilung dieser Behauptung, Platon oder Aristoteles genau wieder zu lesen und ebenso die historiographischen und philosophiehistorischen Arbeiten zum Thema). Zwar finden sich tatsächlich keine Hinweise auf den Versuch so etwas wie die Homoehe zu institutionalisieren, und es scheint zur Zeit unanfechtbar, dass Homosexualität in Athen nicht als Identifikationskategorie für bestimmte „Individuen" fungierte (der Begriff Individuum auf die Athenische Polis angewandt ist selbst ebenso wie derartige Annahmen ein platter – kein „kontrollierter" – Anachronismus); und doch kann Platons Theorie zum homosexuellen Eros nicht als völlig losgelöstes Fabulieren eines einfallsreichen und gespaltenen Autors gesehen werden, der ohnehin nie im eigenen Namen spricht. Es ist vielmehr bezeichnend, dass er gerade diese Theorie einem Komiker in den Mund legt, der nicht nur, in den *Vögel*, Platons Lehrer dem Gelächter preisgab,[9] sondern auch

---

[9] Darüber hinaus ist „Sokratisches" auch nicht persifliert eingebaut und umgekehrt finden wir mehr als eine Persiflage auf Sokrates bei Platon selbst, sogar im Phaidon (als es um die Seelenwanderungstheorie geht) und jedenfalls im Symposion in der Alkibiades-Rede, aber auch in der Rede des Sokrates selbst, wenn er von den ideellen Kindern spricht, die aus einer richtigen Verbindung zwischen zwei Männern hervorgehen, oder im Theaitetos, wenn es um die sokratische Hebammenkunst und

den Tropus von der Machtausübung durch die Frauen, mit dem Unterschied, dass Aristophanes in den *Ekklesiazousai* die Machtübernahme der Frauen als komödiantischen Topos zum Besten gab, während Sokrates/Platon in der *Politeia*, der „Verfassung unserer Wünsche", die Beteiligung der Frauen an der Machtausübung als sinnvoll und wünschenswert darstellt. Das sind eindeutige Verweise und zudem Möglichkeiten der zeitlichen und örtlichen Verortung, die zu erinnern nicht stumpfes Sammeln ist, sondern sich methodologisch geziemt.

Anachronismus und Arten des „Widerstands"

Meine Auffassung, die Platonische Erostheorie sei weniger eine Theorie vom nicht vollzogenen Geschlechtsakt oder vom zurückgehaltenen „platonischen" Eros als vielmehr eine Sublimierungstheorie im keineswegs nur losen Sinne Freuds, stößt nach wie vor, und zwar nicht nur bei Nicht-SpezialistInnen, auf Widerstand. Dass und inwiefern diese beiden Aspekte – Abstinenz und Sublimierung im Sinne Freuds – in Platons/Sokrates' Erostheorie miteinander aufs Engste verknüpft sind, werde ich kurz skizzieren und damit die weitere Beantwortung meiner Frage nach den Vorteilen einer gezielt anachronistischen Leseweise im Kontext diverser Arten von Widerstand versuchen.

Sublimierung nach Freud ist der triebtheoretisch erklärbare Prozess der Hervorbringung neurotischer Symptome im nicht notwendig pathologischen Sinn; es ist eine Kompromissbildung zwischen den strengen Anforderungen des Überich und dem wilden Ansinnen des Es, ohne die kulturelle und künstlerische Hervorbringung der Menschen nicht existierten. Freud arbeitete in einer Zeit, in der erste Homosexuellenbewegungen sich gegen Verfolgung und Ächtung formierten. Einige ihrer Exponenten bezogen sich dabei auch auf Platons *Symposion*, in dem die meisten Redner gerade homosexuellen Männern besondere kulturelle Leistungsfähigkeit attestieren, während Frauen hinsichtlich ihrer kulturellen Leistungen gar nicht erst erwähnt werden, vielmehr wird der Geburtsakt zum Vorbild für die mannmännlicher Zeugung und Hervorbringung von Ideen, was – in den Mund der Priesterin Diotima gelegt – ebenfalls eine Ironie enthält: Ganz entgegen die angebliche „Ideenlehre" Platons, in der das

---

die Abtreibung von Winden geht (die Schleiermacher bekanntlich, die Ironie erkennend, mit „Windeier" übersetzte.)

mimema (Nachahmung, Abbild) stets ein Abklatsch des *eidos* (Vorbilds) ist, wird hier die Nachahmung zur sublimeren Form, die das Modell in den Schatten stellt, womit deutlich wird, das (heterosexuelle) Frauen sich aufgrund der Zeugung im Leib durch mangelnde Sublimierung auszeichnen würden.[10] Von Lesben ist in der Diotima-Rede aber nicht die Rede, während Platon sie in der Aristophanes-Rede des *Symposion* extra benennt, allerdings ohne dass darüber weiter konferiert würde). Im Bezug auf die kreative Sublimierung homosexueller, dann homoerotisch miteinander in der Schöpfung *(poiêsis)* bzw. Geburt von Ideen verbundener Männer kommt dieser Aspekt, wenn auch nicht unter diesem Freudschen Namen, in fast allen Reden des *Symposions* her/vor, am deutlichsten im Sinne von Platons Erostheorie in der Aristophanes-Rede, in der Diotima-Rede und in der Alkibiades-Rede.

In der *Politeia* und im *Symposion* finden wir zwei *logoi* über den Eros, welche mit geradezu entgegen gesetzten Einschätzungen, ja Bewertungen des Eros einhergehen: In der *Politeia* wendet sich die einhellige Staatsräson gegen den Eros, der aus der von Platon / Sokrates eingenommenen Perspektive dieser Staatsräson als Tyrann bezeichnet wird, und zwar nicht nur, weil es hier um die Charakterisierung des Tyrannen, seines Regimes und der diesem zugeneigten Menge geht, sondern weil der Eros die Leute für die Staatsräson unkontrollierbar macht; dagegen stehen die vielstimmigen Lobreden auf Eros im *Symposion*, in dem Platon eine vielschichtige Erostheorie inszeniert und philosophisch-dichterisch entwickelt; eine Erostheorie, der die herkömmliche und zum nicht mehr weiter hinterfragten Dogma erstarrte Rede von der „Platonischen Liebe" in keiner Weise gerecht wird.

Diese von Platon vielschichtig und widersprüchlich dargestellte Erostheorie steht in engem Zusammenhang mit der Erostheorie vor allem des *Phaidros* aber auch anderer Dialoge. Die im herkömmlichen Verständnis von „Platonischer Liebe" vorherrschende Vorstellung dagegen ist eine, welche die Erostheorien, die Platon im *Symposion* und im *Phaidros* entwickelt, erdrückt, nivelliert und domestiziert, und zwar noch wirkmächtiger als dies die politologische Vernunft oder Staatsräson in der *Politeia* zu tun vermag, die Eros als tyrannisch bezeichnet bzw. den Tyrannen als von (einem tyrannischen) Eros beses-

---

[10] Zur Kritik an dieser zum Dogma erstarrten Sichtweise unter Hervorhebung der „Zirkularität der Mimesis" in Platons Werk siehe Pechriggl, 2009 (b).

sen. Wenn wir hier nicht den Erosbegriff differenzieren und von einem „politischen" und zugleich „unsublimierten", von *hybris* geprägten Eros ausgingen, stünde das in unerklärbarem Widerspruch zu den anderen Erostheorien Platons. (Platon, Politeia 572d-573b) Das platt anachronistische Dogma von der „Platonischen Liebe" ist die Vorstellung von einer a priori Sex-losen, mehr asexuellen denn abstinenten Liebe zum Ideellen, die den Sex und das sexuelle Begehren nicht einmal neurotisch geißelt, sondern von vorne herein leugnet. Das ist bekanntlich genau jene Theorie des Lysias, die Sokrates im *Phaidros* als plump und steril erweisen wird (so plump und unästhetisch, dass er sich während der Nachahmung dieser Rede verhüllt). Aber wichtiger noch: Es geschieht in dieser neoplatonisch-christlich geprägten Rezeption genau das mit der Sexualität, was die Staatsräson in Platons *Nomoi* nur erst den homosexuellen Praktiken vorbehalten hatte: Sie müssen tabuisiert werden und nicht verboten, denn ein Verbot erkennt diskursiv die Existenz dessen an, was durch das Verbot untersagt wird. (Platon, Nomoi 838de) Die Sublimierung dagegen geht anders vor und kennt unterschiedliche Qualitäten.

Wir müssen, wenn wir eine Sublimierungstheorie bei Platon freilegen wollen, die Frage stellen, warum das, was in der philosophisch-literarischen Entwicklung der Erostheorie, wie Platon sie vornehmlich im *Symposion* vornimmt, gleichsam die zu sublimierende Wurzel des Eros darstellt, nämlich das sexuelle Begehren, wieso also gerade dessen Ausblendung das Wesen der „Platonischen Liebe" ausmachen soll. Die Antwort kann auf die bigotten, sexualitätsfeindlichen Intentionen und Kontexte der Instituierung der „platonischen Liebe" verweisen, aber sie kann auch vielschichtiger ausfallen. (Um der Vielschichtigkeit der Texte und des Werks gerecht zu werden, wäre es sogar sinnvoll, auch jene im Geist zu behalten, die in dieser Ausblendungsgeschichte einer spätestens seit Ficino tradierten Platonischen Liebe am Werk ist.)

Jeder Mensch ist ein Gefangener und zugleich ein Beförderter seiner Zeit, manche mehr, manche weniger, und die Brille oder das Interpretament der gesellschaftlich-geschichtlichen Bedeutungen bzw. der begrifflichen Wahrnehmungen zwingt uns im Umgang mit der Vergangenheit notwendig Anachronismen auf, von denen wir, aufgrund von Habitus und mangelnder Hinterfragbarkeit dieser Raster, zumeist gar nichts wissen. Nun gibt es aber – ganz abgesehen vom reflektierenden Bewusstsein des „hermeneutischen Zirkels" – den, diesen Zirkel auch institutionell sprengenden Aspekt des Widerstandes gegen tradierte Rezeptionsmuster, aus dem heraus wir sie durchbrechen, aus dem heraus wir die Widersprüche, die sie im Text entstehen lassen und zugleich verdecken, oft überhaupt erst bemerken. Dadurch vermögen wir neue Fenster auf einen alten Text zu öffnen.

Gegen den tradierten Habitus vermögen wir diesen Durchbruch oft nur, weil wir aus einem gesellschaftlich-politisch geführten Konflikt heraus die Kraft dazu aufbringen, und weil die Widersprüche im Text bzw. seiner Zeit oftmals Analogien aufweisen zu den gegenwärtigen Widersprüchen in der von uns kritisierten Ideologie (sei es die Homophobie, die Frauenfeindlichkeit, die Sexualitätsfeindlichkeit etc.), gegen die wir ebenfalls – politisch, philosophisch, ästhetisch und historisch – Widerstand leisten. Ideologie ist ja nicht nur Rationalisierung oder Verschleierung von Herrschaftsverhältnissen, sie ist immer auch Verschleierung dieser Rationalisierung bzw. Verschleierung selbst, in Geschichte und Gegenwart, und sie ist immer auch mit einer Selbsttäuschung verbunden, die im Werk(en) der Kritik langsam einsehbar wird, insofern der Begriff der Ideologie in der Philosophie immer schon jenen der Ideologiekritik nach sich zieht und umgekehrt.[11]

Erst wenn wir uns historiographisch oder geschichtsphilosophisch mit der Frage nach dem Anachronismus befassen und zum Beispiel das Verbot des Anachronismus analog zur Verneinung in der Psychoanalyse als „Widerstand" betrachten („Sublimierungstheorie ist es *k*eine...", Anachronismus!...), werden wir uns seiner gewahr, begeben uns auf seine Spur (wieso gerade dieser und nicht ein anderer Anachronismus?), und lernen ihn – wenn nötig – zu vermeiden bzw. gezielt einzusetzen. In dieser Bewegung des Erkennens unserer anachronistischen Zugangsweise lernen wir etwas über uns und über die Zeit bzw. den historisch zu uns gekommenen Text. Ein bloßes Anachronismus-Verbot kann so auch als Immunisierungsstrategie zur Aufrechterhaltung eines ideengeschichtlichen Fortschrittsglaubens verstanden werden, der es nicht zulässt, dass manche Begriffe, Theorien oder Begriffsgefüge im Großen und Ganzen schon seit 2500 Jahren vorliegen und erst nach dieser Zeitspanne aufgegriffen und im Zuge einer anderen Neuerung (die Entdeckung des Unbewussten, die Traumdeutung) aktualisiert werden.

---

[11] Man denke nur an Marx' witzigen Untertitel *Die heilige Familie oder Kritik der kritischen Kritik ..." (Marx, 1972)*

Zugleich machen wir bei der Arbeit mit antiken Philosophemen und Philosophien die Erfahrung eines Unbehagens mit gegensätzlichen Deutungen, mit Ausblendungen in Texten und mit den allmählich für uns wahrnehmbaren Widersprüchen, die sich aus diesen Ausblendungen ergeben. Diese Erfahrung des Unbehagens und das Sträuben, das sie nach sich zieht, markiert einen affektiv virulenten Widerstand, macht ihn für uns erkennbar und erlaubt uns eventuell seinen methodologisch sinnvollen Einsatz.

Was sind nun die Widerstände, die sich – durchaus naiv anachronistisch – bei heutigen InterpretInnen einstellen, wenn ihnen die Platonische Erostheorie ohne die traditionelle Weglassung der die Homosexualität und die Bisexualität betreffenden Passagen vorgestellt wird, ohne die übliche Ausblendung oder Trivialisierung der sexuellen Aufgeladenheit der immer wieder kehrenden homoerotischen Topoi in den Dialogen Platons, vom *Protagoras* über den *Theaitetos* zum *Symposion* und anderen? Es sind typische Äußerungen der Entwertung, der Leugnung, der Empörung, an denen wir erkennen, dass wir einen sensiblen Punkt getroffen haben. Nach einem Vortrag über die Bezüge auf Philosopheme Sapphos in Platons *Phaidon*, im *Symposion* und im *Phaidros* (Symposion der International Assocation of Greek Philosophy, Rhodos 2000) wurde diese Bezugnahme seitens einiger Zuhörer_innen schlichtweg in Abrede gestellt, auch nach wiederholter Angabe der Textstelle und Unterstützung durch meine Kollegin Natalie Ernoult, eine Althistorikerin, die ebenfalls zu Platon forscht. Abschießend wurde mir von einem Mann im Publikum vorgeworfen, ich würde „aus unserem Sokrates einen Päderasten machen".

Wieso diese Erzählungen aus der Rezeptionsgeschichte und das Beispiel eines Symposions im Jahr 2000? Diese Episoden helfen mir aufzuzeigen und zu verstehen, dass tradierte Ausblendungen und Verstellungen in der Rezeptionsgeschichte gerade der extrem symbolträchtigen und ideologisch eingesetzten Texte und Philosopheme Platons überhaupt nur durch akute gesellschaftlich-politische Konflikte aufgebrochen werden *können*. Wir müssen die Texte ihrer tradierten politischen Verwendung entreißen, aber wir können nicht beanspruchen, selbst ganz frei von dieser Verwendungsintention zu sein, ja es ist zu erkennen, dass gerade ein politisch-widerständiges Erkenntnisinteresse dem Aufbruch dieser verfestigten Muster dienen kann, vorausgesetzt es wird selbst ideologiekritisch hinterfragt. Auch deshalb scheint mir das Explizit-Machen, die analytische Erhellung der Anachronismen, die wir ohnehin unweigerlich begehen, ebenso wichtig wie die „neo-positivistische" Verankerung in dem, was ich einen „methodologischen Textrealismus" nenne.

Die insbesondere von Ficino an einsetzende Ausblendung von Teilen der Aristophanes-Rede, und zwar von genau jenen brisanten, die männliche wie auch weibliche Homosexualität betreffenden Teilen, ist extrem störend für das Verständnis des Platonischen Eros-Begriffs, weshalb sie umso persistenter behauptet und abgesichert werden muss, so dass die Wiedereingliederung dieser Teile nicht von selbst geschieht.

Es mag sein, dass StudentInnen, die in einer sexuell aufgeklärten und für unterschiedliche Liebesarten offenen Zeit und Gesellschaft leben (hier gibt es gewiss keine Globalgeschichte), den Text unzensuriert lesen und alle Teile der Aristophanes-Rede verstehen, auch in ihrer Rolle als konstituierende Elemente des gesamten platonischen Eros-Begriffs. Doch damit die Ausblendung allgemein benennbar und als solche anerkannt wird, bedarf es eines Konflikts, und dieser Konflikt der Sichtweisen wie auch der gegenläufigen zeitlichen Linearitäten macht den gezielt eingesetzten Anachronismus zu einem unverzichtbaren Element umsichtiger, bisweilen dekonstruktiver Analyse. Zum einen als Unterbrechung, *epochê*, einer illusionären Zeitlosigkeit oder logischen Kontinuität, durch die eine dauerhafte Ausbeldung zentraler Textelemente ideell aufrechterhalten wird, etwa nach dem Motto: „der Platonische Eros ist ewig, er war immer so und er wird immer so sein: a-sexuell, jenseits der Geschlechter, jenseits der Geschlechtlichkeit, die ja stets – zumindest phantasmatisch – auf Fortpflanzung und damit auch auf Sterblichkeit der Lebewesen verweist..." Zum anderen wird der Anachronismus zum Werkzeug, mit dem festgefahrene Entwicklungslinearitäten, die irgendwann in der Rezeptionsgeschichte konstituiert wurden, durchbrochen werden können.

Zurück zu den Elementen der platonischen Erostheorie

Der Eros und die Frage nach Homo-/Hetero-/Bisexualität werden in der *Politeia* und den *Nomoi (Gesetzen)* nicht untersucht, sondern propagandistisch be- bzw. entwertet. Der Eros wird in der *Politeia* als Tyrann beschrieben, der die Bürger vom rechten Weg abbringt (dem des Gehorsams und der Unterwerfung unter die Vernunft-Herrschaft der Philosoph_innen), in den *Nomoi* geht es um die im Sinne der politischen Einhelligkeit möglichst wirksame Tabuisierung der homosexuellen Praktiken. Dagegen wird der Eros im *Symposion* gewürdigt, und je differenzierter und philosophischer die Reden, desto expliziterer wird die Darstellung aller Formen des Eros. Geschlechtsspezifische Arbeitsteilung findet ebenso Erwähnung wie die Anatomie der Geschlechts- oder besser der Schamteile (insbesondere die Rede des Aristophanes kann hier auch wie ein witziger Aufklärungsversuch gelesen werden); die Rede der Diotima reicht vom impliziten politischen Tabu der Homosexualität über dessen Wendung in eine geistige Zeugung, die dann philosophische *poiêsis* wird nach dem Vorbild von „Sapphos unsterblichen Kindern". Die Rettung des (homophilen) Eros in der Sublimierung geht einher mit der allmählichen Ausblendung der (Homo)Sexualität als Stamm des männlich-homophilen Eros, nachdem dieser leibliche „Stamm" in den vorhergehenden Reden besungen, gewürdigt bzw. im abschließenden Auftritt des Alkibiades in seiner Ambivalenz gefeiert und zugleich auf Distanz gehalten wird, in der Person des geliebten (ermoneos) Sokrates und als gefährliches Phänomen, das den narzisstischen Politiker (fast) zu Fall bringt.

Die Triebtheorie Freuds und das, was ich – bewusst anachronistisch – als die Triebtheorie Platons bezeichne, stehen in Wechselwirkung zueinander. Sie tun dies nicht losgelöst, für sich stehend, sondern in einer nicht nur zeitlich verwobenen Rezeptionsgeschichte, in der Rezeption einmal mehr als Erinnerung *sui generis* die Autor(inn)en bzw. ihre Texte assimiliert oder gar berufsdogmatisch verzerrt, dann wieder möglichst akkurat philosophiehistorisch arbeitet, in zahlreichen Durchläufen („Wiederholen und Durcharbeiten") zwischen Vergangenheit und Gegenwart hin und her gehend, bis das je begonnene Puzzle (hier die widersprüchlichen Erostheorien bei Platon) allmählich zu einem zusammenhängenden Begriffsbild wird.

Ich komme abschließend zu einem zentralen Punkt in der Verbindung der Elemente in beiden Sublimierungstheorien, nämlich zur Beziehung zwischen Eros und Thanatos. Er gibt dem Anachronismus einer Platon-Lektüre ausgehend von Freud, der sich auf *Platon* bezog, erst seinen vollen Sinn. Denn erst die Dialektik von Eros und Thanatos und die Frage nach dem Weiterleben in den leiblichen (= sterblichen) oder in den „unsterblichen Kindern" macht die Sublimierung sowohl bei Platon als auch bei Freud aus.

Die Sublimierungstheorie ist Reflexion nicht nur über den Eros, sondern auch über die Angst, Angst vor dem Tod, dem Verschwinden im Eros bzw. in der Unlust nicht erwiderter Liebe, dem Verschwinden im anderen, dem Verschwinden aus dem Leben; „aus den Augen - aus dem Sinn" ist ein Diktum, mit dem wir oftmals die Liebestrauer für abgeschlossen erklären wollen, ohne zu bemerken, dass dieser Abschluss erst gelungen ist, wenn wir im Ansichtig-Werden des ehemals geliebten Wesens keinen Schmerz mehr verspüren.

Ich hoffe nachvollziehbar gemacht zu haben, dass die Brüche in der aktuellen Wahrnehmung oder Konzeption von Problemen (hier und jetzt) ein neues Licht werfen auf alte Brüche und Konflikte (damals und dort): Geschlecht/Eros/Sex, Geburt/Tod, Eros/Thanatos, Hetero-/Bi-/Homosexualität im Sublimierungsgefüge, in dem alle Elemente einander in ihrer Konflikthaftigkeit bedingen.

Bibliographie

classics@: An online journal, Volume 7 : Les femmes, le féminin et le politique après Nicole Loraux, eds. The Center for Hellenic Studies of Harvard University, online edition of July 2011, 15 S.
http://chs.harvard.edu/CHS/article/display/3369 (Juni 2015).
Benjamin, Walter. Das Passagen Werk, hg. von R. Thiedemann. Frankfurt/M.: Suhrkamp, 1983.
Flasch, Kurt. Philosophie hat Geschichte, Band 1: Historische Philosophie. Beschreibung einer Denkart. Frankfurt/M.: Vittorio Klostermann, 2003.
Kelsen, Hans. „Die platonische Liebe". In: Imago, XIX, 1933, Heft 1, 35-98.
Marx, Karl. „Die heilige Familie oder Kritik der kritischen Kritik gegen Bruno Bauer und Konsorten". In: Marx Karl, Engels Friedrich, Werke Band 2, (MEW) Berlin 1972, 3 – 223.
Pechriggl, Alice. Utopiefähigkeit und Veränderung. Pfaffenweiler: Centaurus, 1993.
Pechriggl, Alice. „Wie un/dogmatisch ist Kelsens Platon? Drei Annäherungen an *Die Illusion der Gerechtigkeit*". In: Walser Robert, Jabloner Cle-

mens, Zeleny Klaus (H.), Griechische Philosophie im Spiegel Hans Kelsens. Wien: Manz, 2006, 31 – 49.

Pechriggl, Alice. Eros. Stuttgart: UTB, 2009 (a).

Pechriggl, Alice. Chiasmen. Antike Philosophie von Platon zu Sappho – von Sappho zu uns. Bielefeld: transcript, 2009 (b).

Platon. Sämtliche Werke gr. dt. nach d. Übers. V. F. Schleiermacher, ergänzt, hg. v. Karlheinz Hülser. Frankfurt / Main und Leipzig: Insel 1991.

Tamboukou, Maria. „Truth telling in Foucault and Arendt: Parrhesia, the Pariah and Academics in Dark Times". In: Journal of Education Policy, 27 (6) 2012, 849 – 865.

https://www.academia.edu/1838068/_2012_Truth_telling_in_Foucault_an d_Arendt_Parrhesia_the_Pariah_and_Academics_in_Dark_Times._Journal_o f_Education_Policy_27_6_849-865.doi_abs_10.1080_02680939.2012.694482 (Juni 2015)

Vlastos, Gregory. Studies in Greek Philosophy, Vol. II: Socrates, Plato and Their Tradition, edited by Daniel W. Graham, Princeton University Press, 1995.

EDIT ANNA LUKÁCS

DAS WISSEN GOTTES IN DER THEOLOGISCHEN LEHRE AN DER UNIVERSITÄT WIEN (1385-C. 1420): SKIZZE EINES FORSCHUNGSPROJEKTS BEGLEITET VON DER EDITION EINES DISPUTATION-FRAGMENTS

Als sich die Lehrenden der Universität Wien am Ausgang des 14. Jahrhunderts für den Kompatibilismus einschlägig die zukünftigen kontingenten Dinge entschieden haben, wussten sie nicht, dass diese These bis in die Modernität prägend wirken wird (Marenbon 2005, 14). Sie waren schlechthin bemüht, sowohl den unfehlbaren Charakter des Wissens Gottes als auch die Freiheit des menschlichen Willens miteinander zu vereinbaren. Die Zwanghaftigkeit einer solchen Stellungnahme besaß ihre Wurzel anderswo als an der frisch gegründeten Universität Wien. Viele den orthodoxen Glauben in Frage stellende Bekenntnisse über das Wissen Gottes wurden an der Universität Oxford in den 1330er-Jahren formuliert (Genest 1992, 33-60; Schabel 2000, 223-258). Als Heinrich Totting von Oyta und Heinrich Langenstein nach ihren Pariser Studien die Theologische Fakultät in Wien gegründet haben (Uiblein 1963; derselbe 1999) und zu lehren anfingen, entstand diese tatsächlich als eine neue, ins komplexe Wissensnetzwerk der beiden einflussreichsten Universitäten Oxford und Paris eingebundene Entität.

Folglich waren die ersten Lehrenden der Universität Wien Gründer, Fortsetzer und Erneurer. Über diese Einstellungen hinaus besaßen sie noch eine Ursprünglichkeit: das einheitliche Bekenntnis bestimmter Thesen, so dass in der Forschung oft von einer „Wiener Schule" (Hohmann 1977; Prügl 2009) die Rede ist. Konkret bedeutete dies nicht nur die akademisch-gemeinschaftliche Profess mancher Thesen, sondern die quasi-Kommutativität des Unterrichtsmaterials, insbesondere der *Sentenzenkommentare*, an der Theologischen Fakultät, das von Jahr zu Jahr, von Autor zu Autor verglichen nur winzige individuelle Abweichungen aufweist (Courtenay im Druck). Noch konkreter heißt das, dass dieselbe akademische Schrift in verschiedenen Handschriften von unterschiedlichen Lehrenden unterzeichnet vorkommen kann.

74

Diese "gemeinsame" Doktrin, ihre Bildung und Inhalte haben vor allem Historiker in der zweiten Hälfte des 20. Jahrhunderts beschäftigt; es wurde aber, außer einiger Monographien (Shank 1988, Steneck 1976), kaum analysierendes Interesse dem Forschungsobjekt geschenkt. Jedoch gibt es derzeit eine Zuwendung zu den Anfängen der Universität Wien (Brinzei-Schabel 2015, Schabel im Druck). Das FWF Projekt V356 "Oxforder Theologie des 14. Jahrhunderts an der Universität Wien: Die Doktrin des göttlichen Wissens zwischen 1384 und ca. 1420" fügt sich in dieses Wiederaufleben ein, indem es sich mit einer zentralen Problematik des ausgehenden Mittelalters – der Vollkommenheit des Wissens Gottes – in ihren internen und externen Zusammenhängen beschäftigen will.

Inhalt (1): Das Wissen Gottes, 14. Jahrhundert

Die Kultursprache, zugleich die akademische Sprache des Mittelalters, das Latein besaß verschiedene Wörter zur Benennung des Wissen: (1) *scientia* (Wissen(schaft)); (2) *cognitio* (Erkenntnis); (3) *notitia* ((Grund)Kenntnis). Alle drei Wörter, mit kleinen Unterschieden, wurden für Gott verwendet. Die Tatsache, dass das Wissen als Erfahren, als Wahrhaft-Erkennen grundsätzlich ein Habitus ist und als solcher zwecklos im Falle Gottes wäre, wurde im Christentum nicht thematisiert. Zu wissen war eine bei Gott und Menschen eindeutig geteilte Aktivität, die für Gott in der Bibel mehrfach behauptet wurde (Schmutz 2002, 1295).

Die heftigsten Auseinandersetzungen um das göttliche Wissen fanden zweifellos im 14. Jh. statt, als die Stellungnahmen rund um den Mittelpunkt des mittelalterlichen Wissens, Gott und sein eigenes Wissen, mehrere Bereiche der Theologie anrührten. Die Debatten stellten nicht nur den Begriff des Wissens Gottes in Frage, sondern die Ethik der menschlichen Handlungen, die Christologie, die in der Bibel und im Koran niedergeschriebene Wahrheit, die gesprochene und geträumte Wahrheit – die Wahrheit überhaupt. Diese verschiedenen theologischen Problemlagen können unterschiedlichen philosophischen Bereichen zugeordnet werden (Michon 2004, 10): Metaphysik, Sprachlogik, Epistemologie, Ethik, Anthropologie.

Das Wissen Gottes wurde an und für sich und bezüglich der Welt hinterfragt. Der "erstes Wissen" genannte Teil des Wissens Gottes war mit Gott selbst beschäftigt: Was für einen Ideengehalt, welche Eigenschaften müssen dem ersten Wissen von Gott zugeschrieben werden? Welchen Status besitzt das Wissen Gottes über sich selbst in seinem Wissen? Diese rein theoretischen Fragen wurden über die Welt weiter konjugiert, oft als ein Unterschied der christlichen zur arabischen Philosophie: Kann/muss Gott eine Idee von den einzelnen Dingen und Geschehnissen der Welt besitzen, oder teilt dies die substantielle Einheit seines Wissens auf? Stünde die Beschäftigung mit "sekundären Ursachen" im Gegensatz zur Vollkommenheit Gottes? Sobald die Kenntnis von weltlichen Dingen und Geschehnissen Gott zugeschrieben wurde, entstanden weitere Schwierigkeiten: Ist Gottes Wissen von temporären Dingen ewig oder temporär? Wenn ewig, werden die Dinge selbst ewige Existenz besitzen. Wenn temporär, wird Gottes Wissen parallel zu dem des Menschen gestellt, d.h. herabgestuft, unvollkommen, in Antinomie mit dem Wesen des denkenden Subjekts. Eine für das 14. Jahrhundert spezifische Entwicklung betraf die im göttlichen Verstand anwesenden Ideen. Infolge des Universalienstreits hat der Nominalismus (Wilhelm von Ockham, Gregor von Rimini, u. a.) den Ideen ihre Vermittlerrolle im kognitiven Prozess weggenommen, sie aus dem göttlichen Verstand entfernt, und schlechthin als individuell Existierende positioniert. Diese Auffassung hat ein neues epistemologisches Modell generiert, wo Gott keine schöpferische Rolle der einzelnen Dinge via die Ideen besitzt. Folglich verfügen Gott und Mensch über exakt dasselbe kognitive Vermögen (Schmutz 2002, 1296-1297).

Die hier geschilderten Positionen skizzieren die Schwierigkeiten, auf die mittelalterliche Denker gestoßen sind, als sie Vergängliches und Ewiges, Universales und Individuelles miteinander zu verbinden, bzw. überhaupt ein vollkommenes Wissen zu denken versuchten. Diese generellen Problematiken wurden in Oxford noch zugespitzter diskutiert.

Inhalt (2): Das Wissen Gottes, Oxford, 14. Jahrhundert

Den Auftakt zum 14. Jahrhundert in Oxford bildete die In-Frage-Stellung des notwendigen Charakters der Vergangenheit (Gelber 2004). Als Wilhelm von Ockham das Wissen Gottes über kontingente Ereignisse unschlüssig dargestellt hat, wurde die Debatte auf die

Zukunft angewandt (Perler 1988[a] und 1988[b]). Alle uns heute mehr oder weniger bekannte Oxforder Denker dieser Periode haben sich mit den Begriffen des Wissens, der Freiheit und der Notwendigkeit auseinandergesetzt: Thomas Bradwardine (Leff 1957), Wilhelm Crathorn, Richard FitzRalph (Dunne, Nolan 2013), Robert Holcot, Thomas Buckingham (Genest 1992), Richard Kilvington, Adam Wodeham (Courtenay 1978).

Ockhams genannter Lehrsatz hat unvermeidlich den Weg für eine Reihe von theologisch undogmatischen Stellungnahmen eröffnet. Diesen unterliegt eine bipolare Matrix des Wissens Gottes: Gott besitzt weiterhin ein bestimmtes, notwendiges Wissen über die vergangenen und die gegenwärtigen Sachen, aber ein unbestimmtes Wissen über zukünftige Sachbestände. Diese Matrix wird bei Thomas Bradwardine umgewandelt: Gott besitzt bestimmtes Wissen über vergangene und zukünftige Dinge, aber ein unbestimmtes über gegenwärtige. Die *subtilitates anglicanae* – das Idiom kommt im *Philobiblon* des Richard de Bury vor – bezeichnen die theologischen Konsequenzen, die sich aus der Kontingenz des Wissens Gottes über künftige menschliche Handlungen ableiten lassen: 1. die göttliche Täuschung (*deceptio divina* bei FitzRalph, Wodeham, Holcot); 2. die Rechtfertigung im falschen Glauben (*in fide falsa* bei FitzRalph, Wodeham, Holcot); 3. die Verdammung im richtigen Glauben (*in credulitate vera* bei FitzRalph, Holcot, Wodeham); 4. der täuschende oder getäuschte Christ – FitzRalph, Holcot; 5. die Unmöglichkeit der Offenbarung im Christ (*in Verbo* bei FitzRalph, Bradwardine) (Genest 1992, 44-48). Zwei von diesen Thesen, 1 und 4, haben ausschließlich mit Gottes Wissen oder mit Gottes Wissen als Trinität zu tun; die anderen lassen eine Beziehung Gottes zum Geschöpf vermuten.

Diese „Klügeleien" zeigen im Hintergrund nicht wie weitgehend inoffizielle Stellungnahmen an den Universitäten erfunden werden konnten, sondern einfach die Tatsache, dass in einer Argumentation die logischen Konsequenzen gezogen werden mussten, auch wenn diese absurd, kontradiktorisch oder theologisch unorthodox waren. Diese Thesen müssen folglich als mächtiger Erfolg der akademischen Praktiken an der Universität Oxford, insbesondere der Disputation (Lukács im Druck) betrachtet werden.

Inhalt (3): das Wissen Gottes, Wien, 14.-15. Jahrhundert

Die Universität Wien wurde im Jahr 1365 gegründet, und 1384 mit einer Theologischen Fakultät ausgestattet neu ins Leben gerufen (Lenzenweger 1984). Zwischen 1365 und 1384 wurde an der Universität nur ein Curriculum für Artisten angeboten, was ungefähr der heutigen Ausbildung an der Philosophischen Fakultät entspricht. Was und von wem wurde zu dieser Zeit an der Universität Wien unterrichtet? Die Universitätsakten dieser Periode sind lückenhaft, daher bleiben unsere Informationen auch sehr sparsam. Albert von Sachsen (Berger 2010) tritt als die erste wichtigste Persönlichkeit der Artistenfakultät hervor, von dem eine bedeutende Anzahl von aristotelischen Kommentaren erhalten ist, gefolgt von Conrad von Rothenburg und Iodocus Gossolt.

Von den zum Großteil der Sprachlogik und der Philosophie der Natur gewidmeten Schriften der Wiener Universitätslehrer wurden nur die Ethikkommentare eingehender studiert (Flüeler 2004, Ders. 2008). Die philosophischen Werke aus der Frühzeit der Fakultät weisen eindringlich auf eine Besonderheit hin: Eine Mehrzahl von philosophischen *quaestiones*, Kommentaren, Vorlesungen (*lectura*), Noten (*puncta*), Glossen, Auslegungen (*expositio*) wurde anonym, nur Wien als Ort nennend überliefert (Markowski 2000). Die hohe Anzahl dieser *opera Wiennensia* – um 150 – lässt sich durch die mittelalterliche Häufigkeit anonymer Überlieferung nicht erklären. Die Tendenz könnte als spezifisch für Wien, als eine Neigung zum Teilen des Wissens, der Doktrin, der Schriften identifiziert werden, eine Neigung, die die Wiener Philosophen mit den Theologen gemeinsam besessen haben sollen.

Mit der Einrichtung der Theologischen Fakultät wird an Information über die Geschehnisse in den Wänden der Universität gewonnen, auch wenn dem Unterricht und der intellektuellen Aktivität erst ab dem Jahr 1396 vollständiger nachgefolgt werden kann. In den für das theologische Curriculum produzierten akademischen Schriften, vornehmlich in den systematische Theologie ergründenden *Sentenzenkommentaren* verliert wohl die Philosophie an Gesamtgewicht, gewisse philosophisch-theologische Sachverhalte werden aber umfangreicher, bis zu ihren weitreichenden Konsequenzen ausgeführt. Das mag der Grund dafür sein, dass sie in der aktuellen Forschung sogar von

78

den Philosophiehistorikern den Aristoteles-Kommentaren der Artistenfakultät bevorzugt werden.

In den *Sentenzenkommentaren* der ersten zwei Generationen Wiener Universitätslehrer kann viel Interesse am Wissen Gottes nachgewiesen werden. Diese Kommentare waren im 14. Jahrhundert bereits aus Fragen zusammengesetzt, anhand derer die ursprünglich in vier Bücher geteilte Lehre von Peter Lombard diskutiert wurde. Die zehnte Frage zum Buch I der *Sentenzen* des Pariser, Prager und darauf Wiener Universitätstheologen Heinrich Totting von Oyta widmet sich der Kontingenz der Zukunft und deren Wissen bei Gott: "Ob das Zustandekommen eines kontingenten, künftigen Ereignisses mit dem Vorwissen Gottes und einer gesonderten, dem Geschöpf die Zukunft enthüllenden Offenbarung vereinbar ist". Oyta verteidigt in dieser Frage den bereits erwähnten Kompatibilismus, der schematisch wie folgt dargestellt werden kann:

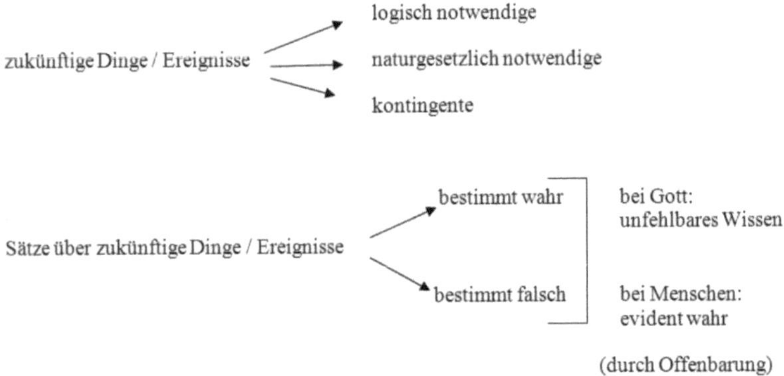

Oyta legt außerdem viel Gewicht auf die Einheit und Einfachheit des göttlichen Wissens, eine Position, die in den anonymen Disputationen der Theologischen Fakultät auch vorkommt. Oytas These richtet sich ausdrücklich gegen Thomas Bradwardines Aufteilung des göttlichen Wissens (Bradwardine 1618, 220-224; Ders. 2013, 139-144). Außerdem zitiert er umfangreicher Adam Wodeham; erwähnt Thomas Buckingham, Walter Burley, Richard Kilvington und weitere Oxforder Autoren. Die Auflistung der bei Oyta angeführten Referenzen bestätigt die Beschäftigung mit zeitgenössischen Autoren. Unter den zitierten

Autoritäten erscheinen die Oxforder Theologen als fiktive Diskussionspartner *par excellence*.

Eine partielle Übernahme und Fortsetzung dieses Kommentarstücks des Heinrich Totting von Oyta bildet die der "Wiener Gruppe" zugeschriebene "Frage über das Vorwissen Gottes über kontingent zukünftige Ereignisse" (Schabel im Druck). Nikolaus Dinkelsbühl, Johannes Berwart von Villingen und Peter Czech von Pulkau, die drei Autoren kopieren sogar Sätze mit Prädikaten in der ersten Person Singular von ihren Vorgängern, Heinrich Totting von Oyta und Heinrich Langenstein, erweitern zugleich ihre philosophischen Thesen, ohne den Lehrsatz umfassend zu ändern. Die Beurteilung von Thomas Bradwardine hat sich beispielsweise verwandelt: Bradwardine wird nicht nur negativ, sondern auch positiv dargestellt. Was heißt genau dieser Wechsel für die Substanz der Doktrin? Die subtilen Änderungen in der Einschätzung der Autoritäten und der These, die nicht immer gleichzustellen sind, bilden eine spannungsvolle Perspektive für die Untersuchung des Wissenstransfers- und der Wissensbildung an der Universität Wien.

An der Theologischen Fakultät gingen den *Sentenzenkommen-taren* die Bibelkommentare im akademischen Curriculum voraus und wurden im Laufe des ganzen Curriculums von der Aktivität der Disputation begleitet. Während die disputierten Fragen zunehmend als Entwürfe gewisser, später in den *Sentenzenkommentaren* desselben Autors behandelter Fragen betrachtet werden und daher zu einem philosophisch-theologischen Forschungsgegenstand wurden, werden Bibelkommentare für philosophische Zwecke nur sehr selten gelesen. Trotzdem eignet sich die Gattung der spätmittelalterlichen Bibelkommentare durch ihren Gewinn an Breite der darin erwogenen Themen für eine philosophisch-theologische Analyse, und zwar auch für ihre Diskussionen des Wissens Gottes.

Der berühmteste Wiener Bibelkommentar wurde von Heinrich Langenstein zur Genesis verfasst. In diesem umfangreichen Kommentar – ungefähr 300 Seiten – diskutiert der Autor nicht nur Themen aus der Kosmologie, der Astronomie oder der Biologie (Steneck 1976), sondern auch das Wissen Gottes. Langenstein widmet dem Problem der kontingent zukünftigen Dinge eine umfangreiche Diskussion, in der er wie sein akademischer Genosse Oyta die Kontingenz der Zukunft und die Notwendigkeit der Vergangenheit verteidigt, den Begriff

80

eines getäuschten Christus aber, den er bei Robert Holcot gefunden hat, verwirft (ÖNB Cod. 3902, 176^v-184^r).

Das Wissen Christi bildet ein bedeutendes Filialgebiet des Wissens Gottes, das man vornehmlich in den Bibelkommentaren bzw. in den Kommentaren zu den Evangelien und den Paulusbriefen findet. Ein Beispiel solcher Diskussionen wird im Matthäuskommentar von Nikolaus Dinkelsbühl (Madre 1965, 52-62) ermittelt. Die Abschrift der Vorlesungen, die Dinkelsbühl über das Matthäusevangelium gehalten hat, bildet eine Mischung aus Kommentar und systematischer Diskussion in Form von Fragen. Was das Wissen Gottes angeht, schlägt Dinkelsbühl eine Fünfteilung vor (ÖNB Cod. 4397, 224^r):

1. einfaches Wissen (*simplicis notitia*),
2. das Wissen durch Sicht – Gottesschau (*notitia visionis*),
3. das Vorwissen (*praescientia*),
4. das verneinende Wissen (*notitia reprobationis*),
5. das bejahende Wissen (*notitia approbationis*).

Das Wissen Christi wird hingegen in vier Teile zerstückelt (ebenda 235^r-238^v):

1. das göttliche Wissen (*scientia divina*),
2. das Wissen durch Sicht – Gottesschau (*scientia visionis*),
3. das „eingeflößte Wissen" – eingegossene Erkenntnis (*scientia infusa*), und
4. das menschliche Wissen – Erfahrung (*scientia humanitatis*).

Diese zwei Schemen, bei Dinkelsbühl auch kurz gefasst, müssen eindringlicher analysiert werden. Während Gottes Wissen selbst mit *notitia* repräsentiert wird und nur sein Vorwissen *scientia* ist, besteht das Wissen Christi ausschließlich aus *scientia*. Was bedeuten diese Unterschiede? Warum wurde die traditionelle Dreiteilung des Wissens Christi (Ernst 1971) durch das göttliche Wissen erweitert? In welchem Verhältnis steht diese Kategorisierung zur Konzeptualisierung des Wissens Gottes in den weitbekannten *Sentenzenkommentaren* von Dinkelsbühl und zur Einfachheit des Wissens Gottes bei Heinrich Totting von Oyta? Die Struktur der göttlichen Noetik muss nicht nur als eine Frage des Wissenstransfers zwischen Universitäten, sondern auch zwischen Generationen von Theologen, bzw. nicht zuletzt als individuell ausgearbeitete Thesensammlung erfasst werden.

Die in dieser und anderer Hinsicht auch unerforschten Bibelkommentare der Wiener Schule bilden die offenste, kontingenteste Zukunft der Erforschung der Doktrin des Wissens Gottes.

Inhalt (4): Disputationen an der Universität Wien anhand eines Beispiels

Wie bereits erwähnt, hat die Aktivität der öffentlichen Fragestellung und Ausführung – der Disputation – das Curriculum an der Theologischen Fakultät in seiner ganzen Länge begleitet. Man nahm an Disputationen bereits als Bachelor im Publikum teil; man disputierte, um den Doktorgrad zu erwerben (*actus vesperiarum*); man disputierte als Lehrer bzw. Professor während des ganzen akademischen Jahres weiter. Man stellte Fragen (*quaestiones*) über beliebige Themen (*de quolibet*); als Kandidat auf den Meistergrad musste man beliebige Fragen der Assistenz beantworten können; man hat sowohl die Bibel als auch die Sentenzen in Form von Fragen analysiert: Im ausgehenden Mittelalter ist die Frageform in alle Lehrformen insbesondere im Bereich der Theologie eingedrungen, ohne die Doktrin, die offiziellen Thesen, die orthodoxen Glaubenssätze kritisch in Frage zu stellen.

Die Fragestellung war also als erstes eine Form (Weijers 2013, 159-164), die in den Statuten der Universität Wien für beide Fakultäten der Humanwissenschaften, der Artisten und der Theologen, explizit gefördert wurde (Kink 1854, 80-127 und 213-220). Als zweites rahmte die Fragestellung unterschiedliche Lehrinhalte ein. Es konnte das schwierige Unterrichtsmaterial am Nachmittag eingehender als im Laufe des Kommentierens am Vormittag diskutiert werden, während die vom Lehrer nicht angesprochenen Themen auch frei (*de quolibet*) zur Diskussion gestellt werden konnten. Beide Typen von Fragen sind in handschriftlicher Überlieferung erhalten, von der der Großteil in der Österreichischen Nationalbibliothek zu finden ist (Courtenay 2011).

Der Codex 4503 der Österreichischen Nationalbibliothek ist eine Handschrift, die ursprünglich dem gleichzeitig mit der Theologischen Fakultät gegründeten Collegium ducale gehört hat. Das Collegium ducale bot Unterkunft für Professoren und Raum für den akademischen Unterricht und besaß außerdem eine Bibliothek (Aschbach 39-40). Handschriften, die ehemals dem Collegium ducale gehört haben und sich derzeit im Besitz der Österreichischen Nationalbibliothek befinden, enthalten vornehmlich Unterrichtsmaterial von der und für die Universität Wien. Im Codex 4503 gibt es drei Schriften, die ihrem Titel nach mit der Universität Wien, zwei davon explizit mit dem Collegium ducale zu verbinden sind. Es handelt sich um Predigten, die zwischen 1424 und 1431 an der Universität Wien gehalten wurden (159^r-301^v); um zwei Reden (*vocatio*), die im Collegium ducale vorgetragen wurden (121^r-127^r); und um im Collegium ducale gehaltene Disputationen (10^r-120^v und 127^v-150^v). Vermutlich haben die Disputationen auch wie die Predigten in den 1420er-Jahren stattgefunden. Vor und nach den zwei Reden (121^r-127^r) sind zwei Reihen von Quaestiones eingelegt, von denen die eine fünfunddreißig (10^r-120^v), die andere elf Fragen (127^v-150^v) enthält.

Die längere Liste (Anhang 1) gibt ein detailliertes Bild von den Themen, die die Theologen wahrscheinlich mehrere Jahre hindurch beschäftigt haben. Die Moraltheologie nimmt den ersten Platz ein, gefolgt von der systematischen Theologie, insbesondere der Soteriologie und von der Sakramentenlehre. Die Trinitätslehre und die Christologie mit jeweils einer Frage sind darunter kaum von Bedeutung. Die moraltheologischen Fragen, auf Sünde und Verdienste konzentriert, bilden eine für die Zeit der hussitischen Reformbewegungen charakteristische Sammlung. Die die systematische Theologie betreffenden Fragen sind konsequent auf die Beziehung Gott-Mensch eingestellt und häufig mit Freiheit und Notwendigkeit beschäftigt. Beispielsweise:

Frage (3): Ob der freie Wille die gleiche Einstellung auf das Gute und das Böse besitzt.

Frage (4): Ob Gottes ewige Bestimmung (*dispositio*) für die zu schöpfenden äußeren Dinge zwingend sein kann.

Frage (7): Ob Gottes potentielle Omnipräsenz zwingend seine wesentliche Omnipräsenz erwirkt.

Frage (26): Ob Gott in seiner tatsächlichen Abhängigkeit von der Schöpfung alle Geschöpfe als Ideen umschließt.

Frage (33): Ob es möglich ist, dass der zum Schutz des Menschen bestellte Engel ihn in seinem aufgenommenen Körper schützt.

Ein weiteres Beispiel zum Ansatz der theologischen Probleme unter dem doppelten Gesichtspunkt von Gott und der Welt schildert die Rationalität Gottes in der Inkarnation. Die Frage 24 aus ÖNB Cod. 4503 illustriert genau dieses Interesse: „Ob das für die Erneuerung des menschlichen Geschlechts zu Mensch gewordene Wort Gottes in der suppositalen Einheit (*in unitate suppositi*) das irrationale Geschöpf hätte aufnehmen können". Der unten (Anhang 2) transkribierte Text dieser disputierten Frage bildet ein Fragment in zweierlei Hinsicht. Einerseits enthält es nur die These derjenigen Person, die auf die Frage antwortet (*respondens*), und nicht die ihres Gegners (*opponens*). In den meisten schriftlich erhaltenen Quaestiones kommt nur der eine Teil vor, was im Vergleich zur mündlichen Praxis des binären, von einem Meister regulierten Disputierens zum Verlust der Lebhaftigkeit der Debatte führt. Andererseits werden die Argumente nicht entfaltet, nur skizziert; und es werden keine Autoritäten zitiert.

Die inhaltliche Relevanz der Frage 24 ist doppelt gestuft. Zum einen wird die Möglichkeit einer Inkarnation Christi als irrationales Geschöpf hinterfragt. Die Potentialität der Inkarnation war über die anderen Personen der Dreifaltigkeit (Warum ist nicht eher der Vater oder der Heilige Geist zu Mensch geworden?) bzw. über Frauen (Hätte Christus als Frau geboren werden können?) bereits konjugiert, und zwar seit den *Sentenzen* des Peter Lombard (Buch III, Dist. 1, Kapitel 6 und 2). Die Kühnheit der Wiener Frage liegt in der Potentialität einer Einigung Gottes mit einem irratonalen Geschöpf und damit in der Verlegung der Grenzen der irdisch-göttlichen Verwirklichung. Zum anderen wird hier die Ausgewogenheit der Befreiung problematisiert: Kann das menschliche Geschlecht durch einen zum Unmenschen gewordenen Gott auch erlöst werden? Die Antwort zielt auf eine solche Möglichkeit. Es stellt keinen Gegensatz zum Wesen Gottes dar, dass er ein irrationales Geschöpf bekleidet. Die Bezugnahme auf die Allmacht Gottes (*omnipotentia*) und das Ausschließen des inneren Widerspruchs (*contradictio*) charakterisieren jede theologische Argumentation, die sich mit rein theoretischen oder imaginären Themen auseinandersetzt.

Nach der Formulierung der These-Antwort folgen zwei Korollare. Der erste Korollar trifft eine Unterscheidung zwischen „seligmachender" Union (*unio sanctificativa*), die aufgrund der Gnade, der Erkenntnis und der Liebe besteht, und der hypostatischen oder personalen Union (*unio hypostatica*) Gottes mit dem Geschöpf in der Person Christi. Die hypostatische Union ist implizit mit der suppositalen Vereinigung gleichzusetzen. Der erste Union-Typ soll wertvoller sein, weil es das Geschöpf mit Gott verbindet, während der zweite Typ das nicht notwendigerweise tut (Lang 1966, 85-90). Dementsprechend kann die suppositale Union Gott mit dem irrationalen Geschöpf verbinden, weil die „seligmachende" Union das rationale Geschöpf mit Gott vollkommen verbinden kann. Der zweite Korollar entwirft eine weitere Matrix: Für Gott ist es möglich, sich mit der rationalen, ohne Erkenntnis und Liebe bestehenden Natur zu einigen, nicht aber mit der ohne Gnade bestehenden Natur, d.h. mit dem Sündenstand. Diese Schlussfolgerung wird dann reduzierter wieder gedeutet. Der Autor differenziert Gottes Einigung mit der menschlichen Natur, der einzeln unterschiedliche Gründe unterliegen, und separat auch erwirkt werden können.

Diese Quaestio definiert dementsprechend die Voraussetzungen der Erlösung des Menschen und reziprok dazu die äußeren Grenzen des göttlichen Wesens neu. Die Wurzeln dieses Wandels sind in der Christologie des Heinrich von Langenstein bereits vorhanden (ebenda), nur gewinnen hier die Schlussfolgerungen durch eine potentielle Vergangenheit (eine andere Erlösungsgeschichte) an Gewicht. Die Rationalität soll nicht mehr eine maßgebliche Rolle in der Inkarnation spielen: Hätte sich Gott als irrationales Geschöpf verwirklicht, wäre seine Rationalität nicht eingebüßt. Die noetischen Implikationen einer solchen Stellungnahme sind verschiedenartig: die gegenseitige Isolation der göttlichen und menschlichen Rationalität bzw. Erkenntnis, da es keine Menschwerdung Gottes gibt, und, so frappant es sein mag, die Annäherung des göttlichen Wesens an die Irrationalität. Die Relevanz dieser Wiener Frage erkennt man nicht zuletzt, sondern perspektivenmäßig, im Hintergrund des ausgehenden Mittelalters.

Methode und Projektziele

Das FWF-Projekt V356 "Oxforder Theologie des 14. Jahrhunderts an der Universität Wien: Die Doktrin des göttlichen Wissens zwischen 1384 und ca. 1420" setzt sich zum Ziel, die Diskussionen über das Wissen Gottes im Unterricht an der jungen Theologischen Fakultät der Universität Wien zu erforschen und als Tradition, Wandel bzw. Innovation zu begreifen. Auf welchen Gewinn hofft man bei einem so stufenartigen, langsamen Vorgehen, das das Arbeiten mit Katalogen, Handschriften und Abschriften annehmen lässt, außer einer Archäologie des Wissens im doppelten Sinne des Wortes?

Die Randgewinne, die durch dieses Projekt in verschiedenen Bereichen (Theologie, Philosophie, Geschichte) erwartet werden, besitzen tatsächlich einen archäologischen Charakter: Wissenstransfer zwischen Universitäten und zwischen zwei Generationen von Wissenschaftlern, Charakteristika des Unterrichts an der jungen Universität Wien, philologische Daten zu Handschriften. Ohne in die Falle einer modernisierenden Analyse der mittelalterlichen Tatbestände zu geraten (Marenbon 2005, 163-170), ist es immerhin nicht uninteressant und irrelevant, zusammenfassend auch einige zeitgenössische Interessen in Bezug auf die oben skizzierten Themen zu pointieren, um die Idee einer mittelalterlichen Isolation der Problematik noch einmal auszuschließen.

Zwei Aspekte des Projekts können in diesem Zusammenhang genannt werden: die Sprachlogik und die möglichen Welten. Der eine Aspekt, die Anwendung der Sprachlogik in der Theologie, war bei den Oxforder Autoren des 14. Jh. besonders prägend. Ihren Einfluss auf die Wiener Akademiker zu beobachten oder einfach die Anwendung der Sprachlogik bei den Wiener Universitätstheologen zu analysieren wird ohnehin einen aktuell relevanten Beitrag leisten. Der andere Aspekt wird von den am Rande der Beschäftigung mit der Zukunft entstehenden Entitäten aufgefüllt, wie mögliche Welten und mögliche Geschichten. Sie unterliegen intensiver Auseinandersetzung namentlich in der modernen Physik. Welche Unterschiede und Gemeinsamkeiten wären zwischen mittelalterlichem und modernem Ansatz zu erkennen? Diese Aspekte schildern mindestens zwei Gründe dafür, warum nicht nur in der Geschichtsforschung, sondern in der Aktualität der Philosophie auch dem Wissen Gottes als komparative und kompetitive Entität ein Platz zukommen soll.

Anhang 1: Eine Frageliste aus ÖNB Cod. 4503, 10ʳ-120ᵛ.

(1) "Utrum culpa secundum se magis meretur supplicium quam iusta praemium"
(2) "Utrum Pater et Filius sint unum principium spirans Spiritum Sanctum"
(3) "Utrum liberum arbitrium se aequaliter habeat ad bonum et ad malum"
(4) "Utrum dispositio Dei aeterna sit necessitas aliqua respectu productibilium ad extra"
(5) "Utrum vita contemplativa sit eligibilior quam activa"

(6) "Utrum per suffragia Ecclesiae remitti valeant propterea gaudorum poenae"

(7) "Utrum Deum esse praesentem ubique secundum potentiam necessario inferat ipsum esse ubique secundum essentiam"

(8) "Utrum resurrectio generalis hominium fiet secundum differentiarum etatum et sexuum"

(9) "Utrum angelus posset aliud corpus assumere in quo exerceat opera vitae"

(10) "Utrum omnium hominum generalis futura resurrectio fiet per miraculum et subito"

(11) "Utrum gaudium beatorum post resurrectionem corporum maius aliunde finiatur"

(12) "Utrum aliqua creatura natura cultu latrie licite sit veneranda"

(13) "Utrum propter vitare proximorum scandala homo teneatur praetermittere tam temporalia quam spiritualia bona"

(14) "Utrum sit homini possibile cuilibet temptationi carnis mundi et daemonis resistere"

(15) "Utrum sicut soli praedestinati sunt vera membra Ecclesiae Christi, sic omnes reprobati sint membra diaboli"

(16) "Utrum quilibet dampnificans alium in se sua non sit vere poenitens ante talis rei restitutionem"

(17) "Utrum quilibet contritus peccatorum teneatur statim habita opportunitate omnia sua peccata proprio suo sacerdoti confiteri"

(18) "Utrum in qualibet parte animae Christi tempore passiorum vere fuerit tristitia vel dolor"

(19) "Utrum omnia Decalogi praecepta obligent ad opera positiva et caritate formata"

(20) "Utrum de necessitate salutis quilibet adultus viator omnes articulos fidei explicite credere teneatur"

(21) "Utrum in consecrationis Eucharistiae sacramento fiat substantiae panis in corpus et vini in sanguinem Christi vera transsubstantiatio"

(22) "Utrum panis in corpus et vini in sanguinem Christi fiat conversio in verborum consecrationis"

(23) "Utrum indulgentiae, quas prelati Ecclesiae de meritis Christi et sanctorum dare habunt, valent tantum quantum sonant"

(24) "Utrum verbum Dei pro humani generis reparatione incarnatum in unitate suppositi potuit assumere creaturam irrationalem"

(25) "Utrum usus et fruitio sint operationes liberae voluntatis"

(26) "Utrum Deus ad creaturam relatus realiter omnium creatorum sit contentivus idealiter"

(27) "Utrum sicut omne mendatium sic et periurium sit de rigore novae legis ut mortale praesumendum"

(28) "Utrum si primus parens in statu innocentiae perstitisset Dei Filius incarnatus fuisset"

(29) "Utrum omnis homo descendens ab Adam per concubitam maris et femine contraxerit peccatum originalem"

(30) "Utrum ad deletionem peccati mortalis sufficiat minimus motus contritionis"

(31) "Utrum peccator pro quolibet peccato mortali possit satisfacere propria satisfactione"

(32) "Utrum peccatum veniale ex circumstantia possit fieri mortale"

(33) "Utrum possibile sit angelum ad custodiam homini deputatum ipsius in assumpto corpore custodire"

(34) "Utrum sicut angeli mali sui obstinationem superbiendo, ita boni angeli sui in bono beatificam confirmationem diligendo Deum meruerit"

Anhang 2: Fragment einer disputierten Frage aus ÖNB Cod. 4503, 83ʳ⁻ᵛ und 92ʳ⁻ᵛ: "Utrum Verbum Dei pro humanis generis reparatione incarnatum in unitate suppositi potuit assumere creaturam irrationalem"

Quod sic arguitur: Omnia illa possunt Deo attribui et divinae suae omnipotentiae quae non implicant contradictionem et quae sibi non derogant. Sed Verbum Dei incarnatum esse pro salute generis humani et assumere irrationalem creaturam in unitate suppositi sunt huiusmodi, igitur quaestio est vera bona.

Corollarium I: Unio sanctificativa quae est cum Deo per gratiam, cognitionem et amorem est donum maius quam unio hypostatica creaturae ad Verbum in se nude considerata. Probatur quia prima unio facit creaturam esse Filium Dei, sed secunda unio non necessario hoc facit, ut nota est ex dictis.

Corollarium II: Quamvis verum potuerit assumere naturam rationalem Deum non cognoscentem, nec amantem, non tamen [est possibile naturam rationalem a nobis assumptam peccare]. Prima pars est: Quia unio hypostatica et dilectio Dei et cognitio Dei sunt diversarum rationum et una non includat aliam, igitur Deus potest unam facere sine alia in quacumque creatura, sed secunda pars non est ex dictis.

Literatur

Aschbach, Joseph. *Geschichte der Wiener Universität im ersten Jahrhunderte ihres Bestehens*, Bd. 1. Wien: Verlag der K.K. Universität, 1865.

Berger, Harald. "Personen, Lehrveranstaltungen und Handschriften aus der Frühzeit der Universität Wien". In: Kurt Mühlberger, Meta Niederkorn-Bruck (Hrsg.). *Die Universität Wien im Konzert europäischer Bildungszentren, 14.-16. Jahrhundert*. Wien: Böhlau, 2010, S. 27-36.

Bradwardine, Thomas. *De causa Dei contra Pelagium et de virtute causarum*. London: Billius, 1618.

Ders. *De causa Dei contra Pelagium et de virtute causarum. Auszüge Lateinisch-Deutsch*. Göttingen: V&R unipress, 2013.

Brinzei, Monica, Schabel, Chris. "The Past, Present, and Future of Late Medieval Theology: The Commentary on the *Sentences* by Nicholas of Dinkelsbühl, Vienna, ca. 1400". In: Philipp W. Rosemann (Hrsg.). *Medieval Commentaries on the* Sentences *of Peter Lombard*, Bd. 3. Leiden: Brill, 2015, S. 174-266.

Courtenay, William J. *Adam Wodeham. An Introduction to His Life and Writings*. Leiden: Brill, 1978.

Derselbe. "Theological Disputations at Vienna in the Early Fifteenth Century. Harvard MS Lat. 162". In: *Bulletin de philosophie médiévale*, Bd. 53, 2011, S. 385-401.

Derselbe. "From Dinkelsbühl's Questiones Communes to Vienna Group Commentary. The Vienna 'School', 1415-1425". In: Monica Brinzei (Hrsg.). *Nicholas of Dinkelsbühl and the* Sentences *at Vienna in the Early XVth Century*. Turnhout: Brepols, im Druck.

Dunne, Michael W., Nolan, Simon. *Richard FitzRalph. His Life, Times and Thought*. Dublin: Four Courts Press, 2013.

Ernst, Johannes Theodorus. *Die Lehre der hochmittelalterlichen Theologen von der vollkommenen Erkenntnis Christi. Ein Versuch zur Auslegung der klassischen Dreiteilung: visio beata, scientia infusa und scientia acquisita*. Freiburg: Herder, 1971.

Flüeler, Christoph. "Ethica in Wien anno 1438. Die Kommentierung der aristotelischen "Ethik" an der Wiener Artistenfakultät". In: F.P. Knapp u.a. (Hrsg.). *Schriften im Umkreis mitteleuropäischer Universitäten um 1400*. Leiden: Brill, 2004, S. 92-138.

Derselbe. "Teaching Ethics at the University of Vienna: The Making of a Commentary at the Faculty of Arts (A Case Study)". In: István P. Bejczy (Hrsg.). *Virtue Ethics in the Middle Ages. Commentaries on Aristotle's* Nicomachean Ethics, *1200-1500*. Leiden: Brill, 2008, S. 277-346.

Gelber, Hester Goodenough. *It Could Have Been Otherwise: Contingency and Necessity in Dominican Theology at Oxford, 1300-1350*. Leiden: Brill, 2004.

Genest, Jean-François. *Prédétermination et liberté créée à Oxford au XIVe siècle. Buckingham contre Bradwardine*. Paris: Vrin, 1992.

Hohmann, Thomas. *Heinrich Langensteins 'Unterscheidung der Geister', Lateinisch und Deutsch. Texte und Untersuchungen zur Übersetzungsliteratur aus der Wiener Schule*. München: De Gruyter, 1977.

Kink, Rudolph. *Geschichte der kaiserlichen Universität zu Wien*. Bd. 2. Statutenbuch der Universität. Wien: Gerold & Sohn, 1854.

Lang, P. Justin. *Die Christologie bei Heinrich von Langenstein. Eine dogmenhistorische Untersuchung*. Freiburg: Herder, 1966.

Leff, Gordon. *Bradwardine and the Pelagians. A Study of His* De causa Dei *and His Opponents*. Cambridge: Cambridge University Press, 1957.

Lenzenweger, Joseph. "Die Gründung der theologischen Fakultät an der Universität Wien (1384)". In: E.C. Suttner (Hrsg.). *Die Katholisch-Theologische Fakultät der Universität Wien 1884-1984*. Berlin: Duncker & Humblot, 1984, S. 1-18.

Lukács, Edit Anna. "The *sophistae in parviso* and the Oxford Calculators: When Disciples Overcome Their Masters". In: Almut-Barbara Renger, Jeonghee Lee-Kalisch. *Meister und Schüler. Master and Disciple. Tradition, Transfer, Transformation*. Weimar: VDG, im Druck.

Madre, Alois. *Nikolaus von Dinkelsbühl. Leben und Schriften*. Münster: Aschendorff, 1965.

Marenbon, John. *Le temps, l'éternité et la préscience de Boèce à Thomas d'Aquin*. Paris: Vrin, 2005.

Markowski, Mieczysław. "Repertorium Philosophicorum Operum Wiennensium inde ab anno 1365 usque ad annum 1500 quae in codicibus manu scriptus bibliothecarum Europae asservantur". In: *Acta Mediaevalia*, Bd. 13, 2000, S. 241-264.

Michon, Cyrille. *Préscience et liberté. Essai de théologie philosophique sur la Providence*. Paris: Vrin, 2004.

Oyta, Heinricus Totting de. *Quaestiones Sententiarum* Liber I, Quaestio 10 "Utrum quodlibet futurum contingenter fore stare possit cum divina praescientia et revelatione distincta de futuro facta creaturae". Im Druck.

Perler, Dominique. *Prädestination, Zeit und Kontingenz. Philosophisch-historische Untersuchungen zu Wilhelm von Ockham's 'Tractatus de praedestinatione et de praescientia Dei respectu futurorum contingentium'*. Amsterdam: Grüner, 1988[a].

Derselbe. "Notwendigkeit und Kontingenz. Das Problem der 'futura contingentia' bei Wilhelm von Ockham". In: Olaf Pluta (Hrsg.). *Die Philosophie im 14. und 15. Jahrhundert. In memoriam Konstanty Michalski*. Amsterdam: Grüner, 1988[b].

Prügl, Thomas. "Bibeltheologie und Kirchenreform – Die Errichtung der Wiener Fakultät und ihre theologische Positionierung im Spätmittelalter". In: Johann Reikerstorfer, Martin Jäggle (Hrsg.). *Vorwärtserinnerungen 625 Jahre Katholisch-Theologische Fakultät der Universität Wien*. Göttingen: V&R unipress, 2009, S. 377-398.

Schabel, Chris. *Theology at Pars, 1316-1345. Peter Auriol and the problem of divine foreknowledge and future contingents*. Aldershot: Ashgate, 2000.

Derselbe. "Henry Totting of Oyta, Henry of Langenstein, and the Vienna Group on Reconciling Human Free Will with Divine Foreknowledge". In: Paul J.J.M. Bakker u.a. (Hrsg.). *Philosophical Psychology in Late-Medieval Commentaries on Peter Lombard's Sentences*. Turnhout: Brepols, im Druck.

Schmutz, Jacob. "Science divine" "Science du Christ". In: Claude Gauvard, Alain de Libera, Michel Zink (Hrsg.). *Dictionnaire du Moyen Age*. Paris: PUF, 2002, S. 1294-1298.

Shank, Michael H. *"Unless You Believe, You Shall Not Understand". Logic, university, and society in late medieval Vienna*. Princeton: Princeton University Press, 1988.

Šmahel, František. "Die Verschriftlichung der Quodlibet-Disputationen an der Prager Artistenfakultät bis 1420". In: F.P: Knapp (Hrsg.). *Schriften im Umkreis mitteleuropäischer Universitäten um 1400*. Leiden: Brill, 2004, S. 63-91.

Steneck, Nicholas H. *Science and Creation in the Middle Ages. Henry of Langenstein (d. 1397) on Genesis*. Notre Dame: University of Notre Dame Press, 1976.

Uiblein, Paul. "Beiträge zur Frühgeschichte der Universität Wien". In: *Mitteilungen des Instituts für Österreichische Geschichtsforschung*. Bd. 71, 1963, S. 284-310.

Derselbe. *Die Universität Wien im Mittelalter. Beiträge und Forschungen*. Wien: WUV-Univ.-Verl., 1999.

Weijers, Olga. *In Search of the Truth. A History of Disputation Techniques from Antiquity to Early Modern Times*. Turnhout: Brepols, 2013.

Rodica Pop

From the "egotism of suffering" to the "instable compassion". A philosophical and theological perspective on Dostoevsky's female characters

Introduction. The place of the woman in Dostoevsky's world

In Nikolai Berdiaev's opinion (Berdiaev 1992, 72-73), women did not represent a point of interest of particularly great importance for the Russian writer, taken autonomously, but they rather were elements that contributed to the outlining and crystallisation of some male characters: "Dostoevsky's anthropology is exclusively masculine. The woman is only important as an element along the destiny of the man. The feminine principle represents only a motif of the tragedy of the masculine spirit, an inner temptation of it. (...). There is nowhere to be found a feminine figure that has value in itself. The woman is just an inner masculine tragedy. (...). The woman is only a hindrance on the way, is not important in and by herself, but simply represents an internal phenomenon of the masculine destiny"[1] (Ibid, 74). So, what we are to understand from Berdiaev's words is that Dostoevsky's women do not have a destiny of their own and are only present in order to emphasise a certain trait of the man, to envelop his destiny, to stir his passion, for the general atmosphere; the destiny of man is the destiny of the individual, of the principle of human entity that, to Dostoevsky, is predominantly masculine.

Nikolai Berdiaev does no dwell too much on the matter but, from what has been stated so far, we might think that he does operate a sort of valorisation of the man in relation to the woman and he somehow tries to establish the superiority of the man. Women have, indeed, a discreet presence in the economy of Dostoevsky's novels, but their manifestations have an extraordinary impact on the men. Placing a woman on the same level as that of a man would have been an improper, unauthentic and mediocre approach. We know very well that the mediocre common conscience imposes a hierarchy. To state that the woman is superior or inferior to the man is just as inappropriate as comparing the importance of water to that of air. In Orthodox spiritu-

---

[1] The translation into English of all quotes belongs to us.

ality, Saint John Chrysostom is uncompromising on the matter: equality generates tensions but this does not mean in any way that one is inferior and the other one is superior. Each one is called to fulfill different attributions in life, so that the whole should work harmoniously. The way in which Dostoevsky created his feminine characters reveals a knowledge of this theology.

Had Dostoevsky defined women starting from the man, the woman would have necessarily been negative. Also, her image would have been false if she had been studied in her own order, placed inside herself. This is the mistake that Simone de Beauvoir made in her book "The Second Sex", to quote one particular case. Dostoevsky, though, sees beyond these models. He passes on to the spiritual realm of the revealed charisms of the feminine archetype. "This is the truth - Paul Evdokimov says - because it includes and explains all the forms of the feminine. It alone transcends the clichés of faithful wives, pious widows and, generally, of women reduced to the mono-dimension of the domestic, that represents only a purely historical point of reference: patriarchy, the reign of the masculine" (Evdokimov 1995, 24). The prominent feminine characters in Dostoevsky's novels - yet, we shall focus our attention on the two novels we mentioned, *The Idiot* and *Crime and Punishment* - manage to stay in the foreground, without us even realising it. By imagining Dostoevsky preoccupied with the feminine element to the same extent as that of man's, Berdiaev would expect women to display behaviours comparable to those of men: to present revolutionary plans, to wish to rule the world and to commit murder in the name of ideas. Dostoevsky knows that women are just as capable of acquiring intellectual ideas as men, that they can intellectualise everything exceedingly, that they can build, shoulder to shoulder with men. Still, he also knows that all these aspects would invalidate them of their very essence, for "the woman is called to bring femininity to culture, in an irreplaceable manner." (Ibid, 191).

Mircea Eliade comes with yet another observation, which is very interesting and radically different from other critics' or exegetes', observation places him among the readers who do not view Dostoevsky's work from a spiritual perspective, even though it appeals to the "austere" character of Dostoevsky's literature. He remarks that all writers up to the Russian writer "every one, but absolutely every single one of them, had believed that the human soul experiences the extremes (damnation, absolution) through women. Does it then not seem as exceptional Dostoevsky's appearance, his titanic break from European tradition, his courage to create people who suffer, hope, crash or find salvation without women?" (Eliade 2003, 86). It is true that the dramas Dostoevsky's men go through are not caused by love pains, by the exhilarating duet in the presence of a woman or by the suffering caused by a woman's leaving. "For Dostoevsky, man becomes firstly a victim of his own destiny - Eliade says. His characters: people who suffer directly, artlessly; who know the abyss of existence in their own lives; not through love, through sharing a living together with someone else. Love led to so much cruelty and disaster in European literature - idea explained by Goethe's saying: to each woman, the man she lives with is a demon. The drama and the suffering originate in man's incapacity to bear an absolute love; from the demoniac created by two people together, in the presence of each other. The woman and love had played here initial data: man alone, facing destiny, the nothingness" (Eliade 2003, 88). It is true, with one twist: the ending of the novel *Crime and Punishment* announces a love story between Raskolnikov and Sonia, a love of perfect beauty. And another observation: Eliade uses the term "man", leaving us to think that he talks of the actual man, calling him thus in relation to the woman. All suspicions that we are dealing with, radical misogyny included aside, we prefer to interpret Eliade's words in a different key. Man, designating by this term either the man or the woman, appears on their own in the face of destiny, of God, confronted alone with challenges, each trying to raise to their Creator or go down into the immensity of Evil. Yet neither is it the cause their own fall. When they remain truly alone, they are swallowed by Hell - as in the case of Nastassyia Filippovna. When they support each other and use the force of love in order to be healed, they can taste heaven - and this is the case with Sonia and Raskolnikov.

I. NASTASSYA FILIPPOVNA BARASHKOVA OR ON THE "EGOISM OF SUFFERING"

Indeed, Dostoevsky did not create another Anna Karenina, but his Nastassya Filippovna is above the former, and, probably, even more important than Myshkin himself. The reader's sensation is that everything gravitates around this woman. All characters have a "business to sort out" with her. Via the subject bringing them together, each character highlights one trait of her character. It is as if Myshkin's returning o Russia from the hospice in Switzerland had no other purpose than that of representing something fundamental in Nastassya's destiny, that is to deepen the crisis she was in and to give her a reason to throw herself into the arms of death. After she got murdered, he went back where he had come from. He had nothing else to do from then on.

All scenes are depicted as leading to their encounter, to insert her detailed in the storyline, while putting our patience to the test. It is the dialogue on the train between Myshkin and Rogozhin, where the latter makes a first account of the all-consuming passion that this young woman inspired in this young man, "because of whom your father handed you the punishment out". Then, there is the discussion between General Yepanchin and Gavrila Ardalyonovich, where she is presented as a commodity that can be bought, used as a trade coin, a woman of low morality. Then, there is the strong impression Nastassya Filippovna's picture made on Prince Myshkin: "What an extraordinary face! (...) And I am convinced that her fate is not at all common. She is full of joy but one can see she had her share of suffering, can't they? Her eyes give her out and, look, her delicately shaped cheek bones, these two little dots under the eyes, where the cheeks bend. She is full of pride, of vanity even, maybe, but I could not say whether she is good or bad at heart." (Dostoevsky 1962, 69-70).

The impact was so powerful that the prince knew he was attracted as if by magic towards that face of "rare beauty", that he secretly kissed, „making sure that nobody could see him", that face that "held in it a secret that now seemed even more disturbing. A pride with no boundaries, blended with contempt, hatred at times, seems this face to indicate, while at the same time, how much kindness, trust and sincerity beamed from it." (Ibid, 127-128). This contrasting mix of beauty, pride, disdain, intelligence and kindness caused in Prince Myshkin's heart an authentic sentiment of love and pity, that will dominate him throughout the novel and will justify every scandalous gesture he decides to do for Nastassya Filippovna.

All the details regarding this character that do no manifest themselves yet, but are only mentioned in the first part of the novel, are meant to create expectancy, tension, impatience and a desire from the reader's part to get to know her. From our point of view, Nastassya proves to be just as much a main character as Myshkin, who has the task of taking everyone's mask off, because only an "idiot" would be capable of telling, with naive sincerity, everything he sees and thinks about his fellow creature. All the other characters gravitate around these two, either as rivals, or as lovers, all are related in one way or another to Nastassya or Myshkin, although we tend to believe that, even when someone has an issue to deal with Myshkin, it is still Nastassya they are really interested in.

In the novel *Crime and Punishment*, we observe the same thing. Although the book is obviously a story of a murder, that is about Raskolnikov and his ideas on the liberties of man, in subsidiary we are presented with the torments of an anguished soul, saved by the humblest of figures, Sonia Semyonovna Marmeladova. Actually, what we are presented with is the mystery of devoutness. With exceptional craftsmanship, Dostoevsky contrasts over and over again, as in the case of Nastassya, ugliness and beauty, darkness and light, "mud and diamonds", in order to unveil every character's traits and the logic of the relationships (Riurikov 1957, 521). He insists every time - and maybe more in the case of Sonia Marmeladova (let's not forget here Svidrigailov, from the same novel, in whose person are combined a sexual promiscuity hard to understand, with an altruistic nature, full of warmth and understanding of the fellow creature in distress) - to notice and describe the double-faced behaviour of humans, in the strong belief that even the most innocent of consciousness can be affected by indignity and wretchedness: "You tell me, - Raskolnikov asked Sonia - how can this abomination and filth coexist in your soul with such opposing, hallowed feelings?" (Dostoevsky 1957, 294). Paradoxically, even though she practises the most contemptable and promiscuous occupation in the world - prostitution, even though she lives in poverty and misery, although she is not protected, is small and lacks charm, nobody can doubt her bright inner life and everybody around her waits from her a moral confirmation in the form of a gesture, a word or actual support, because, even though each of them has something bad to say about her, condemn her through meaningful glances or allusions about the „notebook" she keeps, they are all aware of the goodness of her heart, „as it was obvious prostitution had touched her only in a mechanical fashion; not a drop of debauchery had trickled into her soul yet : she was pure, as denoted by her entire being" (Ibid, 295). Or, as Nichifor Crainic says, "in her heart, the image of Jesus Christ is not yet crumbled" (Crainic 1998, 59).

We notice that Dostoevsky attributes to women a role of high responsibility: at the end of the day, it is from her that we find solutions to the problems of men, and that is because (Raskolnikov liked to linger and think (Dostoevsky 1957, 379), and this is the exact reason of his damnation) nothing can have a manipulative effect on her, because she, "understands matters with her soul" (Ibid, 377). That is Sonia's secret, her ability to find a solution to the unbearable anguish Raskolnikov goes through, thanks to her limitless faith and love, to her readiness to sacrifice herself so much as to giving up her own role in society, thus risking to lose herself because of that "immorality that confuses the mind and petrifies the heart" (Ibid, 295).

I.1. Nastassya Filippovna, seduced and abandoned

Fatality marks the destiny of Nastassya Filippovna since early childhood. Her mother died in a fire and her father soon followed her to the grave, one month later, her younger sister leaving this world a little while later. She is raised on the expense of an extremely wealthy man, of ultrarefined tastes, delicate and a great admirer and connoisseur of feminine beauty (Dostoevsky 1962, 73), Afanasi Ivanovich Totsky. So keen and trained was his eye, that he saw Nastassya's potential when she was still 12 years old (a time when she was a delightful, joyful, clever little girl, who "promised to become a woman of rare beauty" (Ibid, 75), moment in which he decided to invest in her upbringing. After four years of "multicultural education" (Ibid), Nastya is taken to another one of Totsky's properties, into a new little cottage, a modest one but full of things the girl enjoyed: books, instruments, paintings and a little female dog. She had at her disposal a lady butler and a maid. At the age of 16, Nastassya Filipppovna was perfect to be at the disposal of her experienced seducer. In this pleasant place (the property was called Otradnoye - a quiet, plentiful, enjoyable place to be), Totsky spent each summer for four years, "living a quiet, charmed, happy life" (Ibid, 76).

The author does not tell us what Nastassya thinks about this experience she was driven into without being warned. What we do know though is that, when Totsky decided to get married - and on top of it all, to someone else! - Nastassya Filipppovna showed a face of hers that was completely new to her seducer. Totsky got to receive in Petersburg a Nastassya Filippovna who was completely new and different, one who put him in a difficult spot: "she knew and understood extraordinarily many things- so many that he was amazed; where could she have gathered so much knowledge and information, come to such accurate ideas on so many things?" (Ibid, 77). Nothing in this new persona reminded of Nastya the "coy, with indefinite corners of the soul, sometimes full of charming joyfulness, other times silent and meditative, wondered or suspicious, in tears, in a state of troubled restlessness," (Ibid). Now, she is determined to ruin any plans of marriage just for spite and not because she would have any other feelings than those of "nauseating disgust", "even to only mock at you, because my turn to laugh heartily has finally come" (Ibid).

Such a reaction speaks volumes of the impact Totsky's abuse had on her in her teenage years, Totsky, a man whose single interest was that of treating her as a luxury item that he could use any time his heart weak in the face of beauty desired. He is sufficiently intelligent or, at least, versed enough, to realise that what he is confronted with is a human being at least special, with strong emotions and who should have had a say in what she had gone through against her will: "It often happened that strange thoughts came to him when he looked at her: a deep, mysterious light invited understanding its depth like an enigma" (Ibid, 80). Now, that he finds himself in the presence of another Nastassya, a "scandalous" one, he understands he treated too lightly this "easy conquest of an unversed soul; but lately, he had been forced to ask himself many times whether he might be wrong judging Nastassya the way he did" (Ibid).

In Petersburg, Nastassya gets a house and everything she needs and, yet, she lives a simple, modest life, surrounded by a small number of acquaintances. Totsky's plan to give her over to another man fails because she rejects courtship from anybody, even princes, hussars, diplomatic secretaries, poets, novelists, "as if she had a stone for a heart". For five years in a row, Nastasya accepts no man in her life; not even Totsky can find an "open door". Lebedev says on the train that "not even the officers, boisterous as they are, dare say any improper thing about her, because nobody would believe them" (Ibid, 37).

On the day Myshkin makes his appearance, Nastassya Filippovna is turning 25. At some point during the party, she is supposed to give the answer Ganea expects from her, that is whether she accepts or not his proposal to marry him. This proposal was cooked up by Totsky hand and glove with General Yepanchin and Gavrila Ardalyonovich, after the seducer had had an "honest" discussion with Nastassya, during which he admitted to his guilt, explainable by a fact that could not be cancelled, that is he is an "incorrigible womaniser, incapable of resisting temptations" (Ibid, 81). As a result, he asks her to deliver him from this bond and accept the idea that he is to marry Gavrila Ardalyonovich. Nastassya leaves the impression that she agrees, in principle, but that she needs time to think things through until her birthday, when she will give her final response. The problem is Nastassya feels she is being set up and each member of the trio will have something to gain out of this: Totsky could go ahead and marry someone else, Yepanchin is interested in having a taste of Nastassya's charms, whereas Ganea has been proposed a generous amount of money (a kind of a dowry for Nastasia) for this affair, his only concern in life being to get out of ruck.

So, everything seems to point to things settling down. Nastassya's life seems to have gone back into place. In reality though, she has never given up her plan to take her revenge, "feeding her soul with choler", considering that the offence she took could not be cancelled by mere forgiveness. She considers herself irreparably compromised, destroyed, with no chances of rehabilitation in society and, especially, in relation to herself. The story will show us that she cannot move further, take her life in her own hands because she lives in the past, she blames herself and punishes herself over and over again, until the instinct of self-punishing becomes stronger than that of self-preservation. The only way to revenge she could appeal to would be to attract the guilty ones (as the story unfolds, we can see that, besides Totsky, there are other characters who practise sexual abuse, although in different ways: general Yepanchin, who plans to make her his mistress, Ganea who wishes to marry her for money etc.) in the dramatic swirl of her own downfall. This seems to be the only thing she can still find satisfaction in. The birthday party is the moment she planned to initiate her personal vendetta.

I.2. "You have no guilt, Nastassya Filippovna, and I adore you!"

The meeting between Nastassya and Myshkin takes place in Gavrila Ivolghin's house, where the prince lives and where the woman has arrived to visit her "fiancé". It is here that a first scandalous scene occurs for Nastassya planned in detail how exactly to claim revenge, using her opponents' own weapons.

Ganea's family consider her an "immodest woman". And not only they, but the entire society knows her story so the Ivolghins' diagnosis is a form of unappealable doom. Starting from here on, we have a chance to truly understand Nastasya Filippovna. That she is sparkingly beautiful, there is no doubt in anybody's mind. And yet, no man finds it proper to see her as anything else than a hetaera, in any other way than by waving banknotes in front of her proud, sad eyes, in any other manner than as something that could be bought. The offence, the in-dignity are so great, that public self-flagellating repeatedly and in pub-lic seems to be her only source of solace or of paradoxical satisfaction, that because she considers herself very guilty for not having been able to oppose sexual abuse. She believes her wound could never been healed. That is why she cannot forgive herself in any way. "Because, without a doubt, the elements most opposed, in the highest radical manner to the mechanism of forgiveness, are the feeling of shame and the nostalgia for an unyielding integrity" (Marinov 2004, 143).

Modern psychology could definitely rank her among the maso-chists, the ones who suffer from a personality disorder caused by an intense feeling of self-defeat or self-blaming: "everybody knows who I am" (Ibid, 300), "I am just a lost woman" (Ibid, 244) - are phrases that appear like leit-motifs throughout the book. Continous repeating of these words, either in whispers or shouted out loud, like an incantation or a mantra (and it is not even necessary to be uttered all the time, as it is clearly visible in her nostalgic, sad eyes), is a cry of pain that only Myshkin understands and he even tells her later on: "You have a proud disposition, Nastassya Filippovna, but, maybe, you are so unhappy, that you truly think you are guilty" (Ibid, 242).

Nastassya shows up at the Ivolghins' house defiantly, like a woman of low morals but Myshkin takes that veil off her face and reproaches her that she insists on trying to seem someone else than who she really is. This is one of the few scenes where she has a glimpse of having a chance to have her real face, otherwise covered in humiliation, discovered: "In truth, I am not as I appear to be; he guessed my real nature, she whispered in a voice broken from her ardent desire to be believed, blushing with emotion" (Ibid, 176).

During the party, she will throw everybody's dirty secrets in their faces. But the story does not end here. For five years, she has woven a revenge plan to result in her feeling free and independent from Trotsky. Her life gets more complicated with the appearances of Myshkin. She falls in love with him at the first sight. She feels he is the prince she dreamt of, the one who will rescue and rehabilitate her: "I have dreamt of this for a long time; even since that time, during those five years I lived all alone in his country mansion; many a time, I'd let myself dream and I dreamt that a man just like you, kind, honest, handsome and even as helpless as you, would come my way: You have no guilt Nastassya Filippovna, and I adore you! One could go mad, no less, from so much beauty... and, all of a sudden, this one did come along; every year he would spend two months in the countryside and then he'd go away, leaving me defiled, abased, dishonoured, so that a thousand times I wanted to take my own life, to throw myself in a waterhole" (Ibid, 246). This is what Nastassya's suffering comes down to and this is everything her soul longs for, that is to have someone come and erase with a sponge her entire past- that meaning never to be reminded of it again, as if it had never happened - and love her unconditionally.

Seduced and abandoned by Totsky, she directs her fury against sexuality. That is why she becomes completely abstinent. That is why she instinctively grows attached to Myshkin, who does not desire her the way the other men do, because he cannot „get married" to any woman at all since, according to his own words - "I am a sick man" (Ibid, 70). In accordance, one might expect Nastassya to elope with Myshkin, since she said she finally found him after having waited for so long.

But no, Dostoevsky could not be as common and predictable as in Hollywood movies. His hell is not just a pit, but rather a well segmented space, where the visitor is confronted with various forms and faces of evil as he passes from one cubicle to the next. Nastassya knows what evil is after suffering abuse and she perpetuated it during the five years that followed. "The awareness of evil decanted its toxins" (Evdokimov 1995, 154), and their effect is for the long run.

Dostoevsky takes her to the bottom of hell and abandons her there. We might think that he proves cruel to treat his character in such a way, but we have the opportunity to observe in full detail the manner in which the Russian writer understands to experiment man's option for freedom. If Nastassya had been transformed into a nice housewife who raised her children devotedly (assuming that in the meantime Myshkin had vouchsafed to become a father!), we would have had one of the many models we can find in real life and that cannot become a novel. Normality is not inspiring. That is why, "all his novels are tragedies, experiments of human liberty" (Berdiaev 1992, 42).

Nastassya's story is one of freedom. We believe that Dostoevsky considers that it is within the quality of the story that we may find what ontological quality of the object that the story represents. He found it proper to use the storyline as a means of presenting the concept, as a method to convey authenticity, that appeals more to imagination than to reason. Still, we shall have in view some considerations of the conceptual, theoretical nature, about freedom, good and evil, for sometimes the story cannot be understood without a metadiscourse.

I.3. Duality of man through choices and by entering the realm of Evil

Both Nastassya Filippovna and Sonia Marmeladova seek to follow the road leading from appearance to similitude. This is what the oddysey of the two (souls) characters we selected are about, as they represent two variants or, more precisely put, a path in two stages. What we have here is the most concrete form of irrational liberty (Nastassya) and tsarist liberty (Sonia). It is like we are dealing with one person but dual, this state resulting from the choices she makes.

Nastassya admits that she has "given up on the world. Maybe you find it funny to hear something like that from me, seeing me covered in diamonds and lace, in the company of drunkards and villains. Do not be fooled by it, I barely exist any longer and I know it. God knows what lives inside of me instead of me." Under no circumstances does she speak about an ascetic renouncing the world. In her soul, the building of the Godly Kingdom has not begun yet, although she claims God lives inside of her, instead of her. No, what she says is that she is still alive thanks to God's will, to His divine morsel, due to the Spirit that lives inside every one of us. Otherwise, she is dead and she masochistically savours her downfall into the Thanatos. She picks Rogozhin - who is totally antinomic in character to Myshkin, the man with she fell in love with – because what she sees in him is a younger version of Totsky, whom she wants to punish with her vengeance but, once again, she uses him as an instrument of self-destruction. Rogozhin's gesture of flopping one hundred thousand roubles to buy Nastassya is defining of the character of that individual. It is a new opportunity Dostoevsky provides the woman with, so as she might blame herself again, self-flagellate in public, giving up Myshkin's offer in favour of Rogozhin's: "How could you imagine that I would destroy the life of this innocent infant?" (Dostoievsky 1962, 243). Myshkin is the long awaited prince, whom she has finally found but – misfortune! – she has been tainted in the meantime: "I am but a lost woman" (Ibid, 244), "a whore" (Ibid, 245), "I shall go soliciting, do you hear me, that is where I belong, and if I don't, I'll go ahead be a laundry woman" (Ibid, 250). Modern psychology has recognised such behaviour, where a person is confronted with a problem and lets themselves dominated by it, talks a lot about it, and talks, and talks, lets the steam out", but does nothing to free themselves from it, to overcome it. This process of boiling and persistency in evil generates pleasure. A negative one, of course, but pleasure nonetheless. It is like a drug. It neighbours alcoholism.

In addition to the immense pity, Myshkin, who loves her, also feels a great fright. (Ibid, 471). He understands best that her madness hides a wish for dying, accompanied by a terrifying and unnatural pleasure to harm herself. She does not simply want to die, she wants it to happen in a terrible, shameful and painful way, because that would be the only way she could punish herself fully for the „whore" she considers herself to be. As we have said before, she suffers from incurable injury. Rogozhin is the only person Nastassya Filippovna considers capable of punishing her according to her self-destructive expectations; at first, he buys her for a huge amount of money, once again placing her among lost women ("this misfortunate woman is profoundly convinced that she is the lowest, most deprived person in the world" Lebedev says about her), stirring her self-blaming sentiments; and then, she sees in him a high potential for murder: "Maybe that is why she does not drown herself, because she sees herself ending worse than on the bottom of the lake by staying with me." (Ibid, 301). This is not just one his suppositions. Nastassya actually feels that by thinking to marry him: "Marrying you is like throwing myself into a waterhole." (Ibid, 300). She has hated so intensely and for so long, that she has exhausted all her resources for love. She lived in hell even before dying, if we are to consider hell what Father Zosima from Brothers Karamazov considered it to be, that is an "incapacity to love".

Once on the territory of evil, where she meets Rogozhin - himself an evil force - Nastassya Filippovna gradually turns into a volcanic force of evil nature. She is capable of anything, and that is Totsky's greatest fear. She is completely irresponsible, therefore in the grasp of demons, since the demonic is defined, according to Derrida,, as irresponsibility or non-responsibility. The collision of these two forces led to catastrophe. The culminating moment is, predictably, the murdering of Nastassya.

II.   SONIA SEMYONOVNA MARMELADOVA OR ON "INSATIABLE COMPASSION"

II.1. Sonia sells herself for 30 rubles

Sonia is the daughter of an irresponsible, cowardly, alcoholic clerk, whom Dostoevsky introduces to us from the very beginning of the novel, where this clerk encounters Raskolnikov and tells him the story of his miserable life in full detail. A widower and raising a 12-year-old girl, Semyon Marmeladov remarries Katerina Ivanovna, also a widow, with three small children to care for, poor, and repudiated by her family, desperate, suffering from tuberculosis and neurotic. They all live in utter poverty while the head of the family drinks away all their money, including the money he steals from the household. Sonia, a teenager now, is a seamstress, but is treated unfairly and rudely by her customers who, under the pretext that the clothes are not as they were ordered, refuse to pay: "The State Counsellor Klopstock, Ivan Ivanovich - have you ever heard this name before? - not only hasn't paid for the six Dutch linen shirts to this day, but also insulted her, sent her away thumping his feet and said foul words to her because, - he said - the collar was not the right size and asymmetrical. And back home, the children are starving" (Dostoevsky 1957, 19). This is one of the reasons why Katerina Ivanovna - always irritated, frustrated, discontent, sick - accuses Sonia of not making any financial contribution to the household - "Lazy one, you are staying here, cosy, eat and drink!" (Ibid) - and plainly urges her to become a prostitute: „So what,? Great treasure, no less! Why protect it so?" (Ibid).

One day, when the tension was high again from the same reasons, the children were crying because they were hungry and had nothing to eat, Semyon Marmeladov was "dead drunk" again, Katerina, in a desperate approach and having no solutions left, reminds Sonia about the invitation „three times she has sent her [...] transmitted by our host" Daria Frantsevna, a wretched woman, well-known by the police, who meant no good" to Sonia (Ibid). Thus begins the girl's nightmare. Without saying one word, she gets out of the house and sells herself for 30 rubles, a number that could have been like any other number but which, if we follow Sonia's spiritual advance, we shall see that it is a symbolic one and reminds of the silver coins the Saviour was sold for.

We find out in this first presentation from a "marmelade father" (Vladimir Marinov) how a teenager "quiet by nature, who never answers back and has a soft little voice..., fair-haired, with thin, «pale» cheeks", decides to go through with "you know what" (Ibid), choosing of her own accord to enter the category of the most despised women in order to feed her stepmother's children and to support her father's addiction (father who, after stealing from her wife's chest all of her money, drinks it and, to wake from his hangover, goes to Sonia and asks her last 30 kopecks in order to buy vodka). Only a few days after the encounter between Raskolnikov and Marmeladov, the latter dies, context that facilitates the meeting of the two characters we are focussing on - Raskolnikov and Sonia.

Unlike Nastassya Filippovna, who is introduced in a spectacular, passionate, detailed manner, as she is beautiful, intelligent and magnetic, Sonia Semyonovna is introduced in the story as an element of certain promiscuity, irrespective of her father's words, who wishes to atone the misery of reality. What can we expect from such a woman, after we have been accustomed to the remarkable volcano, of bright, deadly force Nastassya Filippovna was? Sonia is unimportant as a woman, seems to have no opinion of her own, subdues to even the cruellest requests from Katerina Ivanovna, her stepmother. Each appearance of hers in the first three parts of the novel are absolutely insignificant or slightly ridiculous, that if we could overlook the scene in which she appears in the room where her father was on his deathbed, dressed in flashy attire, like a cheap prostitute. She hardly ever says anything, is scared and ashamed.

The author points out very clearly that she knows her place in society, that she is aware of the opinion people have about her occupation and that she cannot defend herself. She considers herself a sinner who has an important mission to accomplish. This is one detail we cannot overlook. It is very obvious that Dostoevsky used her silence to tell us with precision that, in the end, nothing is more important to Sonia than saving those three children from starvation. With prostitution as her sole source of income, Sonia considers it useless to try and defend herself. She just keeps silent. But never had silence said more or had a highest effect than in the case of this pale figure. She is the perfect embodiment of humbleness. She does not defend herself because – as Father Arsenie Boca puts it – "where there is fending oneself, there is no humility, thus, no confessing and no forgiveness" (Boca 2006, 63). From the perspective of the common, small-minded man, she is only a fool who leaves the impression she is unable to protect the little honour that she still has and is incapable of defending her own life from the malignancy of Katerina Ivanovna. Yet, this word has too interesting a charge according to Nicolae Steinhardt, to cast any shadow of a doubt upon Sonia's genuinely positive character: "Let us not forget that the Romanian word "fraier" (fool) comes from the German word, meaning a free man. The free man (which in chivalry is the same thing as the noble man) could not care less whether he was taken for a fool by someone" (Steinhardt 1992, 220).

Nothing from the first scenes anticipates the importance the role Sonia Marmeladova will play in the novel. Three hundred pages go by and she is nowhere presented in any significant manner. On the contrary, right to the end, she never acts in force. The effects of her gestures and plans though are radical and of great effect. Small, quiet and humble, Sonya acts like the water that slightly cuts little by little from the bottom of the boulder whom, in time, gets to knock down. She is full of discreet courage, there from the fear of God, which has the role to "overcome the fear of the world. (...)" (Stăniloae 2002, 137).

II.2. Reason is defeated by the heart

Raskolnikov cannot give himself any explanation as to why he has this uncontrollable desire to visit Sonia. He is not attracted to her. There is no way he could ever be. Sonia is not a beautiful woman. Dostoevsky considers beauty of divine nature and believes that it has a special role, that is of redemptive element. He had depicted a woman whose beauty could bring a whole world up side down - in the words of Aglaia Yepanchina, whereas Sonia is described as having nothing attractive and beautiful at a first glance. The dark, intricate, haunted mind of Raskolnikov, whom Dostoevsky plans to redeem, would not have been drawn to the seductive face of a woman. Beauty, particularly that of a woman is an inscrutable mystery, "a dire, horrendous thing" according to Dimitri Karamazov. It is that "there is a dark, demonic underlay to beauty" (Berdiaev 1992, 37). Raskolnikov was already a prisoner of demonic traps, and an emphatic beauty could not represent the solution to lead him to salvation. Still, even since the instances the drunkard Marmeladov had spoken to him of his daughter who was a prostitute, Raskolnikov felt something warm at heart, understood that something unexplainable connected him to her.

And now, after a period of unbearable torment following the murder, he needs to share the burden of his guilty mind with someone else. Of everybody else he could have done that with, sisters, mother, Razumihin – people who obviously loved him and are supposed to not judge him, but rather protect and support him – Raskolnikov picks a stranger to whom everybody shows disdain as they consider that merely being in her presence is enough to be compromised. Raskolnikov does not need a passionate, sexual kind of love for he is a narcissist. Dostoevsky makes Sonia cross Raskolnikov's path because she can inculcate tender love and security upon him. Through her discreet behaviour, never asking anything from the man she loves but always available, even after being sent away, she guides Raskolnikov exactly where she wants him, to living faith and experiencing powerful penitence. At the end of the story, he even wonders why Sonia never "bothered him with religion, always thinking that she would bring forward the subject of the Holy Gospels and force him into getting religious books". But no, to his "big surprise, he never spoke about all these and had not even proposed to bring him the Holy Gospels" (Dostoievsky 1957, 497).

After they fall in love for real, after they confess love to each other, Raskolnikov feels the touch of God's love and the faith of the woman he loves becomes his own faith. It is there, in the Siberian prison that he understands he is now a free man (Ibid, 491). Dostoevsky provides through Raskolnikov a concrete example of freeing oneself from the tyranny of reason.

II.3. "Do you not feel any pity at all?" (Ibid, 291)

Thus, Raskolnikov pays a first visit to Sonia. In the description of this scene, the most signficant is an exchange of information and ideas that are cot connected to the murder, that will be confessed to during the following encounter. We now find out a lot of things about Sonia Semyonovna who, at he sight of the handsome and mysterious Raskolnikov, "feels terribly awkward, is ashamed and happy at the same time." (Ibid, 287). It is not only a question of intense inferiority complex or modesty but it's just that the girl is falling in love with Raskolnikov. The young man asks her a series of questions about her past but she strongly denies being someone's victim, being forced to harlot by evil Katerina Ivanovna. Nobody is responsible for her sins - she does consider herself a sinner - and defends Katerina fiercely. At first, he makes a remark about her being so thin, transparent and small only to then conclude how much compassion this tiny human being is capable of, who can only get angry as much as canary or a little bird can (Ibid, 290). The observation is not at all casual. Dostoevsky comes back again and again to the details on Sonia's physical proportions in contrast with her exceptional power of love and sacrifice, to show us the character of the Christian wisdom and of the man who can feel absolute, self-sacrificing love: "In Vladimir Marinov's opinion, she represents an attempt [...] of the author to give an actual body to the main characteristic of the Eastern Church: divine wisdom (Sonia is a diminutive from Sofia, which means wisdom in Greek), overwhelmingly bright dome, able to encompass the souls of all sinners under one roof" (Marinov 2004, 109).

Before protecting all sinners, she has to take care of Katerina Ivanovna's children first, woman for whom she feels so much pity and understands so well her aggravations and illness, that she always finds justification for all the cruelty and humiliation she has to suffer from her. We notice that she, Sonia, is the one who virtually takes care of everybody else and that she cannot imagine one reason at least to deny herself this self-imposed duty. She is petrified to hear that Polenka, Katerina's daughter might share her own path: "No! This cannot be, no! [...] God is great, He will not allow…such an abomination!" (Dostoievsky 1957, 293). We can see very clearly from her reaction at the idea of an identical fate of Polenka to her own that she is appalled at the nature of her occupation. She knows how despicable it is and what its unavoidable consequences are - "confuses the mind and petrifies the heart", Raskolnikov would think at some point. Aware of the security provided by the highest authority - that of God - Sonia knows that she can prostitute without peril. Raskolnikov, who was never spared from troubles and hunger, is so impressed by Sonia Semyonovna's person, that he sees her as a monument of suffering. Everybody else are nothings in comparison and his sister should feel honoured to stand by her side. He kneels in front of her and kisses her feet: „It is not you I am bowing down to, but to the whole of human suffering" (Ibid).

Raskolnikov understands perfectly who Sonia really is and, from this moment on, he compares himself to her as a highest moral point of reference. From now on, he knows he cannot dismiss her person any longer, because she represents a living human connected with God. He follows her instinctively, almost against his own will. It is the lack of any explanation to this orientation of his that the whole fascination of his profound transformation lies. Sonia beams out the warmth and divine love that Raskolnikov needs so. Through Sonia, he goes back home, to his origins. It is there, in Sonia, that Gods lives, drawing His prodigal son back by means of tender loving.

II.4. Conflict between love and reason

But, let us go back to the storyline. To Raskolnikov, it seems hard to comprehend how Sonia's soul was not drawn into the "pestilential cesspool" (Ibid, 295) of the practices she adhered to. He attempts an explanation related to her faith, asks her if she prays a lot, thus opening a chapter that will put a definitive mark on him, even though he does not feel ready for that. Sonia's answer - "what would I be without God?" gives him the opportunity to refresh his weaknesses and incapacity to believe. He was under the influence of demons and, despite his longing for God not having been destroyed, the company of evil gives him the chance to grin at Sonia and ruffle her in order to take down the principle that makes her entire sacrifice possible.

"What does **God** do for you?", he asks Sonia. This is the moment love and reason become conflictual to each other. Dostoevsky created a character of a paradoxical combination of practices and character. Therefore, we are obligated to observe that only a person in the shadow of God's gift can go through so much suffering and, in spite of owning nothing (neither financially, nor affectively), can still consider that God provides her with everything she needs.

Sonia's faith cannot be argumented the way Raskolnicov, the intellectual desires. Sonia, who has read only two books that she borrowed from Lebeziatnikov, breaks her hands in anguish because she cannot come with an answer. Tears of distress well up in her eyes, as she considers her soul a carrier of a treasure so high and valuable that nothing rational, not a word she could say would make a discourse satisfactory enough for such an inquisitive person as Raskolnikov. Her relationship with God is a mystery that Raskolnikov is not worthy of (Ibid), although she wishes to reveal it. From this reason, she feels troubled. This is a matter of love and pride at the same time. The pride in her heart tells her she is on the right track but is incapable of defeating him with the weapon of logic, which is not on her side, on the side of true faith. Then, Sonia loves the young man and longs for harmony. Sonia is bothered and offended at Raskolnikov's mean suspicions, although she cannot put the finger on the exact thing that troubles her, yet Dostoevsky provides us with clear proofs that she intuits, infers more than is able to convey. That is why Nikolai Berdiaev said that "one must come closer to the phenomenon of the spirit with a soul full of faith, not to rip it apart with suspicion and scepticism." (Berdiaev 2009, 9).

The ground is set for the actual conversion. Raskolnikov wishes to listen, read by the girl, the scene of Lazarus's resurrection. From her lack of disposition we may conclude how hard it is for her to "open up and expose her inner life" (Dostoevsky 1957, 297), but the young man's persistency will make her go ahead with it anyway. Raskolnikov has a notion that it is in this realm, in this area that he will learn Sonia's secret, what keeps her standing and strong in the face of life. This is one concrete situation where we can see that, no matter how dark the steps in one's life or even destiny may be, Dostoevsky lets us glimpse the light, the hoping. After reading the fragment from the Gospel, a scene full of multiple and contrary significances, Raskolnikov feels this is the moment to reveal his own secret. Even though he will do this much later, from his own perspective, the ground is all set. He asks her to elope with him, although he does not really love her, so not because he thinks of her as his perfect mate, but because she is to him the moral support that he cannot live without. Alone with his megalomaniacal rationalist theories, he is aware that he cannot help himself anymore. Sonia becomes in his eyes the epitome of comfort of the soul. He leans on her, although she seems frail, fragile and vulnerable. We once again make a point out of the idea that Dostoevsky's decision to invest Sonia the weak and powerless with so much force and courage is not in the very least casual.

II.5. The arbitrary choice

Sonia and Raskolnikov are two examples of how exactly man understands to be free. How could Raskolnikov be pervious to an irrational argument? That is because the religious problem of the liberty of the soul is not one that can be solved, as Nikolai Berdiaev (Berdiaev 2009, 141) correctly expects, by mean of rationalist philosophy - "Bergson stated that all rational definitions of freedom lead to its disappearing. [...]. Liberty is life itself, which is not accessible in any other way than through the experience of living, because its inner mystery is impossible to be represented by a category of reason. Rational philosophy ends in a static doctrine of liberty, whereas freedom is dynamic in its very essence, it cannot be conceived otherwise than in motion" (Ibid). This does not mean that we cannot reach the experience of true liberty. The only hindrance could be reason. The revolt of reason - as expressed in the article signed by Raskolnikov, a text that summarises in a way his entire conception about superiority within the human species - is an act of rebellion against God, is related to misunderstanding liberty as a divine gift. Nikolai Berdiaev is right to state that, if we do not view liberty like a mystery of creation when we try to understand life, then, we shall find no justification for all the evil in the world, for the afflictions, suffering and tears of innocent people (Berdiaev 1992, 54).

If Sofia's name - Sonia Semyonovna - is chosen for the purpose of acquiring from the very start a sense of the meaning this young woman will play in this story and Vladimir Marinov also draws our attention to Raskolnikov's name too (Marinov 2004, 231). Raskol means „schism" in Russian while „raskolot", to split, to melt, to rip to pieces. When man strays from God, they end up as in the examples we have provided here, in cruelty, in physical cancellation, in schism.

Sonia appears in Raskolniov's path in order to make him a favour, to lead him to redemption. We find it very interesting that neither her, nor the other people who know the truth about his the murder do him any favours by force. What are we to understand from "by force"? Sonia's belief, for instance, is that Raskolnikov will settle down, will regain freedom only if he admits to his guilt and go through the punishment decided by justice. While of course, repent during this time. These are notions that belong to very intimate and deep human experiences. Sonia, the ignorant and the professional policeman know these things only too well and leave everything go by naturally, as both of them have a glimpse of the spiritual facts inside the murderer's mind, that will lead to true repentance. A good deed imposed by force is not a result of freedom but rather of the inquisition. Only a free soul can be held responsible and enjoy dignified treatment, only a soul that can accept its suffering deserve redemption and ultimate deliverance from evil.

Conclusions

Spiritual liberty has God's will in view at all times and man finds freedom through channels of communication accepted with great difficulty by the intellectual species - the heart. Sonia has an organ to engage in dialogues with God. She understands even the most complicated of matters using her heart. Her soul chose uncoerced to go through the pain of humiliation, retorting to fulfilling the godly command of loving one's neighbour.

Nastassya would have been free from suffering, had she chosen love and forgiveness. Sonia would have been delivered from suffering if she had chosen to give up prostitution, thus failing to feed her family. But Nastassya chose definitive deepening into evil, looking for the good the wrong, false way. Her "egotism of suffering" reached its peak. Sonia made the sentient choice of banishing herself from moral society, thus saving her soul, as she was capable of "insatiable compassion".

Bibliographical references

Berdiaev Nikolai. *Filosofia lui Dostoievski* (*Dostoevsky's Philosophy*). Iasi: The European Institute, 1992.

Berdiaev Nikolai. *Spirit şi libertate. Încercare de filosofie creştină* (*Spirit and freedom. Attempts on Christian Philosophy*). Bucuresti: Paideia, 2009.

Boca Arsenie. *Cărarea Împărăţiei (The Pathway to the Kingdom)*. Arad: Publishing House of Romanian Orthodox Episcopie of Arad, 2006.

Crainic Nichifor, *Dostoievski şi creştinismul rus (Dostoevsky and Russian Christianity)*. Bucuresti-Cluj Napoca: Anastasia and Arhidiecezana, 1998.

Dostoievski Feodor M. *Crimă şi pedeapsă* (*Crime and Punishment*). Bucuresti: State Publishing House for Literature and Art, 1957.

Dostoievski Feodor M. *Idiotul* (*The Idiot*). Bucuresti: Publishing House for Universal Literature, 1962.

Eliade Mircea. "Dostoievski şi tradiţia europeană" ("Dostoevsky and the European Tradition"). In: Eliade Mircea. *Fragmentarium,* Bucureşti: Humanitas, 2003.

Evdokimov Paul. *Femeia şi mântuirea lumii (The Woman and Redemption of World)*. Bucuresti: Christiana, 1995.

Marinov Vladimir. *Figuri ale crimei la Dostoievski (Figures of Crime at Dostoevsky)*. Bucuresti: TREI, 2004.

Riurikov B. "Postface". In: Dostoievski Feodor M. *Crimă şi pedeapsă* (*Crime and Punishment*). Bucuresti: State Publishing House for Literature and Art, 1957.

Stăniloae Dumitru. *Ascetica şi mistica Bisericii Ortodoxe* (*Monasticism and the Mystic of the Orthodox Church*). Bucureşti: The Publishing House of the Institute Biblic and the Mision of the Romanian Orthodox Churche, 2002.

Steinhardt Nicolae, *Jurnalul Fericirii* (*The Diary of Happiness*). Cluj-Napoca: Dacia, 1992.

114

Esther Redolfi Widmann

Die Frau *als* Spannungsverhältnis von Situationsgebundenheit und Freiheit in Simone de Beauvoirs *Eine gebrochene Frau*

Im vorliegenden Beitrag wird Simone Lucie Ernestine Marie de Beauvoirs (*9. Januar 1908 in Paris; †14. April 1986 ebenda) Biografie, Philosophie und Literatur unter dem Aspekt der Darstellung der Frau *als* Spannungsverhältnis von Situationsgebundenheit und Freiheit in *Eine gebrochen Frau* zusammengeführt bzw. untersucht werden. Demnach wird Beauvoirs Entwicklung zur Philosophin und Schriftstellerin umrisshaft beleuchtet werden, gefolgt von der philosophischen Definition der Frau *als* Spannungsverhältnis von Situationsgebundenheit und Freiheit in der Erzählung *Eine gebrochene Frau*.

Die Autobiografie: Beauvoirs erlebtes Spannungsverhältnis von Situationsgebundenheit und Freiheit

Mit ihrer vierbändigen bzw. fünfbändigen Autobiografie (*Memoiren einer Tochter aus gutem Hause*; *In den besten Jahren*; *Der Lauf der Dinge*; *Alles in Allem*; *Die Zeremonie des Abschieds*) hat Simone de Beauvoir ihrer Leserschaft die Möglichkeit geboten, ihrer Genese zur Philosophin und Schriftstellerin nachzuspüren. Dabei gilt es die posthum erschienenen Schriften Beauvoirs (*Briefe an Sartre Band I und Band II*; *Briefe an Nelson Algren*; *Briefe an Élisabeth Lacoin*; *Briefe an Jacques-Laurent Bost*; *Jugendtagebücher*; *Kriegstagebuch*) zu berücksichtigen, da diesen in der retrospektiven Konstruktion besagter Entwicklung eine bedeutende Rolle zuteil wird.

Zum erlebten Spannungsverhältnis von Situationsgebundenheit und Freiheit.

Simone de Beauvoir wurde in einer bürgerlichen Familie geboren und von einer strenggläubigen Katholikin, Françoise Marie Thérèse Lucie Brasseur, und einem kultivierten Atheisten, Georges Charles Joseph Bertrand de Beauvoir, erzogen. Bereits in frühester Kindheit wurde Simone einem Spannungsverhältnis von Glauben und Wissen ausgesetzt. In Anbetracht der prekären finanziellen Verhältnisse, in die die Familie geriet (zur fehlenden Mitgift von Simones Mutter, die infolge des 1909 eingeleiteten Konkurses des einst vermögenden Großvaters nie ausbezahlt worden war, kam der zweite Bankrott von Simones Großvater mütterlicherseits hinzu. Die Schuhfabrik des Großvaters, in der auch Simones Vater als Vizedirektor gearbeitet hatte, schloss ihre Tore und nur dank eines reichen Vetters, der Vizedirektor der Banque de Paris in Holland war, fand Georges Arbeit als Anzeigeredakteur und als untergeordneter Redakteursfunktionär) sowie Beauvoirs Beobachtungen der traditionell-bürgerlichen Rollenverteilung, entschied sie sich, sich niemals mit demselben Schicksal ihrer Mutter abzufinden. In ihrem ersten autobiografischen Band *Memoiren einer Tochter aus gutem Hause* hielt Simone Nachstehendes dazu fest: "Nein, sagte ich mir, während ich einen Tellerstapel in den Wandschrank schob; mein ganzes Leben wird zu etwas führen. Glücklicherweise war ich nicht für das Dasein einer Hausfrau gemacht. Mein Vater war nicht für Frauenemanzipation. […] Not kennt kein Gebot: «Heiraten, meine Kleinen», sagte er oft, «werdet ihr freilich nicht. Ihr habt keine Mitgift, da heißt es arbeiten.» Ich zog bei weitem die Aussicht auf einen Beruf der auf Verheiratung vor; das berechtigte doch noch zu Hoffnungen. Viele Leute hatten große Dinge vollbracht, ich würde eben das gleiche tun. Astronomie, Archäologie, Paläontologie hatten mich nacheinander verlockt, und immer noch spielte ich mit dem Gedanken an eine Schriftstellerlaufbahn" (Beauvoir 2007 (b), 149). Schon bald begann Simone de Beauvoir davon zu träumen, über die Freiheit, die damals ausschließlich Männern zustand, eines Tages selbst verfügen zu können. Erreichen wollte sie dies mithilfe ihrer intellektuellen Fähigkeiten. Beauvoir hatte ihre Studien zielstrebig vorangetrieben (nachdem sie am Cours Désir ihre Lernzeit beendet hatte, wurde ihr erlaubt, zeitgleich am *Institute Sainte-Marie* in Neully Klassische Philologie und am *Institute Catholique* in Paris Mathematik zu studieren) und in ihren Memoiren gab sie preis, dass es letztendlich ein Zeitungsartikel über Léontine Zanta gewesen war, der sie dazu bewogen hatte, sich für eine höhere Studienlaufbahn zu entscheiden: "Sie [Léontine Zanta] hatte den Doktor gemacht. Auf der Photographie sah man sie mit ernstem, ruhevollem Antlitz an ihrem Schreibtisch sitzen; sie lebte mit einer jungen Nichte zusammen, die durch Adoption ihre Tochter geworden war; auf diese Weise war es ihr gelungen, das rein zelebrale Dasein mit den Forderungen des weiblichen Gefühlslebens in Einklang zu bringen. Wie gern hätte ich gesehen, man würde eines Tages über mich dergleichen ehrenvolle Dinge veröffentlichen! Damals konnte man die Frauen, die den Doktor oder das Staatsexamen für das höhere Lehramt gemacht hatten, noch an den Fingern der Hand aufzählen; ich wünschte mir, eine dieser Pionierinnen zu sein" (ebenda, 229f). Als Simone de Beauvoir 1929 Jean-Paul Sartre kennen und lieben lernte, war sie mit ihrem Vorhaben ein gutes Stück vorangekommen. 1924 hatte sie das *Premier baccalauréat* in *lettres;* 1925 das *Baccalauréat* in *philosophie* und *mathématiques èlementaires* erhalten; ab 1925 absolvierte sie zeitgleich ein Mathematikstudium am *Institut Catholique in Paris* und ein Studium der Klassischen Philologie am *Institute Sainte Marie* in Neully. Von 1925 bis 1928 erhielt sie die *certificats* in Klassischer Philologie, Philosophie, Literatur, Mathematik und Latein, Philosophiegeschichte, Allgemeiner Philosophie, Griechisch, Logik und Psychologie. Bevor sie mit der Vorbereitung der *agrégation* begann, hatte sie bereits die *licence* in Philosophie erhalten, für die sie ein Lehrpraktikum am *Lycée-Janson-de-Sailly* absolviert und eine Arbeit mit Léon Brunschvicg über Leibniz verfasst hatte. Dass sie sich nach bestandenem *agrégation*-Examen und einer vielversprechenden Beamtenkarriere gegen eine Ehe, einen Haushalt und Kinder entschied und stattdessen mit Sartre einen Liebespakt – der von 1929 bis zu seinem Tod 1980 währte – einging, könnte im Nachhinein betrachtet, so die Zeitzeugin Claudine Monteil, als kluge Kompromisslösung gedeutet werden: "Sartres Vorschlag eröffnete Simone nach reichlicher Überlegung einen Weg, dessen Schwierigkeiten im Vergleich zum beglückenden Gefühl der Freiheit, das sie darin finden würde, unbedeutend erscheinen. Sie würde alldem entfliehen, vor dem sie sich in ihrer Jugend gefürchtet hatte: dem verschwörerischen Lächeln, den Lügen und der Heuchelei, der ganzen bürgerlichen Komödie der Ehe und ihrer zwangsläufig unmittelbaren Folge – dem Ehebruch. Anstelle dieser Lügen würde ein untrennbares Band sie mit Sartre vereinen" (Monteil 2006, 48f). Simone entging also durch besagtes Liebesabkommen den Zwängen, die damals einer Ehefrau und Mutter auferlegt wurden, ohne auf die Vorzüge einer Partnerschaft verzichten zu müssen. Darüberhinaus ließ es sich Beauvoir nicht nehmen, sich sowohl mit Männern als auch mit Frauen in leidenschaftliche Liebesabenteuer zu stürzen. Dass erwähnter Liebespakt immerzu ein Spannungsverhältnis – und zwar sowohl als leidenschaftliche Liebhaberin als auch als streng erzogene, unzureichend aufgeklärte und durch gesellschaftlich bedingte Normen befangene junge Frau – mit sich brachte, liegt auf der Hand. Dennoch konnte Beauvoir, wenngleich unter Spannung, all dem erfolgreich standhalten und sich als Frau ein Leben lang Unabhängigkeit und Freiheit bewahren. Ein ständig wiederkehrender und mit der Freiheit eng verbundener Begriff, in Beauvoirs Oeuvre – darauf haben etliche Wissenschaftlerinnen und Wissenschaftler aufmerksam gemacht (siehe hierfür die bemerkenswerte, erst kürzlich veröffentlichte Aufsatzsammlung von Stoller, Eva (Hrsg.): *Simone de Beauvoir's Philosophy of Age. Gender, Ethics, and Time*. Berlin: de Gruyter, 2014, die unter anderem Beiträge von Debra Bergoffen, Sara Heinämaa, Gail Weiss u.v.a. enthält) – ist das Alter. Simone hat erstaunlich früh damit begonnen, sich mit dem unausweichlichen Prozess des Alterns auseinanderzusetzen: "Mit vierzig Jahren überlegte ich mir eines Tages: »In den Tiefen des Spiegels lauert das Alter. Und das Verhängnisvolle daran ist, daß es mich überrumpeln wird.« Es hat mich überrumpelt" (Beauvoir 2008 (d), 621). Beauvoir hatte als passionierte Wanderin, Reisende und leidenschaftlich Liebende den körperlichen Alterungsprozess stets als Einschränkung bzw. als Situationsgebundenheit wahrgenommen. Mitschuld an dieser pessimistischen Auffassung könnten sowohl der langjährige Alterungs- und Krankheitsprozess Sartres als auch der ihrer Freundinnen Olga und Wanda Kosakiewicz und Sartres Cousine Camille-Simone Sans (mit Künstlernamen Simone Jolivet) gewesen sein. Beauvoir hatte aus nächster Nähe beobachten können, wie vor allem Frauen mit dem biologischen und gesellschaftlichen Druck des Alters mehr schlecht als recht zurechtkamen. Dennoch darf an dieser Stelle die Vermutung gelten, dass Simone de Beauvoir das Spannungsverhältnis von Situationsgebundenheit und Freiheit, dem sie als junge und bejahrte Frau ausgesetzt war, teils bewusst, teils unbewusst erlebt hat. Unbewusst, als sie ihren legendären Gefühlsausbrüchen (sie geriet sehr schnell von einem Gefühl unendlichen Glücks zu krampfhaften aus Traurigkeit und Verzweiflung verursachten Weinkrämpfen) freien Lauf ließ. Diese dürfen als eine Art Ventil gelten, in dem sie die Möglichkeit sah, den Druck, der sich durch die angestaute Spannung gesammelt hatte, abzulassen. Anders verhielt es sich mit Beauvoirs bewusster Zerrissenheit, der sie mit dem Schreiben und dem Reisen ge-

zielt entgegengewirkt haben könnte. Während Simone mit der schrift-
stellerischen Tätigkeit es immer wieder geschafft hatte, schwierige
Momente ihres Lebens zu meistern, gelang es ihr durch das Reisen,
die nötige Distanz zu gewinnen, um sich von besagtem Spannungsverhältnis zu erholen. Das erlebte Spannungsverhältnis, zusammen mit
dem in ihrem *Jugendtagebuch* notierten Grundsatz "Ma philosophie
soit de la viē" (Beauvoir 2008 (a), 387) wird es im anschließenden Teil
ermöglichen, die These von der Frau *als* Spannungsverhältnis von
Situationsgebundenheit und Freiheit zu formulieren bzw. zu erläutern.

Die Philosophie: Die Frau *als* Spannungsverhältnis von Situationsgebundenheit und Freiheit

In *Das andere Geschlecht* hat Simone de Beauvoir es gewagt, die
kühne Frage: "Was ist eine Frau?" (Beauvoir 2008 (b), 9) zu stellen.
Auf der Suche nach einer Antwort beschreibt Beauvoir die Frau als ein
Wesen, welches zwangsläufig einer von der Gesellschaft vorgefertig-
ten Rolle gerecht werden muss. Diesem Zwang kann die Frau – so
Beauvoir – einzig und allein mit der bewussten Inanspruchnahme ihrer
Freiheit entgehen. Die Voraussetzungen, über die die Frau dafür verfügen sollte, sind das Anerkennen und Akzeptieren der Faktizität ihrer
Situation sowie die bewusste Entscheidung diese „neu erworbene"
Freiheit gezielt einzusetzen. In Beauvoirs Essay *Für eine Moral der
Doppelsinnigkeit* hatte sie schon ansatzweise damit begonnen, die
absolute menschliche Freiheit in Frage zu stellen: "Die in einem Harem eingesperrte Mohammedanerin [verfügt] über keine Möglichkeit,
sich gegen die sie unterdrückende Kultur zu wenden, und sei es auch
nur in Gedanken, im Staunen oder im Zorn. Ihr Verhalten wird ganz
und gar durch diese Gegebenheit bestimmt und kann nur aus ihr heraus beurteilt werden, und es ist durchaus möglich, daß sie in ihrer Situation, die wie jede menschliche Situation begrenzt ist, ihre Freiheit
voll und ganz zu bestätigen vermögen. Sobald jedoch eine Befreiung
möglich erscheint, ist der Verzicht auf eine Ausnützung dieser Möglichkeit ein Verzicht auf die Freiheit, ein Verzicht, der Unredlichkeit
bedeutet und eine positive Schuld ist" (Beauvoir 2007 (a), 100). Dies
führte Beauvoir alsbald zur Konzipierung des Begriffs der *situierten
Freiheit* bzw. der *situierten Freiheit der Frau*, zu dem sie *In den besten Jahren* folgenden Disput, der zwischen ihr und Sartre stattgefun-

den hatte, festhielt: "An den folgenden Tagen diskutierten wir Teilprobleme, vor allem das Verhältnis zwischen Situation und Freiheit. Ich hielt dafür, daß hinsichtlich der Freiheit, wie Sartre sie definierte – nicht stoische Resignation, sondern aktives Überwinden des Gegebenen –, die Situationen einander nicht gleichwertig sind. Welche Möglichkeit zur Überwindung hat die Frau, die in einen Harem gesperrt ist? Sogar diese Abgeschlossenheit könne man auf verschiedene Weise erleben, sagte Sartre. Ich blieb hartnäckig und gab schließlich nur halben Herzens nach. Im Grunde hatte ich recht" (Beauvoir 2008 (c), 373). Eine korrelierte Angelegenheit, die aus einer näheren Untersuchung der Situation der Frau in Erscheinung tritt, ist die der Ambiguität. Diese tritt nämlich bei der Frau als eine *"doppelte Doppelsinnigkeit"* auf, und zwar gesellt sich zur ontischen Ambiguität – als Existenz, als Seinsmangel – jene, die ihr als *"Zweitwesen,"* als *"Uneigentliche,"* als *"Andere,"* samt all den daraus resultierenden Konsequenzen, aufgedrängt wird. Die Folgen erläutert Beauvoir in den ersten Seiten von *Das andere Geschlecht*: "Die Menschheit ist männlich, und der Mann definiert die Frau nicht als solche, sondern im Vergleich zu sich selbst: sie wird nicht als autonomes Wesen angesehen. [...] Sie ist nichts anderes als das, was der Mann bestimmt. [...] Sie wird im Bezug auf den Mann determiniert und differenziert, er aber nicht in Bezug auf sie. Sie ist das Unwesentliche gegenüber dem Wesentlichen. Er ist das Subjekt, er ist das Absolute: sie ist das Andere" (Beauvoir 2008 (b), 12). Daraus lässt sich schließen, dass sich die Frau wie vorausgeschickt, unausbleiblich in einer Welt zurechtfinden muss, deren Werte sie als die *Andere* weder konstituiert noch mitgeprägt hat. Hinzu kommt, so Beauvoir, dass sich die Frau dieser Herausforderung mit einem Körper stellen muss, der sich maßgeblich von dem des Mannes unterscheidet. Mit Beauvoirs Worten: "Die Frau ist schwächer als der Mann, sie hat weniger Muskelkraft, weniger rote Blutkörperchen, eine geringere Atemkapazität: sie läuft weniger schnell, hebt weniger Gewichte, und es gibt fast keinen Sport, in dem sie es mit dem Mann aufnehmen könnte; sie kann sich ihm nicht im Kampf stellen. Zu dieser Schwäche kommen Unausgeglichenheit, mangelnde Kontrolliertheit und Anfälligkeiten hinzu: das sind Tatsachen. Ihr Zugriff auf die Welt ist also eingeschränkter; sie ist weniger energisch und ausdauernd im Verfolgen von Entwürfen und entsprechend weniger imstande, sie auszuführen. Demnach wäre ihr individuelles Leben weniger reich als das des Mannes" (ebenda, 59f). Dass der Körper der Frau für Beauvoir ein wesentliches Element ihrer Situation, die sie in der Welt einnimmt, darstellt, reicht aber keinesfalls aus, um diese eingehend zu definieren. Denn – so Beauvoirs gesellschaftlich-kontingente Auffassung der Situation der Frau –, da die Gesellschaft keine Spezies ist, lassen sich die Sitten weder aus der Biologie ableiten, noch begründet die Physiologie Werte, sondern es sind biologische Gegebenheiten, die Werte (und dabei spielen die Sitten: Erziehung, Verlobung, Jungfräulichkeit, Eheleben, ungewollte und gewollte Mutterschaft, die Medizin, der gesellschaftliche Stellenwert des Alters und des Todes sowie die Religion und die Ökonomie eine Rolle) annehmen. Und dies kann – dazu äußert sich Simone de Beauvoir stets unmissverständlich – weder eine Rechtfertigung noch eine Erklärung für all die gesellschaftlichen Nachteile, die daraus für die Frau entstehen, sein: "Sobald man eine menschliche Perspektive einnimmt und den Körper von der Existenz her definiert, wird die Biologie eine abstrakte Wissenschaft; wenn das physiologisch Gegebene (etwa die geringere Muskelkraft) eine Bedeutung bekommt, wird sogleich deutlich, daß diese Bedeutung von einem ganzen Kontext abhängt: die »Schwäche« zeigt sich als solche nur im Licht der Ziele, die der Mensch sich setzt, der Instrumente, über die er verfügt, und der Gesetze, die er sich auferlegt. Wenn er die Welt nicht *erfassen* wollte, hätte die Idee des *Zugriffs* auf die Welt keinen Sinn. Wenn bei diesem Erfassen voller Einsatz und Körperkraft nicht erforderlich ist, heben sich unterhalb des brauchbaren Minimums die Unterschiede auf. Wo die Sitten Gewaltanwendung verbieten, kann die Muskelkraft keine Herrschaft begründen: existentielle, ökonomische und moralische Bezüge sind nötig, damit der Begriff *Schwäche* konkret definiert werden kann. Man hat behauptet, die menschliche Spezies sei eine Antiphysis, was nicht ganz richtig ist, denn der Mensch könnte das Gegebene nicht leugnen: gerade in der Art und Weise, wie er es bejaht, konstituiert er dessen Wahrheit. Die Natur hat für ihn nur Realität, sofern sie in sein Handeln einbezogen ist: seine eigene Natur bildet dabei keine Ausnahme. Ebensowenig wie ihren Zugriff auf die Welt kann man die Belastung theoretisch messen, die die Fortpflanzungsfunktion für die Frau darstellt: die Beziehung zwischen Schwangerschaft und individuellem Leben ist bei den Tieren durch den Zyklus der Brunst und der Jahreszeiten natürlich geregelt: bei der Frau ist sie unbestimmt. Allein die Gesellschaft kann darüber entscheiden: je nachdem, ob sie mehr oder weniger Geburten verlangt, je nach den hygienischen Bedingungen, unter denen Schwangerschaft und Niederkunft stattfinden, ist die Unterwerfung der Frau unter die Art mehr oder weniger stark. Wenn man also sagen kann, daß bei den höheren Tieren die individuelle Existenz sich beim Männchen energischer durchsetzt als beim Weibchen, so hängen beim Menschen die individuellen »Möglichkeiten« von der ökonomischen und sozialen Situation ab" (ebenda, 59f).

Die Lebensphasen der Frau sind stets durch psycho-physische Übergänge bzw. durch Brüche mit der Vergangenheit, die oftmals durch gesellschaftlich-kontingente Faktoren erschwert werden, gekennzeichnet. Anders als beim Mann bringen für die Frau beispielsweise die Pubertät, die Einführung in die Sexualität oder zuletzt das Klimakterium einschneidende Veränderungen mit sich. Dennoch ist und bleibt die weibliche Freiheit, wie die des Mannes, eine Transzendenz, die über die eigene Situation hinaus ein frei gewähltes Ziel anstrebt: "Jedes Subjekt setzt sich durch Entwürfe konkret als eine Transzendenz. Es verwirklicht seine Freiheit nur durch deren ständiges Überschreiten auf andere Freiheiten hin. Es gibt keine andere Rechtfertigung der gegenwärtigen Existenz als ihre Ausdehnung in eine unendlich offene Zukunft. [...] Jedes Individuum, dem daran liegt, seine Existenz zu rechtfertigen, empfindet sie als ein unendliches Bedürfnis, sich zu transzendieren. Was nun die Situation der Frau in einzigartiger Weise definiert, ist, daß sie sich – obwohl wie jeder Mensch eine autonome Freiheit – in einer Welt entdeckt und wählt, in der die Männer ihr vorschreiben, die Rolle des Anderen zu übernehmen; sie soll zum Objekt erstarren und zur Immanenz verurteilt sein, da ihre Transzendenz fortwährend von einem essentiellen, souveräneren Bewußtsein transzendiert wird. Das Drama der Frau besteht in diesem Konflikt zwischen dem fundamentalen Anspruch jedes Subjekts, das sich immer als Wesentliche setzt, und den Anforderungen einer Situation, die sie als unwesentlich konstituiert" (ebenda, 25f). Stößt also die transzendente Bewegung der Freiheit der Frau auf ebengenannte Hindernisse biologisch-faktischer oder gesellschaftlich-kontingenter Natur, so entsteht ein Spannungsverhältnis. Nachdem Beauvoir mit dem berühmtesten Satz *"On ne naît pas femme: on le devient"* (Beauvoir 2012, 13) suggeriert, dass die Frau ein *"Werden"* ist, darf diese als dynamische Bewegung der Freiheit bzw. von Transzendenz und Im-

122

manenz und demnach *als* Spannungsverhältnis von Situationsgebundenheit und Freiheit definiert werden. Besagtes Spannungsverhältnis von Situationsgebundenheit (biologisch-faktischer und/oder gesellschaftlich-kontingenter Natur) und Freiheit manifestiert sich im Falle der jungen Frau *als* Spannungsverhältnis von Pubertät, Erziehung und Freiheit; von Sexualität, Erotik, Liebe und Freiheit; von heterosexueller und homosexueller Liebe und Freiheit; von Ehe und Freiheit und von Mutterschaft und Freiheit. Anders bei der bejahrten Frau, bei dem Besagtes *als* Biologie, Alter und Freiheit und als Sexualität, Alter und Freiheit in Erscheinung tritt. Sollte es der Freiheit der jungen und/oder der bejahrten Frau nicht gelingen, sich über biologische und/oder gesellschaftliche Hindernisse hinwegzusetzen, läuft diese Gefahr, in der Immanenz verweilen zu müssen: "Auf die bloße Faktizität seines Daseins reduziert, in seiner Immanenz erstarrt, von seiner Zukunft getrennt, seiner Transzendenz und der Welt, die diese Transzendenz enthüllt, beraubt, scheint ein Mensch [eine Frau] nicht mehr zu sein als eine Sache unter Sachen, die man aus der Gesamtheit der anderen Dinge entfernen kann, ohne daß seine Abwesenheit irgendeine Spur auf der Erde hinterläßt" (Beauvoir 2007 (a), 146f). Findet sich die Frau mit ihrer Immanenz ab, so äußert sich dies in Beauvoirs sogenannten Formen der Unaufrichtigkeit der *Narzißtin,* der *Liebenden* und der *Mystikerin.*

Allerdings stellt Simone de Beauvoir zwei Möglichkeiten, wie die junge und die bejahrte Frau dieser Immanenz bzw. der anschließenden Unaufrichtigkeit entkommen bzw. lernen können, *als* Spannungsverhältnis von Situationsgebundenheit und Freiheit zu existieren, in Aussicht. Für die Bejahrte sieht sie folgenden Ausweg vor: "Viele von der Gesellschaft zurückgestoßene alte Menschen ziehen Gewinn daraus, dass sie sich nicht mehr mühen, ihr zu gefallen. [...] Sie befreit sie von der Heuchelei. [...] »Endlich kann ich ich selbst sein! Ich bin nicht die Frau von Soundso, die Angestellte von Soundso: Ich bin ich.« Sie definierten sich nicht entsprechend ihrer gesellschaftlichen Funktion: Sie fühlten sich als Individuen, die sich in ihrem Verhalten nicht nach irgendwelchen Bestimmungen zu richten brauchen, sondern nach Belieben entscheiden können. «Endlich kann ich alles tun, was ich will», sagten sie. [...] Früher zwang sie der Druck der Gesellschaft dazu; sie taten so, als interessierten sie sich dafür: Jetzt sind sie wirklich sie selbst. Besonders für die Frauen ist das hohe Alter eine Befreiung: Ihr ganzes Leben lang haben sie sich ihrem Mann unterworfen, sich für ihre Kinder aufgeopfert. Nun können sie sich endlich um sich selbst kümmern" (Beauvoir 2008 (e), 636f).

Die junge unabhängige Frau indes sollte ihrer Meinung nach dezidierter, die eigene Freiheit einsetzend, ihr Schicksal in die Hand nehmen. Dennoch darf dies auf keinen Fall bedeuten – und das sowohl im Interesse der Frauen als auch der Männer –, dass gegen die Gesellschaftsverhältnisse, die dies verhindern bzw. erschweren, vorgegangen werden muss. Beauvoir ist der Überzeugung, dass die Frau nur durch Bildung, sexuelle Freiheit, Selbstbestimmtheit bei der Fortpflanzung sowie durch ökonomische Unabhängigkeit frei bzw. unabhängig werden kann.

Diese philosophische Konzeption der Frau wird im letzten Abschnitt zusammen mit Beauvoirs Biografie als zusätzlicher Interpretationsschlüssel dazu dienen, die Darstellung der Frau *als* Spannungsverhältnis von Situationsgebundenheit und Freiheit in *Eine gebrochene Frau* zu beleuchten.

Die Frau *als* Spannungsverhältnis von Situationsgebundenheit und Freiheit in *Eine gebrochene Frau*

Beauvoirs Erzählung *Eine gebrochene Frau* ist 1967 im gleichnamigen Band zusammen mit *Monolog* und *Das Alter der Vernunft* erschienen. Zu den Gründen, die sie dazu bewogen haben, diese drei Stücke zu schreiben, äußerte sie sich in *Alles in allem* wie folgt: "Ich habe kürzlich die Bekenntnisse mehrerer Frauen um die Vierzig erhalten, die um einer anderen willen von ihren Ehemännern verlassen worden waren. Trotz der Verschiedenheit der Charaktere und Lebensumstände gab es doch zwischen allen diesen Berichten interessante Ähnlichkeiten: diese Frauen begriffen nichts von dem, was ihnen zugestoßen war, jede fand die Verhaltensweise ihres Mannes widerspruchsvoll und abwegig, jede hielt die Rivalin für seiner Liebe unwürdig; ihre Welt stürzte in sich zusammen, sie kannten sich schließlich selbst nicht mehr. [Sie] zappelten in völliger Verständnislosigkeit, und mir kam der Gedanke, das Dunkel ihrer Ratlosigkeit zu beschreiben" (Beauvoir 2008 (f), 133). In *Eine gebrochene Frau* schildert Simone de Beauvoir das Schicksal einer fünfundvierzigjährigen Hausfrau, Mutter zweier erwachsener Töchter, die von ihrem Ehemann für

124

eine Jüngere verlassen worden ist. Simone bedient sich hierfür der Tagebuchform und erklärt in ihrer Autobiografie ausführlich, weshalb sie sich dafür entschlossen hat: "Für mich ging es nicht darum, diese banale Geschichte nur einfach in klaren Worten zu erzählen, sondern an dem Tagebuch derjenigen, die in diesem Fall das Opfer war, nachzuweisen, wie sie sich der Wahrheit zu verschließen versucht. Die Schwierigkeit war noch größer [da] [...] Monique ihr ganzes Bemühen darauf richtet, die Wahrheit zu verwischen, indem sie sich selbst belügt, Dinge verdrängt oder entstellt; von Seite zu Seite widerlegt das Tagbuch sich selbst, doch immer nur auf dem Weg über neue Erdichtungen und Vernebelungen. Sie selber schafft das Dunkel, in dem sie so tief versinkt, daß sie zu ihrem eigenen Bild nicht zurückfinden kann. [...] Kein Satz trägt seinen Sinn in sich, keine Einzelheit hat etwas zu bedeuten außer im Zusammenhang dieses Tagebuchs. Die Wahrheit wird niemals eingestanden; sie verrät sich aber, wenn man genau genug hinsieht" (ebenda, 134).

Monique, die „Heldin" dieses Stückes, hat Beauvoir in ihren Memoiren wie folgt beschrieben: "Als Heldin wählte ich eine sympathische Frau mit gleichwohl etwas allzu besitzergreifendem Gefühlsanspruch; nachdem sie auf eine persönliche Karriere verzichtet hat, vermag sie für die ihres Mannes kein Interesse aufzubringen. In intellektueller Hinsicht seiner Frau weit überlegen, hat dieser seit langem aufgehört, sie zu lieben. Er verliebt sich ernstlich in eine Rechtsanwältin, die aufgeschlossener und geistig lebendiger ist als seine Frau, ihm in allem verwandter. Allmählich löst er sich von Monique und beginnt ein neues Leben" (ebenda, 133). Was Simone an dieser Stelle nicht erwähnt, ist, dass sie Monique mit ihren fünfundvierzig eindeutig bejahrter erscheinen lässt. Aller Wahrscheinlichkeit nach spiegelte dies die gesellschaftlichen Verhältnisse – dass Frauen, die aktuell als in den besten Jahren gelten, zu Beauvoirs Zeiten bereits zur älteren Generation gezählt wurden –, wider. Hinzu kommt, dass in der Erzählung das Alter des Ehemannes, der sogar etwas älter als Monique ist, nie thematisiert wird. Dies könnte auf den Umstand zurückgeführt werden, dass das Alter der Frau weniger biologisch, sondern vielmehr gesellschaftlich bestimmt wurde bzw. wird. Dass darüber die Frau damals wie heute, nicht mitbestimmen durfte bzw. mitbestimmt, ist augenscheinlich und bedarf an dieser Stelle keiner weiteren Ausführung. Genannte ist nur eine von unzähligen Situationen, in die Beauvoir die Frau *als*

Spannungsverhältnis von Situationsgebundenheit und Freiheit deutlich in Erscheinung treten lässt. Eine weitere Episode, in der die Transzendenz der Protagonistin eine maßgebliche Einschränkung erfährt, ist die rein biologische Facette des eben Besagten. Denn der Altersunterschied der beiden Frauen bzw. die Jugend, die Energie und die Zukunftsaussichten der Mitstreiterin sind etwas Gegebenes, eine Faktizität. Für Moniques Freiheit ist es unmöglich, sich über dieses Faktum hinwegzusetzen. Ihr bleiben aber zwei Möglichkeiten: entweder entscheidet sie sich, der Wahrheit ins Auge zu blicken, zu handeln und ihr Schicksal endlich in die Hand zu nehmen, oder sie optiert, weiterhin sich selbst etwas vormachend, in ihrer Immanenz zu verweilen. Dass es so weit kommen konnte – so Beauvoir –, steht im engen Zusammenhang mit Moniques Vergangenheit bzw. mit der früheren Entscheidung, sich auf die Rolle der Mutter und Hausfrau beschränkt zu haben. Die Wahl, auf eine eigene Karriere und auf eine finanzielle Unabhängigkeit zu verzichten, hat Monique getroffen, dennoch liegt der Verdacht nahe, dass ihr dies von der Gesellschaft mit Nachdruck aufgezwungen wurde. Die Erziehung eines Mädchens zielt nämlich darauf ab – betont Beauvoir unermüdlich an zahlreichen Stellen von *Das andere Geschlecht* –, aus ihr eine Ehefrau, Hausfrau und Mutter zu machen. Dabei bleibt aber stets zu beachten – und an dieser Stelle gibt sich Simone de Beauvoir gewohnt unnachgiebig –, dass dies in Moniques Augen der Weg des geringsten Widerstandes dargestellt haben muss. Beauvoir wusste nämlich, wovon sie sprach. Als Frau, die sich immerzu vehement geweigert hatte zu heiraten, Kinder in die Welt zu setzen und einen Haushalt zu führen, musste sie zeit ihres Lebens sowohl männlichen als auch weiblichen Anfeindungen standhalten. An dieser Stelle richtet Beauvoir ihr Augenmerk auf die Wahl der Unaufrichtigkeit Moniques, die den einfachen Weg gewählt hat, weder über die Konsequenzen nachdenkend noch gegen gesellschaftliche Vorgaben rebellierend. Weit strenger fällt Beauvoirs Urteil hinsichtlich der erneuten Entscheidung Moniques, sich auf die Rolle der *Liebenden* zu beschränken. Denn als die betrogene Ehefrau mit der Tatsache konfrontiert wird, von ihrem Mann nicht mehr geliebt und endgültig für die jüngere Noëllie verlassen zu werden, entscheidet sie sich untätig zu bleiben d. h. sich in die Unaufrichtigkeit zurückzuziehen. Monique entflieht als Frau dem Spannungsverhältnis nicht, indem sie sich für die Unaufrichtigkeit, für die Rolle der *Liebenden* entscheidet. Die betrogene und verlassene Ehefrau spielt sich vor, alles bzw. sich selbst aus Liebe zu ihren Töchtern und ihrem Mann aufgegeben zu haben. Abermals beweist Beauvoir Strenge, indem sie unmissverständlich darauf hinweist, dass sie dies nicht gelten lässt, denn die Liebe ist und kann niemals aufgezwungen werden. Für Simone, daran sei an dieser Stelle erinnert, basiert die einzig wahre Form der Liebe auf gegenseitiger Anerkennung, die in diesem Fall nicht vorhanden ist. Die Protagonistin erscheint immer wieder *als* Spannungsverhältnis von Situationsgebundenheit und Freiheit bzw. in einer Zerrissenheit, die in der Dialektik von Aufrichtigkeit (ihr Leben selbst in die Hand zu nehmen, sich eine Arbeit zu suchen und sich für die sentimentale und finanzielle Unabhängigkeit zu entscheiden) und Unaufrichtigkeit (sich vorzumachen, dass ihr Mann zu ihr zurückkehren wird und alles wie früher sein wird) entsteht. Monique bzw. einer Freiheit, der es unmöglich ist, die gegebene Situation zu transzendieren, sich also auf ein frei gewähltes Ziel und damit den Zweck eines sich ständig projizierenden Werdens zu erfüllen läuft Gefahr, daran zu zerbrechen. Auch in diesem Fall hegt Beauvoir keine Zweifel: auf den letzten Seiten ihres Buches schildert sie das seelische und körperliche Zerbrechen Moniques und verleiht folglich der Erzählung den Titel *Une femme rompue*, eine gebrochene (zerrissene) Frau.

Im letzten Abschnitt von *Das andere Geschlecht* schreibt Beauvoir, dass die freie Frau erst geboren werden muss. In *Eine gebrochene Frau* hatte sie dies ebenfalls angedeutet, indem sie Moniques junge Konkurrentin als erfolgreich berufstätige, alleinerziehende und finanziell unabhängige Frau beschrieben hat. Die Frau *als* Spannungsverhältnis von Situationsgebundenheit und Freiheit ist und bleibt – ganz in Beauvoirs Sinne – ein nie abgeschlossener Prozess, ein Werden, denn: "Die freie Frau wird gerade erst geboren. Wenn sie soweit ist, daß sie sich selbst erobert hat, wird sie vielleicht Rimbauds Prophezeiung rechtfertigen: »Dichter werden sein! Wenn die endlose Leibeigenschaft der Frau zerschlagen sein wird, wenn sie für sich und durch sich leben wird, weil der […] Mann sie entlassen hat, wird auch sie Dichterin sein! Die Frau wird das Unbekannte finden! Werden ihre Gedankenwelten anders sein als unsere? Sie wird seltsame, unergründliche, abstoßende, köstliche Dinge finden, wir werden sie nehmen, wir werden sie verstehen.« Es ist nicht gesagt, daß ihre »Gedankenwelten« anders sein werden als die der Männer, da die Frau sich befreien wird, indem sie sich mit ihnen gleichsetzt. Es wäre reichlich gewagt, voraussehen zu wollen, in welchem Maße sie besonders belieben wird und in welchem Maße ihre Besonderheiten von Bedeutung bleiben werden. Fest steht nur, daß die Möglichkeiten der Frau bisher erstickt worden, daß sie der Menschheit verlorengegangen sind und daß es in ihrem eigenen Interesse wie auch im Interesse aller höchste Zeit ist, sie ihre Fähigkeiten endlich ausschöpfen zu lassen" (Beauvoir 2008 (b), 881).

Literatur

Beauvoir de, Simone. *Cahiers de jeunesse 1926–1930*. Paris: Gallimard, 2008 (a).

Beauvoir de, Simone. *Simone de Beauvoir Jacques-Laurent Bost. Correspondance croisée (1937 – 1940)*. Paris: Gallimard: 2004.

Beauvoir de, Simone. *Kriegstagebuch. September 1939 – Januar 1941 [Journal de guerre, Septembre 1939 – Janvier 1941, 1990]*. Hamburg: Rowohlt, 1994.

Beauvoir de, Simone. *Eine transatlantische Liebe. Briefe an Nelson Algren 1947 – 1964 [Lettres à Nelson Algren. Un amour transatlantique, 1947-1964, 1997]*. Hamburg: Rowohlt, 1999.

Beauvoir de, Simone. *Für eine Moral der Doppelsinnigkeit [Pour une morale de l'ambïguité, 1947]*. In: Beauvoir de, Simone: *Soll man de Sade verbrennen? Drei Essays zur Moral des Existentialismus*. Hamburg: Rowohlt, 2007 (a).

Beauvoir de, Simone. *Das andere Geschlecht. Sitte und Sexus der Frau [Le deuxième sexe, 1949]*. Hamburg: Rowohlt, 2008 (b).

Beauvoir, Simone de. *Le deuxième sexe II*. Paris: Gallimard, 2012.

Beauvoir de, Simone. *Memoiren einer Tochter aus gutem Hause [Mémoires d'une jeune fille rangée, 1958]*. Hamburg: Rowohlt, 2007 (b).

Beauvoir de, Simone. *In den besten Jahren [La force de l'âge, 1960]*. Hamburg: Rowohlt, 2008 (c).

Beauvoir de, Simone. *Der Lauf der Dinge. [La force des choses, 1963]*. Hamburg: Rowohlt, 2008 (d).

Beauvoir de, Simone. *Eine gebrochene Frau [La femme rompue, 1967]*. In: *Eine gebrochene Frau*. Hamburg: Rowohlt, 2007, S. 89-185 (c).

Beauvoir de, Simone. *Das Alter* [La Vieillesse, 1970]. Hamburg: Rowohlt, 2008 (e).

Beauvoir de, Simone. *Alles in allem [Tout compte fait, 1972]*. Hamburg: Rowohlt, 2008 (f).

Beauvoir de, Simone. *Die Zeremonie des Abschieds [La cérémonie des adieux, 1981]*. Hamburg: Rowohlt, 2004.

Beauvoir de, Simone. *Briefe an Sartre Band 1: 1930 – 1939 [Lettres à Sartre 1930 – 1939, 1990]*. Hamburg: Rowohlt, 2008 (g).

Beauvoir de, Simone. *Briefe an Sartre Band 2: 1940 – 1963 [Lettres à Sartre 1940 – 1963, 1990]*. Hamburg: Rowohlt, 1998.

Lacoin, Élisabeth. *Zaza: 1907-1929: amie de Simone de Beauvoir. Correspondence et carnets de Elisabeth Lacoin*. Paris: L'Harmattan, 2004.

Monteil, Claudine. *Die Schwestern Hélène und Simone de Beauvoir*. München: Nymphemburg, 2006.

CORNELIA EȘIANU

KUNST UND OFFENBARUNG BEI FRIEDRICH SCHLEGEL

Vorliegende Studie untersucht das Verhältnis von Kunst und Offenbarung bei Friedrich Schlegel vor dem Hintergrund der allgemeinen Frage, ob das Geistige noch Relevanz für die praktische Philosophie heute hat. Sie konzentriert sich dabei auf die Formulierung einer Antwort, die Kunst als Offenbarung des Geistigen im Menschen versteht. Es ist die These Schlegels, dass die Philosophie das Bedürfnis des Menschen nach dem Geistigen nicht stillen kann. Es ist aber die Philosophie selbst, die den Menschen zum Begriff der Offenbarung führt. Zwar vermag sie den Menschen zum Leben anzuleiten, ist aber außer Stande, dessen Leben zu ersetzen. Angesichts des „entgeisteten" Lebens des modernen Menschen wird hier ein Motiv schlegelschen Denkens, das Kunst in der Spannung zwischen Moral und Religion betrachtet, erneut aufgenommen und methodisch erforscht.

1. Einleitung

Friedrich Schlegels Philosophie fängt an mit dem Selbstvertrauen, dem Glauben an sich, an ein „*besseres edleres Selbst*" (Schlegel 1964b, 175), und hört auf mit dem höchsten Begriff, dem Glauben an die Offenbarung. Der Glaube ist, so Schlegel, dem Wissen nicht entgegengesetzt, sondern „er ist nur eine eigentümliche Art des Wissens, ein sich selbst beschränkendes, mit Willen sich selbst anhaltendes, beharrendes Wissen"(ebenda, 175). Der Glaube selbst ist „das innerste Leben des Subjektes" (ebenda, 174).

Ihrem inneren Wesen nach ist die Kunst gemäß Schlegel subjektiv – er betrachtet sie in anderem Zusammenhang aber auch objektiv –, denn sie macht die Offenbarung zu ihrem Gegenstand. Kunst wird in diesem Kontext als eine Ergänzung der Wissenschaft an deren Grenze zur Religion verstanden. Mit anderen Worten, Kunst vermittelt zwischen Wissenschaft und Religion.

Jenseits dieser vorerst aus heuristischen Gründen zu verstehenden existierenden Versuche Schlegels zur Systematisierung jeglicher wissenschaftlicher Disziplinen und höherer Künste, die die LeserInnen auf

Hegel und dessen geistesverwandtes Vorhaben verweisen mögen, ist die Frage nach dem Begriff der Offenbarung bei Schlegel zu stellen im Hinblick auf die Erörterung seines Bezugs zur Kunst. Einige Antworten auf diese Fragen zu geben wird in vorliegendem Aufsatz versucht, ohne allerdings die Problematik damit als erschöpft beantwortet ansehen zu können oder zu wollen.

2. Philosophie und Offenbarung

Offenbarung bedeutet Enthüllung (gr. *apokálypsis*), Erscheinung (gr. *epifaneia*, lat. *revelatio, manifestatio*). Gott lässt (sich) sehen, lässt (sich) erkennen, enthüllt (sich), spricht im Alten Testament. Eine begriffliche Prägnanz erlangt der Terminus „Offenbarung" allmählich erst durch das Christentum. Im Neuen Testament erfolgt die Gotteserkenntnis wesentlich durch Christus, den Mittler der Gotteserkenntnis, dessen Offenbarungs-Funktion vor allem dort benannt wird, wo die von der Philosophie kommende Frage nach der Erkenntnismöglichkeit der Transzendenz Gottes auftaucht (Ritter 1984, 1105f).

Als einer der zentralen Begriffe der Theologie bedeutet Offenbarung in einem allgemeinen Sinne die Selbstmitteilung oder Kundgabe Gottes an die Menschen. Gott offenbart sich selbst in sehr allgemeinen Ereignissen (*allgemeine Offenbarung*), die von allen beobachtbar sind, wie z.B. die Existenz des Universums und seine Übereinstimmung mit den Naturgesetzen, oder in gewissen, besonderen historischen Ereignissen (*besondere Offenbarung*). Diese Ereignisse sind in dem Sinne eine Offenbarung, dass Gott sie hervorgebracht hat und sie etwas von ihm zeigen. Es ist hervorzuheben, dass das Wort „Apokalypse" ursprünglich zur Bibel gehörte und von keinem griechischen Weisen verwendet wurde (ebenda, 1105). Erst mit F.H. Jacobi wird der Begriff „Offenbarung" zu einem Begriff der spekulativen Philosophie (ebenda, 1122).

Friedrich Schlegel wird nicht müde, in seinen Schriften immer wieder zu betonen, dass das Göttliche oder die Gottheit, mit der, in seiner Sicht, und anders als bei Kant, das Sittengesetz zusammenhängt (Schlegel 1964b, 102), sich begrifflich nicht erfassen lässt. Es ist dies eine Behauptung, die Schlegel zu seiner Zeit z.B. mit Friedrich Heinrich Jacobi teilte. „Begreifen", so interpretiert Hegel Jacobi, „heißt Bedingungen des Bedingten erkennen. Das Übernatürliche ist gerade das, was keine Bedingungen hat, nicht begriffen werden kann, ist nur als Tatsache für uns, ist für uns nur auf eine unmittelbare, nicht vermittelte Weise" (Hegel 1986, 167). Zwar strebt die Philosophie in Schlegels Sicht nach „positiver *Erkenntnis*", nach „wissenschaftlicher *Bestimmung*" und „*Erklärung* des Göttlichen", aber diese Aufgabe kann „nie vollendet werden", denn das Höchste, dessen Erkenntnis zwar „das heiligste Bedürfnis des menschlichen Geistes" (Schlegel 1964a, 166) ist, lässt sich dennoch begrifflich nicht erfassen. Schlegel argumentiert diese Idee dahingehend, dass die Erkenntnis eines unendlichen Gegenstandes *wie der Gegenstand selbst unendlich* ist. Das bedeutet aber, dass diese Erkenntnis auch nicht „in bestimmten Worten völlig ausgesprochen" und auch „nie in den engen Grenzen eines Systems eingeschlossen und zusammengefasst werden" (ebenda, 166) kann. Die Conclusio scheint daher für ein denkendes Wesen recht niederschmetternd zu sein: „Jeder, der über das Ich des göttlichen Wesens nachgedacht hat, hat früher oder später denn doch das Geständnis abgelegt, dass die vollkommene Erkenntnis dieses unendlichen Gegenstandes unerreichbar sei" (Schlegel 1958, 8).

Somit wird ein Problem diagnostiziert. Es ist in Schlegels Augen ein Problem der Philosophie – solange sich diese (nur) als Wissenschaft versteht –, angesichts dessen sie ihr Unvermögen zeigt. Erinnert sei daran, dass der Begriff der Wissenschaft noch zu Schlegels Zeit der von Aristoteles überlieferte ist. Wissenschaft wird als Erkenntnis aus Prinzipien bzw. Grundsätzen begriffen. Sie wird als kategorisch-deduktives System von Erkenntnissen gefasst, das durch die Bestimmungen der „Allgemeinheit", „Notwendigkeit" und „Wahrheit" charakterisiert wird. „Wissenschaft, so ferne wir sie in dem Menschen betrachten, ist ein gründliches Erkenntniß eines Dings, oder die Fertigkeit des Verstandes, alles, was man behauptet, aus unwiedersprechlichen Gründen darzuthun. Leben die Menschen ewig; so behalten sie auch ihren Verstand. Dieser muß mit seinen Fertigkeiten gewiß nicht ab, sondern vielmehr zunehmen" (Zedler 1998, 1346f). Das „Hohe in den Wissenschaften" ist dasjenige „welches, wo man nicht zuvor viel andere Sachen verstanden, nicht begriffen werden kann" (ebenda, 1406).

Schlegel unterscheidet in seiner *Logik*-Vorlesung von 1805-1806 zwischen theoretischen und praktischen Wissenschaften. Unter den theoretischen Wissenschaften nimmt die Theologie, oder die Wissenschaft von dem höchsten Wesen, die bedeutendste Stelle ein. Andere sind Geschichte, Physik und Mathematik, aber auch Philosophie und Philologie. Zur näheren Darstellung der Begriffe Wissenschaft und Wissenschaften im Sinne von Erkenntnis und Lehre. Doch wie Ernst Behler in seiner Friedrich-Schlegel-Monographie ausführt, war Philosophie für Schlegel „ein nie zu vollendender Weg des Denkens, der auch im Alter nicht zum Abschluß gekommen war" (Behler 1996, 145f). Philosophie stellt sich für Schlegel mehr als ein „*Suchen*", ein „*Streben* nach Wissenschaft als eine Wissenschaft selbst"(Schlegel 1964a, 166) dar. Die Philosophie spielt aber für Schlegel in letzter Instanz die Rolle einer Wegbereiterin für die Theologie. Die Aufgabe der Philosophie ist es nach Friedrich Schlegel, uns zum Unendlichen zu führen, uns „von dem Scheine des Endlichen und dem Glauben an die Dinge zu befreien und uns zu einer Ansicht der unendlichen Fülle und Mannigfaltigkeit erkennen lehren" (Schlegel 1964a, 335). In seinen Kölner Vorlesungen über die Philosophie äußerte er folgende Überzeugung:

> Die Philosophie lehrte uns, daß alles Göttliche sich nur andeuten, nur mit Wahrscheinlichkeit voraussetzen lasse, und daß wir daher die Offenbarung für die höchste Wahrheit annehmen müssen (Schlegel 1964b, 174).

Die „Wiederherstellung des verlornen göttlichen Ebenbildes im Menschen", wie es am Anfang der *Vorrede* zu seinen *Vorlesungen über die Philosophie der Geschichte* heißt, entwickelt sich für Schlegel zum „nächste(n) Gegenstand" und zur „erste(n) Aufgabe der Philosophie" (Schlegel 1971a, 3). Gemäß der Behauptung von Ludwig Wirz war die Idee des Unendlichen, die Sehnsucht nach Gott, in Schlegels ganzem Leben allbeherrschend (Wirz 1939, 5); sie blieb für den Philosophen Schlegel das wichtigste Reflexionsobjekt, das in diesem Zusammenhang auch seine Überlegungen zum Thema Offenbarung legitimiert.

2.1. Der Begriff der Offenbarung im Schlegelschen Diskurs

Eine wesentliche Frage bezieht sich auf die Bedeutung dieses Begriffs für den Philosophen und Literaturkritiker Schlegel, da angenommen werden muss, dass die „Offenbarung" bei Schlegel nicht strikt dem religiösen oder theologischen Universum verhaftet bleibt, speziell wenn auch bedacht wird, dass „der bedeutendste Kritiker der deutschen Romantik", wie Ernst Behler ihn nennt, einen eigenartigen Umgang mit Termini, sei es nun philosophischer oder anderer Art, aufwies. Zwar spricht Schlegel über die Offenbarung in seiner Theorie der Gottheit im Rahmen seiner Kölner Vorlesungen über die Philosophie von 1804-1806 und gewissermaßen ausführlicher zu einem späteren Zeitpunkt, nämlich 1812, nach seiner Konversion zum Katholizismus, in seiner veröffentlichten Rezension über F.H. Jacobis Schrift *Von den göttlichen Dingen und ihrer Offenbarung* von 1812, doch Schlegels Theorie der Gottheit liegt eine philosophische Theorie der Offenbarung zugrunde, deren wichtigste Züge bereits in seiner Theorie des Menschen angeführt wurden. Der Gedanke liegt daher nahe, dass dieser Begriff von Schlegel vor allem in einer umfassenderen Bedeutung gebraucht wird, so dass die Möglichkeit der Überschneidung mit anderen Diskursen – von dem literatur- und sprachkritischen über den philosophischen und ästhetischen bis hin zum theologischen und religiösen Diskurs – erhalten bleibt.

Allerdings, wie kommt Schlegel zur Notwendigkeit der Annahme einer Idee der Offenbarung, der Mitteilung eines Höchsten, das im weiteren Sinne z.B. auch als die Bedeutung eines Sprach- oder Kunstgebildes, als das Göttliche in der Natur oder im Menschen, oder allgemein im Sinne einer in einem gewissen Augenblick hervorschauenden, dem Ich aber lange verborgen gebliebenen Struktur aufgefasst werden kann? Offensichtlich auf jene Art, dass er zunächst ihre logische Möglichkeit aufgrund von subjektiven Wahrnehmungen herausarbeitet und infolgedessen ihre Wirklichkeit für nicht widerlegbar annimmt. Einen erhellenden Hinweis hierzu könnte folgende Textpassage aus Schlegels Kölner *Vorlesungen über die Philosophie* geben:

> Wenn wir uns beim Nachdenken nicht leugnen können, daß alles in uns ist, so können wir uns das Gefühl der Beschränktheit, das uns im Leben beständig begleitet, nicht anders erklären, als indem wir annehmen, daß wir nur ein Stück von uns selbst sind. Dies führte geradewegs zu einem Glauben an ein Du, nicht als ein (wie im Leben) dem Ich Entgegengesetztes, Ähnliches (Mensch gegen Mensch, nicht Tier, Stein gegen den Menschen), sondern überhaupt als ein Gegen-Ich, und hiermit verbindet sich denn notwendig der Glaube an ein Ur-Ich. Dieses Ur-Ich ist der Begriff, der eigentlich die Philosophie begründet. Hier in diesem Punkte greifen alle Radien der Philosophie zusammen. Unser Ich, philosophisch betrachtet, enthält also eine Beziehung auf ein Ur-Ich, und ein Gegen-Ich; es ist zugleich ein Du, Er, Wir. (Schlegel 1964a, 337)

Es ist die Philosophie – hier nun im Sinne von reflexiver Tätigkeit des Subjekts verstanden –, die uns „lehrte", „dass wir [...] die Offenbarung für die höchste Wahrheit annehmen müssen" (Schlegel 1964b, 174). Unser Ich, ein Stück von uns selbst, befindet sich in einer Art Dreiecksbeziehung mit einem Gegen-Ich und einem sogenannten Ur-Ich, mit denen er sich zugleich zu identifizieren scheint. Dem Ich liegt das Ur-Ich zugrunde. Dieses Ur-Ich ist alles, außer ihm ist nichts. Alles ist nur ein Teil der unendlichen Ichheit. Alles, was wir außer uns wahrnehmen, ist ein lebendiges Gegen-Ich, ein Du. Dieses Du bezeichnet Schlegel als „das Reelle in der Anschauung", das eigentlich als ein Kunstwerk, als ein Zeichen rezipiert wird, das in der Sprache seinen Ort antrifft, von wo er sich dem Ich zeigen und von diesem auch wahrgenommen werden kann:

> Jede Kraft, sobald sie in ein Verhältnis zu uns tritt, d.h. sobald wir sie denken, wahrnehmen, und zu erforschen und zu ergründen suchen, wird sie ein Du; dies ist das Reelle in der Anschauung.

> Der Stoff ist nichts in der Anschauung. Das, was ihr allein Realität gibt, ist das Wesen, die Bedeutung, der Sinn desselben, ist die Sprache, die uns dunkel anspricht, worin sich uns das Du verständlich machen will. Das innere Wesen und die Natur der Pflanzen und Tiere sind die Worte und Sprache gleichsam, welche das entfernte, verschlossene Du zu uns redet. Durch die Bedeutung wird uns auf diese Weise, was sonst nichts sagender Stoff ist, zum Wort und Bilde des uns tief verborgenen, jedoch verwandten Geistes (Schlegel 1964a, 338f).

Zur Notwendigkeit der Idee einer Offenbarung des Höchsten gelangt Schlegel durch Reflexion. Schlegel unterscheidet weiter mehrere Arten von Offenbarung, von denen die erste, wie er annimmt, in der Geschichte der Menschheit – also in einem doch etwas besonderen, sprich anthropologischen Diskurs – an deren Anfang in Form einer Mitteilung der Vernunft durch die „Einwirkung eines höhern Geistes" (Schlegel 1964b, 36) stattgefunden hat.

Indem er sich auf die christliche Philosophie stützt, unterscheidet der späte Schlegel in seiner Jacobi-Rezension drei Arten von Offenbarung: Die erste Art ist die Selbstoffenbarung und Manifestation der Gottheit im Logos, im *ewigen* Wort, die Schlegel auch die metaphysische nennt. Bezüglich der ersten Art von Offenbarung merkt Schlegel an, dass Philosophien, die die Dreieinigkeit und die Lehre vom Logos anerkennen, „nicht aus der Vernunft allein geschöpft, sondern außer der Vernunft immer noch eine andere übernatürliche Erkenntnisquelle aufgestellt und anerkannt" haben, wie z.B. die eigentliche Eingebung, die künstlerische Begeisterung, die Platonische Erinnerung oder die geistige Anschauung. Die zweite Art der Offenbarung ist die *innere*, welche die moralische genannt wird, weil sie sich „in der Stimme des Gewissens und im *sittlichen Gefühl* kund gibt" (Schlegel 1975, 444). Die dritte ist die geschichtliche Offenbarung, die „*positive,* im Christentum *gegebene*". Für Schlegel ist diese dritte Art von Offenbarung die wichtigste, denn durch sie gewinnen die ersten zwei an „Haltung, Festigkeit und Zusammenhang". Die geschichtliche Tatsache der Erlösung ist für den späten Schlegel „der Mittelpunkt aller Menschengeschichte" und bringt „erst einen Zusammenhang und Sinn in das Ganze" (ebenda, 444).

Es ist eben die Vernunft als das Allgemeine, Notwendige im Menschen, die für Schlegel nicht das Produkt einer höher organisierten Form der Materie, sondern das Ergebnis des Geistes ist. Auf die Mitteilung der Vernunft erfolgte eine zweite, die sogenannte „eigentliche" Offenbarung, die von Schlegel als eine „Mitteilung der Begeisterung" bezeichnet wird. Der Grund für die Notwendigkeit dieser zweiten Offenbarung, so wird argumentiert, besteht in einer Unzulänglichkeit der Vernunft, die sich in der Regel nur „zu einer negativen Idee des Unendlichen" erheben kann. Das ist eine Feststellung, zu der Schlegel offensichtlich auf dem diffizilen Weg seiner Auseinandersetzung mit der kritischen Philosophie Kants und vor allem mit dessen Konzept einer reinen Vernunft gebracht wurde.

2.2. Exkurs zu Schlegels Kant-Analyse

In Friedrich Schlegels *Geschichte der alten und neuen Literatur* (1812-1814) heißt es über Kant:

> Das Größte was Kant geleistet hat, bleibt immer, wie er gezeigt, dass die Vernunft in sich selbst streitend und an und für sich leer und ohne Inhalt sei; mithin nur in ihrer Anwendung auf die Erfahrung und im Gebiete derselben gültig, eine Erkenntnis von Gott oder göttlichen Dingen durch sie zu erreichen, also nicht möglich sei (Schlegel 1961, 398).

Gleich im Anschluss an diese Anerkennung, die Schlegel Kants kritischer Philosophie zukommen lässt, setzt auch dessen Kritik ein:

> Statt aber nun anzuerkennen, dass diese [Erkenntnis von Gott – C.E.]
> nur durch innere Wahrnehmung erlangt werde, dass die höhere Phi-
> losophie eine Erfahrungswissenschaft sei, statt der Vernunft auch
> hier im Gebiete der übersinnlichen Erfahrung dieselbe zweite, ord-
> nende und dienende Stelle anzuweisen, stellte er statt dessen den-
> noch die Vernunft, obwohl unter der ihr gar nicht anstehenden Mas-
> ke des Glaubens wieder auf den Thron (ebenda, 398).

Kants Lösung, „Gott" als Postulat in seiner *Kritik der praktischen Vernunft* einzuführen (Kant 1968, 124f), überzeugt Schlegel, wie später auch Schelling, nicht. *„Unser Resultat"*, behauptet Schelling, „fordert eine Erweiterung der Philosophie selbst, … namentlich daß ein anderes als bloß rationales, daß ein reales Verhältniß des menschlichen Bewußtseyns zu Gott begriffen werden könne" (Schelling 1996, 204). Der „neuere Rationalismus", dessen Grundlage Kants Unternehmen darstellt, die Religion auf eine Forderung, auf ein Postulat der praktischen Vernunft zu bauen, lässt, wie Schelling interpretiert,

> nur soviel als wirkliche Religion und Offenbarung gelten, als
> nothwendig ist zur Bestehung Gottes des Vollstreckers des morali-
> schen Gesetzes; was darüber hinaus ist, erklärt dieser Rationalismus
> für bloße Philosophie alexandrinische, neuplatonische oder über-
> haupt orientalische (ebenda, 201).

In Friedrich Schlegels Rezension der bereits angeführten Schrift von Jacobi heißt es:

> Der Kantische glauben sollende und glauben wollende, oft auch
> nicht recht wollende oder könnende *Vernunftglauben* – ein trotziges
> und verzagtes Wesen, wie das menschliche Herz in der Schrift ge-
> nannt wird – war auf keine Weise geeignet, dauerhaften Eingang und
> festen Grund in den Gemütern zu fassen. Es war ja dieser Glauben
> offenbar nichts anders als die Vernunft selbst, welche, nachdem sie
> aus dem vordern Hauptgebäude der Kantischen Philosophie feierlich
> ausgestoßen worden, durch die Hintertür (*jure postliminii*) unter der
> falschen Maske des Glaubens und der Religion wieder hereinge-
> schlichen kam, und unter einem neuen Namen ihr altes Wesen und
> Unwesen weiter trieb (Schlegel 1975, 442).

Schlegels Kritik an Kant ist diskussionswürdig, steht hier jedoch nicht zur Debatte. Mit Schlegels Kant-Diskussion habe ich mich näher in meiner Dissertation beschäftigt (Eşianu 2013, 33f). Festgehalten soll allerdings werden, dass es dieser Sachverhalt ist, der Schlegel zur Ausarbeitung einer Theorie des Bewusstseins antreibt und seine eigene Philosophie, die Lebensphilosophie seiner späteren Jahre, auch als

Gottesphilosophie bezeichnet, in der das Thema der Offenbarung wieder zur Sprache kommt, möglich machen wird. Jacobi selber, so Schlegel, habe seinerseits „auf die Offenbarung und eine eigentümliche Ansicht derselben wohl vielfach hingedeutet" (Schlegel 1975, 442). Trotzdem ist Schlegel deswegen nicht als ein Vernunftfeind oder Irrationalist abzustempeln, wie z.B. ein Georg Lukács mit Bezug auf die Romantiker, hauptsächlich auf Schelling, zu argumentieren versucht hat (Lukacs 1955).

Zwar ist die Vernunft für Schlegel das Vermögen zu denken, sie ist „die notwendige Grundform des menschlichen Bewusstseins", aber sie ist nicht „das Höchste", denn, wie der Romantiker in seinem Sprachduktus hervorhebt, „mit der bloßen Vernunft würde sich der Mensch nie zu dem Höheren, Göttlichen erheben" können. Die Vernunft ist „nichts als ein abstraktes Verbindungsvermögen, im Endlichen und mit dem Endlichen". Schlegel verwirft die Kantische Unterscheidung zwischen Vernunft und Verstand und kehrt zur Bedeutung von Verstand im Sinne von Nous, nämlich Geist, zurück. In seinem Aufsatz *Von der Seele* von 1823 kommentiert er seine eigene Verstandes- und Vernunftkonzeption folgenderweise:

Der Verstand ist das auf das Einzelne, Individuelle, Bestimmte und Positive gerichtete Denken, es mag dieses Wirkliche und Positive, Gegebene, nun ein Zeitliches und Vergängliches sein oder das Ewige. Eben daher gibt es zweierlei Arten von Verstand, einen irdischen und gemeinen, einen erleuchteten, geistigen und göttlichen; je nachdem der Verstand, der immer einen bestimmten Gegenstand hat, auf das eine oder das andere gerichtet ist. Den ersten mag man der Vernunft weit unterordnen; der zweite ist über sie so erhaben, als die volle Anschauung des Ewigen über das leere Selbstdenken. Die Vernunft ist aber das Vermögen, alle möglichen Gedanken und Begriffe nach einem innern Gesetz der Notwendigkeit untereinander zu verknüpfen, entgegenzustellen und zu vergleichen, welches sich nach allen Seiten gränzenlos fortsetzen lässt, wenn Gränze und Ziel nicht anders woher gegeben sind; sie ist mit einem Worte das unendliche Denken oder das ins Unendliche fortgesetzte Verknüpfen der selbsterzeugten, nach eigener Freiheit zusammengestellten oder getrennten Gedanken und Begriffe. Sie ist nicht das dem Wirklichen, Positiven außer uns, es mag nun ein Einzelnes oder das Ewige sein, hingegebne Denken, sondern ein freies, inneres Selbstdenken und eben deswegen ist auch das Denken des Denkens, die Erfassung des eignen Denkens auf der Tat, oder die Reflexion, der Vernunft und nicht dem Verstande eigen (Schlegel 1975, 605f).

Was Schlegel deutlich bekämpft, ist die Bevorzugung der Vernunft in einem restriktiven Sinne zuungunsten anderer menschlicher Vermögen wie z.B. der Einbildungskraft, des Verstandes oder des Willens. So bezeichnet Schlegel die vollständige Isolierung und Trennung der menschlichen Kräfte, welche laut ihm doch nur gemeinsam, d.h. in „freier Vereinigung" gesund bleiben können, als „die eigentliche Erbsünde der modernen Bildung" (Schlegel 1967, 58). So liest man bei Schlegel, dass selbst „unsere größten Denker [...] nicht ganz frei von Abgötterei mit der Vernunft (sind)" (ebenda, 58). Schlegel zitiert Jacobi als denjenigen, der gegen „solche despotische Eingriffe [...] die Rechte des Herzens in Schutz" (ebenda 58) nimmt. Der Romantiker plädiert somit gegen die „Alleinherrschaft" der Vernunft in der Philosophie. Vernunft und Offenbarung werden von ihm aber als entgegengesetzte Begriffe behandelt. In dieser Hinsicht stimmt er, wie er selbst behauptet, mit Jacobi überein, dass „der Gegensatz zwischen Vernunft, es sei nun der natürlichen oder der wissenschaftlichen, und der Offenbarung als der wichtigste und entscheidendste für die gesamte Philosophie gilt" (Schlegel 1975, 442). Es ist dies ein Kennzeichen der gesamten Aufklärungsphilosophie.

Erinnert sei in diesem Rahmen daran, dass für Kant selbst der „Offenbarungsglaube" identisch mit der positiven Religion und dem zufällig gegebenen „statutarischen" Kirchenglauben ist. Jeder Offenbarungsglaube muss in seinem Kern mit der reinen moralischen Vernunftreligion übereinstimmen, sich vor ihr rechtfertigen und sie befördern (Kant 1968, 102f). Für Fichte, der sich Kant anschließt, ist Offenbarung eine „durch die Causalität Gottes in der Sinnenwelt bewirkte Erscheinung, wodurch er sich als moralischen Gesetzgeber ankündigt" (Fichte 1964, 48). Die so verstandene Offenbarung sei zwar denkmöglich, aber keine empirische Erscheinung könne als Offenbarung nachgewiesen werden. Zwar lässt Schlegel die moralische Offenbarung gelten, hebt jedoch hervor, dass diese nur durch die geschichtliche Offenbarung „Haltung, Festigkeit und Zusammenhang" gewinne. Schlegel, könnte man sagen, weist den Standpunkt der kritischen Philosophie gegenüber der Offenbarung nicht kategorisch zurück, sondern meint nur, er sei unzureichend, denn der Mensch besitze „Organe für die höhere Welt, für Gott und die göttlichen Dinge" (Schlegel 1975, 452). Eine in der Tat komplexe Situation!

2.3. Die Mitteilung der Begeisterung

In seiner Theorie der Gottheit nimmt Schlegel zwei Arten der Offenbarung an, die erste, die Mitteilung der Vernunft, und die zweite, die Mitteilung der Begeisterung. Diese zweite und eigentliche Offenbarung (welche eigentlich die dritte ist, wie Ernst Behler auslegt), die Mitteilung der Begeisterung, ist für Schlegel identisch mit dem „Anfang des Höhern im Menschen" (Schlegel 1964b, 34). Sicher wäre es hier nötig, eine genauere Differenzierung zwischen der zweiten und dritten Art von Offenbarung bei Schlegel vorzunehmen, doch das ginge über den Rahmen des vorliegenden Essays hinaus. Außerdem ist die Bedeutung des Begriffs „Offenbarung" für unsere Fragestellung vielmehr in einem weiten Sinne – so wie er auch in der Epoche aufgefasst wurde – zu verstehen. Erwähnt soll aber werden, dass sich von diesem Punkte aus ein interessanter Bogen zu Mircea Eliade und seiner Theorie des Mythos herstellen lässt. Mit seinen Untersuchungen zu den religiösen Vorstellungen archaischer Gesellschaften scheint sich Eliade auf die Spuren dieser von Schlegel so genannten „mißverstandenen Offenbarung" zu begeben, während er in seinem Buch *Kosmos und Geschichte* die von Schlegel als dritte bezeichnete Art von Offenbarung (die Menschwerdung Gottes – die höchste Hierophanie in der Sprache von Eliade, die Offenbarung in der Geschichte) näher untersucht. Die sich in der Natur offenbarende Gottheit, der Pantheismus, ist vor allem für den späten Schlegel nicht mehr das Wahre. Eliade spricht allerdings nicht von Pantheismus, wenn er sich auf die ältesten religiösen Vorstellungen bezieht, sondern von „Pan-Ontismus" (z.B. der Inder). Aber beide Autoren erwähnen die Möglichkeit einer Verbindung von Polytheismus und Monotheismus, d.h. insofern sich die vielen Gottheiten einer höheren unterordnen lassen. Schlegel sieht das mit Bezug auf die indische (jedoch nicht griechische) Mythologie gegeben (Schlegel 1958, 25). In seinem Buch *Das Heilige und das Profane* spricht er von dem einen höchsten Wesen der archaischen Völker, das, obwohl es ein „ferner Gott" (Eliade 1984, 108f) ist und also im Leben des Volkes nur noch eine unbedeutende Rolle spielt, in Notsituationen dennoch angerufen wird.

Mit der Begeisterung entsteht im Menschen die positive Idee des Unendlichen oder der Gottheit. „Kein Mensch entbehrt der Vernunft", sagt Schlegel und merkt weiter an: „aber wohl vermisst man bei vielen diese höhere Begeisterung, die auf der positiven Idee der Gottheit beruht" (Schlegel 1964b, 34). Begeisterung beschreibt Schlegel als „das, was den Menschen von dem Endlichen zu dem Unendlichen erhebt und ihm den Blick in die höhere göttliche Welt öffnet". Mit anderen Worten: Die positive Idee des Unendlichen oder der Gottheit entsteht im Menschen, so Schlegel, durch Begeisterung. Begeisterung ist ein Zustand, „der uns aus dem niedern Bewußtsein über die Schranken hinaus in das hohe, freie, unendliche hinaufhebt" (Schlegel 1964a, 393). Sie ist ein Gefühl, „Leidenschaft für das Unendliche" (ebenda, 394). Schlegel verwendet synonym zu Begeisterung als Offenbarung auch die Termini „Ahndung", „Erleuchtung" und „Enthusiasmus-Genie" (Schlegel 1971b, 58).

An dieser Stelle ist der Aufsatz von Friedrich Stolberg über die Begeisterung anzuführen, der 1782 im Erstdruck im „Deutschen Museum" erschien und dessen Autor von Schlegel besonders geschätzt wurde. Dieser erwähnt ihn lobend in seiner *Geschichte der alten und neuen Literatur* von 1812-1814 (Schlegel 1961, 400) und schreibt eine positive Rezension über Stolbergs Schrift *Geschichte der Religion Jesu Christi* (Schlegel 1975, 86f).

Die Begeisterung wird hier als eine Kraft beschrieben, die nur einige Menschen ergreift, die aber fast alle Menschen durch die „Ergriffenen" erfahren haben. Sie ist „ein seltenes Geschenk der Natur" und kann nur vom „Vorurteil und Ideentand" verhindert werden. Sie ist im Grunde eine Macht, „eine Stimme der Natur" (Stolberg 1970, 34) und wird durch drei Charakteristika gekennzeichnet: 1) „Sie ist wenigen gegeben." 2) „Sie ist unabhängig von dem, den sie besucht, und steht ihm niemals zu Gebot." 3) „Sie wirkt durch ihre Geweihten auf andre sicher und schnell" (ebenda, 34). Man könnte fast sagen, dass sich hier um eine Art geistige Droge handelt, die ihre Wirkung wellenartig ausübt und jede und jeden erfasst, der sich in ihre Bahn begibt, aber auch mit „dem Strome der Zeit" (ebenda, 36) nicht aufhören wird. Stolberg stellt sie in Form einer Person dar, die nicht geleitet und beeinflusst werden kann. „Ihren Lieblingen begegnet sie mit dem größten Eigensinn" (ebenda, 35), denn indem sie „auf ihren Flügeln Einen erhebt, wehet sie in ihrem Fluge tausend an" (ebenda, 36). Das physische Attribut der Begeisterung ist jenes der Wärme, das mit der „innige(n) Liebe im Herzen" (ebenda, 41) gedacht werden muss. Der wahre

Dichter ist jener, dem diese Eigenschaft zugeschrieben werden kann. Ihm „schenkt" die Begeisterung „das Original" (ebenda, 38). Der Dichter „gibt nur die Übersetzung, eine Übersetzung, welche weniger als andre das Original erreicht!" Die Natur gibt jedem Begeisterten ihr Geschenk „nur auf Augenblicke". Stolberg erklärt das so: „Ich meine den schnellen Blick, welcher dem Begeisterten richtige Verhältnisse zeigt, ehe er sie berechnen kann – die schöpferische Kraft, welche idealische Welten schafft und zerstört – Ahnungen von Ideen, von Wahrheiten, von Empfindungen, die außer dem Gesichtskreise des gewöhnlichen Zustandes des Menschen liegen." Eben diese Kraft – die „von jeher für etwas Göttliches gehalten ward" (ebenda, 42) – macht den Dichter zum Visionären, während der Philosoph – wie Stolberg betont – ein Forscher ist.

Auch Schlegel erklärt Begeisterung nicht aus der Vernunft. Zu der positiven Idee der Gottheit kann sich die Vernunft nicht erheben, behauptet Schlegel. Den *lebendigen Gott* selbst kann man durch Vernunft nicht erkennen. „Die positive Idee der Gottheit [...] muß dem Menschen eigentlich *offenbart* werden" (Schlegel 1964b, 33).

3. Kunst als Offenbarung des Geistigen im Menschen

Kunst ist eine spezifische Tätigkeit des menschlichen Geistes und leitet sich aus dem menschlichen Trieb nach Darstellung ab. Aus dem Trieb nach Darstellung geht die Forderung nach dem Schönen hervor.

Schlegel betrachtet die Kunst in zweierlei Hinsicht: diese ist objektiv und subjektiv. Mit der Wissenschaft teilt Kunst ihre objektive Form, insofern sich diese als ein sich auf bestimmte Ziele hinbewegendes methodisches und systematisches Experimentieren versteht. Mit der Religion teilt Kunst ihr inneres Wesen, die Offenbarung. Der Materie nach, sagt Schlegel, haben Poesie und Kunst „kein anderes Objekt als *Religion* und *Moral*. [...] Aller Kunst-Sinn wird sich beziehen auf Liebe und Natur, mithin auf *Religion*. Das Besondere aber, der Charakter, die Leidenschaften, Gefühle, die die Kunst darstellt pp., bezieht sich auf die Moral." Die Kunst ist demnach „die *materielle Poesie* in Ton, Farbe oder Wort" (Schlegel 1964a, 61). Sie ist für Schlegel der Ort, an dem sich das Göttliche dem Menschen offenbart. Kunst wird als „eine sichtbare Erscheinung des Reichs Gottes auf

Erden" (Schlegel 1964b, 55), „ein Zweig der göttlichen Magie, welche den Zweck hat, das himmlische sichtbare Reich Gottes herzustellen, die Natur zu verklären, die Erde ihrer Fesseln zu entledigen und sie zu vollenden" (ebenda, 55) beschrieben.

Kunst ist Mittel zur Darstellung der Offenbarung, dient aber auch einer lebendigen Auffassung des Glaubens. Da Offenbarung, wie Schlegel ausführt, für den sinnlichen Menschen „eigentlich eine zu erhabene Erkenntnis" ist, so tritt die Kunst sehr gut ins Mittel, um durch sinnliche Darstellung und Deutlichkeit dem Menschen die Gegenstände der Offenbarung vor Augen zu stellen (Schlegel 1964b, 174).

Auf die Frage, welche Kunstgattung sich in Schlegels Sicht am besten eignet, die Offenbarung zu ihrem Gegenstand zu haben, ist folgendes hervorzuheben: Als „die universellste Kunst aller Künste" ist die Poesie das beste Medium zur Erscheinung der Allheit (Schlegel 1981, 30). Aber auch die Malerei eignet sich dazu, denn der Maler erforscht die Gottheit in der Natur (Schlegel 1959, 77). So ist das Göttliche in der Natur nicht nur „das Leben und die Kraft allein, sondern das Eine und Unbegreifliche, der *Geist*, das *Bedeutende*, die Eigentümlichkeit" (ebenda, 77). Die ursprüngliche Bestimmung der Malerei war es, so Schlegel, die Geheimnisse der Religion „noch schöner und deutlicher zu offenbaren, als es durch Worte geschehen kann" (Schlegel 1959, 79). Die Malerkunst sei aber „zur bloßen Technik herabgesunken" und ihre ursprüngliche Idee ganz verloren gegangen" (ebenda, 81). Die Konvergenz zwischen der schönen Idee und der technischen Perfektion ist zur Ausnahme geworden.

Schlegel betrachtet auch eine weitere Kunstgattung, die Musik, als Begeisterung, als Sprache des Gefühls, als „die einzige universelle Sprache", die „in das innerste Herz des Bewußtseins eingreift" (Schlegel 1964b, 58). So kann die „wahre Musik" nie etwas anderes darstellen als „die unendliche Fülle und Einheit, worin das ganze volle Bewusstsein des Menschen erwacht" (ebenda, 58).

Begeisterung gehört jedoch für Schlegel zu dem, was den Künstler, mehr als die Kunst und die Werke, ausmacht (Schlegel 1967, 154). Der Künstler ist ein „wahrer Sprecher Gottes" (Schlegel 1981, 30). Das innere Organ dafür ist die Fantasie oder die Einbildungskraft, welche „ein übernatürliches Vermögen – [...] allemahl Offenbarung, Begeisterung, Erleuchtung" (Schlegel 1971b, 171) ist. Diese steht im Gegensatz zur Vernunft, denn sie ist ein ganz freies Denken. Sie strebt nach dem Bildlichen und vermeidet das Abstrakte (Schlegel 1964b, 359).

Kunst als Darstellung des Unendlichen meint jedoch nicht „Darstellung der Resultate, sondern der Art und Weise, wie es entstanden ist" (Schlegel 1964a, 102). Die Darstellung soll das in dem anderen produzieren, „was derjenige in sich hat, der darstellt" (ebenda, 103). „Das Absolute selbst ist indemonstrabel" (Schlegel 1963, 512). Das Absolute ist das Unsagbare; es ist sprachlich nicht einholbar. So muss die Sprachwerdung der Unendlichkeitserfahrung, wie Ulrike Zeuch in ihrem Buch schlussfolgert, stets unabgeschlossen bleiben (Zeuch 1991, 205). Das Wort darf nichts Bestimmtes meinen. Gefordert wird demnach eine Sprache der Uneigentlichkeit, die für etwas Unbestimmtes steht, was sie selbst nicht ist. Unter diesen Umständen wird die Bedeutung der Allegorie und des Symbols begreiflich. Die Darstellung des Unendlichen, Göttlichen ist eine Darstellung des Undarstellbaren, ein offenes Tor zum Universum.

4. Schluss

Es kann festgehalten werden, dass in Schlegels Sicht Kunst, nicht weniger als Religion, dem Menschen das Göttliche anzudeuten hat. Kunst, vor allem die gute oder wahre Kunst in Schlegels Sprache, deren Zweck er als „die Bedeutung" (Schlegel 1964b, 174) erläutert, ist eine Offenbarung, und zwar eine Offenbarung des Unendlichen durch die Allegorie, denn nur diese ist nach Schlegel in der Lage, das Endliche mit dem Unendlichen zu verbinden. „Eine Hieroglyphe, ein göttliches Sinnbild" soll jedes „wahrhaft" (Schlegel 1959, 151) zu nennende Kunstobjekt sein. Die metaphysische Dimension der Kunst eröffnet dem Menschen den Weg zum Unendlichen. Sie ermöglicht ihm, ähnlich wie in der Religion, die Erhebung zum Absoluten, zum Göttlichen im Menschen.

Im Sich-Zeigen des Geistigen in der Kunst und durch die Kunst ist heute noch immer ein Weg zu erahnen, auf dem der harmoniebedürftige Mensch seine Humanität zu erwirken vermag: eine Humanität, die, wie Schlegel in seiner *Lessing*-Abhandlung hervorhebt, „die innige Freude und herzliche Teilnahme an der Freiheit und dem Verstande andrer, der Wunsch diese Geistesfreiheit, so viel an uns ist,

144

zu erregen und zu entwickeln" ist. Diese Humanität ist aber gleichzeitig auch „die stets bereitwillige Mitwirkung dazu, und die rege Aufmerksamkeit auf alle Mittel, die dahin führen." (Schlegel 1975b, 73). Das heißt aber in letzter Instanz, dass das Göttliche im Menschen als das Geistige auf imaginative Art und Weise erkennbar werden zu lassen, aber es gleichermaßen auch zu achten, möglich ist.

Bibliographie:

Behler, Ernst. *Friedrich Schlegel mit Selbstzeugnissen und Bilddokumenten.* Reinbek bei Hamburg: Rowohlt, 1996.

Eliade, Mircea. *Das Heilige und das Profane. Vom Wesen des Religiösen.* Aus dem Französischen von Eva Moldhauer. Frankfurt am Main: Insel Verlag, 1984.

Eşianu, Cornelia. *Poesie – ein Bedürfnis der Philosophie? Der Lösungsversuch eines Problems bei Friedrich Schlegel.* Wien: Universität (Dissertation). 2013.

Fichte, Johann Gottlieb. *Versuch einer Critik aller Offenbarung. 1792.* In: Ders. *Werke 1791 – 1794.* Bd. 1. Stuttgart-Bad Cannstatt: Fromann-Holzboog, 1964.

Hegel, Georg Wilhelm Friedrich. *Vorlesungen über die Geschichte der Philosophie. Teil 4. Philosophie des Mittelalters und der neueren Zeit.* In: Ders. *Vorlesungen. Ausgewählte Nachschriften und Manuskripte.* Bd. 9. Hamburg: Meiner Verlag 1986.

Kant, Immanuel. *Kritik der praktischen Vernunft.* 1788. In: Ders. *Werke.* Bd. 5, Berlin: Walter de Gruyter & Co, 1968.

Kant, Immanuel. *Die Religion innerhalb der Grenzen der bloßen Vernunft.* In: Ders. *Werke.* Bd. 6, Berlin: Walter de Gruyter & Co, 1968.

Lukács, Georg. *Die Zerstörung der Vernunft. Der Weg des Irrationalismus von Schelling zu Hitler.* Berlin: Aufbau-Verlag, 1955.

Ritter, Joachim. Gründer, Karlfried. Gottfried, Gabriel. *Historisches Wörterbuch der Philosophie.* Bd. 6. Basel/Stuttgart: Schwabe & Co Ag, 1984.

Schelling, Friedrich Wilhelm Joseph. *Philosophie der Mythologie. Nachschrift der letzten Münchener Vorlesungen 1841.* Stuttgart-Bad Cannstatt: Fromann-Holzboog, 1996.

Schlegel, Friedrich. *Wissenschaft der europäischen Literatur. Vorlesungen, Aufsätze und Fragmente aus der Zeit von 1795 – 1804.* In: Ders. *Kritische-Friedrich-Schlegel-Ausgabe,* Bd. 11. München. Paderborn. Wien: Schöningh/Thomas, 1958.

Schlegel, Friedrich. *Ansichten und Ideen von der christlichen Kunst.* In: Ders. *Kritische-Friedrich-Schlegel-Ausgabe,* Bd. 4. München. Paderborn. Wien: Schöningh/Thomas, 1959.

Schlegel, Friedrich. *Geschichte der alten und neuen Literatur.* In: Ders. *Kritische-Friedrich-Schlegel-Ausgabe,* Bd. 6. München. Paderborn. Wien: Schöningh/Thomas, 1961.

Schlegel, Friedrich. *Philosophische Lehrjahre 1796 – 1806, nebst philosophischen Manuskripten aus den Jahren 1796 – 1828. 1.* Bd. 18. München. Paderborn. Wien: Schöningh/Thomas, 1963.

Schlegel, Friedrich. *Philosophische Vorlesungen (1800 – 1807).* In: Ders. *Kritische-Friedrich-Schlegel-Ausgabe,* Bd. 12. München. Paderborn. Wien: Schöningh/Thomas, 1964 (a).

Schlegel, Friedrich. *Philosophische Vorlesungen (1800 – 1807).* In: Ders. *Kritische-Friedrich-Schlegel-Ausgabe,* Bd. 13. München. Paderborn. Wien: Schöningh/Thomas, 1964 (b).

Schlegel, Friedrich. *Charakteristiken und Kritiken 1. (1796 – 1801).* In: Ders. *Kritische-Friedrich-Schlegel-Ausgabe,* Bd. 2. München. Paderborn. Wien: Schöningh/Thomas, 1967.

Schlegel, Friedrich. *Philosophie der Geschichte. In achtzehn Vorlesungen gehalten zu Wien im Jahre 1828.* In: Ders. *Kritische-Friedrich-Schlegel-Ausgabe,* Bd. 9. München. Paderborn. Wien: Schöningh/Thomas, 1971 (a).

Schlegel, Friedrich. *Philosophische Lehrjahre 1796 – 1806; nebst philosophischen Manuskripten aus den Jahren 1796 – 1828. 2.* In: Ders. *Kritische-Friedrich-Schlegel-Ausgabe,* Bd. 19. München. Paderborn. Wien: Schöningh/Thomas, 1971 (b).

Schlegel, Friedrich. *Studien zur Philosophie und Theologie.* In: Ders. *Kritische-Friedrich-Schlegel-Ausgabe,* Bd. 8. München. Paderborn. Wien: Schöningh/Thomas, 1975. (a)

Schlegel, Friedrich. *Charakteristiken und Kritiken 2. (1802 – 1829).* In: Ders. *Kritische-Friedrich-Schlegel-Ausgabe,* Bd. 3. München. Paderborn. Wien: Schöningh/Thomas, 1975. (b)

Schlegel, Friedrich. *Studien des klassischen Altertums.* In: Ders. *Kritische-Friedrich-Schlegel-Ausgabe,* Bd. 1. München. Paderborn. Wien: Schöningh/Thomas, 1979.

Schlegel, Friedrich. *Fragmente zur Poesie und Literatur 1.* In: Ders. *Kritische-Friedrich-Schlegel-Ausgabe,* Bd. 16. München. Paderborn. Wien: Schöningh/Thomas, 1981.

Stolberg, Friedrich Leopold. "Über die Begeisterung". In: Ders. *Über die Fülle des Herzens. Frühe Prosa.* Stuttgart: Reclam, 1970.

Wirz, Ludwig. *Friedrich Schlegels philosophische Entwicklung.* Bonn: Hanstein, 1939.

Zedler, Johann Heinrich. *Grosses Vollständiges Universal-Lexikon,* Bd. 57. Graz: Akademische Druck- u. Verlagsanstalt, 1998.

Zeuch, Ulrike. *Das Unendliche – höchste Fülle oder Nichts? Zur Problematik von Friedrich Schlegels Geist-Begriff und dessen geistesgeschichtlichen Voraussetzungen.* Würzburg: Königshausen und Neumann, 1991.

BRIGITTA KEINTZEL

LIEBE ALS VERSÖHNUNG ODER LIEBE ALS GERECHTIGKEIT? HEGEL UND LEVINAS IM DIALOG[1]

I. Warum Hegel und Levinas?

Wir sind gewohnt, das Phänomen Liebe mit ethischen, sexuellen, sozialen, kulturellen und religiösen Einsichten zu verbinden. Die philosophische Herausforderung ist hier beträchtlich. Sie besteht darin, divergierende Ansprüche in ein Verhältnis zueinander zu bringen und gleichzeitig notwendige Differenzierungen vorzunehmen. Liebe tritt nicht nur mit dem Anspruch auf, individuelle Bedürfnisse zu befriedigen, sie tritt auch mit dem Anspruch auf, in das Leben der Gesellschaft einzugreifen. Inhärent ist diesen Ansprüchen ein gemeinsamer Bezugspunkt, der unterschiedlich betrachtet werden kann.

Die hohe Bewertung des Begriffs Liebe für philosophische Theorieproduktion ist sowohl bei einem der herausragenden Denker der Moderne, nämlich Georg W. F. Hegel, als auch einem der herausragenden Denker nach der Shoa, nämlich Emmanuel Levinas, eindeutig. Wie kaum andere Denker ihrer Zeit haben sowohl Hegel als auch Levinas Liebe ins Zentrum ihrer Überlegungen gestellt. Verblüffend ist nicht nur die Eindeutigkeit des jeweiligen Unterfangens, verblüffend ist auch die unterschiedliche Einordnung des Themas Liebe in den jeweiligen philosophischen Ansatz. Betont Hegel einen Zusammenhang zwischen Liebe und Versöhnung, bringt Levinas Liebe und Gerechtigkeit in ein gedankliches Naheverhältnis. Anders als bei Hegel ereignet sich bei Levinas Liebe nicht als Vereinigung und Versöhnung, sondern als Entzug. Nach Levinas bleibt Liebe den Zielen der Gerechtigkeit verpflichtet, sie kann auf diese aber nicht reduziert werden. Nach Hegel besitzt Liebe gerade in ihrer Eigenschaft, Differenzen unterschiedlicher Positionen abzuschwächen, ihnen ihre Absolutheit

---

[1] Wichtige Arbeiten zum vorliegenden Beitrag entstanden im Rahmen des abgeschlossenen Forschungsprojektes P18281 und des aktuellen Forschungsprojektes V345 gefördert vom österreichischen Fonds der Wissenschaften.

abzusprechen, sie – um ein modernes Wort zu gebrauchen – zu relativieren, einen Anspruch darauf, als gerecht anerkannt zu werden.

Verschieden sind Hegel und Levinas nicht nur in der philosophischen Bewertung, sondern auch in der zeitlichen Zuordnung. Nach Hegel weist Liebe, ebenso wie der Begriff Geist in die Vergangenheit. In Hegels Verständnis verlangt das triebhafte Moment der Liebe (als Synonym für erotisches Begehren und ebenso für gesellschaftsbildendes Werden) nach einem zeitlich nachträglichen Begreifen. Das aktuelle, in die Zukunft weisende Liebesgeschehen ändert nach vollbrachtem Vollzug gewissermaßen seinen Zeitindex und wird als vergangenes Geschehen schließlich begreifbar. Zukunft und Vergangenheit werden in diesem Modell komplementär gedacht und bilden die Grundlage für den begrifflichen Zusammenschluss von Liebe und Versöhnung. Dieser Zusammenschluss besitzt nicht nur Rückwirkungen für intersubjektive, sondern auch für gesellschaftliche Verhältnisse.

Vielleicht kann an dieser Stelle Levinas' Formulierung von einem „Ausstieg aus dem Begriff" verständlich gemacht werden. Diese Formulierung meint nämlich nicht, wie oft irrtümlich angenommen worden ist, eine Bankrotterklärung an das begriffliche Denken, sondern sie meint einen Ausstieg aus einer begrifflichen Operation, um eine neue und damit auch eine andere Perspektive auf das dialektische Denken zu gewinnen. Diese neue Perspektive zeigt sich gerade in Levinas' philosophischem Verständnis der Liebe. Liebe ereignet sich nach Levinas – unter Bezugnahme auf Franz Rosenzweig – in ihrer Unvorhersehbarkeit. Sie ist nicht ein Element des Wissens, sondern sie ermöglicht Wissen. Dieses Wissen gründet in der Einsicht, dass die Einstellung den Sachverhalt bestimmt und nicht – wie Hegels Perspektive nahelegt – die Betrachtung auf den Sachverhalt die Einstellung. Um sich aber von einer beliebigen Vielfalt von Einstellungen abzugrenzen, ging Levinas einen Schritt weiter. Er behauptete nämlich, dass die Einstellung, mit der wir Philosophie betreiben, eine zentrale Bedeutung besitzt. Diese Einstellung ist präreflexiv. Sie besteht darin, dass der Andere immer schon vor dem Selbst da war, und deswegen nicht nur vorzeitig, sondern auch ethisch primär ist. Das „Ich" gründet also nicht in einem „Wir", wie es die sozial-ontologische Perspektive Hegels naheliegt, sondern in einem „du warst schon vor mir da und dennoch wirst du mich nicht töten". Diese Vorrangstellung der/des Anderen besitzt Rückwirkungen auf das Verständnis von Freiheit: Freiheit konkretisiert sich nach Levinas in einer asymmetrischen Verantwortung und Stellvertretung und nicht im Wechselverhältnis zwischen subjektivem Anspruch und intersubjektiver Praxis. Nicht die Gleichzeitigkeit von Anspruch und empirisch überprüfbarer Notwendigkeit, sondern das Spannungsverhältnis zwischen sinnlichem Bedürfnis und ethisch geprägtem Begehren stellt für Levinas die Grundlage für sein gesamtes Oeuvre dar. Der sich daraus ergebende Dialog ist Gegenstand der folgenden Überlegungen.

II. Hegel

Liebe war für Hegel das zentrale Thema. Die Beschäftigung mit ihr hatte seine Entwicklung und Professionalisierung als Philosophen maßgeblich beeinflusst. Die philosophische Entfaltung des Liebesbegriffs war bei Hegel die *via regia*, die von den Frühschriften zur Entwicklung seiner philosophischen Methode führte. In Hegels Frühwerk besaß Liebe eine *„existentielle Bedeutung“* (vgl. u. a.: Rózsa 2013, 113). Sie wurde als lebensnotwendiges Mittel beschrieben, um die Qualität des Lebens und Erlebens zu erfahren. In späteren Schriften war Liebe nicht nur Mittel zum Zweck, sondern auch Zweck für sich. Dies hatte zur Folge, dass die philosophische Entfaltung des Themas Liebe von der philosophischen Methode beiseite gedrängt wurde. An die Stelle der existentiellen Beschreibung des Phänomens Liebe trat die philosophische Reflexion am methodischen Leitfaden des Themas Liebe.[2]

Die Grundintention in beiden Betrachtungsweisen war es, sinnliches Bedürfnis und ethisches Streben in einen begrifflichen Zusammenhang zu bringen. In Weiterentwicklung zu Kant lautete die Devise: Das, was die Menschen im Innersten zusammenhält, ist nicht primär der gemeinsame Wille nach Rechten, Pflichten und Werten, das gemeinsame Wissen über ethische und epistemologische Möglichkeiten und Grenzen, sondern das, was die Menschen im Innersten zusammenhält, ist ihr Bestreben, Beziehungen einzugehen.[3] Im An-

---

[2] Judith Butler bemerkt hier: „Später [nach dem sogenannten „Systemfragment von 1800“; Anm. d. Verf.] scheint die Liebe zu weichen, wird beiseite gedrängt oder stillschweigend in seine Schriften über den Geist integriert“ (Butler 2014, 20f.).

[3] In den Frühschriften wurden diese Beziehungen im Zusammenhang mit dem Topos Liebe als vereinigende und nicht als Differenz setzende und damit dialektische beschrie-

schluss an Schiller und Hölderlin ging es dem frühen Hegel in seiner Frankfurter Auseinandersetzung mit Kant vor allem auch um eine gleichwertige Verbindung von Ethik und Ästhetik, die er als philosophisch-utopisches Konzept in Gestalt von Liebe und Schönheit beschrieb. In der zentralen Frage nach der Verwirklichung dieser Utopie entstand allerdings eine Aporie (Plotnikov 1999, 143ff). Sie zeigte sich in der Frage, wie reale Beziehungen zwischen Personen und damit einhergehend Veränderungen und Neubeginn über das Primat der Vereinigung überhaupt gedacht werden konnten, wenn Liebe als Urbild und Vorbild des zeitlosen Schönen beschrieben wurde. Dadurch blieb die Deutung des Realen dürftig, da die Liebesgemeinschaft nicht zeitlich veränderbar und damit dynamisch gedacht werden konnte. Ignoriert bzw. nicht dezidiert beschrieben wurden geschlechtsspezifische Merkmale. 1797/98 deutete Hegel Liebe noch als geschlechterübergreifendes Lebensprinzip: „Wahre Vereinigung, eigentliche Liebe findet nur unter Lebendigen statt, die an Macht sich gleich und also durchaus füreinander Lebendige, von keiner Seite gegeneinander Tote sind; [...] An Liebenden ist keine Materie, sie sind ein lebendiges Ganzes; Liebende haben Selbständigkeit, eigenes Lebensprinzip – [das] heißt nur: sie können sterben" (Hegel 1970 a, 245f). Der bei Hegel in den Frühschriften angelegte Gedanke der Wechselseitigkeit im Vorgang der Liebe impliziert „ein sich auf den Anderen einlassen, und damit auch die Fähigkeit zu Trennungsschmerz und Trauer" (Nagl-Docekal 2008, 118), er impliziert auch die Fähigkeit zur Erinnerung, die mit körperlicher Scham gleichgesetzt wird: „Ein reines Gemüt schämt sich der Liebe nicht, es schämt sich aber, daß diese nicht vollkommen ist, sie wirft es sich vor, daß noch eine Macht, ein Feindliches ist, das der Vollendung Hindernisse macht. Die Scham tritt nur ein durch die Erinnerung an den Körper, durch persönliche Gegenwart, beim Gefühl der Individualität – sie ist nicht eine Furcht für das Sterbliche" (Hegel 1970 a, 247).

---

ben. Otto Pöggeler betont, dass bereits in den Frühschriften Vernunft und Liebe strukturanalog gedacht wurden (Pöggeler 1990, 87). Nach Panajotis Kondylis beinhaltet Liebe bereits im Tübinger Fragment ein „pathologisches Prinzip". Diese Widersprüche in der Tübinger Zeit führt Kondylis auf eine unterschiedliche Interpretation der Liebe bzw. des Verhältnisses zwischen Sinnlichkeit und Vernunft auf der Ebene der Moral und jener der Metaphysik zurück (Kondylis 1979, 255ff.).

Der Umstand, dass ein liebendes Lebendig-sein zeitliche Veränderungen impliziert, machte Hegel – nicht zuletzt auch in Auseinandersetzung mit Hölderlin[4] – auf die geistigen und kulturellen Wurzeln der Erinnerung aufmerksam. Hilfreich mag hier auch Hegels Beschäftigung mit jüdischer Religion gewesen sein. Eine Einsicht, die Hegel in der Schrift *Der Geist des Judentums* (1798-1800) besonders herausstrich, war nämlich die Aufwertung der Erinnerung. Religion könne nicht in Geschichtswahrheiten gründen. Wichtig sei vielmehr, „wie sie in der Phantasie und in dem erinnernden Leben der Juden vorhanden war" (Hegel 1970 a, 289, Jaeschke 2003, 90; weiterführend: Hamacher 1978, 136ff). Allerdings, wichtig ist es hier zu betonen, dass nicht nur die Berücksichtigung der Erinnerung sondern auch die Berücksichtigung der Versöhnung in der *Phänomenologie des Geistes* Hegel es ermöglicht hat, Problemstellungen der Vereinigungsphilosophie auf eine neue Ebene der Betrachtung zu bringen.

In der *Phänomenologie des Geistes* besitzt Versöhnung – ebenso wie Erinnerung - eine subjektive und eine objektive Ausprägung. In dieser Doppelfunktion gibt Versöhnung einen methodischen Rahmen vor, innerhalb dessen die inhaltliche Ausrichtung der *Phänomenologie des Geistes* erfolgt. Versöhnung ist nicht nur ein Element des Denkens, sie ist auf die emotionalen und kulturellen Wurzeln der Menschheit und damit auch auf vorreflexive Voraussetzungen angewiesen. Ein Subjekt kann sich nur dann mit einem Etwas oder Jemand versöhnen, wenn diesem Vorhaben die Einstellung vorausgeht, dass Differenzen mittels Versöhnung gemildert oder gänzlich aufgehoben wer-

---

[4] Dieter Henrich sieht sowohl in Hölderlins als auch in Hegels Denken das Motiv der Erinnerung als wesentlich. Bei Hegel allerdings ist nach Henrich Erinnern immer ein „Verwandeln, – Er-Innerung als Überholen des An-sich-seins des Vergangenen, – eine neue Weise, es zu setzen als zugehörig dem erinnernden Ich oder dem Allgemeinen der Intelligenz" (Henrich 1971, 35). Was das Verhältnis Hegel und Hölderlin zum Thema Erinnerung anbelangt, betont Johann Kreuzer, dass das Thema sowohl in Hegels *Phänomenologie des Geistes* als auch in Hölderlins Verfahrensweise des poetischen Geistes zentral ist und dass „der logische Kern spekulativer Darstellungen auf Zeitrelationen beruht" (Kreuzer 2002, 154). Die Tatsache, dass Denken und Erinnerung sich Hegel zufolge in einen unauflöslichen Zusammenhang befinden, betont besonders Thamar Rossi Leidi mit dem Argument, dass erst Erinnerung eine Brücke zwischen dem Vergangen und Zukünftigen schaffe (Rossi Leidi 2009, 257). Die sich daran anknüpfende Frage nach der Mehrwertigkeit von Erinnerung, die jenseits von zerstörender und bestimmender Negation geschichtsbestimmend wirkt, ist eine Frage, die mit Levinas weiterführend gestellt werden kann, aber hier nicht Gegenstand der weiteren Erörterungen sein kann.

den können. Die Voraussetzung für Versöhnung ist nach Hegel das Festhalten an der Notwendigkeit an einer negativen emotionalen Grundeinstellung gegenüber übergeordneten allgemeinen sozialen, religiösen und/oder politischen Funktionseinheiten, auf Grund dessen der Mechanismus der Versöhnung bzw. der Relativierung von unterschiedlichen Positionen überhaupt erst greifen kann.

Mit der Behauptung, dass Leiden die negative Einstellung des Bewusstseins prägt, leitet Hegel zum Geist-Kapitel in der *Phänomenologie des Geistes* über, indem er Sophokles Antigone mit den Worten zitiert: „(I)ndem wir leiden anerkennen wir, dass wir gefehlt". Dieses Leiden besitzt eine geschlechtsspezifische Färbung. Nach Hegel sind es nicht die Söhne und wehrfähigen Männer, sondern Frauen, die einen Eltern- und oder Geschwisterverlust erfahren haben, die die Hauptverantwortung für die ethische Grundlage eines modernen Gemeinwesen bilden. Hier zeigt sich eine interessante Parallele zu Levinas, die weiter unten noch zu beschreiben sein wird. Vorläufig kann festgehalten werden, dass in der Entgegensetzung von „menschlich-männlichem" und „göttlich-weiblichem" Gesetz nach Hegel das moderne Gemeinwesen eine ethische Grundlage erhalten hat. Das menschlich-männliche Gesetz manifestiert sich in Kreons Verkündigung, den toten Polyneikes bei Androhung der Todesstrafe nicht bestatten zu dürfen. Kreons Verweigerung, seine Verfehlung anzuerkennen, geschieht im Zeichen eines moralischen Egoismus, der in Hegels Sichtweise von einem erotischen Egoismus nur bedingt unterschieden ist. Das weiblich-göttliche Gesetz manifestiert sich in Antigones Liebesgebot, als Schwester den Bruder und Sohn ihrer Mutter zu bestatten. Antigones Liebesgebot fordert Erinnerung, aber auch Versöhnung kategorisch ein. Nicht nur ihre als zweimalige vollzogene Bestattung bezeugte Erinnerung, sondern auch ihre Bereitschaft, für diese Tat ihr eigenes Leben zu opfern, und, last, not least, ihre versöhnende Einstellung zur Gesellschaft, mit der sie in den Tod geht, unterstreichen die Besonderheit ihres Charakters. Hegel, der, wie bereits hingewiesen, Antigone mit den Worten zitierte: „(I)ndem wir leiden, anerkennen wir, daß wir gefehlt", setzt Antigones Maxime mit dem Stadium des absoluten Wissens gleich.[5] In dieser Lesart ist das dominierende Subjekt in der *Phänomenologie des Geistes* Antigone.

---

[5] Meine Schlussfolgerung, die ich mit George Steiner teile, lautet hier, dass Antigones Imperativ der Erinnerung eine Unbedingtheit artikuliert, die die Zerrissenheit des moder-

Verfehlen, Leiden, sich Erinnern und schließlich sich Versöhnen geben in der Phänomenologie des Geistes die dialektische Richtung vor, die Hegels Verständnis von Liebe in der *Phänomenologie des Geistes* bestimmen und auch den Schlusspunkt, nämlich das Kapitel „Das absolute Wissen" bilden. Hegel beschreibt diesen Schlusspunkt als sich wechselseitig relativierende Erinnerungen an subjektiven Einstellungen und objektiven, geschichtlich geprägten Verhältnissen: „Ihre Aufbewahrung nach der Seite ihres freien, in der Form der Zufälligkeit erscheinenden Daseins ist die Geschichte, nach der Seite ihrer begriffenen Organisation aber die Wissenschaft des erscheinenden Wissens; beide zusammen, die begriffene Geschichte, bilden die Erinnerung und die Schädelstätte des absoluten Geistes [...]" (Hegel 1970 b, 591).

Die semantische Verknüpfung von Versöhnung mit Erinnerung, wie sie in der *Phänomenologie des Geistes*, entwickelt[6] worden ist, kann nicht darüber hinwegtäuschen, dass, wie Erzsébet Rózsa zu Recht hervorhebt, Versöhnung im Verständnis von Hegel eine ambivalente Struktur beinhaltet, nämlich als „Strukturierungsprinzip des Geistes" und „als praktisches Verhaltensmuster in kunstphilosophischen Texten" (Rósza 2005, 386). Dabei sind es gerade Hegels ästhetische Einsichten zum Thema Liebe, die eine Anschlussfähigkeit an Levinas erlauben. Besonders in den ästhetischen und existentiell geprägten Einsichten, wie in den *Theologischen Jugendschriften* und in den *Vorlesungen über die Ästhetik* dargelegt, beschreibt Hegel Liebe als ein intersubjektives Verhältnis, das die Infragestellung des eigenen

---

nen, nach Hegel männlichen Bewusstseins dominiert (Steiner 1990, 58; v. d. Verf.: 2010, 209f.). Dieser Imperativ der Erinnerung verbindet präreflexives mit begrifflichem Wissen, der erst im Stadium des absoluten Wissens als versöhntes Wissen sich gewissermaßen „offenbart". Valentina Ricci betont, dass in Hegels *Phänomenologie des Geistes* erst durch Erinnerung die Verschränkung von psychologischen Einsichten mit gedanklichen und schließlich auch geschichtlichen Zusammenhängen vollzogen werden kann (vgl. Ricci 2013).

[6] Weiterführend: Erzsébet Rózsa's umfangreiche Studie zu *Versöhnung und System* (2005). Unberücksichtigt allerdings bleibt in dieser Studie der Stellenwert der Versöhnung gerade in Hegels *Phänomenologie des Geistes*, die für den vorliegenden Artikel zentral ist. Robert Bernasconi betont ein unklares Verhältnis zwischen Versöhnung und Verzeihung in der *Phänomenologie des Geistes*, da die Gesamtstruktur des Werkes in ein versöhnendes Ja mündet, wohingegen Verzeihen eine Wechselwirkung verlangt (Bernasconi 2005, 62f.).

Selbstbezugs zur Voraussetzung hat. „Liebe kann nur stattfinden gegen das Gleiche, gegen den Spiegel, gegen das Echo unseres Wesens" (Hegel 1970 a, 243). *Was* hier Levinas mit dem frühen Hegel verbindet, ist die Einsicht, dass „Liebe unendliches Leben ist" (Butler 2014, 35). Was hier ebenso Hegel mit Levinas verbindet, ist die Betonung der Asymmetrie und nicht die Betonung der Wechselseitigkeit als zentrales Merkmal der Liebe. Der Gedanke, dass Liebe eine Bedeutung gerade auf dem Hintergrund der Verschränkung von Kunst und Wirklichkeit besitzt, wird von Hegel in den Ästhetischen Vorlesungen der Berliner Zeit aufgegriffen.

Hegels Kritik an der Verknüpfung von Pathos, Liebe und Männlichkeit offenbart ebenfalls überraschende Affinitäten zu Levinas' Kritik an der heldischen Männlichkeitskonstruktion abendländischen Denkens. So schreibt Hegel in den *Vorlesungen über die Ästhetik*: „Was jedoch die Helden des Mittelalters mit den Heroen des Altertums gemeinschaftlich haben, ist die *Tapferkeit*. Doch auch diese erhält hier eine ganz andere Stellung. Sie ist weniger der natürliche Mut, der auf der gesunden Tüchtigkeit und von der Bildung ungeschwächten Kraft des Körpers und Willens beruht und der Durchführung objektiver Interessen zur Stütze dient, sondern sie geht von der Innerlichkeit des Geistes, von der Ehre, der Ritterlichkeit aus und ist im ganzen phantastisch, indem sie sich den Abenteuern der inneren Willkür und den Zufälligkeiten äußerer Verschlingungen oder den Impulsen der mystischen Frömmigkeit, überhaupt aber der subjektiven Beziehung des Subjekts auf sich unterwirft" (Hegel 1970 e, 175). Die Affinität zu Levinas ist hier deswegen verblüffend, da Levinas ins Zentrum seiner Kritik die Figur des kriegsbereiten, „heroischen", in der Regel männlichen Selbst gestellt hat (s. u. a.: Levinas 2002 [1961], 446 [p.284]). Die, so ließe sich auch mit Hegel – zumindest im Kontext seiner ästhetischen Überlegungen – argumentieren, von einem Übermaß an Ehre und „innerer Willkür" geprägt sei, wodurch der Bezug zur Vielgestaltigkeit des Realen abhanden gekommen sei. Weniger einverstanden allerdings war Levinas mit den Schlussfolgerungen, die Hegel daraus gezogen hatte. Diese bestanden zum einen darin, Liebe als semantische Verlängerung der Vernunft zu begreifen, wie dies in den Jugendschriften implizit enthalten ist und in späteren Werken explizit gemacht wird. So schreibt Hegel dazu beispielsweise in der *Philosophie des Rechts*: „Die Liebe [...] der ungeheuerste Widerspruch, den der Verstand nicht lösen kann, indem es nichts härteres gibt, als diese Punktualität des Selbstbewusstseins, die negiert wird, und die ich doch als affirmativ haben soll. Die Liebe ist die Hervorbringung und die Auflösung des Widerspruchs zugleich" (Hegel 1970 c, §158; weiterführend: Nagl-Docekal 2008, 116). Zum anderen bestand seine Schlussfolgerung darin, Liebe im Ausgang vom Selbst mit einem christlich geprägten Begriff der Versöhnung in einen Zusammenhang zu bringen,[7] die, wie Levinas unter Bezugnahme auf Franz Rosenzweig an Hegel kritisiert hat, die jüdische Beteiligung an dieser Denktradition leugnet: „Wir waren davon ausgegangen von dem Widerstand der Seienden gegen die Totalisierung von einer Mannigfaltigkeit, die kein Ganzes konstituiert, von der Unmöglichkeit ihrer Versöhnung im Selben"[8] (Levinas 2002 [1961], 425 [p. 270]).m

III. Levinas

Gerade in der Auseinandersetzung mit der abendländischen Tradition bezeichnet Levinas in gedanklicher Nähe zu Franz Rosenzweigs *Stern der Erlösung* Hegel als einen philosophischen Denker der „Einheit" und als einen Denker einer Geschichte, „die ihre Erfüllung in der Vereinigung" findet, als „Odyssee" oder als „Heimweh" (ebenda, 370 ff. [p. 232]). Beide – sowohl das homerische Epos als auch das Begehren nach dem Ursprung – stehen nach Levinas nicht für die Möglichkeit, sondern für die Unmöglichkeit, Versöhnung zu erlangen, da eine Versöhnung im Ausgang vom Selbst eine unmögliche „Versöhnung im Selben" bleibt (ebenda, 425 [p. 270]). Der Wunsch oder die Sehnsucht, die in der Vergangenheit wurzelnden Ursprünge gedanklich wieder erreichen zu können, widersetzt sich nach Levinas dem Voranschreiten einer Zeit, die niemals kontinuierlich voranschreitet: „Es bedarf eines Bruches der Kontinuität und einer Fortsetzung durch den Bruch hindurch. Das Wesentliche der Zeit besteht darin, ein Drama zu

---

[7] Nach Levinas resultiert gegenüber der Tradition eine durch die totalitären Einbrüche des 20. Jahrhunderts bedingte Problemkonstellation, die eine Neubestimmung von Versöhnung und Gerechtigkeit in theologischer und/oder atheistischer Perspektive erforderlich macht (vgl.: Ansorge 2002, 36-58).

[8] Ähnlich Bernasconi in seiner Einschätzung: „Nevertheless the fundamental difference remains that Hegel's discourse is governed by «the horizons of a reconciliatory return to self and absolute knowledge», whereas in Levinas there is no return" (Bernasconi 2005, 53).

sein, eine Mannigfaltigkeit von Akten, in denen der folgende Akt jeweils den Knoten des vorhergehenden löst" (ebenda, 414f. [p. 260]).

Um das Neue in der Zeit, die „Unvorhersehbarkeiten von Geschichte" philosophisch beschreiben zu können, muss anerkannt werden, dass nicht das Sein der Zeit Neues hinzufügt, sondern umgekehrt Zeit dem Sein Neues hinzufügt (ebenda, 414 [p. 260]). Dies ereignet sich nicht schematisch kontinuierlich, sondern diskontinuierlich. Die Unmöglichkeit, Zeit kontinuierlich zu denken, sondern sie diskontinuierlich zu erfahren, ordnet das Verhältnis zwischen Geschichte und Neubeginn neu. Der Neubeginn entfaltet sich vom Anderen her und ist mit einem ethischen Anspruch verknüpft. Dieser Andere verlangt nämlich nicht bloß die Legitimität seines eigenen Ichs, sondern durch die Konfrontation mit einem bereits vorhandenen Ich, mehr als ein Ich. Dieses Mehr, diesen Überschuss des Ichs, der sich in der Begegnung mit dem anderen Gesicht manifestiert, nennt Levinas das Verlangen nach Gerechtigkeit: „Aber ein Prinzip bricht in dem Augenblick durch diesen Schwindel und dieses Beben hindurch, in dem das Antlitz sich präsentiert und Gerechtigkeit verlangt" (ebenda, 425 [p. 270]). Durch die Begegnung mit dem anderen Gesicht wird nach Levinas nicht nur ein Bedürfnis nach persönlicher Selbstvergewisserung produziert, sondern gleichzeitig auch ein Mehrwert, den Levinas Ethik nennt. Als ethischer Anspruch beeinflusst die Begegnung mit dem anderen Gesicht das Verständnis von Zeit, die primär als Neubeginn und nicht als Vollendung eines bereits vorhandenen Zeitgeschehens zu denken ist. Nach Levinas gelingt es die ästhetische Begegnung mit dem anderen Gesicht als ethischen Mehrwert zu denken, indem der Prosa der Fruchtbarkeit (und der Produktivität) die Liturgie der Vergebung gegenüberstellt wird: „Dieser Neubeginn des Augenblicks, dieser Triumph der Zeit der Fruchtbarkeit über das Werden des sterblichen und alternden Seienden, ist die Vergebung, das eigentliche Werk der Zeit" (ebenda, 413 [p. 259]).

Levinas zufolge strebt sinnliche Liebe nicht nach idealer Vereinigung mit dem Objekt ihrer Liebe[9], sondern sie besteht in einer „unüberwindlichen Dualität der Seienden" (Levinas 1989 [1946-47], 57). Diese „unüberwindliche Dualität der Seienden" erlaubt auch, wie im

---

[9] Herta Nagl-Docekal weist hier zurecht hin, dass Eins-sein auch bei dem jungen Hegel nicht als nivellierende Verschmelzung, sondern als „Einheit von zugleich Differenten und Different bleibenden" (In: Nagl-Docekal 2008, 114).

folgenden zu zeigen ist, einen gedanklichen Zusammenhang zwischen Liebe und Gerechtigkeit.

Levinas, der sich in seinen Überlegungen auf einen in der jüdischen Tradition angelegten Gedanken der Alterität beruft, bezieht sich nicht auf ein in der platonischen Tradition angelegtes präexistentes Ganzes und damit auch nicht auf eine „Dualität komplementärer Bezugspunkte" (ebenda, 56f.)[10]. Liebe darf nicht in Analogie bzw. nach Maßgabe der Erfordernisse einer vermittelnden und vereinigenden Vernunft begriffen werden.

Indem Begehren nach Levinas sich nicht – im Sinne des platonischen Mythos – damit begnügt, die andere Hälfte einer vermeintlich ursprünglichen Einheit wiederzufinden bzw. zu erkennen, ist Begehren nicht der Stillstand des Denkens, sondern Voraussetzung für Denken, und Denken ebenso Voraussetzung für Begehren. In Abgrenzung zu Hegel ist Levinas' Verständnis von Geschlechterliebe mit der Infragestellung von Parmenides' Identifizierung von Sein und Denken eng verknüpft. Denken der Geschlechter heißt nicht Denken ihrer Einheit, sondern Denken ihrer Pluralität: „Der Unterschied der Geschlechter ist eine formale Struktur, die die Wirklichkeit in einem formalen Sinn einteilt und die die eigentliche Möglichkeit der Wirklichkeit als einer vielfältigen bedingt, und zwar gegen die Einheit des Seins, die Parmenides proklamiert" (ebenda, 56). In Levinas' Verständnis kann Eros bzw. sinnliches Begehren keinen Beitrag zu einem platonischen „Ideal der Vereinigung" leisten, vielmehr führt Begehren zu einer Vertiefung der Differenz zwischen den Geschlechtern: „Zu sagen, dass die geschlechtliche Dualität ein Ganzes voraussetze, hieße, von vornherein die Liebe als Verschmelzen zu setzen. Die Leidenschaftlichkeit der Liebe besteht jedoch in einer unüberwindbaren Dualität der Seienden. Es ist ein Verhältnis zu dem, das sich für immer entzieht. Das

---

[10] Wohlmuth betont hier, dass Liebe sich vielmehr als probates Mittel erweist, um aus dieser komplementären Dualität auszuscheren (Wohlmuth 2000, 51). Liebe in Levinas' Verständnis ist, wie Susanne Sandherr im Anschluss an Levinas ausführt, ein „*Nach oben fallen*" und nicht so sehr ein „*Zusammenfallen*" (Sandherr 1999, 147). Eine andere Position dazu vertritt Sabine Gürtler. Sie interpretiert in der Studie *Elementare Ethik – Alterität, Generativität und Geschlechterverhältnis bei Emmanuel Levinas* Mutterschaft als Modell „*an-archischer Verantwortung*" und Vaterschaft als Modell „generativer Transzendenz", die deren leiblich unterschiedliche Verantwortung in ein komplementäres Verhältnis zueinander bringt (Gürtler 2001, 317 f. u. 393ff.).

Verhältnis neutralisiert nicht *ipso facto* die Anderheit, sondern bewahrt sie" (ebenda, 57 u. Sandford 2002, 141).

Levinas' Einwand lautet hier, dass Liebe als Verzeihung und damit auch in meiner Lesart als Versöhnung dann für die Vernachlässigung der Gesellschaft verantwortlich ist (Levinas 1995 [1954], 31; Bernasconi 1998, 91), wenn sie auf dem Modell einer Intimität zu zweit beruht und dann auch für den Ausschluss des Dritten verantwortlich ist. Um nun zu verstehen, in welcher Weise Levinas ein Verständnis von Liebe gewinnt, das sowohl eine schöpferische „Intimität zu zweit" als auch eine Voraussetzung für das Zusammenwirken von politischen und ethischen Verhältnissen zum Ausdruck bringt, erweist sich ein Blick auf die Frühschriften als sinnvoll. Wenn Levinas 1954 in „Ich und Totalität" betont, dass eine intime Gesellschaft die übrige Gesellschaft ausschließt: „Wir sind unter uns. Sie schließt den Dritten aus. [...] Das intersubjektive Verhältnis der Liebe ist nicht Beginn, sondern Negation der Gesellschaft." (Levinas 1995 [1954], 32f.), dann ist für Levinas klar, dass erst die „Krise der Liebe" die „wirkliche Gesellschaft" (ebenda, 37) entdecken lässt.

Das demokratische Potential des Politischen würde ebenfalls durch eine Reduktion des Ethischen auf das sexuelle Motiv geschmälert werden. Dennoch beinhaltet die Intimität des sexuellen Paares eine Gerechtigkeit, gerade wenn im Antlitz der/s Anderen die Perspektive des Dritten – als die/den kulturell verallgemeinerbaren Andere/n – nicht geleugnet wird. Liebe zu Zweit greift auf soziale und politische Belange über, gerade wenn in einer Beziehung von Angesicht-zu-Angesicht, die Perspektive der dritten Person nicht unsichtbar bleibt. Im Anschluss an Levinas' Beharren auf das notwendige Spannungsverhältnis zwischen Ethik und Politik[11] kann hier schlussgefolgert werden, dass Liebe gerade kraft des Gegensatzes zwischen sinnlichem Bedürfnis und ethischem Begehren sich bestimmt. Die Nivellierung dieses Gegensatzes würde das Ende der Liebe, in Levinas' Worten das Ende der „Ambiguität der Liebe" bedeuten.

---

[11] Einen Überblick dazu gibt Robert Bernasconi in dem Aufsatz „Wer ist der Dritte?" (1998, 110ff.). Die wechselseitigen Verschränkungen zwischen Ethik und Politik, aber auch die daraus resultierenden Fallstricken hat Howard Caygill in der Studie *Levinas & the Political* (2002) herausgearbeitet.

Die Figur des Dritten[12] begründet die Notwendigkeit der ethischen Haltung (Levinas 1991 [1982], 132). Sie ist gewissermaßen eine permanente Infragestellung einer Intimität zu zweit, aber auch eine permanente Infragestellung eines religiösen Supranaturalismus. Nicht eine übernatürliche Offenbarung, sondern eine im Diesseits verwurzelte Erfahrung unterstreicht die Notwendigkeit einer ethischen Erfahrung, die danach verlangt, Individuation als Verantwortung für den Anderen und zwar im hier und jetzt zu begreifen (ebenda, 134). Liebe als ethisches Geschehen darf seine Ursache nicht in einer selbstbezogenen Liebe haben, die den Anderen als Verlängerung des eigenen Ichs begreift. Sie artikuliert sich vielmehr als Begehren mit einer „Strenge der moralischen Forderung"[13], die in der ethischen Haltung einer „Asymmetrie der Subjektivität" als Voraussetzung für die Möglichkeit von Gerechtigkeit gründet.

Dieser in Levinas' Frühschriften implizit enthaltene Zusammenhang zwischen Liebe und Gerechtigkeit wird in den Spätschriften explizit gemacht. So kann festgehalten werden, dass die späten Arbeiten sein Verständnis von Liebe radikalisieren und ethisch vertiefen. Besonders in den Spätschriften wird Liebe vor allem als „Gebot" und auch als „Befehl" beschrieben (Levinas 1991 [1982], 140). Damit wird Liebe in semantische Nähe zur Gerechtigkeit gerückt. Gerecht ist Liebe deswegen, weil sie eine Wahrheit nicht von einem Menschen, sondern von zwei Menschen, die gleichermaßen an diesem Geschehen beteiligt sind, abbildet, indem beide bereit sind, egologische Ansprüche an das individuelle Liebesglück zu hinterfragen, ohne bedürfnisgeleitete, sinnliche Ansprüche des eigenen Körpers zu leugnen oder hintanzustellen. Diese sinnlichen Ansprüche sind nach Levinas nur dann vereinbar mit einer ethischen Forderung, wenn sexuelle Differenzen

---

[12] Thomas Bedorf (2003, 75) betont zu Recht, dass die Figur des Dritten nicht einfach empirisch dazu tritt, sondern das Angesicht vielmehr doppelgesichtig ist. Unter Bezugnahme auf Stéphane Moses (1993) vertieft Pascal Delhom (2000, 201) diesen Gedanken, indem er betont, dass es neben dem Dritten keinen Vierten gibt, da der Dritte das Ich für die Pluralität der Menschen öffnet. Auch Matthias Flatscher betont, dass der Dritte als der „Andere-im-Plural" mit der Forderung nach einer institutionalisierbaren Gerechtigkeit verbunden ist, „die gleichermaßen nach singularitätssensiblen und dennoch universalisierbaren Antworten sucht" (Flatscher 2015, 194ff.).

[13] „Das Begehren des Unendlichen hat nicht die gefühlsbetonte Selbstgefälligkeit der Liebe, sondern die Strenge der moralischen Forderung" (In: Levinas 1999 [1957] 207 [p. 177]).

160

nicht vergessen werden.[14] Erst kraft dieser beschränken sich sinnliche Ansprüche und ethische Forderungen nicht gegenseitig, sondern bereichern sich diese.

IV. Hegel und Levinas

Anliegen von Hegel war es, der empirischen Vielgestaltigkeit des modernen Lebens und damit einhergehend dem Zersplittern und Zerfallen des modernen Bewusstseins in unterschiedliche Lebensbereiche durch das Zusammendenken von Liebe mit Versöhnung entgegenzusteuern. In diesem Modell ist Liebe nicht nur gefühltes, sondern vor allem auch gewusstes Wissen. Dieses gewusste Wissen erreicht in der *Phänomenologie des Geistes* im Stadium des absoluten Wissens seine höchste Stufe. Wenn Hegel in der Vorrede zur *Phänomenologie des Geistes* seine Kritik festhält: „Daran mitzuarbeiten, daß die Philosophie der Form der Wissenschaft näherkomme – dem Ziele, ihren Namen der *Liebe* zum *Wissen* ablegen zu können und *wirkliches Wissen* zu sein –, ist es, was ich mir vorgesetzt" (Hegel 1970 b, 14), so meint diese im griechischen Denken angelegte Programmatik, dass Liebe sich nach Maßgabe unseres Verständnisses von Realität entfalten müsse. Levinas hingegen erblickt in Hegel nicht den Gegenspieler, sondern den Vollender dieser griechischen Denktradition. Freilich unbeantwortet bleibt hier die Frage, ob Vollendung nicht gleichzeitig auch Überwindung und Befreiung von den Altlasten der Vergangenheit bedeuten könnte. Auch hier ist es wichtig zu betonen, dass Levinas Hegels Zugang nicht bloß infrage stellt. Zu sehr war er sich des Momentes bewusst, dass eine Infragestellung von Hegels Systemgedanken letztlich diesen bestätigen würde. So kann Levinas' Verständnis von Liebe nicht als dialektisch zu interpretierende Kritik verstanden werden. Vielmehr stellt er Hegels Liebesbegriff eine andere, jüdisch geprägte Zugangsweise voran und eben nicht hintan.

Nach Ephraim Meir fasste Levinas das Judentum „als eine Unruhe im Ich auf, das einen Rückzug von der Verantwortung für den Anderen nicht zulässt. [...] Die jüdische Erfahrung des Anderen geht der Philosophie Levinas voraus und speist sie" (Meir 2011, 24). Sie geht nicht nur einer philosophischen Denkoperation voraus, sondern auch der Wahrnehmung des eigenen Bewusstseins: „Die Besetzung des Ichs

---

[14] Weiterführend: Luce Irigaray 1991[1984].

durch den Anderen geht dem Bewusstsein und der Vernunft voraus. Ethische Offenheit kommt vor dem universalen, philosophischen Diskurs. Dialog oder besser Ansprache kommt vor der Logik. [...] Er setzt Jerusalem vor Athen, ohne jedoch Athen zu verdrängen" (ebenda, 20).

Levinas' Annahme ist hier, dass Philosophie nur dann der griechischen Denktradition des Phänomens Liebe gerecht werden kann, wenn diesem Denken die Einsicht vorausgeht, dass Wissen zuerst im Dienste der Liebe erfolgt. Dieses erste, ethisch inspirierte Wissen, nennt Levinas „Weisheit der Liebe im Dienste der Liebe" (Levinas 1998 [1974], 207)[15]. Diese besitzt eine doppelte Ausrichtung auf Wahrheit, nämlich als „Zweideutigkeit der Liebe" (Levinas 2002 [1961], 370-372 [p. 232-233]) und als Mehrdeutigkeit der Geschichte. Im Gegensatz zu Hegel, der im Prozess der Versöhnung nicht nur intersubjektive, sondern auch geschichtliche Verhältnisse aufhebt und dadurch Geschichte in ein randunscharfes Verhältnis zu moralischer Rechtfertigung bringt, sieht Levinas (mit Rosenzweig) im Gedanken der Rechtfertigung der Geschichte ein Problem (weiterführend: Bernasconi 2005, 62ff.). Geschichte kann auch durch die Berücksichtigung der liebenden Einstellung ihrer Akteure den Prozess der Wahrheit nicht abbilden. Denken und Beschreiben sind nicht raum- und zeitlose Kategorien, sondern Kinder ihrer Zeit. Dem heterogenen Geschehen Geschichte wird nicht durch eine liebende Einstellung, sondern durch differenzierte und heterogene Einstellungen Bedeutung verliehen. In dieser Perspektive erlangt Wahrheit eine transzendente, vielleicht auch prophetische Dimension, da sie in die Geschichte hineinragt, sich darin aber nicht erschöpft. Auch Liebe besitzt eine prophetische Dimension, die über die Faktizität ihres Seins hinausweist. Zur Diskussion steht demzufolge nicht die philosophische Beschreibung des Seins der Liebe, sondern ihr darüber Hinausweisen, gewissermaßen das „Jenseits des Seins im Sein der Liebe".

Anstelle Levinas' Verständnis von einer „Ambiguität der Liebe" stellt Hegel ins Zentrum seiner Betrachtungen eine Ambiguität der Freiheit, nämlich eine Ambiguität, die sich als changierendes Wech-

---

[15] Acht Jahre später hat Levinas im Gespräch mit Raúl Fornet und Alfred Gómez den Begriff Liebe deutlich distanzierter betrachtet hat: „Das Wort ‚Liebe' mag ich nicht sosehr, es ist so abgegriffen und mißbraucht. Lassen Sie uns von einem Aufsichnehmen des anderen Schicksals sprechen" (Levinas 1995 [1982], 132).

162

selverhältnis zwischen Anspruch und lebensweltlichen Notwendigkeiten zeigt. Die Diskrepanz zwischen Sein und Sollen erachtet Hegel als „Ursprung des Bösen" (Hegel, 1970 d, 292 [§ 472]) und Liebe besitzt auf der Grundlage dieser Diskrepanz eine Korrekturfunktion. Die Abgründe und Irrwege der menschlichen Seele sollen durch das Phänomen Liebe gemildert und auch ethisch korrigiert werden. In diesem Modell ist Liebe Antwort und nicht, wie bei Levinas, Anlass für die Forderungen der Freiheit.

Als Herausforderung haben Levinas und Hegel die Frage begriffen, wie eine subjektphilosophische Entfaltung des Themas Liebe einem Verantwortungsverhältnis in der Praxis entsprechen kann. Levinas' Feststellung einer „Zweideutigkeit der Liebe", die entgegen dem Aristophanischen Mythos nicht nach einer Rückkehr, sondern nach einer „Gleichzeitigkeit von Bedürfnis und Begehren, von Begierde und Transzendenz" (Levinas 2002 [1961], 372 [233]) verlangt, verweigert eine begrifflich exakte Unterscheidung zwischen Bedürfnis und Begehren. Daraus ergibt sich die mit Levinas nicht leicht zu beantwortende Frage, ob es verbindliche Maßstäbe geben kann (und soll), um das Verhältnis von Gerechtigkcit und ethischer Liebe (caritas) zu definieren. Levinas' Statement, dass „*caritas* ohne Gerechtigkeit nicht möglich ist, und dass Gerechtigkeit ohne *caritas* entartet" (Levinas 1995 [1982], 153), deutet den Sinn des Politischen in der „Gerechtigkeit des Vergleichens", die „notwendigerweise nach der Barmherzigkeit" kommt. [16]

---

[16] Weber 1994, 121. Weiterführend: Stegmaier 2005, 25-44. Eva Buddebergs (2012, 5, 722) Feststellung, dass Levinas keinen „Pflichtenkatalog" und „auch keine klar definierten Tugenden" formuliert hat, erlaubt nur bedingt ihre Schlussfolgerung, dass er keine politische Theorie der Gerechtigkeit entworfen habe, sondern verweist vielmehr auf ein intersubjektiv verengtes Politikverständnis. In dem Gespräch mit Elisabeth Weber hält Levinas fest: „In meinem Denken gibt es einen genau bestimmten Sinn des Politischen. Er besteht in der Tatsache, daß wir nicht zu zweit, sondern mindestens zu dritt sind. […] Sobald es aber einen Dritten gibt, muß ich vergleichen, das Unvergleichbare des Antlitzes mit aller nur möglichen Behutsamkeit vergleichen. Die Gerechtigkeit des Vergleichens kommt notwendigerweise nach der Barmherzigkeit. Sie verdankt der Barmherzigkeit alles, aber sie verneint sie ständig. Darin liegt schon das Politische" (Weber 1994, 121). Mit seinem Verständnis des Politischen fordert uns Levinas auf, tradierte Sichtweisen über das Politische infrage zu stellen. Im Ausgang von Franz Rosenzweig geht es Levinas darum, deutlich zu machen, dass auch theoretische Philosophie politische Implikationen besitzt und politische Ziele nicht unabhängig von theoretischen und auch nicht unabhängig von religiös angeleiteten Positionen zu betrachten sind. Die Art und Weise, wie

Zusammenfassend kann festgehalten werden, dass Levinas einen Perspektivenwechsel zu Hegels mehrstufigem Liebesbegriff, der in Versöhnung gipfelt, vollzogen hat. Mit seinem Verständnis von Liebe beansprucht Levinas, komplementäre Sichtweisen, die sinnliche und kognitive Aspekte der Liebe in ein Verhältnis zueinander bringen, zu überwinden.

Argumentiert haben beide dafür, dass Eros bzw. sinnliche Liebe und ethische Liebe einen gemeinsamen Kontext besitzen, ohne dass ethische Liebe auf Eros reduziert werden kann. Ausgehend von diesen Überlegungen finden sich in den *Theologischen Jugendschriften* und in den *Vorlesungen zur Ästhetik* Einsichten, die eine argumentative Brücke zu Levinas erlauben, wie weiter oben skizziert wurde. Beide argumentieren für ein Verständnis von Liebe, das im Ausgang von Kant in der Relativierung von selbstbezogenen Interessen und Neigungen gründet. Mit unterschiedlicher Schwerpunktsetzung haben Hegel und Levinas die epistemische Leerstelle des selbstbezogenen Ichs mit phänomenologischen Gesichtspunkten bereichert und auf unterschiedliche Weise mit geschlechtsspezifischen Attributen versehen. Antigones *ungeschriebene Gesetze* können als Ergänzung zu Kants kategorischem Imperativ gelesen werden. Die Einsicht zu sittlichem Handeln erfolgt nicht nur als Ergebnis einer begrifflichen Operation, sondern gleichzeitig als Liebesakt: Handle so, dass die Maximen deiner Handlung verallgemeinerbar sind, indem du Liebe nicht nur als Bereicherung deines Selbstgefühls begreifst, sondern auch als Einschränkung deiner Selbstliebe und als Infragestellung des Absolutheitsanspruches einer ich-zentrierten Ausrichtung.

---

wir Erkenntnis definieren, definiert ebenso die Gegenstände der Erkenntnis und damit auch das Verhältnis sowie die Beziehungen und Kooperationen, die wir im Prozess der Erkenntnis mit den Gegenständen unserer Erkenntnis eingehen. Aus der Tatsache, dass auch theoretische Philosophie politische Implikationen besitzt, folgert Levinas, dass der Ursprung der theoretischen Philosophie und der politischen Theorie im Ethischen liegt. Ethik befindet sich demzufolge in einem asymmetrischen Verhältnis zu Philosophie und Politik. Unter Bezugnahme auf Hannah Arendt leitet Judith Butler aus Levinas' theoretischer Behauptung, dass Beziehungen asymmetrisch sind, eine Richtschnur für politische Normen und Strategien als Modi der Kohabitation ab (Butler 2012, 5, 696 u. 699).

Literatur

Ansorge, Dirk. „Vergebung auf Kosten der Opfer? Umrisse einer Theologie der Versöhnung. In: SaThZ 6 (2002), S. 36-58.

Bedorf, Thomas. *Dimensionen des Dritten*. München: Fink, 2003.

Bernasconi, Robert. „Wer ist der Dritte? Überkreuzung von Ethik und Politik bei Levinas. In: Bernhard Waldenfels, Iris Därmann (Hg.). *Der Anspruch des Anderen. Perspektiven phänomenologischer Ethik*. München: Fink, 1998, S. 87-110.

Bernasconi, Robert. „Hegel and Levinas: the possibility of forgiveness and reconciliation". In: Katz, Claire. *Critical Assessments of leading philosophers 2, Levinas and the history of philosophy*. London: Routledge, 2005, p. 49-68.

Bertaux, Pierre. *Friedrich Hölderlin* [1807]. Frankfurt a. M.: Suhrkamp, 1981.

Buddeberg, Eva. „*Du wirst nicht töten* – Lévinas Ethik der Verantwortung als erste Philosophie". In: *Deutsche Zeitschrift für Philosophie* 60 (2012) 5, S. 705-724.

Butler, Judith. „Gefährdetes Leben, Verletzbarkeit und die Ethik der Kohabitation". In: *Deutsche Zeitschrift für Philosophie* 60 (2012) 5, S. 691-704.

Butler, Judith. *Fühlen, was im anderen lebendig ist: Hegels frühe Liebe*. Ostfildern: Hatje Cantz, 2014.

Caygill, Howard. *Levinas & the Political*. London: Routledge, 2002.

Delhom, Pascal. *Der Dritte. Levinas' Philosophie zwischen Verantwortung und Gerechtigkeit*. München: Fink, 2000.

Flatscher, Matthias. „Das Verhältnis zwischen dem Ethischen und dem Politischen. Überlegungen zu Levinas' Figur des Dritten". In: Alfred Bodenheimer, Miriam Fischer-Geboers (Hg.). *Lesarten der Freiheit*. Freiburg: Alber, 2015, S. 182-214.

Gürtler, Sabine. *Elementare Ethik – Alterität, Generativität und Geschlechterverhältnis bei Emmanuel Levinas*. München: Fink, 2001.

Irigaray, Luce. *Éthique de la différence sexuelle*. Paris: Éditions de Minuit, 1984.

Hamacher, Werner. „Einleitung". In: G. W. F. Hegel. *„Der Geist des Christentums". Schriften 1796–1800*. Frankfurt a. M.: Ullstein, 1978, S. 11-333.

Hegel, Georg Wilhelm Friedrich. *Frühe Schriften*. In: Ders. *Werke*, Bd. 1. Frankfurt a. M.: Suhrkamp, 1970 (a).

Hegel, Georg Wilhelm Friedrich. *Phänomenologie des Geistes* [1807]. In: Ders. *Werke*, Bd. 3. Frankfurt a. M.: Suhrkamp, 1970 (b).

Hegel, Georg Wilhelm Friedrich. *Grundlinien der Philosophie des Rechts* [1820]. In: Ders. *Werke*, Bd. 7. Frankfurt a. M.: Suhrkamp, 1970 (c).

Hegel, Georg Wilhelm Friedrich. *Enzyklopädie der philosophische Wissenschaften* [1830]. In: Ders. *Werke*, Bd. 10. Frankfurt a. M.: Suhrkamp, 1970 (d).

Hegel, Georg Wilhelm Friedrich. *Vorlesungen über die Ästhetik II*. In: Ders. *Werke*, Bd. 14. Frankfurt a. M.: Suhrkamp, 1970 (e).

Henrich, Dieter. *Hegel im Kontext*. Frankfurt a. M.: Suhrkamp, 1971.

Jaeschke, Walter. *Hegel-Handbuch*. Weimar: J. B. Metzler, 2003.

Keintzel, Brigitta. „Antigones Stimme und das Schweigen der Dialektik". In: Dies., Burkhard Liebsch (Hg.). *Hegel und Levinas*. Freiburg: Alber, 2010, S. 201-223.

Keintzel, Brigitta. „Gewissen und Urteil – Hegel und Levinas im Vergleich". In: Sandra Lehmann, Sophie Loidolt (Hg.). *Urteil und Fehlurteil*. Wien: Turia+Kant, 2011, S. 153-167.

Kondylis, Panajotis. *Die Entstehung der Dialektik*. Stuttgart: Klett Cotta, 1979.

Kreuzer, Johann (Hg.). *Hölderlin Handbuch*. Stuttgart: J. B. Metzler, 2002.

Levinas, Emmanuel. *Die Zeit und der Andere*, übersetzt von Ludwig Wenzler. Hamburg, 1989 [*Le Temps et l'Autre*. Montpellier, 1946-47].

Levinas, Emmanuel. „Die Philosophie und die Idee des Unendlichen" [1957], übersetzt von N. N. Krewani. In: Ders. *Die Spur des Anderen – Untersuchungen zur Phänomenologie und Sozialphilosophie*. Freiburg i. Br.: Alber, 1989, S. 185-208.

Levinas, Emmanuel. *Totalität und Unendlichkeit. Versuch über die Exteriorität*, übersetzt von W. N. Krewani. Freiburg, 2002 [*Totalité et Infini. Essai sur l'extériorité*. La Haye, 1961].

Levinas, Emmanuel. *Jenseits des Seins oder anders als Sein geschieht*, übersetzt von Thomas Wiemer. Freiburg: Alber, 1998 [Autrement qu'être ou au-delà de l'essence. Paris, 1974].

Levinas, Emmanuel. „Ich und Totalität" [1954], „Das nicht-intentionale Bewußtsein" [1983], „Philosophie, Gerechtigkeit und Liebe" [1982], übersetzt von Frank Miething. In: Ders. *Zwischen uns – Versuche über das Denken an den Anderen*, übersetzt von Frank Miething. München: Hanser, 1995 [*Entre nous. Essais sur le penser-à-l'autre*. Paris, 1991].

Levinas, Emmanuel. *Ethik und Unendliches*. Gespräche mit Phillippe Nemo, übersetzt v. Dorothea Schmidt. Wien: Passagen, 1982.

Meir, Ephraim. *Differenz und Dialog*. Münster: Waxmann, 2011.

Nagl-Docekal, Herta. „Philosophische Reflexionen über Liebe und die Gefahr ihrer Unterbestimmung im zeitgenössischen Diskurs". In: Dies., Friedrich Wolfram (Hg.). *Jenseits der Säkularisierung. Religionsphilosophische Studien.* Berlin: Parerga, 2008, S. 111-141.

Plotonikov, Nikolaj. „Vereinigung als ‚Vervollständigung'. Hegels Konzeption einer praktischen Philosophie in Verbindung mit seiner Frankfurter Auseinandersetzung mit Kant". In: Martin Bondeli, Helmut Linneweber-Lammerskitten (Hg.). *Hegels Denkweg in der Berner und Frankfurter Zeit.* München: Fink, 1999, S. 143-166.

Pöggeler, Otto. „Hegels philosophische Anfänge". In: Christoph Jamme, Helmuth Schneider (Hg.). *Der Weg zum System. Materialien zum jungen Hegel.* Frankfurt a. M.: Suhrkamp, 1990, S. 68-111.

Ricci, Valentina. „The Role of *Erinnerung* in Absolute Knowing: History and Absoluteness". In: Dies., Sanguinetti, Federico (eds.). *Hegel of Recollection: Essays on the Concept of ‚Erinnerung' in Hegel's System.* New Castle: Cambridge, 2013, p. 1-20.

Rossi Leidi, Thamar. *Hegels Begriff der Erinnerung.* Frankfurt a. M.: Peter Lang, 2009.

Rózsa, Erzsébet. *Versöhnung und System – Zu Grundmotiven in Hegels praktischer Philosophie.* München: Fink, 2005.

Rózsa, Erzsébet. „Liebe als Frühmotiv bei Hegel". In: Kerstin Andermann, Andreas Jürgens (Hg.). *Mythos – Geist – Kultur*, München: Fink, 2013.

Rózsa, N.. „Die Liebe und ‚das Gefühl der Versöhnung'". In: *Hegel-Jahrbuch,* 1990, S. 133-139.

Sandherr, Susanne. „*Nach oben fallen* – Die Alteritätskonzeption von Emmanuel Levinas als Impuls für den feministisch-theologischen Diskurs". In: Josef Wohlmuth (Hg.). *Emmanuel Levinas – eine Herausforderung für christliche Theologie.* Paderborn: Schoeningh, 1999, S. 143-161.

Sandford, Stella. „Levinas, feminism and the feminine". In: Simon Critchley, Robert Bernasconi (eds.). *The Cambridge Companion to Levinas.* Cambridge: University Press, 2002, p. 139-160.

Stegmaier, Werner. *Levinas.* Freiburg: Herder, 2002.

Stegmaier, Werner. „Die Bindung des Bindenden. Levinas' Konzeption des Politischen". In: Pascal Delhom, Alfred Hirsch (Hg.). *Im Angesicht der Anderen. Levinas' Philosophie des Politischen.* Zürich: diaphanes, 2005, S. 25-44.

Steiner, George. *Die Antigonen. Geschichte und Gegenwart eines Mythos,* übersetzt von Martin Pfeiffer. München: dtv, 1990 [*Antigones: How the Anti-*

gone Legend has Endured in Western Literature, Art, and Thought. Oxford, 1986].

Weber, Elisabeth. *Jüdisches Denken in Frankreich. Gespräche*, Frankfurt a. M.: Suhrkamp, 1994.

Wetzel, Michael. „Nachwort". In: Emmanuel Levinas. *Stunde der Nationen. Talmudlektüren*, übersetzt von Elisabeth Weber. München: Fink, 1994 [*L'heure de la nation*. Paris, 1988].

Wohlmuth, Josef. „Egalität und Differenz der Geschlechter in philosophischer Perspektive – Dargestellt an Emmanuel Levinas". In: Anne Jensen (Hg.). *Was verändert feministische Theologie?*. Münster: LIT, 2000, S. 47-62.

BRIGITTE BUCHHAMMER

**RELIGION UND GESCHLECHTERGERECHTIGKEIT
FEMINISTISCH-PHILOSOPHISCHE REFLEXIONEN
IM ANSCHLUSS AN HEGEL**

Einleitung

Dieser Aufsatz geht der Frage nach, welches Potential im Kontext von *Religion* vorhanden ist für das Engagement für mehr Geschlechtergerechtigkeit in Kirchen und Gesellschaft. Was kann Philosophie und im speziellen feministische Religionsphilosophie dazu beitragen, eine solide *philosophische* Argumentationsbasis zu erarbeiten für eine adäquate Auseinandersetzung einerseits mit römisch-katholisch-lehramtlichen Stellungnahmen[1] zu Geschlecht, Geschlechtsrollen, Familie und Sexualität und andererseits mit feministisch-theologischen Konzeptionen?[2]

Die *Pastoralkonstitution über die Kirche in der Welt von heute: „Gaudium et spes"* vom 7. Dezember 1965 beginnt mit den programmatischen Worten: „Freude und Hoffnung, Trauer und Angst der Menschen von heute, besonders der Armen und Bedrängten aller Art, sind auch Freude und Hoffnung, Trauer und Angst der Jünger Christi, und es findet sich nichts wahrhaft Menschliches, das nicht in ihrem Herzen seinen Widerhall fände." (Gaudium et spes DH 4301, Pkt. 1) Trauer und Angst der Menschen: Vor allem Frauen und Kinder zählen zu den am meisten benachteiligten Menschen auf der Welt. Frauen haben unter den Menschen mit den schlechtesten Lebensbedingungen den größten Anteil. „Der Bericht der Vereinten Nationen stellt indes fest, dass die Feminisierung von Armut zu einem weltweit anwachsenden Phänomen geworden ist und dass 70 % der 1,3 Milliarden weltweit ärmsten Menschen Frauen sind (...). Die verheerende Statistik des Ernährungs- und Gesundheitszustandes sowie der Sterblichkeitsrate von Kindern ist sowohl im globalen Süden als auch im globalen Norden mit der allgemei-

---

[1] In meinem Essay setze ich mich kritisch-würdigend mit der römisch-katholischen Tradition auseinander.

[2] Eine kritische philosophische Auseinandersetzung mit rezenten Theorien aus dem Bereich der Gender-/Queerstudies habe ich in meinem Aufsatz (Buchhammer 2014, 80 ff) und in meinem Buch (Buchhammer 2011) erarbeitet.

nen Armut von Frauen verbunden." (Jaggar 2001, 79) Eine der dringendsten Aufgaben des zeitgenössischen Feminismus sowie der praktischen Philosophie besteht laut Jaggar in einer Kritik am aktuellen Neoliberalismus, am Aufzeigen von dessen erschreckenden Auswirkungen auf die Situation der meisten Frauen auf der Welt und in der Analyse der Auswirkungen der wirtschaftlichen Entscheidungen der wohlhabenden Industriestaaten auf die Frauen in den Ländern des Südens (siehe ebenda 76). Amartya Sen (siehe Sen 1990) fasst seine Analyse in dem Satz zusammen: More than 100 million women are missing, mehr als 100 Millionen Frauen, getötet durch extreme Armut, Gewalt, Hunger, Krankheit und systematische Vernachlässigung. Inwieweit liegen die Wurzeln dieser Gewalt gegen Frauen in traditionellen hierarchischen Familienstrukturen?

Hierarchische Familienstrukturen werden oftmals auch in Verlautbarungen der römisch-katholischen Kirche verteidigt. In den lehramtlichen Texten steht der Begriff der Naturordnung im Zentrum der Argumentation: Es gehe darum, die normative Natur, die Natur in ihrer Finalität ernst zu nehmen. (Persona humana DH 4583). Die normative Bedeutung der ausschließlich Mann und Frau vorbehaltenen Institution der Ehe als Grundlage von Familie, Gesellschaft und Kirche wird aus der Natur abgeleitet, und damit wird gefordert, sie als gottgewollt anzuerkennen. Der Geschlechtscharakter der Menschen wird von der Natur des Leibes hergeleitet. Philosophisch kann man aber anknüpfen zB. an Konzeptionen des Menschen in *Gaudium et spes*, wo davon gesprochen wird, dass Menschen nach „einem erfüllten und freien Leben, das des Menschen würdig ist" streben (Gaudium et spes DH 4309) Dieses Dokument fordert: „(...) (D)ie gesellschaftliche Ordnung und ihr Fortschreiten müssen sich unaufhörlich am Wohl der Personen ausrichten (...)." (ebenda, DH 4326) Hier kommt alles darauf an, welches philosophische Konzept von Personalität zu Grunde liegt. Mit Hegel werde ich zeigen, dass es in den Debatten um Geschlechtergerechtigkeit zielführend ist, von einem Begriff des Menschen als *geistbegabtes* Lebewesen auszugehen. Ich weise in diesem Zusammenhang auf die bekannte Wendung Hegels vom Menschen als sich wissendem Tier hin: „Der Mensch ist Tier, doch selbst in seinen tierischen Funktionen bleibt er nicht als in einem Ansich stehen wie das Tier, sondern wird ihrer bewußt, erkennt sie und erhebt sie, wie z.B. den Prozeß der Verdauung, zu selbstbewußter Wissenschaft. Dadurch löst der Mensch die Schranke

170

seiner ansichseienden Unmittelbarkeit auf, so daß er deshalb gerade, weil er weiß, dass er Tier ist, aufhört, Tier zu sein, und sich das Wissen seiner als Geist gibt." (Hegel 1970c, 112) In diesem spekulativen Satz ist ausgesagt, dass der Mensch zwar Organismus ist, wie andere Organismen auch, doch indem er dies weiß, ist er über das bloße Organismus-Sein hinaus und anerkennt sich als Geist. Das Subjekt begreift sich als leiblich daseiendes Vernunftwesen. In der Vorrede zur *Phänomenologie des Geistes* schreibt Hegel: „Die lebendige Substanz ist ferner das Sein, welches in Wahrheit Subjekt oder, was dasselbe heißt, welches in Wahrheit wirklich ist, nur insofern sie die Bewegung des Sichselbstsetzens oder die Vermittlung des Sichanderswerdens mit sich selbst ist." (Hegel 1970a, 23) Die Weltstellung des Menschen als geistbegabtes Lebewesen besagt, dass der Mensch zwar von Natur aus da ist, aber in der Natur nicht aufgeht. Zur Natur des Menschen gehört es, über bloße Natur immer schon hinaus zu sein. Von dieser Konzeption des Menschen als Selbstbewusstsein her sind auch Sexualität[3] und Geschlechts-Identität als Thema der Freiheit, dh. des Handelns, in den Blick zu nehmen. -

Jose Casanova engagiert sich, so wie das *Council for Research in Values and Philosophy*, für eine Erneuerung der Kirche in der gegenwärtigen Welt und er sieht die drängende Aufgabe für die Kirche, sich der Frage der Geschlechtergerechtigkeit auf dem höchsten Reflexionsniveau zu öffnen. George F. McLean schreibt in seiner Einleitung in „Disjunctions in the 21st Century": „Jose Casanova issues a highly critical appraisal of the growing disjunction between societal and Church morality in connection with three morally contested issues: the ordination of women, the official pronouncements of the Church hierarchy on issues of gender and sexual morality, and the societal moral outrage produced by the clerical sexual abuse of children. – Casanova cites in this regard the continuing significance of three issues: ordination of women, gender and sexual morality and the common moral outrage at the perceived concern of the Church to protect its own institutional reputation over the safety of its children." (In: Charles Taylor, José Casanova, George F. McLean 2012, 11).

Sieht man sich die Verlautbarungen des vatikanischen Stuhls näher an, so zeigt sich ein Mangel an sorgfältiger Auseinandersetzung mit einer bereits jahrzehntelangen Forschungstätigkeit im Bereich der Gen-

---

[3] In meinem Essay (Buchhammer 2008) habe ich diese Thematik näher entfaltet.

der-Studies. Herta Nagl-Docekals Einschätzung der aktuellen lehramtlichen Stellungnahmen zu Geschlechterfragen scheint mir überzeugend zu sein: „As one takes a closer look at the harsh critique voiced by Church authorities claiming that any appropriation of the concept of 'gender' is in clear contradiction to the teachings of the Catholic Church, it seems evident that there exists a decisive lack of information on the part of these critics. Obviously, they have failed to study with adequate care the discourse they claim to refute. One of their frequently employed strategies is to focus on some over-simplified articulations of feminist concerns that can, indeed, be easily dismissed as theoretically deficient. But it is certainly not a viable mode of proceeding to seek an easy target while neglecting the more sophisticated arguments that have been developed in the international debate since the early 1970s. In view of this shortcoming, it seems desirable to establish – by means of philosophical argument – a consistent reconstruction of core elements of the concept of 'gender' in order to provide a sound basis for a theological approach that seeks to discuss the ideas shaping the modern world in their most elaborate forms." (Nagl-Docekal 2012, 155)

Dass es zielführend ist, von einem philosophisch entfalteten Begriff des Menschen aus an die Frage nach Geschlechtergerechtigkeit im Kontext von Religion und Kirchen heran zu gehen, will ich in diesem Aufsatz aufzeigen. Die Verkürzungen im Begriff des Menschen, die zu Benachteiligung und Diskriminierung von Frauen, homo-, trans- und intersexuellen Menschen führen, aufzuzeigen und kritisch argumentativ zurück zu weisen, ist wesentliches Anliegen einer feministischen Religionsphilosophie. Beruht das im römisch-katholischen Lehramt vorherrschende Frauenbild auf einem Geschlechteressentialismus, also auf einem reduktionistischen Begriff des Menschen? Andererseits: Gerät nicht auch der Gender-/Queer-Diskurs in die Gefahr reduktionistischer Verkürzungen des Begriffs des Menschen? Geschlechteressentialistische Konzeptionen leiten aus körperlichen Geschlechtsmerkmalen Charaktereigenschaften ab. Diesen biologistischen Auffassungen stehen konstruktivistische Reduktionismen gegenüber, wonach behauptet wird, auch die biologische Ausstattung unserer Leiblichkeit sei Effekt des Diskurses (zB. Judith Butler). Gegen den Geschlechteressentialismus führen Gender-/Queer-Theoretiker_innen ins Treffen, im Sprechen über Körperlichkeit würden immer schon spezifische Bedeutungen von dem angelegt, was in der gegenwärtigen historischen Situation als ge-

172

schlechtlicher Körper gelte. Gender Identity ließe sich nicht aus politischen und kulturellen Vernetzungen und Interpretationen heraus lösen, in denen sie ständig hervorgebracht und aufrechterhalten werde. Menschen werden gemäß der angeführten Reduktionismen entweder als bloß von der leiblichen Seite her bestimmt gedacht oder bloß als gesellschaftlich konstruiert. Feministische Religionsphilosophie kann hier ein Differenzierungsangebot in die Debatte einbringen. Sie erachtet es als ihre Aufgabe, die Reduktionismen im Begriff des Menschen, die sowohl in (feministisch-)theologischen als auch in Gender-/Queer-Konzeptionen generiert werden, kritisch in den Blick zu nehmen.

Pamela Sue Anderson schreibt: „Essentially philosophy of religion done by feminists (...) has as its focus that which makes up our fundamental nature and our relationships to that we find undeniable. That we are born, we love, suffer, long for love with endures, and we die." (Anderson 2004, XI).

In meinem Essay skizziere ich kurz die Aufgabe von Philosophie und von feministischer Philosophie auf dem Boden von Hegels Philosophie. In einem weiteren Schritt zeige ich an Hand einiger feministisch-theologischer Positionen auf, inwiefern hier durch das Fehlen einer theoretisch-systematischen Grundlage Reduktionismen generiert werden. Mit einer sehr knappen Darstellung von Hegels Theorie des Menschen möchte ich dessen Bedeutung für feministisch-philosophische Problem- und Fragestellungen in den Blick rücken. Mit feministisch-philosophischen Anknüpfungen an Hegels Religionsphilosophie will ich meinen Aufsatz beenden. Auf die vielen in der Fachliteratur erörterten Problemstellungen in Bezug auf Einzelthemen der hier erörterten Theoriestücke Hegels werde ich nicht eingehen, da es mein Anliegen ist, die Aktualität Hegels, die systematische Relevanz seiner Theorie des Menschen und seiner Religionsphilosophie für feministische Religionsphilosophie heraus zu arbeiten.

1. Aufgabe von Philosophie und feministischer Philosophie

1.1. „Philosophie ist, ihre Zeit in Gedanken erfaßt" (Hegel 1970b, 26)

Hegel hat unermüdlich auf Krisenphänomene seiner Zeit hingewiesen. Inwieweit können wir uns heute auf Hegel beziehen hinsichtlich unserer kritischen Auseinandersetzung mit unserer Zeit, mit den vielfältigen Formen von Entsolidarisierung überall auf der Welt, mit politischen Verfallsformen, mit Reduktionismen im Begriff des Staates, der Freiheit, der Gerechtigkeit, Verkürzungen im Begriff des Menschen, die stets zu Ungerechtigkeit, Diskriminierung und Menschenverachtung führen? Hegel bezeichnet die Aufgabe von Philosophie so: „Philosophie ist, ihre Zeit in Gedanken erfasst" (ebenda, 26). Damit meint Hegel die kritische, denkende Auseinandersetzung mit unserer Zeit. Die so begriffene Philosophie hat die Grundlagenfragen zu stellen. Sie hat ihren Gegenstand mit Kunst und Religion gemeinsam, sie ist eine der Gestalten des absoluten Geistes, „in denen der Geist sich auf sich zurückwendet, sein Bewußtsein über sich selbst gewinnt und eben darin absoluter Geist ist: Selbstbewußtsein des absoluten Geistes", wie Jaeschke zusammenfassend formuliert. (Jaeschke 2003, 474) Kunst, Religion und Philosophie sind die drei Gestalten des absoluten Geistes, denen vermögenstheoretisch die drei Formen Anschauung, Vorstellung und begreifendes Denken des subjektiven Geistes entsprechen. Hegels Lehre vom absoluten Geist beruht auf der Anstrengung, das Selbstbewusstsein der Freiheit darzustellen. In den drei Gestalten des absoluten Geistes geht es immer auch um einen adäquaten Begriff des Menschen, der menschlichen Freiheit, um die Frage nach der Welterfahrung der Menschen. Absolute Wahrheit umfasst die Sinnfragen des Lebens. Es geht darum, dass „Freude und Hoffnung, Trauer und Angst der Menschen", dh. „alles Menschliche in unserem Herzen seinen Widerhall findet", wie Gaudium et spes es ausdrückt. Auf dem Boden des absoluten Geistes geben die Menschen sich die Bestimmung dessen, was sie für das Wahre halten (siehe Hegel 1970e, 70) – im Sinne Hegels: eine immer subtilere Ausdifferenzierung des Begriffs der Freiheit und damit die philosophische Entwicklung eines adäquaten Begriffs des Menschen. Was heißt es, als Mensch in der Welt zu sein? Dabei handelt es sich um Fragen der Gerechtigkeit, um Solidarität im mitmenschlichen Zusammenleben. Das Absolute ist etwas, das nicht mehr bedingt ist durch etwas Anderes: die Forderung der Achtung der Menschenwürde jedes Menschen ist absolut, gilt universell, im Sinne von Kants Theoriestück des kategorischen Imperativs, das man hier intrapolieren kann, dh. jederzeit ist überall auf der Welt die Menschenwürde jedes Menschen zu achten. Ein Zentralbegriff bei Hegel ist der Begriff der Freiheit. Wie ist ein sinnvoller Begriff von Freiheit und Gerechtigkeit zu entwickeln, der als Maßstab dienen kann zur kritischen Prüfung aller herrschenden Verhältnisse – dies systematisch zu erkunden ist Aufgabe der praktischen Philosophie im Sinne Hegels.

Inwieweit können feministisch Philosophierende sich auf Hegel beziehen hinsichtlich der Entwicklung eines adäquaten Begriffs des Menschen und eines Konzepts von Geschlechtergerechtigkeit im Kontext von Religion?

1.2. Warum heute noch feministische Philosophie?

Pamela Sue Anderson schreibt: „In certain fields of study, feminism is thought to be a thing of the past: discrimination against women is no longer a live issue. (…) However, it is undeniable that feminism is not finished." (Anderson 2004, XIII) Mechthild Bereswill führt aus: "Die Frage 'Was ist und wozu heute noch feministische Theorie?' (…) ist aus meiner Sicht nie abschließend zu beantworten: Feminismus ist im besten Fall eine offene und kontroverse Dynamik, die kritisches Denken über Gesellschaft herausfordert und politische Interventionen (er)findet, die den Naturalisierungen des Sozialen ebenso entgegentreten wie der Durchsetzung eines am Homo Oeconomicus orientierten Menschenbilds. Zudem hat das unabgeschlossene Projekt des Feminismus sich so lange nicht überlebt, wie Gewalt-Verhältnisse und Geschlechterverhältnisse augenscheinlich korrespondieren und dies weltweit immer noch zu wenig begriffen und bearbeitet wird." (Bereswill 2013, 15) Sabine Hark fragt: „Sind wir uns den Feminismus heute noch schuldig? Ist er ein unabgeschlossenes Projekt? Ein Luftschloss? Orientiert an den Herausforderungen, die der globalisierte Kapitalismus stellt?" (Hark 2013, 4) Die Autorinnen dieses genannten Heftes der *feministischen studien* sind der Überzeugung, „dass wir noch immer in einer Welt leben, in der feministische Kernthemen global gesehen so aktuell und ungelöst sind wie je und insofern einer Theoretisierung bedürfen." (ebenda, 4) Silvia Bovenschen: „Bist du eine Feministin? werde ich von einer jungen Frau gefragt. Ja, bin ich (und) füge hinzu, dass ich das für eine Frage der Intelligenz halte." (ebenda, 6) Ich halte mit einer gewissen Beharrlichkeit am Terminus und Programm Feminismus fest. So lange die Ziele feministischer Bemühungen nicht verwirklicht sind, ist Feminismus notwendig. Ich beziehe mich auf Alison Jaggar, die in vielen ihrer Arbeiten über Frauenarmut schreibt: Gegenwärtig stellen Frauen einen überproportional großen Anteil der

Bevölkerungsgruppen mit den schlechtesten Lebensbedingungen. Ihre Armutssituation wird durch Gewalt, sexuelle Ausbeutung und politische Marginalisierung weiter verschlimmert. (Jaggar 2001, 79 f) Feministische Aufgabe hat auch darin zu bestehen, kritisch zu untersuchen, wie unsere eigenen Länder an der Verarmung und politischen Marginalisierung von Frauen in der südlichen Hemisphäre beteiligt sind. Die neoliberale globale Wirtschaft hat den Frauen enorm geschadet, wenn auch nicht *nur* den Frauen und nicht *allen* Frauen. Armut und Gewalt an Frauen sind die dringendsten Themen feministischer Anstrengungen. (Jaggar 2001, 76)

Ute Gerhard führt aus: „Das Feministische an der feministisch motivierten Forschung war und ist immer ein emanzipatorisches, d.h. es beinhaltete Aufklärung und die Kritik hegemonialer Wissens- und Herrschaftsformen und die Infragestellung gesellschaftlicher Missstände und Ungerechtigkeiten im Blick auf die Beziehung der Geschlechter; aber nicht nur auf diese, sondern im Wissen um und sensibilisiert für die sich verschränkenden Unrechtserfahrungen und gesellschaftlichen Positionierungen auch im Blick auf andere Formen sozialer Ungleichheit und Diskriminierung." (Gerhard 2013, 58) Es geht, wie Ute Gerhard schreibt, darum, „Frauen in allen Lebensbereichen, in Staat, Gesellschaft und Kultur und vor allem auch in der Privatsphäre, gleiche Rechte und Freiheiten sowie gleiche Teilhabe an politischer Macht und gesellschaftlichen Ressourcen zu verschaffen. Das heißt, im Zentrum der Bestrebungen liegt (...) die Einlösung demokratischer Prinzipien der Freiheit und Gleichheit aller Menschen und die Anerkennung ihrer gleichen Menschenwürde – Prinzipien, die seit der Französischen Revolution als Kennzeichen einer rechtsstaatlichen demokratischen Ordnung gelten." (Gerhard 2009, 6)

Das Bestreben feministischer Praxis zielt auch auf eine Veränderung gesellschaftlicher und politischer Verhältnisse insgesamt unter dem Aspekt der Gerechtigkeit. Feminismus ist andererseits aber auch eine Gesellschafts*theorie*, die gesellschaftliche und politische Strukturen kritisch analysiert. Sie entwickelt Prinzipien für mehr Gerechtigkeit; es geht um Kritik an *jeglicher* Form von Unterdrückung und Diskriminierung, zB. auf Grund der ethnischen Zugehörigkeit, der Hautfarbe, des Alters, aufgrund von Krankheit und Behinderung, der Religionszugehörigkeit, der sexuellen Orientierung. (siehe Gerhard 2008, 15 f)

Das Wort *Feminismus* bezeichnet also eine soziale Bewegung und Theorie, mit dem Ziel, einerseits Geschlechterverhältnisse überall auf der Welt zu demokratisieren, aber es geht auch um das Engagement für mehr Gerechtigkeit in viel umfassenderem Sinn.

Herta Nagl-Docekal grenzt den Terminus *Feministische Philosophie* ab von dem Wort *Frauenforschung*, denn der Terminus Frauenforschung ist irreführend und macht nicht klar, dass es darum zu gehen hat, beide Geschlechter zu thematisieren. Feministische Philosophie ist *kein* Philosophieren von Frauen/für Frauen/über Frauen, sondern ein Engagement für mehr Gerechtigkeit hinsichtlich des Geschlechter*verhältnisses*. (Nagl-Docekal 2008a, 454)

Welche Mittel kann Philosophie zur Verfügung stellen, um die Unterordnung der Frauen, und die Diskriminierung homo-, trans- und intersexueller Menschen sichtbar werden zu lassen und zu problematisieren?

Feministische Philosophie ist *Philosophieren am Leitfaden des Interesses an der Befreiung der Frauen*, dies ist die pointierte These von Herta Nagl-Docekal. (Nagl-Docekal 1990, 11) Das Faktum, „dass Frauen in allen Lebensbcreichen diskriminiert werden, bildet hier den Ausgangspunkt des Denkens". (Nagl-Docekal 2008a, 454) Von diesem feministisch-philosophischen Ansatz her muss selbstverständlich auch die Geschlechterungerechtigkeit, die sich aus der Diskriminierung auf Grund der sexuellen Orientierung oder auf Grund von Trans- und Intersexualität ergibt, thematisiert und kritisch aufs Korn genommen werden.

Wichtig ist es, zu prüfen, ob das entwickelte philosophische Instrumentarium zur Kritik an Geschlechterklischee-Vorstellungen auch für eine kritische Analyse der gesellschaftspolitischen Zusammenhänge *in anderen Ländern* Gültigkeit beanspruchen kann. Schon 1990 widmete sich ein Band der *beiträge zur feministischen theorie und praxis* dem Thema Rassismus im Feminismus. „Der Titel ‚Geteilter Feminismus' bedeutet (...) die Erkenntnis, daß es nicht *einen* Feminismus gibt, und daß innerhalb der [feministischen] Bewegung rassistisch, antisemitisch, fremdenfeindlich ausgegrenzt wird." (beiträge Nr. 27, 1990, 5)

Herta Nagl-Docekal schlägt vor, auf die *Kontextbezogenheit* genau acht zu geben. Sie schreibt: „Ich denke, gerade unter dem Vorzeichen der sich global verdichtenden Verbindungen ist eine Sensibilisierung für die jeweils besonderen regionalen Ausgangsbedingungen unverzichtbar, um die Gefahr einer ‚Nivellierung von Differenz' zu vermeiden. Als

Desiderat erscheint mir daher die (weitere) Ausbildung einer Kultur aufmerksamen Zuhörens." (Nagl-Docekal 2010, 117) Feministische Aufgabe besteht in einer *Kultur aufmerksamen Zuhörens*.

Pamela Sue Anderson spricht von vier feministischen Tugenden, four intellectual virtues: reflective critical openness, care-knowing, strong objectivity and principled autonomy. (Anderson 2004, 89 f) Ich möchte nur einen Aspekt heraus greifen. Eine der von Anderson fokussierten Tugenden ist *Care-knowing*. "Feminism involves *critical self-reflection* on the interactive practice of caring. And this means an *ability to listen to, and register, what the other says or, simply, needs*. (…) Like reflective critical openness, care-knowing is developed as a disposition for practical wisdom." (ebenda, 92) Zunächst ist es wichtig, sich zu vergegenwärtigen, was mit *caring* gemeint ist. Das selbstzerstörerische Klischee von caring ist, "a woman bound up with an oppressive construction of femininity. There is the self-destructive stereotype of the (…) self-sacrifying woman whose 'care' allows her to be clearly exploited by her husband, or by other men with whom she may have a social personal relationship. We cannot deny that religious ethics have often reinforced the exploitative, stereotypical case of the caring woman." (ebenda, 93) Der zentrale Kern der Tugend des care-knowing besteht darin, wie Pamela Sue Anderson ausführt: "As a cognitive disposition, care-knowing (…) is shaped intellectually by imaginatively *listening to* and reflexively registering the perspectives of others, especially as developed by one's interactive practices with these others." (ebenda, 93) Sie spricht von caring about, caring for, taking care and caring about caring. (siehe ebenda, 93)

2. Feministisch-theologische Kernargumente

Zunächst möchte ich knapp einige zentrale Positionen des römisch-katholischen Lehramtes skizzieren, an denen feministisch-theologische Kritik sich entzündet. Die lehramtlichen Texte argumentieren in zweierlei Hinsicht: Einerseits leiten sie in ihrer Geschlechtertheorie den ‚Geschlechtscharakter' der Menschen aus der Natur der Leiblichkeit ab. Dies birgt die Gefahr eines reduktionistischen, essentialistischen Begriffs des Menschen in sich: Frauen werden auf ein ihnen gemeinsames Wesen festgelegt und nicht als vernunftbegabte Personen, die durch die Kompetenz der Freiheit, Autonomie, Entscheidungs- und Handlungsfähigkeit ausgezeichnet sind, anerkannt. Hier ist Philosophie gut beraten, argumentative Spannungen innerhalb der vatikanischen Texte aufzuzeigen. Es legt sich nahe, jene Passagen aufzugreifen und philosophisch weiter zu entfalten, in denen vatikanische Verlautbarungen mit einem Konzept von Personalität und Geistbegabtheit des Menschen operieren, wie zB. in *Gaudium et spes*: „Es ist nämlich wirklich beklagenswert, daß jene Grundrechte der Person noch immer nicht überall unverletzlich gewahrt werden; wenn man etwa der Frau die Möglichkeit verweigert, frei den Gatten zu wählen und den Lebensstand zu ergreifen oder zu derselben Bildung und Kultur zu gelangen, die dem Mann zuerkannt wird." (Gaudium et spes, DH 4329)

In *Mulieris Dignitatem* äußert Papst Johannes Paul II. sich über die Würde der Frauen. Er hebt dabei den personalen Charakter des Menschen heraus: Männer und Frauen sind gleichermaßen Personen und als solche Vernunftwesen (animal rationale). Was den Menschen Gott ähnlich macht, ist die Tatsache, dass er Vernunftwesen ist, Person ist. Der Kirchentext sieht sehr richtig die Würde des Menschen in seiner Personalität verankert, in der Tatsache, dass Menschen geistbegabte Lebewesen sind. Dann aber, im Widerspruch zu dieser Position, führt der Text ein paar Seiten später aus, dass Männer und Frauen ein unterschiedliches in ihnen angelegtes Wesen hätten, das sie in einem Prozess der Selbstverwirklichung allmählich entfalten müssten. Dabei wird der Ansatz, der vom Personalitätsprinzip, von der Freiheit und Handlungskompetenz des Menschen ausgeht, verlassen und es werden Individuen reduziert auf ein in ihrer Natur angelegtes Geschlechtswesen. Die Frau ist anders, aber gleich an Würde. In Bezug auf welchen Maßstab ist hier gesagt, dass die Frau ‚anders' ist? Der Maßstab für Menschsein ist dabei der Mann. Dies widerspricht dem Konzept der *gleichen Würde aller Menschen*, die sich biblisch in dem Bild der gleichen Gotteskindschaft aller Menschen ausdrückt.

Der andere Argumentationszusammenhang beruht auf der Betonung der Treue zu einer Tradition, die nur im männlichen Körper eines Menschen die wahre Christusmäßigkeit, ja die wahre Gottebenbildlichkeit erblickt. Die ablehnende Haltung hinsichtlich des Priesteramtes für die Frauen begründet Papst Johannes Paul II. damit, dass er ausführt, der Priester sei Zeichen, das wahrnehmbar sein muss und leicht verstanden werden soll. Er handelt in persona Christi, indem er die Stelle Christi einnimmt und sogar sein Abbild wird. „Die Ökonomie der Sakramente ist in der Tat auf natürlichen Zeichen begründet, auf Symbolen, die in die menschliche Psychologie eingeschrieben sind: Die ‚sakramentalen Zeichen', sagt der hl. Thomas, ‚repräsentieren das, was sie bezeichnen, durch eine natürliche Ähnlichkeit'. Dasselbe Gesetz der Ähnlichkeit gilt ebenso für die Personen wie für die Dinge: wenn die Stellung und Funktion Christi in der Eucharistie sakramental dargestellt werden soll, so liegt diese ‚natürliche Ähnlichkeit', die zwischen Christus und seinem Diener bestehen muß, nicht vor, wenn die Stelle Christi dabei nicht von einem Mann vertreten wird: andernfalls würde man in ihm schwerlich das Abbild Christi erblicken. Christus selbst war und bleibt nämlich ein Mann. (...) Nichtsdestoweniger ist die Menschwerdung des Wortes in der Form des männlichen Geschlechts erfolgt. Dies ist natürlich eine Tatsachenfrage." (Apostolisches Schreiben Nr. 117, 1994, 22) Die Männlichkeit Christi ist der Kern des Heilsplanes, so argumentiert dieser Kirchentext. Ist es nicht aber so, dass der Priester vernünftigerweise nur Zeichen in moralischer Hinsicht sein kann? Sein Handeln im Geist der Nächstenliebe soll von den Gläubigen ‚leicht verstanden werden' können! Ist es nicht so, dass mit natürlicher Ähnlichkeit im Grunde nur die Natur des Geistes gemeint sein kann, und das ist die Liebe, die Geisteshaltung engagierter Mitmenschlichkeit?

Nun haben sich verschiedene Strömungen feministischer Theologie heraus gebildet, die sich kritisch mit der Haltung des römisch-katholischen Lehramtes Frauen gegenüber auseinander setzen. Viele dieser Bemühungen bleiben aber in bestürzender Weise einem Geschlechteressentialismus verhaftet. Das Problem feministisch-theologischer Anstrengungen besteht meines Erachtens darin, dass diese sehr verständlichen Bestrebungen um Aufhebung der Diskriminierung eigentlich nicht heraus kommen aus dem Beharren auf dem Geschlecht: Menschen werden auch da nicht als Personen in ihrer individuellen Begabung und Entscheidungskompetenz anerkannt, sondern auf ihre Geschlechtlichkeit reduziert. Im Insistieren auf dem Geschlecht Gottes wird Gott auf Geschlechtlichkeit reduziert; im Rahmen solch einer reduktionistischen Position werden auch Menschen nicht primär von ihrer Personalität her gefasst, sondern reduziert auf Geschlechtlichkeit.

Feministische Theolog_innen im Kontext der röm.-katholischen Kirche kritisieren die in den Dokumenten des vatikanischen Lehramtes zum Ausdruck gebrachte Diskriminierung von Frauen aufgrund ihrer Zugehörigkeit zum weiblichen Geschlecht und den menschenverachtenden

Umgang mit homosexuellen Menschen. Beruht das im römisch-katholischen Lehramt vorherrschende Frauenbild auf einem Geschlechteressentialismus, dh. auf einem biologistisch verkürzten Begriff des Menschen, wie der kritische feministische Einwand lautet? Entspringt der „contra-naturam-Einwand" gegen Homosexualität einem reduktionistischen Menschenbild?

Feminist_innen monieren auch, dass viele vatikanische Verlautbarungen mit einem problematischen Begriff von *Religion* operieren, was sich zB. darin zeigt, dass die Lehrerlässe fordern, aus Treue zur Tradition müsse von Gott in männlichen Prädikaten gesprochen werden, zB. Gott muss als Mann vorgestellt werden, als Vater, Herr, König, Herrscher; Jesus muss Menschen-Sohn genannt werden (siehe zB. das lehramtliche Dokument *liturgiam authenticam*); dabei wird die Heilsbedeutung an den Geschlechtsleib Christi gebunden.

Feministische Theologiekonzeptionen üben Kritik an traditionellen kirchlich übermittelten Gottesbildern, am pointiertesten zusammengefasst in der These Mary Dalys: „If God is male then the male is God." (Daly 1973, 19) Die Vorstellung eines männlichen Gottes kann Grundlage sein für gesellschaftspolitische Geschlechterungerechtigkeit, so die These feministischer Theologinnen.

Manche Theolog_innen ersetzen die Vorstellung vom männlichen Gott durch Göttinnenbilder: Schwester, Mutter, Sophia, ja gar die Jesa Christa. Einige suchen einen Ausweg und möchten von Gott nur mehr in naturischen Bildern sprechen: Gott als Windhauch, als Brunnquell, oder, wie Mary Daly, Gott als Sei-en. Bezüglich der Gottesprädikate führt Elisabeth Schüssler-Fiorenza zB. aus, dass es durchaus wünschenswert sei, weibliche Gottesbilder zu verwenden, aber immer im Bewusstsein der via eminentiae, sodass eine Vermehrung von Bildern und Symbolen möglich wäre. (Schüssler-Fiorenza 2004b, 245 f) Dorothee Sölle (Sölle 1981, 225 f) stellt an das Gottesprädikat des „Vaters" folgende Fragen: Kann dies nicht ein autoritäres Menschenbild zur Folge haben? Bringt eine autoritäre Religion, die absoluten Gehorsam gegenüber diesem Vater-Gott fordert, nicht Barbarei hervor? Ist es tatsächlich sinnvoll, das Wort „Vater" anzuwenden, wenn Gott und Befreiung zusammen gedacht werden? Welche Elemente eines Vaterprädikates sind für eine Befreiungstheologie unverzichtbar? Sölles Kritik am Vaterbild entzündet sich an einer Gehorsamkeitsideologie, die den Begriff Gehorsam aufs schlimmste missbraucht hat. Das geschichtliche Zentralereignis ist für sie die Shoah. Gehört nicht Gehorsam zu einem jener Begriffe, die nach der Shoah nicht mehr heil werden können, fragt Sölle. Gehorsam definiere sich heute an den Sachzwängen der Wirtschaft, der Politik, der Militarisierung. Die Relikte einer repressiven religiösen Erziehung formen Menschen zu einem Gehorsam, „aus dem alle personalen, auf Vertrauen und Hingabe bezogenen Züge, verschwunden sind." (ebenda, 1981, 224) Sölle sieht eine Gemeinsamkeit zwischen dem religiösen Begriff von Gehorsam und dem technokratischen: beiden gemeinsam ist die Anerkennung einer höheren Macht, die Selbstbestimmung ausschließe, die Unterwerfung unter die Herrschaft dieser Macht verlange, die keine Legitimation braucht. „Die Haupttugend der autoritären Religion ist Gehorsam, die Kardinalsünde Auflehnung im Gegensatz zu humanitärer Religion, (...)". (ebenda, 224)[4] Warum, so Sölle, sollen wir einen Gott verehren, der sich auf dem empirisch erfahrbaren sittlichen Niveau der derzeit von Männern bestimmten Kultur befindet und dieses Niveau nicht transzendiert? Welche Gottesprädikate könnten zum Ausdruck bringen, dass Menschen auf Beziehung angelegte Wesen sind, der Autonomie fähige Individuen? Familiale Prädikate können dann sinnvoll sein, wenn damit Vertrauen und Verbundenheit zum Ausdruck kommt, wie Sölle ausführt.

Viel Kritik seitens feministischer Theolog_innen entzündet sich an der Christologie. Kann ein männlicher Erlöser Frauen erlösen, so die brennende Frage feministischer Theologiekonzepte. Wenn das Christus-Symbol benutzt wird, um Frauen zu unterdrücken und Geschlechterungerechtigkeit zu legitimieren: weist dies nicht auf einen inhärenten Mangel des Symbols selber hin, so die Frage seitens feministischer Theologinnen.

Das nachvollziehbare und wichtige Bestreben feministischer Theologie besteht nach Schüssler-Fiorenza darin, „die Verfilzung von Rassismus, Hetero-Sexismus, Klassismus und Nationalismus in modernen wissenschaftlichen und kirchlich-theologischen Diskursen kritisch theoretisch zu bedenken". (Schüssler-Fiorenza 2004a, 331) Aufgabe feministischer Theologie liegt ihrer Auffassung nach in der kritischen Befragung des biblischen Gottesverständnisses, den daraus abgeleiteten Herr-

---

[4] Es sei hier nur kurz erwähnt, dass der Begriff Gehorsamkeit (Wortbedeutung des Hinhörens) auch gänzlich anders gefasst werden könnte, zB. als Einübung in die Tugend des Zuhörens, als Entwicklung einer „ability to listen to, and register, what the other says or, simply, needs" (Anderson 2004, 92)

182

schaftsstrukturen und Unterordnungsverhältnissen, der *himmelschreien-den Ungerechtigkeit*, die an Frauen und anderen unterdrückten Menschen verübt wurde, viel zu oft unter Berufung auf den Gott der heiligen Schriften und eine kirchliche Tradition, die Frauen diskriminiert, ausgrenzt und ihnen Gerechtigkeit und Nächstenliebe verweigert. Feministische Theologie hat sich zu engagieren für ein menschenwürdiges Leben für alle Menschen auf der Welt. Ihre Vision einer (geschlecher)-gerechten und solidarischen Kirche ist die einer *Ekklesia der Frauen*. „Dadurch dass *ekklesia*, mit dem Genitiv ‚Frauen' qualifiziert wird, der auf die Nicht-BürgerInnen der Moderne verweist, soll ins öffentliche Bewusstsein gehoben werden, dass weder Kirche noch Demokratie das sind, was sie zu sein vorgeben: ekklesia – der radikal demokratische Kongress von mündigen VollbürgerInnen." (ebenda, 334)

Eher vatikannahe versucht Hanna-Barbara Gerl-Falkovitz (Gerl-Falkovitz 2008, 230 ff) eine feministische Konzeption zu entwickeln, in deren Zentrum ein von der philosophischen Richtung der Phänomenologie her akzentuierter Personbegriff steht. Ganz im Sinne des Differenzfeminismus macht sie sich stark für die Anerkennung des vom Mann unterschiedenen Wesens der Frau, plädiert für eine frauliche Kultur, frauliche Ästhetik, eine Kultur gemeinsamer fraulicher Regeln. Frauen sind *andersartig, aber gleichwertig* (mit dieser Formulierung übernimmt sie die Lehrmeinung des Vatikans), sagt aber kritisch in Richtung Lehramt: Weil Frauen gleichwertig, aber andersartig sind, dürfen sie nicht unterdrückt werden.

Konterkariert wird dieses feministisch-theologische Engagement für Geschlechtergerechtigkeit durch das Fehlen einer theoretisch-systematischen Grundlage, die eine kritische Differenzierung der Begrifflichkeit, auf die feministisch-theologische Ansätze ihre Ausführungen stützen, erlauben würde. Es gilt, philosophisch-systematisch sorgfältig zu argumentieren, um wegzukommen von den Reduktionismen, die durch die angeführten Konzeptionen feministischer Theologie und römisch-katholisch-amtskirchlicher Argumentation generiert werden. Um diese Arbeit leisten zu können, erscheint mir dir Erarbeitung einer feministischen Religionsphilosophie unverzichtbar.

3. Feministische Relektüre von Hegels Theorie des Menschen

Kann Hegels philosophische Lehre vom Menschen ein Angebot darstellen für feministische Philosophie, um die in den Gender-Studies einerseits und den kirchlichen Erlässen andererseits generierten Reduktionismen im Begriff des Menschen kritisch zurückweisen zu können? Ein neuerliches close-reading von zentralen Kernthesen Hegels erscheint mir in diesem Zusammenhang zielführend.

Die Abhandlungen in der Enzyklopädie zum subjektiven Geist (Hegel 1970 d) skizzieren den immanenten Prozess der Selbsterkenntnis des subjektiven Geistes. Erkenne dich selbst: damit ist gemeint „die Bedeutung der Erkenntnis des Wahrhaften des Menschen wie des Wahrhaften an und für sich – das Wesen selbst als Geistes." (ebenda, § 377, 9) In den Ausführungen der Lehre vom subjektiven Geist geht es Hegel um die Frage: „Wie verstehe ich den Sinn von Menschsein überhaupt, welche Bedeutung haben die einzelnen menschlichen Fähigkeiten für diesen Gesamtsinn?" (Fetscher 1970, 17) Hegels Theorie des Menschen ist erfassbar durch seine Lehre vom Geist. Das Wesen des Geistes ist Aktivität, actus, Handeln. Geist ist Freiheit, wie Hegel klar und präzise in § 382 schreibt: Das Wesen des Geistes ist Freiheit. Die Substanz des Geistes ist Freiheit. „Die wirkliche Freiheit ist also nicht etwas unmittelbar im Geiste Seiendes, sondern etwas durch seine Tätigkeit Hervorzubringendes." (Hegel 1970d, 27) Das, was der Mensch qua Geist ist, muss er handelnd hervorbringen. Die Entwicklungsschritte, die das Lehrstück des subjektiven Geistes entfaltet, sind *diejenigen*, die der Geist von seinem An-sich-Sein in der natürlichen Seele über die fühlende und die wirkliche Seele bis hin zum Sich-selbst-Erfassen als Freiheit durchmacht. Die notwendigen Schritte sind: 1) die Seele, 2) das Bewusstsein und 3) der Geist als solcher. Auf dem ganzen Entwicklungsgang des Geistes liegt sein Ziel darin, bei sich, dh. frei zu sein. Auf der Ebene des subjektiven Geistes ist Geist, dh. Freiheit, noch nicht vollendet. „Der Mensch ist existierender aktualer Geist, und er hat von daher gar nicht die Wahl, ob er sich mit seiner natürlichen Unmittelbarkeit identifizieren will oder nicht: er kann es nicht, denn er hat sich qua Geist an sich schon über die Natur hinaus bestimmt, er ist beispielsweise an sich schon dazu bestimmt, ein geistig selbstbestimmtes Wesen und nicht einfach ein wesentlich immer fremdbestimmter Naturgegenstand zu sein." (Hoffmann 2004, 403)

Im Menschen kehrt der Geist aus der Natur zu sich selber zurück. Der Geist im Medium der Seele ist von der Natur bestimmt. Die Entwicklung der Seele weist eine zunehmende Emanzipation aus der Natur der eigenen Leiblichkeit und der außermenschlichen Natur (Klima, geographische Gegebenheiten, etc.) auf. Der Weg des Geistes im Medium der Seele geht aus von der an die Naturbestimmungen gebundenen Seele. Aus dieser unmittelbaren Verbundenheit mit der Natur tritt der Geist als Seele in den Gegensatz und Kampf mit der Natur. Der Geist siegt über die Leiblichkeit, im Medium der Seele wird der Leib durch den Geist zum Zeichen der Seele herabgesetzt, der Leib wird zur Darstellung der Seele. Schon im Medium der Seele leistet der Geist jene schrittweise Negation des Natürlichen, ein Sich-Distanzieren-Können. Seele ist die Fähigkeit im Menschen, durch die Menschen in der Lage sind, sich selbst herauszuarbeiten als freier Geist, als Wille. Den gedanklichen Weg von der Natur zum Geist im Medium der Seele macht die Anthropologie zu ihrem Thema. „Der erste Teil von Hegels Philosophie des Geistes, die Lehre vom subjektiven Geist, beschäftigt sich mit dieser spezifischen conditio humana, mitten in naturaler Unmittelbarkeit zur Freiheit bestimmt und erkennendes Wesen zu sein. Wie überall, so ist auch hier die Bestimmung des Geistes nicht die, die Natur einfach abzuleugnen, sondern sie als aufgehoben gesetztes Moment des eigenen Seins und darin in gewisser Weise auch als Mitte des geistigen Lebens anzusehen. Für den Geist erreicht die Natur eine Transparenz, die sie für sich nicht hat." (ebenda, 404)

Der Philosophie des Geistes geht es um die Frage, was den Menschen ausmacht. In der Anthropologie zeigt Hegel auf, dass der ganze Mensch, als Geist, an die Leiblichkeit gebunden ist, das ganze Ich ist in der Leiblichkeit zu Hause. Als natürliche Seele arbeitet der Geist sich aus den Bestimmtheiten heraus, zB. Unterschiede der Hautfarbe sind beim Menschen der denkenden und handelnden Umgangsweise unterstellt. „Aus der Abstammung kann aber kein Grund für die Berechtigung oder Nichtberechtigung der Menschen zur Freiheit und zur Herrschaft geschöpft werden. Der Mensch ist an sich vernünftig; darin liegt die Möglichkeit der Gleichheit des Rechtes aller Menschen – die Nichtigkeit einer starren Unterscheidung in berechtigte und rechtlose Menschengattungen." (Hegel 1970d, § 393, 57 f) Der Unterschied der Abstammung ist ein bloß natürlicher und hat für ihn als Geist keine bestimmende Relevanz.- Menschen finden sich mit einer individuellen Naturbestimmtheit vor: Temperament, Talente, Physiognomie, etc. Zu diesen Naturvorgegebenheiten können und müssen Menschen qua Geistbegabtheit handelnd Bezug nehmen. Auch die natürliche Geschlechtsausstattung ist der geistigen Person als Aufgabe des Handelns aufgegeben. Diese Überlegungen Hegels sind für feministische Philosophie doch sehr spannend hinsichtlich der Problematisierung von Reduktionismen.

Der Geist des Menschen ist zugleich leiblich. Aber wir *haben* nicht nur einzelne Empfindungen, sondern wir *wissen* zugleich darum. Wir können Empfindungen festhalten – in der Erinnerung. Andererseits werden geistige Bestimmtheiten, um empfunden zu werden, verleiblicht. „Hiernach unterscheidet sich eine Sphäre des Empfindens, welches zuerst Bestimmung der Leiblichkeit (...) ist, die dadurch Empfindung wird, daß sie im Fürsichsein der Seele innerlich macht, erinnert wird, - und eine andere Sphäre der im Geiste entsprungenen, ihm ungehörigen Bestimmtheiten, die, um als gefundene zu sein, um empfunden zu werden, verleiblicht werden." (ebenda § 401, 100) Als individuelle Seele *habe* ich einen Leib, ich *bin* nicht bloß Leib, es ist mein Leib. Wichtig ist die Unterscheidung von Empfindung und Gefühl. Empfindungen sind immer einzelne, vorübergehende Bestimmungen, Veränderungen der Seele. Die Seele, wie Hegel sie hier fasst, ist an sich reflektierende Ganzheit. Die fühlende Seele fasst diese einzelnen Empfindungen, diese Vielheit in eine Einheit zusammen. Die fühlende Seele ist einerseits noch an ihre Natürlichkeit gefesselt, andererseits beginnt sie sich von ihrer Natürlichkeit zu distanzieren: sie steht zwischen ihrem unmittelbaren Naturleben einerseits und dem objektiven freien Bewusstsein andererseits. Die fühlende Seele ist das Medium der Individualität: dies ist noch nicht die denkende, begriffene Einheit, sondern die gefühlshafte Zusammenfassung der Vielheit der Empfindungen zur Einheit: Ich bin ein ganz Einfaches, wie Hegel hier die fühlende Seele skizziert. Die fühlende Seele ist die Einheit des Selbstgefühls, die Individualität, aber erst gefühlshaft, noch nicht denkend begriffen. Bei der unmittelbaren Einheit mit ihrer Leiblichkeit kann die Seele nicht stehen bleiben, die Seele muss „ihre Identität mit ihrem Leibe zu einer durch den Geist gesetzten oder vermittelten machen, ihren Leib in Besitz nehmen, ihn zum gefügigen und geschickten Werkzeug ihrer Tätigkeit bilden, ihn so umgestalten, daß sie in ihm sich auf sich selber bezieht, daß er zu einem mit ihrer Substanz, der Freiheit in Einklang gebrachten Akzidens wird." (ebenda, § 410, 190) Der Leib ist die Mitte, durch die ich mit der Außenwelt in Kontakt treten kann. Um dies zu können, muss mein Leib gebildet werden: diese Durchdringung meines Leibes durch die Seele ist ein Bildungsprozess. Dazu bedarf es der Übung, der Gewohnheit. Der

Geist im Medium der wirklichen Seele hat sich den Leib als sein Kunstwerk gemacht: Der Leib als Kunstwerk der Seele – das ist die wirkliche Seele. „Die Seele ist in ihrer durchgebildeten und sich zu eigen gemachten Leiblichkeit als *einzelnes* Subjekt für sich, und die Leiblichkeit ist so die *Äußerlichkeit* als Prädikat, in welchem sich das Subjekt nur auf sich bezieht. Diese Äußerlichkeit (...) ist deren Zeichen. Die Seele ist als diese Identität des Inneren mit dem Äußeren, das jenem unterworfen ist, wirklich; sie hat an ihrer Leiblichkeit ihre freie Gestalt, in der sie *sich* fühlt und *sich* zu fühlen gibt, die als das Kunstwerk der Seele menschlichen (...) Ausdruck hat." (ebenda, § 411, 192) Mit wirklicher Seele meint Hegel die Seele, die sich verwirklicht im Leib. Am Beispiel des Antlitzes macht er dies deutlich: Das Antlitz ist in eminenter Weise Ausdruck der Seele. Aber auch Hände und Sprache sind Ausdruck der Individualität des Menschen. Hegel spricht von dem über den ganzen Leib ausgegossenen geistigen Ton, was den Körper als Äußerlichkeit des Geistes ausweist. (siehe ebenda, § 411, 192) Der Leib ist ein unvollkommenes Zeichen des Geistes, die Sprache ist der vollkommene Ausdruck des Geistes. Im Medium der wirklichen Seele befreit der Geist sich zum Ich: Sehr bildhaft sagt Hegel: *Das Ich ist der Blitz, der durch die Naturseele schlägt und ihre Natürlichkeit verzehrt.* Im Ich ist die Natürlichkeit, dh. das Wesen der Seele, aufgehoben, das Ich weiß um die Natürlichkeit der Seele. Als subjektiver Geist zeigt der Geist sich in seinem geistigen Entstehen. Er integriert als Seele die Natur der Leiblichkeit, als Ich begreift das Individuum seine Leiblichkeit als Aufgabe für das Handeln. „Das Geistige steht für Hegel nicht abstrakt neben der Leiblichkeit, sondern es durchdringt sie." (Jaeschke 2003, 356)

Der nächste Schritt ist die Lehre vom Menschen als Bewusstsein, die Hegel in dem Enzyklopädie-Kapitel *Phänomenologie des Bewusstseins* abhandelt. Der Geist macht im Medium des Bewusstseins wieder eine stufenweise Entwicklung durch in der Beziehung auf die Welt und die Menschen. Das Bewusstsein erfasst in seinem Entwicklungsprozess seine Kompetenz der Gegenstandskonstitution, es weiß im Gegenstand sich selbst und wird zum Selbstbewusstsein: „Ich weiß von dem Gegenstande als dem meinigen (...), ich weiß daher darin von mir." (Hegel 1970d, § 424, 213) Weiters sagt Hegel: „Die Freiheit und die Vernunft besteht darin, daß ich mich zu der Form des Ich=Ich erhebe, daß ich alles als das Meinige, als Ich erkenne, daß ich jedes Objekt als ein Glied in dem Systeme desjenigen fasse, was ich selbst bin, - kurz darin, daß ich in *einem und demselben* Bewußtsein *Ich* und die *Welt* habe, in der Welt mich selber wiederfinde und umgekehrt in meinem Bewußtsein das habe, was *ist*, was *Objektivität* hat."(ebenda, § 422, 212) Dieses Selbstbewusstsein durchläuft nun wieder einzelne Entwicklungsstufen: Es begibt sich in die äußere Welt und sucht Befriedigung in der Welt. Die erste Stufe der Entwicklung des Selbstbewusstseins ist die Begierde. Es ist auf ein äußeres Objekt gerichtet, in dem es sich zu befriedigen sucht. (siehe ebenda, § 426, 215) Individuen erfahren sich auf dieser Stufe als Lebewesen, die zB. Hunger empfinden. Das Subjekt schaut im Objekt „seinen eigenen Mangel, seine eigene Einseitigkeit an, sieht im Objekt etwas zu seinem eigenen Wesen Gehöriges und dennoch ihm Fehlendes." (ebenda § 427, 217) zB. Tiere, die in der Jagd zu Nahrungszwecken erlegt werden. Das Objekt der Begierde wird verzehrt, die Begierde befriedigt. Das Objekt wird negiert, das Subjekt erhält sich. „Die Begierde ist somit in ihrer Befriedigung überhaupt zerstörend wie in ihrem Inhalte nach selbstsüchtig, und da die Befriedigung nur im Einzelnen geschehen, dieses aber vorübergehend ist, so erzeugt sich in der Befriedigung wieder die Begierde."(ebenda § 428, 218) Das Selbstbewusstsein erfährt sich wieder als hungrig, die Begierde wird erneut entfacht. Die Geschlechtsbeziehung auf dieser Stufe sieht so aus, dass das Selbstbewusstsein die andere Person als bloßes Objekt der Begierde erfasst, bloß zur Befriedigung der eigenen Bedürfnisse. Das Verhältnis der Begierde zum Gegenstand ist auf dieser Stufe noch selbstsüchtig und zerstörerisch. Deshalb muss die Entwicklung des Selbstbewusstseins weiter gehen. Das Selbstbewusstsein trifft auf ein anderes Selbstbewusstsein: „(E)s ist ein Selbstbewußtsein für ein Selbstbewußtsein." (ebenda, § 430, 219) Auf dieser Entwicklungsstufe wird das Selbstbewusstsein ein anerkennendes Selbstbewusstsein. Es erfasst sich als freies Selbstbewusstsein und will vom anderen Selbstbewusstsein als freies anerkannt werden. Es kommt zu einem Kampf um Anerkennung, das Selbstbewusstsein muss lernen, das andere Selbstbewusstsein auch als ein freies, geistiges Individuum anzuerkennen. „Nur so kommt die wahre Freiheit zustande; denn da diese in der Identität meiner mit dem anderen besteht, so bin ich wahrhaft frei nur dann, wenn auch der andere frei ist und von mir als frei anerkannt wird. Diese Freiheit des einen im anderen vereinigt die Menschen auf innerliche Weise, wogegen das Bedürfnis und die Not dieselben nur äußerlich zusammenbringt. Die Menschen müssen sich daher ineinander wiederfinden wollen." (ebenda, §

188

431, 220) Das entwickelte Selbstbewusstsein ist das affirmative Wissen seiner selbst im Anderen, dh. das andere Selbstbewusstsein wird anerkannt als ebenso freie Person. Beide anerkennen einander als freie Personen. Dieses Anerkennen des anderen Selbstbewusstseins als frei, dies ist die Substanz der Sittlichkeit. Hegels Konzept des Selbstbewusstseins ist daher in eminenter Weise intersubjektiv. Dieses Erfassen seiner selbst und des Anderen als frei, dh. die an und für sich seiende Allgemeinheit des Selbstbewusstseins (dass Menschen freie, handlungskompetente Personen sind und unveräußerliche Würde haben): dies zu erfassen bezeichnet Hegel als Vernunft. Indem das Selbstbewusstsein sich als Allgemeines erfasst, das Besondere aufhebt, wird es Vernunft. Das Selbstbewusstsein begreift sich nun als unendliche Allgemeinheit, als an und für sich seiende Freiheit, und dies Begreifen ist der Geist.

Der letzte Prozess des subjektiven Geistes im Rahmen der Enzyklopädie, das, was Hegel mit *Psychologie* bezeichnet, ist jene Sphäre, in der der Mensch weiß, dass er Geist ist. Auch hier gibt es wieder einen Entwicklungsgang zu durchlaufen: Der Weg des Geistes ist es 1) theoretisch zu sein, 2) Wille, praktischer Geist zu sein und 3) als freier Geist sich gegenständlich zu sein. Theoretischer und praktischer Geist hängen aber zusammen, denn auch das Handeln bedarf des Denkens. Als Wille tritt der Geist in die Wirklichkeit. Indem der Wille sich selber den Inhalt gibt, ist der Wille bei sich, ist er frei. Frei zu sein ist sein bestimmter Begriff. Der freie Wille, der den freien Willen will und seinen Inhalt zu entäußern hat – der Wille muss die Freiheit zu seiner Bestimmtheit machen, zu seinem Inhalt und Dasein. Dieser Begriff der Freiheit muss in die Wirklichkeit hineingebildet werden, in die Institutionen des Staates – dies ist der objektive Geist. Die Idee der gleichen Freiheit aller Menschen, „nach welchem das Individuum als solches einen unendlichen Wert hat, (...), d.i. daß der Mensch an sich zur höchsten Freiheit bestimmt ist" (ebenda, § 482, 302) – dieses Wissen, dass der Mensch absolute Würde hat, muss nun eingebildet werden in die Wirklichkeit, in die Institutionen des Staates, national und international – dies ist der objektive Geist. Freiheit ist nicht beschränkt darauf, dass man tun kann, was man will. „Der gewöhnliche Mensch glaubt, frei zu sein, wenn ihm willkürlich zu handeln erlaubt ist" (ebenda) – aber dadurch bin ich von Bedürfnissen aller Art abhängig. In dieser Willkürfreiheit bin ich nicht wirklich frei. Erst indem der Wille sich selbst zum Gegenstand hat, ist er für sich, was er an sich ist. *Erst der Wille, der sich selbst als freien*

Willen erfasst, begreift und sich selbst als freien Willen will: das ist der an und für sich freie, wahrhaft freie Wille. Hier ist die Sittlichkeit Inhalt des Willens. Man könnte dies ausformulieren mit Kants kategorischem Imperativ: die Menschenwürde jedes Menschen jederzeit überall auf der Welt zu respektieren, Menschen als Zweck an sich selbst anzuerkennen, sie niemals bloß als Mittel zu instrumentalisieren. Das meint Hegel mit dem wahrhaft freien Willen, der den freien Willen will.

Was bedeutet diese Auffassung des Menschen als freier Wille nun für feministische Philosophie? Hegel spricht diese Fähigkeit des freien Willens jedem Menschen zu, das ist nicht geschlechtlich konnotiert. Er schreibt kritisch gegen Sklaverei: In solchen Gesellschaften, so Hegel, wo es Sklaven gibt, ist der Begriff des Menschen als freier Wille verletzt. Ein nicht-verkürzter Begriff des Menschen bedeutet, dass der Mensch frei ist und als freie Person anerkannt wird.

Hegel entfaltet in seiner Rechtsphilosophie einen spannenden Begriff der *Person.* Dass der Geist sich als freies Ich zum Zweck hat, darin ist der Mensch Person. Das Höchste des Menschen ist es, Person zu sein. Als Person weiß ich mich frei in mir selbst. Hegel formuliert hier sein Rechtsgebot: „Sei eine Person und respektiere die anderen als Personen." (Hegel 1970b, § 36, 95). Er betont die reziproke Zuschreibung des Person-Seins: Jeder andere Mensch ist ebenso Person wie ich, ich anerkenne im anderen Menschen die gleiche Personalität wie in mir. Ich fasse mich in der Form der Allgemeinheit auf, dh. ich anerkenne mich als Person, dies ist es, worin aber alle Menschen als gleiche anerkannt werden müssen: dass sie Person sind. Hegel sagt nun: „Der Mensch gilt so, weil er Mensch ist, nicht weil er Jude, Katholik, Protestant, Deutscher, Italiener, usf. ist. Dieses Bewußtsein (...) ist von unendlicher Wichtigkeit" (ebenda, § 209), nämlich dieses Bewusstsein, dass jeder Mensch, weil er Mensch ist, als Person anerkannt werden muss, zB. auch unabhängig von Geschlechtszugehörigkeit oder sexueller Orientierung. Es geht um wechselseitig respektierte absolute Anerkennung von Personsein. Darin finden wir die Universalität der Person, das Allgemeine, die absolute Gleichheit in der Relation der reziproken Anerkennung. Vieweg führt erläuternd dazu aus: „Verhältnisse wie Knechtschaft, Sklaverei oder Despotismus können somit von vornherein nicht als Formen der Freiheit gelten, sowohl der Knecht als auch der Herr sind nicht frei, sie sind in demselben Verhältnis der Unfreiheit, das von ihnen Unterschiedene, der Andere ist kein Freier." (Vieweg 2012, 102) Der

Kern von Hegels Freiheitsbegriff liegt in der reziproken Anerkennung der Personen als Personen. Hegels Theorie der Person ist strikt intersubjektiv zu begreifen: Der Kern der Personalität ist Intersubjektivität.

Vehement kritisiert Hegel Sklaverei und Unterdrückung, Diskriminierung von Menschen als Unrecht. Den Menschen als bloßes Naturwesen zu betrachten, als bloßes Lasttier in der Sklaverei, als Sexware und Sexobjekt heute in der Pornoindustrie zB., dies ist dem Begriff des Menschen als Person nicht angemessen. Von dem Begriff des Menschen als Person, als freiem Willen her ist Sklaverei Unrecht; *dieser Begriff der Person, gefasst als freier Wille, ist der kritische Maßstab, mit dem alle Unrechtsverhältnisse kritisch zurückgewiesen werden können.* Meine Personalität, meine Menschenwürde, ist unveräußerlich. Hegel gibt dann Beispiele an von Veräußerung der Persönlichkeit: Sklaverei, Leibeigenschaft. Weil Menschen Personen sind und unveräußerliche Menschenwürde besitzen, haben Sklaven „ein absolutes Recht, sich frei zu machen (...).“ (Hegel 1970b, Zusatz zu § 66, 144) Hier ist ein Recht auf Widerstand angesprochen bei Hegel. Ein Mensch, der seiner Menschenwürde beraubt wird, der verachtet wird, diskriminiert, instrumentalisiert, wie ein Lasttier, auf seine reine Naturalität reduziert wird, hat das Recht, Widerstand zu leisten, ja sogar ein absolutes Recht, wie Hegel hier ausführt. Gegen jede Art von Instrumentalisierung und Versklavung schreibt Hegel: „Nur weil ich als Freies im Körper lebendig bin, darf dieses lebendige Dasein nicht zum Lasttiere mißbraucht werden. (...) Der Leib ist das Dasein der Freiheit, und ich empfinde in ihm.“ (ebenda, 111) Meinem Körper von anderen angetane Gewalt ist mir angetane Gewalt. Niemand darf einem Menschen körperliche Gewalt antun.

Gerade in Bezug auf Gewalt gegen Frauen ist dies ein sehr bedeutsamer Punkt, was Frauenhandel, Vergewaltigung, aber auch das zur Ware machen des weiblichen Körpers anbelangt.

Im Zentrum dieser Überlegungen Hegels steht sein Konzept der *sittlichen Substanz.* Diesen Bereich differenziert er wieder in verschiedene Sphären der Sittlichkeit: Familie, bürgerliche Gesellschaft und Staat. Welche Formen von Familie, bürgerlicher Gesellschaft und Staat sind für ein freies, geistbegabtes Individuum adäquate Formen, die die Freiheit ermöglichen, nicht aber Freiheit zerstören?

Der Begriff des Geistes ist vorrangig durch den Begriff der Sittlichkeit, der sittlichen Substanz bestimmt. Der wirkliche Geist, so Hegel, ist die Vermittlung von sittlicher Substanz und Individuum. Die Sittlichkeit darf die autonome Vernunft nicht außer sich haben, sondern die Menschen selber müssen die sittliche Substanz hervorbringen. Die sittliche Substanz ist die „absolute Einheit der Einzelheit und der Allgemeinheit der Freiheit", wie Hegel in der Enzyklopädie weiter ausführt. (Hegel 1970d, § 515) In der Rechtsphilosophie bezeichnet Hegel die Sittlichkeit als „die Idee der Freiheit, als das lebendige Gute, das in dem Selbstbewußtsein sein Wissen, Wollen und durch dessen Handeln seine Wirklichkeit, so wie dieses an dem sittlichen Sein seine an und für sich seiende Grundlage und bewegenden Zweck hat, - der zur vorhandenen Welt und zur Natur des Selbstbewußtseins gewordene Begriff der Freiheit." (Hegel 1970b, § 142) Die sittliche Substanz ist niemals unabhängig von den Individuen zu denken. Es kommt alles darauf an, dass der autonome Geist als Substanz und Subjekt verwirklicht wird. Im Kontext der Anerkennungsvollzüge drückt Hegel das, was mit sittlicher Freiheit gemeint ist, so aus, dass die wahre Freiheit nur in der Anerkennung der anderen Person als mir gleich an Freiheit zustande kommt. Das Wesen, die Substanz des Geistes, ist Freiheit. Diese Substanz des Geistes, die Freiheit, muss nun handelnd von den Menschen in die Wirklichkeit ihrer gemeinsam gestalteten Welt eingebildet werden, hineingearbeitet werden: in die Institutionen des Staates und international. Das Wissen der Menschen, dass ihr Zweck die Freiheit ist, das Wissen von dieser Idee ist die Wirklichkeit des Menschen. Die Zwecktätigkeit des Willens zielt darauf ab, seinen Begriff, die Freiheit, in die Welt einzubilden, so dass der Wille in der durch den Willen hervorgebrachten Welt bei sich ist.

Hegel fasst die sittliche Substanz als das Wir, in dem Menschen sich weltgestaltend zusammen schließen: Sittliche Substanz: Ich, das Wir und Wir, das Ich ist. Menschen müssen sich auf andere Menschen einlassen und mit ihnen zusammen Gemeinschaft gestalten „Das Selbstbewußtsein erreicht seine Befriedigung nur in einem anderen Selbstbewußtsein." (Hegel 1970a, 144) In diesem Wir müssen die einzelnen Individuen als Personen in ihrer Autonomie anerkannt werden (die Sittlichkeit hat ja im Selbstbewusstsein ihre Wirklichkeit).

Ein sinnvoller Begriff von sittlichem Gemeinwesen hat die Autonomie *und* die Gemeinschaftsbedürftigkeit der Individuen anzuerkennen. Es gilt zu berücksichtigen, dass menschliches Leben nicht wirklich gelingen kann, wenn Menschen einerseits bloß atomistisch nebeneinander existieren, andererseits die Individuen in ihrer Besonderheit und Einmaligkeit negiert werden.

4. Hegels Religionsphilosophie unter feministischer Perspektive

Subjektiver und objektiver Geist sind der Weg, auf dem der Geist sich entfaltet und sich als Freiheit begreift und verwirklicht. Erst als absoluter Geist ist Geist seinem Begriff vollkommen angemessen. Auf der Stufe des absoluten Geistes haben Menschen in einem Lernprozess sich selber vollständig als Geist erfasst: im Medium der *Anschauung* (Kunst), der *Vorstellung* (Religion) und des *Begriffs* (Philosophie). In der Sphäre des absoluten Geistes wendet der Geist sich auf sich zurück, gewinnt sein Bewusstsein über sich und ist eben darin absoluter Geist: Selbstbewusstsein des absoluten Geistes. Kunst, Religion und Philosophie sind die drei Gestalten des absoluten Geistes, denen vermögenstheoretisch die drei Formen Anschauung, Vorstellung und begreifendes Denken des subjektiven Geistes entsprechen. Den Lernprozess des Geistes skizziert Hegel auch in seiner Geschichtsphilosophie. Im Gang des Geistes, der in der Geschichte webt, ist Freiheit der Endzweck. Der Endzweck der Welt ist das Bewusstsein des Geistes von seiner Freiheit, es kommt darauf an zu begreifen, dass der Mensch *als Mensch* frei ist. Die Idee der gleichen Freiheit aller Menschen ist, wie Hegel hervorhebt, mit dem Christentum in die Welt gekommen, „nach welchem das Individuum als solches einen unendlichen Wert hat, indem es Gegenstand und Zweck der Liebe Gottes, dazu bestimmt ist, zu Gott als Geist sein absolutes Verhältnis, diesen Geist in sich wohnen zu haben, d.i. daß der Mensch an sich zur höchsten Freiheit bestimmt ist." (ebenda, § 482) Das heißt, das Wissen des Menschen, dass ihr Zweck die Freiheit ist, dh. dass die Menschen diese Idee *sind*, sie haben sie nicht bloß.

In der Religionsphilosophie geht Hegel zunächst der Frage nach: Was ist Religion überhaupt? Er macht Religion für sich zum Thema philosophischer Betrachtungen. Wo ist der Ort der Religion?

In der Sphäre des absoluten Geistes „verhält sich der Geist nicht mehr zu etwas anderem und Beschränktem, sondern zum Unbeschränkten und Unendlichen, und das ist ein unendliches Verhältnis, ein Verhältnis der Freiheit und nicht mehr der Abhängigkeit, da ist sein Bewußtsein absolut frei und selbst wahrhaftes Bewußtsein, weil es Bewußtsein der absoluten Wahrheit ist." (Hegel 1970f, I, 11) Religion ist der Standpunkt des Bewusstseins der Wahrheit, und diese Wahrheit ist näherhin bestimmt als *Freiheit, freier* Geist.

Auch Gott ist Geist, Geist, der sich *entäußert* in die Gemeinschaft hinein. „Es ist also eine Beziehung von Geist zu Geist. Dieses Verhältnis von Geist zu Geist liegt der Religion zu Grunde." (ebenda, 102) Geist ist nur wirklich, wenn er sich entäußert. Der menschliche Geist entäußert sich in die Welt hinein durch Denken und Handeln. Gott als Geist entäußert sich in die bestimmten Religionen im Laufe der Religionsgeschichte. Der Entwicklungsgang des Geistes durch die Gestaltungen der bestimmten Religionen, dh. der in der Geschichte entstandenen Glaubensgemeinschaften, ist ein Lernprozess des Geistes. Die letzte Stufe der Entwicklung des Geistes im Medium der Religion bezeichnet Hegel als absolute Religion, und zwar warum: Im Christentum als der absoluten Religion ist Gott als Geist aufgefasst, und damit auch der Mensch als Geist, in der subtilsten Weise von Freiheit und Menschenwürde, die nur möglich ist. In der absoluten Religion weiß Gott sich im *Denken* der Menschen. Vollendet ist die Religion, wenn sie ihren Begriff verwirklicht hat: wenn die Einheit, die Versöhnung von göttlichem und endlichem Wesen, Gegenstand des religiösen Bewusstseins wird.

Wo ist der Ort der Religion im Menschen? Hier skizziert Hegel eine ungemein spannende Anthropologie: die Sphäre des Gefühls, der Anschauung, Vorstellung und des Denkens. Gott ist Geist, der Mensch ist Geist. Die Vernunft ist der Boden des Geistigen. Geist, Vernunft, ist eine Kompetenz *im* Menschen. Gott als Geist offenbart sich im Medium des Geistes, dh. er offenbart sich *im* Menschen. Der Geist im Menschen ist der Ort der Entäußerung, der Offenbarung dessen, was Geist ist. Dieser Grundbegriff des Geistes ist das, was sich in der ganzen Religionsgeschichte entfaltet. Der Geist offenbart sich dem Geist, der Geist gibt Zeugnis dem Geiste. Gott weiß sich selbst im endlichen Geist. Geist ist nichts bloß Innerliches, sondern muss sich manifestieren, sich entäußern, muss in die Wirklichkeit hineingebildet werden. In diesem Zusammenhang ist Hegels Theorie der Gemeinde entscheidend wichtig.

4.1. Hegels religionsphilosophische Konzeption von Gemeinde

Geist ist gemäß Hegel immer ein Selbstbewusstsein für ein Selbstbewusstsein. Herbert Scheit führt in seinem Werk ‚Geist und Gemeinde' aus: „Geist ist also von vornherein und wesentlich ein ‚dialogisches', ja ein ‚gesellschaftliches' Phänomen und braucht daher die Auseinandersetzung, aber auch die Anerkennung eines ihm gleichgestellten Partners. Weil dies für den Begriff des ‚Geistes' gilt, dass er ‚nie allein' ist, sondern nur in einer Pluralität und Gemeinschaft, gilt dies auch für Gott als absoluten Geist: er ist ‚nur Geist, insofern er für den Geist ist.'" (Scheit 1973, 154) Die höchste Bestimmung des Menschen als autonomes Individuum liegt darin, die *spröde Spitze der Partikularität*, die Eigeninteressen, die Vorstellung, isolierter Einzelner zu sein, zu überwinden und sich zu öffnen für die Gestaltung einer solidarischen und gerechten Gemeinschaft, für ein Miteinander-Leben mit anderen Menschen, die in gleicher Weise als Geist anerkannt werden.

Wenn die Sphäre des absoluten Geistes die Frage ist: Was ist der Mensch? Der Mensch als Geist ist dies, sich zu entäußern in die Gemeinschaft hinein, als autonomes Individuum sich zu öffnen für ein Miteinander-Leben mit anderen Menschen, die ebenso in gleicher Weise als Geist anerkannt werden. Das Verharren auf der Vereinzelung – dies ist im Sinne Hegels das Böse, die Sünde wider den Geist. Hegel spricht vom Ich, das Wir ist: „Ich, das wir, und Wir, das Ich ist." (Hegel 1970a, 145) Was der Gemeinde zum Bewusstsein kommt, ist dies: „Die Subjektivität, die ihren unendlichen Wert erfaßt hat, hat damit alle Unterschiede der Herrschaft, der Gewalt, des Standes, selbst des Geschlechts aufgehoben: vor Gott sind alle Menschen gleich. In der Negation des unendlichen Schmerzes der Liebe liegt auch erst die Möglichkeit und Wurzel des wahrhaft allgemeinen Rechts, der Verwirklichung der Freiheit." (Hegel 1970f, II, 303) Der Geist der Gemeinde ist die Liebe zwischen den einzelnen Individuen, die so nicht mehr bloß Einzelne sind, sondern als Individuen im Geist verbunden sind zu einer Gemeinschaft. Dieser Geist der Zusammengehörigkeit entspricht dem Begriff des Geistes selbst: „So ist diese Liebe der Geist als solcher, der Heilige Geist." (ebenda, 305) Hegel interpretiert in diesem Zusammenhang den theologischen Begriff der ‚Sünde wider den Geist'; er versteht diese als Sünde wider die Liebe, die darin liegt, sich dem Lieben zu verweigern, indem man sich in sich verschließt und damit auch die Anderen in die Vereinzelung, Vereinsamung treibt. Diese Überlegungen bestimmen auch Hegels Verständnis von Kirche – diese ist für ihn die reale Gemeinde. Die Lehre der Kirche ist die Lehre von der Versöhnung, gedacht als Versöhntsein des Individuums mir Gott. Dies bedeutet, wie gesagt, dass die *spröde Spitze der Subjektivität* mit dem Allgemeinen vermittelt ist. Diese Vermittlung muss nun auch im Handeln der Menschen vollzogen werden, darin sieht Hegel die Bedeutung des Kults.

4.2. Bedeutung des Kults

Kultus ist ein praktisches Verhältnis. „Der Kult als die Praxis der Gemeinde ist daher der Genuß der Versöhnung; in ihm erfährt der Mensch als diese besondere Persönlichkeit seine ‚Göttlichkeit', d.h. er weiß sich als absoluter Endzweck." (Scheit 1973, 215) Der Kult ist Liebe, indem der Mensch mit dem Absoluten identisch wird. Scheit deutet Hegels Begriff des Kults in einer sehr umfassenden Weise, die sich nicht auf liturgische Handlungen, Gottesdienst und Sakramente beschränkt: Der Kult macht vor allem die Struktur von Praxis im eigentlichen Sinn deutlich – es geht primär um „die ‚Rekonstruktion' des natürlichen Willens zu einem Willen, der das Allgemeine und Vernünftige will." (ebenda, 216) Die Aufgabe der Gemeinde besteht so in der wechselseitigen sittlichen Sensibilisierung der Menschen, in der wechselseitigen Erziehung der Menschen zur sittlichen Autonomie. Daher muss der Kult die gesamte sittliche Lebensführung des Menschen umfassen. „Der bloß religiöse Kult wäre immer noch eine bestimmte und damit beschränkte Praxis; deshalb muß er sich zu einem sittlichen Leben umsetzen, um der ‚Kultus im Elemente der Freiheit' sein zu können." (ebenda, 226) Die Sittlichkeit ist damit der Widerschein des Göttlichen in der Welt, die Gegenwart Gottes in der endlichen Wirklichkeit. (siehe ebenda, 226) Im Kultus „stehe ich auf der einen und Gott auf der anderen Seite, und die Bestimmung ist nun, mich in Gott und Gott in mich zusammenzuschließen und diese konkrete Einheit hervorzubringen". (Hegel 1970f, I, 202) In dieser Gewissheit des absoluten Geistes ist enthalten das schon vom absoluten Inhalt wissende Selbstbewusstsein, das sich als geistig und frei weiß. Im Kultus begreift das Ich, dass es sich dazu erziehen soll, ein geistiges Wesen zu sein. Kultus ist Selbsterziehung: dass ich mich als geistiges, dh. freies Wesen begreife und mich für die Gemeinschaft öffne, dh. für die Anerkennung der Anderen als ebenso geistige Wesen in ihrer – unserer – Gottebenbildlichkeit. Das Gute, das ewig sich vollbringt: dies bedeutet die Erhebung zum Absoluten, indem ich meine *spröde Spitze der Subjektivität* aufhebe und mich auf die Gemeinschaft hin öffne, der Liebe öffne.

Der Kultus ist die Praxis des Begreifenlernens, dass wir freier Geist sind, mit der Kompetenz des freien Willens und der Menschenwürde ausgestattet. Wichtig ist, dass der Mensch sich als unendliche Persönlichkeit weiß, also die unveräußerliche Personwürde jedes Menschen anerkennt.

Die Versöhnung im Kultus bedeutet, dass das Subjekt seinem Begriff gemäß ist, dh. dass der Mensch sich darüber klar wird, dass er Geist und daher frei ist: dass er für sich unendlichen Wert hat und Gegenstand der unendlichen Liebe Gottes ist. In der absoluten Religion, im Christentum, ist im Bild der Trinität für die Vorstellung die Versöhnung Gottes und des Menschen so konzipiert: In Christus ist Gott Mensch und der Mensch Gott; doch der Mensch ist nur insofern Gott, als er die Natürlichkeit und Endlichkeit seines Geistes aufhebt und sich zu Gott erhebt. Die Versöhnung Gottes und des Menschen, die in Christus vorgestellt wird, ist eine Versöhnung, die jedem Menschen zukommt. In Christus ist der Mensch schlechthin erlöst und versöhnt: „Der Mensch, als endlicher für sich betrachtet, ist zugleich auch Ebenbild Gottes und Quelle der Unendlichkeit in ihm selbst; er ist Selbstzweck, hat in ihm selbst unendlichen Wert (...) (D)er Mensch ist jetzt als Mensch nach seiner allgemeinen Natur in Gott angeschaut; jeder Einzelne ist ein Gegenstand der Gnade Gottes und des göttlichen Endzwecks: Gott will, dass alle Menschen selig werden. Ganz ohne Partikularität, an und für sich hat also der Mensch, und zwar schon als Mensch unendlichen Wert, und eben dieser unendliche Wert hebt alle Partikularität der Geburt und des Vaterlandes auf." (Hegel 1970f, II, 404) Jeder einzelne Mensch ist in seiner absoluten Menschenwürde anzuerkennen.

Die höchste Form des Kultus liegt darin, das Verharren auf dem Egoismus aufzuheben. Der Mensch wird im Kultus befähigt, sein Herz zu öffnen für Gott und für die Mitmenschen, für die Gestaltung eines sittlichen Gemeinwesens. Jede Person ist zunächst ein starres, sprödes, selbständiges Fürsichsein, doch auf dieser Spitze ereignet sich ein dialektisches Umschlagen: „Es ist der Charakter der Person, des Subjekts vielmehr, seine Isolierung, Abgesondertheit aufzuheben. Die Sittlichkeit, Liebe, ist, seine Besonderheit, besondere Persönlichkeit aufzuheben, zur Allgemeinheit zu erweitern. (...) In Freundschaft, Liebe gebe ich meine abstrakte Persönlichkeit auf und gewinne sie dadurch als konkrete." (ebenda, II, 233)

Geist ist Hegel gemäß immer ein Selbstbewusstsein für ein Selbstbewusstsein. Hegel spricht vom Ich, das Wir ist und Wir, das Ich ist. Geist ist Geist in Gemeinschaft. Daher muss der Kultus die gesamte sittliche Lebensführung des Menschen umfassen – er muss Kultus im Element der Freiheit sein. Der heilige Geist ist die ewige Liebe. Was ist Liebe im Sinne Hegels? Das Wesen des Geistes, für die Empfindung ausgedrückt, ist die Liebe.

4.3. Philosophische Idee der Liebe in Hegels Werk

Hegel erläutert den Begriff der Liebe, den er zur Deutung der Trinität heranzieht, unter Bezugnahme auf die zwischenmenschliche Erfahrung: „(D)ie Liebe ist ein Unterscheiden zweier, die doch füreinander schlechthin nicht unterschieden sind. Das Gefühl und Bewußtsein dieser Identität ist die Liebe, dieses, außer mir zu sein: ich habe mein Selbstbewußtsein nicht in mir, sondern im Anderen, aber dieses Andere, in dem nur ich befriedigt bin, meinen Frieden mit mir habe – und ich bin nur, indem ich Frieden mit mir habe; habe ich diesen nicht, so bin ich der Widerspruch, der auseinander geht -, dieses Andere, indem es ebenso außer sich ist, hat sein Selbstbewußtsein nur in mir, und beide sind nur dieses Bewußtsein ihres Außersichseins und ihrer Identität. Dies Anschauen, dies Fühlen, dies Wissen der Einheit – das ist die Liebe. Gott ist die Liebe, d.i. dies Unterscheiden und die Nichtigkeit dieses Unterschieds." (ebenda, II, 222)

Was sind die Konsequenzen dieses Konzepts von Liebe für unser menschliches Zusammenleben? Was sind die Konsequenzen für eine feministische Religionsphilosophie?

Unter der Perspektive der Hegelschen Deutung des christlichen Liebesbegriffs, die den Aspekt der wechselseitigen Anerkennung in den Vordergrund rückt, ist jegliche Diskriminierung von Menschen auf Grund der Geschlechtszugehörigkeit, der ethnischen Zugehörigkeit, der sexuellen Orientierung, usw. als strikt unhaltbar zurück zu weisen. In Hegels Philosophie ist Liebe als symmetrische Anerkennungsform begriffen – im Sinn der Anerkennung der anderen Person als Wesen mit unveräußerlicher Würde und der Anerkennung ihrer je individuellen Besonderheit. Für Hegel ist Liebe durch vollständige Reziprozität gekennzeichnet: „(N)ur in der Liebe allein ist man eins mit dem Objekt, es beherrscht nicht und wird nicht beherrscht." (Hegel 1970g, 239 ff) Gott ist Geist, der Mensch ist Geist, und der Geist ist Liebe. Die neue Gemeinschaft ist eine Beziehung von unverwechselbaren Individuen, die nicht länger als Individuen leben, sondern verbunden sind im Geist der Liebe und Freundschaft.

Der Geist ist freier Wille und Liebe und Freiheit ist das höchste Gut.

Wo bleibt dieser Gemeinschaftsgedanke, wenn wir aus der Religion herausgehen? Diese Umsetzung in die Praxis, wo kommt das vor? An diesem Punkt wird Hegels Theorie des Staates relevant. Im Medium der Religion ist die Kirche die Gemeinschaft. Im Bereich außerhalb der Religion – was ist das säkulare Pendant dazu für das Hinausgehen aus der Vereinzelung hin in die menschliche Gemeinschaft? „In der Religion ist der Mensch frei vor Gott; (...) Der Staat ist nur die Freiheit in der Welt, in der Wirklichkeit. Es kommt hier wesentlich auf den Begriff der Freiheit an, den ein Volk in seinem Selbstbewußtsein trägt; denn im Staat wird der Freiheitsbegriff realisiert, und zu dieser Realisierung gehört wesentlich das Bewußtsein der an sich seienden Freiheit. Völker, die nicht wissen, daß der Mensch an und für sich frei sei, leben in der Verdumpfung sowohl in Ansehung ihrer Verfassung als ihrer Religion. Es ist ein Begriff der Freiheit in Religion und Staat. Dieser eine Begriff ist das Höchste was der Mensch hat, und er wird von dem Menschen realisiert. Das Volk, das einen schlechten Begriff von Gott hat, hat auch einen schlechten Staat, schlechte Regierung, schlechte Gesetze." (Hegel 1970f, I, 237)

4.4. Denkende Erkundung der religiösen Tradition

Eine andere Form der Versöhnung besteht darin, dass der Inhalt der Religion sich im Denken bewähren muss. Gott ist Geist, der Mensch ist Geist, es ist *ein* Geist. Das Wissen von Gott als Geist ist immer auch Wissen vom Menschen als Geist. Geist muss sich entäußern in die Welt der Menschen, in die Institutionen seines Zusammenlebens: Recht, Familie, Staat, Politik, Medizin, Erziehung, Kunst, Wissenschaft, Wirtschaft, etc. „(E)in Geist geht durch die Wirklichkeit und durch das philosophische Denken." (ebenda, 53), so Hegel. Die Narrative der Religion müssen denkend erkundet werden. Deshalb ist Theologie gut beraten, sich auf einen Dialog mit Philosophie einzulassen, um auf dem höchsten geistigen Niveau zu arbeiten. Die Erzählungen der heiligen Schriften sind eingehüllt in ein Sprachkleid der jeweiligen Zeit, in der diese Erzählungen entstanden sind. Durch dieses Sprachkleid durchzudringen zum geistigen Kern der Erzählung – das ist die Aufgabe des Denkens auf dem Boden des Geistes, das ist Aufgabe der Philosophie. Für Hegel stellt sich das Bestehen der Gemeinde als ein fortdauerndes, ewiges Werden dar, da der Geist „dies ist, sich ewig zu erkennen". (ebenda, II, 320) In diesem Sinn hält Hegel fest: „Gott will nicht engherzige Gemüter und leere Köpfe zu seinen Kindern haben." (Hegel 1970e, S. 27) Damit sind Glaubensgemeinschaften zur beständigen Selbstkritik aufgefordert – zur jeweils neuen, denkenden Aneignung ihrer Tradition. Die Aufgabe der Philosophie liegt darin, den Inhalt der Vorstellung in begriffliches Denken zu übersetzen. Der Inhalt ist der gleiche in Kunst, Religion und Philosophie, dieser muss aus der religiösen Vorstellung ins Denken übersetzt werden, dialektisch aufgehoben werden, weil Menschen sich denkend mit religiösen Inhalten auseinander setzen müssen. Die religiösen Narrative müssen ins Denken übersetzt werden, weil Menschen die Kompetenz des Denkens haben.

5. Hegels Relevanz für feministische Religionsphilosophie

Kann Hegels Theorie des Menschen ein Angebot darstellen für feministische Philosophie? Hegel fasst den Menschen primär von der Geistbegabtheit her, der Mensch ist geist- und vernunftbegabtes Lebewesen, dh. das was der Mensch ist, muss er handelnd und sprechend aus sich selber machen. Wenn Kirchendokumente vom „Wesen der Frau" sprechen, und feministische Theologiekonzeptionen zB. von einer Frauenkirche, dann besteht ein Problem in dem Singular „die Frau": dabei wird individuelle Vielfalt ausgeblendet, wie Nagl-Docekal einleuchtend darlegt. „All jene Dimensionen im Leben einer Frau, die nicht unmittelbar mit der allen Frauen zugedachten trans-historischen Geschlechtsrolle zu tun haben – die sehr verschiedenartigen Begabungen und Interessen der einzelnen Frauen - werden als nicht wirklich relevant ausgeblendet. So erweist sich der Singular ‚die Frau' als der Abgrund, in den Vielfältigkeit versenkt wird. Das bedeutet nichts weniger, als dass den Frauen die volle Anerkennung als Menschen verweigert wird – die Entfaltung von Individualität bleibt (...) ein Prärogativ der Männer. Dazu eine ‚laientheologische Frage': Liegt nicht im Gedanken der Gotteskindschaft aller Einzelnen die Forderung eines Ernstnehmens der Individuen in ihrer jeweiligen Einzigartigkeit?" (Nagl-Docekal 2008b, 130).

Manche römisch-katholische Dokumente leiten aus der leiblichen Beschaffenheit von Menschen Charaktereigenschaften, Tugenden, Wesensmerkmale ab. Freilich werden Menschen mit bestimmter leiblicher Ausstattung geboren. Es ist jedoch ein biologistischer Reduktionismus, ein Geschlechteressentialismus, aus der leiblichen Beschaffenheit von Menschen Charaktereigenschaften abzuleiten. Die körperliche Ausstattung, mit der wir geboren werden, legt uns nicht wesensmäßig fest, denn Menschen verfügen über die Kompetenz, sich handelnd mit der eigenen leiblichen Ausstattung auseinander zu setzen. Aus körperlichen Merkmalen Tugenden ableiten zu wollen, stellt einen Reduktionismus dar. Die Aufgabe für uns Menschen als geistbegabte Personen besteht darin: erstens mit unserer Leiblichkeit handelnd umzugehen; zweitens sich mit den geschichtlich überlieferten, kulturellen Deutungen dieser Leiblichkeit handelnd auseinander zu setzen.

Die Auseinandersetzung mit zentralen Theoriestücken in Hegels Philosophie regt dazu an, den Grundgedanken des Christentums erneut philosophisch auszudeuten.

Hegels Relevanz in Bezug auf feministische Religionsphilosophie möchte ich an Hand eines Zitates von Herta Nagl-Docekal näher beleuchten: Hegel unterstreicht in seiner Religionsphilosophie die christliche Lehre von der Gotteskindschaft jedes Menschen. "Theological tradition has emphasized all along that each human being must be perceived, and respected, as a child of God. In this regard it seems helpful, indeed, to adopt core conceptions of modern philosophy which explain, through careful argument, the dignity and singularity of the human being. One consequence of such a philosophical reading is of particular relevance here: (…) the thesis that all humans are of equal dignity is incompatible with a naturalistic approach to the social order in general and women in particular. From this perspective, the main thrust of feminism no longer appears as alien to Christianity; rather, the question arises: how can one claim to be a Christian while rejecting the feminist concern for equal treatment of women and men?" (Nagl-Docekal 2012, 184) Das Nächstenliebe-Gebot meint in ganz besonderer Weise Frauen, da es offensichtlich ist, dass Frauen überall auf der Welt die schlechtesten Lebensbedingungen haben. Alle Formen von Paternalismus, Demütigung und Diskriminierung sind zurück zu weisen. Nagl-Docekal: "Women face a grim social reality - "one which affects their children as well – the reason lies in the respective construction of gender roles, i.e., in a social order that denies women the chance to be economically independent." (ebenda, 184)

Bezugnehmend auf Hegels Religionsphilosophie ist es bedeutsam zu zeigen, dass der biblische Aufruf zu Gerechtigkeit und Solidarität impliziert, dass Frauen voll als Personen anzuerkennen sind, wie Nagl-Docekal unterstreicht. (ebenda, 184)

Nagl-Docekal betont die Problematik naturalistischer Reduktionismen im Blick auf Frauen: "Modern culture, most notably the area of advertising, has increasingly shaped a portrayal of women from the perspective of sexual availability. Also, fashion has gradually adopted a pornographic style. The sharp increase in both international trafficking of women and sexual violence is a further component of the same picture. The use of rape as a means of warfare, which has been practiced extensively in recent conflicts, represents only one step further down that road. What all these phenomena have in common is that women are being treated as objects rather than respected as subjects who are entitled to decide on their own whom they would like to get involved with. This is the point that needs to be made in order to support any public challenge of these features of the contemporary world – a point that can be shown to be well-founded in the Bible." (ebenda, 185 f)

Mit Hegels Interpretation von Religion, Kultus und der Aufgabe der Kirchen, der Gemeinde haben feministische Religionsphilosophinnen ein brauchbares Instrument, um Diskriminierung von Frauen, homo-, trans- und intersexuellen Menschen, jede Form von Gewalt gegen Frauen und benachteiligte Gruppierungen zurückzuweisen. Hegels Theorie von Religion ist für feministische Religionsphilosophie ein geeignetes Konzept, da hier Gott und der Mensch als Geist begriffen werden: Geist ist Liebe und Liebe ist symmetrische Anerkennung. Die Aufgabe, die sich hier von der Religion her ergibt, ist die Pflicht zur Zurückweisung jeglicher Gender-Hierarchie und Diskriminierung. Hegels Theorie der Liebe kann begriffen werden als philosophische Ausbuchstabierung des Nächstenliebegebotes, das uns zur Aufgabe macht, dass „Trauer und Angst der Menschen", die auf Grund der Zugehörigkeit zum weiblichen Geschlecht diskriminiert und benachteiligt werden, „im Herzen der Christ_innen ihren Widerhall finden". (Gaudium et spes DH 4301, Pkt. 1)

Bibliographie

Anderson Pamela Sue. Feminist Philosophy of Religion. An epistemological approach. In: Pamela Sue Anderson and Beverley Clack (ed.), Feminist Philosophy of Religion. London and New York: Routledge 2004, p. 87 – 101.

beiträge zur feministischen theorie und praxis. Geteilter Feminismus. Heft Nr. 27, 1990.

Bereswill, Mechthild. „Ein unabgeschlossenes Projekt." In: Was wollen sie noch? feministische studien. Zeitschrift für interdisziplinäre Frauen- und Geschlechterforschung, 31. Jg., Mai 2013, Nr. 1.

Buchhammer, Brigitte. „Religion und Homosexualität. Eine Relektüre von Hegels Religionsphilosophie." In: Nagl-Docekal Herta, Kaltenbacher Wolfgang und Nagl Ludwig (Hg.), Viele Religionen – eine Vernunft? Ein Disput zu Hegel. Wiener Reihe Themen der Philosophie. Band 14, in Zusammenarbeit mit dem Istituto Italiano per gli Studi Filosofici. Wien-Berlin: Böhlau/Akademie Verlag, 2008.

Buchhammer, Brigitte. Feministische Religionsphilosophie. Philosophisch-systematische Grundlagen. Wien-Berlin: Lit, 2011.

Buchhammer, Brigitte. „Feministische Religionsphilosophie – ein innovatives Projekt." In: Ethik, Freiheit und Liebe. Zum 70. Geburtstag von Herta Nagl-Docekal, Labyrinth. An International Journal for Philosophy, Value Theory and Sociocultural Hermeneutics, Vol. 16 (2), Winter 2014, 66 – 91. Axia Academic Publishers, 2014.

Daly, Mary. Beyond God the Father. Boston 1973.

Fetscher, Iring. Hegels Lehre vom Menschen. Stuttgart-Bad Cannstatt: Friedrich Frommann/Günther Holzboog, 1970.

Gerhard, Ute. „Feminismus heute?" In: Elisabeth Moltmann-Wendel (Hg.), Feministische Theologie. Wo steht sie? Wohin geht sie? Eine kritische Bilanz. Neukirchen-Vluyn: Neukirchener, 2008.

Gerhard, Ute. Frauenbewegung und Feminismus. Eine Geschichte seit 1789. München: Ch. Beck, 2009.

Gerhard, Ute. „In den Brüchen der Zeit. 30 Jahre feministische studien. In: feministische studien. Zeitschrift für interdisziplinäre Frauen- und Geschlechterforschung. 31. Jg., Mai 2013, Nr. 1.

Gerl-Falkovitz, Hannah Barbara. „Personalität in Mann und Frau." In: Putallaz/Schumacher (Hg.), Der Mensch und die Person. Darmstadt, 2008.

Hark, Sabine. „'Feministin sein bin ich mir schuldig'. 30 Jahre *feministische studien* - Einleitung." In: feministische studien. Zeitschrift für interdisziplinäre Frauen- und Geschlechterforschung. 31. Jg., Mai 2013, Nr. 1.

Hegel, G.W.F. Phänomenologie des Geistes. Frankfurt/M.: Suhrkamp, 1970 (a).

Hegel, G.W.F. Grundlinien der Philosophie des Rechts. Frankfurt/M.: Suhrkamp, 1970 (b).

Hegel, G.W.F.Vorlesungen über die Ästhetik I. Werke 13. Frankfurt/M.: Suhrkamp, 1970 (c).

Hegel,G.W.F. Enzyklopädie der philosophischen Wissenschaften III. Werke 10. Frankfurt/M.: Suhrkamp, 1970 (d).

Hegel, G.W.F. Vorlesungen über die Philosophie der Geschichte. Werke 12. Frankfurt/M.: Suhrkamp, 1970 (e).

Hegel, G.W.F. Vorlesungen über die Philosophie der Religion I + II. Werke 17. Frankfurt/M.: Suhrkamp, 1970 (f).

Hegel, G.W.F., Entwürfe über Religion und Liebe. In: Frühe Schriften. Werke 1. Frankfurt/M.: Suhrkamp, 1970 (g).

Hoffmann, Thomas Sören. Georg Wilhelm Friedrich Hegel. Eine Propädeutik. Wiesbaden: Marix, 2004.

Jaeschke, Walter. Hegel Handbuch. Leben-Werk-Wirkung. Stuttgart: Metzler, 2003.

Jaggar, Alison. „Eine feministische Kritik der angeblichen Verschuldung des Südens." In: Hobuß, Steffi, Schües Christina, Zimnik Nina, Hartmann Birgit, Patrut Julia (Hg.), Die andere Hälfte der Globalisierung. Menschenrechte, Ökonomie und Medialität aus feministischer Sicht. Frankfurt/M.-New York: Campus, 2001.

Nagl-Docekal, Herta (Hg.). Feministische Philosophie. München: Oldenbourg, 1990.

Nagl-Docekal, Herta. Artikel „Feministische Philosophie", in: Metzler Lexikon Philosophie. 3. Auflage. Stuttgart-Weimar: Metzler, 2008 (a).

Nagl-Docekal, Herta. „Philosophische Reflexionen über Liebe und die Gefahr ihrer Unterbestimmung im zeitgenössischen Diskurs." In: Nagl-Docekal Herta, Wolfram Friedrich (Hg.), Jenseits der Säkularisierung. Berlin: Parerga, 2008 (b).

Nagl-Docekal, Herta. In: Maria Isabel Pena Aguado, Schmitz Bettina (Hg.), Klassikerinnen des modernen Feminismus. Aachen: ein-Fach, 2010, S. 112 – 181.

Nagl-Docekal, Herta. „Issues of Gender in Catholicism: How The Current Debate Could Benefit From A Philosophical Approach." In: Charles Taylor, José Casanova, George F. McLean (Hg.), Church and People: Disjunctions in a Secular Age. Christian Philosophical Studies, I. Washington: The Council for Research in Values and Philosophy, 2012, p. 155 – 186.

Scheit, Herbert. Geist und Gemeinde. Zum Verhältnis von Religion und Politik bei Hegel. München: Pustet, 1973.

Schüssler-Fiorenza, Elisabeth. „Feministische Theologie zwischen Moderne und Postmoderne." In: Dethloff Klaus, Langthaler Rudolf, Nagl-Docekal Herta und Wolfram Friedrich (Hg.), Orte der Religion im philosophischen Diskurs der Gegenwart. Schriften der Österreichischen Gesellschaft für Religionsphilosophie. Band 5. Berlin-Wien: Böhlau/Akademie Verlag, 2004 (a).

Schüssler-Fiorenza, Elisabeth. Grenzen überschreiten. Der theoretische Anspruch feministischer Theologie. Ausgewählte Aufsätze. Münster: Lit, 2004 (b).

Sen Amartya. More than 100 Million Women are missing. In: The New York Review of books, 37. Jg., Heft 20, 1990.
http://www.nybooks.com/articles/archives/1990/dec/20/more-than-100-million-women-are missing/?insrc=toc

Sölle, Dorothee. Vater, Macht und Barbarei. In Concilium 17 (1981) 225 ff.

Strahm-Bernet, Silvia. Jesa Christa. In: Doris Strahm/Regula Strobel (Hg.), Vom Verlangen nach Heilwerden. Christologie in feministisch-theologischer Sicht. Fribourg/Luzern: Edition Exodus, 1991.

Charles Taylor, José Casanova, George F. McLean (Hg.), Church and People: Disjunctions in a Secular Age. Christian Philosophical Studies, I. Washington: The Council for Research in Values and Philosophy, 2012.

Vieweg, Klaus. Das Denken der Freiheit. Hegels Grundlinien der Philosophie des Rechts. München: Wilhelm Fink, 2012.

Lehramtliche vatikanische Verlautbarungen:

Gaudium et spes. Pastoralkonstitution über die Kirche in der Welt von heute. 7. Dezember 1965. In: Heinrich Denzinger/Peter Hünermann (Hg.), Kompendium der Glaubensbekenntnisse und kirchlichen Lehrentscheidungen. Lateinisch-Deutsch. Freiburg/Rom/Wien: Herder 1991 (Abgekürzt: DH) DH 4301 – 4345.

Apostolisches Schreiben von Papst Johannes Paul II. über die nur Männern vorbehaltene Priesterweihe. Verlautbarungen des Apostolischen Stuhls Nr. 117, 22. Mai 1994.

Mulieris dignitatem. Apostolisches Schreiben von Papst Johannes Paul II. über die Würde und die Berufung der Frau anlässlich des Marianischen Jahres. Verlautbarungen des Apostolischen Stuhls Nr. 86, 15. August 1988. In: Heinrich Denzinger/Peter Hünermann (Hg.), Kompendium der Glaubensbekenntnisse und kirchlichen Lehrentscheidungen. Lateinisch-Deutsch. Freiburg/Rom/Wien: Herder 1991. DH 4830 – 4841.

Persona humana, Erklärung der Glaubenskongregation zu einigen Fragen der Sexualethik. Seelsorge und Homosexualität. In: Heinrich Denzinger/Peter Hünermann (Hg.), Kompendium der Glaubensbekenntnisse und kirchlichen Lehrentscheidungen. Lateinisch-Deutsch. Freiburg/Rom/Wien: Herder 1991. DH 4580 – 4584.

ANNE SIEGETSLEITNER

SUSAN STEBBING AND THE VIENNA CIRCLE ON MORAL PHILOSOPHY[1]

Susan Stebbing, who is rarely mentioned in the history of analytic philosophy, was a prominent figure in the Unity of Science movement and maintained relationships with leading members of the Vienna Circle. This paper compares Stebbing's conception of moral philosophy to those of Carnap, Neurath, and Schlick.

At first glance, the conceptions of moral philosophy held by Stebbing and the Vienna Circle differ widely, as Stebbing rejects the logical empiricist standard view of moral philosophy generally ascribed to the Vienna Circle. What we now call normative or substantial ethics – and what is ruled out by the standard view – is an essential part of moral philosophy in Stebbing's conception. A closer look reveals, however, that Schlick shares this view. He practiced normative and applied ethics on a eudaimonistic basis.

The discrepancies further diminish once more general questions are addressed. Stebbing, Carnap, Neurath and Schlick endorse the perspective of scientific humanism. They are convinced that it is the task of humanity itself to improve human life conditions and that science is one of the most valuable means to this improvement.

Therefore, Stebbing is close to the Vienna Circle in her conception of moral philosophy once the Vienna Circle is no longer reduced to a general rejection of normative ethics, and scientific humanism is taken into account. New insights may be gained by reconsidering the Ethical Movement.

I. Introduction

Susan Stebbing (1885–1943) was the first female professor of philosophy in Great Britain, a leading figure of the so-called Cambridge School of Analysis, co-founder of the journal *Analysis,* and president of the Mind Association as well as of the Aristotelian Society. Despite

---

[1] SWIP UK Panel at the Joint Session of the Mind Association and Aristotelian Society, University of Warwick, UK, July 11, 2015

her importance, she is rarely mentioned in the history of analytic philosophy (see Chapman 2013 as a recent exception). Therefore, it is not common knowledge that Stebbing was also a prominent figure in the Unity of Science movement and that she maintained relationships with Rudolf Carnap, Otto Neurath, and Moritz Schlick, the "triumvirate" of the Vienna Circle.

The aim of my paper is to compare Stebbing's conception of moral philosophy to those of Carnap, Neurath, and Schlick. As this cannot be done thoroughly in a short paper, I will concentrate on a few fundamental aspects. In a first step, I will outline the logical empiricist standard view of moral philosophy generally ascribed to the Vienna Circle and compare it to Stebbing's conception. At this first glance, the Vienna Circle and Stebbing seem to hold very different views. In the following sections I will show, however, that the discrepancies are not so fundamental once more general questions are addressed. Stebbing shares interesting and hitherto disregarded convictions with Carnap, Neurath, and Schlick, ones which are worth reconsidering.

II. A First Glance: The Logical Empiricist Standard View of Moral Philosophy and Stebbing's Conception

The standard view of logical empiricist moral philosophy is held to be characterized by the acceptance of descriptive empirical research – but this research is not regarded as genuine moral philosophy – and the rejection of normative and substantial ethics. Metaethics remains the only legitimate way of doing moral philosophy. This is generally considered to be the view of the Vienna Circle.

How does Stebbing relate to this? She states her conception very clearly in *Men and Moral Principles* (1944). In this publication, she not only expresses a high opinion of moral philosophy, calling it the "most difficult of philosophical studies" (p. 3), but also ascribes to this discipline more than analysis (p. 4). Although logic, rationality, and clarity may be important for moral life, as she demonstrates in *Logic in Practice* (1931) and *Thinking to Some Purpose* (1939), she contends in *Men and Moral Principles* that moral philosophers "must be concerned with the ways in which men live" (p. 4). What we now call normative or substantial ethics – and what is ruled out by the standard view – is an essential part of moral philosophy in Stebbing's conception. To be more specific, it is an important task "to formulate ideals worth living for and to attempt to make clear principles which may afford guides for action" (p. 4). In *Ideals and Illusions* (1941) Stebbing lays out her grave concerns about the pain and misery of human beings and ponders which ideals might change the world for the better. She contends that some ideals are evil and some rest on illusions. Moral philosophy should provide counterpoint ideals, good ideals without illusions, as we might put it.

In short, at first glance, the conceptions of moral philosophy held by Stebbing and the Vienna Circle differ widely. But let us now take a second look by starting a closer comparison with Carnap's thinking, followed by Neurath's and Schlick's.

III. A Second Look: Taking Scientific Humanism and Dissenting Opinions into Account

Carnap (1891–1970) is the member of the Vienna Circle whose conception of moral philosophy is closest to the standard view. In his well-known article "Überwindung der Metaphysik durch logische Analyse der Sprache" ("Elimination of Metaphysics Through Logical Analysis of Language", 1931/32) one finds nearly all features of this view.[2] In the English-speaking world, this perspective was widely spread by Ayer's *Language, Truth, and Logic* (1936) and Carnap's own *Philosophy and Logical Syntax* (1935). The later contains the published version of three lectures given by Carnap at the University of London during his first visit to Great Britain in 1934.

As an interesting aside, Carnap gave these lectures on none other than Stebbing's invitation, which he also mentions in his autobiography. However, apart from a brief acknowledgement of her person, he does not report any interesting discussions with her, as he does, for example, for Russell, Ogden and Ayer (Carnap 1963, pp. 33–34). Given Stebbing's expertise and renown, this oversight seems more than a little curious.

---

[2] Prior to this position, Carnap was more closely associated with phenomenological and Neo-Kantian approaches regarding questions of value (see e.g. Mormann 2006, Siegetsleitner 2014a).

That aside, as far as the logical empiricist standard view is concerned, Carnap and Stebbing obviously do disagree. However, this is not the end of the story.

On a more general level, the Vienna Circle shared a humanistic version of morality and moral philosophy, which can already be found in the Circle's manifesto *Wissenschaftliche Weltauffassung. Der Wiener Kreis. (Scientific Conception of the World: The Vienna Circle*, Neurath/Hahn/Carnap 1929). Later it was formulated by Carnap in his autobiography as a combination of three views: (1) All that "can be done to improve life is the task of man himself"; (2) humanity is able to avoid much of contemporary suffering and improve life conditions; (3) science is one of the most valuable means to this improvement (Carnap 1963, p. 83). Carnap understood his logical work as a contribution to this kind of humanism. This general scientific humanism was certainly shared by Stebbing, as can be seen, for example, through her conviction that morality does not require otherworldly sanctions or religion (see e.g. her "Ethics and Materialism" 1939).

Nevertheless, it is possible to subscribe scientific humanism without endorsing the standard view, as is the case with Stebbing. In conclusion, Stebbing and Carnap share the humanistic approach but not the standard view.

I will now turn to Otto Neurath (1882–1945). When Neurath had to flee from the Netherlands to England in 1940, it was Stebbing and others who succeeded in getting him released from an internment camp and helped him to start a new life in Oxford (see Sandner 2011). Stebbing had been engaged in Neurath's major project, the Unity of Science movement, since 1935, which is how they had become friends.

In their philosophical and moral outlook, Neurath and Stebbing not only share an enthusiasm for the philosophy of science but also the conviction that science and philosophy could make a major difference to people's living conditions and happiness. Their philosophical work has a moral purpose with scientific humanism as the common background. Both worked against harmful speculations. Neurath sees Stebbing as an ally when he points out: "It is not only by accident that L. Susan *Stebbing* wrote on the one hand a book criticizing highly metaphysical speculations of modern physicists and on the other hand her

Thinking to some Purpose and her *Ideals and Illusions*" (Neurath 1941, p. 132).

Whereas, however, Stebbing admitted that normative ethics plays an important role in accomplishing this task, Neurath was very reluctant to accept this idea. Although both were concerned about the miserable living conditions of men and women, Neurath restricted his academic work to providing tools for the social sciences in order to describe and finally improve these circumstances. This effort is once again rooted in scientific humanism, but Neurath still endorsed the logical empiricist standard view of moral philosophy. Nevertheless, he let Carnap know: "In our movement I sometimes have the feeling that some members avoid discussing problems of decision, action etc and are using analysis as a kind of escape from life. THAT IS NOT MY APPROACH" (Neurath to Carnap, 22 September 1945, Wiener Kreis Archief, Haarlem, no. 223, cited from Siegetsleitner 2014a, p. 250, n. 329). Stebbing certainly did not avoid such discussions, nor did Schlick.

Moritz Schlick (1882–1936), the founder of the Vienna Circle, deviates from the standard view in fundamental respects. His position is very close to the moral philosophy of Stebbing, with whom he got acquainted at a conference in London in 1932. In a letter to Carnap he admits that she is the most reasonable philosopher he had met in London (Schlick to Carnap, 3 December 1932, Archives of Scientific Philosophy, Hillman Library, University of Pittsburgh, Rudolf Carnap Collection, no. 029-29-01, see Friedl/Rutte 2013, p. 148, n. 5).

Schlick followed the ideal of a wise man, suggesting a worthwhile way of life to people. His first book, *Lebensweisheit* (*The Wisdom of Life*, 1908), already deals with ethical questions. In 1930 he published *Fragen der Ethik* (*Problems of Ethics*, English translation 1939), which mostly is about moral psychological issues. The last chapter, however, proclaims a moral principle on a eudaimonistic basis: "Be ready for happiness!" (Schlick 1939, p. 187) On the same basis, his posthumously published work *Natur und Kultur* (*Nature and Culture*, 1952) discusses questions of politics, war, economics, law as well as technology. It belongs in the category of applied ethics. This demonstrates that Schlick and Stebbing not only share the general outlook of scientific humanism but also the legitimacy of normative ethics, therein differing from the logical empiricist standard view of moral philosophy.

What may come as a surprise to some, Schlick used the expression "applied ethics". "Applied ethics" was a common term in the so-called Ethical Movement which was of particular importance to Stebbing and the Vienna Circle.

IV. A short Remark on the Ethical Movement

The Ethical Movement was initiated in the last decades of the 19th century. Its aim was a secular humanist moral life, moral education and philosophy. In 1890 the movement launched the *International Journal of Ethics*, known as *Ethics* today (see Siegetsleitner 2014b). Stebbing gave ethical lectures at the Sunday meetings of the South Place Ethical Society (e.g. on 10 December 1939 and 19 April 1942); Carnap and Schlick were members of the Ethical Community in Vienna. All of them took an active part in this movement. This important relationship is still in need to be taken into consideration when we scrutinize the relationship between Stebbing and the Vienna Circle, especially when it comes to moral philosophy.

V. Summary

In summary, the conceptions of moral philosophy held by Stebbing and the Vienna Circle differ widely at first glance, as Stebbing rejects the logical empiricist standard view of moral philosophy. A closer look reveals, however, that even Schlick does so, as well. Moreover, Stebbing, Carnap, Neurath, and Schlick share the perspective of scientific humanism. Therefore, Stebbing is close to the Vienna Circle in her conception of moral philosophy once the Vienna Circle is no longer reduced to a general rejection of normative ethics, and scientific humanism is taken into account. New insights may be gained by reconsidering the Ethical Movement.

References

Ayer, A. J. 1936: *Language, Truth, and Logic*. London.

Carnap, R. 1931/32: "Überwindung der Metaphysik durch logische Analyse der Sprache", in: *Erkenntnis* 2 (4), pp. 219–241.

Carnap, R. 1935: *Philosophy and Logical Syntax*. London.

Carnap R. 1963: "Intellectual Autobiography", in: Schilpp, P. A. (ed.): *The Philosophy of Rudolf Carnap*. Chicago, La Salle, pp. 1–84.

Chapman, S. 2013: *Susan Stebbing and the Language of Common Sense*. London.

Friedl, J./Rutte, H. 2013: "Form and Content. An Introduction into Philosophical Thinking. Editorischer Bericht", in: Friedl, J./Rutte H. (eds.): *Moritz Schlick. Erkenntnistheoretische Schriften 1926–1936*. Wien, New York, pp. 147–168.

Mormann, Th. 2006: "Werte bei Carnap", in: *Zeitschrift für philosophische Forschung* 60 (2), pp. 169–189.

Neurath, O. 1941: "Universal Jargon and Terminology", in: *Proceedings of the Aristotelian Society. New Series* 41, pp. 127–148.

Neurath, O./Hahn, H. /Carnap R. 1929: *Wissenschaftliche Weltauffassung. Der Wiener Kreis*. Wien.

Sandner, G. 2011: "The German Human Climate and Its Opposite: Otto Neurath in England, 1940–45", in: Grenville A./Reiter, A. (eds.): *Political Exile and Exile Politics in Britain after 1933*. New York, Amsterdam, pp. 67–85.

Siegetsleitner, A. 2014a: *Ethik und Moral im Wiener Kreis. Zur Geschichte eines engagierten Humanismus*. Wien, Köln, Weimar.

Siegetsleitner, A. 2014b: "On Friedrich Jodl's 'Morals in History'", in: *Ethics* 125, pp. 211–213.

Schlick, M. 1908: *Lebensweisheit. Versuch einer Glückseligkeitslehre*. Munich.

Schlick, M. 1930: *Fragen der Ethik*. Vienna. (English translation as *Problems of Ethics*. New York 1939)

Schlick, M. 1952: *Natur und Kultur*. Vienna.

Stebbing, S. 1931: *Logic in Practice*. London.

Stebbing, S. 1939a: *Thinking to Some Purpose*. Harmondsworth.

Stebbing, S. 1939b: "Ethics and Materialisms", in: *Ethics* 50 (1), pp. 35–44.

Stebbing, S. 1941: *Ideas and Illusions*. London.

Stebbing, S. 1944: *Men and Moral Principles*. London.

Susanne Moser

Werte und Gefühle:
Max Scheler und Ronald de Sousa im Vergleich

Begehre ich etwas, weil es einen Wert hat, oder bekommt etwas erst einen Wert dadurch, dass ich es begehre? Gibt es so etwas wie objektive Werte, nach denen ich mein Begehren richte, oder hängt alles von meiner subjektiven Wertschätzung ab? Diese Frage steht im Zentrum der im 19. Jahrhundert in Deutschland entstandenen Wertphilosophie, der Axiologie. Mit dem Zusammenbruch der großen metaphysischen Systeme und ihrer Wertordnungen und dem Aufkommen verschiedener einander widersprechender Weltanschauungen wurde die Frage virulent, ob es nicht doch noch so etwas wie objektive Werte geben könnte und nicht alles nur der subjektiven Beliebigkeit unterworfen sei.

Heutzutage werden die axiologischen Entwürfe von Husserl, Scheler, oder Hartmann jedoch kaum mehr wahrgenommen[1] und wenn man dennoch über Werttheorien spricht, kann es sein, dass man sich „als Vertreter der Großväter-Ideologie der ‚ewigen Werte' verdächtig" macht.[2] Die heutigen Debatten über Werte stehen im Spannungsfeld zwischen einem nahezu inflationären Sprachgebrauch von Werten und einer – insbesondere im deutschsprachigen Raum zu verzeichnenden – Ablehnung des Wertbegriffs als Ausdruck eines subjektiven Willens zur Macht und einer kapitalistischen Ökonomie, die jegliche Werte von der Beliebigkeit subjektiver Marktnachfrage und damit vom

---

[1] Regina Polak, Herausgeberin der Europäischen Wertestudie 1990-2010, spricht davon, dass „die historischen wertphilosophischen Entwürfe – von Husserl, Scheler, Hartmann – in ihrer Studie unberücksichtigt bleiben, „dass sie in der gegenwärtigen Debatte kaum eine Rolle spielen (Polak 2011, 60).

[2] „Wer heute in einem philosophischen Institut etwas über Werttheorien ankündigte, machte sich entweder als Vertreter der Großväter-Ideologie der ‚ewigen Werte' verdächtig, oder erschiene vielen als Marx-Exeget, der die Geheimnisse des Verhältnisses von Gebrauchswert und Tauschwert zu lüften verspricht." (Schnädelbach 1983, 197); siehe auch Yvanka B. Raynova, "The European Values: A 'Dictatorship' or a Chance for Union?" (Raynova 2015, 333 ff; vgl. Raynova 2010, 11ff).

214

jeweiligen Preis abhängig macht.[3] Im angloamerikanischen Raum hingegen findet die Auseinandersetzung mit Werten auf einer Ebene statt, welche die Wahrnehmung von Werteigenschaften thematisiert und zwar in Analogie zur Sinneswahrnehmung (McDowell 2009, 225) und unter Einbeziehung von Gefühlen (Döring 2009, 433). So wie wir wahrnehmen, dass etwas grün ist, so können wir auch wahrnehmen, dass etwas wertvoll ist.[4] (Reicher 2005, 35) Dabei geht man davon aus, dass uns diese Werteigenschaften auf eine zumindest ähnliche Art und Weise gegeben sind. Meinungsverschiedenheiten und Streit wären nicht möglich, wenn wir nicht eine gewisse Übereinstimmung voraussetzen würden. Auch verweise die Struktur unserer Sprache auf den engen Zusammenhang zwischen Gefühlen und Werten: Ausdrucksweisen wie „beneidenswert", „beschämend", „bewundernswert", „erfreulich" „ärgerlich" oder „empörend" sind Wertprädikate, die Gefühle wie „Neid", „Scham", „Bewunderung", „Freude", „Ärger" und „Empörung" enthalten und uns etwas darüber aussagen, wie wir die uns umgebende Welt wahrnehmen und bewerten.

Ziel meines Beitrages ist es, die Wertphilosophie Max Schelers unter dem Blickwinkel der Wiederaufnahmen axiologischer Fragestellungen innerhalb der zeitgenössischen Gefühlsforschung erneut einer Diskussion zu unterziehen. In diesem Sinne werde ich eine Verbindung zu Ronald de Sousa herstellen, der wie Scheler darum bemüht ist, den Zusammenhang zwischen Gefühlen und Werten aufzuzeigen. Wenn die Frage der Rationalität von Gefühlen einer Klärung zugeführt werde, könne dies nach De Sousa „vielleicht auch

---

[3] Hannah Arendt kritisiert, dass Güter und Tugenden der traditionellen Philosophie in der Wertphilosophie zu Werten werden: Der Wert ist das, was früher Tugend oder Gut geheißen hat. Arendt verbindet damit die Befürchtung, dass „jedes zu einem Wert gewordene Gut oder jede in einen Wert transformierte Tugend ihren Preis hat, nämlich dasjenige, wofür ihr Besitzer bereit wäre, sie einzutauschen" (Hannah Arendt. *Elemente und Ursprünge totaler Herrschaft*. München, Zürich: Piper 2013, 319).

[4] Für Reicher gibt es eine Analogie zwischen Sinnesqualitäten und Wertqualitäten. So wie wir sagen können, dass etwas dann grün ist, wenn es die Eigenschaft hat, Wesen mit unserem Wahrnehmungsapparat als grün zu erscheinen, so sei es auch bei den Wertqualitäten: „‚x ist wertvoll' hieße dann etwa so viel wie: „x hat die Eigenschaft in Wesen mit unserem Wertsinn unter günstigen Bedingungen ein positives Wertgefühl auszulösen" (Reicher 2005, 35).

wichtige Fragen in der Theorie der Werte erhellen". (De Sousa 2009, 34) Anhand der *Euthyphron*-Frage[5], ob wir etwas lieben, weil es liebenswert ist, oder es liebenswert nennen, weil wir es lieben, geht er der Frage nach, ob es so etwas wie ein „objektives" Begehren gibt, das sich an objektiven Werten orientiert. Im Zentrum seiner Untersuchungen steht die Rolle der Gefühle bei der Wahrnehmung von Werten. Dabei geht er davon aus, dass Gefühle rational sind und uns etwas über die Objekte in der Welt, bzw. über ihre Eigenschaften aussagen können: „Eine häufige Leistung unserer Gefühle besteht im Erfassen von Eigenschaften einer bestimmten Art, die ich als ‚axiologische' bezeichnen werde," erklärt er. (De Sousa 2009, 11) Für Max Scheler hingegen steht die Werterfassung im Vordergrund, wobei er zwischen dem Fühlen von Gefühlen und dem Fühlen von Werten unterscheidet. Dadurch wird der Blick frei für einen differenzierteren Zusammenhang von Gefühlen und Werten. Unsere Bedürfnisse und unser Begehren hängen von unseren Werten ab, die ihrerseits wiederum vom geschichtlichen und kulturellen Kontext, dem Ethos, mitbestimmt werden. Schelers detaillierte Auseinandersetzung mit der Bedeutung von Werten für unsere Wahrnehmung und unsere Sichtweise der Welt kann wichtige Impulse sowohl für die zeitgenössische Gefühlsforschung als auch für die gegenwärtigen Versuche einer Renaissance der Wertphilosophie geben.

Im Beitrag sollen sowohl die Unterschiede als auch die Gemeinsamkeiten von De Sousa und Scheler aufgezeigt werden. Im ersten Teil werden folgende Fragen erörtert: Welche Objekte sind uns in der Gefühls- bzw. Wertwahrnehmung wirklich gegeben? Sind es Werteigenschaften, so wie De Sousa annimmt, oder die Werte selbst, wie Scheler meint? Wie ist das Verhältnis zwischen Werten und Werteigenschaften zu verstehen? Welcher Bezug besteht zwischen Werten und Gütern? Im zweiten Teil wird die subjektive Seite des Begehrens, bzw. des Strebens thematisiert. Hier soll geklärt werden, ob es objektive Werte, an denen sich das Begehren orientiert, geben kann und welche Rolle dabei die Bedürfnisstruktur des Menschen spielt. Im dritten

---

[5] Im Dialog *Euthypron* stellt Sokrates die Frage, „ ob wohl das Fromme, weil es fromm ist, von den Göttern geliebt wird, oder ob es, weil es geliebt wird fromm ist?" (Platon 1991, 10a) Konkret gehe es, so Ronald de Sousa, um die Frage: Lieben die Götter die Frömmigkeit, weil sie fromm ist, oder nennen wir lediglich alles fromm, was ihnen gefällt? (De Sousa 2009, 33)

Teil geht es um die Werterfassung selbst. Wie werden uns Werte, bzw. Werteigenschaften konkret zugänglich? Kann es so etwas wie ein direktes Wertfühlen geben, wie Scheler meint, oder muss die Wertwahrnehmung über die Erfassung von Werteigenschaften verlaufen, wie dies De Sousa analog zur Sinneswahrnehmung annimmt? Anhand von De Sousas Konzept der Schlüsselszenarien und Schelers Annahme eines historisch gewachsenen Ethos werden dann die sozialen und kulturellen Aspekte der Werterfassung genauer analysiert.

1. Werteigenschaften

1.1 Eigenschaften von Gütern

In seinem Hauptwerk *Der Formalismus in der Ethik und die materiale Wertethik* betont Scheler, dass es niemals genüge, einen Wert über Merkmale und Eigenschaften von Gütern erschließen zu wollen. So wenig wie Farbnamen auf bloße Eigenschaften von körperlichen Dingen gehen, so dürfen die Werte nicht „auf die Eigenschaften der dinglich gegebenen Einheiten, die wir Güter nennen" zurückgeführt werden. (Scheler 2007, 7). Die Werte manifestieren sich zwar in den Gütern: „Erst in den Gütern werden Werte ‚wirklich'"[6], sind aber mit ihnen nicht identisch. (Scheler 2007, 16) Es sei auch tatsächlich so, dass uns in der natürlichen Einstellung zunächst einmal Güter gegeben sind, an denen wir bestimmte Eigenschaften wahrnehmen (Scheler 2007, 55). Um zu zeigen, dass Güter, als Träger von Werten, nicht mit Werten gleichgesetzt werden dürfen, gibt Scheler einige Beispiele. So hänge der Wert des sinnlich Angenehmen nicht von den wechselnden Eigenschaften verschiedener Früchte, einen Wohlgeschmack hervorzurufen, ab. Auch die ästhetischen Werte wie lieblich, reizend, erhaben und schön würden nicht die Eigenschaften von

---

[6] Scheler betont, dass zwischen Gütern, d.h. Wertdingen und bloßen Werten, die Dinge haben, d.h. „Dingwerten" unterschieden werden müsse. (Scheler 2007, 15) Bei diesen handle es sich um Wertgegenstände, um Sachen, über die wir willkürlich verfügen. Der Unterschied werde darin erkennbar, dass ein Gut zerstört werden könne, ohne dass das Ding mit zerstört wird, das den realen Gegenstand darstelle, z.B. ein Kunstwerk dessen Farben verbleichen. Auch können Dinge geteilt werden, während ein Gut durch die Teilung zerstört werden würde.

Dingen bezeichnen, die Träger dieser Werte seien.[7] Vielmehr müssten uns die Werte bereits gegeben sein, um die betreffenden Dinge als schön, lieblich, oder reizend bezeichnen zu können. Je mehr sich der Mensch jedoch von seinen Trieben und Bedürfnissen leiten lasse, desto mehr sind die Werte für ihn nur als Zeichen für Güterdinge gegeben, die für seine leiblichen Bedürfnisse wichtig sind. Je mehr die Persönlichkeit entwickelt sei, desto mehr seien auch die geistigen Werte gegeben. Für Scheler ist jede Bildung einer Güterwelt – wie immer sie auch erfolgt – durch irgendeine Rangordnung der Werte bereits geleitet, wie z. B. die Bildung der Kunst einer bestimmten Epoche: „Sie steckt ihr einen Spielraum des Möglichen ab, außerhalb dessen eine Bildung von Gütern nicht erfolgen kann." (Scheler 2007, 18)

Dass uns die Werte unabhängig von den Gütern und ihren Eigenschaften gegeben seien, zeige sich, so Scheler, darin, dass es immer wieder Situationen gebe, in denen wir Werte erfassen, ohne diese an Eigenschaften von Gütern festmachen zu können. Ein Mensch könne peinlich und abstoßend oder angenehm und sympathisch wirken, ohne dass wir noch anzugeben vermögen, woran das liege. Wir können in ein Zimmer eintreten, das uns unangenehm berührt, ohne genau zu wissen warum. Bei jeder „Milieuerfassung erfassen wir z.B. zugleich zunächst das unanalysierbare Ganze und an diesem seinen Wert." (Scheler 2007, 13) Der Wert schreitet gleichsam voran als erster Bote. Auch würden wir Kunstwerke als schön erfassen, ohne noch im entferntesten zu wissen, an welchen Eigenschaften des betreffenden Bildinhaltes dies liege. In solchen Fällen offenbare sich klar, wie unabhängig im Sein die Werte von ihren Trägern, den Gütern, seien: „Weder die Erfahrung des Wertes noch der Grad der (...) Evidenz (...) erweist sich von der Erfahrung der Träger dieser Werte irgendwie abhängig." (Scheler 2007, 13) Die Wertnuance eines Gegenstandes ist das Primärste, das wir erfassen. „Sein Wert schreitet ihm gleichsam voran; er ist der erste ‚Bote' seiner besonderen Natur." (Scheler 2007, 13) Daher ist alles primäre Verhalten zur Welt nicht ein Verhalten des sinnlichen Wahrnehmens, sondern immer gleichzeitig und primär ein emotionales und wertnehmendes Verhal-

---

[7] „Erst wo wir bereits die Dinge unter einen anderen Begriff stellen, der kein Wertbegriff ist, also etwa nach den gemeinsamen Eigenschaften lieblicher Vasen oder Blumen, oder edler Pferde fragen, besteht die Aussicht solche gemeinsamen Eigenschaften anzugeben." (Scheler 2007, 8)

218

ten. Er betont, dass erst „ein künstliches Wegnehmen (…) von dem ursprünglich Gegebenen vermöge eines ausdrücklichen Nichtvollzuges gewisser Akte des Fühlens, Liebens, Hassens, Wollens usw. wertfreie Objekte ergibt".[8] (Scheler 2007, 200)

Für Scheler ist die Welt immer schon mit Werten erfüllt. Werte geben der Welt eine qualitative Note, sozusagen eine Färbung. „Wenn man also Werte überhaupt unter eine Kategorie subsumieren will, so muss man sie als Qualitäten bezeichnen." (Scheler 2007, 249). Scheler nimmt an, dass wir über die Akte des Fühlens und des Liebens einen Zugang zu den Werten haben. Wenn dieser Zugang gestört ist, so z.B. bei einer schweren Depression, dann wird alles nur mehr als grau in grau erlebt. Es kommt zu einem Wert- und damit zum einem Sinnverlust.[9] Werte stellen in diesem Sinne Wahrnehmungsfilter, bzw. Wahrnehmungsermöglichungen dar. Nur wenn ich bestimmte Werte fühle, kann ich bestimmte Phänomene in der Welt überhaupt wahrnehmen.

Werte sind für Scheler „selbständige Phänomene, die mit weitgehendster Unabhängigkeit von der Besonderheit des Inhalts, sowie von dem Realsein oder Idealsein – resp. dem Nichtsein (…) ihrer Träger erfasst werden." (Scheler 2007, 187) Scheler spricht von einem „Sein der Werte" und von Werten als Tatsachen, die allerdings nur durch eine bestimmte Erfahrungsart erfasst werden können, nämlich dem Wertfühlen. (Scheler 2007, 189) Er nimmt an, dass wir Werte genauso erfassen können, wie empirische Tatsachen. In diesem Sinne können Wertaussagen wahr oder falsch sein, je nachdem ob das Urteil mit dem Sachverhalt übereinstimmt. „Werte sind Tatsachen, gehörig zu einer bestimmten Erfahrungsart, und es gehört darum zum Wesen der Wahrheit eines solchen gültigen Satzes, dass er mit diesen Tatsachen übereinstimmt." (Scheler 2007, 189) Wenn wir Wertaussagen vornehmen, wie „A ist gut" oder „A ist schön" dann beziehen wir uns genauso auf Tatsachen, wie wenn wir sagen

---

[8] Dass die Werte nicht irgendwie hinzu gebracht werden, zeige sich daran, dass es für den nichtgeschulten sehr schwer sei wertfrei zu beobachten und damit von den „primär stets mitgegebenen Wertqualitäten (…) abzusehen" (Scheler 2007, 201)

[9] Es ist auffällig, dass Kleinkinder keinen Sinnverlust kennen. Sie entdecken die Welt von ihrer Wertseite her, allmählich eröffnet sich ihnen die ganze Farbigkeit der Welt. Kinder fühlen die Wertqualitäten in ihrem Umfeld besonders stark und intensiv.

„A ist grün" oder „A ist hart". Der Unterschied bestehe „lediglich in der Materie des Prädikates" (Scheler 2007, 185).

1.2. Die Rationalität von Gefühlen

In *Die Rationalität des Gefühls* setzt sich De Sousa mit der Frage auseinander, ob Gefühle rational sein können. Rationalität enthält für ihn „die Idee der Adäquatheit oder der Angemessenheit von Denken und Handeln an die objektive Realität." (De Sousa 2009, 33) Gefühle müssen, um rational sein zu können, etwas mit der Realität zu tun haben, sie müssen etwas über die objektive Welt aussagen. Dieser Gedanke ist nicht selbstverständlich, wurden Gefühle doch lange Zeit als rein subjektiv und sehr oft auch als irrational angesehen. Immanuel Kant und David Hume zum Beispiel nahmen an, dass den Gefühlen jegliche Gerichtetheit nach außen hin fehle[10] und wir deshalb durch unsere Gefühle nichts über die Welt erfahren können, sondern nur über uns selbst.[11] Erst Franz Brentano rückte im Anschluss an die Scholastiker die Welterschließungsfunktion der Gefühle wieder in den Vordergrund, indem er allen psychischen Phänomenen eine Intentionalität, d.h. einen Objektbezug zuschrieb.[12]

---

[10] Hume nahm an, dass ein Affekt keine repräsentative Eigenschaft besitzt, „ durch die er als Abbild eines anderen Etwas charakterisiert würde. Bin ich ärgerlich, so hat mich der Affekt tatsächlich ergriffen, und in dieser Gefühlserregung liegt so wenig eine Beziehung zu einem anderen damit gemeinten oder dadurch repräsentierten Gegenstand, als wenn ich durstig oder krank oder über fünf Fuß groß wäre" (Hume 1978, 153). Da Gefühle nicht auf die Welt bezogen sind, sind sie nach Humes Meinung nicht wahrheitsfähig und entziehen sich damit grundsätzlich der rationalen Kritisierbarkeit. Anhand der Gefühle können wir nichts über die Welt erfahren, nur über uns selbst, weshalb er sie auch als Selbstwahrnehmung bezeichnet.

[11] Kant sieht in den Gefühlen „eine Beziehung bloß aufs Subjekt, da sie für sich selbst Gründe sind, ihre eigene Existenz in demselben bloß zu erhalten und so ferne im Verhältnis zum Gefühle der Lust betrachtet werden, welches letztere schlechterdings kein Erkenntnis ist noch verschafft, ob es zwar dergleichen zum Bestimmungsgrund mag" (Brentano 1959, 9).

[12] Brentano sieht jedes „psychische Phänomen durch das charakterisiert, was die Scholastiker des Mittelalters die intentionale (auch wohl mentale) Inexistenz eines Gegenstandes genannt haben und was wir, obwohl mit nicht ganz unzweideutigen Ausdrücken, die Beziehung auf einen Inhalt, die Richtung auf ein Objekt (worunter hier nicht eine Realität zu verstehen ist), oder die immanente Gegenständlichkeit nennen würden. Jedes enthält etwas als Objekt in sich, obwohl nicht jedes in gleicher Weise" (Brentano 1973, 124).

220

Daran anknüpfend prägte Anthony Kenny den Begriff des „formalen Objektes"[13], der auch für De Sousa eine zentrale Rolle spielt.

Das Formalobjekt bildet den Maßstab der Richtigkeit eines Gefühls.[14] „Der Begriff des Formalobjektes ist auf jeden Zustand anwendbar, der einen Inhalt hat, welcher hinsichtlich seiner Richtigkeit beurteilbar ist: Es ist dann, aufgrund seiner Definition, der Maßstab der Richtigkeit für diesen Zustand", unterstreicht De Sousa. (De Sousa 2009, 206) Beim formalen Objekt handelt es sich also nicht um das konkrete Objekt, mit dem wir konfrontiert sind. Die Furcht vor einer Schlange hat diese zwar zum Objekt; der Neid auf den Nachbarn gilt ebendiesem als dem Objekt der Emotion, aber um von Furcht oder Neid sprechen zu können, bedarf es mehr als eines Objektes der Furcht oder des Neides. Ronald de Sousa weist darauf hin, dass es für jede Emotion eine Eigenschaft zweiter Ordnung gibt, nämlich das Formalobjekt. Er erläutert: „Das Formalobjekt ist in dem Sinne eine Eigenschaft zweiter Ordnung, dass es supervenient durch eine andere Eigenschaft oder andere Eigenschaften hervorgebracht wird: Etwas ist zum Beispiel furchterregend, weil es gefährlich ist. Doch manchmal werde ich ungenauer – und natürlicher – so sprechen, als ob die formale Eigenschaft einfach eine Eigenschaft des Gegenstandes sei. In diesem ungenauen Sinne ist ein Gefühl teilweise *angemessen*, wenn der Gegenstand tatsächlich eine Fokuseigenschaft besitzt, dank deren das Formalobjekt zum Gegenstand passt." (De Sousa 2009, 206). Für De Sousa stellen die formalen Objekte „unabhängige Dimensionen der Bewertung" dar, die er *axiologisch* nennt. (De Sousa 2009, 286)

Die strikte Trennung der psychischen Tätigkeiten in Erkennen, Fühlen und Wollen, so wie Kant sie angenommen hatte, wurde von Brentano verworfen (ebenda. 12). Seine Klassifizierung der psychischen Phänomene erfolgt in drei Klassen: 1. Vorstellung, 2. Urteil, 3. Gemütsbewegung, Interesse oder Liebe, in welcher er das Fühlen und Wollen zusammenfasst (ebenda, 33).

[13] „Die mittelalterlichen Scholastiker formulierten Einschränkungen (...) indem sie sagten, das formale Objekt der Furcht sei ein zukünftiges Übel oder das des Neides das Gut eines Anderen. Sie folgen darin Aristoteles, der in seiner *Rhetorik*, wenngleich nicht in dieser Terminologie, eine Liste formaler Objekte vorlegt" (Kenny 2009, 81).

[14] Könnten wir vor Depression hüpfen? Uns aus Freude krümmen? Lächeln vor Neid? Aus Güte wüten? Vor Stolz kichern? Die Antwort, die uns Ronald de Sousa darauf gibt ist: „Ja aber nicht *wirklich*" (De Sousa 2009, 203).

1.3. Axiologische Eigenschaften

Doch was versteht De Sousa genauer unter dieser unabhängigen axiologischen Dimension? Zunächst weist er darauf hin, dass es sich hierbei nicht um eine konkrete Eigenschaft eines Gegenstandes handelt. Vielmehr handle es sich um eine axiologische Eigenschaft, also eine Werteigenschaft, die erst durch eine Art Bewertung zustande komme: Der Gegenstand ist furchterregend, *weil* er gefährlich ist. Doch wie erfolgt die Bewertung? Erfolgt sie über ein Urteil?[15] Oder nimmt das Gefühl diese Bewertung automatisch vor? Ist eine Werteigenschaft genauso erfassbar wie die Eigenschaft eines Blattes, grün zu sein? De Sousa geht auf all diese Fragen nicht ein. Stattdessen führt er den Begriff Axiologie ein und spricht davon, dass die Klasse der formalen Objekte des Gefühls eine Gattung bilden, die er unter dem Titel ‚Axiologie' zusammenfasst. (De Sousa 2009, 237) Bei diesem Begriff handle es sich um eine fast vergessene Terminologie, die noch in alten Lehrbüchern zu finden sei, wo zwischen zwei ethischen Dimensionen, nämlich der axiologischen und der deontologischen unterschieden worden sei: „Axiologie war die Theorie dessen, was bedeutend und wertvoll ist, die Deontologie lehrte, wie man handeln soll." (De Sousa 2009, 278)

Bei der axiologischen Dimension geht es also um die Frage, ob etwas von Bedeutung ist, ob etwas wichtig und wertvoll ist. Jemand ist beneidenswert, *weil* er über etwas verfügt, was man selber gerne hätte, etwas ist ärgerlich, *weil* Jemand meine Pläne durchkreuzt, etwas ist erfreulich, *weil* es mir neue Perspektiven eröffnet, Jemand ist bewundernswert, *weil* er Eigenschaften besitzt, die ich auch gerne hätte. Die axiologischen Eigenschaften, bzw. die formalen Objekte, stehen also in einem Begründungszusammenhang, durch welchen die Angemessenheit des Gefühls gerechtfertigt wird.

Die Frage die sich nun stellt ist, ob es sich bei den formalen Objekten um Werte handelt. In der gegenwärtigen Metaethik werden die formalen Objekte – in Anschluss an Brentano – als intentionale Ob-

---

[15] In der zeitgenössischen Gefühlsforschung ging man ursprünglich davon aus, dass diese Bewertung über ein Urteil verläuft. Viele Phänomene, so z. B. die Tatsache, dass ich immer noch Angst verspüre, obwohl ich klar erkenne, dass keine Gefahr mehr vorliegt, führten dazu, ein komplexeres Zusammenspiel von Wahrnehmung, Bewertung und körperlichen Prozessen anzunehmen. Siehe dazu: „Philosophie der Gefühle: Neuere Theorien und Debatten" (Moser 2013, 20-33).

jekte von Emotionen verstanden und mit Werteigenschaften gleichgesetzt. Vendrell Ferran bezeichnet diese axiologischen Qualitäten, „die dafür verantwortlich sind, dass sich uns die Welt als ein Horizont mit bestimmten Schattierungen präsentiert, die uns eine Orientierung ermöglichen, (...) im Anschluss an die deutschsprachige Tradition mit Brentano als ‚Werte'". (Vendrell Ferran 2013, 73) Christine Tappolet vertritt ebenfalls die These, dass es sich bei den formalen Objekten von Emotionen um Werte handelt. „Die Emotionen spielen die gleiche Rolle hinsichtlich von Werten, wie es Wahrnehmungen in bezug auf Formen und Farben tun. In günstigen Fällen, würden uns also Emotionen erlauben, Bewußtsein von Werten zu haben." (Tappolet 2009, 455, 456) Auch Kevin Mullikan nimmt an, dass Werteigenschaften Eigenschaften seien, „die wir dank unserer Emotionen erkennen können. Emotionen (...) erschließen uns Werteigenschaften. (Mulligan 2009, 462)

Axiologische Eigenschaften verkörpern also Werteigenschaften und Wertprädikate und werden in bestimmten Bereichen der gegenwärtigen Wertphilosophie und philosophischen Gefühlsforschung als Werte bezeichnet. Dahinter steht die Annahme, dass die axiologischen Eigenschaften uns die Welt von ihrer qualitativen Seite her erschließen. Abgesehen vom Problem der Werterfassung – erfolgt diese über Gefühle oder über eine eigene Art des Wertfühlens[16] – stellt sich die Frage, ob über Wertprädikate hinaus auch Werte wie Freiheit, Gleichheit oder Würde zugänglich gemacht werden können. Bedarf es hier nicht eines komplexeren Begriffszusammenhanges und – um mit Hegel zu sprechen – einer Arbeit am Begriff? Spielen hier nicht ideengeschichtliche Faktoren eine Rolle, durch welche erst ein Bewusstsein für bestimmte Werte geschaffen wird. Stellt die Auseinandersetzung mit Werten und der Versuch, sie in Begriffe zu fassen, nicht den zentralen Kern des Philosophierens überhaupt dar? Und wenn dies so ist, wieso wurde dann so lange der Zusammenhang von Werten und Gefühlen nicht wahrgenommen, ja mehr noch, das Gefühl für jede Begriffsarbeit als hinderlich angesehen?

---

[16] Vendrell Ferran weist darauf hin, dass Tappolet Scheler irrigerweise die These zuschreibt, „dass die Gefühle Werte erfassten. (...) Scheler aber trennt auf das Schärfste das Fühlen von Werten und die Gefühle als Antwortreaktionen auf im Fühlen gegebene Werte (Vendrell Ferran 2013, 84).

1.4 Ethische und weltanschauliche Dimensionen

In dem Moment wo ethische, kulturelle und politische Dimensionen ins Spiel kommen, wird die Eins-zu-eins Verknüpfung zwischen Emotionen und axiologischen Eigenschaften problematisch. De Sousa weist darauf hin, dass die Vielfalt an möglichen Formalobjekten es schwierig mache, Gefühle angemessen zu bewerten. Darin sieht er einen der Gründe, warum der Beitrag des Gefühls zum ethischen Leben so komplex sei. (De Sousa 2009, S. 206). Morallehren wie z.B. der Emotivismus nehmen an, dass ethische Urteile auf Gefühlen gründen, doch verbleibe der Emotivismus in einem reinen Subjektivismus. De Sousa hingegen erfasst die Gefühle als „die Basis eines Bewertungssystems, mittels dessen sie selbst kritisiert werden können". (De Sousa 2009, S. 484) Wenn Gefühle axiologische Wertungen sind und wenn diese nun ihrerseits axiologisch bewertet werden sollen, liegt hier nicht ein Zirkelschluss vor? De Sousa verneint dies mit dem Hinweis, dass dies nur dann der Fall wäre, wenn man von den Gefühlen verlange, „dass sie den alleinigen Rechtfertigungsgrund für die Werte liefern, mittels deren sie später beurteilt werden sollen." (De Sousa 2009, S. 484)

De Sousa spricht das Phänomen an, dass Gefühle in einem Bewertungszusammenhang stehen. Die Angemessenheit von Gefühlen hängt davon ab, ob die Bewertung, die im formalen Objekt stattfindet, auch tatsächlich zutrifft. Diese Bewertungen sind jedoch ihrerseits abhängig von einem Begründungs- und Rechtfertigungszusammenhang, wie Kevin Mullikan aufzeigt: „Zu begreifen, was es heißt, dass etwas ‚F-wert' ist (beispielsweise bewundernswert) wenn F dazu verwendet wird, eine Emotion zuzuschreiben (beispielsweise Bewunderung), ist oft gleichbedeutend damit, den Rechtfertigungsübergang von der erwähnten Emotion zur Anwendung des Prädikats zu beherrschen." (Mullikan 2009, 479). Das Aushandeln von Vereinbarungen darüber, was Bewertungsprädikate wirklich bedeuten und wie sie angewendet werden sollen, müsse mitberücksichtig werden. Damit wird das Gebiet von Ethik und Verhaltensregelungen betreten: Verhalten ist nicht nur von biologischen Faktoren abhängig, sondern auch von sozialen und ethischen Vorgaben. Eine zentrale Funktion von Emotion liegt darin „anzuzeigen oder zu signalisieren,

224

was in einem Milieu von menschlichen wie auch nichtmenschlichen Wesen einen positiven oder negativen Wert hat." (Mullikan 2009, 490)

Was einen Wert hat oder nicht ist abhängig davon, welche Wertvorstellungen in einer Gesellschaft vorherrschen. Diese bestimmen, welche Gefühle in welchen Situationen angemessen sind. Neue Weltanschauungen oder ein politischer Machtwechsel können Gefühle buchstäblich von einem Tag auf den anderen grundlegend verändern.[17]

2. Begehren

2.1. Begierden

Die Begierden spielen bei De Sousa eine wichtige Rolle, da er versucht, über sie zu einer Art Wertrangordnung zu gelangen. Die Frage, ob es so etwas wie objektiv wertvolle Objekte des Begehrens gebe, sagt er, sei schon immer im Zentrum seiner Überlegungen gestanden. Sie habe ihn ständig zur Euthyphron-Frage zurückkehren lassen: „Begehren wir etwas, weil es begehrenswert ist, oder ist es begehrenswert, weil wir es begehren?" (De Sousa 2009, 294) Eine moderne Antwort, so De Sousa, laute, dass alles vom subjektiven Begehren und unseren Präferenzen abhängt. Damit habe er sich jedoch nicht zufrieden gegeben. De Sousa ist also auf der Suche nach so etwas wie objektiven Werten. Diesen nähert er sich über das Begehren und den Wunsch an. So wie Wahrheit das Formalobjekt der Überzeugung sei, so der „Wert oder *Begehrenswertigkeit* (...) das Formalobjekt des Wünschens." (De Sousa 2009, 206). Bei den „objektiven" Begierden komme so „etwas wie Wertwahrnehmung" vor. (De Sousa 2009, 365). Das Begehren ist für ihn insofern objektiv,

---

[17] Ferdinand von Schirach, der Enkel des Reichsjugendführers und Gauleiter von Wien, Baldur von Schirach, fragt sich in seinem 2014 erschienen Buch *Die Würde ist antastbar* warum sein Großvater, der aus einem großbürgerlichen Haus kam und ein behütetes, weiches Kind war, sich begeisterte „für das Dumpfe und Laute? (...) Wieso begreift er, der gerne über Goethe schrieb und Richard Strauss zum Patenonkel eines Sohnes machte, nicht schon bei der Bücherverbrennung, dass er jetzt auf der Seite der Barbaren steht?" (Schirach 2014, 43) Mangelnde Bildung oder Armut könne nicht der Grund dafür gewesen sein, dass er die rassistischen Werte des Nationalsozialismus mit Begeisterung annahm (Schirach 2014, 40).

weil es der Gegenstand-mit-seinem-Wert ist, worauf sich das Begehren richtet. (De Sousa 2009, 369) De Sousa spricht hier erstmals explizit von Werten. An den „objektiven" Begierden würden wir die Dauer schätzen und dass sie eine moralische oder ästhetische Bedeutung haben. Man würde es als schmerzhaft empfinden, wenn sie allzu flüchtig wären und zwar deshalb, weil sie „einem objektiven Wert zu entsprechen" scheinen. (De Sousa 2009, 293) Bewunderung, Liebe, das Empfinden von Schönheit zählt er genauso dazu wie das *ludische Begehren*, das für ihn eine Form des „müßigen Spieles" darstellt, dem Aristoteles den Namen der *Kontemplation* gegeben habe und das als Vorfahre jener Lüste gelten könne, die Platon *reine* Freuden nannte. (De Sousa 2009, 351)

De Sousa nimmt eine Rangordnung der Begierden an, die drei Stufen enthält. Auf der untersten Stufe setzt er das subjektive oder – wie er es nennt – *konsumatorische* Begehren an. Dieses steht für ihn in enger Verbindung mit den biologischen Funktionen des Menschen. Genau genommen, so De Sousa, würden die Grundbedürfnissen, die vier „Fs": *food, fighting, fucking, flight*, also Essen, Kämpfen, Geschlechtsverkehr und Flucht, gar keine wirklichen Gefühle benötigen. (De Sousa 2009, 311). Gefühle seien zwar tief in der Biologie verwurzelt, würden aber „geistig-psychische" Phänomene darstellen. (De Sousa 2009, 176) Diejenigen Begierden, die eine ästhetische oder moralische Bedeutung haben, siedelt er auf einer zweiten Stufe an, wobei die ludischen Begehren des müßigen Spieles und der Kontemplation den krönenden Abschluss der dritten Stufe bilden. Spirituelles Begehren nach Heiligkeit hingegen lehnt er vollkommen ab. Hier verlässt er seine sonst wertrealistische Sichtweise[18] und nimmt mit Jean-Paul Sartre an, dass Gefühle intentionale Strategien sein können, „die reale Welt (…) auf magische Weise" zu verän-

---

[18] Der Wertsubjektivismus nimmt an, dass der Wert eines Gegenstandes in seinem Wertgehalten-werden besteht, der Wertrealismus hingegen, „dass Werte die intentionalen Objekte affektiver Akte sind, auf die bezogen diese Akte angemessen oder unangemessen sind. Allerdings werden die Werte hier nicht in Abhängigkeit von Subjekt und Objekt verstanden, sondern es wird ihnen eine von Mensch und Gegenstand unabhängige Existenz zugeschrieben" (Ferran 2013, 82).

226

dern.[19] (De Sousa 2009, 83) In diesem Sinne erfassen religiöse Gefühle keineswegs etwas Reales, sie stellen vielmehr eine Möglichkeit dar, die bestehende Welt für das Subjekt zu verändern und sie in einem anderen Licht erscheinen zu lassen. Für De Sousa sind Religionen Wahnvorstellungen, die von gesellschaftlicher Billigung getragen sind. (De Sousa 2009, 395)

Über eine Rangordnung der Begierden versucht De Sousa eine Antwort auf die Frage zu erhalten, ob sich unser Begehren nach objektiven Werten richtet, oder ob es rein subjektiv ist. Auffällig ist, dass er auf der untersten Ebene des Begehrens annimmt, dass wir es gar nicht mit Gefühlen und Werten zu tun haben, sondern mit reinen Instinkten und Trieben, was sehr problematisch ist. Noch problematischer erscheint jedoch, dass De Sousa bei den religiösen Gefühlen seine wertrealistische Sichtweise verlässt und den religiösen Gefühlen jeglichen Rationalitätsgehalt abspricht. Dadurch wird er nicht nur seiner eigenen Argumentationslogik untreu, sondern begibt sich auf das Feld der Theologie, dem er in keiner Weise gerecht wird. Bei ästhetischen, moralischen und kontemplativen Gefühlen spricht er jedoch sehr wohl davon, dass sich unser Begehren an objektiven Werten orientiert. Hier nimmt er eine Wertrangordnung vor, die sich nach der Dauerhaftigkeit richtet.

2.2 Wertrangordnung

Im Gegensatz zu De Sousa, der über die Begierden zu einer Wertrangordnung zu kommen hofft, setzt Scheler bei einer Rangordnung der Werte selbst an, die folgende vier Wertebenen enthält. Auf der ersten Ebene befinden sich die Werte des Angenehmen und Nützlichen, die für alle Sinnenwesen gelten. Auf der zweiten Ebene sind die Vitalwerte bzw. Lebenswerte, Gesundheit, Wohlbefinden, Sicherheit. Auf der dritten Ebene siedelt er die geistigen Werte an, wie Schönheit (Ästhetik), Wahrheit (Wissenschaft) und das Recht (Gesetze, Rechtsordnung, Staat). Auf der vierten Ebene befinden sich die Werte des Heiligen, das für ihn eine nicht weiter definierbare Einheit gewisser Wertqualitäten ausmacht. Keinesfalls dürfe jedoch darunter das verstanden werden, was bei verschiedenen Völkern an Dingen,

---

[19] De Sousa betont zwar, dass Magie normalerweise nicht funktioniere. „Wenn sie es doch tut, nenne ich das erfolgreiches *bootstrapping*" (De Sousa 2009, 83).

realen Personen und Institutionen als heilig gegolten habe. (Scheler 2007, 107).

Als Kriterien für die Wertrangordnung von Gütern gibt Scheler Dauerhaftigkeit, Teilnahmemöglichkeit möglichst Vieler, Fundierungscharakter und Befriedigung an. (Scheler 2007, 88). Anders gesagt: Ein Gut ist umso wertvoller, je dauerhafter es ist, je mehr Menschen daran teilhaben können, ohne es aufzubrauchen, je mehr dieses Gut alle anderen Güter befördert und ermöglicht und je mehr Befriedigung es gibt.

Für Scheler wird durch die objektive Wertrangordnung der Rahmen dafür abgesteckt, wonach unser Streben und Begehren sich richtet, bzw. richten sollte. Seine Absicht besteht darin, eine materiale Wertethik im Gegensatz zu Kants formaler Ethik zu entwickeln. Entscheidend ist für ihn die Frage, welche Werte überhaupt dem Streben von Menschen zugrunde liegen und damit „den möglichen Spielraum für ihre Zwecksetzungen abgeben". (Scheler 2007, 37) Ob jemand sittlich richtig handle hängt nach Scheler von seinen Werten ab, die seinem Streben zugrunde liegen. Für die hochstehende sittliche Natur eines Menschen sei es charakteristisch, dass bereits sein unwillkürliches Streben und Begehren entsprechend einer Vorzugsordnung verlaufe, die der objektiven Rangordnung der Werte entspreche. Die Vorzugsordnung werde hier „zur inneren Regel des Automatismus des Strebens selbst und schon der Art und Weise, wie die Strebungen an die zentrale Willenssphäre gelangen." (Scheler 2007, 38)

Unsere subjektive Wertrangordnung weicht davon jedoch häufig ab. Ja vielfach ist sie uns selbst gar nicht bewusst. Scheler schlägt ein Gedankenexperiment vor, indem wir auf unsere (fiktiven) Strebungen achten. Dies sei eine „subjektive Methode", um uns zur Klarheit zu bringen, welcher Wert für uns der höhere sei. (Scheler 2009, 34) Wen würden wir in einer Gefahr zuerst retten? Welche Speise würden wir von zwei uns angebotenen wählen? Im Vorziehen sei uns gegeben, welcher Wert für uns der höhere ist. Denn häufig würden wir unsere Werte erst im konkreten Erstreben derselben erkennen. Auch die Größe der Befriedigung eines Strebenes zeige uns, wie hoch für uns der Wert ist, den wir erstreben. Hier spricht Scheler eine ganz spezielle Problematik an: Unsere Werte sind uns zumeist gar nicht bewusst gegeben. Wie ein Eisberg, der größtenteils unter dem

Meeresspiegel liegt, so befinden sich unsere Werte meist unterhalb unserer Bewusstseinsschwelle. Oft kennen wir unsere Bedürfnisse gar nicht und wissen nicht wirklich, was uns wichtig ist.

2.3. Werte und Bedürfnisse

Für Scheler hängen auch unsere Bedürfnisse von einer Wertrangordnung ab. Im Gegensatz zu De Sousa nimmt er an, dass es keine „angeborenen Bedürfnisse" gibt. (Scheler 2007, 364) Im Unterschied zu Trieben wie Hunger, Durst und Schlaf, stehen Bedürfnisse für ihn immer in einem Wertebezug. Scheler nimmt an, dass jedes Bedürfnis erst einer Bedürfnisweckung bedarf, bei der es zum Einen darum geht, den Wert dieses Gutes überhaupt fühlbar zu machen und zum Anderen das Bewusstsein und die Überzeugung dafür zu schaffen, dass dieses Gut vorhanden ist, bzw. sein könnte. Scheler lehnt die schon auf John Locke zurückgehende Bedürfnistheorie des Wertes und der Wertschätzung ab, wonach etwas nur deshalb wertvoll ist, weil es ein Bedürfnis befriedigt: „Wertvollsein von etwas heißt nicht, dass ein bloßer Mangel (...) beseitigt, dass eine Wertleere sozusagen ausgefüllt, dass ein Loch zugestopft werden könne." (Scheler 2007, 364)

Genauswenig wie der Wert für Scheler eine Folge eines Bedürfnisses ist, so ist er auch niemals nur die Folge eines Strebens. Für ihn ist ausgeschlossen, dass Wert „nur das jeweilige X eines Strebens oder Widerstrebens" ist (Scheler 2009, 32). Vielmehr wird jedes Streben erst durch das Fühlen eines Wertes überhaupt möglich. „Denn nur in einem Wertfühlen (resp. Vorziehen, resp. Lieben und Hassen) und seinen Inhalten ist jegliches Streben unmittelbar fundiert. (...) Damit ist schon ein Doppeltes gesagt: Dass alles Wollen „von etwas" bereits das Fühlen des (positiven oder negativen) Wertes dieses „Etwas" voraussetzt, dass niemals also der Wert erst eine Folge dieses Wollens sein kann." (Scheler 2007, 33) Werte, so Scheler, würden uns förmlich zu den Strebenszielen hinziehen und, so gesehen, sei Motivation eine unmittelbar erlebte Kausalität und zwar im ausgezeichneten Sinne „Zugkausalität". (Scheler 2007, 357) Daraus folgt für ihn, dass die Gegenstände, denen wir uns zuwenden, bereits durch unsere Werthaltungen vorselektiert sind. Die praktische Welt, so Scheler, „trägt bereits das Gesicht, das Antlitz, die Wertstruktur der ‚Gesinnung' des Trägers dieses Wollens." (Scheler 2007, 134)

3.   Werterfassung

3.1. Wahrnehmung von Gefühlen

Ronald De Sousa stellt bei der Gefühlswahrnehmung eine Analogie zur Sinneswahrnehmung her, wobei er sich von folgender Frage leiten lässt: „Wie weit kommen wir mit der Vorstelllung, dass Gefühle eine Art Wahrnehmung sind?"(De Sousa 2009, 248) Zunächst weist er darauf hin, dass unsere sinnliche Wahrnehmungsfähigkeit von verschiedenen Faktoren abhängt. Ganz entscheidend dabei ist, dass unsere Sinneswahrnehmung vom Sinnesorgan selbst abhänge. Wenn dieses nicht funktioniere, gibt es auch keine entsprechende Wahrnehmung. Am Beispiel des Sehsinnes gibt er folgende Faktoren an, von denen eine angemessene Wahrnehmung abhängig ist: Erstens von den primären Eigenschaften, wie sichtbaren Qualitäten (Töne würde da nicht dazugehören), zweitens von Umweltfaktoren, wie Licht, drittens von unserem körperlichen und psychischen Zustand, viertens von der Geschichte unserer Erfahrungen und unseren gegenwärtigen Überzeugungen, sowie fünftens von sozialen und ideologischen Faktoren. Unser Wahrnehmungsapparat funktioniere dann normal, wenn unsere Empfänglichkeit für die Faktoren zwei bis fünf abnehmend sei, d.h. wenn wir uns von ihnen nicht oder kaum beeinflussen lassen. Bei unseren Gefühlen, so De Sousa, werden wir hingegen von allen fünf Faktoren beeinflusst. Dies sei zum Einen eine Folge dessen, „dass wir keine Gefühlsorgane haben" und der Körper eine weit größere Rolle spiele als bei der Sinneswahrnehmung. (De Sousa 2009, 254). Zum Anderen hänge es damit zusammen, dass wir viel stärker von unserer persönlichen Erfahrung (Faktor 4) abhängig seien und von sozialen und ideologischen Faktoren (Faktor5) beeinflusst werden.

Entsprechend seiner Ausgangsthese, dass Gefühle rational seien und uns daher etwas über die objektive Welt aussagen können, gibt De Sousa die Faktoren an, welche hinderlich dabei sein könnten. Trotz seiner Annahme, dass die formalen Objekte der Gefühlswahrnehmung axiologische Eigenschaften sind, entsteht hier der Eindruck, als ob es möglich wäre, durch Gefühle die Realität unabhängig von Wertvorstellungen zu erfassen, ja mehr noch, die Betonung der Verzerrung bzw. Entstellung der Gefühlswahrnehmung durch Ideologien, lässt vermuten, dass De Sousa tatsächlich annimmt, dass axiologische Eigenschaften Ähnliches darstellen, wie Farben, die nur richtig wahrgenommen werden müssen. Man bräuchte dann nur eine Art Realitätstest durchführen, indem man nachmisst, ob es sich wirklich um die entsprechende Farbe handelt.

3.2. Intentionales Fühlen

Scheler unterscheidet zwischen Gefühlen und Fühlen. Nur das Fühlen ist für ihn intentional, d.h. auf etwas gerichtet. Das worauf es gerichtet ist, sind entweder Gefühlszustände oder Werte. Der auf Franz Brentano zurückgehende Begriff der Intentionalität beinhaltet den Gedanken, dass es kein psychisches Erleben gibt, das nicht eine intentionale Beziehung zu etwas hat: „Kein Hören ohne Gehörtes, kein Glauben ohne Geglaubtes, kein Hoffen ohne Gehofftes, kein Streben ohne Erstrebtes, keine Freude ohne etwas, worüber man sich freut und so im übrigen." (Brentano 1921, 15) Immer muss beides gegeben sein, mein subjektiver Vollzug und das objektive Vorliegen von etwas, das sich mir von sich aus erschließt. Beides korreliert miteinander im Erlebnisakt. Verschiedene Akte erschließen verschiedene Gegenstände, so im Akt des Wertfühlens die Werte. „Dieses Fühlen hat daher genau dieselbe Beziehung zu seinem Wertkorrelat wie die ‚Vorstellung' zu ihrem ‚Gegenstand'; eben die intentionale Beziehung. Hier wird nicht das Fühlen unmittelbar mit einem Gegenstand, oder mit einem Gegenstand durch eine Vorstellung hindurch (…) äußerlich zusammengebracht, sondern das Fühlen geht ursprünglich auf eine eigene Art von Gegenständen, eben die ‚Werte'" (Scheler 2007, 265) Entsprechend dem Korrelationsapriori muss umgekehrt auch die Erfahrungsart mitgegeben sein. So wie es das Gehörte nicht ohne das Hören gibt, so gibt es auch keine Werte ohne Wertfühlen: „Jede Behauptung der Existenz einer Gegenstandsart fordert aufgrund dieses Wesenszusammenhanges auch die Angabe einer Erfahrungsart, in der diese Gegenstandsart gegeben ist. Insofern sagen wir: Werte müssen ihrem Wesen nach einem fühlenden Bewusstsein erscheinbar sein." (Scheler 2007, 272) Für Scheler gehören Fühlen und Werte untrennbar zusammen, deshalb weist er einen unabhängig von einem fühlenden Wesen vorhandenen Ideen-

und Werthimmel ebenso zurück wie die Behauptung, dass Werte gesetzt werden oder ‚gelten'.[20]

In Anlehnung an Blaise Pascal nimmt Scheler an, dass es ein spezielles Organ des Wertfühlens gibt, nämlich das Herz. Dieses sei nicht nur dazu fähig Werte zu erfassen, sondern diese auch auf eine bestimmte Art und Weise zu ordnen: Es gibt eine Ordnung, bzw. Logik des Herzens, „eine apriorische ‚Ordre du coeur' oder logique du coeur', wie Blaise Pascal treffend sagt". (Scheler 2009, 59) Hierbei handle es sich um eine Erfahrungsart, deren Gegenstände dem ‚Verstande' völlig verschlossen seien; für die dieser so blind sei wie das Ohr und das Hören für die Farbe, „eine Erfahrungsart aber, die uns echte objektive Gegenstände und eine ewige Ordnung zwischen ihnen zuführt, eben die Werte; und eine Rangordnung zwischen ihnen." (Scheler 2007, 262) Scheler stellt der reinen Logik eine reine Wertlehre zur Seite und nimmt einen Apriorismus des Emotionalen an, der uns im intentionalen Fühlen zugänglich wird.

3.3. Das emotionale Leben bei Scheler

Scheler siedelt das emotionale Leben entsprechend seiner Wertrangordnung auf vier verschiedenen Ebenen an: Gefühlsempfindung auf der Ebene des Angenehmen, Lebensgefühle auf der Ebene des Vitalen, Gefühle im eigentlichen Sinne auf der geistigen Ebene und Persönlichkeitsgefühle auf der Ebene des Heiligen.

Auf der untersten Ebene befinden sich die Gefühle, die er stark mit körperlichen Prozessen in Verbindung bringt. Gefühle scheinen zunächst körperlichen Phänomenen, nämlich Gefühlszuständen zu entspringen, die durch irgendeinen Gegenstand in der Vorstellung oder Wahrnehmung verursacht wurden und im Körper eine Erregung hervorriefen. Zum Einen kann das Fühlen dieses Gefühlszustandes nun auf verschiedene Art und Weise erfolgen, so kann ich meinen Schmerz erleiden oder vielleicht sogar genießen, zum Anderen bedarf es eines nachträglichen Reflexionsprozesses, um Klarheit darüber zu erreichen, wodurch dieser Gefühlszustand überhaupt ausgelöst

---

[20] „Die Behauptung, dass Werte (...) ‚gälten' verdient Zurückweisung" (Scheler 2007, 195). „Es gibt keine Wesen und Werte ‚an sich', wenn ‚an sich' sagen soll, dass Akte erst sekundär und nachträglich hinzutreten – und eine ontische Unabhängigkeit von Akt und Wesen bestünde." (Scheler GW 11, 225, zitiert nach Sander 1996, 77).

wurde. Appetit und Ekel sind für Scheler keine Triebimpulse, sondern „wertgerichtete Funktionen des vitalen Fühlens. Sie sind daher völlig verschieden sowohl vom Hungern, jenem mit Organempfindungen brennender und stechender Schmerzbetonung begleiteten ungerichteten Drängen (…) als vom Eßtrieb und seines Gegenteiles, des Brechimpulses, die Folgen des Appetites und des Ekels sind." (Scheler 2007, 252). Bei starkem Hunger könne man sich vor der Speise ekeln, bei sehr geringem aber trotzdem Appetit haben. Die Gefühlszustände sagen nichts über die äußere Welt aus. Scheler versteht Zorn als körperlich „in mir" aufsteigend und dann automatisch ablaufend: „Sicher ‚erfasse' ich in diesem Zorne nichts". (Scheler 2007, 265) Hier spricht Scheler das von Paul Ekman angesprochene Phänomen des Refraktärzustandes an, in dem wir ganz von dem Gefühl durchdrungen sind und die Welt um uns entweder gar nicht, oder nur in der mit unserem Gefühl in Einklang stehenden Art und Weise wahrnehmen. (Ekman 2010, 56) Erst nachträglich können wir versuchen, denkerisch eine Verknüpfung herzustellen zwischen unserem Gefühl und dem jeweiligen Auslöser und versuchen, die Situation besser zu verstehen. Für Scheler sind alle sinnlichen Gefühle mittelbarer Natur: „Immer sind es erst dem Gegebensein des Gefühls nachträgliche Akte des Beziehens, durch die die Gefühle mit dem Gegenstand verknüpft sind". (Scheler 2007, 263)

Während die sinnlichen Gefühle ausgedehnt und im Körper lokalisiert sind, steht das vitale Lebensgefühl auf der zweiten Ebene zwar noch mit dem Körper in Verbindung, ohne jedoch eine bestimmte Ausdehnung in ihm zu haben. „Behaglichkeit und Unbehaglichkeit, z.B. Gesundheits- und Krankheitsgefühl, Mattigkeit und Frische können nicht in analoger Weise nach ihrer Lokalisierung und ihrem Organ bestimmt werden, wie wenn ich frage: Wo tut es Dir weh? Wo empfindest Du Lust?" (Scheler 2007, 351) In ihnen fühle ich mich matt und krank, wobei dieses „mich" darauf verweise, dass es sich im Unterschied zu den Gefühlen der höheren Ebenen immer noch um Leibgefühle handle.

Auf der dritten, der geistigen Ebene sind wir auf bestimmte Bereiche bezogen wie Gesellschaft, Freunde, Beruf, Kunst, Kultur, Staat. Hier freuen wir uns über etwas, sind über etwas traurig, sind von etwas berührt oder über etwas begeistert.

Die Gefühle, welche der höchsten Ebene entsprechen, sind für Scheler die Seligkeit und die Verzweiflung. Zum Wesen dieser Gefühle gehöre, dass sie einerseits keinen Bezug mehr zu irgendwelchen Handlungen des Ichs haben, andererseits aber, dass sie entweder gar nicht erlebt werden, oder von der gesamten Persönlichkeit erfasst werden. „Wie in der Verzweiflung ein emotionales ‚Nein!' im Kerne unserer Personenexistenz und unserer Welt steckt – ohne dass die ‚Person' dabei auch nur Reflexionsobjekt ist – so in der Seligkeit – der tiefsten Schicht des Glücksgefühls – ein emotionales ‚Ja!'" (Scheler 2007, 356) Dieses Gefühl werde nicht mehr „über" etwas ausgelöst, wir können nur selig oder verzweifelt „sein". Seligkeit und Verzweiflung erfüllen vom Kern der Person her unsere ganze Existenz.[21]

Scheler unterscheidet das Fühlen von Gefühlen oder Stimmungen vom intentionalen „Fühlen von Werten, wie angenehm, schön, gut. Erst bei letzterem gewinnt das Fühlen neben seiner intentionalen Natur auch noch eine kognitive Funktion, die es in den beiden ersten Fällen nicht besitzt. (Scheler 2007, 264) Er schreibt den Gefühlen keine Erkenntnisfunktion zu. Für ihn stehen sie auch nicht in direktem Zusammenhang mit Werten, sondern nur indirekt, indem sie eine Antwortreaktion hervorrufen. Ja mehr noch, die Werte, die sich im intentionalen Fühlen erschließen, fordern in bestimmten Fällen regelrecht eine gefühlsmäßige Antwort. Wenn wir uns über etwas freuen, über etwas ärgern oder über etwas traurig sind, zeigt dieses „über" an, dass die Gegenstände hier nicht einfach nur wahrgenommen werden, sondern vor mir stehen „bereits mit im Fühlen gegebenen Wertprädikaten behaftet. Die in den betreffenden Wertverhalten liegenden Wertqualitäten fordern von sich aus gewisse Qualitäten derartiger emotionaler ‚Antwortreaktionen". (Scheler 2007, 265) Wenn die Forderung der Werte nicht erfüllt werde, dann leiden wir daran, so z.B. sind wir traurig, wenn wir uns über ein Ereignis nicht so freuen können, wie es sein gefühlter Wert verdient, oder nicht so trauern können, wie es der Todesfall eines geliebten Menschen fordert. Für Scheler handelt es sich hierbei um Sinnzusammenhänge, die zu verstehen die Voraussetzung für alles empirische Forschen und die Er-

---

[21] Scheler spricht davon, dass diese Gefühle „aus dem Quellpunkt der geistigen Akte selbst – gleichsam – hervorzuströmen und alles jeweilig in diesen Akten Gegebene der Innen- und Außenwelt mit ihrem Lichte und ihrem Dunkel zu übergießen" scheinen. (Scheler 2007, 356)

fassung jeglicher „Verständnisgesetze fremden Seelenlebens" bildet. (Scheler 2007, 265)

Für Scheler legen die Sinnzusammenhänge fest, welche Werte welche Gefühle nach sich ziehen, bzw. nach sich ziehen sollten. Worin sie genau bestehen, darin lässt er uns jedoch im Dunklen. Er betont, dass es möglich ist, der Forderung der Werte nicht nachzukommen, also nicht angemessen gefühlsmäßig zu reagieren. Wir können sehr wohl die Schönheit einer Landschaft erfassen, ohne uns darüber zu freuen, auch wäre es möglich, die Ungerechtigkeit einer Situation festzustellen, ohne mit Empörung zu reagieren.

Schelers Unterscheidung zwischen Wertfühlen und Gefühlen hat Einzug in die zeitgenössische Gefühls- und Werteforschung gefunden. Vendrell Ferran weist darauf hin, dass Kevin Mulligan seine ursprüngliche Theorie der Werte zu Gunsten eines Wertrealismus revidiert hat, der sehr stark von Scheler beeinflusst ist. „Im Anschluss an Scheler argumentiert Mulligan für die Unterscheidung zwischen dem Fühlen von Werten einerseits und den Gefühlen als Antwortreaktionen auf die im Fühlen gegebenen Werte andererseits." (Vendrell Ferran 2013, 85) Wie Scheler auch, so schreibe Mulligan nur dem Fühlen die erkenntnistheoretische Funktion der Werterfassung zu.

3.4. Werterschließung durch Liebe

Die Neuerschließung von Werten erfolgt für Scheler erst auf der höchsten Wertrangebene, der Ebene der Liebe und des Heiligen. Hier fühlen wir die Werte nicht mehr „über etwas" wie bei den Antwortreaktionen der Gefühle, sondern unmittelbar in Form von spontanen Akten der Liebe und des Hasses. „In Liebe und Haß tut unser Geist etwas viel Größeres als ‚antworten' auf schon gefühlte und eventuell vorgezogene Werte." (Scheler 2007, 268) Im Akt der Liebe findet eine Erweiterung des Wertehorizontes statt. Die Liebe spielt eine entdeckerische Rolle, wodurch wir neue, höhere, uns bisher noch unbekannte Werte erfassen können.[22] Das Phänomen, dass einem

---

[22] An dieser Stelle möchte ich darauf hinweisen, dass die Liebe als ein wesentlicher Faktor der Werterschließung schon von der antiken Philosophie erkannt wurde. Philosophie als Liebe zur Weisheit beinhaltete von Beginn an das Anliegen, den Menschen höhere und höchste Werte erkennbar und zugänglich zu machen. Siehe dazu meinen Artikel „Vom Wert der Liebe" (Moser 2014).

Menschen plötzlich neue Werte zugänglich werden, sich förmlich neue Welten erschließen, wird damit erklärbar.

Viele Gefühle zu haben, muss nicht bedeuten, über ein weites Wertespektrum zu verfügen. Insbesondere die höchsten Werte stehen für Scheler nicht mit herkömmlichen Gefühlen in Verbindung, sondern werden direkt über die Liebe erfasst. Scheler eröffnet durch das Wertfühlen eine neue Dimension emotionaler Erfahrungen, insbesondere im Bereich der geistigen Werte und des Heiligen. Die Erforschung dieser Dimension könnte zu völlig neuen Erkenntnissen führen und Erklärungen dafür bringen, warum manche Menschen in ihrem Umfeld mehr spüren als andere und dass manche darüber hinaus auch einen Zugang zur Ebene der Spiritualität haben.[23]

Der Arzt und Psychotherapeut Viktor Frankl hat sich in der Entwicklung seines eigenen therapeutischen Ansatzes, der Logotherapie und Existenzanalyse, stark vom Werk Max Schelers inspirieren lassen. In seinen Lebenserinnerungen schreibt er: " Vollends wurde ich durch Max Scheler aufgerüttelt, dessen *Formalismus in der Ethik* ich wie eine Bibel bei mir trug." (Frankl 2002, 42) Ähnlich wie Scheler sieht Frankl in der Liebe den grundlegenden Akt der Werterfassung und der Erweiterung des Blickfeldes: „Die Liebe erhöht beim Liebenden die menschliche Resonanz für die Fülle der Werte. (...) Der ganze Kosmos wird für ihn weiter und tiefer an Werthaftigkeit, er erglänzt in den Strahlen jener Werte, die erst der Liebende sieht; denn bekanntlich macht Liebe nicht blind, sondern sehend – wertsichtig." (Frankl 1998, 167) Frankl war als Arzt immer wieder mit selbstmordgefährdeten Menschen konfrontiert, die keinen Wert mehr im Leben sahen. Durch das Vertrauen und die liebevolle Zuwendung im therapeutischen Gespräch wird es möglich, dass die Werthaftigkeit der Welt wieder gefühlt und die eigenen Möglichkeiten wahrgenommen wurden.[24]

---

[23] In den Neurowissenschaften versucht man diese Phänomene sowohl in der High-Sensitivity-Forschung als auch in der Neurotheologie zu erforschen, wobei es Hinweise auf einen Zusammenhang gibt zwischen erhöhter Sensibilität und spirituellen Erfahrungen.

[24] Dass Psychotherapie die Wiederherstellung der Liebesfähigkeit zum Inhalt hat, davon handeln viele therapeutische Diskurse. So heißt es etwa bei Sigmund Freud: „Jede psychoanalytische Behandlung ist ein Versuch, verdrängte Liebe zu befreien, die in einem Symptom einen kümmerlichen Kompromißausweg gefunden hatte." (Freud 1999, 118.) und in einem Brief Freuds an C. G. Jung lesen wir: „Ihnen wird

Sowohl Scheler als auch Frankl betonen die Rolle der Vorbildwirkung. Häufig würden wir Werte erst dadurch erfassen, dass wir sie an Anderen erleben. Es gehe darum, Auswege zu finden, die Andere bereits gegangen sind und die nun als Vorbilder fungieren.

3.5. Soziale und kulturelle Einflussfaktoren

Sowohl Scheler als auch De Sousa verweisen auf die historische und kulturelle Abhängigkeit des Werterfassens. Darüber hinaus hängt der jeweilige Wertehorizont jedoch auch von individuellen Faktoren ab. Während bei De Sousa Gefühle stark von in der Kindheit liegenden Schlüsselszenarien abhängen, unterscheidet Scheler prinzipiell zwischen einer gesellschaftlichen und einer persönlichen Ebene.

3.5.1. Ethos und ordo amoris

Das persönliche Erleben von Werten ist für Scheler zunächst an historische „Formen des Ethos" geknüpft, d.h. an den Wertehorizont der jeweiligen Gesellschaft in der man lebt. (Scheler 2007, 314) Der Mensch ist durch das gesellschaftliche Umfeld jedoch nicht ein für allemal festgelegt. Vielmehr hat er die Möglichkeit einer persönlichen Entwicklung, die darin besteht, ein eigenständiges Wesen, eine Person zu werden. Der Mensch ist, „solange er will, was Eltern und Erzieher oder irgendeiner der Umgebung will", und solange er ohne darüber nachzudenken einfach mitmacht, in der „Form der Ansteckung, des Mittuns, im weitesten Sinne der Tradition" (Scheler 2007, 489) noch unmündig und keine Person. Insbesondere Kinder sind zunächst stark von ihrem Umfeld abhängig. Erst später, wenn sie im Stande sind, zur Gesellschaft auf Distanz zu gehen und ihre eigenen Gefühle und Werte zu reflektieren und die der Anderen in Frage zu stellen, werden sie nach Scheler zu Personen. Für ihn bildet die Person die Basis sowohl für die Erweiterung des eigenen Wertehorizontes, als auch für die Herzensbildung. Scheler spricht in dieser Hinsicht von einem *ordo amoris,* von einer „Ordnung der Liebe", die den Rahmen vorgibt, der dem Einzelnen zur Verfügung steht. Der

---

nicht entgangen sein, daß unsere Heilungen durch die Fixierung einer im Unbewußten regierenden Libido zustande kommen (Übertragung) (...). Es ist eigentlich eine Heilung durch Liebe." (siehe McGuiere/ Sauerländer, 1974, 13).

Mensch ist jedoch auch hier nicht endgültig festgelegt, sondern hat die Chancen, seine je eigene Bestimmung, d.h. sein „Wertidealbild" zu verwirklichen. Dieser ideale *ordo amoris* stellt einen Maßstab dar, der nicht von außen als normatives Ideal, sondern als unsere je eigene Möglichkeit zu verstehen ist. (Scheler 2011, 348) Scheler leitet daraus eine gesellschaftliche Forderung ab, nämlich die „Solidarität und Verantwortlichkeit für die Erkenntnis und Verwirklichung dieser idealen Bestimmung" für jede einzelne Person. (Sander 2003, 76)

3.5.2. Schlüsselszenarien

Im Gegensatz zu Scheler betont De Sousa viel stärker die familiäre und gesellschaftliche Prägung des Individuums in der Kindheit. Für ihn hängt das, was wir gefühlsmäßig wahrnehmen von einem langen Sozialisationsprozess ab, in dem wir lernen mit unseren Gefühlen umzugehen, ja mehr noch, welche Gefühle wir in welcher Situation haben sollen und in welchem Ausmaß. Anhand des Konzeptes der Schlüsselszenarien stellt er eine Verbindung her zwischen biologischen und kulturellen Faktoren und versucht die Genese von Gefühlen und ihren formalen Objekten aufzuzeigen. Er macht deutlich, dass eine Emotion nicht nur eine individuelle Kreation, sondern in ihrem Kern „gesellschaftlich" ist, d.h. sie hat mit unseren Beziehungen zu anderen Menschen zu tun. Gefühle sind eben nicht, wie Freud annahm, einfach biologische Triebe, sondern Beteiligungen an der Welt. Wir machen uns mit dem Gefühlsvokabular vertraut, „indem wir es mit Schlüsselszenarien assoziieren lernen. Anfangs, solange wir klein sind, beziehen wir diese Szenen aus unserem alltäglichen Leben, später verstärkt aus Geschichten, Kunst und Kultur. Noch später werden sie, in Lesekulturen, ergänzt und verfeinert durch Literatur." (De Sousa 2009, 298) Der Mensch lernt schon als Säugling, wie er auf das Verhalten anderer zu reagieren hat. Das zunächst angeborene Lächeln bei Babies löst Reaktionen beim Erwachsenen aus, nämlich Zuwendung. Blinde Kinder verlieren die Ausdruckskraft ihres Lächelns, weil es keine Bestätigung findet. Aus Reaktionsdispositionen (angeborenes Lächeln) werden Emotionen (freudiges Lächeln bei Zuwendung) aufgebaut. Im Laufe der Entwicklung lernen Kinder, die Reaktionen der Anderen zu identifizieren. Erziehung besteht unter anderem darin, im Kontext der jeweiligen Szenarien dem Kind Namen dafür zu geben was es erlebt und

238

ihm die Gefühle, die es empfindet zu erschließen. De Sousa betont, dass schon Aristoteles darauf hingewiesen habe, dass es einen zentralen Bestandteil der Moralerziehung ausmache, die richtigen Emotionen zu fühlen. (De Sousa 2009, 300)[25] Dabei kommt es zu starken Differenzierungen hinsichtlich Geschlecht und gesellschaftlichem Status. Das emotionale Repertoire wird mit der Zeit immer größer. Mit drei Jahren erfassen Kinder, dass gewisse Typen von Ereignissen bestimmte Emotionen verursachen, mit vier und fünf Jahren, welche Geschichten zu welchen einfachen Gefühlen gehören. Schuld und Verantwortlichkeit werden von 6-Jährigen nicht immer gut verstanden, sodass sie nicht immer nachvollziehen können, wer in Geschichten, in denen derartige Empfindungen angebracht wären, wann was fühlt. Manche Emotionen, so De Sousa, seien denkabhängiger als andere und können ohne komplexe sprachliche Fähigkeiten gar nicht erfasst werden.

De Sousa nimmt also an, dass wir in unseren Gefühlen und damit in unserer Wertwahrnehmung von den jeweiligen Erfahrungen in unserer Kindheit stark geprägt sind. Ja mehr noch, unsere Einbettung in einen gesellschaftlichen und kulturellen Kontext ermöglicht uns überhaupt erst, bestimmte Gefühle zu entwickeln und dadurch bestimmte Werte zu erfassen. Aus Reaktionsdispositionen, die evolutionär angelegt sind, werden durch Zuwendung und Verstärkung dauerhafte Reiz-Reaktionspaarungen hergestellt. Wenn dies wirklich der Fall ist, wie können wir dann für bestimmte Gefühle, wie z.B. rassistische, kritisiert werden, wenn wir in einem rassistischen Umfeld leben, fragt De Sousa? Zunächst stellt er fest: „Rassistische Gefühle sind eindeutig schlechte Gefühle." (De Sousa 2009, 501) Aber warum haben wir sie dann überhaupt, wenn sie so schlecht sind, fragt er weiter? Waren sie vielleicht evolutionäre „Abfallprodukte von Schlüsselszenarien, welche unerlässlich waren für die Entwicklung brauchbarer Gefühle?" (De Sousa 2009, 502) Noch komplizierter wird das Ganze dann, wenn ich mir die Frage stelle „wieviel von meinen Gefühlen von mir kommt und wieviel bloß aufgesaugte gesellschaftliche Ideologie ist." (De Sousa 2009, 512) Durch die Of-

---

[25] In diesem Sinne weist Aristoteles darauf hin, dass wir lernen müssen, bei denjenigen Dingen Lust und Unlust zu empfinden, „bei denen man soll, das nämlich ist die richtige Erziehung" (Aristoteles 2011, 1104b10).

fenheit der Gefühle für Nachahmung und Ideologie drohe mir immer die Nicht-Authentizität, denn wenn meine Erfahrung von Werten ihren Ursprung in Schlüsselszenarien in meiner Kindheit hat, dann gibt es keine Garantie, dass meine Werte etwas anderes als bloße Projektionen jener damaligen Erfahrung sind. De Sousa schließt daraus: „Ohne solche Erfahrung könnte es gar kein Wertbewusstsein geben. Halten wir uns aber an sie, sind wir in projektiver Subjektivität befangen." (De Sousa 2009, 521) Dies habe zur Folge, dass die Welten des Wertes unreduzierbar verschieden seien, was eine Axiologie, die so unerschütterlich wäre wie die Wahrheit und so universell wie die Logik, unmöglich mache. Letztendlich endet er damit, dass die Welt tragisch reich sei an Werten von unversöhnlicher Pluralität und die philosophische Analyse des Gefühls „zu einer tragischen Sicht des Lebens" führe. (De Sousa 2009, 526)

Von den Gefühlen ausgehend, münden De Sousas Überlegungen in wertphilosophischen Fragestelllungen. Gibt es so etwas wie universelle Werte? Wenn ja, wieso gibt es dann so eine unversöhnliche Pluralität von Werten? Gibt es etwas, das uns dabei helfen könnte, Ideologien nicht auf den Leim zu gehen? Die Antwort, die De Sousa hier gibt, ist eines Philosophen würdig: Bewusstseinsbildung. Schlicht seinen Gefühlen zu folgen sei jedenfalls nicht der Königsweg zur Authentizität. (De Sousa 2009, 383) Viel mehr müssen wir in einer Art Lebensprüfung den erfahrenen Gehalt von Gefühlen transformieren, reformieren und von Selbsttäuschung befreien. Hier verschmelze, so De Sousa, die philosophische mit der psychologischen Analyse, so dass jede die therapeutische Kraft verstärke, welche die andere verspreche. (De Sousa 2009, 423)

3.5.3. Kritik der Gefühle

Worin liegen nun die Kriterien der Lebensprüfung? Das von De Sousa angesprochene rassistische Gefühl kann nur aus dem Blickwinkel einer bestimmten Wertordnung, nämlich derjenigen eines liberalen, an den Werten von Menschenwürde, Freiheit und Gleichheit orientierten Menschen kritisiert werden. Es besteht jedoch eine Spannung zwischen De Sousas Suche nach objektiven Werten und dem gleichzeitigen Zurückweisen derjenigen philosophischen Ansätze, die über eine objektive Wertordnung verfügen. De Sousas Nahverhältnis zu Platon ist aus vielen Bezugnahmen zu Platons Dialogen ersichtlich. Zugleich lehnt er Platons Wertordnung entschieden ab. Keinesfalls möchte er als idealistisch erscheinen, als jemand, welcher der Illusion eines Ganzen oder Wahren anheimfällt. Der Kantsche Ansatz bietet ihm auch keinen Ausweg, da Kant zum Einen nur rein pflichtbestimmte Motive, die über jeden Verdacht, durch eine Neigung, also ein Gefühl bestimmt zu sein, erhaben sind und zum Anderen weil das Universalisierungsgebot des kategorischen Imperativs auf einer logischen Verallgemeinerung beruhe. Zwar sind, so De Sousa, die Gefühle rational, aber „Gefühlen fehlt das logische Rückgrat, den strengen Anforderungen der Logik Genüge zu tun, ganz so wie man von einem Weichtier nicht erwarten kann, dass es rennt." (De Sousa 2009, 487) Auch der klassische Utilitarismus bringe diesbezüglich nichts zuwege, da er die Empfindungen des Ungehaltenseins, die der Rassist bei ‚Rassenschande' empfindet, gegen die Gefühle der so Diskriminierten aufrechne. Aber das Gefühl des Rassisten könne gar nicht aufgewogen werden, weil es „überhaupt nicht wert ist, irgendwie in Betracht gezogen zu werden." (De Sousa 2009, 501)

Dennoch gibt De Sousa die Hoffnung nicht auf. Er nimmt eine Erweiterung des Ethischen vor, in der eine Eliminierung projektiver Gefühle möglich ist unter dem Motto: „Empfinde die Dinge, wie sie wirklich sind." (De Sousa 2009, 500) Die emotionale Verantwortung zeige sich darin, dass man die rein subjektiv-projektiven von den objektiven und damit wahrnehmungsähnlichen Gefühlen abtrenne. So werde eine Kritik der Gefühle möglich. De Sousa versucht mit seiner axiologischen Perspektive ein Kriterium dafür zu geben, welche Gefühle schlecht sind und welche nicht. Ganz im Sinne seines Wertrealismus stellt für ihn das Kriterium der Beurteilung das Erfassen der Realität dar. Gefühle können danach beurteilt werden, was sie für uns beim Erfassen der Realität leisten können. Danach sollte ihr Wert nach dem Modell des epistemischen Werts von Überzeugungen aufgefasst werden. (De Sousa, 501) Hier greift De Sousa auf seine Ausgangsthese zurück, dass Gefühle objektiv und damit rational sein können. Allerdings nimmt er die Möglichkeit der Selbsttäuschung an, die dann vorliegt, wenn wir uns etwas vormachen und uns in etwas auf fast magische Weise hineinsteigern. De Sousa betont zwar, dass Magie normalerweise nicht funktioniere, wenn sie es aber doch tut, dann nennt er das „erfolgreiches *bootstrapping*." [26] (De Sousa 2009, 83). Ein gesellschaftliches *bootstrapping* liegt für ihn im Falle rassistischer Gefühle vor: „Wenn die Gefühle axiologisch betrachtet werden, gibt es am Unbehagen des Rassisten oder der Rassistin nichts, das uns irgendetwas über den objektiven Wert sagt, um den es in der Situation geht: Die Empfindungsweise der Rassistin hat nur mit der Rassistin selbst zu tun." (De Sousa 2009, 502)

Hier verlässt De Sousa, ebenso wie bei den religiösen Gefühlen, seine wertrealistische Argumentationslinie. Warum rassistische Gefühle jeglicher Rationalität entbehren sollten, darüber lässt er uns völlig im Unklaren, wobei er die lange wissenschaftliche Auseinandersetzung mit Rassentheorien überhaupt nicht in Betracht zieht. De Sousas Untersuchungen sind von der Absicht getragen denjenigen Ideologien, die in der Menschheitsgeschichte so viel Unheil angerichtet haben, etwas entgegen zu setzen. Dazu müsste er sich jedoch über die Ebene der Gefühle hinaus, den Werten selbst in stärkerem Maße zuwenden.

Schlussfolgerung

Sowohl De Sousa als auch Scheler thematisieren den Zusammenhang von Gefühlen und Werten. De Sousa geht von den Gefühlen aus, um zu den Werten gelangen. Indem er aufzeigt, dass Gefühle rational sind, d.h. angemessene Reaktionen auf objektive Sachverhalte darstellen, hofft er einen Beitrag zu einer objektiven Werttheorie leisten zu können. Gefühle können die Realität direkt erfassen, sie können den Gegenstand in seinem Wert erfassen, in seiner axiologischen Dimension. Seine Ausgangsfrage, ob wir etwas begehren, weil es einen Wert hat, oder ob es einen Wert erst durch unser Begehren erhält, beantwortet er dahingehend, dass es Gegenstände gibt, die unabhängig von unserem Begehren einen Wert haben, wie z.B. das Spiel oder die Kontemplation. Auf der Ebene religiöser und weltanschaulicher Gefühle verlässt De Sousa jedoch seinen wertrea-

---

[26] De Sousa weist darauf hin, dass der Begriff *bootstrapping* von Clark Glymour in die Wissenschaftstheorie eingeführt worden sei, um zu beschreiben, dass bei der Rechtfertigung einer Hypothese die Belege eine Rolle spielen, die ihre Einführung motivierten. Der Ausdruck meine einen Prozess, der seine eigene Rechtfertigung liefere (De Sousa 2009, 22).

listischen Standpunkt. Bei religiösen Gefühlen spricht er von *boots-trapping*, einer magisch hergestellten Wirklichkeit, ähnlich einer Halluzination. Religionen stellen für ihn kollektive Wahngebilde dar. Bei rassistischen Gefühlen spricht er hingegen von rein subjektiven Projektionen, die überhaupt nichts über die Realität aussagen. De Sousa wird hierbei nicht nur seiner Argumentationslinie der prinzipiellen Rationalität von Gefühlen untreu, sondern unterschätzt auch die Rationalität von Rassentheorien, die auf eine lange wissenschaftliche Tradition zurückblicken können. Ebenso zeugt De Sousas Abwertung religiöser Gefühle von eine zu sehr vereinfachenden Sicht auf Religionen und deren rationalem Gehalt.

Für Scheler geht die Wertwahrnehmung jeder Sinnes-, und Gefühlswahrnehmung voraus. Die Erfassung von Werten erfolgt über das Fühlen, das Scheler strikt von Gefühlen unterscheidet. Gefühle stellen für ihn Antwortreaktionen auf im Fühlen erfasste Werte dar. Gefühle verfügen über keine Intentionalität und können damit auch nicht auf Werte gerichtet sein. Sie erstrecken sich von Gefühlszuständen über Leibgefühle und geistige Gefühle bis hin zu Persönlichkcitsgefühlen. Welche Gefühlsreaktionen angemessen sind, das ergibt sich für Scheler aus dem Sinnzusammenhang. Das Fühlen hingegen ist intentional auf Werte gerichtet. In der Liebe erschließen sich uns nicht nur die Werte, vielmehr findet hier eine Erweiterung unseres Wertehorizontes, unseres *ordo amoris*, statt. Dieser ist nämlich nicht für immer festgelegt, sondern kann erweitert werden. Eingebettet ist das individuelle Werterfassen bei Scheler in den jeweiligen Ethos, d.h. in die gelebten Sittlichkeit und den Wertehorizont einer gegebenen Gesellschaft.

Bei De Sousa spielt die kindliche Sozialisation eine große Rolle. Nach dem von ihm entwickelten Konzept der Schlüsselszenarien lernen wir in der Kindheit, wie wir auf bestimmte Situationen gefühlsmäßig zu reagieren haben. Diese in der Kindheit erlebten Schlüsselszenarien bleiben dann oft auch im Erwachsenenalter handlungswirksam. De Sousa scheint wenig Spielraum dafür offen zu lassen, dass diese Gefühlsreaktionen später revidiert werden können. Der Prozess, in dem wir lernen, angemessen mit Gefühlen umzugehen, endet nicht in der kindlichen Sozialisation, sondern dauert ein ganzes Leben an. Zum Einen können wir lernen, besser mit unseren Gefühlen umzugehen, so z.B. mit unserem Ärger oder unserer Wut, zum Anderen können sich uns im Laufe des Lebens neue Werte erschließen, was dazu führt, dass wir nunmehr andere Gefühle als bisher als angemessen ansehen.

Sowohl für De Sousa als auch Scheler spielen ethische Fragestellungen eine zentrale Rolle. Eines von De Sousa Hauptanliegen besteht darin, ein Kriterium dafür zu finden, dass rassistische Gefühle schlecht sind. Dieses Kriterium findet er im Realitätstest. Gefühle sind angemessen, wenn sie der Realität entsprechen. Dem rassistischen Gefühl entspricht für De Sousa jedoch nichts in der Realität. Er sieht darin, ebenso wie bei religiösen Gefühlen, rein subjektive Projektionen und Wahnvorstellungen. De Sousa verlässt auf der religiösen und weltanschaulichen Ebene seine wertrealistische Position, was ihn letztendlich dazu führt, sein Projekt, über Gefühle zu einem Bewertungssystem für Gefühle zu gelangen, als zum Scheitern verurteilt anzusehen. Übrig bleibt eine tragische Weltsicht, die von dem Verlangen erfüllt ist eine objektive Wertordnung zu finden und dem Eingeständnis, dass wir – nicht zuletzt aufgrund der Schlüsselszenarien – dazu verurteilt sind, in einer Welt pluraler, unversöhnlicher Werte zu leben.

Scheler setzt hingegen voraus, dass es eine objektive Wertrangordnung gibt, die jedoch nicht – wie bei Platos Ideenhimmel – unabhängig von einem fühlenden Bewusstsein existiert. Diese erstreckt sich von den Werten des Angenehmen und Vitalen über die geistigen und gesellschaftlichen Werte hin bis zum Wert des Heiligen. Persönlichkeitsentwicklung im Sinne eines möglichst breiten Spektrums des Wertfühlens steht im Vordergrund von Schelers Überlegungen, also bis hin zum Fühlen des Heiligen, wodurch sich eine Seligkeit einstellt, welche die ganze Person erfüllt. Verzweiflung hingegen sieht er als Zeichen der Ablehnung dieses Wertes an. Scheler sieht es als Aufgabe der ganzen Gesellschaft, dem Einzelnen dazu zu verhelfen seinen *ordo amoris*, d.h. seine Liebes- und Werterfassungsfähigkeit zu erweitern und damit die Welt immer stärker von ihrer Wertseite her zu erschließen.

Scheler und De Sousa sind von sehr ähnlichen Anliegen getragen. Beide thematisieren die Notwendigkeit einer Wertordnung, beide setzen sie mit dem emotionalen Leben des Menschen in Verbindung. Beide nehmen eine Wertrangordnung vor, die im Grunde genommen sehr ähnlich ist. Beide setzen, ausgehend von den Überlebenswerten und vitalen Werten, geistige und moralische Werte auf einer höheren Stufe an. Dennoch kommen sie zu ganz unterschiedlichen Ergebnissen. Während Scheler an der Möglichkeit einer Persönlichkeitsentwicklung festhält, die sich an einer objektiven Wertordnung orientieren kann, schreckt De Sousa – in Erinnerung an die Totalitarismen des 20. Jahrhunderts und die vielen religiösen Konflikte – davor zurück, die von ihm in Ansätzen entwickelte Wertrangordnung weiter zu übernehmen. Stattdessen sieht er einen Pluralismus von Werten, die er als Quelle unlösbarer Konflikte versteht, wobei er mit der Einsicht endet, dass der Weg, über die Gefühle zu einer Ethik und zu einem Bewertungssystem von Gefühlen zu gelangen, nicht zielführend ist.

Unabhängig davon, dass bei beiden Philosophen verschiedene Fragen offen bleiben, ist eines klar: Jede zukünftige Werteforschung muss sich auf die eine oder andere Art mit den Gefühlen auseinandersetzen. Umgekehrt wird es im Rahmen der Gefühlsforschung immer wichtiger, mit der Werteforschung zusammenzuarbeiten. Schelers differenzierte Auseinandersetzung mit dem emotionalen Leben, seine Unterscheidung zwischen Gefühlszuständen, Gefühlen, Fühlen und Lieben ermöglicht es in Regionen vorzudringen, die bisher ausgeblendet oder überhaupt verworfen wurden. Scheler ist daher insbesondere aus der Sicht einer religiösen Werteforschung von Interesse, weil er eine Erfahrungsart annimmt, die über die Sinnes-, und Gefühlwahrnehmung hinaus, Zugang zu diesen Werten ermöglicht.

Literaturangaben

Aristoteles. *Nikomachische Ethik*. Hamburg: Felix Meiner Verlag, 1985.

Brentano, Franz. *Psychologie vom empirischen Standpunkt*. Band1. Hamburg: Felix Meiner Verlag, 1973.

Brentano, Franz. *Psychologie vom empirischen Standpunk.*, Band 2. Hamburg: Felix Meiner Verlag, 1959.

Brentano, Franz. *Vom Ursprung sittlicher Erkenntnis*. 2. Auflage. Herausgegeben von Oskar Kraus. Leipzig: Felix Meiner, 1921.

Döring, Sabine (Hg.). *Philosophie der Gefühle*. Frankfurt am Main: Suhrkamp, 2009.

Ekmann, Paul. *Gefühle lesen*. Heidelberg: Spektrum Akademischer Verlag, 2010.

Frankl, Viktor E. *Ärztliche Seelsorge*. Frankfurt am Main: Fischer Taschenbuch Verlag, 1998.

Frankl, Viktor E. *Was nicht in meinen Büchern steht – Lebenserinnerungen*. Weinhein-Basel: Beltz Verlag, 2002.

Freud, Sigmund: *Der Wahn und die Träume in W. Jensens ‚Gradiva'*, in: Ders.: *Gesammelte Werke*, Frankfurt a.M.: Fischer 1999, Bd. VII, 118

Hume, David. *Traktat über die menschliche Vernunft*. Band 2. Hamburg: Meiner, 1978.

Kenny Anthony. „Handlung, Emotion und Wille", in: Döring, Sabine (Hg.). *Philosophie der Gefühle*. Frankfurt am Main: Suhrkamp, 2009.

McDowell, John. *Wert und Wirklichkeit*. Frankfurt am Main: Suhrkamp, 2009.

McGuiere, William/Sauerländer, Wolfgang (Hrsg.): *Sigmund Freud – C.G. Jung. Briefwechsel*. Frankfurt a.M.: Fischer 1974.

Meinong, Alexius. *Zur Grundlegung der allgemeinen Werttheorie*, in: Alexius Meinong, *Abhandlungen zur Werttheorie*, Band 3 der Alexius Meinong *Gesamtausgabe*, Herausgegeben von Rudolf Haller und Rudolf Kindinger, Graz, 1968, S. 469-656.

Moser, Susanne, „Vom Wert der Liebe", in: *Labyrinth*, Vol. 16, Nr. 2., Wien, Axia Academic Publishers, 2014. S. 20 – 47.

Moser, Susanne, „Philosophie der Gefühle: Neuere Theorien und Debatten", in: *Actual Challenges in Philosophy*, 2/2014, S. 20 - 33

Mulligan,Kevin. „Von angemessenen Emotionen zu Werten", in: Döring, Sabine (Hg.). *Philosophie der Gefühle*. Frankfurt am Main: Suhrkamp, 2009.

Polak, Regina (Hg.). *Zukunft. Werte. Europa. Die Europäische Wertestudie 1990-2010: Österreich im Vergleich*. Wien, Köln, Weimar: Böhlau, 2011.

Platon. *Euthyphron*. Frankfurt am Main und Leipzig: Insel Verlag, 1991.

Raynova, Yvanka B. „The European Values: A 'Dictatorship' or a Chance for Union?", in idem (ed.), *Community, Praxis and Values in a Postmetaphysical Age. Studies on Exclusion and Social Integration in Feminist Theory and Contemporary Philosophy*, Vienna: Axia Academic Publishers, 2015, S. 333-350.

Raynova, Yvanka B. *Être et être libre: Deux „passions" des philosophies phénoménologiques*, Frankfurt am Main: Peter Lang, 2010.

Reicher, Maria E. „Wertgefühle", in: Fruwirth, Andera, Reicher, Maria E. Wilhelmer, Peter (Hg.) *Markt – Wert – Gefühle*. Wien: Passagen Verlag, 2005.

Sander, Angelika. *Mensch – Subjekt – Person. Die Dezentrierung des Subjekts in der Philosophie Max Schelers*. Bonn: Bouvier Verlag, 1996.

Sander, Angelika. „Normative und deskriptive Bedeutung des *ordo amoris*", in: Bermes, Christian, Henckmann, Wolfhart. Leonardy Heinz (Hg) *Vernunft und Gefühl. Schelers Phänomenologie des emotionalen Lebens*, Würzburg: Königshausen und Neumann, 2003, S. 63-80.

Sartre, Jean-Paul. *Skizze einer Theorie der Emotionen*, in: Sartre, Jean-Paul, *Die Transzendenz des Ego. Philosophische Essays 1931-1939*, Hamburng: Gallimard, 1994.

Schirach, Baldur von. *Die Würde ist antastbar*. München: Piber 2014.

Scheler, Max. *Der Formalismus in der Ethik und die materiale Wertethik*, Adamant Media Corporation, 2007.

Scheler, Max. *Gesammelte Werke 11: Schriften aus dem Nachlass*, Bd.2: *Erkenntnislehre und Metaphysik*. Hrsg. v. Manfred Frings, Bern 1979.

Scheler, Max. *Schriften aus dem Nachlass*, Bern und München: Francke Verlag, zitiert nach Manfred S. Frings, *Der Ordo Amoris bei Max Scheler*, in: *Zeitschrift für philosophische Forschung*, Bd. 20 H1, (Jan-Mar., 1966)

Schnädelbach, Herbert. *Philosophie in Deutschland 1831-1933*. Frankfurt am Main: Suhrkamp, 1983.

Schnädelbach, Herbert. *Was Philosophen wissen und was man von ihnen lernen kann*. München: C.H. Beck, 2013.

Wiggins, David,. „Ein vernünftiger Subjektivismus", in: Döring, Sabine (Hg.). *Philosophie der Gefühle*. Frankfurt am Main: Suhrkamp, 2009.

ANKE GRANESS

DIE GESCHICHTE DER PHILOSOPHIE UND AFRIKA
ZUR MARGINALISIERUNG VON TRADITIONEN

Einleitung

Philosophiegeschichte ist nicht nur ein Teilgebiet der akademischen Philosophie im Sinne einer Wissenschaftsgeschichte, sondern wird zugleich als philosophische Tätigkeit selbst betrachtet. Auch wenn Philosophiegeschichtsschreibung genau genommen ein sekundärer Diskurs ist, der Texte über philosophische Texte, Konzepte, Begriffe und Debatten sowie deren Autoren und Autorinnen produziert, entsteht im Schreiben einer Philosophiegeschichte ein neuer Diskurs, der die vorangegangenen Debatten zwar beinhaltet und bewahrt, aber auch verändert. Gegenwärtig stellt die Beschäftigung mit der Philosophiegeschichte in der akademischen Philosophie, sowohl im Studium als auch in der Forschung, den Hauptteil philosophischer Arbeit dar. Wie anhand der Existenz einer unglaublich großen Anzahl an Bänden zur Geschichte der Philosophie (auch immer mehr Bänden in populärwissenschaftlicher oder unterhaltender Absicht bis hin zum Comic) deutlich wird, ist die Auseinandersetzung mit Themen, Texten, Begriffen und Konzepten unserer Vorväter (und einiger weniger Mütter) die Hauptbeschäftigung gegenwärtiger Philosophen_innen.[1] Und auch die Reflexion auf zentrale Themen unserer Zeit wie Fragen einer Umweltethik, einer Technik- und Medienethik, Fragen von Armut und Gerechtigkeit, Fragen, die die Kognitionswissenschaften aufwerfen oder die Biotechnologie, erfolgt stets in enger Bezugnahme auf Konzepte aus der Geschichte der Philosophie – ob nun als Autoritätsbeweis für Argumente oder in Absetzung zu älteren Konzepten. Mit gutem Grund kann somit behauptet werden, dass die Geschichte der Philosophie konstitutiv für den Gegenstand und die Disziplin der Philosophie geworden ist. Philosophiegeschichte formt unser Verständnis von Philosophie, den

---

[1] Ulrich Johannes Schneider hat in seinem Buch *Philosophie und Universität. Historisierung der Vernunft im 19. Jahrhundert* (Hamburg 1999) allein aus dem 19. Jahrhundert über 300 Philosophiegeschichten angeführt!

philosophischen Kanon und unsere Lehrpläne an philosophischen Instituten.

Dabei ist jeder Prozess des Schreibens einer Philosophiegeschichte ein ausschließender: Denker_innen, Theorien, Konzepte oder Begriffe werden in die Erzählung ein- oder ausgeschlossen je nach jeweils vorherrschendem Philosophieverständnis, welches durch Zeit und Raum durchaus variieren kann, letztlich aber durch vorangegangene Erzählungen der Philosophiegeschichte meist schon vorgeprägt ist. Der Prozess der Philosophiegeschichtsschreibung schafft einen bestimmten Kanon an philosophischen Arbeiten und Autoren_innen, welcher wiederum das zukünftige Verständnis von Philosophie als Art des Denkens und akademische Disziplin bestimmt. Wir befinden uns hier also gewissermaßen in einem Denkzirkel. So weist der französische Philosophiehistoriker Lucien Braun darauf hin, dass das, was wir Philosophiegeschichte nennen, letztlich ein Auswählen und Ordnen von Texten ist mit nicht zu unterschätzenden Konsequenzen:

"Immer schon gab es Lektüren, die durch Auslese, Auswahl, Klassifizierung die Texte in neuen Ensembles zusammenstellten: das ist es, was wir Philosophiegeschichte nennen. Die Resultate dieser Lektüren, solcher konstituierenden Realitäten, belasten alle späteren Lektüren. Das Gewicht dieser Trägheit macht sich beispielsweise in der Annahme geltend, einen Text als philosophisch anzusehen, nicht weil die gegenwärtige Evidenz ihn als solchen auswiese, sondern weil die Überlieferung ihn als solchen nimmt." (Braun 1990, 3)

Das "Gewicht dieser Trägheit", wie Braun es nennt, determiniert also alle folgende Lektüre. An diesem Punkt wird deutlich, wie entscheidend die Aufnahme eines Textes, eines Konzepts, eines Autors oder einer Autorin in die große Erzählung der Philosophie ist – oder eben der Ausschluss aus eben dieser Erzählung. Dabei sind Ausschluss, Abgrenzung und Auswahl die die Philosophiegeschichtsschreibung dominierenden Motive, ja vielleicht sogar der Philosophie selbst, insbesondere dann, wenn diese mit einem absoluten Wahrheitsanspruch in Verbindung gebracht wird. Bis heute wird die Geschichte der Philosophie als Beweis dafür angeführt, dass Philosophie eine sehr spezifische, abgegrenzte und sich abgrenzende Tätigkeit ist (vgl. Schneider 1990, 14), eine Tätigkeit bzw. eine Fähigkeit zu der nicht jede/r in der Lage ist.

Im Falle Afrikas hatten solch ausschließende Tendenzen eine besonders verheerende Wirkung: Bis heute sind sie mitverantwortlich für die Geringschätzung Afrikas als Quelle von Wissen, Wissenschaft und kulturellen Errungenschaften – wie eben auch der Philosophie. In Anbetracht der Tatsache, dass der Besitz von Philosophie bis heute im Allgemeinen als Merkmal für einen hohen gesellschaftlichen Entwicklungsstand gilt und das Fehlen philosophischer Reflexion gleichgesetzt wird mit dem Verharren auf einem 'primitiven', 'archaischen' Niveau gesellschaftlicher Entwicklung, Philosophie mithin als Qualität gilt, die einige Gesellschaften anderen als überlegen erscheinen lässt, ist die Frage nach dem Beginn der Philosophie ebenso wie die nach eigenen philosophischen Traditionen in den verschiedenen Regionen der Welt nicht allein eine akademische, sondern hat wichtige politische Konnotationen.

Hier ist die dominante abendländische Version der Philosophiegeschichtsschreibung ein gutes Beispiel für das, was heute oft mit dem Begriff "epistemische Ungerechtigkeit" ("epistemic injustice", Miranda Fricker 2007) bezeichnet wird. Für Fricker ist epistemische Ungerechtigkeit ein Unrecht, dass jemandem in seiner Funktion als ein Wissender angetan wird (Fricker 2007, 1). Sie manifestiert sich u.a. in Skepsis, falschen Interpretationen, in Ignoranz oder auch in einem gänzlichen Verstummen. Das Verstummen eines ganzen Kontinents bzw. das Verschweigen der Beiträge eines ganzen Kontinents zur Philosophiegeschichte der Menschheit ist sicherlich ein sehr eindrückliches Beispiel epistemischer Ungerechtigkeit.

Auf den Ausschluss Afrikas aus der Philosophiegeschichtsschreibung soll nun etwas näher eingegangen werden.

1. Afrika in der Geschichte der Philosophie

Jahrhundertelang wurde die Fähigkeit der Afrikaner_innen zu Logik und rationalem Denken in Frage gestellt. Die Beschreibung des vorkolonialen Afrika als "unhistorisch"[2] und "primitiv"[3] – auch

---

[2] GWF. Hegel's Beschreibung Afrikas in seinen *Vorlesungen über die Philosophie der Geschichte* (veröffentlicht 1837, gehalten 1822/23 bis 1830/31), in denen er die Einwohner Afrikas als weder zu Bildung noch Entwicklung fähig, als gefangen in Aberglauben und Fetischismus, ohne jegliche Sittlichkeit und Moral beschreibt, sind sehr bekannt und wurden breits häufig zitiert. So heißt es hier: "Darum verlassen wir hiermit Afrika, um

250

durch herausragende Vertreter der deutschen Aufklärung und Philosophie – war sicher eines der Haupthindernisse für eine vorurteilslose und gründliche Erforschung der Geschichte des philosophischen Denkens in dieser Region der Welt. Afrika wurde nicht als Quelle philosophischen Denkens in Betracht gezogen und somit auch nicht als Teil der Weltphilosophie betrachtet. Insbesondere die Region südlich der Sahara galt als frei von jeglicher philosophischer Tradition, was sich bis heute in Fragen wie "Gibt es überhaupt Philosophie in Afrika? Und was ist das Afrikanische an der afrikanischen Philosophie?" widerspiegelt.

Allerdings war das nicht immer so. Abgesehen von antiken Quellen, die insbesondere Ägypten und seiner Wissenschaft eine maßgebliche Rolle bei der Entstehung von Philosophie und Wissenschaft im antiken Griechenland beimessen (vgl. u.a. Aristoteles[4]), bezogen sich Werke zur Geschichte der Philosophie noch bis zum Ende des 18. Jahrhunderts auf die chaldäische, persische, arabische, indische, chinesische oder ägyptische Philosophie als Vorgänger und Wurzel abendländischer Philosophie. Auch phönizische, äthiopische und japanische Philosophie werden gelegentlich erwähnt. Philosophen

---

späterhin seiner keine Erwähnung mehr zu tun. Denn es ist kein geschichtlicher Weltteil; er hat keine Bewegung und Entwicklung aufzuweisen, und was etwa in ihm, das heißt, in seinem Norden geschehen ist, gehört der asiatischen und europäischen Welt zu. Karthago war dort ein wichtiges und vorübergehendes Moment; aber als phönizische Kolonie fällt es Asien zu. Ägypten wird im Übergange des Menschengeistes von Osten nach Westen betrachtet werden, aber es ist nicht dem afrikanischen Geiste zugehörig. Was wir eigentlich unter Afrika verstehen, das ist das Geschichtslose und Unaufgeschlossene, das noch ganz im natürlichen Geiste befangen ist, und das hier bloß an der Schwelle der Weltgeschichte vorgeführt werden mußte." (Hegel 1994, 234)

[3] "Im Allgemeinen müssen wir sagen, daß im inneren Afrika das Bewußtsein überhaupt noch nicht zu der Anschauung eines festen Objektiven, einer Objektivität gekommen ist. Die feste Objektivität heißt Gott, das Ewige, das Rechte, die Natur, die natürlichen Dinge. ... Die Afrikaner aber sind noch nicht zu dieser Anerkennung des Allgemeinen gekommen; ihre Natur ist die Gedrungenheit in sich: was wir Religion, Staat, an und für sich Seiendes, schlechthin Geltendes nennen, alles dies ist hier noch nicht vorhanden. Die weitläufigen Berichte der Missionare bestätigen dies vollkommen, und nur der Mohammedanismus scheint das einzige zu sein, was die Neger noch einigermaßen der Bildung annähert." (Ebd., 217)

[4] "Daher entstanden auch die mathematischen Wissenschaften in Ägypten, denn dort gestattete man dem Priesterstand, Muße zu pflegen." (Aristoteles, Metaphysik, I. Buch (A) 981b; vgl. Aristoteles 1987, 19) Griechische Philosophen, wie Thales, Anaximander und Parmenides, auch Platon haben in Ägypten studiert.

und Philosophiehistoriker wie Braun (1990, orig. 1973), Schneider (1999), Bernasconi (1997) und Park (2013), um hier nur einige zu nennen, zeigen, dass der Ausschluss Afrikas, insbesondere Ägyptens, aus der Philosophiegeschichte im Wesentlichen gegen Ende des 18. Jahrhunderts erfolgte.[5] Park sieht einen grundlegenden Wandel in der Philosophiegeschichtsschreibung zwischen 1780 bis 1830 vonstattengehen, ein Wandel, der vor allem mit einem Ausschluss Afrikas und Asiens aus der Geschichte der Philosophie und einem Fokus auf das antike Griechenland als alleiniger Quelle der Philosophie einher geht. Davor war es üblich, auf die Vorläufer griechischer Philosophie zu verweisen, so u.a. noch in Diderots *Encyclopédie* (1764) und Jacob Bruckers *Historia critica philosophiae a mundi incunabilis ad nostram usque aetatem deducta* (5 Bände, 1742-44; 2. Auflage 6 Bände, 1766-67) — eine der Hauptquellen Diderots. Brucker beschreibt verschiedene Völker und deren Philosophie, u.a. die Ägypter und Äthiopier, und bezeichnet die Ägypter noch explizit als Philosophen.

Schneider stellt in seiner *Archäologie der Philosophiegeschichte* (1990) fest, dass die beiden letzten philosophiehistorischen Werke, die noch eine nennenswerte Beschreibung von Völkern und Kulturen vor dem antiken Griechenland beinhalten, die *Allgemeine Geschichte der Philosophie* (1787) von Johann August Eberhard und das *Lehrbuch der Geschichte der Philosophie* (1796) von Johann Gottlieb Buhle sind (Schneider 1990, 75). Er betrachtet, ebenso wie Bernasconi, Dietrich Tiedemanns *Der Geist der spekulativen Philosophie* (1791-7) und Wilhelm Gottlieb Tennemanns *Geschichte der*

---

[5] Sehr bekannt in diesem Zusammenhang ist Martin Bernals *Black Athena* (1987, dt. *Schwarze Athene* 1992). Bernal argumentiert, dass ein neuer Blick auf das antike Griechenland im Wesentlichen gegen Ende des 18. Jahrhunderts entstand. Er unterscheidet zwischen zwei verschiedenen Geschichtsmodellen: dem arischen Modell (die griechische Zivilisation wurde von Indo-Europäischen Siedlern aus Zentraleuropa gegründet) und dem antiken Modell (Ägypter und Phönizier haben das antike Griechenland maßgeblich geprägt – eine Ansicht, die in der Antike noch weit verbreitet war). Das antike Modell wurde erst ab etwa 1820 zunehmend durch das arische verdrängt, als die Romantik sowie Konzepte von Fortschritt ebenso wie Rassismus die Diskurse zunehmend zu dominieren begannen. Damit einher ging die Ablehnung eines ägyptischen und phönizischen Einflusses auf die griechische Zivilisation, so Bernal. Seine Theorie blieb nicht unwidersprochen und wurde teils heftig kritisiert (siehe Lefkowitz and Rogers 1996).

252

Philosophie (1798-1819)[6] als die ersten bedeutenden Werke, in denen als Quelle der Philosophie einzig die griechische genannt wird.[7] Der entscheidende Grund für diesen Wandel in der Philosophiegeschichtsschreibung ist laut Schneider ein neues Philosophieverständnis, das Philosophie als ein wissenschaftliches, rationales Denken versteht, das an ein Individuum – den Philosophen – gebunden ist. So ist für Tiedemann Thales der erste Philosoph, da er der erste war, der "seine Lehre als *Erkenntnisse aus Gründen, hergenommen von Erfahrungen, oder Vernunft*begriffe vorgetragen habe." (Schneider 1999, 76-77) Dies ist ein Meilenstein in der Philosophiegeschichtsschreibung, den Schneider so zusammenfasst:

"Durch die theoretische Definition von Philosophie zum einen als durch Vernunft begründete Lehre und zum anderen durch die Forderung, dafür als Beleg nur die auf den Lehrenden bezogene Nachricht gelten zu lassen, wird alle vorgriechische Philosophie aus der Philosophiegeschichte verbannt." (Schneider 1999, 77)

Diese "ahistorische Zäsur", wie Schneider es nennt, die zudem den Einfluss von Spekulation und Religion, von Mythos und Vernunft marginalisiert zielt auf einen "geschlossenen Überlieferungszusammenhang", der auf der Garantie basiert, immer einen Urheber, einen Autor benennen zu können. (Schneider 1999, 78) Damit wird Autorenschaft zu einem entscheidenden Kriterium für die Aufnahme in die Philosophiegeschichte.

Diese Wende zur Autorenschaft wurde zugleich begleitet von dem Versuch, Philosophie und Philosophiegeschichte auf eine wissenschaftliche Basis zu stellen. Wie Braun und Schneider argumen-

---

[6] Der Beginn der Geschichte der Philosophie als akademischer Disziplin war stark von deutschen protestantischen Gelehrten geprägt, wie z.B. Christoph August Heumann, Jacob Brucker, Dietrich Tiedemann, und Wilhelm Gottlieb Tennemann, deren Werke grundlegend waren für ein modernes Verständnis der Disziplin, ihrer Methoden und Funktion. Schneider schreibt: "Es handelt sich bei Tennemanns Werk nicht um irgendeine Philosophiegeschichte, sondern um das Projekt der Philosophiegeschichte überhaupt. Hier formuliert sich zum erstenmal ein historisches Interesse an der Philosophie: es wird ein *beobachtender Blick* auf sie gerichtet." (Schneider 1990, 11) Und Lucien Braun stellt fest: "L'histoire de la philosophie est, au moment de sa modification radicale, chose allemande, chose protestante" (Braun 1973, 94).

[7] Park sieht diese Verschiebung etwas früher, nämlich bereits in Christoph Meiners *Geschichte des Ursprungs, Fortgangs und Verfalls der Wissenschaften in Griechenland und Rom* (1781) und *Grundriss der Geschichte der Menschheit* (1785).

tieren, führt die Verwissenschaftlichung des historischen Denkens im 18. Jahrhundert dazu, dass es auch zu einer Standardisierung des Konzepts der Philosophie kam, d.h. zu einer Vereinheitlichung der Vergangenheit der Philosophie auf der Grundlage eines bestimmten methodischen Konzepts. Zudem begann die Idee eines kontinuierlichen Fortschritts zu immer umfassenderem Wissen auch die Philosophiegeschichtsschreibung zu beherrschen. In diesem Verständnis sind frühere Philosophien Stufen auf dem Weg zur Wahrheit und die Entwicklung philosophischer Konzepte eine kontinuierliche Geschichte des Fortschritts. Bereits Tennemanns Schilderung der Philosophiegeschichte orientiert sich an dem Grundgedanken, dass Philosophiegeschichte Fortschritte und Rückschritte mache, auch Irrtümer umfasse, aber ganz grundlegend einem bestimmten Ziel zustrebe nämlich der "Selbsterkenntnis der Vernunft" und der "letzten Begründungen" einer philosophischen Wissenschaft — ein Gedanke, der dann im Hegelschen System letztlich seine Vollendung fand. Ein solches Herangehen geht ohne Zweifel mit Reduktionen bzw. Ausgrenzungen einher, nämlich der Einschränkung dessen, was als Vergangenheit und Geschichte des (philosophischen) Geistes überhaupt angenommen wird. Wer zur "Selbsterkenntnis der Vernunft" beigetragen hat, ist letztlich eine Frage der Definition. In Hegels *Geschichte der Philosophie*, seiner Version des Gangs der Vernunft durch die Weltgeschichte, wird das Denken in Asien und Arabien als Vorgeschichte betrachtet, der Beginn der Philosophie wird in Griechenland angesetzt und die höchste Entwicklung erreicht die Vernunft dann letztlich in Westeuropa – mit einer Tendenz des Übergangs in die Kolonien der neuen Welt, also Nordamerikas. Afrika oder Lateinamerika werden ebenso ausgeschlossen wie das Denken der Frauen. Die Marginalisierung bzw. der Ausschluss von Denktraditionen und Schulen aus der Geschichte der Philosophie ist also kein neues Phänomen; die Entstehung des "Anderen der Vernunft", eine Tendenz des Ausschließens bereits im Ansatz der großen Erzählung der Philosophiegeschichte zu verorten.[8]

---

[8] Dabei finden solche Ausschlusstendenzen nicht nur mit Blick auf Regionen außerhalb Europas statt, sondern auch innerhalb Europas – und das nicht nur im Hinblick auf den Ausschluss weiblichen Denkens. Es gibt eine ganze Reihe von Ländern (insbesondere an den Rändern Europas), die in Standardwerken zur Geschichte der Philosophie im Prinzip

Diese Art einer teleologischen großen Erzählung der Geschichte der Philosophie hat das Philosophieren der letzten 200 Jahre grundlegend bestimmt, ebenso wie unser heutiges Verständnis von dem, was Philosophie ist. Vorannahme der genannten Autoren ist, dass Philosophie einen Anfang und ein Ziel hat. Mag es auch unterschiedliche Auffassungen über das Ziel der Entwicklung der (philosophischen) Vernunft gegeben haben, der Anfang war schnell gefunden: die griechische Philosophie als die erste "echte" Philosophie und somit der Anfang aller Philosophie. Folgt man dieser Auffassung, muss sich, wie Heit schreibt, vor *zweieinhalbtausend Jahren* im nordöstlichen Mittelmeerraum etwas Erstaunliches zugetragen haben (Heit 2007, 7 und 256): nämlich ein kultureller Wandel von universaler Bedeutung. Aufgrund günstiger Umstände wie Klima, technische Entwicklung, Schriftkultur hätten die Griechen den Schritt von der kindlichen Phantasie des homerischen Mythos zur umsichtigen Reife der Vernunft gewagt und damit den Grundstein der abendländischen Kultur und Philosophie gelegt. Diese These hat sich vom Ende des 18. Jahrhunderts bis heute weitgehend erhalten, wobei nicht selten als Argument angeführt wird, dass der Begriff Philosophie selbst aus dem Griechischen stamme. Im Griechenland des 5. Jahrhunderts BCE entstand, so das Argument, das erste freie und selbständige Denken in Abgrenzung von Mythos und Religion. Das menschliche Streben nach Wissen nahm hier seinen Ausgangspunkt und ein Prozess der Rationalisierung setzte ein, der zu einem Aufblühen der Wissenschaften führte. Quellen und Voraussetzungen, aus denen die Griechen wiederum schöpften, werden in dieser Argumentation kaum mit in Betracht gezogen.[9]

---

keine Rolle spielen, u.a. Bulgarien, Rumänien oder Griechenland nach der klassischen Antike, oder auch Spanien und Portugal.

[9] Allerdings gibt es auch eine Gegentendenz, für die Karl Jaspers mit seiner These von der »Achsenzeit« (ca. 800 bis 200 v.Chr.) exemplarisch stehen mag. Hier wird der philosophische Aufbruch der Griechen im größeren Zusammenhang einer universalgeschichtlichen Transformation, die sich gleichzeitig in China, Indien, Iran und im Nahen Osten vollzog, betrachtete. Andere Autoren wie Martin L.West *(Early Greek Philosophy and the Orient),* Martin Bernal *(Black Athena),* George James *(Stolen Legacy)* und Walter Burkert *(Die Griechen und der Orient)* weisen den hier angelegten Eurozentrismus ebenfalls zurück und betonen die Bedeutung der ägyptischen, orientalischen und afrikanischen Einflüsse auf Griechenland. Der Absolutheit des griechischen Modells wurde und wird auch in der sogenannten Afrozentrismusdebatte (siehe Cheikh Anta Diop und seine

Die auf Thales und das antike Griechenland eingeengte Debatte lässt außer Acht, dass auch die Geschichte Griechenlands eine der Interferenzen und Überlagerungen, also keine reine, 'nicht-kontaminierte' Geschichte ist. Oder wie Lucien Braun es ausdrückt:

"Was wir von der griechischen und lateinischen Antike wissen, ist das Ergebnis einer langsamen und geduldigen Arbeit der Wiederherstellung und der immer von neuem wiederholten Lektüre. Es wäre müßig, die Antike beschwören zu wollen, wie sie an sich gewesen ist. Sie ist eben das, was Gelehrte und Philologen, was Hegel, Nietzsche, Heidegger und andere über sie gesagt haben, ausgehend von Fragmenten, Texten und Spuren, die selbst wiederum eine Geschichte haben.

Diese lange Arbeit, die nach und nach die Antike für uns wiederhergestellt hat und immer noch dabei ist, sie wiederherzustellen, schafft vielfältige Interferenzen die oft schwer zu entwirren sind. Immer exakter stellen wir die Quellen fest, vergleichen, argumentieren und interpretieren wir. Indem wir dies tun, konstituieren wir die Geschichte – gleichzeitig aber rationalisieren wir sie, vor allem unter dem Einfluß der Philologie, welche anderen Ansprüchen gehorcht als die Philosophiegeschichte, indem wir nämlich die Irrtümer der Geschichte, ihre irrigen Lesarten und ihre Legenden unterdrücken." (Braun 1990, 9)

Geleitet durch neue theoretische, soziale und politische Bedürfnisse vergleichen und interpretieren wir die Texte immer wieder neu und bewerten sie auf dieser neuen Basis. So wird die Geschichte der Antike immer wieder neu geschrieben, unter neuen Perspektiven und Aspekten, die zu unterschiedlichen historischen Zeitpunkten eine unterschiedliche Bedeutung haben. Unser heutiges Verständnis der Antike ist somit das Ergebnis einer Rekonstruktion, die wiederum Geschichte konstituiert.

Aus der Konstruktion eines eindeutigen Anfangs entstehen bereits die ersten Probleme, denn sie kann zwar harmlos idealistisch formuliert werden, aber ebenso rassistische oder nationalistische Ressentiments beinhalten, wie das Absprechen der Fähigkeit zu Logik und

---

Nachfolger Theophile Obenga, Molefi Kete Asante, Maulana Karenga) in Frage gestellt. Hier wird der Ursprung der Philosophie ins antike Ägypten und somit nach Afrika verlagert. Auch Autoren wie Enrique Dussel (2013) oder van Binsbergen (2009-10) betrachten Ägypten als eine der Quellen der Weltphilosophie betrachten.

256

Philosophie und die Annahme einer Unmündigkeit der afrikanischen
Völker, auf denen letztlich auch die Vorstellung von der zivilisatori-
schen Mission Europas, von der "Bürde des weißen Mannes", d.h.
dem Umdeutung des Kolonialismus zu einem humanitären Akt, beruhen. So sind es auch philosophische Theorien, die Kolonialismus
und Neokolonialismus ideologisch möglich gemacht und legitimiert
haben. Unter diesem Aspekt sind Fragen nach dem Anfang von Philosophie und Wissenschaft und eigenen philosophischen Traditionen
in den verschiedenen Regionen der Welt durchaus erinnerungspoli-
tisch aufgeladen.

Der Prozess der Philosophiegeschichtsschreibung geht also einher
mit einem Kanon formenden Prozess, d.h. dem Ein- oder Ausschließen von Theorien, Konzepten und Begriffen, sowie Autoren und
Autorinnen. Jede Geschichtsschreibung erfolgt unter bestimmten
subjektiven Kriterien, die sowohl von individuellen Vorlieben bzw.
dem individuellen Verständnis des Forschungsgegenstandes, als auch
von gesellschaftlichen Gegebenheiten, wie vorherrschenden Weltanschauungen oder Ideologien und selbstverständlich Machtkonstella-
tionen abhängen. In den letzten Jahren ist es vor allem das Verdienst
der Postkolonialismus-theorien, Fragen von Interesse und Macht im
Rahmen der Definition von Begriffen, Geschichte etc., gerade auch
im kolonialen und postkolonialen Kontext, genauer untersucht zu
haben. Im Kontext der Philosophiegeschichtsschreibung sind es aber
auch Arbeiten wie die von Lucien Braun, der in seiner *Geschichte
der Philosophiegeschichte* eine diskurskritische Analyse liefert, oder
von Franz Wimmer, der in seinem Buch *Interkulturelle Philosophie*
(1990) den Umgang von Philosophiehistorikern mit dem Fremden
beschreibt. Beide machen deutlich, dass Philosophiegeschichtsschreibung Teil eines Bedeutung produzierenden Prozesses ist, der
zu einem Herrschaftsdiskurs werden kann, wie im Fall der Konstruktion eines einzigartigen Ursprungs der Philosophie im antiken Griechenland.

Fragen der Kanonbildung sind also zentrale Fragen, denen in der
Auseinandersetzung mit unserem Fach und eben auch der Philosophiegeschichtsschreibung mehr Raum gegeben werden muss, die
aber im Wesentlichen (zumindest in der vorherrschenden euro-
amerikanischen Philosophie) kaum gestellt werden. Aber wie entsteht ein philosophischer Kanon? Wer gehört hinein und wer nicht?

Wie schreibt man eine Philosophiegeschichte? Dies sind weiterhin aktuelle, bildungspolitische Fragen, die auch unsere zukünftige Forschung bestimmen. Wir müssen uns fragen bzw. die Frage gefallen lassen, wer diejenigen sind, die aus der großen philosophischen Erzählung bisher ausgeschlossen wurden und warum. Wir müssen uns fragen, welche Geschichten noch nicht erzählt wurden und erzählt werden müssen. Und wir müssen uns ebenso fragen, welche Bedeutung die vorliegenden Erzählungen für uns heute haben und wie wir Philosophiegeschichte weiter schreiben wollen. Gerade die letzteren Fragen sind von immenser Bedeutung hinsichtlich philosophischer Curricula: Wen und welche Theorien müssen/wollen wir unterrichten bzw. was soll gelesen werden? Bzw. warum muss jede/r Philosophiestudent/in den Namen des amerikanischen Philosophen John Rawls und dessen Theorie der Gerechtigkeit kennen, den des kenianischen Philosophen Henry Odera Oruka und sein Konzept einer globalen Gerechtigkeit aber nicht?

Und mit dieser Frage wären wir beim Problem des weiterhin fortbestehenden Ausschlusses afrikanischer Philosophen und Philosophinnen aus fast allen internationalen philosophischen Debatten der Gegenwart, einschlägigen Publikationen und Lehrplänen.

2. Mechanismen des Ausschlusses heute

Die Bedeutung von Philosophen_innen und ihrer Konzepte wird gemeinhin gemessen an ihrem Beitrag zum "Fortschritt des Denkens", der innovativen Kraft ihrer Konzepte, dem Einfluss, den sie auf ihre Nachfolger hatten oder die von ihnen ausgehenden Inspirationen für weiterführende Debatten. Aber ist es wirklich der Fall, dass allein die Qualität von Gedanken und der Beitrag zum menschlichen Fortschritt (ein durchaus kontrovers diskutiertes Konzept) allein die Bedeutung eines Denkers / einer Denkerin bestimmen? Ich denke, die folgenden Faktoren beeinflussen die Wahrnehmung der Bedeutung eines Philosophen / einer Philosophin bzw. eines philosophischen Konzepts heute deutlich – und sind mit für die anhaltende Ignoranz gegenüber wissenschaftlichen und philosophischen Traditionen ebenso wie dem Schaffen der Gegenwart in Afrika (wie in anderen Regionen des globalen Südens) verantwortlich:

1. Die kanonbildende Kraft der Universitäten

Ein Kanon besteht aus einer Auswahl an Personen, Arbeiten oder Inhalten, die als eine Art Maßstab oder Standard bestimmt werden und sich als solche vor anderen auszeichnen. Ein Kanon geht davon aus, notwendige, zeitlose und universal gültige Konzepte zu umfassen. Aber wie funktioniert ein Prozess der Kanonbildung? Wie erlangen Personen oder Werke den Status eines "Klassikers"? Neben Autoritäten wie Fachleuten, Kritikern oder Verlegern sind es heute vor allem die Universitäten, die über Lehrpläne und die Finanzierung von Forschungsthemen über eine sehr spezielle kanonbildende Kraft verfügen. Werden Studenten_innen dazu verpflichtet, bestimmte Kurse zu belegen und bestimmte Themen bei Prüfungen abrufbar zu haben, wird es schwierig, andere Interessengebiete zu verfolgen oder überhaupt erst zu entwickeln. Eine an einem bestimmten Kanon orientierte Lehre und Forschung kann fast so effektiv sein wie das Einsetzen einer Zensur, denn einem Kanon zu folgen bedeutet immer, die Aufmerksamkeit auf bestimmte Probleme oder Theorien zu lenken – und von anderen weg. Es bedeutet, bestimmte Autoren_innen zu fördern – und andere nicht. Die Grundfrage in diesem Zusammenhang ist allerdings auch, ob es neben der Originalität der Gedanken und Konzepte eines betreffenden Autors / einer Autorin eine Rolle spielt, ob sein/ihr akademischer Grad aus Princeton oder von der Universität Nairobi stammt, ob das Geschlecht, die Religion, Hautfarbe oder familiäre Hintergrund einen entscheidenden Unterschied bei der Auswahl machen.

Für Philosophie aus Afrika und afrikanische Philosophen_innen bedeutet der historische Ausschluss aus der Philosophiegeschichte, dass sie auch heute kaum in philosophischen Übersichts- und Einführungswerken erwähnt werden und somit das Fortbestehen eines allgemeinen Mangels an Wissen über die Entwicklung der Philosophie in Afrika in Vergangenheit und Gegenwart, welcher wiederum zu einer Nichtbeachtung in neuen Publikationen ebenso wie in der Lehre führt – und damit zu einem sich wiederholenden Zirkel. Denn Universitäten wählen die Themen ihrer Lehre in Übereinstimmung mit gesellschaftlichen Bedürfnissen, finanziellen Zwängen und nicht zuletzt - in einer hoch kompetitiven akademischen Welt - auch in Übereinstimmung mit bestimmten aktuellen Moden und Trends. Im

Kanon zu sein bedeutet ernst genommen zu werden; Dem Kanon nicht anzugehören dagegen bedeutet nicht wahrgenommen zu werden und damit auch das Fehlen finanzieller Ressourcen für die Forschung, denn allzu oft wird der Ausschluss einer Person oder Theorie aus dem Kanon gleich gesetzt mit 'hat keine Bedeutung' für die jeweilige Wissenschaft. Allerdings kann ein so verstandener Kanon bzw. die Eingrenzung von Wissenschaft auf kanonische Personen und Theorien nur lähmend für die Entwicklung philosophischen Wissens sein.

2. Der Ort der Publikation

Neben den Universitäten haben Verlage (und zunehmend wissenschaftliche Zeitschriften), also der Ort, an dem die Werke eines bestimmten Autors /einer Autorin erscheinen, einen entscheidenden Einfluss auf die Wahrnehmung. Die Wahl des Verlages beeinflusst das Publikum, das erreicht werden kann, ganz abgesehen von der heutigen Praxis, die Förderung von Wissenschaftlern_innen von der Anzahl ihrer Veröffentlichungen in begutachteten Zeitschriften abhängig zu machen. Trotz erheblicher Verbesserungen durch die elektronische Vernetzung der Welt und dem dadurch gegebenen leichteren Zugang zu Verlagen und Zeitschriften für afrikanische Autoren_innen, ist deren Zugang zu Publikationen in Verlagen mit großem Namen oder zu open access Publikationen in Zeitschriften durch hohe Druckkostenzuschüsse oder Autorenbeiträge, die weder ihre jeweiligen akademischen Institutionen noch sie persönlich aufbringen können, weiterhin beschränkt. Hier macht es einen großen Unterschied, ob ein/e Autor/in in Europa oder Nordamerika angesiedelt ist und auf entsprechende Budgets zugreifen kann oder nicht.

Die andere Seite des Problems ist, dass Arbeiten, die in Afrika verlegt werden, in Europa und Nordamerika kaum zugänglich sind. Auch dies begrenzt die Wahrnehmung von Autoren_innen aus Afrika in anderen Teilen der Welt. So ist u.a. das oben bereits erwähnte Konzept globaler Gerechtigkeit des kenianischen Philosophen Henry Odera Oruka in Europa auch deshalb unbekannt, da er im Wesentlichen alle seine Arbeiten in Kenia publiziert hat. Als kenianischer Philosoph in einer in jeder Hinsicht marginalisierten Position (örtlich und hinsichtlich der vorherrschenden Auffassung von der ideenge-

260

schichtlichen Bedeutung Afrikas) blieben seine Arbeiten ebenso wie die anderer interessanter Philosophen_innen aus Afrika lange Zeit unbekannt. Dies sagt allerdings noch nichts über die Qualität der jeweiligen Theorien aus.

3. Finanzielle Ressourcen

Und damit wären wir beim vielleicht einflussreichsten Faktor: den finanziellen Ressourcen. Die Situation akademischer Philosophen_innen in Afrika ist zum großen Teil eine prekäre: die Gehälter an afrikanischen Universitäten sind aufgrund der Armut vieler afrikanischer Staaten oft ausgesprochen gering. Das macht es nicht gerade attraktiv, sich für eine akademische philosophische Karriere zu entscheiden (Nachwuchsprobleme), bringt es aber zudem auch mit sich, dass viele afrikanische Akademiker_innen neben ihrer Stelle an der Universität noch ein weiteres Kleinunternehmen betreiben (vom Handel, über Landwirtschaft bis hin zum Betreiben eines Pubs). Andere arbeiten für NGO's oder geben Privatunterricht. Die Breite solcher Aktivitäten ist groß. Hier befinden sich die heutigen Philosophen_innen Afrikas in guter Gesellschaft: bis zum 18. Jahrhundert gab es auch in Europa kaum akademische Philosophen, die von der Philosophie leben konnten und Philosophie als Beruf ausübten. Die meisten Gelehrten, die heute als einflussreich gelten, dienten der Kirche, dem Staat oder einem Aristokraten. Einige waren auch Handwerker wie Jakob Böhme, der Schuhmacher oder Spinoza, der Linsenschleifer. Und sowohl Kant als auch Hegel verdienten ihren Lebensunterhalt zunächst als Hauslehrer, bevor sie eine Universitätsstelle antreten konnten. Auch wenn es jahrhundertelang üblich gewesen sein mag, Philosophie neben einem anderen Beruf zu betreiben – heute ist der Umstand, dass sich viele afrikanische Akademiker_innen nicht allein auf ihre akademische Arbeit konzentrieren können, ein klarer Nachteil und einer der Hauptgründe für die Migration hochqualifizierter Akademiker_innen nach Nordamerika oder Europa.[10]

---

[10] Einige der besten philosophischen Köpfe haben heute Afrika den Rücken gekehrt und arbeiten nun zumeist im akademischen Betrieb der USA. Dazu gehören u.a. Kwasi Wiredu, Dismas Masolo, Souleymane Bachir Diagne, Oyeronke Oyewumi, Nkiru Nzegwu.

4. Die Sprache

Heute findet der internationale wissenschaftliche Diskurs – auch in der Philosophie - vorrangig auf Englisch statt. Dies hat nicht nur zu einer Marginalisierung ehemals als Wissenschaftssprachen anerkannter Sprachen wie Französisch, Italienisch oder Deutsch geführt, sondern ebenso zu einer Marginalisierung von Weltsprachen (hinsichtlich der Anzahl der Sprecher) wie Arabisch, Chinesisch oder Spanisch. Natürlich gibt es zahlreiche Vorteile einer wissenschaftlichen Weltsprache, wie die weite Verbreitung wissenschaftlicher Ergebnisse, die heute noch über neue Kommunikationsmedien erheblich unterstützt wird. So argumentiert der belgische Philosoph Philippe van Parijs, dass ein solcher Prozess der Verbreitung von Kompetenz durch eine *lingua franca* sehr zu begrüßen ist, insbesondere auch, da er dem Kampf um größere weltweite Gerechtigkeit eine wichtige Waffe an die Hand gibt, nämlich ein billiges Medium für die Kommunikation und Mobilisierung (Van Parijs 2011).

Allerdings gibt es auch klare Nachteile einer einzigen Wissenschaftssprache. Zum einen war in der Menschheitsgeschichte eine *lingua franca* immer die Sprache einer hegemonialen Macht. Latein und Arabisch sind Beispiele dafür und im Falle des Englischen ist das koloniale Erbe sogar noch offensichtlicher. So wird die Tendenz, Englisch als neue Weltsprache der Globalisierung zu betrachten, zu Recht als eine Art Neokolonialismus kritisiert (siehe hier die berühmte Kritik von Ngũgĩ wa Thiong'o 1993). Zum anderen haben Muttersprachler einer solchen *lingua franca* selbstverständlich gegenüber Nicht-Muttersprachlern klare Vorteile. Und zum dritten werden Diskurse, die in anderen Sprachen geführt werden, klar marginalisiert. Schon heute gibt es die Tendenz alles, was nicht ins Englische übersetzt wurde, für irrelevant zu halten. Aber gerade in der Philosophie sollte eine größere Sensibilität gegenüber Übersetzungsfragen und dem Wert eines sprachlichen Pluralismus bestehen, gehört die Untersuchung des Verhältnisses zwischen Sprache und Denken doch zu einer der philosophischen Kernfragen.

Für afrikanische Philosophen_innen ist die Wahl ihrer akademischen Sprache ebenso wichtig wie für Philosophen_innen heute weltweit. Dabei ist die Ausgangslage meist noch etwas komplizierter als für z.B. österreichische Philosophen_innen, denn hineingeboren in eine afrikanische Sprachfamilie und aufgewachsen möglicherweise neben der eigenen Muttersprache mit einer weiteren afrikanischen *lingua franca* wie dem Kiswahili, ausgebildet in den Kolonialsprachen Französisch oder Portugiesisch (wenn nicht bereits im Englischen), durchlaufen sie weit mehr sprachliche Umbrüche. Diese große sprachliche Breite ist dabei natürlich auch eine Ressource und Chance.

Philosophische Konzepte entstehen nicht nur in einem spezifischen historischen, kulturellen, sprachlichen und politischen Kontext (um nur einige wenige zu nennen, die auf Inhalt und Methode des Philosophierens Einfluss haben), sie entstehen auch unter ganz bestimmten finanziellen und technischen sowie institutionellen Bedingungen, welche alles andere als philosophischer Natur sind. Trotzdem sind diese materiellen Bedingungen relevante Faktoren hinsichtlich der Frage, ob eine Person oder ein bestimmtes Konzept von der internationalen Gemeinschaft der Philosophen wahrgenommen wird oder nicht. Für den Wert eines philosophischen Arguments als solches ist es irrelevant, wo es entwickelt wurde – für seine Wahrnehmung, Akzeptanz und Aufnahme in den internationalen Diskurs ist der Ort seiner Entstehung allerdings ausgesprochen wichtig – wenn nicht sogar entscheidend.

3. Bedeutung und Herausforderungen der Philosophiegeschichtsschreibung in Afrika

Afrika ist bis heute im Wesentlichen von allen Überblickswerken zur Geschichte der Philosophie ausgeschlossen.[11] Wenn diese Region behandelt wird, dann meist als eine Art Vorgeschichte der Philosophie und unter dem Begriff "traditionelles Denken".[12] Die Abwertung Afrikas, insbesondere das Afrika südlich der Sahara (Nordafrika

---

[11] Eine Ausnahme ist das *Oxford Handbook of World Philosophy* von Garfield und Edelglass (2011).

[12] Ein interessanter Fall ist in diesem Zusammenhang die *Encyclopédie philosophique universelle* (1989). Sie besteht aus drei Teilen: 1. Philosophie occidentale; 2. Pensée asiatique (Inde, Chine, Japon); 3. Conceptualisation des societés traditionelles (Afrique, Amerique, Asie du Sud-Est, Océanie). Die Abstufung der Begriffe von abendländischer Philosophic über asiatisches Denken bis hin zu Konzepten traditioneller Gesellschaften macht die unterschiedlichen Wertungen mehr als deutlich.

wird im Rahmen der Geschichte der arabisch-islamischen Philosophie mit behandelt), bezieht sich allerdings nicht nur auf das Vermögen zur Philosophie, sondern Afrika bzw. die Bewohner des Kontinents werden hinsichtlich ihrer eigenständigen Geschichtlichkeit in Frage gestellt. Bis heute wird die Geschichte Afrikas zumeist als Geschichte der auf Afrika einwirkenden Kräfte erzählt. Insofern geht die Frage nach der Geschichte der Philosophie in Afrika eigentlich über die Disziplin der Philosophie weit hinaus, oder wie Dismas Masolo es in seinem Buch *African philosophy in search of identity* auf den Punkt bringt: "The history of African philosophy is therefore the history of Africa in a very special way" (Masolo 1994, 44). Es ist die Geschichte eines Befreiungskampfes (konzeptionell wie institutionell) und der Selbstvergewisserung der eigenen Position im Rahmen der Weltgeschichte. Die Kolonisierung Afrikas, die einher ging mit einem Ausschluss des Kontinents aus der Weltgeschichte und einer Inferiorisierung seiner Bewohner, betraf auch deren Fähigkeit ein Wissender zu sein – auch im Zusammenhang mit der Philosophie. Aus diesem Grund steht die Disziplin der Philosophiegeschichtsschreibung hier immer auch im Zusammenhang mit dem Projekt einer "conceptual decolonisation"[13], einer Dekolonisierung des Bewusstseins. Dies erklärt sowohl die Bedeutung als auch die Schwierigkeit der Philosophiegeschichtsschreibung in Afrika, denn jeder Versuch in diese Richtung ist von Beginn an bereits politisch aufgeladen.

Allerdings, während die Philosophiegeschichtsschreibung in Europa eine lange Geschichte besitzt und bereits in Platons Dialogen mit der Schilderung der Lehren anderer Denker einsetzt, ist sie in Afrika eine noch relativ junge Disziplin. Im Gegensatz zu den vielen Bänden zur Philosophiegeschichte Europas oder auch Asiens gibt es bis heute noch keine umfassende Philosophiegeschichte Afrikas.

---

[13] Das Projekt einer "conceptual decolonisation" oder "decolonisation of the mind", d.h. begrifflichen Dekolonisierung bzw. Dekolonisierung des Bewusstseins hat eine lange Geschichte, die bis in die Mitte des 19. Jahrhunderts führt, wo lateinamerikanische Intellektuelle wie Andrés Bello und José Marti die auch nach der formalen politischen Unabhängigkeit fortbestehende koloniale Mentalität ihrer Mitbürger kritisierten. Für afrikanische Intellektuelle, wie den Schriftsteller Ngũgĩ wa Thiong'o oder den Philosophen Kwasi Wiredu (1996) ist der Kampf gegen eine fortbestehende mentale und intellektuelle Abhängigkeit von den ehemaligen Kolonialländern ein zentrales Thema.

Dafür gibt es viele Gründe, einige wurden in den vorherigen Abschnitten bereits erläutert.

Die umrissene Problemlage prägte auch das Schaffen der Philosophen_innen in Afrika im 20. Jahrhundert: Sie konnten nicht selbstverständlich auf ein philosophisches Erbe zurückgreifen und mussten sich zudem mit den Hinterlassenschaften des Kolonialismus und Vorurteilen des Rassismus auseinandersetzen. Vorurteile dieser Art sind in modifizierter Form bis heute anzutreffen und haben eine selbstverständliche Auseinandersetzung – jenseits eines Legitimationsdiskurses - zu philosophischen Fragen in Afrika fast unmöglich gemacht. So ist es nicht verwunderlich, dass die Frage „Was ist afrikanische Philosophie?" in den 1950er bis zum Anfang der 1990er Jahre die philosophischen Debatten in Afrika bestimmte. Eine kritische Vergewisserung über den Philosophiebegriff betraf den Versuch der Selbstbegründung einer bewussten, grundlegenden Orientierung des Denkens und Handelns. Dreh- und Angelpunkt dieser Debatte war die Frage nach der Universalität von Philosophie einerseits bzw. der Art und Weise ihrer kulturellen Gebundenheit andererseits.

Ein weiterer naheliegender Grund für das Fehlen einer umfassenden afrikanischen Philosophiegeschichte ist der Umstand, dass die Befreiung Afrikas vom Kolonialismus, betrachtet im Maßstab der Menschheitsgeschichte, letztlich erst kürzlich erfolgt ist, im wesentlichen um das Jahr 1960 herum und später. Die Befreiung Südafrikas vom Apartheidregime liegt gerade einmal 25 Jahre zurück. Eine eigenständige wissenschaftliche und eben auch philosophische Tätigkeit ist somit nach der Unterbrechung durch den Kolonialismus erst seit wenigen Jahrzehnten wieder möglich. Und auch die postkoloniale intellektuelle Entwicklung, insbesondere an Bildungsinstitutionen, war und ist eng an die ehemaligen Kolonialmächte gebunden. Was die akademische Philosophie betrifft wurden bis weit in die 1960er Jahre hinein alle Philosophen_innen an europäischen oder amerikanischen Universitäten ausgebildet. Der Grund dafür ist einfach: Obwohl die ersten Universitäten nach westlichem Vorbild[14] in Südafri-

---

[14] Ich möchte hier ausdrücklich darauf verweisen, dass die ältesten Universitäten der Welt auf afrikanischem Boden entstanden, nämlich die Universität Al-Qarawiyyin in Fès, Marokko (gegründet 859) und die Al-Azhar Universität in Kairo, Ägypten (gegründet etwa 972). Auch im Afrika südlich der Sahara gab es lange vor der Gründung von Universitäten nach westlichem Vorbild eigene Bildungszentren und Universitäten, wie die

ka bereits 1829 (Cape Town) und in Sierra Leone 1872 gegründet wurden, erfolgte die Mehrzahl der Gründungen erst in den 1950er Jahren und später. Ausnahmen sind die Makerere Universität in Uganda, gegründet bereits 1922 als Ableger der London University für Ostafrika, und die ersten Universitäten in Ghana und Nigeria, die 1948 gegründet wurden. Die neu gegründeten Universitäten besaßen zwar durchweg theologische Fakultäten, aber keine philosophischen. An der Makerere Universität wurde im Studienjahr 1965/66 das erste Philosophieprogramm eingeführt und in der Folge das *Department of Religious Studies* umbenannt in *Department of Religious Studies and Philosophy*. (vgl. Odera Oruka 1997, 231) In Nairobi wurden Philosophieprogramme 1969 eingeführt, an den Universitäten in Malawi und Lusaka (Sambia) sogar erst 1980. (vgl. Odera Oruka 1997, 229) Zuvor wurde Philosophie lange Zeit ausschließlich an theologischen Seminaren gelehrt. Das erste Philosophiedepartment wurde 1961 an der Universität Addis Ababa (Äthiopien) gegründet, später an der Universität Lagos (Nigeria) im Jahr 1966, an den meisten afrikanischen Universitäten allerdings noch wesentlich später, meist erst in den 1980er Jahren (z.B. an der Universität Nairobi[15]) und durch eine Abspaltung von den theologischen Fakultäten. Zuvor war ein Studium der Philosophie an afrikanischen Universitäten kaum möglich, insbesondere die Promotion im Fach ausgeschlossen. Die ersten akademischen Philosophen_innen Afrikas im 20. Jahrhundert durchliefen also eine euro-amerikanische Ausbildung und schrieben und lehrten Philosophie in europäischen Sprachen. Das ist bis heute im Wesentlichen so geblieben: alle Universitäten in Afrika südlich der Sahara sind am französischen, englischen, portugiesischen oder amerikanischen Bildungssystem orientiert und lehren in ehemaligen Kolonialsprachen; die Lehrpläne sind vielfach ein Spiegelbild der Philosophie an europäischen oder amerikanischen Universitäten. Dies hat enorme Auswirkungen: Die Beschreibung und Rekonstruktion vor-

---

Sankorè Universität im 15. und 16. Jahrhundert in Timbuktu, Mali, die zu ihrer Zeit für die islamische Welt ein wichtiges Zentrum der Bildung war.

[15] An der Universität Nairobi war es dem Engagement des kenianischen Philosophen Henry Odera Oruka zu verdanken, dass das *Department of Religious Studies and Philosophy* geteilt und 1980 ein eigenes *Philosophy Department* gegründet wurde. Allerdings wurde diese für die Philosophie so positive Entwicklung im Jahr 2005 wieder rückgängig gemacht und beide Departments wurden wieder zum *Department of Religious Studies and Philosophy* vereinigt.

kolonialer Denksysteme und philosophischer Konzepte erfolgt ebenso wie die Beschreibung der heutigen Wirklichkeit und die Diskussion philosophischer Probleme und Fragen in den meisten Teilen Afrikas in europäischen Sprachen, die in vielen Ländern zur *lingua franca* und damit auch Bildungssprache wurden. Somit wird Philosophie (und alle anderen Wissenschaften) zumeist auf der Basis von Begriffen und Konzepten, die auf westlichen *épistémen* beruhen, betrieben – ein Bruch bzw. ein Problem, das von afrikanischen Kollegen_innen kritisch reflektiert wird (siehe u.a. Wiredu 1996).

Neben den institutionellen Voraussetzungen und mit der Erfahrung von Kolonialismus und Rassismus einhergehenden Brüchen sollen hier noch zwei weitere Umstände benannt werden, die das Schreiben einer Philosophiegeschichte in Afrika vor besondere Herausforderungen stellt:

1. Die orale Traditionsvermittlung in Teilen Afrikas

Eine Besonderheit besteht darin, dass in einigen Teilen Afrikas die Schrift bei der Übermittlung von Geschichte und Wissen keine Rolle gespielt hat, sondern eine orale Traditionsvermittlung vorherrschend war. Es gibt also einen Mangel an Texten und damit ein Quellenproblem. Philosophiegeschichtsschreibung in ihrer dominanten europäischen Variante ist letztlich ein Diskurs, der sich in Texten über Texte und den Umgang mit diesen Texten ausdrückt. Die Frage nach dem Umgang mit oralem Erbe hat sich so bisher nicht gestellt bzw. wurde nicht als philosophische Frage betrachtet. Zudem bindet eine noch immer vorherrschende Meinung das Argumentations- und Reflexionsniveau der Philosophie ganz klar an die Voraussetzung der Schriftlichkeit. In schriftlosen Kulturen sei ein derartiger Grad an Reflexion schlicht nicht zu erreichen (siehe Goody 1990 oder Havelock 1992). Aber Philosophiegeschichtsschreibung in Afrika wird sich sowohl mit den vorhandenen schriftlichen Quellen (Ägypten, Äthiopien, arabisch-islamische Quellen, Ajami-Literatur, und natürlich den Texten ab dem Ende des 18./Beginn des 19. Jahrhunderts) als auch mit mündlichen Quellen (Begriffe, Konzepte, ethische und kosmologische Vorstellungen u.a.) auseinander setzen müssen. Dabei sind eine Reihe von methodischen Fragen zu klären: Wie kann man sich philosophischen Traditionen in einer oralen Gesellschaft annähern? Wie können diese dokumentiert werden? Was ist die Stellung des Autoren/der Autorin im Rahmen einer Philosophiegeschichte? Sind Konzepte ohne explizite Autorenschaft Bestandteil einer Philosophiegeschichte?

Die Disziplin der Geschichte der Philosophie, die in der europäischen Tradition eine rein textbasierte Disziplin ist, muss hier neue Wege gehen, wobei eine kritische Reflexion auf das Verhältnis zwischen schriftlichen und mündlichen Traditionen natürlich die Grundvoraussetzung bildet. Afrikanische Kollegen_innen können hier Pionierarbeit leisten.

2. Der Einfluss des Kolonialismus

Die umfassende Kolonisation des Kontinents (bis auf Äthiopien war vom Ende des 19. Jahrhunderts bis 1951 der gesamte Kontinent europäischen Mächten unterworfen) hat zu einem fundamentalen Bruch in der Geistesgeschichte Afrikas geführt. Kolonialismus bedeutet neben der Zerstörung der ökonomischen und politischen Strukturen des kolonisierten Gebietes und deren Ersetzen durch Strukturen kolonialer Verwaltung immer auch eine Infragestellung, eine Beeinträchtigung oder gar eine Zerstörung historisch gewachsener kultureller und religiöser Werte, Regeln, Institutionen und Traditionen. Und zwar auf zweierlei Weise: zum einen durch die Zerstörung der sozialen (politisch-ökonomischen) Wurzeln einer Kultur, zum anderen durch den Versuch des Kolonisators, dem Unterworfenen seine eigenen, als höherwertig betrachteten, kulturellen Errungenschaften aufzuzwingen. Die Abwertung des Kolonisierten und dessen Kultur verbunden mit dem Postulat, dass einzig der Kolonisator im Besitz der "Norm der Geschichte" sei, ist eine notwendige Komponente zur Vervollkommnung der Kolonisation. Der Einfluss und die Auswirkungen von Sklaverei, Kolonialismus und Rassismus können beim Schreiben einer Ideengeschichte Afrikas nicht ignoriert werden.

Wir haben es also beim Schreiben einer Philosophiegeschichte Afrikas mit einer ganzen Anzahl von Brüchen und sehr spezifischen Herausforderungen zu tun, die allerdings ganz zentrale philosophische Fragen berühren: Die Bedeutung der Sprache für das Philosophieren, das Verhältnis zwischen Oralität und Schriftlichkeit, die Frage nach dem Warum und Wie der Rekonstruktion von Philosophiegeschichte, ihrer Aufgaben, Funktion und Rolle sowohl im gesellschaftlichen als auch akademischen Rahmen. Aufgrund der beschriebenen schwierigen Lage ist es kein Wunder, dass eine umfassende Geschichte der Philosophie bis heute nicht gewagt wurde, auch wenn Philosophie nunmehr an vielen afrikanischen Universitäten eine mehr oder weniger etablierte Disziplin ist und die Forschungen der letzten Jahre das reiche kulturelle und intellektuelle Erbe des Kontinents immer besser dokumentieren, oder wie Barry Hallen es ausdrückt: "What is becoming increasingly clear, as more and more meaningful research is done on precolonial Africa, is that philosophy in the African historical context does have a voluminous, rich, distinctive, original, and multicultural heritage." (Hallen 2009, 22) Das Schreiben einer umfassenden Philosophiegeschichte Afrikas wird somit zu einem immer dringenderen Anliegen.

Auch wenn das Schreiben einer Geschichte der Philosophie in Afrika vor sehr spezifischen Herausforderungen steht, so ist es doch zugleich eine unter philosophiehistorischen Aspekten einmalige Chance. Die Aufgabe, eine Geschichte der Philosophie in Afrika zu schreiben, führt uns, wie wir weiter oben gesehen haben, zu Fragen von ganz grundlegender Bedeutung für die Philosophie (siehe Verhältnis Oralität – Schriftlichkeit oder auch die Bedeutung der Sprache). Zudem stellt sie grundlegende Fragen im Zusammenhang mit der Entwicklung von Philosophie, wie die Frage danach, was philosophisches Denken in verschiedenen historischen, kulturellen und sozio-ökonomischen Kontexten antreibt oder nach den Interessen, die hinter jeder Philosophiegeschichtsschreibung stehen. Interessant ist zudem, dass die Entwicklung einer Philosophiegeschichtsschreibung in Afrika momentan quasi direkt vor unseren Augen stattfindet, d.h. Debatten darüber, wer und was in den Kanon der Philosophie in Afrika hinein gehört oder nicht, werden unter den afrikanischen Kollegen_innern heute geführt. Erste Tendenzen der Ausgrenzung sind allerdings auch hier bereits zu verzeichnen: Da die Philosophie der Gegenwart von Philosophen dominiert wird, zeichnet sich z.B. eine Marginalisierung der Philosophinnen und ihrer Konzepte bzw. philosophischer feministischer Theorien ab, der es möglichst heute schon entgegenzuwirken gilt.

4. Anstatt einer Conclusio

Anstelle einer abschließenden *Conclusio* möchte ich hier auf das am Anfang aufgeworfene Problem epistemischer Ungerechtigkeit zurückkommen. Wie kann epistemische (Fricker 2004) oder kognitive Ungerechtigkeit ("cognitive injustice", de Sousa Santos spricht hinsichtlich der Ignoranz gegenüber Wissenssystem des Südens auch von einem *Epistemicide*, 2014) korrigiert werden? Die akademische Philosophie wird heute stark von euro-amerikanischen Denkern_innen beeinflusst und geprägt, von deren Konzepten, Begriffen und Methoden. Beiträge aus anderen Regionen der Welt, aus anderen Kulturen (historischen wie auch gegenwärtigen) werden selten in Betracht gezogen. Ein Problem ist dabei bereits, dass diese monokulturelle Reduktion und Einschränkung des philosophischen Diskurses dabei meist nicht einmal als Mangel oder Defizit wahrgenommen wird.

Sicher liegt es nicht in unserer Hand, in naher Zukunft die politisch-ökonomischen Strukturen zu verändern, auf denen epistemische Ungerechtigkeit basiert. Aber als Philosophen_innen und Akademiker_innen liegt es durchaus in unseren Händen, unser Herangehen an philosophische Fragestellungen, Themen und Konzepte zu modifizieren und damit einen Beitrag für mehr akademische Gerechtigkeit in unseren jeweiligen Arbeitsfeldern zu leisten. Folgendes scheint mir hierbei von Bedeutung:

Erstens müssen sich Philosophen_innen selbstkritisch ihrer eigenen Kontextualität bewusst werden und deren Auswirkungen auf das eigene Denken und die eigenen philosophischen Konzepte. Hier können euro-amerikanische Philosophen_innen im Übrigen viel von ihren Kollegen_innen aus anderen Regionen der Welt lernen. Afrikanische Philosophen_innen sind sich der Verankerung ihres Denkens in ihrem jeweiligen historisch, politisch-ökonomisch, kulturell-religiös und sprachlich geprägten Kontext überaus bewusst, während euro-amerikanische Philosophen_innen oft unter Vernachlässigung einer Reflexion auf ihre eigene kontextuelle Gebundenheit universalgültige Theorien schaffen wollen.

Zweitens sollte es zum Grundprinzip akademischer Arbeit werden, ernsthafte Anstrengungen zu unternehmen, um Perspektiven aus anderen kulturellen, religiösen und politisch-ökonomischen Kontexten einzubeziehen und einen wirklichen interkulturellen Austausch philosophischer Ideen und Konzepte anzustreben.

Im speziellen Fall der Philosophiegeschichte bewegt sich die Herausforderung auf drei Ebenen:

- eine vertiefte Erforschung der Quellen der Philosophie in den verschiedenen Regionen der Welt (Vergangenheit)
- einer Untersuchung der Mechanismen, die zum fortwährenden Ausschluss von Denktraditionen führen (Gegenwart)
- und eine Reflexion auf die Frage: Wie wollen wir die Geschichte der Philosophie in Zukunft erzählen? (Zukunft).

Ziel muss es sein, eine neue Offenheit gegenüber philosophischen Traditionen und dem philosophischen Schaffen der Gegenwart in den verschiedenen Regionen der Welt zu entwickeln, um den 'westlichen' philosophischen Monolog zu unterbrechen und durch einen Dia- oder Polylog der verschiedenen Traditionen zu ersetzen, der sich letztlich nicht nur in der Forschung, sondern auch in der Gestaltung unserer Lehrpläne widerspiegeln muss.

Literaturliste

Aristoteles. 1987. *Metaphysik*. Stuttgart: Philipp Reclam Jun.

Asante, M. K. 2000. *The Egyptian Philosophers: Ancient African Voices from Imhotep to Akhenaten*. Chicago: African American Images.

Asante, M. K. 2010. 'Egypt'. In Irele and Jyifo 2010, I:335-338.

Bernal, M. 1987. *Black Athena: The Afro-Asiatic Roots of Classical Civilisation*. London: Free Association Books. (Dt.: 1992. *Schwarze Athene: die afroasiatischen Wurzeln der griechischen Antike; wie das klassische Griechenland "erfunden" wur*de. München: List.

Bernasconi, R. 1997. Philosophy's paradoxical parochialism: the reinvention of philosophy as Greek. In K. Anssell-Pearson, B. Parry, & J. Squires (Ed). *Cultural readings of imperialism*. London: Lawrence & Wishart, pp. 212-26.

Boele van Hensbroek, P. 1999. *Political discourses in African thought, 1860 to the Present*, Westport, Connecticut / London: Praeger.

Braun, L. 1990. *Geschichte der Philosophiegeschichte*. Ulrich Johannes (Ed) Schneider. Darmstadt: Wissenschaftliche Buchgesellschaft. [French original: *Histoire de l'histoire de la philosophie*. Paris: Ophrys 1973]

Bilolo, M. 1991. 'Die klassische ägyptische Philosophie. Ein Überblick'. In *Philosophie, Ideologie und Gesellschaft in Afrika, Wien 1989*. edited by Christian Neugebauer. Frankfurt am Main: Peter Lang, 199-212.

Diop, CA. 1954. *Nations nègres et culture: de l'antiquité nègre égyptienne aux problèmes culturels de l'Afrique noire d'aujourd'hui*. Paris: Présence Africaine.

Diop, C. A. 1974. *The African Origin of Civilization: Myth or Reality*. New York: L. Hill. (Contains translations of sections of *Antériorité des civilisations négres and Nations nègres et culture*).

Dussel, E. 2013a. *Ethics of liberation in the age of globalization and exclusion*. Durham, North Carolina: Duke University Press.

Dussel, E. 2013b. Agenda for a South-South Philosophical Dialogue. In *Human Architecture: Journal of the Sociology of Self-Knowledge*. Vol. 11: 1, Article 3. Available at: http://scholarworks.umb.edu/ humanarchitecture/ vol11/iss1/3

Fricker, M. 2007. *Epistemic injustice: power and the ethics of knowing*. Oxford: Oxford University Press.

Garfield, JL. & Edelglass, W. (Ed). 2011. *Oxford handbook of world philosophy*. New York: Oxford University Press.

Goody, J. 1986. *The logic of writing and the organization of society*. Cambridge: Cambridge University Press.

Graness, A. 2015. Is the debate on 'Global Justice' a global one? Some Considerations in View of Modern Philosophy in Africa. In *Journal of Global Ethics*, Vol. 11:1, pp. 126-140. DOI: 10.1080/ 17449626.2015.1010014.

Hallen, B. 2009. *A short history of African philosophy*. 2nd ed. Bloomington: Indiana University Press; first edition: 2002.

Havelock, EA. 1988. *The muse learns to write: reflections on orality and literacy from antiquity to the present*. New Haven CT: Yale University Press.

Hegel, GWF. 1994. *Vorlesungen über die Philosophie der Weltgeschichte*. Band I: Die Vernunft in der Geschichte, Hrsg. J. Hoffmeister, Hamburg: Felix Meiner Verlag.

Hegel, GWF. 1982. *Vorlesungen über die Geschichte der Philosophie*. Leipzig: Verlag Philipp Reclam jun.

Heit, H. 2007. *Der Ursprungsmythos der Vernunft: zur philosophischen Genealogie des griechischen Wunders*. Würzburg: Königshausen & Neumann.

Irele, F. A. and B. Jyifo (eds.) 2010. *The Oxford Encyclopedia of African Thought.* New York: Oxford University Press.

Jacob, A. (Ed). 1989. *Encyclopédie philosophique universelle.* Paris: Presses Universitaires de France.

Karenga, M. 2004. *Maat: The Moral Ideal in Ancient Egypt.* Los Angeles: University of Sankore Press.

Kimmerle, H. 1991. *Philosophie in Afrika–Afrikanische Philosophie: Annäherungen an einen interkulturellen Philosophiebegriff.* Frankfurt am Main: Campus Verlag.

Kimmerle, H. 1994. *Die Dimension des interkulturellen: Philosophie in Afrika–afrikanische Philosophie.* Amsterdam: Rodopi.

Kimmerle, H. 2005. *Afrikanische Philosophie im Kontext der Weltphilosophie.* Nordhausen: Traugott Bautz Verlag.

Kresse, K. 2007. *Philosophising in Mombasa: knowledge, Islam and intellectual practice on the Swahili coast.* Edinburgh University Press.

Lefkowitz, M. & Rogers, GM. (Ed). 1996. *Black Athena revisited.* Chapel Hill: The University of North Carolina Press.

Masolo, D. A. 1994. *African Philosophy in Search of Identity.* Bloomington: Indiana University Press.

Ndjana, H. M. 2009. *Histoire de la philosophie africaine,* Paris: L'Harmattan.

Ngũgĩ wa Thiong'o. 1993. *Moving the Centre: The Struggle for Cultural Freedoms.* London: James Currey Publishers.

Obenga, T. 1990. *La Philosophie africaine de la période pharaonique 2780-330 avant notre ère,* Paris: L'Harmattan.

Odera Oruka, H. 1997. *Practical Philosophy. In Search of an Ethical Minimum.* Nairobi/Kampala: East African Educational Publishers.

Park, PKJ. 2013. *Africa, Asia, and the history of philosophy: racism in the formation of the philosophical canon, 1780-1830.* Albany: State University of New York Press.

Santos, Boaventura de Sousa. 2014. *Epistemologies of the South. Justice against Epistemicide.* Boulder/London: Paradigm Publishers.

Schneider, U.J. 1990. *Die Vergangenheit des Geistes. Eine Archäologie der Philosophiegeschichte.* Frankfurt: Suhrkamp Verlag.

Schneider, U.J. 1999. *Philosophie und Universität. Historisierung der Vernunft im 19. Jahrhundert.* Hamburg: Felix Meiner Verlag.

Van Binsbergen, W. 2009-2010. 'Before the Pre-Socratics'. Special issue of *Quest: An African Journal of Philosophy/Revue Africaine de Philosophie* 23-24:1-2.

Van Parijs, P. 2011. *Linguistic Justice for Europe and for the World.* Oxford: Oxford University Press.

Wimmer, F. 1990. *Interkulturelle Philosophie. Geschichte und Theorie.* Band 1, Wien: Passagen-Verlag.

Wiredu, K. 1996. *Cultural Universals and Particulars: An African Perspective.* Bloomington, Indiana University Press.

ELISABETH LIST

CARE, CARE WORK AND LIFE

Of course, it is only care work that can be an issue for economy, be it political economy or specifically feminist economy. Care work has become the most present topic for feminist economists, and also in their accounts the moral and affective components of care remain in the background. But just these are essential for care that cannot be treated in terms of economy, be it feminist or otherwise. Looking at dictionaries, we learn, that care means carefulness, assistance and support, to be considered, to support, attending the need of the other, to provide und to look for someone, care and diligence, prudence and cautiousness.

In short: Caring is a social act and activity. It is addressed to somebody, attached to somebody who needs help, to care for her or him. Caring is social action. What are its specific properties? It means a relation of attention and affection. What can be said about it in an economic frame of thinking?

Not much. Caring is focused on those people in charge of caring. It is about relating with this people, being in touch with them. A theoretical framework of economy that reduces relation to others to acts of exchange of goods and commodities must by definition fail to deal with care properly.

More than that: A conceptual framework taking production and its organization as its main topic, even its exclusive one, give a full picture of the human condition? To doubt this seems to question the adequacy of the whole project of the Marxism project to reflect of what it means to be a human being. What would be an adequate framework or mode of conceptualization of that issue? I will not give an answer to this question.

From a feminist perspective it is the concrete, embodied person in need of care that is of concern that is not present in an economic process.

Therefore I propose to take the issue of life as central to the feminist approach – as well as for a Marxist one. The required transformation of Marxist thinking would require a fundamental change of the way how the issue of relatedness to others can be made visible and how that could be made part of the Marxist view of the world.

We can start with Marx. What is clear from reading Marx' first volume of *Kapital* is that he is fully aware of the questions raised by feminists. What he calls concrete and materialist, is the day-to-day requirements and necessities of life.

To live and to survive the first necessities are food, nourishment and housing. To fulfill these primary needs humans must actively intervene with the surrounding nature. It means to establish an efficient exchange with nature, that means she has to work so that she can get from nature what she and her family needs to survive.

This is the point of departure of Marx´ Critique of political economy. Because the issues of exchange of goods for survival have the priority for Marx, the issue of relatedness to the other disappears from his image of the economic condition.

Now there is another question: What is nature? Looking for relevant information about nature I went to the section on Nature in the library of our philosophical department, and I discovered that 90 percent of the books in this section in the library where books about Physics. So philosophers seem to see nature as a huge reservoir of materials, material for technologists.

What is nature?

If you look back in the history of philosophy, you will find a much more plausible definition of nature. For instance in Aristotles' work. According to him "Natura" is what is born – nascere –, which flourishes, and dies. That means that humans themselves are of this kind, they are part of nature as life process. They are living creatures, who are born, are cared for, leading their life, and die. And as in all species of mammals, his or her life is bound to the presence of others who take part in his and her life in many respects.

I take the position of Aristotles. What we can call nature, are all forms of living, "Formen des Lebendigen", as we say in German. Human life is a form of living, a peculiar form of living among many other leaving creatures, it is embedded in a whole network of living.

From a materialist point of view being a living form is the essential feature of what it means to be human. The Marxist concept of materialism however is more specific and more narrow. It takes as the primary feature of human life one specific aspect of this form of life – the capacity and at the same time necessitiy to survive by enganging together into an interaction with the surrounding forms of nature to acquire the necessary goods and *that means to work to materially reproduce his or her bodily life.* This is evidently true, but this form of reproduction is essentially depending on a network of relationships with other humans. As feminists know, we are social beings.

Marx' image of the human being does not succeed to overcome the traditional intellectualist image of humans as "men of reason", which has been frequently been the target of feminist criticism. On the other hand, he did, what philosophers mostly have not done, he conceived of the human being as a living creature. For many philosophers, for many people, especially academics and educated people, this has long been more or less as a triviality. We are living creatures, so what?

A triviality: Something one takes for granted, but not a relevant issue for further considerations.

Is it really a triviality? Indeed, it has long been as something taken for granted, but in the last decades it has become clear that the question of life is no longer a triviality, but more and more problematic, because there are tendencies and developments in the field of what Wolf Haug calls "High-Tech-Capitalism" that endanger this elementary level of life conditions, endanger and even destroy it. Living structures are open for control, manipulation, and, a consequence, take the form of a commodities at the market place. The main forces to install a perfect control of all forms of life are today technology and science.

It is not necessary to tell the whole story of the adventures and failures of *Prometeus unbound,* as Landes poetic Phrase for the adventures of Technology and Science in their conquest for the domination of life (Landes 1973). Its relentless striving to control the whole universe of Nature in the name of human success, and that meant in modern times the striving for profit, has resulted in the last century in a series of social and cultural disasters:

- The pollution of environment, rivers, lakes, seas, fields and woods,

- The destructive results of war industries and wars,

- The deadly dangers of atomic energy,

to name just the most dramatic ones.

All this phenomena have in the last decades given rise to a forceful movement of ecological and feminist critique, a critical assessment of the developments of the industrial and postindustrial capitalist system.

Marx at his time had a rather optimistic attitude toward both natural sciences and technology. We should not blame him for that, because in his lifetime the positive accomplishments of scientific and technological developments were more visible and convincing. Now, times have changed and this is a signal for a necessary transformation of the design of the Marxian project. And surely the presence of a strong feminist voice will contribute to this endeavor.

What kind of Transformation?

To start with a question: Why was the relation between Marxism and Feminism been regarded as an "unhappy marriage"?

The reason for that was the issue of social reproduction. Marx ignored the role and the contribution of women's work to the whole business of social reproduction. This can be shown in detail from the writings of Marx and Marxists. As for example Silvia Federici (Federici 2012) has done. What could be done about it? The design of Marxist theory, as most theories we know, has a certain hegemonic structure. One example: The debate about the so-called "Hauptwiderspruch" and "Nebenwiderspruch". There may be more than one topic of relevance, but one of them must have priority from the Marxist theoretical perspective. This topic is for Marx the question of wage labour in Capitalism. This is the main point of Marx and his Political Economy.

One example: There is in biology not only the race for "survival of the fittest", as a certain form of Darwinism wants to have it. Recent developments in the life sciences have shown, that also principles of cooperation are at work in the process of evolution. The human body is a good example for that. Parts of our organism have evolved as living forms in their own, before they where integrated in the human organism. Our organism not only is hosting millions of bacteria and other microorganism, but is living by them. It does not follow the one "principle of life".

Prominent biologists have therefore stopped to seek the *one* theory of life, but instead tell the story about the history of the multiplicity of life forms. This is a significant shift away from hierarchical thinking, resembling some positions of postmodernity. A shift away from universalist "master theories".

Now let's go back to the controversy of feminism and Marxism. Refering to the mentioned talk of "Hauptwiderspruch" and "Nebenwiderspruch", some people might argue, that the right way to „fight" would be to overturn the old hierarchy and have it the other way, making Womens´ issue the main cause, and the Marxist issue a secondary issue. We instead should give up the style of hierarchic thinking we know from the classical theories. We should stop thinking in hicrarchies and in theories of this type. We should turn from abstract theories to concrete practice. We should begin to understand that it is as irrelevant as it is wrong to quarrel about which principle should have priority. Debates about the priority of principles are not about nature, but about power, hegemony.

When we turn to concrete practice we are confronted with problems in concrete situations of activities, be it activities of production or social reproduction calling for a solution, a solution through concrete situated action or interaction. What counts here is to find a solution for the practical problem at hand. This solution might call for an answer from a feminist point of view, if it is a question of social reproduction like care, or it might call for actions in terms of class struggle or production in the Marxist framework of critique.

In short: It is the concrete historical moment of involving, intervening in a problematic context that decides which perspective to take. *In this sense, feminism is a perspective, a perspective of action, maybe a struggle, and not a theory.* Feminists will take the perspective of Marxist political economy, if the problem at hand requires it. If we understand that both Marxism and Feminism are historically situated, seeing them in this way, there is no contradiction between

Marxism and Feminism. But to see that means to say farewell to universal knowledge claims on both sides. This is of course difficult for those who are deeply committed to one of these "Master Theories". Also Marxist Thinking is bound to such a type of a "master theory".

To sum up: The Transformation required is to give up such claims of theoretical hegemony.

References

Federici Silvia. *Aufstand aus der Küche. Reproduktionsarbeit im globalen Kapitalismus und die unvollendete feministische Revolution*. Münster: Edition Assemblage, 2012.

Landes David S. *Der entfesselte Prometheus. Technologischer Wandel und industrielle Entwicklung in Westeuropa von 1750 bis zur Gegenwart*. Köln: Kiepenheuer und Wietsch, 1973.

BIRGE KRONDORFER

FEMINISTISCHE EINWÜRFE ZU ANARCHIE UND AUTONOMIE
AKTUELLE PARADOXIEN VON ‚SELBST'-BESTIMMUNG

> Was in der postmodernen Kultur hauptsächlich zur Macht der
> Macht beiträgt, ist der Wille, in erster Person Erfolg zu haben, an-
> erkannt und bewundert zu werden, in den Augen anderer mit der
> eigenen Einmaligkeit zu existieren. (Muraro 2014, 75)

Ein Anarchismus, der ‚Regierung' grosso modo ablehnt, kann nicht mehr ‚unschuldig' proklamiert werden. Unsere Gesellschaften lassen sich reflektieren als solche, wo der Anarchismus hinter der Maske von Recht und Ordnung schon an der Macht ist und das Schauspiel von Recht und Ordnung eine obszöne Karnevaleske darstellt (Zizek 2011). „Die bequeme anarchistische Geste, sich angesichts des staatssozialistischen Zusammenbruchs im Recht fühlend auf die Schulter zu klopfen, ist nur zu einem Teil angebracht. [...] Denn heute sind nicht nur skurrile ‚Anarchokapitalisten', sondern überhaupt die Offenheit libertärer Ideale für eine der brutalsten Formen des Kapitalismus erklärungsbedürftig. Die meisten ehemals libertär inspirierten ‚68er' sind mittlerweile zu TrägerInnen des Neoliberalismus mutiert, zentrale libertäre Begriffe wie Selbstbestimmung, Kreativität und Autonomie werden nicht selten antikollektivistisch gewendet und kooptiert" (Kastner o.J.). Das Libertäre durchzieht die westlichen Gesellschaften (Konsum- und sexuelle Freiheit, selbstbestimmte (Gender-) Identitäten etc.), aber völlig eingeschrumpft auf einen Individualismus, der mit Struktur-, Gesellschaft- und Politikkritik nichts zu tun hat.

„Angesichts des Ungeheuerlichen, das sich uns groß und mächtig aufzwingt und gerade dabei ist, das Gewebe der Welt zu zerstören", schreibt eine Autorin des Buches ‚Macht und Politik sind nicht dasselbe' (Zamboni 2012, 152), möchte sie über das Wenige sprechen, das ihr und uns zur Verfügung steht. Dabei geht es um ein politisches Begehren, von dem ein Subjekt besetzt ist, um den Einsatz der Leidenschaften, der persönlichen Beziehungen, des Denkens und dass dadurch, dass dieses sich ereignet, das Subjektive überschritten wird. „In anderen Worten: Das Begehren nach Politik ist ein ‚Mehr' gegenüber den Notwendigkeiten unseres Lebens. Es ist diskontinuierlich in Bezug auf die objektiven Kräfte der Realität und schafft darin den kleinen Spalt einer Öffnung. Es ist etwas Unvorhergesehenes in der Welt der Fakten. Dass wir diese Liebe zur Politik spüren, kann uns auch dann passieren, wenn alles, wirklich alles, ihr entgegenzustehen scheint" (ebenda, 153). Lange Zeit, seit Mitte des 19. Jahrhunderts in anarchistischen Strömungen, seit Mitte des 20. Jahrhunderts in autonomen Bewegungen – und minoritär bis heute – war Selbstbestimmung[1] wesentlicher Kristallisationspunkt einer politischen Modellierung, die Kräfte im Prozess des Umsturzes der gesellschaftlichen Situation intensivieren wollte, verknüpft mit der Befreiung der Einzelnen.

Im Folgenden[2] wird zum einen der feministische Topos der Selbstbestimmung in den Konzepten von Anarchie und Autonomie gegen- und ineinander verhandelt und zum weiteren wird ‚Selbstbestimmung' bzw. ‚Autonomie' als Kategorie am Horizont des verschwindenden Politischen befragt. Ist sie heute (noch) brauchbar für etwas Unvorgesehenes, für „den kleinen Spalt einer Öffnung"?

(Fem)Anarchismus, Autonome Frauen – Herrschaftslosigkeit oder Selbstgesetzgebung

Einerseits scheinen die Zugänge der beiden politischen Lehren und Aktionsformen im Grunde ganz ähnlich zu sein: in der Kritik an (staatlichen) Institutionen, in der basisdemokratischen Organisierung, in der Ablehnung aller Regierungsstrukturen, in der Negation jeglicher Hierarchie und der Positivierung der Selbstbestimmung, in der Selbstverwirklichung und im Begehren nach Freiheit. Louise Michel (1830-1905), anarchistische Kombattantin der Pariser Kommune (1871) schrieb: „Ich sah unsere Genossen am Werk, und nach und nach kam ich zu der Überzeugung, dass selbst die Redlichsten, könnten sie die Macht ausüben, den Schurken ähnlich würden, die sie einst bekämpften. Ich sah die Unmöglichkeit, dass sich die Freiheit mit einer wie auch immer gearteten Macht vereinbaren lässt. Ich fühlte, wenn die Revolution irgendeine Regierungsform annimmt, ist es um sie gesche-

---

[1] Nicht zu verwechseln mit Selbstdeklaration, wie es heute in queer-feministischen Kreisen angesagt ist (vgl. Staritz 2014).

[2] Der Text besteht in Teilen aus meinen Beiträgen „Short cuts zu einer Utopie" (2014) und „Selbstorganisierung im Widerstreit von Autonomie und Allianzen" (2012).

hen; und wenn Institutionen der Vergangenheit, die schon zu verschwinden schienen, doch bestehen bleiben – dann tragen sie nur ein anderes Etikett."[3] Jene historischen Anarchistinnen, die sich der Frauenfrage und der Gefahr der Übernahme von herkömmlicher Regierung bewusst waren, da diese nicht nur eine Unterwerfung unter strukturelle Gewalt bedeutet, sondern sie auch wiederholt, können retrospektiv als Vorläuferinnen des autonomen Feminismus gesehen werden.

Historische Hintergründe und ideelle Gemeinsamkeiten

Auch die Kritik des Feminismus an der Arbeiterbewegung als Gesamtsubjekt gesellschaftlicher Progression, wird in der Geschichte des Anarchismus vorgezeichnet, wenn man die Entstehung des Anarchismus innerhalb der Arbeiter(innen)-Bewegung mit einbezieht, die geprägt war von Grabenkämpfen zwischen Kommunisten und Anarchisten. Seit Mitte des 19. Jahrhunderts entwickelte sich im frühkapitalistischen Nordwesten Europas als Gegenbewegung der Sozialismus. „Rasch formten sich aus den Diskussionen und Flügelkämpfen zwei Hauptströmungen heraus, die sich auf der radikalen Seite der Bewegung an zwei Namen festmachen lassen: Karl Marx für den autoritären und Michael Bakunin für den anti-autoritären Flügel der Arbeiterbewegung. Der Anarchismus hat [...] den größeren Anspruch an die moralischen und ethischen Werte der Menschen gestellt. Seine Ansprüche an eine unteilbare Freiheit für ALLE Menschen, sowie die kompromisslose Ablehnung jeglichen Elitedenkens und jeder Form von ‚vorübergehenden' Zugeständnissen an Machtstrukturen" (Degen, Knoblauch 2006) standen der kommunistischen Fixierung auf den Staat und das Proletariat als Befreiungsträger diametral gegenüber: „Wer Herr der Geschichte ist und ihr den Rhythmus des Fortschritts aufzwingt, wer das sichere und unaufhaltsame Fortschreiten der kommunistischen Zivilisation bestimmt, das sind nicht die ‚Halbstarken', das ist nicht das Lumpenproletariat, das sind nicht die Bohemiens, die Dilettanten, die langhaarigen und frenetischen Romantiker, sondern das sind die großen Massen der klassenbewussten Arbeiter, die stählernen Bataillone des bewussten und disziplinierten Proletariats" (Gramsci 1919). Die perspektivische Differenz zeigt sich auch in einem Slogan von

---

[3] Zit. aus: http://www.anarchismus.at/anarchistische-klassiker/louise-michel/68-louise-michel-warum-ich-anarchistin-wurde

Louise Michel: „Nicht die Paläste sollen brennen, sondern die hässlichen und verpesteten Hütten."[4] Und sie zeigt sich, zumindest ideell, auch in Schnittstellen zu einem selbstorganisierten Feminismus, weil „es beiden nicht darum geht, ein festes Programm voranzutreiben, sondern darum, Räume zu schaffen, wo man sich freiheitlich auseinandersetzen kann über das, was man eigentlich möchte. [...] Da sehe ich auch viele Parallelen zum Feminismus. Es geht mir nicht um eine Gleichstellung von Frauen in Bezug auf das, was die Männer bisher schon gemacht haben, sondern, was mich interessiert sind Ideen von Frauen darauf hin, was man anders machen kann. Da sehe ich viele Parallelen zum Anarchismus, der ja eben auch nicht den Ansatz hatte, dass sich die Arbeiter in das bestehende parlamentarische System integrieren, [...] dass es darum geht, zu verhandeln, wie man das Politische überhaupt anders denken kann und wie man Regeln auf eine andere Weise finden kann, als durch die bestehenden staatlichen Strukturen" (Schrupp 2013).

Auch an Motiven von Emma Goldmann (1869-1940), einer weiteren großen Anarchistin, kann die Distanzierung von der kommunistischen / sozialistischen Anrufung des Rechts auf Erwerbsarbeit sowie die feministische Kritik an Gleichstellungspolitik, die sich gegen die Einpassung an das (Wirtschafts- und Arbeits-) System wendet, anknüpfen. „Freiheit und Gleichheit für die Frau! [...] Auch meine Hoffnungen richten sich auf dieses Ziel, jedoch glaube ich, dass die Emanzipation der Frau, wie sie heute interpretiert und auch gelebt wird, nicht dorthin führen kann. Es ist heute für die Frau notwendig geworden, sich von der Emanzipation zu emanzipieren, will sie wirklich frei sein. [...] Die Emanzipation hat der Frau wirtschaftliche Gleichberechtigung gebracht; d.h. sie kann sich ihren eigenen Beruf und ihr eigenes Handwerk wählen; da sie jedoch nach wie vor physisch nicht in jedem Fall in der Lage ist, es mit dem Mann aufzunehmen, muß sie oft alle ihr zur Verfügung stehenden Kräfte aufwenden, [...] um den Marktwert zu erreichen. Und nur ein Bruchteil ist erfolgreich, denn nachweislich wird den Lehrerinnen, Ärztinnen, Rechtsanwältinnen, Architektinnen und weiblichen Ingenieuren weder das gleiche Vertrauen wie ihren männlichen Kollegen entgegengebracht, noch werden sie gleich bezahlt. Und die, die tatsächlich die so verlockende Gleichstellung erreichen, erreichen sie größtenteils auf Kosten ihres physischen

---

[4] Zit. aus: http://www.anarchismus.at/anarchistische-klassiker/louise-michel

und psychischen Wohlergehens. Wieviel Unabhängigkeit ist erreicht, wenn die Masse der arbeitenden Frauen und Mädchen die Borniertheit und den Mangel an Freiheit zuhause eintauscht gegen die Borniertheit und den Mangel an Freiheit in der Fabrik, den Ausbeutungsbetrieben, im Kaufhaus oder Büro? Dazu kommt die Belastung vieler Frauen, die nach einem harten Arbeitstag sich auch noch um Heim und Herd kümmern müssen. [...] Was für eine herrliche Unabhängigkeit! Kein Wunder, daß so viele junge Mädchen, die ihre ‚Unabhängigkeit' hinter dem Ladentisch, der Näh- oder Schreibmaschine gründlich satt haben, jede Möglichkeit zu heiraten sofort wahrnehmen."[5] Bestürzend diese Ähnlichkeit der prekären Situation des Lebens- und Arbeitszusammenhangs der meisten Frauen heute und vor 100 Jahren. Aktuell geht es längst nicht mehr um ein Recht auf Arbeit als Projekt der Selbstverwirklichung und Unabhängigkeit, auch wenn das allerorten behauptet wird, sondern die Frauen werden in der EU aus Gründen der Wettbewerbsfähigkeit durch Ausnützung aller Humanressourcen dazu angehalten, am Arbeitsmarkt teilzunehmen – egal unter welchen Bedingungen.

AnarchistInnen und feministisch Bewegte teilen die Wahrnehmung, dass „wenn ich mich an die Welt halte, so wie sie ist, diese Welt schon vollständig den Vorstellungen und der Macht anderer unterliegt, und mir nur die Alternative zwischen der Anpassung und der Entfremdung bleibt. Aber für diejenigen, die bereit sind, zu erfinden, ist die Welt neu und groß, sie ist nicht schon besetzt, und es ist nicht notwendig, an Quoten und Aufteilungen zu denken" (Muraro 1991). Es geht um die Möglichkeit, andere imaginäre und konkrete Bezugsrahmen zu erinnern und zu setzen. Im historischen Teil einer frauenfreundlichen Lektüre „Freiheit pur. Die Idee der Anarchie, Geschichte und Zukunft" (Stowasser 1995) wird u.a. das Patriarchat als Herrschaftsform kritisch reflektiert und unter dem Titel ‚Mama Anarchija – Vom weiblichen Urgrund der Freiheit' vom Matriarchat als d e r Form einer herrschaftslosen Gesellschaft gesprochen.[6] „Die Frau war und blieb in dieser Kultur als Schöpferin auch die Handlungsträgerin der Geschichte. Insofern waren diese Gesellschaften zwar matrifokal und matrilinear [...], aber die Idee einer Herrschaft wie sie uns geläufig ist,

---

[5] Zit. aus: http://www.marxists.org/deutsch/referenz/goldman/1911/aufsaetze/frau.htm
[6] Das Problem von Remythologisierung / projektive Erfindung matriarchaler Ursprungsgeschichte wird hier nicht diskutiert. Es würde den Argumentationsrahmen sprengen.

passte offenbar ebensowenig zu dem ‚kreativen Grundprinzip' des Matriarchats wie Gewalt, privilegierte Klassen oder privater Grundbesitz" (ebenda, 150). Der Autor fragt sich, wie mit dem Begriff des ‚Matriarchats' umzugehen sei, steckt doch auch darin die ‚Herrschaft'. Erklärend wird argumentiert, dass unsere Sprache einerseits einfach keinen adäquaten Begriff für diese Gemeinschaftsform hat und dass zum anderen die im altgriechischen Wort ‚arché' steckende Bedeutung ‚Anfang, Prinzip, Ursprung' hier zum Tragen kommt. „Am Anfang war die Mutter [...]. Und das trifft die Sache" (ebenda). An dieser Stelle läßt sich – wiewohl sie sich selbst nicht in einem Naheverhältnis zum Anarchismus verorten – eine Verbindung zu den (italienischen) Denkerinnen der sexuellen Differenz andenken, insofern sie politisch auf die ‚symbolische Ordnung der Mutter' rekurrieren. Im Zentrum dieser feministischen Philosophie „steht nicht die Mütterlichkeit als ethische oder psychologische Qualität, sondern die Beziehung zur Mutter als symbolische Form, die ihrerseits soziale Formen hervorbringt, die eher durch sprachliche Vermittlung als durch Gesetze gekennzeichnet sind."[7] Wenn sich Frauen (und Männer) in die Genealogie der Mutter begeben, wenn die weibliche Autorität über die gesellschaftlich konstituierte Macht gestellt wird – „wenn ich im Symbolischen kreativ bin –, dann ist das eine andere Welt, aber auf die Art und Weise, die am praktischsten und realistischsten ist" (Muraro 1991).

Vergegenwärtigungen und Divergenzen

Unterschieden jedoch waren und sind Anarchistinnen vom autonom-feministischen Zugang durch die dauernde Operation in gemischtgeschlechtlichen Zusammenhängen. Bezogen auf den spanischen Bürgerkrieg z.B. und die in diesem Zusammenhang enstandene Bewegung der Mujeres Libres, der 20000 Frauen angehörten, wird beschrieben, dass die emanzpierten Frauen „schon damals ihre Forderungen nicht nur gegenüber der reaktionär-patriarchalen Gesellschaft durchzusetzen hatten, sondern zunehmend gezwungen waren, sich in ihrem eigenen politischen Milieu Gehör, Verständnis und Respekt zu verschaffen. [...] Und so mancher [...] Anarchist dürfte es als selbstverständlich angesehen haben, dass er Abend für Abend auf anarchisti-

---

[7] Zit. aus: http://www.traum-symbolika.com/foren-austausch/manuskripte-frauen/luisa-muraro-die-symbolische-ordnung/

sche Meetings, Streikversammlungen oder libertäre Debattierclubs gehen konnte, während seine companera daheim Küche und Kinder zu hüten hatte" (Stowasser 1995, 49). Auch die anarchistische Bewegung existiert nicht jenseits der Andrarchie. Um nur ein weiteres geschichtliches Beispiel unter vielen zu zitieren: „Die sich Anfang der 1920er Jahre gründenden syndikalistischen Frauenbünde sahen sich zudem dem Vorwurf der Spaltung, des Dualismus und des Separatismus ausgesetzt. Die stetige Sabotage männlicher Anarchisten brachte die Bünde schon Mitte der 1920er zum Erliegen" (Wamper 2011). Wie entsprechenden Internetforen zu entnehmen ist, existieren bis heute ,Frauenprobleme' in männlich dominierten anarchistischen Gruppen. Auch fällt der Mangel an eigenständigen feministisch-anarchistischen Manifestationen auf, aktuelle originäre Positionen sind schwierig auszumachen, es wird auf altbekannte Anarchistinnen zurückgegriffen, bzw. auf feministische / queere Texte verwiesen.[8] Heute reklamieren Anarchisten feministisches Gedankengut als genuin anarchistisch, sie verdrehen auch die Diskussion um den Anarchafeminismus hin zum überheblichen männlichen Gestus gegen den Separatismus der autonomen Frauenbewegung. Und statt sich mit dem Sexismus in den eigenen Reihen zu beschäftigen, setzt sich der bereits historische Vorwurf der Spaltung bis heute fort (nach ebenda). Darin unterscheiden sich anarchistische Zirkel nicht von anderen linken Kontexten: auch revolutionäre Frauen müssen einen doppelten Kampf führen, für das allgemeine Ziel und gegen die eigenen Genossen. Selbstbestimmung, Selbstorganisation und Solidarität, hohe anarchistische Güter, obliegen einer männlich-hegemonialen Mentalität der Genossen.

Im Fokus der radikal frauenbewegten Kämpfe stand jedoch immer das Patriarchat, auch als Grundlage des Kapitalismus, bzw. die Männerherrschaft. Um dieser zu entgehen, gründete sich im Laufe der Entwicklung der Zweiten Frauenbewegung der autonome Flügel als eigenständige Organisierung von Frauen, mit Frauen, für Frauen. Auch die unterschiedliche Benennung verweist auf grundlegende Differenzen im Zugang zum selbstbestimmten politischen Raum und zur ideengeschichtlichen Basis. Autonomie heißt Selbstgesetzlichkeit,

---

[8] Vgl. die Plattform: http://www.anarchismus.at/anarcha-feminismus/ anarchafeministisches. Silke Lohschelder, Mitautorin des solitären Einführungsbandes in den Anarchafeminismus (2009), warnt sogar vor einer Einverleibung des Feminismus in den Anarchismus.

Anarchie wird allgemein mit Herrschaftslosigkeit übersetzt. Autonomie, feministisch gewendet, ist weder individualistisch, noch als „bloße Abgrenzung von bestehenden Verhältnissen zu verstehen. Als solche aufgefasst wäre sie rein negativ bestimmt oder Autarkie (Selbstgenügsamkeit). Selbst wenn es darum geht, von Beherrschung frei zu sein, ist damit noch keineswegs die Frage danach gestellt [...], wofür wir frei sein sollen und worin diese Freiheit besteht. In dieser positiven Bestimmung des ‚für' bedeutet Autonomie die permanente Bewegung gemeinsamer Setzung unserer Regeln" (Krondorfer et al 1991, 14). Herrschaftslosigkeit hingegen, gefasst als reine Freiheit, bleibt immer abstrakt; ihre Konkretion stößt notwendig an Grenzen, u.a. an die Ambivalenz von sozialer und individueller Befreiung. Oder an jene, dass kein Gebilde ohne Macht auskommt, und es von daher sinnvoll ist, dieses Phänomen zu reflektieren, bevor es hinterrücks zur Herrschaft mutiert. Denn „die subjektive Tugend, die bloß von der Gesinnung aus regiert, bringt die fürchterlichste Tyrannei mit sich" (Hegel 1924). Einen selbstreflektierten Anarchismus plagt, wie andere systemkritische Bewegungen auch, das Problem, dass es ein Leben außerhalb der Verhältnisse nicht gibt. Selbst die Kritik muss sich immer auf das beziehen, was sie angreift; im anarchistischen Fall der Abschaffung des Staates „muss sich der Anarchist über die Bedingung der Möglichkeit für seine Zweifel täuschen: Wenn er die Autorität des Staates in Zweifel stellt, hat er diese immer schon vorausgesetzt" (Rinderle 2005, 26). Eine Schwierigkeit bleibt also das Problem der Voraussetzung einer jeden Setzung. Es existiert keine Gründung, aber auch keine Begründung ohne Setzung; auch keine Eigengesetzlichkeit oder Gesetzlosigkeit existiert ohne ‚Gesetzmäßigkeit'.

Das verweist auf die zweite Bedeutung von ‚arché' als ‚Anfang', die m.e. einen semantischen Mangel bei den meisten AnarchistInnen darstellt; sie übersetzen arché zumeist mit Herrschaft und unterschlagen damit einen wesentlichen Teil der herkünftigen Bedeutung. Was aber impliziert ‚Anfangslosigkeit', bzw. was wird hier nicht mitbedacht? Wenn jeder Anfang negiert werden muss, entsteht, ähnlich dem Problem der Voraussetzung, die Dynamik eines Regresses ad infinitum; damit ist in Folge auch die Frage des bisherigen anarchistischen Scheiterns angesprochen, nämlich wie die erkämpften Errungenschaften zu bewahren sind, wenn Setzungen oder Satzungen nicht gelten dürfen. Umgekehrt kann dem Anarchismus affirmativ unterstellt werden, dass er in der Ablehnung der Anerkennung des (bewussten) Anfangs einen jeden Anfang auflösen will, weil er im Kern die Problematik der Identität von ‚Herrschaft' und Anfang unbewusst erkennt und ablehnt. Ein bekannter anarchistischer Theoretiker schrieb bereits zu Beginn des letzten Jahrhunderts: „Die Anarchisten müssen einsehen: ein Ziel läßt sich nur erreichen, wenn das Mittel schon in der Farbe dieses Zieles gefärbt ist. Nie kommt man durch Gewalt zur Gewaltlosigkeit. Die Anarchie ist da, wo Anarchisten sind, wirkliche Anarchisten, solche Menschen, die keine Gewalt mehr üben. Die Anarchie ist nicht eine Sache der Zukunft, sondern der Gegenwart; nicht der Forderungen, sondern des Lebens. [...] Die alten Gegensätze von Zerstören und Aufbauen fangen an ihren Sinn zu verlieren; es handelt sich ums Formen des nie Gewesenen" (Landauer 1901).

Auch die autonome Frauenbewegung wollte noch nie Dagewesenes durch eine radikale Distanznahme zu institutionalisierter Politik, ihre Artikulation ungehörter Stimmen, ihre Streitbarkeit wider die Herrschaft, ihr Ringen um Freiheit zu neuen Lebens- und Liebensformen, ihre Kämpfe gegen Gewalt, Ausbeutung und Unterdrückung, ihre Proklamation einer bis dato unvorhergesehenen Autonomie, ihre Verwehrung gegen Stellvertretungsansprüche und Vereinnahmung durch Parteipolitik, ihre Umdeutung von Geschichte, Sprache und Denktradition. Doch „der feministische Selbstbestimmungsbegriff war kein Freibrief für das Ausagieren geschichtsloser Individualität an sich, sondern wurde im Zusammenhang mit der Veränderung jener Rahmenbedingungen verknüpft, die von anderen – sei es von androzentrischen Institutionen wie Kirche, Staat, Medizin oder von androzentrischen Interessenlagen – vorgegeben, gesetzt und kontrolliert wurden" (Trallori 2008, 158). Die Politik der Subjektivität verband sich in der Neuen Frauenbewegung mit emanzipatorischer Gesellschaftspolitik und kulturrevolutionären Entwürfen. Doch diese Geschichte liegt wie hinter Nebelschwaden verdeckt, denn das Hohelied der Autonomie lässt sich heute nicht mehr so ohne Weiteres anstimmen, es wurde vom neoliberalen Diskurs vereinnahmt und bis zur Unkenntlichkeit umgetrimmt. Es wird direkt auf die ständige ‚Selbstbestimmung' abgezielt. Selbstbestimmung und Selbstkontrolle sind wie in einem Vexierbild ineinander verzahnt. Die Neoliberalisierung ist zu diagnostizieren als eine Regierungsform, die unter dem Diktat der Wirtschaftlichkeit agiert und dies in die Sprache der Selbstverwirklichung gegossen hat. Die Freiheit der Selbstbestimmung wird heute zum Zwang dazu und so wird jede/r durch sich selbst zum Instrument einer Selbstregierung, die zugleich Prozess einer ‚innovativen' Subjektivierung ist. Jede ist selbst verantwortlich, wenn es ihr an Autonomie, Initiative, Flexibilität, Mobilität mangelt. Pointiert gesagt: Heute lässt sich sozusagen ‚Autonomie' nicht verweigern. Übertragen auf die politische Sphäre bedeutet dies, dass zivilgesellschaftliche Selbstbestimmung als Mitbestimmung nicht mehr eingeklagt werden muss, da alle zur Partizipation aufgerufen sind; Inklusion ist das Schlagwort der Zeit, Systemkonformität ist ihr Effekt.[9]

Demokratie, Selbstbestimmung und Freiheit

Die Einsicht, dass es weniger um scheinkonsensuale Prozesse denn um dissensuale Haltungen geht, wird auch in neueren radikaldemokratischen Theoremen und Entwürfen geteilt, die hier kursorisch eine Referenz finden, da die realexistierende Demokratie in Gefahr ist, zum Restposten einer neoliberal durchseuchten Globalisierung zu verkommen, in welcher der maskulinistische Ökonomismus zur eigentlichen Regierung mutiert ist und die res publica zum Verschwinden bringt. Anders ausgedrückt: die postideologische liberale Demokratie ist der Zwilling der spätkapitalistischen Marktideologie mit deren Effekten der Politikabstinenz, des Sozialabbaus, der Privatisierung, der Individualisierung, der Selbsttechnologisierung, der Zeitverknappung, des Mainstreamings, der ‚freien' Konsumenten, der Prekarisierung … .

---

[9] In den 1990er Jahren kam es durch kritische Theorie geprägten Feministinnen überhaupt nicht in den Sinn ‚Inklusion', die heutzutage bei fast allen minoritären Gruppen auf der Agenda steht, für einen positiven Wert zu halten. Im Gegenteil, es ging um Systemveränderung und das Problem der weiblichen Nicht/Anerkennung in diesem. „Es [...] geht darum [...] aus der Berechenbarkeit von Opposition und Kritik auszusteigen. Gegen jeden Systemzwang unberechenbar zu werden, Frauen trauen sich das nicht nur nicht zu – der jahrhundertealte Irrationalismus-Vorwurf wirkt – sondern sie wollen es auch nicht. Sie wollen einsteigen, was zu sagen haben, gesehen werden, die Stimme erheben. Es ist ein fatales Paradox. Wie soll frau ein System verändern, wenn diese Veränderung einzig darauf zielt, dass sie in diesem System endlich mal zur Geltung kommen will [...]" (Treusch-Dieter 2014, 26)?

Die Aufgabe einer emanzipativen Politik heute bestünde darin, die verschiedenen Stimmen des Protestes zu verbinden, ohne sie ihres Eigensinns zu berauben. Radikale Demokratie hielte uns vielmehr dazu an, den Dissens und den Antagonismus auszuhalten, denn die kleinste politische Einheit ist nicht das Individuum, sondern eine antagonistische Beziehung (Ernesto Laclau, nach Heil/Hetzel 2006, 7ff). Authentische politische Praxen folgen nicht einfach etablierten Regeln, sondern bemühen sich um deren permanente Setzung und Entsetzung. Denn Politik erschöpft sich nicht im parlamentarischen Disput, sondern beginnt erst dort, wo diejenigen Anteile der Bevölkerung, die nicht institutionell repräsentiert sind, die Einrichtung eines Anteils der Anteilslosen fordern. Widerstreit ist die Voraussetzung von Demokratie und die Möglichkeitsbedingung von politischer Kommunikation. Den Anderen erkenne ich erst dann wirklich an, wenn ich die Auseinandersetzung mit ihm aufnehme, nicht dagegen, wenn ich ihn bloß akzeptiere und damit vergleichgültige (Jacques Rancière, nach ebenda). Demokratie muss zum Synonym dafür werden, dass die ‚Mitte der Macht' leer bleibt. Diese ‚leere Mitte' ist ein anderer Name für die Perspektivität und Partikularität jeder Position im politischen Prozess, oder mit anderen Worten: für die Unmöglichkeit jeder im substantialistischen Sinne verstandenen Universalität. Das bedeutet die Abweisung aller Versuche, die leere Mitte mit totalisierenden Inhalten zu besetzen (Claude Lefort, nach ebenda). Es geht immer um die Offenheit einer ‚kommenden Demokratie'; einer Demokratie ohne Ausnahme, die genau dort Einspruch erhebt, wo die Diskurse über Menschenrechte und Demokratie zum obszönen Alibi verkommen. Die Demokratie denken heißt insofern primär ‚den Erstbesten denken, irgendwen, einen Beliebigen.' Das bedeutet auch, eine gefahrvolle Freiheit der einschläfernden Ruhe einer Unterjochung vorzuziehen (Jacques Derrida, nach ebenda).

Unvereinbar ist diese Perspektive mit jenen im aktuellen Regime propagierten permanenten Wahloptionen, libertären Individualitäten und postmodernen Selbstbezeichnungen. Die Technik neoliberaler Herrschaftsführung, in avancierten sozialwissenschaftlichen Studien ‚Gouvernementalität'[10] genannt, funktioniert im suggestiven Zugriff

---

[10] Im Anschluss an Michel Foucault, der diesen Begriff geprägt und bereits seit den späten 1970er Jahren in vielen Schriften ausgearbeitet hat, z.B. in „Gouvernementalität" (2003, 796 ff)

auf die Subjekte, indem diese zu ‚autonomen' Entscheidungen, Selbstkontrolle und freier Produktivität gefordert sind. Herrschaft und Eigenregie sind identisch geworden; keine/r spricht mehr von Fremdbestimmtheit, da diese ununterscheidbar mit Selbstbestimmung verkuppelt ist. „Die ‚Kunst des Regierens' – wie Foucault Gouvernementalität auch genannt hat – besteht in modernen Gesellschaften also nicht in erster Linie darin, repressiv zu sein, sondern in ‚nach innen verlagerter' Selbstdisziplinierung und Selbstbeherrschung. Analysiert wird eine Ordnung, die den Menschen, den Körpern, den Dingen nicht nur aufgezwungen wird, sondern von der sie gleichzeitig aktiver Teil sind. Nicht die Frage nach der Regulierung autonomer, freier Subjekte steht im Mittelpunkt der Problematisierung gouvernementaler Regierungstechniken, sondern die Regulierung der Verhältnisse, durch die sogenannte autonome und freie Subjekte überhaupt erst zu solchen werden" (Lorey 2006). Zur Frage steht, was gegenwärtig unter ‚weiblicher Freiheit' eigentlich noch verstanden werden kann, wenn „die selbstbestimmten Entscheidungen [...], die den Frauen heute aufgedrängt werden, sie nicht mehr zu gesetzestreuem Verhalten [zwingen], sondern zu innerer Gleichschaltung. Sie zielen auf ihr Denken und Wünschen" (Samerski 2003, 213). Die bizarre Situation für feministische Politiken, die Selbstbestimmung von und für Frauen nach wie vor reklamieren, bestünde nun darin, die ‚freie Wahl' zu verweigern, da verschiedenste Lebenswirklichkeiten wie „die Supermutti, die erfolgreiche Unternehmerin und die Notstandshilfe-Empfängerin durch diese herrschaftlichen Subjektivierungsweisen" (Sauer 2008, 26) produziert werden. Wie lässt sich da für eine (widerständige) Handlungsmöglichkeiten votieren, wenn jede Handlungsfähigkeit bereits kontaminiert, jede Option bereits kooptiert ist?

Da Frauen (noch) nicht gänzlich in der ‚schönen neuen Welt'[11] angekommen bzw. aufgesogen sind, bleibt die denkwürdige Lage, von einer mit nichts zu legitimierenden sozialen und symbolischen Ungleichheit ausgehend, doch die Un(gleich)artigkeit als Hoffnung auf Alternativen zu rechtfertigen. Veränderungen lassen sich nicht nur

---

[11] Womit selbstredend die postindustrielle nordwestliche Hemisphäre gemeint ist; inklusive des allgemeinen nicht wahrgenommenen Aspekts, „dass kapitalistische Gesellschaften ein massives Männerproblem haben, [was] die derzeitige so genannte Finanzkrise [zeigt], die vor allem eine Krise männlicher Versager in den Chefetagen von Banken und Unternehmen ist" (Sauer ebenda, 25).

durch Forderungen ans bestehende System erreichen, sondern hier käme die Politik der Subjektivität, wenn auch modifiziert, nämlich als politische Selbstreflexion, wieder zum Tragen. In ihrer Positionierung als „integrierte Außenseiterinnen" hätten Frauen die Aufgabe „über das Regiertwerden, die eigene Regierung anderer und die Selbstregierungstechniken herrschaftskritisch" nachzudenken (Holland-Cunz 2005, 150). Sie hätten die eigene dialektische Verortetheit in Mitregierungs- und Selbstregierungsdynamiken zu eruieren, die in ihrer Gleichzeitigkeit von beherrschtem Außenseiterinnen-Status und ihrer Teilnahme an der Herrschaftlichkeit liegen.

Denn, wie die innerfeministische Kritik am weiblichen Egozentrismus längstens bemerkt hat, sind auch Frauen zu Mittäterinnen eines neokolonialistischen Kapitalismus und weltabgewandte Nutznießende dieser Herrschaftsweise geworden. „Der Autonomiebegriff der Neuen Frauenbewegung war anfangs ein Kampfbegriff gegen die Kolonialisierung und Vereinnahmung der Frau, außerdem eine Herausforderung zur Schaffung von Organisationsformen, die frei von geistiger, psychischer und physischer Dominanz des Mannes sein sollten, schließlich die Herausforderung, den Blick und das Interesse auf andere Frauen zu richten, die wir meist übersehen hatten. Ein Autonomiestreben [hingegen], das erstrangig das eigene Ich im Auge hat und die anderen dazu benutzt, diesem Ich Nahrung zu geben, pervertiert zu [...] einem Autonomiebegriff, der offenbar besonders im westlichen Feminismus immer wieder missverstanden [wird] als individuelle Unabhängigkeit [...], als Recht auf individuelle Wahlmöglichkeiten" (Thürmer-Rohr 1994, 23f). Das ist der Abgesang politischer Selbstbestimmung hin zur Mentalität der Selbstbedienung.

Sicher, jedes Subjekt ist, ob es das erträgt oder nicht, SysteminsassIn, doch das Bemühen, sich zur Vorherrschaft dieses Systems in Distanz zu begeben, muss (wieder) unaufgebbare Aufgabe werden. Und welche sonst, wenn nicht sozietäre Minderheitspositionen, haben den Blick vom Rande; sie können den Bindestrich zwischen Innen und Außen als dessen Differenz artikulieren, sozusagen die Kritik – in ihrem Ursinn als das Handwerk des Unterscheidens (Platons kritiké techne) – verkörpern. Und nicht nur, aber gerade die Frauen, die in dem Paradox existieren, zwar die Mehrheit zu sein, jedoch nicht das

Allgemeine zu repräsentieren[12] – eine permanente Verletzungsgeschichte – wären in der Lage der Ent-Setzung, bzw. der Widersetzlichkeit.

Widerständige Selbstorganisierung wäre eine Einholung von Widerstreit als Konstituenz einer Demokratie, die Widersprüche nicht ignoriert, sondern als Voraussetzung und Ziel ihrer selbst wahrnimmt (vgl. Krondorfer 2008). Welche Formen für eine politische Selbstorganisierung in je historischen Situationen angemessen erscheinen – Revolte, Verweigerung, Ungehorsam, Desertion, Dissidenz, Subversion, Gegen-Verhalten, Demonstrationen – ist abhängig von den jeweiligen gesellschaftlichen Kräfteverhältnissen und obliegt der Urteils- und Bewegungskraft der AkteurInnen. Das setzt ein Verständnis von Autonomie voraus, das Selbstbestimmung nicht im Singular, sondern im Gemeinsamen verortet, das, was Hannah Arendt zeitschreibens das Politische genannt hat: das Gespräch der Unterschiedenen zur gemeinsamen Weltgestaltung. Das bedeutet keine Universalisierung des eigenen, immer partikulären Standpunkts und keine leere Toleranz, deren Geste immer ein verdecktes Hierarchieverhältnis impliziert. Die Aufgabe besteht darin, im Prozess der Aus-ein-ander-setzung weder sich und schon gar nicht die jeweils anderen, ohne die m/ein auf diese Art und Weise des In-der-Welt-Seins nicht existierte, aufzugeben. Das (Wider-) Sprechen, das Austauschen im Gegeneinander der unterschiedlichen Perspektiven der Welterfahrung erst bildet politische Urteilskraft und ermöglicht im Miteinander Weltgestaltung. Jede Sache hat so viele Seiten, wie Menschen an ihr beteiligt sind, und Wirklichkeit kann nur erfasst werden, wenn sie zeigen, dass die Welt sie

---

[12] „Dass der empathische Menschenbegriff in wesentlichen Teilen inhaltsleer geblieben ist und schließlich dem reduktionistischen Platz machen musste, merkt man spätestens, wenn man die Nivellierung der Geschlechterdifferenz betrachtet, die er mit sich bringt. [...] Es wurde...ein die Geschlechter vereinigender Gattungs- und Menschenbegriff ‚erfunden', [... dem] der männliche Erscheinungsteil untergeschoben [wurde] und unter dieser Verinhaltlichung wurden dann beide Geschlechter subsumiert [...] Man konnte [...] auf die Frau als Arbeitskraft nicht verzichten, man wollte sie aber nicht als Frau in der Organisation beschäftigen. [...] Gleichberechtigung von Mann und Frau kann nicht heißen, die Geschlechterdifferenz in einen leeren (moralisch) empathischen Menschenbegriff zu nivellieren, [...] Gleichberechtigtheit heißt vielmehr Organisationsformen [...] zu finden, [die] die Geschlechterdifferenz ernst nehmen. Davon sind wir noch weit entfernt" (Heintel, Götz 1999, 162ff).

etwas angeht, was Hannah Arendt Weltbegabtheit nennt (vgl. Grunenberg et al 2007). Durch das miteinander Sprechen werden die Dinge nicht einfacher, sondern widersprüchlicher, mannigfaltiger und dabei geht es nicht um ein fertiges Ergebnis, denn dieser Prozess impliziert die Erkenntnis, dass ein Weiterkommen ein immer wieder Anfangen bedeutet. Weltsicht, die nicht eindimensional sein will, setzt ein Verständnis von der Wirklichkeit der Welt voraus, als etwas „was Vielen gemeinsam ist, zwischen ihnen liegt, sie trennt und verbindet, sich jedem anders zeigt" (Arendt 1993, 52).

Die Suche nach dem ‚kleinen Spalt einer Öffnung', es könnte die Suche nach dem sein, was als die menschliche Fähigkeit zur Freiheit des Anfangens und eines Handelns in unselbstgenügsamer Macht zu benennen wäre. „Wenn man den Unterschied zwischen Macht und Nichtmacht im Unterschied zwischen Handeln und Nichthandeln sieht, dann ist Macht nicht mehr nur das, was von außen auf uns einwirkt bzw. das wir anderen von außen aufoktroyieren [...]. Wenn Macht nicht an Instrumente, Mittel, Werkzeuge und andere materielle Voraussetzungen gebunden ist, außer an den Mut, hervorzutreten und sich zu positionieren und an die Fähigkeit, andere einzubinden, Bündnisse zu suchen und zu halten, dann würde ‚vorenthaltene Macht' soviel bedeuten, wie die Unmöglichkeit oder Unfähigkeit, mit anderen zu handeln, und ‚Machtunterlegenheit' soviel wie Vereinzelung: Mangel an Menschen, Mangel an Zustimmung, Mangel an Dialog" (Thürmer-Rohr: o.J.). Selbstbestimmung ist hier deutlich abgegrenzt von Autarkie und Individualismus. Das Ringen um Autonomie, das einst emphatische ‚Von-sich-ausgehen-Dürfen' wird durchquert hin zu einem empathischen ‚Von-sich-absehen-Können'. Nach Hannah Arendt ist der Sinn der Politik die Freiheit. Allerdings ist diese Freiheit abhängig von den anderen; nicht nur gemeint als Begrenzung von Freiheit, sondern als deren Ermöglichung durch die anderen. „‚Wären Souveränität und Freiheit wirklich dasselbe, so könnten Menschen tatsächlich nicht frei sein, weil Souveränität, nämlich unbedingte Autonomie und Herrschaft über sich selbst, der menschlichen Bedingtheit der Pluralität widerspricht', bemerkt Arendt. [...] Nicht-Souveränität ist die Bedingung demokratischer Politik, die Bedingung der Verwandlung eines Ich-will in ein Ich-kann und somit der Freiheit. Politische Freiheit braucht andere und ist räumlich durch deren Gegenwart begrenzt. Freiheit ist kein subjektives Selbstverhältnis; sie ist angewiesen auf eine bestimmte Art von Verhältnis zu anderen in jenem durch Pluralität bestimmten Raum, den Arendt ‚gemeinsame Welt' nennt" (Zerilli 2010, 35f). Nicht Selbstbezug, sondern Selbstüberschreitung eröffnet den kleinen Spalt.

Bibliographie

Arendt, Hannah. *Was ist Politik?* München: Piper, 1993.

Degen, Hans-Jürgen, Knoblauch, Jochen. *Anarchismus. Eine Einführung.* Stuttgart: Schmetterling, 2006. Zit. nach: http://www.theorie.org/titel/ 585_anarchismus

Gramsci, Antonio. „Der Staat und der Sozialismus". (1919). Zit nach: Jens Kastner: *„Langhaarige und frenetische Romantiker".* Gramsci und der Anarchismus. In: http://www.postanarchismus.net/texte/kastner_gramsci.htm

Grunenberg, Antonia, Thürmer-Rohr, Christina. „Gespräch über den Mythos Hannah Arendt. ‚Dass man miteinander streitet'" (2007). http://www.taz.de/!5191992/

Hegel, Georg Wilhelm Friedrich. *Vorlesungen über die Philosophie der Geschichte* (Kapitel 51, 1924). Zit. aus: http://gutenberg.spiegel.de/ buch/1657/51

Heil, Reinhard, Hetzel, Andreas. (Hrsg.) *Die unendliche Aufgabe. Kritik und Perspektiven der Demokratietheorie.* Bielefeld: transcript, 2006.

Heintel, Peter, Götz, Klaus. *Das Verhältnis von Institution und Organisation. Zur Dialektik von Abhängigkeit und Zwang.* München/Mering: Rainer Hampp, 1999.

Holland-Cunz, Barbara. *Die Regierung des Wissens. Wissenschaft, Politik und Geschlecht in der ‚Wissensgesellschaft'.* Opladen: Barbara Budrich, 2005.

Kastner, Jens. *„Langhaarige und frenetische Romantiker".* Gramsci und der Anarchismus. http://www.postanarchismus.net/texte/kastner_gramsci.htm

Krondorfer, Birge, Bauer, Sabine, Pechriggl, Alice, Perko, Gudrun. „Das es-Sie-können. Mögen". In: Verein zur Förderung von Frauenbildungsprojekten (Hrsg.). *Autonomie in Bewegung. 6. Österreichische Frauensommeruniversität. Texte, Reflexionen, Sub-Versionen.* Wien: Promedia, 1991, S. 12-20.

Krondorfer, Birge. „Pluralität ist Konsens? Oder: noch keine Pluralität nirgends". In: Birge Krondorfer, Miriam Wischer, Andrea Strutzmann

(Hrsg.). *Frauen und Politik. Nachrichten aus Demokratien.* Wien: Promedia, 2008, S. 226-237.

Krondorfer, Birge. „Selbstorganisierung im Widerstreit von Autonomie und Allianzen. Gegen Deutungshoheiten zu und in politischen Kollektivierungsversuchen". In: Birge Krondorfer, Hilde Grammel (Hrsg.). *Frauen-Fragen. 100 Jahre Bewegung, Reflexion, Vision.* Wien: Promedia, 2012, S. 362-371.

Krondorfer, Birge. „Short cuts zu einer Utopie". In: *aep informationen.* Nr. 3, 2014, S. 11-17.

Landauer, Gustav. „Anarchische Gedanken über Anarchismus". (1901). Zit aus: http://www.anarchismus.de/allgemeines/ positionen.htm

Lohschelder, Silke, Dubowy Liane M., Gutschmidt, Inés. *Anarchafeminismus – Auf den Spuren einer Utopie.* Münster: Unrast, 2009.

Lorey, Isabell. *Gouvernementalität und Selbst-Prekarisierung.* (2006). In: http://eipcp.net/transversal/1106/lorey/de

Muraro, Luisa. *Politisch ist... die Politik der Frauen!* 1991. In: http://www.bzw-weiterdenken.de/2015/07/politisch-ist-die-politik-der-frauen/

Muraro, Luisa. *Stärke und Gewalt.* Rüsselsheim: Christel Göttert, 2014.

Rinderle, Peter. *Der Zweifel des Anarchisten. Für eine neue Theorie von politischen Verpflichtungen und staatlicher Legitimität.* Frankfurt am Main: Vittorio Klostermann, 2005.

Samerski, Silja. „Entmündigende Selbstbestimmung. Wie genetische Beratung schwangere Frauen zu einer unmöglichen Entscheidung befähigt". In: Graumann, Sigrid; Schneider, Ingrid (Hrsg). *Verkörperte Technik – Entkörperte Frau. Biopolitik und Geschlecht.* Frankfurt am Main: Campus, 2003. Zit. nach L. N. Trallori in ebenda, S. 161.

Schrupp, Antje. *Die Liebe der Frauen zur Freiheit. Anarchismus und Feminismus.* Interview von Johanna Demory und Bernd Drücke 2013. http://www.graswurzel.net/379/antje.shtml

Sauer, Birgit, „Es gibt kein feministisches Außen. Plädoyer für eine linke feministische Politik". In: Kulturrisse. Zeitschrift für radikaldemokratische Kulturpolitik: Heft 4, 24-27 2008.

Staritz, Nikola. *Ich bin, also bin ich. Wie die Kritik an Geschlechter-Kategorien zur unreflektierten Identitätspolitik werden kann.* (2014). In: http://www.malmoe.org/artikel/alltag/2818

Stowasser, Horst. *Freiheit pur. Die Idee der Anarchie, Geschichte und Zukunft.* Frankfurt am Main: Eichborn, 1995 (downloadbar von Mamanarchija.net).

Thürmer-Rohr, Christina. *Verlorene Narrenfreiheit*. Berlin: Orlanda Frauenverlag, 1994.

Thürmer-Rohr, Christina. *Das feministische Problem mit der Macht. Und die Provokation durch Hannah Arendts Machtbegriff.* (o.J.) In: https://www.gender.hu-berlin.de/de/veranstaltungen/archiv /zif-1990-2004/pdf_dokumente

Trallori, Lisbeth N. „Selbstbestimmung – Neue Technologien – Neoliberalismus. Enteignungen und Verfremdungen". In: Krondorfer, Birge et al. (Hrsg). *Frauen und Politik. Nachrichten aus Demokratien.* Wien: Promedia, 2008, S.157-164.

Treusch-Dieter, Gerburg. „Frei vom Körper, jenseits der Geschlechterdifferenz. Die Knoten des Sozialen lösen" (1992). In: Edith Futscher, Heiko Kremer, Birge Krondorfer, Gerlinde Mauerer (Hrsg.) *Gerburg Treusch-Dieter Ausgewählte Schriften.* Wien: Turia + Kant, 2014, S. 19-49.

Wamper, Regina. http://www.kritisch-lesen.de/rezension/der-doppelte-kampf

Zerilli, Linda M.G.. *Feminismus und der Abgrund der Freiheit.* Wien, Turia + Kant, 2010

Zizek, Slavoj. *Die bösen Geister des himmlischen Bereichs: Der linke Kampf um das 21. Jahrhundert.* Frankfurt am Main: S. Fischer, 2011.

UTTA ISOP

INSTITUTIONELLE GEWALT: DIE LUST AM HIERARCHISIEREN – EINSCHLIESSEN – AUSSCHLIESSEN[1]

„Viele Leute haben bereits die Dilemmata und Komplizenschaften von radikalen Bewegungen und Diskursen in akademischen Institutionen aufgezeigt. Beispielsweise sind akademischer Feminismus und Postkolonialismus voller Widersprüche, die in den unhinterfragten und nur selten bekämpften Hierarchien und Machtbeziehungen in der Universität oder dem College leben. Unsere Analysen von kulturellen Texten sind oftmals scharf und klug, scheinen aber niemals unsere institutionellen Kontexte, Diskurse und Prozesse zu betreffen: unsere Beziehungen zu den Kolleg*, den Studierenden, den Administrator* und weiteren Personen."
(Aruna Srivastava 1998, Übersetzung durch Utta Isop)

„Der Entwurf der Autonomie (…) fordert über die Frage von Sex, Gender und Begehren hinaus – radikal die Abschaffung der Hierarchien als Teilung der jeweiligen Gesellschaft in Macht und Nicht-Macht, in 'höhere' und 'niedere' Statusgruppen, in mit Rechten und nicht mit Rechten ausgestattete Menschen u.v.m. Die Politik der Autonomie tritt für die Abschaffung von eindeutigen Identitätspolitiken ein, in denen die einen eingeschlossen, die anderen stigmatisiert, ausgegrenzt, marginalisiert, diskriminiert oder getötet werden. Demgegenüber geht es um die Institutierung der Gleichheit auf der Ebene der Macht der Gesellschaft, die keineswegs ein Naturzustand ist: als Möglichkeit der politischen Partizipation aller in der Anerkennung der jeweiligen anderen und letztlich für die Freiheit aller." (Gudrun Perko 2005, 89)

1) Einführung

1.1) Die Lust am Hierarchisieren, Einschließen, Ausschließen

Institutionelle Gewalt vollzieht sich als strukturelle einerseits durch das Einschließen und Hierarchisieren von Menschen innerhalb einer Institution und andererseits durch das Ausschließen von Men-

---

[1] Da ich eine feministisch-queere Position im Verhältnis zu Normierungen und Identifizierungen vertrete, verwende ich, gerade um die Vielfalt an geschlechtlichen Lebensformen zu betonen, sowohl *, als auch _, als auch das große I oder das kleine i. Die Vereinheitlichung der Schreibweise durch den Unterstrich empfinde ich als Normierung, der mit queeren Ansprüchen nicht vereinbar ist.

schen außerhalb derselben. Institutionelle Gewalt geht ebenso wie andere Formen struktureller Gewalt mit Traumatisierung, Verletzungen und Kränkungen nicht spurlos an den Betroffenen vorüber. Genauer gesagt, durch das Abschließen von Ressourcen einer Institution vor Menschen außerhalb derselben und entsprechend der Hierarchien auch innerhalb erfolgen Degradierung, Entwertung und Markierung von Personen. Ein Teil von uns ist in Institutionen eingeschlossen. Wir kommen nicht heraus, aus der Universität, dem Ministerium, der Bildungseinrichtung, dem Betrieb, dem Medium, der Firma, in der wir arbeiten. Jahrzehnte des Genießens und Leidens kommen und gehen. Wir schließen uns und andere ein und aus. Wir hierarchisieren und kränken uns selbst und andere. Wir zahlen mit Selbstaufgabe, Aushöhlung, Enthüllung, Verzicht und Leben. Die Institution fordert viel. Von manchen fordert sie alles. Und wir wandeln als institutionelle Hüllen unter den Menschen. Wir kommen nicht heraus, weil wir nicht wissen, wohin wir gehen sollen. Gibt es doch wenige freie Lohnarbeitsplätze, die Bezahlung und Anerkennung versprechen. Und droht doch Arbeitslosigkeit, wenn wir einmal die schützenden und einschließenden Barrieren der Institutionen und Betriebe verlassen.

Ein anderer Teil von uns ist ausgeschlossen. Wir warten Jahrzehnte auf die einmalige Gelegenheit, einen Fuß in die Institution, in den Betrieb zu bekommen. Wir zahlen mit zeitaufwändiger Geduld, Zuwendungsakten und energieverschleißenden Geschenken an den Grenzen, Rändern, Öffnungen und zugänglichen Personen der Institutionen, Betriebe und Subkulturen. Wir versuchen, die schwer zugänglichen Institutionen und Währungen aus dem opaken Inneren der Institutionen und Betriebe für unser Eingelassen-Werden zu nutzen. Dienlich zu sein, als würdig und wertvoll für die Institution erkannt und belohnt zu werden, darauf sind all unsere Anstrengungen gerichtet, hat die Institution, der Betrieb einmal unser Begehren geweckt. Kumulieren doch alle Ressourcen und Aufmerksamkeiten innerhalb und zwischen den großen Institutionen und Betrieben, mit kleinen subkulturellen Ausläufern als Vermittlung. Und dann bleiben wir nicht nur auf unserem Begehren, gesehen zu werden, sondern auch noch auf der Notwendigkeit, Geld zu verdienen, sitzen, außerhalb der Institutionen und Betriebe. Oftmals rechtfertigen wir die Prozesse des Hierarchisierens, Einschließens und Ausschließens

dadurch, dass nicht ausreichende Ressourcen innerhalb von Institutionen und Gesellschaften für alle vorhanden seien. Ich vertrete hier
eine entgegengesetzte These, nämlich , dass es sich bei den Prozessen des Hierarchisierens, Ein- und Ausschließens nicht nur um notwendige Auseinandersetzungen rund um institutionelle Ressourcen
handelt, sondern auch um libidinöse, sexuelle Prozesse, die in den
sexuellen Praktiken ihren Platz finden sollen, aber in den Prozessen
des Zugangs zu institutionellen überlebensnotwendigen Ressourcen
einer Gesellschaft kulturtechnisch minimiert werden sollten. Ich
vertrete hier die These, dass die institutionellen Prozesse des Hierarchisierens, Einschließens und Ausschließens mit Prozessen der Lust
verbunden sind, die mit der „Mordlust" wie Sigmund Freud sie nannte verknüpft sind. So wie sich in der Frage „schön oder nicht schön?"
(Youtube 2015), die auf sozialen Medien gestellt wird, die Frage
„sein oder nicht sein?" verbirgt, wie die Kommentare zu den geposteten Videos und Fotos verraten, so steckt in den Prozessen des Hierarchisierens, Einschließens und Ausschließens meiner These nach
ein Stück transformierter Mordlust. Freud leitet diese aus dem Gebot
„Du sollst nicht töten" ab:

> „Ein so starkes Verbot kann sich nur gegen einen ebenso starken Im
> puls richten. Was keines Menschen Seele begehrt, braucht man nicht
> zu verbieten, es schließt sich von selbst aus. Gerade die Betonung des
> Gebotes: Du sollst nicht töten, macht uns sicher, dass wir von einer
> unendlich langen Generationsreihe von Mördern abstammen (…) Un
> ser Unbewusstes führt die Tötung nicht aus, es denkt und wünscht sie
> bloß. (…) Wir beseitigen in unseren unbewussten Regungen täglich
> und stündlich alle, die uns im Wege stehen, die uns beleidigt und ge
> schädigt haben. (…) Ja, unser Unbewusstes mordet selbst für Kleinig
> keiten; wie die alte athenische Gesetzgebung des Drakon kennt es für
> Verbrechen keine andere Strafe als den Tod, und dies mit einer gewis
> sen Konsequenz, denn jede Schädigung unseres allmächtigen und
> selbstherrlichen Ichs ist im Grunde ein crimen laesae majestatis."
> (Sigmund Freud 1999, 35f.)

Wohlgemerkt vertrete ich die These, dass es sich um kulturtechnisch vielfach transformierte Mordlust handelt, die in den Prozessen
des Hierarchisierens, Einschließens und Ausschließens wirkt. Und
ich vertrete diese These, weil ich argumentiere, dass Lust keine gesellschaftliche Legitimation von Prozessen des Hierarchisierens,
Einschließens und Ausschließens liefern kann. Im Gegensatz zu den
Legitimationen der knappen Ressourcen, der Bildung, des Talents,

der Leistung, der Herkunft, des Geschlechts und was da noch der vielfältigen Legitimationen für Hierarchien in Institutionen mehr sind, ist es gesellschaftlich aktuell unmöglich zu argumentieren, dass wir Prozesse des Hierarchisierens, Einschließens und Ausschließens in Institutionen und Betrieben in erster Linie deshalb leben, weil sie uns Lust bereiten. Es geht mir also mit dieser Fokussierung auf die Lust an den Prozessen des Hierarchisierens, Einschließens und Ausschließens darum, Hierarchien in Institutionen und Gesellschaften zu delegitimieren. Prozesse des Hierarchisierens, Einschließens und Ausschließens sollen in kulturtechnisch eigens dafür geschaffenen Räume der sado-masochistischen Lust konsensuell gelebt werden und aus den Institutionen zu Verwaltung lebensnotwendiger Güter wie Bildung, Gesundheit, Technik und vielen mehr weitestgehend verschwinden. Mit der Setzung von gesellschaftlichen Orten für Mordlust und Sado-Masochismus in freier Einvernahme, öffne ich die Institutionen lebensnotwendiger Güter für das Begehren nach egalitären Praktiken und Demokratisierung in Betrieben und Gesellschaften.

Der jüngste Welterfolg von „Fifty Shades of Grey" macht diese Lust am Hierarchisieren, Einschließen, Ausschließen und ihre sexuellen Bezüge sehr deutlich, auch wenn der Roman leider diese Prozesse innerhalb der Institutionen und Betriebe nicht in Frage stellt.

1.2) „Fifty Shades of Grey" veranschaulicht diese Lust am Hierarchisieren, Einschließen, Ausschließen

Der jüngste Welterfolg der belletristischen Romantrilogie „Fifty Shades of Grey" von E.L. James (2012) veranschaulicht sehr gut die sexuellen Komponenten der lustvollen Prozesse des Hierarchisierens, Einschließens und Ausschließens. Er macht auch die Bedeutung dieser Prozesse für die Positionierung von Individuen innerhalb von Institutionen und Betrieben deutlich. Wenn die eher sadistisch veranlagte männliche Hauptfigur eine leitende Position innerhalb der von ihm selbst geschaffenen und am Markt sehr erfolgreichen Konzerne einnimmt, so stellt der Roman einen deutlichen Zusammenhang zwischen dieser sozialen Position und der Lust zu kontrollieren, zu beherrschen, zu dominieren und Schmerzen zuzufügen, die sich auch im Sexuellen äußert, her. Neben dem geringen Bedürfnis nach Schlaf und der geringen Beziehungsorientierung der männlichen Hauptfigur wird diese Lust, die Prozesse des Hierarchisierens, Einschließens, Ausschließens zu kontrollieren und zu prozessieren geradezu als der Kern des Erfolgs am Markt dargestellt. Die weibliche Hauptfigur, Anastasia Steele, hat im Verlaufe der Romantrilogie Teil an der Persönlichkeitstransformation von Christian Grey, durch welche die sadistischen und beziehungsabgewandten Aspekte dieser Persönlichkeit in sexuell-lustvolle und beziehungsorientierte Strukturen verwandelt werden. Die weibliche Hauptfigur übernimmt es, die Prozesse des Hierarchisierens, Einschließens und Ausschließens im Privatleben und in der Liebesbeziehung zu bestimmen. Sie stellt allerdings in keiner Weise die Hierarchien im Konzern in Frage, sondern mildert allenfalls die sadistischen Tendenzen der männlichen Hauptfigur. Sehr schön und anschaulich werden hier die Verbindungen zwischen der Lust an den Prozessen des Hierarchisierens, Einschließens, und Ausschließens innerhalb der Institutionen und Konzerne mit den sexuellen Prozessen in sogenannten „privaten" Beziehungen herausgearbeitet. Dieser romanhaften Veranschaulichung entsprechen bis zu einem gewissen Grad die sozialpsychologischen Studien von Erin E. Buckels und Delroy Paulhus.

1.3) Führungskräfte benötigen überproportional häufig Narzissmus, Machiavellismus, Psychopathie und sadistische Lust

Die sozialpsychologischen Studien („Everyday Sadists Take Pleasure In Others' Pain") von Erin E. Buckels und Delroy Paulhus (2013) weisen auf die alltäglichen sado-masochistischen Prozesse in Institutionen und Betrieben hin: "These people aren't necessarily serial killers or sexual deviants but they gain some emotional benefit in causing or simply observing others' suffering."(Buckels 2013) Gemeinsam mit anderen Forscher*innen zeigt Paulhus auf, dass Führungskräfte überproportional häufig über die sadistisch orientierten beschriebenen Persönlichkeitsstrukturen des Narzissmus, des Machiavellismus und der Psychopathie verfügen. Besonders bedeutsam ist für diese sozialpsychologischen Begriffe des alltäglichen Sadismus, des Machiavellismus, des Narzissmus und der Psychopathie, dass sie keine klinischen Begriffe sind, dass sie also nicht mit „Pathologisierung" einhergehen. Im Gegenteil stellen diese Prozesse alltägliche Phänomene im Rahmen hierarchischer Institutionen und Betriebe dar (Susanne Wedlich 2013). Meine These ist, dass die Prozesse des Hierarchisierens, Einschließens und Ausschließens zu kontrollieren, anzuleiten und diese selbst zu vollziehen sozialpsychologische Persönlichkeits- und Beziehungsstrukturen wie die von Paulhus beschriebenen, benötigen. Gefühlskälte in Bezug auf andere, Ich-Bezogenheit, Lust an der Manipulation, Lust am Dominieren und Selbstüberschätzung erleichtern, so meine These, das Kultivieren der Lust an Prozessen des Hierarchisierens, Einschließens und Ausschließens. Das heißt selbstverständlich nicht, dass diese Prozesse ausschließlich bei Führungspersonen in hierarchischen Institutionen und Betrieben zu finden sind, sondern, dass sie an diesen Spitzenpositionen des Entscheidungsgeschehens besonders deutlich ausgeprägt sind. Institutionen und Betriebe vollziehen an allen Positionen Prozesse des Einschließens, Ausschließens und Hierarchisierens, jedoch so meine These, lassen sich Quantitäten und Qualitäten dieser Prozesse unterscheiden. Es lassen sich, so meine These, Organisationsformen mit weniger und weniger grausamen Prozessen des Hierarchisierens, Einschließens und Ausschließens von Organisationsformen mit mehr und grausameren Prozessen unterscheiden. Dies führt dann im weiteren zu meiner These, dass sich egalitärere von weniger egalitären Praktiken unterscheiden lassen, so wie sich als Leitgedanke Differenzen von Hierarchien unterscheiden lassen müssen, denn worauf sonst zielt Kritik? Hier wird also nur kurz ein Ausblick auf mein analytisches und philosophisches Projekt geboten, das darin besteht, die Unterscheidung von Hierarchien und Differenzen als orientierenden Leitgedanken zu etablieren, hierarchischere von weniger hierarchischen Organisierungsformen zu unterscheiden und egalitäre von weniger egalitären Praktiken trennen zu können. Dies alles stellt keine Selbstverständlichkeit dar.

2) Hauptteil

2.1) Institutionelle Gewalt

Nach Max Weber bezieht sich institutionelle Gewalt „auf die durch dauerhafte Unterwerfungsverhältnisse und durch physische Sanktionen abgestützte Verfügungsmacht, die den Inhabern bestimmter Positionen eingeräumt wird. Prototyp ist der Hoheits- und Gehorsamsanspruch des Staates gegenüber den Bürgern", der mit dem „Monopol legitimer physischer Gewaltanwendung" ausgestattet ist. (Florian Grotz und Dieter Nohlen 2006, 222) Kerstin Brückweh (2006, 275ff.) formuliert ganz ähnlich: „Die physische Gewalt geht mit der institutionellen Gewalt einher, die als eine 'durch physische Sanktionen abgestützte Verfügungsmacht, die den Inhabern hierarchischer Positionen über Untergebene und Abhängige eingeräumt ist', definiert werden kann. Prototyp institutioneller Gewalt ist nach Peter Waldmann in der Moderne der Hoheits- und Gehorsamsanspruch, mit dem der Staat dem einzelnen gegenübertritt." Ulrich von Hagen (2013) erweiterte den Begriff der institutionellen Gewalt um die symbolische Gewalt von Pierre Bourdieu, die gesellschaftliche Herrschaftsverhältnisse in „natürliche" transformiert. Weiters integrierte von Hagen das Konzept der „aktuellen und eventuellen Gewaltsamkeit" von Max Weber in den Begriff der institutionellen Gewalt, sodass eine neuere Definition dieses Begriffs wie folgt lautet:

"Der Begriff der institutionellen Gewalt (…) geht insofern über das direkte, personelle Verständnis von Gewalt hinaus, als er nicht allein auf eine spezifische Modalität sozialen Handelns, sondern auf dauerhafte Abhängigkeits- und Unterwerfungsverhältnisse abstellt. Man kann ihn definieren als eine durch physische Sanktionen abgestützte Verfügungsmacht, die den Inhabern hierarchischer Positionen über Untergebene und Abhängige eingeräumt ist. (…) Prototyp institutioneller Gewalt in der Moderne ist der Hoheits- und Gehorsamsanspruch, mit dem der Staat dem einzelnen gegenübertritt." (Ulrich von Hagen 2013)

Mir geht es nun einerseits darum, am Begriffskern der „dauerhaften Abhängigkeits- und Unterwerfungsverhältnisse" festzuhalten, diese aber um die Fokussierung auf die performativen Prozesse des Hierarchisierens, Einschließens und Ausschließens zu erweitern. Andererseits möchte ich dem Konzept der institutionellen Gewalt auch die geschlechterkritische und sexualtheoretische Perspektive auf die Lust an diesen Prozessen des Hierarchisierens, Einschließens und Ausschließens hinzufügen. Marquis de Sade macht in seinen Werken wie kaum ein anderer die Lust an den Prozessen des Hierarchisierens, Einschließens und Ausschließens deutlich. In seinen Romanen sind es meist „Inhaber hierarchischer Positionen", die ihre Lust durch gewalttätige und erzwungene sexuelle Akte von Seiten ihrer Untergebenen und Abhängigen generieren. Der Erfolg Juliettes und das Unglück Justines entstehen geradezu dadurch, dass sie, beziehungsweise, dass sie nicht, die Prozesse des Hierarchisierens, Einschließens und Ausschließens lustvoll praktizieren. Das Verdienst de Sades ist es gezeigt zu haben, dass diese gesellschaftlichen Prozesse des lustvollen Hierarchisierens, Einschließens, und Ausschließens gleichzeitig systematische Prozesse des Kränkens, des Verletzens, des Tötens und Mordens darstellen:

> „Es ist zweifellos peinlich, einerseits die schrecklichen Unglücksfälle schildern zu müssen, von denen die sanfte und empfindsame Frau (Justine) überhäuft wird, die aufs Beste der Tugend gehorcht und andererseits zeigen zu müssen, wie die Leute glücklich sind, die diese selbe Frau quälen und zu Tode hetzen. Aber der Schriftsteller, der genug Philosoph ist, um die Wahrheit sagen zu können, steht über diesen Unannehmlichkeiten und wird durch die Notwendigkeit zur Grausamkeit gezwungen, (…) Denn wie oft sehen sie nicht, daß Bösewichte für ihre Missetaten nur süßen Lohn ernten? (…) Und aus diesen Gründen werden wir mit der zynischesten Sprache, den unsittlichsten und gottlosesten Ideen das Verbrechen beschreiben, wie es ist, das heißt, stets triumphierend, immer zufrieden und beglückt und die Tugend wird man gleicherweise immer unglücklich, bekümmert und gepeinigt sehen. (…) In Tränen gebadet, wendet sich Justine an ihren Beichtvater und schildert ihm ihre Lage mit der Leidenschaft ihres Alters. Sie war weiß gekleidet, ihre Haare waren nachlässig in ein großes Tuch eingeschlagen. Ihre zart entwickelte Brust blieb dem Auge des Lüstlings durch einen doppelten Gazeschleier verborgen. Ihr hübsches Gesicht war bleich durch die Aufregung und Tränen standen ihr in den Augen, was ihr Gesicht noch interessanter machte. Man konnte unmöglich schöner sein." (Marquis de Sade)

Der investigative Journalismus wie er in Österreich etwa von Florian Klenk im Falter in Bezug auf Polizei, Justiz, Gefängnisse und Ministerien betrieben wird, um sogenannte „Missstände" aufzuklären, führen sehr anschaulich vor Augen, welche Formen institutionelle Gewalt in hierarchischen Strukturen annehmen kann. Die Verwahrlosung von Gefangenen, der sexuelle Missbrauch in Heimen und Unterbringungen von Jugendlichen mit und ohne Behinderungen, die Übergriffe in psychiatrischen Krankenhäusern oder Pflegefamilien, der Machtmissbrauch in Vorstandsgremien, Ministerien und Banken, basieren auf den institutionellen und betrieblichen Prozessen des Hierarchisierens, Einschließens und Ausschließens und deren Legitimation. Institutionelle Gewalt kann überhaupt nur geübt werden, weil die mit ihr einhergehenden Akte des Hierarchisierens, Einschließens und Ausschließens als legitim gelten entweder aufgrund der Funktionalität, der Leistung, der Qualitätssicherung, der Bildung, der Arbeitsteilung oder der ökonomischen Ressourcenknappheit.

Um ein weiteres aktuelles Beispiel für das Zelebrieren, das Darstellen, das Performieren institutioneller Gewalt anzusprechen, möchte ich die medialen Angebote von diversen Shows nennen, die, aus welchen Gründen auch immer, Menschen auswählen, zurücksetzen und ausschließen. Wenn Millionen von Menschen die Auswahl- und Selektionsprozesse in Fernsehformaten wie „Germanys next Top Model", „Deutschland sucht den Superstar" und zahlreichen anderen Reality Shows verfolgen, so liegt es nahe, dass sich mit den in diesen Formaten vor sich gehenden Selektionsprozessen lustvolle und zerstörerische Dynamiken in den Zuschauer*innen realisieren (Monika Preuk 2014). In den Formaten dieses „Sadismus-Fernsehens" besteht die Lust darin, dass eine andere Person ausgeschlossen und gekränkt wird und nicht die beobachtende oder durchführende Person.

So plädiere ich hier dafür, den Begriff der institutionellen Gewalt von Ulrich von Hagen wie folgt abzuändern: „Der Begriff der institutionellen Gewalt geht insofern über das direkte, personelle Verständnis von Gewalt hinaus, als er nicht allein auf eine spezifische Modalität sozialen Handelns *in Form der performativen Prozesse des Einschließens, Ausschließens und Hierarchisierens*, sondern *auch* auf dauerhafte Abhängigkeits- und Unterwerfungsverhältnisse abstellt. Wir können ihn definieren als eine durch *Sanktionen und Lust* abgestützte Verfügungsmacht, die den Inhabern hierarchischer Positionen über Untergebene und Abhängige eingeräumt ist. (…) Prototypen institutioneller Gewalt in der Moderne sind der Hoheits- und Gehorsamsanspruch, mit dem der Staat dem einzelnen gegenübertritt, sowie die Dynamiken des Kapitals, die den Gehorsam in den Betrieben durchsetzen."

2.2) Zur Kontingenz von Hierarchien und deren Legitimationen nach Cornelius Castoriadis

Die Gefahr, ausschließlich ökonomische Ursachen für die Prozesse des Einschließens, Ausschließens und Hierarchisierens in Institutionen und Betrieben anzunehmen, arbeitet in gewisser Weise bereits einer Legitimation dieser Prozesse in die Hand, die Knappheit sei die Ursache und bedinge die Notwendigkeit der Prozesse des Einschließens, Ausschließens und Hierarchisierens. Dem halte ich entgegen, dass auch der Faktor der Lust an diesen Prozessen eine nicht unbedeutende Rolle spielen mag. Und diese These, dass die Prozesse des Einschließens, Ausschließens und Hierarchisierens nicht nur aus ökonomischen Motiven sondern auch aus Lust an diesen Prozessen vollzogen werden, lässt diese Prozesse möglicherweise etwas weniger legitim erscheinen. Ausgehend von diesen Versuchen, Prozesse des Einschließens, Ausschließens und Hierarchisierens zu legitimieren, komme ich hier auf die Thesen von Cornelius Castoriadis (2014, 153-164) zur kontingenten Institutierung von Lohn- und Einkommenshierarchien zu sprechen. Vor dem Hintergrund der Fragestellung, wie gesellschaftliche Selbstverwaltung umsetzbar ist, ohne dass sofort wieder staatliche und betriebliche Bürokratien und Hierarchien sich herausbilden, die zur de facto Auflösung und Vereinnahmung der Selbstverwaltung führen, diskutiert Castoriadis Hierarchien als jenen Aspekt, der „fast immer ausgeklammert" wird. Auch in den aktuellen Neoliberalismus- und Kapitalismuskritiken werden Hierarchie- und Institutionenkritik ausgeklammert. Castoriadis konstatiert, dass kaum Diskussionen sowohl über die Macht- und Befehlshierarchie als auch über die ökonomischen Hierarchien der Löhne und Einkommen geführt werden. Selbstverwaltung impliziert für Castoriadis die Infragestellung beider Formen von Hierarchien. Die Existenz von Befehls-, Lohn-, und Einkommenshierarchien werden durch folgende Arten von Legitimationen gerechtfertigt: 1) durch Wissen/Qualifikation/ Knappheit an entsprechenden Spezialkenntnissen 2) durch Talent 3) durch Verantwortung. Ich würde dieser Liste an Rechtfertigungen noch 4) durch ökonomische Knappheit hinzufügen, da sich die Lust an Hierarchien nicht wirklich zur Legitimation eignet. Diese Legitimationen haben ideologischen Charakter, da sie rechtfertigen sollen, was bereits existiert. Castoriadis analysiert, dass diese Begründungen für Hierarchien nicht zusammenfallen, sondern einander widersprechen und deshalb nicht wirklich alle gemeinsam für eine Befehls- und Einkommenshierarchie gelten können:

„(G)roße Wissenschafter haben keinerlei 'Verantwortung', während Arbeiter mit geringem 'Wissen' tagtäglich die Verantwortung für Leben und Tod hunderter oder tausender von Menschen tragen. (…) ist der Versuch, diese verschiedenen Kriterien 'zusammenzufassen' oder zu 'gewichten' notwendigerweise und zwangsläufig reine Willkür. Ebenso willkürlich und ohne den leistesten Schatten einer möglichen Rechtfertigung ist schließlich der Übergang von einer solchen Skala, vorausgesetzt, sie ließe sich erstellen, zu einer Differenzierung der Entgelte." (Castoriadis 2014, 156)

Die Befehls- und Einkommenshierarchien etwa beruhen nicht auf 1) Wissen, Qualifikationen und bestimmten Spezialkenntnissen, so Castoriadis, denn ansonsten müssten die Institutionen und Betriebe von Wissenschaftern geleitet werden und diese auch am meisten verdienen (unter der Veraussetzung, dass Wissenschafter*innen tatsächlich über das meiste Wissen verfügen). 2) Das Talent, eine Sache gut zu machen, kann ebenfalls nicht zur Differenzierung von Befehls- und Einkommenshierarchien führen, da Führungspersonen ja ihren gesamten Einsatz auf die Durchsetzung in Konkurrenzkämpfen, auf die libidinöse Bindung an Vorgesetzte und auf die Analyse von sich formierenden Machtverhältnisse aufwenden müssen. Da bleibt keine Zeit, um eine „Sache gut zu machen". 3) Die Verantwortung, so Castoriadis, könne ebenfalls keine überzeugende Legitimation für die Ausbildung von Befehls- und Einkommenshierarchien darstellen, da „Verantwortung" immer nur in den untersten Bereichen von Bürokratien, Befehlsketten, Institutionen und Betrieben auszumachen sei. An „höheren" Positionen in Hierarchien sowie in gesellschaftlich komplexen Zusammenhängen ließen sich „Verantwortungen" ungefähr wie die Frage, wer für den Reichtum sorge, nicht an Einzelpersonen, sondern nur am Zusammenwirken großer Menschenmassen in Institutionen festmachen:

„Auch hier besteht kein Zusammenhang zwischen der Logik des Arguments und dem tatsächlichen Geschehen. Ein Schrankenwärter oder ein Fluglotse haben täglich das Leben von hunderten von Personen in der Hand und bekommen dafür nur einen Bruchteil dessen bezahlt, was ein Vorstandsmitglied der SNCF und von Air France verdient, von dem kein einziges Leben abhängt. (…) Ganz generell kann man gar nicht genug auf die Doppelzüngigkeit und Unaufrichtigkeit all dieser Rechtfertigungen hinweisen (...)" (Castoriadis 2014, 159)

Castoriadis spricht von einer *„Rechtfertigungsideologie der Hierarchie"*, kritisiert aber in weiterer Folge ebenso die Erklärungen marxistischer und nicht-marxistischer Wirtschaftswissenschaften für eine Einkommenshierarchie. Sowohl die wirtschaftswissenschaftliche Begründung, dass sich der Lohn danach bemesse, „was eine Arbeitsstunde eines zusätzlichen Arbeiters dem Produkt hinzufüge" als auch, dass sich der Lohn nach dem Arbeitswertgesetz (den Produktions- und Reproduktionskosten der Ware Arbeitskraft) richte, können allenfalls eine Erklärung von Einkommensunterschieden geben, aber keine Rechtfertigung, so Castoriadis. Die Existenz unterschiedlicher Qualifikationen wird sowohl von den marxistischen Wirtschaftswissenschaften als auch vom Mainstream der Wirtschaftswissenschaften vorausgesetzt, ohne diese bereits bestehenden Hierarchien in Frage zu stellen oder die Frage nach ihrer Rechtfertigung auch nur zu streifen:

> „All diese Theorien können also bestenfalls 'erklären', dass wenn anfangs eine hierarchische Differenzierung besteht, sie sich über diesen Mechanismus fortpflanzen wird. Fügen wir hinzu, (...) dass es keinen Grund mehr gibt, warum derjenige, der bereits auf Kosten der Gesellschaft eine Ausbildung erhalten hat, die ihm eine interessantere, weniger mühselige Arbeit garantiert, davon ein zweites Mal in Form eines höheren Einkommens profitieren sollte." (Castoriadis 2014, 162)

Castoriadis kommt ebenfalls auf, wie er es nennt, den „Kern des Hierarchieproblems" zu sprechen, der für ihn aus „sehr grundlegenden soziologischen und psychologischen Faktoren" besteht. Auf allen Ebenen gesellschaftlicher, institutioneller und betrieblicher Hierarchien stoßen wir auf breite Akzeptanz von Befehls- und Einkommenshierarchien wie auch auf deren verschiedene ideologische Legitimationen. Hierzu skizziert er einige Überlegungen und Thesen, warum Befehls- und Einkommenshierarchien auf derart breite Zustimmung stoßen. Soziale Bewegungen wie die Arbeiterbewegung beispielsweise weisen bei ihrer Entstehung oftmals egalitäre Praktiken und Strukturen auf. Zentrale Motive dafür, Hierarchisierungsprozesse zu vollziehen und zu akzeptieren, ortet Castoriadis in den Belohnungsstrukturen „Konsumsteigerung, Einkommenssteigerung und sozialer Aufstieg" kapitalistischer Gesellschaften. Dennoch lässt sich für mich nicht überzeugend argumentieren, dass Massen von Menschen die Prozesse des Einschließens, Ausschließens und Hierarchisierens lediglich behavioristisch im Hinblick auf Belohnungen, die nur ein Bruchteil der Menschen tatsächlich erreichen, auch tatsächlich vollziehen. Meiner Thesen nach müssen hier zusätzlich, wie die Psychoanalyse sexualtheoretisch argumentiert, libidinöse Prozesse der Lust beim Vollziehen der Prozesse des Einschließens, Ausschließens und Hierarchisierens selbst und deren Legitimation am Werk sein. Castoriadis benennt das nicht in dieser Weise, aber er deutet es an:

> „Doch gibt es zweifellos noch einen tiefgründigeren, schwerer zu formulierenden Faktor, der in diesem Zusammenhang die Hauptrolle spielt. Die erfolgreich voranschreitende Bürokratisierung der Gesellschaft war gleichzeitig und zwangsläufig auch der Triumph einer imaginären Vorstellung von Gesellschaft – der alle mehr oder weniger verpflichtet sind – als hierarchischer Pyramide oder System solcher Pyramiden. Um es deutlich zu sagen: es erscheint dem Menschen von heute geradezu unmöglich, sich eine Gesellschaft vorzustellen, in der die Einzelnen wirklich gleich an Rechten und Pflichten wären, in der die individuellen Unterschiede etwas anderem entsprächen als unterschiedlichen Positionen in einer Befehlskette oder Einkommensskala." (Castoriadis 2014, 163)

Psychoanalytisch spielt für Castoriadis das Bedürfnis überhaupt zur Person zu werden und eine Form von Identität ausbilden zu können für diese Akzeptanz von Befehls- und Einkommenshierarchien eine bedeutende Rolle. Erst durch den Platz in einer hierarchischen Struktur erlange ich eine Vorstellung meiner selbst und werde im bürokratischen Kapitalismus zu etwas „halbwegs Bestimmtem". Dabei lässt er den Aspekt der Lust an den Prozessen des Einschließens, Hierarchisierens und Ausschließens außer Acht. Für eine radikale Kritik der Hierarchie, wie Castoriadis sie fordert, ist aber der Ansatz, die Dimension der Lust an diesen Prozessen des Einschließens, Ausschließens und Hierarchisierens zu betonen, deshalb aussichtsreich, weil dadurch die unmittelbar auf dem Fuße folgende Legitimation durch Lust sich nicht so einfach gestaltet. Hier soll keiner Lustfeindlichkeit das Wort geredet werden, sondern einem bewussten Umgang mit diesen Prozessen der Lust in gesellschaftlich eigens dafür reservierten egalitären Räumen außerhalb des Zugangs zu überlebenswichtigen Ressourcen in Institutionen und Betrieben. Der Ansatz der BDSM-Bewegungen erscheint mir deshalb für eine radikale lusttheoretische Kritik von Hierarchien so fruchtbar, weil die Lust an diesen Prozessen mit explizitem, ausgesprochenem, bewussten Bekenntnis, Erkenntnis, Verbalisierung und einer Schaffung von spezifischen Räumen für die lustvollen Prozesse des Einschließens, Ausschließens und Hierarchisierens dem impliziten, nicht-bekennenden und nicht freiwilligen sado-masochistischen Genießen innerhalb von Institutionen und Betrieben von einem ethischen Gesichtspunkt aus gesehen so weit voraus ist. Die Notwendigkeit zu den sozialen, mentalen und materiellen Ressourcen in Institutionen und Betrieben Zugang zu bekommen, zwingt die meisten Menschen in nicht reflektierte, nicht zurückzuweisende, oktruierte Prozesse des Einschließens, Ausschließens und Hierarchisierens in Institutionen und Betrieben. Als Kulturtechnik oder egalitäre Praxis schlage ich deshalb die Trennung dieser libidinösen Prozesse des Einschließens, Ausschließens und Hierarchisierens von den überlebensnotwendigen Zugängen zu Ressourcen in Institutionen und Betrieben vor. Dafür aber mit voller Reflexions- und Erkenntniskraft sich diesen Prozessen in an Zustimmung gebundene freie Räume für libidinöse Prozesse des Einschließens, Hierarchisierens und Ausschließens hinzugeben, um mit umso schärferer Analysekraft und egalitärem Bewusstsein an einer Verringerung von Herrschaft, Hierarchie und Gewalt innerhalb der überlebensnotwendigen Institutionen und Betriebe einzutreten. Diese Trennung würde in etwa einer kulturtechnischen sozialen Praxis entsprechen, wonach kriegerische Auseinandersetzungen und die Lust am Töten in der Phantasie vollzogen werden, wie auch die damit verwandten Prozesse des Einschließens, Ausschließens und Hierarchisierens in eigens dafür vorgesehenen sozialen Räumen vollzogen werden, um den Menschen in den restlichen sozialen Räumen so wenig wie möglich davon aufzuzwingen. Durch dialektisch-kathartische Prozesse in Phantasiewelten, Rollenspielen, Videospielen könnten in einem viel expliziteren Diskurs die Lust an Gewalt, am Töten, an Prozessen des Einschließens, Ausschließens und Hierarchisierens einerseits explizit, bekennend und reflektiert ausgelebt werden, um an anderer Stelle in jenen Institutionen und Betrieben, die Zugang zu überlebensnotwendigen Ressourcen bieten, darauf verzichten zu können. Das hieße wie in den Ausführungen von Castoriadis Institutionen und Betriebe und letztlich Gesellschaften mit so wenig Befehls- und Einkommenshierarchien zu organisieren wie möglich, ahnend, dass diese keinerlei „sachliche Funktion" für gesellschaftliche Organisierung inne haben. Das hieße auch wie

312

Castoriadis sagt, Selbstverwaltung so zu organiseren, dass Befehls- und Einkommenshierarchien so weit als möglich wegfallen und egalitäre Praktiken zum Abbau von Herrschaft, Hierarchie und Gewalt das Zentrum gesellschaftlicher Bemühungen bilden.

2.3) Kränkungen - zur Dysfunktionalität von Hierarchien durch Krankheit und fehlende Achtung

„Gesellschaften mit einem hohen Grad an Ungleichheit werden von einem antiegalitären Geist durchweht, und der produziert schlecht funktionierende Institutionen." (Robert Misik 2010) resümiert Robert Misik in seiner Rezension des Buches „Gleichheit ist Glück" von Richard Wilkinson und Kate Pickett. Gemäß der EpidemiologInnen Kate Pickett, Michael Marmot und Richard Wilkinson legen eine Fülle empirischer Studien nahe, dass die Kränkung, Abwertung und Erniedrigung durch unterschiedliche Einkommensverteilungen und durch hierarchisch organisierte Statuspositionen bedeutsam zu Erkrankungen von Menschen innerhalb von Institutionen und Gesellschaften gesamt beitragen[2]. Beispielsweise zeigten die Whitehall Studien an mehreren zehntausend britischen BeamtInnen, dass Personen in den unteren Hierarchien signifikant häufiger erkrankten und früher starben als Personen in den oberen Hierarchien. Der psychosoziale Zusammenhang zwischen der sozialen und/oder ökonomischen Position und der Gesundheit eines Menschen verläuft über die Faktoren des Selbstvertrauens, der Entspannung, der Sicherheit und der Sensibilität für den eigenen sozialen Status und die damit einhergehenden Disprivilegierungsformen. Hierarchien in Einkommen und sozialen Positionen innerhalb von Institutionen, die stets mit Vergleichen, Bewertungen und Abwertungen und den damit verbundenen emotionalen Folgen von Scham, Ekel und Kränkungen verbunden sind, führen statistisch zu Krankheiten und zum Unbehagen aller beteiligten Personen. Niemand, auch, diejenigen, die teil-

---

[2] „Aufgaben, die einen gesellschaftlichen Bewertungsdruck erzeugten (etwa eine Gefährdung der Selbstachtung oder des sozialen Status), die also eine mögliche negative Bewertung der Leistung durch andere einschlossen, vor allem bei Aufgaben, deren Bewältigung nicht absehbar war, erzeugten höhere und gleichmäßigere Veränderungen der Kortisolwerte als Stressoren ohne diesen spezifischen Druck" (Wilkinson, Pickett 2010, 53)

weise von Disprivilegierungsstrukturen profitieren, bleiben von dieser institutionellen Kultur des Wertens und Abwertens, des Hierarchisierens, Ein- und Ausschließens emotional unberührt. Dennoch erhöhen sich die Kortisolwerte, die den Stress eines Menschen messen, bei Personen in den unteren Hierarchien und Einkommensstufen wesentlich deutlicher als bei anderen und führen nachweislich zu höherer Morbidität und Mortalität. Oder wie Wilkinson es ausdrückt: „Wir haben Dutzende Studien ausgewertet, sie sprechen alle dieselbe Sprache: Massive Ungleichheit macht eine Gesellschaft ganz generell dysfunktionaler." (Richard Wilkinson 2010)

In der organisationssoziologischen und herrschaftssoziologischen Literatur (Andrea Maurer 2004, 25ff.) liegt eine funktionale Bedeutung von Hierarchien in der Entlastung der Vorgesetzten von der Achtung, dem Respekt, der Anerkennung und der Zustimmung ihrer Untergebenen. Die Handlungsketten in Betrieben und Institutionen sollen an zeitlicher Geschwindigkeit und Effizienz gewinnen, indem die Vorgesetzten nicht auf die Zustimmung und die Achtung der Mitarbeiter*innen angewiesen sind. In dieses Argument nicht integriert ist das Ausmaß an Zeit- und Effizienzverzögerung, das sich durch Widerstand von unten, geschönte Rückmeldungen, mangelnden Informationsfluss von unten nach oben, Privatisierungs- und Aneignungsprozesse auf Seiten der Vorgesetzten und nicht von unten kontrollierbare Korruptions- und Missbrauchshandlungen auf Seiten der Vorgesetzten ergibt. Aus dem Widerspruch einer im Anspruch, sich als demokratisch verstehenden Gesellschaft einerseits und hierarchischen Institutionen und Betrieben andererseits, folgen die Versuche, Scheinpartizipation und Scheindemokratie zumindest punktuell auch in hierarchischen Institutionen und Betrieben zu simulieren. Diese „strategischen Einbindungen" (Wilk/Sahler 2014) sollen über den geringen Gestaltungsspielraum, die nicht vorhandenen Möglichkeiten, Einfluss zu nehmen, die auf der Motivation der Mitarbeiter* lasten, hinwegtäuschen. Der geringe Gestaltungsspielraum ergibt sich aber nicht nur aus ökonomischen Zwängen, sondern auch aus hierarchischen Strukturen, die das Ausmaß an Einfluss je nach Position innerhalb der Hierarchie erhöhen oder reduzieren. Die Sozialisation innerhalb von Betrieben und Institutionen stellt eine der wesentlichsten Einflussgrößen in Bezug auf die Subjektivierungspraktiken und Organisierungsformen von Menschen dar. So verwundert es

314

beispielsweise auch nicht, dass Flüchtlinge wie Emmanuel Mbolela weniger den Alltagsrassismus als den Rassismus der innerbetrieblichen Arbeitsverhältnisse anprangern. Mich überzeugen die Argumente der Effizienz von Hierarchien als Organisierungsform durchaus nicht, da ich die These vertrete, dass es sich bei den Prozessen des Hierarchisierens, Aus- und Einschließens in erster Linie um libidinöse, sexuelle Prozesse als Selbstzweck handelt. Diese aber werden, sei es aus Gründen der Prüderie und/ oder aus Gründen der Herrschaftslegitimation nicht als Selbstzweck angesehen. Wie aber können Gesellschaften auf Dauer demokratisch sein, wenn ihre Institutionen und Betriebe hierarchisch sind?

2.4) Zur Dysfunktionalität von Hierarchien für die Anliegen sozialer Bewegungen wie der feministisch orientierten Gleichstellungstätigkeit

Hierarchien, Einschlüsse und Ausschlüsse sind dysfunktional, weil sie kränken und krank machen. Sie sind aber noch aus anderen Gründen dysfunktional und dies im Besonderen, wenn es darum geht, die Anliegen sozialer Bewegungen wie postkolonialer, feministischer und queerer innerhalb von Institutionen zur Geltung zu bringen. Hierarchien, wie auch immer sie prozessiert und legitimiert werden, sei es durch unterschiedliche Einkommensverteilung oder soziale Herrschaftsformen (nach Begehren, Geschlecht, Herkunft, Fähigkeit) werden auch innerhalb sozialer Bewegungen wie der feministisch-queeren etwa äußerst selten explizit zur Sprache gebracht und als solche insgesamt in Frage gestellt. Meine Kritik an den Gleichstellungsstrategien vieler sozialer Bewegungen und im Besonderen der feministischen, zielt darauf, dass Gleichstellung in institutionellen Hierarchien nicht erfolgen kann, weil die Positionen eben hierarchisch und nicht horizontal organisiert sind. Die Scheinpartizipation, Scheindemokratisierung, die Verbiegungen und Paradoxien, die durch Gleichstellungsarbeit innerhalb von hierarchischen Betrieben und Institutionen nötig werden, ziehen eine nicht endende Fülle an Ansprüchen immer neu auftauchender „Kategorien von Menschen" nach sich. Sobald ich die Ansprüche einer Gruppe von Personen und ihre Disprivilegierung als legitime Argumentation dafür akzeptiere, innerhalb sozialer und ökonomischer Hierarchien aufzusteigen, ermuntert dies viele weitere Ansprüche aller anderen, nicht beim sozialen Aufstieg erfolgreicher Personen. Die paradoxe Intervention von Einrichtungen, die innerhalb hierarchischer Strukturen für Gleichstellung sorgen sollen, führt einerseits zur Sisyphos-Tätigkeit, Mehrfachdiskriminierungen und intersektionalen Herrschaftsformen gerecht zu werden und andererseits dazu, dass gerade in den Momenten der Durchsetzung von Gleichstellung oftmals eine Entmachtung von Gleichstellungseinrichtungen erfolgt, weil sie ja für kurze Momente die gesamte institutionelle Legitimation von Hierarchien tatsächlich in Frage stellen (Stichwort „faktische Gleichstellung").

2.5) Die Theorien der Intersektionalität unterscheiden nicht zwischen Differenzen und Hierarchien und stellen Einkommens- und Befehlshierarchien nicht direkt in Frage

Eine radikale Kritik von Befehls- und Einkommenshierarchien im Sinne ihrer Abschaffung fehlt in den Theorien der Intersektionalität. Es geht den Theorien und politischen Ansätzen von Intersektionalität um Chancengleichheit für Individuen unterschiedlicher Gruppen innerhalb von Befehls- und Einkommenshierarchien. Die Theorien der Intersektionalität stellen aber nicht die Existenz von Befehls- und Einkommenshierarchien und deren Legitimation direkt und explizit in Frage. „Faktische Gleichheit" ist für Theorien der Intersektionalität keine explizite Bezugsgröße sondern maximal eine implizites Hoffen und Repräsentieren von versteckten Wünschen nach faktischer Gleichheit oder „egalitären Differenzen", wie ich es nenne. Queere Theorien wie die von Gudrun Perko hingegen stellen Hierarchien insgesamt in Frage. Theorien der Intersektionalität geht es um das Beforschen, Benennen und Analysieren von verschiedenen Herrschaftsformen, Formen der Dominanz, Formen der Ungleichheit und deren interdependentes Zusammenwirken von Mehrfachdiskriminierungen. Die sozialwissenschaftlichen Analysen von Diskriminierungen, die durch Herrschaftsstrukturen und performatives Handeln in Institutionen und Betrieben vollzogen und legitimiert werden, stellen dadurch die Institutierung von Befehls- und Einkommenshierarchien implizit in Frage. Dennoch wird weder theoretisch noch in der sozialwissenschaftlichen Praxis die Gesamtheit von Befehls- und

Einkommenshierarchien, sowie deren Legitimation in Frage gestellt. Wenn etwa in Diversity-Theorien damit argumentiert wird, dass die Leistungs- und Profitfähigkeit von Unternehmen sich durch die diverse Zusammensetzung von Personalstrukturen steigern lässt, so ist hier sehr offensichtlich keine grundlegende Kritik an der Zufälligkeit und der Existenz von Befehls- und Einkommensstrukturen zu erkennen. Wenn es darum geht, in Detail-Analysen für bestimmte gesellschaftliche Gruppen, seien es Minderheiten oder Mehrheiten, nicht von diesen durchdrungene Befehls- und Einkommensstrukturen zu öffnen, so schärft sich der Blick für die Prozesse des Ausschließens dieser spezifischen Gruppen. Wenn ich aber analysiere, mittels welcher Prozesse beispielsweise eine behinderte farbige Trans*Person ausgeschlossen und hierarchisiert wird, stelle ich dadurch noch nicht in Frage, dass eine behinderte farbige Trans*Person in der Befehls- und Einkommenshierarchie über einer anderen behinderten farbigen Trans*Person zu stehen kommen kann. Die Forderung nach der Durchlässigkeit von Befehls- und Einkommenshierarchien, sowie Führungspositionen, stellt deren Existenz und Legitimation selbst noch nicht in Frage, suggeriert aber implizit, dass sie es täten. Dies ist meine erste Kritik an den Theorien der Intersektionalität.

Meine zweite Kritik an Theorien der Intersektionalität ist, dass sie nicht zwischen Differenzen und Hierarchien unterscheiden. Theorien der Intersektionalität nehmen wie aktuelle Gender-Theorien generell eine ontologische Untrennbarkeit von Hierarchien und Differenzen an:

> „In recent years, the concept of intersectionality has taken center stage and become a dominant model with which to engage in how differences such as „race", gender, class, sexuality, age, disability and religion interweave and intersect upon individual lives in a modern „risk" society. Intersectionality has become a model upon which to understand, analyse and engage with difference in which difference itself becomes a defining feature of „otherness"." (Kalwant Bhopal and John Preston, in: Spoto 2015, 80)

Dieses Zitat von Bhopal und Preston veranschaulicht, dass Differenzen und Hierarchien in den Herrschaftsformen „race", gender, class, sexuality, age, disability and religion weder analytisch noch strategisch voneinander unterschieden werden. Dass diese Prämisse alle weiteren Analysen zu Ungleichheit, Diskriminierung, Herrschaft, Hierarchie und Gewalt überflüssig macht, stört den Main

Stream der Gendertheorien dabei nicht. Wenn wir nicht zwischen herrschaftsförmigeren und weniger herrschaftsförmigen, zwischen gewaltförmigen und weniger gewaltförmigen, zwischen egalitäreren und weniger egalitären Organisationsformen unterscheiden können, macht die Reflexion und Analyse auf Herrschaft und Diskriminierung jedoch keinen Sinn. Die Möglichkeit der Unterscheidung von Hierarchien und Differenzen und sei es nur in einer Sekunde der Erkenntnis muss gegeben sein, um überhaupt Gesellschaftskritik und die Formulierung von „Anti-Diskriminierung" in Recht und Politik sinnvoll zu machen. Ich argumentiere hier, dass die Theorien der Intersektionalität von der Möglichkeit der Unterscheidung von Hierarchien und Differenzen ausgehen, ohne dies als klare Prämisse zu benennen. Damit tragen sie zur Verschleierung und ideologischen Legitimation von Befehls- und Einkommenshierarchien bei.

2.6) Warum kapitalismusfokussierte Analysen und Neoliberalismus-Kritiken für eine grundlegende Kritik an Hierarchien nicht ausreichen

Theoretische Begriffe der Kapitalismusanalyse tendieren dazu, seien es Klassenverhältnisse oder das Wertverhältnis als Fetisch, andere Formen der Hierarchisierung, der Herrschaft und Diskriminierung ausschließlich in Bezug auf diese kapitalistischen Dynamiken zu denken und nicht als relativ eigenständige, geschweige denn als völlig eigenständige anzusehen. Selbst für die Wertkritikerin Roswitha Scholz, die sich sehr große Mühe gibt, von einem identitätslogischen Denken abzugehen, das alle unterschiedlichen Formen von Hierarchien auf das kapitalistische Wertverhältnis reduziert, bleiben die Dimensionen der Wert-Abspaltung, die sich in Sexismen, Rassismen und Antisemitismen außerhalb des Werts bewegen, doch dialektisch auf den Wert verwiesen. Um es an einem Beispiel durchzudenken: dem Vatikan und der katholischen Kirche. Handelt es sich bei dieser kapitalismusanalytisch um einen Konzern, ein Unternehmen auf dem Markt der Religionen ganz ähnlich anderen Unternehmen auf anderen Märkten? Was das Ausmaß an Kapital und Eigentum betrifft, das die katholische Kirche weltweit umsetzt, würde dieser Schluss naheliegen. Was aber andere Hierarchien wie beispielsweise den Ausschluss von Frauen, das Zölibat, den Ausschluss

318

von wiederverheirateten Geschiedenen, den Ausschluss von Homosexuellen innerhalb der katholischen Kirche betrifft, so sind diese Ausschlüsse und Hierarchisierungen nicht völlig, sondern wenn, nur äußerst partiell durch kapitalistische Logiken zu erklären. Die katholische Kirche ist wie Universitäten auch eine Institution, deren institutionelle Geschichte weit in vorkapitalistische Gesellschaften reicht, auch wenn sie aktuell sehr bedeutsam von neoliberalen und/oder fordistischen Beziehungsverhältnissen durchzogen werden. Die ersten Universitäten wurden ab dem 11. Jahrhundert (1108 Bologna, 1150 Paris...) gegründet. Die heutige Organisationsform der Universitäten geht auf Strukturierungen der frühen Neuzeit im 15. Jahrhundert bis 16. Jahrhundert zurück, in welchem die ordentlichen Professoren der Fakultäten den Senat bildeten und Dekan und Rektor gewählt wurden. Nun lässt sich argumentieren, dass frühkapitalistische Gesellschaftsformen einen massiven Einfluss auf diese Art der Organisierung von Universitäten und ihre zunehmende relative Unabhängigkeit (beispielsweise in Form einer eigenständigen Gerichtsbarkeit) von Kirche und Staat hatten. Dennoch lässt sich diese spezifische institutionelle Form der Organisierung nicht völlig durch kapitalfokussierte Analysen erklären, da die Institutionen selbst relativ autonome Logiken und Geschichten der Hierarchisierung hervorbringen, die sie, je mächtiger eine Institution ist, auch gegen die Logiken des Kapitals verteidigen. Das heißt innerhalb von Universitäten wirken insitutionenspezifische Logiken des Hierarchisierens wie dies Pierre Bourdieu (1987) etwa für die relativ unabhängigen sozialen Felder der Bildung und Kunst insgesamt usw. beschrieben hat, die zwar alle in Beziehung zum ökonomischen Feld stehen, aber nicht auf dieses reduzierbar sind.

2.7) Die BDSM-Bewegung macht die Lust an den Prozessen des Hierarchisierens, des Einschließens und Ausschließens explizit

„The play power dynamics of BDSM mirror the nonconsensual power dynamics of the wider culture. (...) The primary power operation of BDSM is a claiming or borrowing of nonconsensual mainstream power dynamics, which are reproduced as consensual play power in BDSM settings." (freaksexual 2007)

Freaksexual formuliert in ihrem Text „Towards a general theory of BDSM and power" die These, dass die Macht-Dynamik innerhalb der BDSM-Subkultur auf konsensuelle Weise widerspiegelt, was außerhalb der BDSM-Subkultur auf nicht-konsensuelle Weise vollzogen wird. Ich vertrete diese These hier ebenfalls: Prozesse des Hierarchisierens, Einschließens und Ausschließens in Institutionen werden vollzogen, weil sie mit Lust verknüpft sind, so meine These. Allerdings werden sie nicht durch Lust legitimiert oder begründet, sondern durch ökonomisch knappe Ressourcen, durch Leistung, durch Bildung, durch Qualifikation, durch Herkunft und vieles mehr. Diese Legitimationen und Begründungen stelle ich hier radikal in Frage. Ich stelle hier die These auf, dass diese Legitimationen nur einen sehr kleinen Anteil an Begründungen für die gelebten Prozesse des Hierarchisierens, Einschließens und Ausschließens darstellen und dass ein wesentlich größerer Anteil die Lust bei der Ausübung dieser Prozesse darstellt. Über diese Prozesse der Lust beim Hierarchisieren, Einschließen und Ausschließen wird jedoch in den seltensten Fällen ein öffentlicher, institutioneller Diskurs gepflogen. Hierarchien lassen sich auch nicht dadurch legitimieren, dass sie Lust bereiten. Und gerade das ist es, was mich an diesem Argument interessiert, dass sich Hierarchien, Prozesse des Einschließens und Ausschließens gerade nicht durch Lust legitimieren lassen. Nun plädiere ich hier für eine kulturtechnische Revolution in der Hinsicht, dass wir uns diese Lust an den Prozessen des Hierarchisierens, Einschließens und Ausschließens bewusst machen. Und dass wir im Zuge dieser Bewusstmachung gesellschaftliche Institutionen schaffen, welche die lebensnotwendigen Güter wie Bildung, Nahrung, Wohnung, Gesundheit, Kultur und Politik kulturtechnisch so weit als möglich von dieser Lust an den Prozessen des Hierarchisierens, Einschließens und Ausschließens lösen, etwa durch den Einsatz von Losprozessen und die Öffnung dieser Institutionen für alle. Gerade jene Institutionen für Güter, die für das gute Leben aller notwendig sind, sollen von diesen nicht-konsensuellen Hierarchien kulturtechnisch befreit werden. Dafür aber sollen, wie es uns die Subkultur des BDSM lehrt, konsensuelle Räume für die Prozesse des Hierarchisierens, Einschließens und Ausschließens geschaffen werden, in denen unter Zustimmung aller Beteiligten nach wie vor „Chef*in und Sekretär" gespielt und gelebt werden kann.

2.8) Von Identitäten und Differenzen zu Organisierungsformen – von herrschaftsförmigeren Organsierungen zu weniger herrschaftsförmigen Organisierungen

„Let me suggest as a starting-point therefore that the appropriate way to morn this anti-Oedipal non-master may well be the joyfull disrespectful affirmation of positive and multiple differences, even and especially among his followers." (Rosi Braidotti 2007, 68)

Eine sehr große Schwierigkeit in Theorien der Differenz/en stellt für mich die Nicht-Unterscheidung von Hierarchien und Differenzen einerseits und die Nicht-Unterscheidung von herrschaftsförmigeren und weniger herrschaftsförmigen Organisierungsformen andererseits dar. Das Zitat von Rosi Braidotti illustriert diese Nicht-Unterscheidung in der Verwendung des Begriffs der Differenzen und Hierarchien. Wenn wir davon ausgehen, dass sich Differenzen nicht von ihren Bewertungen und Hierarchisierungen lösen lassen, so bleibt wohl tatsächlich nur der Aufruf zur permanenten Selbstreflexion und Selbstkritik bezüglich der stetig von uns vorgenommenen Einschlüsse, Ausschlüsse und Hierarchisierungen, aber keinerlei alternative Organisierung. Wenn wir keine Möglichkeiten sehen, beispielsweise den Prozessen des Losens innerhalb einer Demokratie geringere Herrschaftsförmigkeit zuzuschreiben als den Prozessen der Wahl, so können wir folglich auch keine alternativen Organisierungsvorschläge zum Status quo einer Gruppe oder einer Gesellschaft erarbeiten. Was bleibt ist ein ewiges Konkurrenzieren einer unendlichen Kette von hierarchisierten Differenzen/Identitäten, die sich in der Artikulation ihrer eigenen Verletzungen einerseits und in Selbstkritik andererseits üben, ohne jedoch Verständigungen darüber zu fokussieren, welche Beziehungen, Organisierungen, welche Bündnisse und Formen des Zusammenlebens herrschaftsförmiger und welche weniger herrschaftsförmig sind. „Flächige Machtbegriffe" wie jene Foucaults beispielsweise, erleichtern die Unterscheidung zwischen Differenzen und Hierarchien nicht gerade. Wenn ich davon ausgehe, dass Macht an allen Orten in einer Gesellschaft auf dieselbe Weise ausgeübt wird und nicht zwischen der Machtausübung beispielsweise in sozialen Bewegungen einerseits und in Institutionen andererseits unterscheiden kann, entsteht in gegenwärtigen Philosophien der Eindruck, als ob alle Personen in gleicher Weise gesellschaftlich hierarchisiert oder „normiert" wären. Wenn etwa Butler davon ausgeht, dass der Preis für die Subjekt-Werdung die Unterordnung darstellt: „Lieber will ich in Unterordnung leben als gar nicht" (Butler 2001, 13) und sie davon ausgeht, dass das „Begehren zu sein", das Begehren nach Existenz mit Unterordnung und dem Risiko der Ausbeutung bezahlt werden muss, so gilt das für alle Menschen in gleicher Weise und in jeder nur erdenklichen Organisierungs- und Gesellschaftsform. Eine Diskussion darüber, ob es möglicherweise Organisierungsformen gibt, in welchen geringere Ausmaße an Unterwerfung und geringere Risiken der Ausbeutung gegeben sind, macht unter solchen Prämissen keinen Sinn, was ich als äußerst problematisch empfinde.

3) Schluss

3.1) Von Hierarchien zu Differenzen – für alle, nicht nur für einzelne Gruppen!

Eine grundlegende und umfassende Hierarchiekritik findet sich nur marginal in den einzelnen sozialen Bewegungen, da es meist um die Bearbeitung einer Einzeldiskriminierung, einer spezifischen Herrschaftsform und der Vertretung spezifischer Interessensgruppen geht, ohne jedoch Hierarchien als Ganzes innerhalb der Institutionen, Betriebe und Gesellschaften in Frage zu stellen. Mein Nachdenken geht demgegenüber in die Richtung anarcha-feministischer Traditionen, dass nämlich spezifische Formen der Organisation dazu beitragen können, Hierarchien insgesamt für alle in Differenzen umzuwandeln. Dazu ist aber nötig, erst einmal zwischen Hierarchien und Differenzen zu unterscheiden und die Möglichkeit in Betracht zu ziehen, dass Organisierungsformen lebbar werden, die Differenzen befördern, ohne diese mit Bewertungen, Ab- und Aufwertungen zu versehen, ohne diese also zu hierarchisieren. Ein für mich sehr gangbarer Weg der Organisierung von Differenzen stellt bespielsweise das Losen von sozialen Positionen, politischen und ökonomischen Vertretungsstrukturen dar wie sie etwa der anarchistische Philosoph John Burnheim (1987) in seinem Begriff der „Demarchie" anlegt, in welchem in Form eines Gedankenexperiments das bedingungslose

Grundeinkommen mit Prozessen des Losens in sozialen Feldern der Selbstverwaltung verknüpft werden. Diese Praktiken des Losens gehören für mich sehr eng zu einem queeren Verständnis des Verwischens von eindeutigen Identitäten. Der Zufall im Los kann meiner Auffassung nach Identitäten hervorbringen, deren Legitimität und Immunität als eindeutige auf die vielfältigen gesellschaftlichen Subjektivierungspraktiken hin geöffnet werden. Ich stelle die psychoanalytisch inspirierte These auf, dass die Prozesse des Hierarchisierens, des Ein- und Ausschließens nicht aus funktionalen Gründen der Effizienz und Ressourcenknappheit so bedeutsam für Betriebe, Institutionen und Gesellschaften sind, sondern aus Gründen des Begehrens, Menschen unter- und überzuordnen, sie ein- und auszuschließen. Jedoch besteht über diese „libidinösen Zentren" von Institutionen möglicherweise aus Gründen der Prüderie und der Legitimation nur ein sehr marginalisierter Diskurs. Ich plädiere dafür, das Begehren, Beziehungen des Hierarchisierens, Ein- und Ausschließens zu leben, von den Zugängen zu Ressourcen innerhalb von Betrieben und Institutionen zu lösen und diese im Grunde libidinös-sexuellen Vorgänge in sexuellen Praktiken zu vollziehen, wie es die BDSM-Subkulturen beispielsweise bereits jetzt praktizieren. Jedoch die Betriebe, Institutionen und gesellschaftlichen Beziehungen außerhalb von sexuellen Praktiken so frei als möglich von Prozessen des Hierarchisierens, Ein- und Ausschließens zu halten. Eine Gesellschaft, die demokratisch sein will, kann ihre Betriebe und Institutionen nicht autoritär und hierarchisch organisieren.

3.2) „Wer sind alle?"[3] Vom Wählen zum Losen in einer postfundamentalistischen Gesellschaft nach Oliver Marchart

Wie Oliver Marchart (2013, 390ff.) ausführt, lässt sich für westliche demokratische Gesellschaften auf theoretisch philosophischer Ebene postulieren, dass Demokratie gerade darin besteht, ihre eigene Grundlosigkeit, ihre eigene Begründungslosigkeit und ihre eigene Kontingenz bei der Ausübung von Herrschaft, Hierarchie und Gewalt anzuerkennen. Dies meint der Begriff des „Postfundamentalismus" von Marchart. Daran möchte ich meine These anschließen, dass die Praxis der Wahl und des Wählens am Begriff des selbstbe-

---

[3] http://www.trafo-k.at/projekte/washeisstalle/ 20.07.2015

stimmen Subjekts festhält, das gerade keine Einsicht in die Kontingenz und Gesellschaftlichkeit seiner selbst pflegt. Deshalb stelle ich hier die These auf, dass die Praxis des Losens wie sie beispielsweise Hubertus Buchstein (2009, 445ff.) mit einem europäischen House of Lots vorgeschlagen hat oder wie sie John Burnheim (1987) in seinem Buch „Demarchie" überlegte als gesellschaftliche und egaliäre Praxis dieses postfundamentalistische Bewusstsein von Demokratie auch praktisch vollzieht. Die Praxis des Wählens in der Demokratie jedoch hält am Fundamentalismus der Begründung von Herrschaft, Hierarchie und Gewalt durch selbstbestimmte, individualisierte Gruppen und Interessenseinheiten in einer Gesellschaft fest, die auch tatsächlich über einen Grund und eine Rechtfertigung für ihre Wahl verfügen. Das Losen als egalitäre Praxis in Kommunen, Betrieben, Institutionen, Parlamenten und Regierungen halte ich für in der Lage, das Ausmaß an institutioneller Gewalt zu reduzieren und zur Verringerung von Praktiken des Einschließens, Ausschließens und Hierarchisierens beizutragen. Steht doch am Beginn jedes Prozesses des Einschließens, Ausschließens und Hierarchisierens in Institutionen und Betrieben der Zufall, der als Legitimation zwar gesellschaftlich relevant ist, weil er den Anspruch hat, Herrschaft, Hierarchie und Gewalt zu reduzieren, aber nicht in dem Ausmaß zur ideologischen Rechtfertigung von Hierarchien benutzt werden kann, wie dies bei den von Castoriadis benannten Legitimationsstrategien der Fall ist.

3.3) Egalitäre Praktiken: Wie können Gesellschaften demokratisch sein, wenn ihre Institutionen und Betriebe hierarchisch sind?

Zusammenfassend möchte ich sagen, dass ich hier und in anderen Publikationen (Utta Isop 2009, 2011, 2013, 2014) die Thesen vertrete, dass sich Gewalt, Herrschaft und Hierarchien in Gesellschaften reduzieren lassen. Und das egalitäre Praktiken zur Reduktion von Gewalt, Herrschaft und Hierarchien in Gesellschaften beitragen können. Eine solche egalitäre Praxis stellt für mich beispielsweise das Losen von Vertretungsstrukturen in Institutionen und Betrieben dar. Egalitäre Praktiken sind für mich auch solche, die die lustvollen Prozesse des Hierarchisierens, Einschließens und Ausschließens aus den überlebensnotwendigen Zugängen zu Ressourcen in Institutionen und Betrieben lösen und sie in reflexiven sozialen Räumen der

324

BDSM explizit und bekennend vollziehen. Zu egalitären Praktiken gehört es weiters, Befehls- und Einkommenshierarchien in Institutionen und Betrieben so gering wie möglich zu halten und die Lust auf Hierarchien in die eigens dafür geschaffenen sozialen Räume, Phantasien und Beziehungen zu verweisen. Demokratisch zu werden, bedeutet für Gesellschaften ein dauerndes Bemühen um den Abbau von Herrschaft, Hierarchien und Gewalt, die Reduktion von institutioneller Gewalt, auch und gerade in ihren Institutionen und Betrieben. Wie können Gesellschaften, die sich durch die nicht-demokratischen Prozesse der Wahl selbst konstituieren und deren Institutionen und Betriebe durch Befehls- und Einkommenshierarchien gekennzeichnet sind, demokratisch nennen? Wie können Gesellschaften demokratisch sein, wenn ihre Institutionen und Betriebe hierarchisch, einschließen und ausschließend strukturiert sind?

Bibliographie

Pierre Bourdieu *Die feinen Unterschiede. Kritik der gesellschaftlichen Urteilskraft.* Frankfurt am Main: Suhrkamp, 1987.

Rosi Braidotti *metamorphoses. Towards a materialist theory of becoming.* Oxford: Polity Press, 2007.

Kerstin Brückweh *Mordlust: Serienmorde, Gewalt und Emotionen im 20. Jahrhundert.* Frankfurt: Campus, 2006.

Hubertus Buchstein *Demokratie und Lotterie. Das Los als politisches Entscheidungsinstrument von der Antike bis zur EU.* Frankfurt: Campus, 2009.

Erin E. Buckels und Delroy Paulhus *„Everyday Sadists Take Pleasure In Others' Pain"",* /Association of Psychological Science/ 12.09.2013, online accessed 07.06.2015: http://www.psychologicalscience.org/index.php/news/releases/everyday-sadists-take-pleasure-in-others-pain.html

John Burnheim *Über Demokratie. Alternativen zum Parlamentarismus.* Berlin: Wagenbach Klaus GmbH., 1987.

Judith Butler *Psyche der Macht. Das Subjekt der Unterwerfung.* Frankfurt am Main: edition suhrkamp, 2001.

Cornelius Castoriadis *„Die Lohn- und Einkommenshierarchie"*. In: *Kapitalismus als imaginäre Institution. Ausgewählte Schriften*. Band 6. Hessen: Verlag Edition AV, 2014, S.153-164.

Freaksexual *„Towards a general theory of BDSM and power"*, /Blog freaksexual wordpress, 11.06.2007/, online accessed 29.04.2015: https://freaksexual.wordpress.com/2007/06/11/towards-a-general-theory-of-bdsm-and-power/

Sigmund Freud *„Zeitgemäßes über Krieg und Tod"*. In: *Gesammelte Werke. Werke aus den Jahren 1913-1917*. Frankfurt am Main: Fischer, 1999, S.324-355.

Florian Grotz und Dieter Nohlen *Kleines Lexikon der Politik*. München: Beck, 2006.

Ulrich von Hagen *„Homo militaris – Gestalt insitutionalisierter Gewalt"*, /Bundeszentrale für politische Bildung/ 21.10.2013, online accessed 24.03.2015: http://www.bpb.de/apuz/170815/homo-militaris-gestalt-institutionalisierter-gewalt

Utta Isop *„Institutionelle Gewalt – zur Dysfunktionalität von Hierarchien für Demokratie und Gleichstellung. Neuere Tendenzen queerer Anarchafeminismen"*. In: *aep informationen. Feministische Zeitschrift für Politik und Gesellschaft*, Nr.3/2014, S.46-50.

Utta Isop *„Praktiken der Selbstorganisation. Losdemokratie, Rotationsprinzip und Sorgearbeit"*. In: Fink/Krondorfer/Prokop/Brunner *Prekarität und Freiheit? Feministische Wissenschaft, Kulturkritik und Selbstorganisation*. Münster: Westfälisches Dampfboot, 2013, S.242-252.

Utta Isop *"Enough is enough" – "Ya basta!" Kein Gott, keine Nation, kein Konzern, kein Ehemann"*. In: *Differenzen leben. Kulturwissenschaftlichgeschlechterkritische Perspektiven auf Inklusion und Exklusion*. Bielefeld: Transkript, 2011, S. 171-186.

Utta Isop *„Geschlechterbasisdemokratie. Fünf Forderungen queerer Politik"*. In: A. Pechriggl, K. Mertlitsch, U. Isop, B. Hipfl (Hg.) *Über Geschlechterdemokratie hinaus. Beyond Gender Democracy*. Klagenfurt: Drava Verlag, 2009, S. 45-67.

E.L. James *Fifty Shades of Grey*. New York: First Vintage Books Edition, 2012.

Oliver Marchart *Das unmögliche Objekt. Eine postfundamentalistische Theorie der Gesellschaft*. Frankfurt: Suhrkamp, 2013.

Marquis de Sade *Die Geschichte der Justine oder die Nachteile der Tugend*, /Zeno.org/ Berliner Ausgabe 2014, 3. Auflage Neusatz durch Michael Holzinger, online accessed 17.07.2015: http://www.zeno.org/Literatur/M/ Sade+Marquis+de/Roman/Die+Geschichte+der+Justine+oder+die+Nachteile+der +Tugend/Erster+Band

Andrea Maurer *Herrschaftssoziologie. Eine Einführung*. Frankfurt: Campus, 2004.

Robert Misik *„Plädoyer gegen Ungleichmacherei Vom Glück, in einer Gesellschaft der Gleichen zu leben: Zwei britische Wissenschafter zeigen in einer großen Studie, wie Ungleichheit schadet"*, /Der Standard/, 02. April 2010, online accessed 17.07.2015: http://derstandard.at/1269448828194/Plaedoyer-gegen-Ungleichmacherei

Gudrun Perko *Queer-Theorien. Ethische, politische und logische Dimensionen plural-queeren Denkens*. Köln: Papy Rossa, 2005.

Kate Pickett/ Richard Wilkinson *Gleichheit ist Glück. Warum gerechte Gesellschaften für alle besser sind*. Frankfurt: Tolkemitt Verlag, 2010.

Monika Preuk *„Faszination Ekel: Warum so viele Dschungelcamp schauen"*, /Focus online/, 17.01.2014, online accessed 17.07.2015: www.focus.de/ gesundheit/ratgeber/psychologie/news/von-schadenfreude-bis-sadismus-moderne-form-des-prangers-heisst-dschungelcamp_aid_704499.html

Stephanic Spoto *„Teaching against Hierarchies: An Anarchist Approach"*, Mai 2015, online accessed 20.07.2015: https://www.academia.edu/11729649/ Teaching_Against_Hierarchies_an_Anarchist_Approach

Aruna Srivastava *"Editorial introduction to "Postcolonialism and Its Discontents" issue of ARIEL"*, 1998, online accessed 25.12.2014: http://www.ucalgary.ca/uofc/eduweb/engl392/aruna-ed.html

Susanne Wedlich *„Der Sadist unter uns"*, /Süddeutsche Zeitung/, 22.Oktober 2013, online accessed 07.04.2015: http://www.sueddeutsche.de/ wissen/psychologie-der-sadist-unter-uns-1.1799935

Michael Wilk und Bernd Sahler *Strategische Einbindung: Von Mediationen, Schlichtungen, runden Tischen... und wie Protestbewegungen manipuliert werden*. Lich: Edition AV'88, 2014.

Richard Wilkinson *"Die Mittelklasse irrt"*, /Die Zeit/, 26.März 2010, online accessed 25.12.2014: http://www.zeit.de/2010/13/Wohlstand-Interview-Richard-Wilkinson

Youtube *„Schön oder nicht schön?"* 2015, online accessed 16.07.2015: https://www.youtube.com/watch?v=U-nWcD_Uulo

HEIDE HAMMER

TAKING A BACK SEAT: LÄSSLICHE KLASSENFRAGEN

> „Revolution ist nichts für schwache Nerven. Sie ist etwas für
> Ungeheuer. Du musst verlieren, was du bist, um zu erkennen,
> was du werden kannst." (Hardt/Negri 2010, 347)

In der Motivation, etwas radikal Anderes zu wollen, liegt die Verbindung mit ähnlichen AkteurInnen wesentlich im Unbehagen, einer Unzufriedenheit und erkannten Unerträglichkeit der gegebenen Verhältnisse. Daneben sind wir ein Einrichten in der jeweiligen Situation gewohnt, selbst Wohlfühlen ist durchaus möglich. Umfassendere Wünsche sind eher mit dem Begriffspaar Nähe und Distanz verknüpft: Wie sehr, wie nahe lasse ich das Elend dieser Welt an mich heran? Inwiefern kümmert es mich, dass an den Grenzen der EU Flüchtlinge einen gewaltsamen Tod erleiden oder Teile eines modernisierten Sklavenwesens werden, dessen Ursache die bestehenden Grenzregime und die Abschottung der Wohlstandsinseln sind? Wann nehme ich meine politische und soziale Verantwortung wahr? Wir sind auch Teil einer rechten Politik, einem politischen Handeln und fortwährenden Bemühen, die eigenen Privilegien zu bewahren, ungeachtet der Tatsache, wie viele Menschenleben diese Ordnung kostet. Die Verweigerung der emotionalen Präsenz des globalen Skandals von Hunger, Elend und gewaltsamem Tod liegt weniger in einem Mangel an Wissen, es ist eher ein Mechanismus des Selbstschutzes und auch der Resignation.

Die grobe Unterscheidung von links und rechts, von emanzipatorischen und konservativen politischen Haltungen bleibt somit notwendig und sinnvoll. Marx prägnante Forderung in der Einleitung zur Kritik der Hegelschen Rechtsphilosophie lautet: „*alle Verhältnisse umzuwerfen*, in denen der Mensch ein erniedrigtes, ein geknechtetes, ein verlassenes, ein verächtliches Wesen ist." (385)

Hinter diesen Formulierungen verbirgt sich auch eine politische, eine ethische Entscheidung. Die Lust an der Distinktion, der Einordnung in ein hierarchisches Gefüge, erlaubt uns das zufriedene Einrichten in der bürgerlichen Gesellschaft oder ein Bewegen in ganz unterschiedlichen Nischen und Szenen, doch auch dies skizziert nur einen allzu engen Möglichkeitsraum. Dass in kapitalistischen Verhältnissen die Grenzen des Möglichen zu eng gefasst sind, zeigen uns Ereignisse, die mit einer Bewegung des Widerständigen einhergehen, aus kollektiven Befreiungsprozessen, in der Vorwegnahme jener Bedingungen, die tatsächlich für alle gelten und so Freiheit mit Gleichheit und Gerechtigkeit verbindet, eine eminent ethische Perspektive. Diese kann daher auch nicht im strengen Sinne begründet werden, denn ein individuelles Überschreiten enger Grenzen ist auch im kapitalistischen Modus möglich und erwünscht.

Sandro Mezzadra besteht im Begriff des „Postkolonialen Kapitalismus" auf einer „geographischen Brechung (…) einem fortwährenden Durcheinander der Maßstäbe von Akkumulation, Enteignung und Ausbeutung". Mit dem Ende des Fordismus drängt das Elend der Welt sehr nahe an uns heran, in Gestalt von BettlerInnen vor dem von uns bevorzugten Supermarkt, im Billiglohnland Deutschland, vor dessen Vorbild hiesige GewerkschafterInnen bereits warnen und es haftet an unseren Kleidern aus den Sweatshops Vietnams oder Mexikos.

Die Sinnlosigkeit der Existenz ist für Ungläubige eine unhintergehbare Tatsache und somit geht es darum, wie wir dieses Zusammenleben hier gestalten. Eine Position radikaler Immanenz erlöst uns nicht vor der konkreten Unterscheidung, welche politische Position wir verfolgen. Hannah Arendt antwortet auf die Frage, Was ist Politik, „… der Mensch ist a-politisch. Politik entsteht in dem *Zwischen-den-*Menschen, also durchaus *außerhalb* des Menschen. Es gibt daher keine eigentlich politische Substanz. Politik entsteht im Zwischen und etabliert sich als Bezug." (Arendt 1993, 11) Bei Arendt wird dieser Möglichkeitsraum als öffentlicher und kollektiver Ort gefasst. In diesem Möglichkeitsraum entstehen Beziehungen und werden Bedeutungen erzeugt. Darin kann die Wahrnehmung einer Realität gelingen, die etwas bedeutet, also nicht schon für sich bedeutsam ist, sondern erst durch das kollektive Handeln aktualisiert wird. Der Begriff des Handelns ist bei Arendt wesentlich vom Herstellen und Arbeiten, also dem Bereich der Mittel und Zwecke unterschieden. Darin liegt das jeweils zu aktualisierende Potenzial von Freiheit und Kreativität.

Wenn wir uns eine Gesellschaft der Freien und Gleichen wünschen, oder mit Brecht formuliert, MitkämpferInnen, die „unter sich keine Sklaven und über sich keine Herren" sehen wollen, dann ist es überaus hilfreich, an einer Vervielfältigung der Möglichkeit von mannigfaltigen Wahrnehmungen und Erfahrungen zu wirken.

Ob die gegenwärtige Aufgabe linksradikaler Theoriebildung in einem Changieren, einem Experimentieren zwischen Potentialen der Assoziation – im Sinne Donna Haraways „Affinität statt Identität" - und der eindeutigen Zurückweisung von Argumentationen und Handlungen, die demokratischen, partizipativen, emanzipativen Wünschen entgegengerichtet sind, besteht? Das ist nach Jahrzehnten dahingehender Theoriebildung doch etwas dürftig und es wächst die Ungeduld.

Das Werden, das Prozesshafte, Unabgeschlossene mag für privilegierte Personen ganz hübsch sein und es reicht zumindest für den Gestus des radical chic, um sich gegenüber herkömmlichen Konservativismen abzugrenzen. Die Differenz zur neoliberalen Aufforderung, kreativ und emotional, als gesamte Person in den Arbeitszusammenhang involviert zu sein, ist dennoch groß. Eine Verwechslung mit sozialistischer Kollektivität wird zuverlässig von den engen Grenzen des kapitalistischen Regimes verhindert, dessen Ausschlüsse mal mit Gender und Diversity Konzepten, doch beständig entlang der Kategorien von Nationalität, Klasse, Rasse, Geschlecht oder Ability wirken. Der Anspruch lautet nie für alle, sondern es gilt in Konkurrenz um knappe Güter zu bestehen, zu gewinnen und zu verlieren und das Verhältnis von Siegen und Niederlagen hängt ganz entschieden von ererbten Kapitalien ab.

Der Begriff queer schimmert nach wie vor und wenn er dann auch noch mit Anarchismen kombiniert wird, umso mehr. *queer* wurde in der Kritik an feministischen Positionen geschärft und auch wenn sein Ausgangspunkt im Komplex der Sexualität liegt, geht es wesentlich um eine radikale Kritik an jeglicher Form der Identität.

Vielleicht spricht die Ungeduld des Alters aus ihm oder doch die Einsicht, dass all dies angehäufte positive Wissen, das wiederholte Thematisieren unzuträglicher und in bestimmtem Sinne auch unvernünftiger Bedingungen noch nicht einmal eine bedeutende Verschiebung der gesellschaftlichen Hegemonie bedingt. Alain Badiou setzt sich mit seinem Entwurf einer *Ethik* in eine Traditionslinie, die auf Wahrheit und Wahrhaftigkeit fokussiert. Dazu assoziieren vorsichtig vernünftige Gemüter umgehend einen Rückfall in jene glücklich überwundenen Phasen dogmatischer Theorieproduktion und politischer Gruppen, die trotz penetranten Bemühens weder die Gunst der

Stunde noch die Aufmerksamkeit der (werktätigen) Massen gewinnen konnten. Anders etwa als Judith Butler verwirft er die Konstruktion von Menschenrechten und Butlers vage Zielorientierung zunehmender Demokratisierung. Gerade die wohlmeinende „Ethik der Menschenrechte", der „Respekt der Verschiedenheiten" definiere eine Identität, die den/die Andere/n nur als Objekt der Anpassung und Integration tolerieren kann: (Badiou 2003, 39ff) „Die objektive (oder historische) Grundlage der gegenwärtigen Ethik ist der Kulturalismus, die wahrhaft touristische Faszination für das Vielfache an Sitten, Bräuchen und Überzeugungen. (…) Ja, das Wesentliche der ethischen ‚Objektivität' hängt von einer volkstümlichen Soziologie ab, welche unmittelbar aus dem kolonialen Erstaunen über die Wilden übernommen worden ist, wobei es klar ist, dass die Wilden auch unter uns sind (Drogenabhängige der Vororte, Glaubensgemeinschaften, Sekten …: all der journalistische Kram der bedrohlichen inneren Andersheit); dieser Tatsache stellt die Ethik, ohne ihr Forschungsprogramm zu ändern, *ihre* ‚Anerkennung' und *ihre* Sozialarbeiter gegenüber." (ebenda, 42)

Badiou wendet sich weniger gegen die Konstruktion geschlossener Identitäten als vielmehr gegen jene Form des Universalismus, die wir seit Kants Fassungen der Vernunft zu denken und proklamieren gewohnt sind. Sein Begriff von „Wahrheit" stützt eine eigentümliche Form des Universalismus: „Eine Wahrheit allein ist als solche indifferent in Bezug auf die Verschiedenheiten. (...) Eine Wahrheit ist für alle dieselbe." (ebenda, 43) Die Terminologie ist etwas gewöhnungsbedürftig und gemahnt in ihrer Erwartung an ein künftiges Ereignis an messianische Hoffnung. Mit Lacan illustriert Badiou nicht nur die Gegenstands- und Situationsgebundenheit einer Ethik (etwa die Ethik der Psychoanalyse oder die Ethik der klinischen Situation), sondern auch die konstitutive Bedeutung des Begehrens für das Subjekt des Unbewussten und dieses Begehren ist das Ungewusste schlechthin. (ebenda, 68) Lacans Diktum: „Ich behaupte, daß es nur eines gibt, dessen man schuldig sein kann, zumindest in analytischer Perspektive, und das ist, abgelassen zu haben von seinem Begehren" (Lacan 1996, 380) wird nun pointiert: „Nicht in dem nachgeben, was man über sich selbst nicht weiß." (Badiou 2003, 68)

Trotz des Pathos in der *Ethik* Badious fasziniert das Allgemeine/Universelle der Wahrheit, ebenso wie die „*unvergleichbare[n] Intensitäten der Existenz*". Dieses Ergründen einer Haltung oder Motivation, die Lust an radikalen Veränderungen mögen die tendenziell pragmatischen, vorsichtigen Ausführungen Judith Butlers ergänzen. Badiou nennt politische Ereignisse, die gewöhnlich einer großen Geschichtserzählung folgen - so als wäre mit dem Sturm auf die Bastille, das Winterpalais oder mit der „Nacht der Barrikaden" 1968 tatsächlich eine „Situation geschaffen [worden], die jede Umkehr unmöglich macht" (Marx 1972, 118). Doch folgt sein Blick dem „Gesetzwidrigen" der einzelnen Situationen, er beschreibt „Wahrheitsprozesse" und nennt deren AkteurInnen „Wahrheitspunkte". Daher gewinnt die „Treue" zu einem Ereignis auch diese herausragende Bedeutung, die Frage der Kontinuität, des Festhaltens an der Sehnsucht nach jenem radikal Neuen, das für alle gilt. Diese Sehnsucht ist für Badiou vom „Ungewussten schlechthin", dem Begehren motiviert. Im Ereignis kommt nur die Leere der vorangegangenen Situation zum Sein. Die „Wahrheiten [haben] ihren singulären Durchbruch nur im Webstoff der Meinungen", wir werden also wieder selbst inmitten und als Teil eines Ereignisses diverse Belanglosigkeiten austauschen. Ohnehin verwehrt sich Badiou gegen jegliche Rigidität und politischen Terror. Seine *Ethik* ist vielmehr von einem unerschütterlichen Wohlwollen gegenüber der konkreten Person geprägt: „Denn so feindlich auch immer ein ‚Jemand' einer Wahrheit gegenüber steht, wird er immer in der Ethik der Wahrheiten als fähig vorgestellt, der Unsterbliche, der er [je] ist, zu werden." (Badiou 2003,100)

Butler zeigt im Gegensatz zu Badiou ihre Vorsicht gegenüber einer lediglich affirmativen Verwendung des Terminus „Begehren". Ihre Vorsicht resultiert aus der Präsenz von Gewaltverhältnissen, deren Vernichtungsdrohung „Fragen des Überlebens" (Butler 2009, 313) nahe legt. Sie bleibt damit manchmal „auf die Arbeit des Negativen im Hegelschen Sinne konzentriert", doch die Voraussetzung jeglicher Affirmation ist das Überleben, womit auch die Entscheidung, einem Begehren nach Sicherheit und klaren Kategorisierungen konsequent zu folgen – das Objekt der Unordnung auszulöschen - klar verurteilt werden muss. Butler und Badiou stimmen vermutlich darin überein, *„dass die einzige Sache, die dem Menschen zustoßen kann,* [nicht] *der Tod ist"*. (Badiou 2003, 52) Während Butler jedoch am Axiom des Schutzes der konkreten Person festhält - ohne deren Lebendigkeit jeglicher Verweis auf ihr Begehren zunichte wird, beschreibt Badiou den Universalismus herkömmlicher Ethik als Form des Nihilismus, die „jede breite positive Sicht der Möglichkeiten" untersagt.

Vielleicht befinden wir uns immer noch in einer Kerbe repetitiver Theorieproduktion – in durchaus emanzipativer Absicht – wo doch klar ist, dass kein „Über-Ich der theoretischen Postmoderne" die Verwendung von Begriffen wie Vernunft, Subjekt, Universalität, Demokratie oder Freiheit verbietet. (Butler 2009, 287) Mit Butler besteht die Aufgabe der Wiederaneignung dieser Begriffe in progressiver Absicht, um ein divergierendes Funktionieren dieser Terminologie zu ermöglichen. In vielfältigen Versuchen der Wiederaneignung müssen die konstitutiven Ausschlüsse des Konzepts der Moderne präsent gehalten und ihre zentralen Begriffe auf jene Personen und Gruppen ausgedehnt werden, deren Ausschluss bisher konstitutiv für die Verfasstheit gerade auch demokratischer Gesellschaften ist. Butler erkennt, dass ein solches politisches Vorhaben jene Regierungsform, die das zu erreichen versucht, zugleich in den Ruin führen würde. Eine solche Regierung würde also im Sinne ihrer eigenen Abschaffung wirken. (ebenda, 289) In der Absicht einer radikalen Demokratisierung von Gesellschaft muss der „Sinn für Differenz und Zukünftigkeit" in das Konzept der Moderne integriert werden. (ebenda)

Nun scheinen gesellschaftliche Veränderungen kaum durch die Instanz des Bewusstseins erreicht zu werden. Wir verfügen über eine Vielzahl an guten Argumenten und umfassenden Informationen. Vielmehr geht es um einen Überfluss an Kreativität in einer „Politik der Codes", um der Rigidität und den wahnhaften Geschlossenheitsphantasien rechtsextremer Politik eine Vielfalt von alltäglichen Praktiken, die zu „Imitation und Aufsässigkeit" (Butler 1996, 15ff) motivieren, entgegenzusetzen.

Ein bereits etabliertes Beispiel für die Aufhebung einer – durchaus kämpferisch gefassten - Identität liefert für Michael Hardt und Antonio Negri die revolutionäre kommunistische Tradition: „Das Proletariat ist gemäß dieser Tradition die erste wahrhaft revolutionäre Klasse in der Menschheitsgeschichte, insofern sie darauf aus ist, sich als Klasse selbst abzuschaffen. Die Bourgeoisie versucht sich ständig selbst zu erhalten, wie das schon der Adel und alle anderen herrschenden Klassen früherer Tage taten. (…) Das Projekt zur Abschaffung der Identität übernimmt somit die traditionelle Rolle der *Abschaffung des Eigentums und des Staates.* Damit der revolutionäre Kommunismus zu einem Projekt nicht der Emanzipation, sondern der Befreiung wird – nicht der Emanzipation *der* Arbeit, sondern der Befreiung *von der* Arbeit-, muss er einen Prozess der Selbsttransformation über die Arbeiteridentität hinaus in Gang setzen." (Hardt/Negri 2010, 340)

Auch hierorts gibt es viele Versuche der kollektiven Produktion, des gemeinsamen Tuns. Dieses Tun und Tätigsein scheint aber generell zur zentralen Währung geworden zu sein. In der Vielzahl der Aktivitäten wird Attraktivität gemessen. Die Einförmigkeit der Erfolgsindikatoren korrespondiert direkt mit Konkurrenz und Vereinzelung: Bini Adamzak fasst pointiert: „Trotz WG, Szene, Freundschaft trifft die polit-ökonomische [libidinöse] Anrufung Subjekte als Einzelne: [nicht nur] allein einkaufen, allein abwaschen, allein arbeiten, allein Steuern erklären, immer wieder Prüfung. So betreten die Einzelnen die Arena des Liebesmarktes, die Sphäre libidinöser Zirkulation als Vereinzelte, einander fremde, entfremdete." (Adamzak 2006) Mit Badiou können wir im Medium der Politik, der Kunst, der Wissenschaft oder der Liebe die Intensität der Existenz wählen und es ist wohl als Glücksfall zu betrachten, wenn die notwendige Orientierung auf das zukünftige Ereignis auch hierorts durch gelegentlich ereignishafte Ausbrüche aus der bisherigen Ordnung motiviert ist. Schließlich geht es in einem emanzipatorischen Diskurs um ein Modell der „Solidarität jenseits der Identität". (Steyrl 2007)

Literatur

Adamzak, Bini. „Theorie der polysexuellen Ökonomie". In: *diskurs – Frankfurter Student_Innen Zeitschrift*. Nr. 1, 2006.
http://www.copyriot.com/diskus/061/theorie_der_polysexuellen_oekonomie.htm

Arendt, Hannah. *Was ist Politik? Fragmente aus dem Nachlaß (1950-1959)*. München: Piper, 1993.

Badiou, Alain. *Ethik. Versuch über das Bewusstsein des Bösen*. Wien: Turia + Kant, 2003.

Butler, Judith. „Imitation und Aufsässigkeit der Geschlechtsidentität". In: Sabine Hark (Hrsg.): *Grenzen lesbischer Identitäten*. Berlin: Querverlag, 1996, S. 15-37.

Butler, Judith. *Die Macht der Geschlechternormen und die Grenzen des Möglichen*. Frankfurt/M.: Suhrkamp, 2009.

Hardt, Michael; Negri, Antonio. *Common Wealth: Das Ende des Eigentums*. Frankfurt/New York: Campus, 2010.

Lacan, Jacques. *Die Ethik der Psychoanalyse. Das Seminarbuch VII*. Weinheim, Berlin: Quadriga, 1996.

Marx, Karl; Engels, Friedrich. „Zur Kritik der Hegelschen Rechtsphilosophie. Einleitung". In: Dies. *Werke*. Bd. 1. Berlin: Dietz, 1976, S. 378-391.

Marx, Karl. „Der achtzehnte Brumaire des Louis Bonaparte". In: *Werke*, Bd. 8. Berlin: Dietz, 1972, S. 115-123.

Mezzadra, Sandro. *Wie viele Geschichten der Arbeit? Für eine Theorie des postkolonialen Kapitalismus*. (Übersetzt von Therese Kaufmann und Tom Waibel, 01 2012) http://eipcp.net/transversal/0112/mezzadra/de

Steyerl, Hito. „Die Gegenwart der Subalternen." In: G. Ch. Spivak: *Can the Subaltern Speak?* Einleitung. Wien: Turia + Kant 2007.

http://translate.eipcp.net/strands/03/steyerl-strands02en?lid=steyerl-strands02de#redir

DORIS LEIBETSEDER

„PREKÄRER SEX: EINE QUEER-FEMINISTISCHE DIS/ABILITY ETHIK"

Dieser Essay umfasst zentrale Thesen meiner aktuellen Forschungs-arbeit über eine nicht-normative[1] queer-feministische und dis/ability[2] Ethik, die sich mit den *Neuen Reproduktiven und Genetischen Techno-logien* (NRGT) beschäftigt. Allgemein gesagt, besteht diese Forschung aus zwei Teilen: erstens aus einer angewandten Ethik, die sich mit den reproduktiven Herausforderungen für transgender[3] und intergeschlecht-lichen (intersex)[4] Personen und Menschen mit Dis/Ability beschäftigt und zweitens einer Meta-Ethik, welche die wichtigsten Elemente einer queer-feministischen dis/ability Ethik der Reproduktion beinhält.

In diesem Aufsatz gebe ich erstens eine kurze Beschreibung des ers-ten und zweiten Teils meiner Forschungsarbeit. Zu Beginn erkläre ich, was eine queer-feministische dis/ability Ethik sein soll und gehe näher auf die NRGT ein, indem ich die non-normativen Potentiale der NRGT hervorhebe und die negativen Aspekte der NRGT gegenüberstelle und letztendlich auf die Herausforderungen für transgender und interge-schlechtliche Personen und Menschen mit Behinderungen hinweise. Die Schlussfolgerung aus diesen Aspekten der NRGT zielt auf eine gemein-

---

[1] Mehr zum Thema Queer Theorie und Anti-Normativität in der Ausgabe „Queer Theory and Antinormativity" der Zeitschrift *differences* (2015) 26/1.

[2] Ich verwende den englischen Begriff für Behinderung, da diese Schreibweise mit Querstrich nur mit dem englischen Wort funktioniert. Der Querstrich verdeutlicht, dass die Grenze zwischen Behinderung und Nichtbehinderung oft nicht eindeutig ist.

[3] Transgender und trans* sind Begriffe, die inkludierender sind als "transsexuell", sie beziehen sich auf Personen, die sich nicht wohl fühlen in der Geschlechterrolle, die ihnen bei der Geburt zugeteilt wurde, oder die eine andere Geschlechtsidentität als "Mann" oder "Frau" haben (vgl. Whittle 2006, XI).

[4] "ist eine Übersetzung des englischen Begriffs Intersexuality / Intersex. Da im Englischen nicht Sexualität (wie Hetero- oder Homosexualität = sexuelle Orientie-rung) gemeint ist sondern das körperliche Geschlecht (engl.: sex), und weil der deutsche Begriff ebenfalls neben dem körperlichen Geschlecht auch das soziale Geschlecht (engl.: gender) beinhaltet, bevorzugen wir den Begriff der Interge-schlechtlichkeit." „Intergeschlechtlichkeit ist das was entsteht, wenn körperlich die willkürlich gesteckten Grenzen zwischen Männlichkeit und Weiblichkeit überschrit-ten werden." (http://www.intersexualite.de/ aufgerufen am 20.7.2015)

same Handlungsmacht für Veränderungen in den NRGT. Der zweite Teil, die Meta-Ethik der Reproduktion beschäftigt sich mit den grundlegenden Elementen einer solchen Ethik, wie z.B.: Gerechtigkeit, Anerkennung (Intersektionalität und Ontologie), Universalismus, Interdependenz, Fähigkeiten und transformatives Ethos.

Allgemeine Beschreibung einer queer-feministischen dis/ability Ethik

Eine queer-feministische dis/ability Ethik ist eine Kritik an der angenommenen Neutralität von ethischen Herangehensweisen und deren heteronormativen, kolonialisierenden, „rassisierenden", ethnisierenden und „ablebodied" Perspektiven. Das heißt, diese werden mit den Praktiken der Auflösung des Zweigeschlechtersystems, der Heterosexualität und der traditionellen Familienstruktur und Strategien der Dekolonialisierung, des Anti-Rassismus und der „Anti-Abledbodiedness" konfrontiert. Die Betonung liegt auf nicht-normativen Körpern, Sexualitäten und Fortpflanzungsmöglichkeiten, die zu neuen Verwandtschaftsformen führen und gegen die Dichotomie der Norm/Devianz oder gesund/krank (pathologisch), und gegen ethnische und „rassische" Kategorisierungen arbeitet. Ich fokussiere auf wesentliche Elemente einer queer-feministischen-dis/ability Ethik im foucaultschen Sinne einer postmoralischen Ethik, die sich am Beispiel der NRGT zeigt, und die kollektive Handlungsmöglichkeiten betont.

I. Erster Teil: angewandte Ethik der NRGT

1. Normative NRGT

Je nach Gebrauch der NRGT können deren Ergebnisse normativ bzw. normierend oder non-normative bzw. nicht-normierend sein. In Charis Thompsons Kapitel *Techniques of Normalization* (Thompson 2005, 79-115) werden mehrere Beispiele angegeben, wie die Prozesse und Objekte in den NRGT-Kliniken normalisiert oder routiniert werden (ebenda, 80 f). Diese normalisierenden Prozesse involvieren die Normierung und Performanz von Geschlecht (ebenda, 135 ff). Thompsons Schlussfolgerung daraus ist, dass in den NRGT-Kliniken Geschlechterstereotype benutzt werden, um diese neuartigen soziotechnologischen Vorgänge zu rechtfertigen (ebenda, 141). Auch heben einige Forscher*innen hervor, wie NRGT die traditionelle patriarchale weiße Familie stärken, indem sie die Fortpflanzung von unfruchtbaren weißen heterosexuellen Paaren ermöglichen und gleichzeitig alleinstehende Frauen, lesbische oder schwule Paare, arme Frauen oder Personen, die nicht dem patriarchalen weißen Ideal von Mutterschaft entsprechen, ausschließen (vgl. Roberts 1997, Deomampo 2013a, 517). Preciado beschreibt die Heterosexualität als eine "politisch assistierte Fortpflanzungstechnologie", die vom Staat organisiert und unterstützt wird, weil NRGT zum Beispiel in Frankreich (in Österreich erst seit 2015 für Lesben erlaubt) und vielen anderen Ländern nicht für gleichgeschlechtliche Paare, gewisse heterosexuelle Personen (alleinstehende Frauen), transgender, asexuelle und behinderte Menschen erlaubt sind. Diese Gruppen bilden daher eine reproduktive Minderheit (in Anlehnung an das Wort sexuelle Minderheit, aber ohne die statistische Minderheitsbedeutung), weil es für sie verboten ist, ihr genetisches Material weiterzugeben, da sie es nicht mit einem heterosexuellen Geschlechtsakt vollbringen können. Diese Gruppen sind also politisch sterilisiert und der politische und ökonomische Kampf um den Zugang zu NRGT ist verbunden mit der Entpathologisierung ihrer Leben und mit der Kontrolle über ihr reproduktives Material (vgl. Preciado 2013).[5]

---

[5] "Pour les homosexuels, pour certains transsexuels, pour certains hétérosexuels, pour les asexuelles et pour certaines personnes avec diversité fonctionnelle, provoquer la rencontre de leur materiaux genetiques n'est pas possible á travers la penetration pénis-vagin avec ejaculation. Mais ça ne veut pas dire que nous ne soyons pas fertiles ou que nous n'ayons pas le droit de transmettre notre information génétique. Homosexuels, transsexuels et asexuels, nous ne sommes pas uniquement des *minorités sexuelles* (j'utilise ici "minorite" dans le sens deleuzien, non pas en termes statistiques, mais pour indiquer un segment social politiquement opprimé), nous sommes aussi des *minorités reproductives*. Jusqu'à maintenant, nous avons payé notre dissidence sexuelle par le silence genetique de nos chromosomes. Nous n'avons pas seulement été privés de la transmission du patrimoine économique: notre patrimoine genetique aussi nous a éte confisqué. Homosexuels, transsexuels, et corps considérés comme "handicaps", nous avons été politiquement sterilizes ou bien nous avons été forcés de nous reproduire avec des techniques hétérosexuelles. La bataille actuelle pour l'extension de la PMA <Procréation médicalement assistée> aux corps non-hétérosexuels est une guerre politique et économique pour la dépathologisation de nos formes de vie et pour le contrôle de nos metériaux reproductifs. Le refus du gouvernement de légliser la PMA pour les couples et les individus non-hétérosexuels viendrait soutenir les forms hégémoniques de reproduction et confir-

2. Non-normative NRGT – queere Potentiale

Die queeren Potentiale liegen in den nicht-normativen NRGT, die folgende Aspekte betreffen, wie Ute Kalender erklärt: erstens der Aspekt der Sexualität, da ein heterosexueller Geschlechtsverkehr für die Fortpflanzung mithilfe der NRGT nicht mehr notwendig ist; zweitens den geschlechtlichen Körper betreffend, da der nicht mehr als weiblich für die Reproduktion definiert sein muss (z.B. Schwangerschaft von Transmännern); drittens der Aspekt der Verwandtschaft, weil traditionelle Formen von Familie und Blutsverwandtschaft in Frage gestellt werden (Kalender 2012, 199) und z.B. Regenbogenfamilien mit NRGT hergestellt werden.

NRGT ermöglichen eine neue reproduktive Logik, in der LGBTIQ-(lesbische, schwule, bisexuelle, transgender, intersex, queere) Personen und Menschen mit Behinderungen nicht-genetische und manchmal sogar genetische Verwandtschaften bilden können. In diesen Fällen erfanden die NRGT ein neues Konzept für reproduktive Rechte, weil neue ethische und politische Fragen, vor allem auch mit den genetischen Tests, entstanden sind.

3. Negative Aspekte der NRGT

3.1. Neue Eugenik

Vor allem die Gefahr einer *Neuen Eugenik*, verursacht durch die Präimplantationsdiagnostik (PID), welche die noch nicht eingepflanzten Embryos testet, oder durch im Handel erhältliche nicht-invasive Gen-Tests, die nur einen Tropfen Blut der Mutter brauchen, um ein pränatales DNA-Sequenzing durchzuführen (von Firmen, wie „23andMe" angeboten), oder durch Mitochondrien Ersatztherapie (auch „3-Eltern-Baby" genannt, ist seit Februar 2015 im UK erlaubt) ist gegeben, da sie intergeschlechtliche und/oder behinderte Embryos verhindern. Außerdem können diese genetischen Technologien zu einer Verstärkung der „rassischen" Unterschiede (Roberts 2011), der Heternormativität (Ka-

---

merait que le gouvernement de Hollande perpétue une politique d'hétérosexualisme d'Etat." (Hervorhebung im Original, Preciado 2013).

lender 2012, 206-10) und der „Able-bodiedness" oder „Able-mindedness" führen.

3.2. Bio-Kapital und Bio-Kolonialismus

Der sogenannte "Kinderwunschmarkt" ist hoch kommerziell und SpenderInnen und Keimzellen zirkulieren transnational und ein reproduktiver Tourismus existiert in jene Länder, die billigere NRGT Dienste (z.B. Indien, Spanien, Osteuropa) anbieten, oder in denen mehr (LGBT)-Eingriffe als im Herkunftsland erlaubt sind.

Charis Thompson verglich die kapitalistische Produktion mit der biomedizinischen Reproduktion und kam zum Schluss, dass in der Biomedizin beides, die Produktion und Reproduktion, der Wirtschaft unterliegen (Thompson 2005, 250). Reproduktive Technologien sind weltweit eine multinationale wachsende Industrie. Wie sich die Rolle der biomedizinischen Reproduktion im Lauf der Zeit veränderte, erklärt Preciado: so stand anfangs im Biomachtregime die Kontrolle über die Spermien und Eizellen im Vordergrund, welche wiederum die Kontrolle über die Reproduktion sicherte, jetzt ist lediglich die Reproduktion von Kapital wichtig, also der Profit (Preciado 2008, 32).

Mia Mingus, „eine queere, körperlich behinderte koreanische Frau, die transethnisch und transnational adoptiert wurde"[6], spricht vom medizinischen Industrie-Komplex als einem Profitsystem, dessen Wurzeln in Eugenik, Kapitalismus, Kolonialismus, Sklaverei, Immigration, Krieg, Gefängnissen und reproduktiver Unterdrückung liegen und in ihrer Visualisierung dieses medizinischen Industrie-Komplexes stellt sie die Verbindung zwischen den NRGT und dem *Bio-Kolonialismus* dar[7] (Mingus 2015), der sich in zwei Zielen äußert, nämlich der (ethnischen) Kontrolle über Reproduktion (wer darf sich wie fortpflanzen?) und der (post)kolonialen Ausbeutung zum Zweck des Profitgewinns, z.B. indische Leihmütter (Deomampo 2013a und b), Latinas und Afrikanisch-

---

[6] Deutsche Übersetzung der Autorin von Mingus Website, aufgerufen am 10.3.2015. https://leavingevidence.wordpress.com/about-2/

[7] „Medical Industrial Complex Visual" (Mingus 2015). Mingus gibt an, dass die Skizze nicht allein ihre Arbeit war, sondern ein kollektives Werk, das u.a. aus dem Workshop *"Re-envisioning the Revolutionary Body: Disability, Race, Queerness and the Possibility of Cross-movement Building."* von 2009 mit Cara Page und Patty Berne hervorging.

Amerikanische Frauen in Kalifornien als Leihmütter (Twine 2015) oder osteuropäische Frauen in der Ukraine (Bernard 2014).

Um den Bio-Kolonialismus besser zu verstehen, ist es angebracht, die NRGT näher daraufhin zu untersuchen, wer welche Arbeit in diesen reproduktiven Technologien leistet. Laut Ute Kalender betonen materialistische Feministinnen, dass die Embryos in den Laboratorien materialisierte Produkte von Arbeit sind, was der Annahme widerspricht, dass nur die Klinik die Arbeit vollbringt, und die Frauen nur als Spenderinnen auftreten. Cooper und Waldby (2010) sprechen von der regenerativen Arbeit, weil diese Arbeit der regenerativen Medizin hilft, was wiederum eine euphemistische Bezeichnung für Stammzellen- und Klonforschung ist. Ute Kalender geht einen Schritt weiter und nennt es Rohstoffarbeit, die Rohstoffe herstellt und zur Verfügung stellt (Kalender 2012, 199-204).

In EU-Ländern, in denen die Eizellspende legal ist, (ab 2015 auch in Österreich) werden oft Migrantinnen mit unsicherem Visa- oder Aufenthaltsstatus als bezahlte Spenderinnen beworben. In diesem Fall sind die Rohstoffarbeit und die prekäre Staatsangehörigkeiten/Bürgerrechte miteinander verwoben – z.B. sind es in Spanien oft osteuropäische Migrantinnen (Bergmann 2011). Ute Kalender betont, dass Eizellenspende daher eine Möglichkeit darstellt, als anerkannte und reproduktive Bürgerin gesehen zu werden (Kalender 2012, 205).

Interessanterweise werden "queere" Eizellen besonders wertgeschätzt und tragen zu einer Homonormativität[8] und so wie im Falle von Großbritannien zu einer Homonationalität[9] bei, wenn die Wirtschaft eines Staates von der Biotechnologie profitiert. So zum Beispiel haben lesbische Frauen ein um 20% höheres positives Ergebnis in den NRGT, weil es für sie keine wirklichen Sterilitätsgründe gibt (Kalender 2012,

---

[8] Lisa Duggan gebrauchte dieses Konzept, um die sexuelle Politik des Neoliberalismus zu beschreiben, die Idee der gleichen Rechte der gleichgeschlechtlichen Bewegung in konservative Institutionen aufnimmt (z. B. Heirat und Militär). Das Resultat ist eine konservative gleichgeschlechtliche Politik, die vollkommen mit der neoliberalen Privatisierung übereinstimmt (Duggan 2002, 190). In vielen Fällen entspricht es einer bloßen unkritischen Angleichung an das heterosexuelle System.

[9] Homonationalität geht mit der Homonormativität einher, und bezieht sich darauf, dass sich die gleichgeschlechtliche Bewegung mit dem Staat oder der Nation verbündet hat, um in dessen Institutionen anerkannt zu sein. Wie Jasbir Puar schreibt, äußert sich das in der nationalen Rhetorik der patriotischen Inkludierung (Puar 2006, 67).

204 und Breitbach 2009). Es fehlt für sie nur der reproduktive sexuelle Akt, deswegen nehmen sie die NRGT in Anspruch.

In Großbritannien ist der Zugang zu NRGT für Lesben bereits länger erlaubt und sie werden gezielt von den Kinderwunschkliniken für „Egg-sharing"- Programme beworben, d.h. sie geben mehr Eizellen - als für die eigene Befruchtung notwendig - her und bekommen eine günstigere oder sogar eine gratis Behandlung. Deren Eizelle zählt nun als hochqualitativer Rohstoff. Ute Kalender fragt sich daher, ob queere Personen ihre prekäre Stellung als reproduktive StaatsbürgerInnen verändern können. Meiner Auffassung nach ist hier trotzdem Vorsicht geboten, um nicht der Homonormativität (Anpassung an das heterosexuelle System) oder sogar der Homonationalität (der Staat, der gleichgeschlechtliche Rechte instrumentalisiert) Vorschub zu leisten.

Andere Fragen, die Ute Kalender stellt, betreffen nicht jene Bereiche, die ich mit den Beispielen Homonormativität und Homonationalität als eine queere interne Kritik veranschaulichte, sondern solche Aspekte, die aus einer queeren Ökonomiekritik kommen, so z.B. „Wie ist das Arbeiten rund um die neuen Reproduktions- und Biotechnologien durch Heteronormativität reguliert?" (Kalender 2012, 206). Wer leistet die Rohstoffarbeit in queeren Beziehungen? Sind es eher die Femme-Partnerinnen von Transmännern? Oder sind es die Transmänner selbst, weil sie deren Eizellen vor der geschlechtsanpassenden OP oder vor der Hormoneinnahme einfrieren lassen? Besteht die Gefahr der Etablierung der Lesben als der guten Queers im Unterschied zu Transpersonen (vgl. ebenda)?

Wir sehen, dass wir eine Allianz dieser prekären Personen brauchen, die im Austausch von biomedizinischen Gütern in diesem medizinischen Industriekomplex involviert sind, nämlich von transgender und intergeschlechtlichen Personen, Menschen mit Behinderung und Schwarzen, Farbigen und migrantischen Personen, die Rohstoffarbeiten in den NRGT leisten.

4. Herausforderungen für transgender und intergeschlechtlichen Personen und Menschen mit Behinderungen

4.1. Transgender Personen

Für viele transgender Personen stellt bereits die Krankenversicherung die erste Hürde dar, um NRGT in Anspruch nehmen zu können, denn diese Versicherung ist oft an einen Arbeitsvertrag gebunden und vor allem in den USA sind deswegen viele nicht versichert, obwohl sich die Situation mit „Obama-Care" gebessert hat. Ein weiteres Hindernis liegt darin, dass viele Versicherungen transgender Gesundheitsprobleme nicht inkludieren wollen. In den letzten Jahren ist aber die Anzahl der Versicherungen in den USA, die transgender Angelegenheiten inkludiert, im Steigen (Hanssmann 2014, Plemons 2014).

In vielen Ländern ist für die Änderung der Dokumente die geschlechtsanpassende Operation erforderlich, was einer Sterilisation gleich kommt. 2014 waren es noch 21 Länder in Europa.[10] Der Europäische Menschenrechtsgerichtshof (EGMR) entschied 2015, dass die Forderung nach permanenter Unfruchtbarkeit, die mit einer geschlechtsanpassenden Operation einhergeht, nicht kompatibel mit den Menschenrechten ist.[11]

Falls transgender Personen Zugang zu Kinderwunschkliniken bekommen, werden sie aber oft respektloser als Lesben oder sogar schwule Männer behandelt, wie auch ein kanadischer Zeitungsartikel vom 22. Sept. 2013 von Natalie Stechyson berichtet: „Transgender pregnancy: The last frontier in assisted reproductive technology". In Kanada zahlen transgender Personen eine höhere Gebühr für das Einfrieren ihrer Keimzellen.

Des Weiteren zeigt dieser Artikel anhand von Forschungsberichten aus Europa, dass viele transgender Personen NRGT in Anspruch nehmen möchten. z.B. zeigt eine westeuropäische Studie von 2012, dass sich 40% der Transfrauen Kinder wünschen und mehr als die Hälfte möchten das eigene Sperma benutzen. Aus einer Studie von 2011 zum reproduktiven Wunsch von Transmännern geht hervor, dass mehr als die Hälfte der Transmänner in Belgien sich Kinder wünschen, und 37,5 Prozent hätten ihre Eizellen vor der Transition eingefroren, wenn es damals möglich gewesen wäre (Wierckx et al. 2011).

4.2. Intergeschlechtliche Personen

Viele der intergeschlechtlichen Personen sind – je nach Fall – auf NRGT angewiesen, sei es, weil es die intergeschlechtliche Kondition

---

[10] Trans Rights Europe Map 2014.
[11] Aufgerufen am 10. März 2015. http://tgeu.org/ecthr-ends-absurd-sterilisation-requirement-in-turkish-law/

nicht anders ermöglicht[12] oder weil sich die Reproduktionsfähigkeit durch (Zwangs)-Operationen verringert hat.

Oft wird in der Medizin oder in den Kliniken ein intergeschlechtlicher Nachwuchs befürchtet und die Reproduktion wird daher nicht durchgeführt oder durch genetische Tests werden intergeschlechtliche Embryonen aussortiert.

4.3. Menschen mit Behinderung

Die reproduktive Gleichberechtigung ist für Menschen mit *Dis/Ability* besonders wichtig, da seit langem Zwangssterilisationen an ihnen durchgeführt wurden/werden, entweder weil sie als ungeeignete Eltern oder als asexuell gesehen wurden/werden.

Viele MedizinerInnen sind gegen ihre Fortpflanzung aus Angst davor, dass auch deren Kinder Behinderungen zeigen. Genauso wie bei intergeschlechtlichen Personen werden mittels Gentests Embryos mit Behinderungen aussortiert.

Dis/Ability-AktivistInnen betonen die kollektive Handlungsmacht gegen diesen Selektierungsprozess und beharren wie LGBTI Personen und queere Communities auf dem Recht, NRGT (im Englischen ARGT) in Anspruch nehmen zu dürfen:

"Disability activists have voiced critical concerns about the use of prenatal diagnostic tests and ARGTs to select against the birth of a child with differing abilities. LBGTI people and queer communities offer models of family which centralize intentional relationships and longstanding kinship, challenging the value placed exclusively on biological children while simultaneously affirming our rights to use ARGTs to create families." (Mingus und Berne, 49).

---

[12] Hier zwei Beispiele von intersex Personen aus den Medien, bei denen eine Behandlung gelang, beide aufgerufen am 9.2.2015 http://www.msn.com/en-us/news/world/indian-woman-has-twins-despite-discovery-she-is-mostly-male/ar-AA99zdt und http://www.independent.co.uk/news/science/woman-born-with-no-womb-gives-birth-to-twins-after-treatment-breakthrough-10015506.html?origin=internalSearch (31.1.2015).

5. Schluss: Angewandte Ethik der NRGT

Zusammenfassend gesehen können NRGT als nicht-normative bio-logische Reproduktion für queere und dis/abled Communities benutzt werden. Trotzdem sollen die negativen Aspekte der NRGT beachtet und kritisch analysiert werden: Wer leistet die Rohstoffarbeit und wer wird ausgeschlossen oder hat erschwerten Zugang zu NRGT? Aus dieser Analyse ergibt sich der Handlungsbedarf für Veränderungen in den NRGT, die in Form einer Zusammenarbeit von LGBTIQ-Personen, Menschen mit Behinderungen und RohstoffarbeiterInnen zu einem ge-rechteren Zugang und Umgang mit NRGT führen wird. Diese kollektive Handlungsmacht gilt es ausfindig zu machen.

II. Zweiter Teil: Meta-Ethik der Reproduktion

Dieser Teil dient als Überblick über die aktuellen und wichtigsten Elemente einer queer-feministischen dis/ability Ethik, die sich auf Re-produktion und vor allem auf zwei Grundlagen bezieht: Gerechtigkeit und Ontologie. Das Ziel ist es eine Ethik zu entwickeln, die nicht eine regulatorische Art und Weise vorgibt, sondern die im Gegenteil gegen ihre Instrumentalisierung von normativen Systemen arbeitet.

Die Struktur dieses zweiten Teils ist nun wie folgt gegliedert: An-fangs gebe ich eine nähere Einführung zu einer queer-feministischen dis/ability Meta-Ethik der Reproduktion. Dann gehe ich auf die wichti-gen Fäden dieses ethischen Knotens ein und zwar: Gerechtigkeit, Aner-kennung (Intersektionalität und Ontologie), Universalismus, Interde-pendenz, Fähigkeiten und transformativer Ethos sind.

Von den 1980ern bis in die frühen 2000ern war das heterogene Feld der feministischen Ethik mit vielfältigen Herangehensweisen wie z.B. der marxistischen, existentialistischen, psychoanalytischen, postkoloni-alen, ökologischen Perspektive (Kuusela 2011, 8) ein nützliches Instru-ment, denn sie überdachte „die traditionelle Ethik, die Erfahrungen oder Merkmale von Frauen ignorierte und herunterspielte. Trotz des breiten Feldes und der Diversität einer feministischen Ethik (Pflegeethik, lesbi-sche Ethik, liberale und radikale feministische Ethik) hatte sie primär die gleiche Absicht: die Schaffung einer geschlechtspezifischen Ethik, die als Ziel die Auslöschung der Unterdrückung oder zumindest die Verbesserung der Unterdrückung von jeglicher Personengruppe hat."[13] Wie auch immer: Eine aktuelle queer-feministische dis/ability Ethik der Reproduktion fehlt, obwohl es vereinzelt einige Ideen und Konzepte dazu gibt, die ich später erwähnen werde.

In diesem Artikel bringe ich nach wie vor relevante Theorien aus dem Feld der feministischen Ethik mit den weitreichenden Umrissen einer gegenwärtigen queer-feministischen dis/ability Ethik zusammen. Warum wurde über eine solche queer-feministische Ethik bis jetzt noch nicht geschrieben? Falls Ethik als Moralität aufgefasst wird, ist es nicht überraschend, dass queere TheoretikerInnen sich nicht mit dem ethischen System beschäftigen wollen, das alle Arten der sexuellen Abweichung verdammte (Huffer 2011, 518). Trotzdem lehnten queere Kritikerinnen wie Janet Halley oder Gayle Rubin ethisches Denken nicht ab, aber sie riefen zu einer anderen Ethik auf und auch die anti-normative Basis der Queer Theorie, die selbst zu einer normativen moralischen Kraft wurde, verdeutlichen einen kritischen nietzscheanischen Punkt: in dem moralische Normen verneint werden, wird nicht verhindert werden, dass neue moralische Kräfte zurückkommen (ebenda, 519). Ein anderes Argument gegen eine solche Ethik kommt aus der postmodernen Kritik, in dem sich die Ethik stabiler Konzepte wie „dem Guten", dem „Gerechten", der „korrekten moralischen Handlung", etc. bedient, die eine postmoderne Analyse strikt als endgültig und universelle Wahrheiten ablehnt (Lykke 2010, 157). Trotzdem existiert nun eine Tendenz innerhalb des Postmodernismus und eine, die über Postmodernismus und Konstruktivismus hinausgeht, welche die Destabilisierung des rationalen Universalismus der traditionellen Ethik fordert und daher für eine Öffnung für Ambiguität, Vielfachheit und Vielfältigkeit eintritt (ebenda).

Die frühere feministische Ethik richtete den Fokus auf Geschlecht und damit verbunden klar auf die Unterteilung in Mann und Frau, aber in rezenten Theorien haben sich die Vorstellungen und Konzepte des Begriffs „Geschlecht" geändert hin zu einer weniger fixierten Auffassung und da wir in einer postkolonialen, transnationalen und globalisierten Welt leben, ist es wichtig miteinzubeziehen, dass in manchen Kulturen „Geschlecht" keine fundamentale Kategorie darstellt (Oyewumi 1997) bzw. dass geschlechtliche Normen verschieden sind in unter-

---

[13] Übersetzung der Autorin aus dem englischen Original von Tong und Williams 2009.

schiedlichen Frauengruppen, oder auch, dass dieselben Normen unterschiedliche Gruppen anders beeinflussen (Jaggar 1991, 98). Jaggar betont daher, dass eine feministische Ethik nicht nur inländische sondern auch internationale Themen ansprechen soll.

Die queeren Anteile in dieser Ethik bestehen allerdings nicht nur aus dem Konzept, das Geschlecht keine fixe Identität mehr ist, sondern auch aus der Auffassung einer queeren Politik, die versucht, normative Machtsysteme zu transformieren und das Recht des queeren Selbstausdrucks und der queeren Selbstdefinition zu betonen.

In diese Ethikkonzeption inkludiere ich auch Menschen mit Behinderungen, die Sexualität anders als die heterosexuelle und nichtbehinderte Norm erfahren und deren reproduktive Möglichkeiten und Geschlechtsäußerungen nicht mit den heteronormativen und nichtbehinderten Erwartungen übereinstimmen. Das heißt nicht, dass ich nur auf queere und behinderte Menschen (also eine Person, die zugleich queer und behindert ist) eingehe, sondern auch auf diejenigen, deren Körper, Psyche und Geist andere Möglichkeiten zur Fortpflanzung brauchen als den normativen heterosexuellen Geschlechtsakt.

Die bereits vorher erwähnten Stränge dieses ethischen Knotens helfen mir, dieses verworrene Cat's Cradle (Fadenspiel oder Abnehmspiel, bei dem Fäden in verschiedenen Verknotungen um die Finger gelegt werden) näher zu erklären. Mit Cat's Cradle nehme ich Donna Haraways beliebtes Spiel, das von indigenen Völkern erfunden wurde (z.B. den Navajos in den jetzigen USA) als Metapher für das implodierte Objekt einer queer-feministischen dis/ability Meta-Ethik für NRGT, weil sie damit vorschlägt, wie Schlüsseldiskurse über Technikwissenschaften neu (metaphorisch) dargestellt und verknüpft werden können. Haraways kategorischer Imperativ ist das zu verqueeren, was als Natur gilt (Haraway 1994, 59).[14]

Um diesen großen Knoten zu entwirren, suche ich relevante Fäden oder Stränge der früheren feministischen Ethik heraus und verknote sie wieder mit aktuellen queeren und dis/ability Fäden, sodass ein neuer Knoten, der einer queer-feministischen-dis/ability Ethik der Reproduktion entsteht. Ich erkläre daher einige Ideen und Konzepte der feministi-

---

[14] "how to refigure – how to trope and how to knot together – key discourses about technoscience (…). Queering what counts as nature is my categorical imperative." (Haraway 1994, 59-71).

schen Ethik und zeige, wie sie die weiteren Gedanken zu diesem Thema heutzutage beeinflussten.

1.   Der erste Faden: Gerechtigkeit

Das Hauptziel dieser queer-feministischen dis/ability Ethik ist die reproduktive Gerechtigkeit. „Reproductive Justice exists when all people have the social, political and economic power and resources to make healthy decisions about our gender, bodies and sexuality for ourselves, our families and our communities. Reproductive Justice aims to transform power inequities and create long-term systematic change, and relies on communities most impacted by reproductive oppression. The Reproductive Justice framework recognizes that all individuals are part of communities and that our strategies must lift up entire communities to support individuals" (von Asian Communities for Reproductive Justice 2005). Die reproduktive Gerechtigkeit ist beides, sowohl eine anwendungsorientierte Bewegung als auch ein theoretisches Rahmenkonzept, das seinen Ursprung in den reproduktiven Gesundheitsorganisationen der farbigen Frauen in den USA zu Begin der 1980ern hat (Roberts 1997, Silliaman et al 2004, Ehrenreich 2008). Deswegen richtet die reproduktive Gerechtigkeitsbewegung nicht nur einen starken Fokus auf Geschlecht, sondern auch auf „Rasse" und Klasse. Das Konzept der Gerechtigkeit in diesem Fall ist die Verteilung der Vorteile und Lasten auf eine gerechte Art und Weise (Brunero 2011, CXVII), ähnlich wie John Rawls' Theorie der Verteilungsgerechtigkeit in seinem Werk *A Theory of Justice* (1971), in dem er sich mit der Gerechtigkeit von Institutionen oder den grundlegenden Strukturen der Gesellschaft beschäftigt. Für ihn leitet sich die individuelle Gerechtigkeit von der sozialen Gerechtigkeit ab (Slote 2010). Der prozedurale Charakter der Theorie von Rawls legt die Gewichtung auf das gerechte Verfahren oder den Prozess der Verteilung und nicht auf das Endergebnis. Diese prozedurale Gerechtigkeit ist ausschlaggebend für eine queer-feministische dis/ability Ethik der Reproduktion, denn was hier zählt, ist der Zugang zur Reproduktion und das die Behandlung für alle auf einer fairen, gerechten und gleichen Art und Weise erfolgt.

Für eine Verteilungsgerechtigkeit ist es heutzutage wichtig in Betracht zu ziehen, dass, wie ich bereits im ersten Teil erwähnte, wenn es um die Biomacht (Leben zu produzieren und zu managen) der Reproduktion geht, wir bereits in einem neuen ökonomischen Regime sind, nämlich weg von der Kontrolle über die Reproduktion hin zur Reproduzierung von Kapital mithilfe der Reproduktion, wobei auch der Bio-Kolonialismus in den Technologien Einzug erhalten hat, die die reproduktiven Kontrolle und NRGT betreffen. Deswegen ist es so wichtig eine Allianz der prekären Menschen in diesen reproduktiven Systemen zu bilden. Transgender und intersex Personen, Menschen mit Behinderung, MigrantInnen, farbige Menschen, postkoloniale Subjekte, etc. zählen zu dieser Gruppe und sollen in einer Ethik der der Verteilungsgerechtigkeit besonders berücksichtigt werden.

2. Der zweite Faden: Anerkennung - Intersektionalität und Ontologie

Die nächsten Stränge sind eng mit einander verwoben, denn die Intersektionalität geht aus dem Wesen jeder einzelnen Person hervor. Wie ich im letzten Absatz zeigte, ist nicht nur das Geschlecht, sondern auch die Nicht/Behinderung und „Rasse", Ethnie und Herkunft von Bedeutung für die Verteilungsgerechtigkeit.

Das Konzept der Intersektionalität wurde anfangs von Kimberle Crenshaw (1989) verwendet, um zu erklären, warum Erfahrungen der Schwarzen Frauen viel mehr ausmachen, als nur die Summe von deren Geschlecht und „Rasse" zu sein. Patricia Hill Collins hat diese Idee der Intersektionalität weiterentwickelt, und meint, dass kulturelle Muster der Unterdrückung nicht nur mit einander in Beziehung stehen, sondern aneinander gebunden und durch das intersektionelle Gesellschaftssystem, wie z.B. Geschlecht, „Rasse", Klasse und Ethnie (Collins 2000, 42) beeinflusst werden. „Die Theorie schlägt vor, dass – und versucht zu untersuchen wie – verschiedene biologische, soziale und kulturelle Kategorien wie z. B. Geschlecht, „Rasse", Klasse, Nicht/Behinderung, sexuelle Orientierung, Religion, Kaste, Spezies und andere Identitätssachsen auf vielfältigen und oft gleichzeitigen Niveaus interagieren und so zu einer systematischen Ungerechtigkeit beitragen" (Übersetzung der Autorin. Original von Collins ebenda).

Wir sehen also in den Beispielen der prekären Menschen auf dem Gebiet der Reproduktion, dass die Kategorisierungen und hierarchische Einteilungen eng mit diesen intersektionellen Charakteristiken verbunden sind, die von der Gesellschaft auferlegt sind und scheinbar fix mit deren Wesen gekoppelt ist. Daher kommt nun der Strang der Ontologie mit ins ethische Fadenspiel.

Ontologie

Obwohl der Konstruktivismus die Kategorien Geschlecht und „Rasse" als von der Gesellschaft konstruiert aufdeckte, finden wir reelle reproduktive und ökonomische Ungerechtigkeiten, die mit diesen Intersektionen einhergehen. Daher ist für die ethischen Fragen rund um Reproduktion und NRGT eine erneute Zuwendung zu Körpern und Materialien unabwendbar, so wie es auch in den „Neuen Materialismen" verlangt wird, in denen die Handlungskraft und –macht der Materie auf eine nicht-essentialistische Art und Weise neugedacht wird (Lykke 2010, 204). Karen Barads Idee der Intra-Aktion ist dabei ein wichtiges Beispiel: gegenseitig sich transformierende Wechselspiele, die implizieren, dass es keine Grenzen zwischen biologisch-materiellen und soziokulturellen Aspekten gibt (Barad 2012, 203), was auch zeigt, dass Objekte (oder Materie) genauso performativ konstruiert ist. Barad (ebenda) ruft zu einer „Ethico-Onto-Epistemologie" auf, welche die Verflechtung von Ethik, Wissen und Sein ernst nimmt.

Nochmals näher auf die Rawlssche Verteilungsgerechtigkeit und Ontologie eingehend, ist Nancy Frasers Bedenken Ernst zu nehmen, wenn sie meint, dass wenn Güter vermehrt an Minderheiten verteilt werden, es zu einer Verstärkung des Eindrucks kommt, dass diese Gruppen Defizite haben. Nancy Fraser und Axel Honneth setzen sich für Anerkennung als eine ethische und politische Strategie in diesem Zusammenhang ein (Fraser und Honneth 2003). Auch Butler betont die Anerkennung als Strategie für prekäre Menschen (Willig 2012).

Die reproduktive Anerkennung ist daher zusätzlich zur reproduktiven Gerechtigkeit als geeignetes Mittel zu sehen, um die Intersektionalitäten, die im Wesen oder Sein der Menschen in der jetzigen Gesellschaft liegen, auszugleichen.

3. Der dritte Faden: Universalismus

Der Universalismus wurde lange Zeit vom linken Diskurs im Feminismus verbannt, weil er für imperialistische, kolonialistische und westliche Anliegen ausgenützt wurde, um die normativen Behauptungen der dominanten Kultur zu rechtfertigen. Iris Marion Young streicht hervor, dass die meisten Kritiken des Universalismus epistemologisch sind, d.h. dass die universellen Normen dazu tendieren, ihren besonderen Ursprung zu verdecken. (Young 2001, 80 und MacKenzie 2009, 346).

350

Trotzdem warnen feministische und postkoloniale TheoretikerInnen, wie z.B. Martha Nussbaum, Judith Butler, Paul Gilroy (strategischer Universalismus) und Homi Bhabha davor, universalistische Strategien im politischen Kampf zu schnell abzulegen. (Butler 2000a, 15, MacKenzie, 343). Butler zum Beispiel verteidigt engagiert die Brauchbarkeit von offenen und angreifbaren Universalismen ein einem hegemonischen Kampf (Butler 2000a, 38), wobei die kulturelle Übersetzung eine essentielle Rolle spielt. Das Ziel der kulturellen Übersetzung ist nicht die Assimilierung, sondern eher das Aufdecken von Brüchen oder Gräben im dominanten Universalismus und der Anfang der Entwicklung eines anderen Universalismus mithilfe des Wissens über die fehlerhaften Grundlagen.[15]

Warum Universalismus wichtiger ist als Partikularität, erklärt Madhavi Menon in ihrer Fabel über die Partition von Indien und Pakistan, in der sie sich vorstellt, der Universalismus und die Partition wären Nachbarn. Sie beschreibt den Universalismus folgendermaßen: Er nimmt universell an, dass Differenzen existieren, aber keine einzelne Differenz kann eine Person oder eine Angelegenheit vollständig definieren (Menon 2015, 117). „If partition speaks the language of the particular norm that has to be opposed to the antinorm, then universalism speaks Esperanto. This universal language is not the opposite of Partition; it does not fall prey yet again to the idea of a coherent norm that can and should be opposed. Instead, universalism allows that differences exist in the world and are very real." (ebenda, 120). Nach ihrer Meinung müssen wir, wenn wir den unendlichen Kreis von ontologischen Partitionierungen unterbrechen wollen, universell darüber nachdenken, was wir als Partitionierung bezeichnen, und uns verweigern, die Differenz kohärent, selbst-identisch, oder als die Basis der Identität zu machen (ebenda, 121). „Particulars exist *and* cannot be translated into norms or ontological identities. Universalism is a movement across partitions that does not privilege any one particular as a basis for ontology." (Hervorhebung im Original. Ebenda). Sie gibt als

---

[15] "Indeed, the task will be not to assimilate the unspeakable into the domain of speakability in order to house it here, within the existing norms of dominance, but to shatter the confidence of dominance, to show how equivocal its claims to universality are, and, from that equivocation, track the break-up of its regime, and opening towards alternative versions of universality that are wrought from the work of translation itself" (Butler 2000a, 179).

Beispiel den migrantischen Fluss über die Grenzen an, der die Lüge entlarvt, dass es ontologische Identitäten, basierend auf geographischen Partikularitäten, gäbe (ebenda, 122). „(…)(U)niversalism points out instead the „structural antagonism" that denies wholeness to particularity; it fractures the notion that particularity can be the normative basis of a nation-state or even just of a state of being." (ebenda). Universalismus bringt für Menon die Partikularitäten zusammen, aber in universalistischer Nicht-Fixiertheit, also als das, was sie als das genaue Gegenteil des Aufklärerischen Universalismus sieht, der daraus bestand, eine Partikularität in den Status den Universalen zu erhöhen. „Universalism is the political thing that makes particulars fail to cohere; universalism as the idea that spurs longing across borders; universalism as the notion that allows intellectual ferment: these are the domains of the queer." (ebenda, 134).

Was passiert aber mit der Norm in diesem anderen Universalismus? Menon schließt, dass in diesem Universalismus kein Platz ist für eine Norm oder Anti-Norm, weil die Normativität unmöglich ist. Diese dickköpfige Queerness steht dieser Normativität im Weg, denn die Queerness geht über Identität und Grenzen hinaus, da sie zu restriktiv sind. Queerness findet ihren/seinen Frieden stattdessen in einem Universum der Partikularitäten (ebenda, 136).

Dieser andere Universalismus, der die kulturelle Übersetzung ernst nimmt und der aufdeckt, dass eine einzelne Partikularität als normative Basis angenommen wurde, ist ein wichtiger Faden in unserem ethischen Knoten. Dieser queere Universalismus bringt die Partikularitäten zusammen, aber in einer Nicht-Fixiertheit und ohne Normen und Anti-Normen.

4. Vierter bis sechster Faden: Interdependenz, Fähigkeiten
und transformatives Ethos

Eine queer-feministische dis/ability Ethik basiert auf verbündeten Praktiken von queeren und nicht/behinderten Personen. Diese prekären Personen haben keine gemeinsame Identität aber gemeinsame Erfahrungen, da sie diverse professionelle, geschlechtliche, sexuelle, oder ethnisierte Positionen und Status gleichzeitig oder aufeinanderfolgend einnehmen (Lorey 2010). Daher, so die Schlussfolgerung von Lorey und Butler, ist nur eine Ontologie fähig, die diese Interdependenzen in

Betracht nimmt, und nicht eine Ontologie des Individualismus, diese Prekarität des Lebens anzuerkennen und zuzugestehen.

Auf die Interdependenz innerhalb dieser reproduktiven Prekarität zu fokussieren und zugleich die radikalen Unterschiede zwischen den Individuen anzuerkennen, befähigt die Menschen, politisch zu agieren, ohne die Gemeinschaft auf eine homogene Identität, die auf Vulnerabilität basiert, zu reduzieren.

Fähigkeiten

Nussbaum entwickelt den Fähigkeitenansatz, um den Aspekt der Geschlechtergerechtigkeit in Rawls Konzept zu inkludieren, da er das Geschlecht außer Acht ließ und daher die Gleichheit der Geschlechter unterminiert wurde. Sie weist auch eine Theorie weiblicher Fürsorgeethik zurück, weil sie Bedenken hat, dass Frauen, deren Rollen durch Ungerechtigkeit geformt werden, wiederum auf diese Rolle festgenagelt werden. Sie sieht Fürsorge also nicht, wie Carol Gilligan, als weibliche Form der Moralität, sondern als Konstrukt der weiblichen Unterordnung (Nussbaum 1999,13). Trotzdem glaubt sie, dass Pflege und Mitgefühl im Herzen des ethischen Lebens liegen (ebenda, 14). Das ist auch der Grund, warum sie nicht auf die Fürsorge setzt sondern auf ihre Fähigkeitenliste, um die Geschlechter- und Behinderungsungerechtigkeit herauszufordern. In jenen Schriften, in denen sie den Fähigkeitenansatz entfaltet, argumentiert sie, dass eine minimale Bedingung für soziale Gerechtigkeit darin besteht, dass alle Menschen zehn grundlegende Möglichkeiten wahrnehmen können, die sie in ihrer Liste der zentralen menschlichen funktionsgerechten Fähigkeiten definiert (Nussbaum 2000, 78ff). Diese Liste beinhaltet zwei relevante Punkte für eine queer-feministische-nicht/behinderte Ethik der Reproduktion. In ihrer zweiten grundlegenden Möglichkeit für körperliche Gesundheit inkludiert sie die reproduktive Gesundheit (ebenda, 78) und in ihrer dritten grundlegenden Möglichkeit für körperliche Unversehrtheit streicht sie die Möglichkeiten für sexuelle Befriedigung und für die Wahl in Reproduktionsfragen hervor (ebenda). Sie spricht explizit von Garantien der Nicht-Einmischung mit gewissen Entscheidungen, die spezifisch persönlich sind und für das Selbstsein definierend sind (Nussbaum 1997-98, 277).

Ein klarer queerer Vorteil der Fähigkeitenliste im Unterschied zu den Menschenrechten ist darin zu sehen, dass, wie MacKenzie hervorhebt, dieser Ansatz von Fähigkeiten und Potenzialen nützlich ist, um Subjektivität eher als einen Prozess zu sehen, und nicht als eine stabile und vorherbestimmte Identität (MacKenzie 2009, 353). Wendy Brown warnt davor, dass die Anwendung der Menschenrechte nicht immer einen politischen Nutzen darstellt, da der Anspruch auf Menschenrechte das Potential birgt, Identitätskategorien zu zementieren. Es besteht die Gefahr, dass diese Identitäten nicht emanzipiert werden, sondern als Instrumente der Bevölkerungsregulierung und -verwaltung eingesetzt werden (ebenda). Menschenrechte tendieren zur Naturalisierung und Dekontextualisierung von Identitäten. „Wenn aktuelle Rechtsansprüche verwendet werden, um historische und kontextuelle kontingente Identitäten zu schützen, so wird die Verbindung der universellen Rechtsidiome zur Kontingenz der beschützten Identitäten eine solche sein, dass die Rechte unbeabsichtigter Weise diese Identitäten unterordnen und renaturalisieren, obwohl die Rechte in ihrer Artikulation sie emanzipieren wollten." (Übersetzung der Autorin. Original von Brown 1995, 99).[16]

Transformatives Ethos

Gudrun Perko beschrieb bereits allgemeine Gedanken einer queeren Ethik und rief zu einem affirmativen und transformativen Ethos der Akzeptanz und Anerkennung auf. Ein affirmativer Ansatz bedeutet, dass Werte, Normen und moralische Haltungen, die nicht den eigenen entsprechen oder die vollständig fremd sind, zugelassen werden und ein Dialog zugestanden wird. Transformation bedeutet also die Möglichkeit, seine eigene Imagination, Wahrnehmung und das eigene Denken durch das Andere zu ändern (Perko 2005, 64). Daher ist ein queeres Ethos eine affirmative und transformative Anerkennung, die sich gegen eine soziale Realität richtet, in der Menschen hierarchisch eingeteilt und kategorisiert werden, und diese Hierarchien durch Gesetze, Institutionen, Imaginationen und Positionen verstärkt werden. Ein queeres Ethos nimmt die Existenz von pluralen Lebensweisen an, so wie auch die Möglichkeit

---

[16] "If contemporary rights claims are deployed to protect historically and contextually contingent identities, might the relationship of the universal idioms of rights to the contingency of the protected identities be such that the former operates inadvertently to resubordinate by renaturalizing that which it was meant to emancipate by articulating?" (Brown 1995, 99).[16]

354

der Selbstdefinierung, die Öffnung von verschiedenen und vielfältigen Raumen, Ambiguitäten und Pluralität (Perko, 66).

Bibliographie

Asian Communities for Reproductive Justice. 2005. Aufgerufen am 22.5.2013. http://strongfamiliesmovement.org/what-is-reproductive-justice

Barad, Karen. 2012. *Agentieller Realismus*. Berlin: Suhrkamp Verlag.

Bergmann, Sven. 2011. „Reproduktives Reisen". *Gen-ethischer Informationsdienst* 204, 33-35.

Bernard, Andreas. 2014. *Kinder Machen. Neue Reproduktionstechnologien und die Ordnung der Familie. Samenspender, Leihmütter, Künstliche Befruchtung*. Frankfurt am Main: S. Fischer Verlag.

Bhabha, Homi et al. 1996. "Dialogue". In Alan Read (Hrsg.) *The Fact of Blackness. Frantz Fenon and Visual Representation*. London: Institute of Contemporary Arts. 38-44.

Breitbach, Elmar. 2009. „Großbritannien: Lesbische Frauen sind begehrt". *Die Wunschkinderseite*, aufgerufen am 7.5. 2014, http://www.wunschkinder.net /aktuell/gesellschaft/ausland/lesbische-frauen-sind-begehrt-3344/ (11.06.).

Brown, Wendy. 2011. „Thinking in Time. An Epilogue on Ethics and Politics." In: *The Question of Gender: Joan W. Scott's critical feminism*. Judith Butler, Elizabeth Weed (Hrsg.) Bloomington: Indiana University Press, 312-319.

Brown, Wendy. 1995. *States of injury: Power and freedom in late modernity*. Princeton: Princeton UP.

Brunero, John, et al. 2011. „Important Technical Terms in Ethics". In: *The Continuum companion to ethics*. Christian Miller (Hrsg.) London/New York: Continuum. cvi – cxxx.

Butler, Judith. 2009. *Frames of War: When Is Life Grievable?* London/New York: Verso.

Butler, Judith. 2007. *Kritik der ethischen Gewalt*. Frankfurt am Main: Suhrkamp Verlag.

Butler, Judith. 2004. *Precarious Life. The Powers of Mourning and Violence* London/New York: Verso.

Butler, Judith. 2000a. "Competing universalities". In: *Contingency, hegemony, universality: Contemporary dialogues on the Left*. Judith Butler, Ernesto Laclau, and Slavoj Zizek. London/New York: Verso.

Butler, Judith. 2000b. "Restaging the Universal: Hegemony and the Limits of Formalism". In: *Contingency, Hegemony, Universality: contemporary dialogues on the Left*. By Judith Butler, Ernesto Laclau, and Slavoj Žižek. London/New York: Verso.

Butler, Judith. 1996. „Universality in culture". In: *For love of country: Debating the limits of patriotism*. Joshua Cohen (Hrsg.) Boston: Beacon Press.

Collins Hill, Patricia. 2000. *Black Feminist Thought: Knowledge, Consciousness and the Politics of Empowerment* New York: Routledge.

Crenshaw, Kimberle. 1991. „Mapping the Margins: Intersectionality, Identity Politics, and Violence against Women of Color." *Stanford Law Review* 43/6, 1241-1299.

Cooper, M. und Waldby C. 2010. "From Reproductive Work to Regenerative Labour: The Female Body and the Stem Cell Industries. " *Feminist Theory* 11/3, 3-22.

Deomampo, Daisy. 2013a. "Gendered Geographies of Reproductive Tourism." *Gender & Society* 27/4, 514-537.

Deomampo, Daisy. 2013b. "Transnational Surrogacy in India." *Frontiers* 34/3, 167-188.

Duggan, Lisa. 2002. "The New Homonormaitivity: The Sexual Politics of Neoliberalism". In: *Materializing Democracy: Toward a Revitalized Cultural Politics*. Russ Castronovo und Dana D. Nelson (Hrsg.) Durham: Duke UP.

Ehrenreich, Nancy Ed. 2008. *The Reproductive Rights Reader. Law Medicine, and the Construction of Motherhood.* New York/London: New York University Press.

Franklin, Sara. 2011. "Not a flat world: the future of cross-border reproductive care." Commentary *Reproductive BioMedicine Online* 23, 814-16.

Fraser, N. und Honneth, A. 2003. *Redistribution or Recognition? A Political-Philosophical Exchange* London/New York: Verso.

Gilroy, Paul. 2000. *Between Camps: Nations, Culture and the Allure of Race*. London: Allen Lane.

Golombok, S., Casey, P., Readings, J., Blake, L., Marks, A. & Jadva, V. 2011. „Families created through surrogacy: Mother-child relationships and children's psychological adjustment at age 7." *Developmental Psychology 47*/6, 1579-1578.

Golombok, S., MacCallum, F., Murray, C., Lycett, E. & Jadva, V. 2006. "Surrogacy families: Parental functioning, parent-child relationships and children's psychological development at age 2." *Journal of Child Psychology & Psychiatry* 47/2, 213-222.

Golombok, S., Murray, C., Jadva, V., MacCallum, F.& Lycett, E. 2004. "Families created through surrogacy arrangements: Parent-child relationships in the first year of life." *Developmental Psychology* 40, 400-411.

Hanssmann, Christoph. 2014. "The Lively Clinic and the Classificatory Tome: Trans Health Practice and the Science of the Diagnostic Category" Paper presented at *Interruptions: Sciences, Feminisms, Knowledges* at UC Berkeley. 19. April.

Haraway, Donna J.1994. „A Game of Cat's Cradle: Science Studies, Feminist Theory, Cultural Studies" *Configurations,* 2/1: 59-71.

Haraway, Donna J. 1992/2004. „The Promises of Monsters: a Regenerative Politics for Inappropriate/d Others". In: *The Haraway Reader* Donna Haraway. New York: Routledge. 63-124.

Haraway, Donna J. 1991. „Situated Knowledges: The Science Question in Feminism and the Privilege of Partial Perspective". In: *Simians, Cyborgs and Women: The Reinvention of Nature.* Donna Haraway, London: Free Association Books.183-201.

Huffer, Lynne. 2011. "Are the Lips a Grave?" *GLQ: A Journal of Lesbian and Gay Studies* 17/4, 517-542.

Huffer, Lynne. 2010. *Mad for Foucault. Rethinking the Foundations of Queer Theory.* New York: Columbia University Press.

Huffer, Lynne. 2009. "Foucault's Ethical Ars Erotica" *SubStance* 120/38 (3): 125-147.

Jadva V. und Imrie, S. 2014. "The significance of relatedness for surrogates and their families." In: *We are Family? Perceptions of relatedness in assisted conception families.* T. Feeman, F. Ebtehaj, S. Graham und M. Richards M. (Hrsg.). Cambridge: Cambridge University Press.

Jaggar, Alison M. 2006. Reasoning about Well-Being: Nussbaum's Methods of Justifying the Capabilities. *The Journal of Political Philosophy* 14/3: 301-22.

Jaggar, Alison M. 1991. Feminist Ethics: Projects, Problem, Prospects. In: *Feminist Ethics* Claudia Card. (Hrsg.). USA: University Press of Kansas. 78-105.

Kalender, Ute. 2012. „Queere Potentiale? Zur Queernesss von Reprodukti-onstechnologien aus der Perspektive materialistischer Feminismen und kriti-scher Disability Studies" *Feministische Studien* 2/12, 198-209.

Kuusela, Oskari. 2011. *Key Terms in Ethics*. London/New York: Conti-nuum.

Lorey, Isabell. 2010. „Gemeinsam Werden. Prekarisierung als politische Konstituierung" *Grundrisse* 35, 19-25.

Lykke, Nina. 2010. *Feminist studies: a guide to intersectional theory, methodology and writing*. New York/Abingdon: Routledge.

MacKenzie, Julie. 2009. „Refiguring Universalism" *Australian Feminist Studies*, 24/61, 343-58.

Menon, Madhavi. 2015. „Universalism and Partition: A Queer Theory" *differences: A Journal of Feminist Cultural Studies* 26/1, 117-140.

Mingus, Mia. 2015. "Medical Industrial Complex Visual" aufgerufen am 9.3.2015. https://leavingevidence.wordpress.com/2015/02/06/medical-industrial -complex-visual/ .

Mingus, Mia, und Berne, Patty, s.a. "The Myth of the Norm: Genetic Tech-nologies and the De-Selection of Disabled Bodies: A Reproductive Justice Perspective." *Reproductive Justice Briefing Book* aufgerufen am 15.1.2014. http://www.protectchoice.org/section.php?id=17

Nussbaum, Martha. 2000. *Women and human development: The capabilities approach*. Cambridge: Cambridge University Press.

Nussbaum, Martha. 1999. *Sex and Social Justice*. New York: Oxford UP.

Nussbaum, Martha. 1997-98. „Capabilities and Human Rights" *Fordham Law Review* 66, 273-300.

Oyewumi, Oyeronke. 1997. *The Invention of Women: Making an African Sense of Western Gender Discourses*. Minneapolis: University of Minnesota Press.

Perko, Gudrun. 2005. *Queer-Theorien. Ethische, politische und logische Dimensionen plural-queeren Denkens* Köln: Papy Rossa.

Plemons, Eric. 2014. "Trans- surgery Matters" Paper presented at *Trans-gender Studies Matters* at UC Berkeley, 18. April. https://www.facebook.com/ OurstoriesClub/posts/767387466637662 aufgerufen am 10.3.2015.

Preciado, Paul B. 2013. "Procréation politiquement assistée" *Libération* 27. Sept. 2013, aufgerufen am 5.7.2014, http://www.liberation.fr/societe/ 2013/09/27/procreation-politiquement-assistee_935256

Preciado, Beatriz. 2008. *Testo Yonkie*. Madrid: Espasa.

Puar, Jasbir. 2006. "Mapping U.S. Homonormativities" *Gender, Place, and Culture* 13/1: 67-88.

Rawls, John. 1971. *A Theory of Justice* Cambridge MA: The Belknap Press of Harvard University Press.

Roberts, Dorothy. 2011. *Fatal Invention. How Science, Politics, and Big Business Re-create Race in the Twenty-First century*. New York: the New Press.

Roberts, Dorothy. 1997. *Killing the Black Body: Race, Reproduction and the Meaning of Liberty*. New York: Pantheon Books.

Slote, Michael. 2010. "Justice as a Virtue" aufgerufen am 15.1.2014. http://plato.stanford.edu/entries/justice-virtue/.

Silliman, Jael/Gerber Fried, Marlene/Ross, Loretta/Gutierrez, Elena R. 2004. *Undivided Rights: Women of Color Organize for Reproductive Justice*. Cambridge, MA. : South End Press.

Thompson, Charis. 2005. *Making Parents: The Ontological Choreography of Reproductive Technologies* Cambridge, MA: MIT Press.

Tong, Rosemarie und Williams, Nancy. 2009. *Feminist Ethics* (4.5.) aufgerufen am 20.1.2014. http://plato.stanford.edu/entries/feminism-ethics/ .

Trans Rights Europe Map 2014, aufgerufen am 06.07.2014. http://tgeu.org/trans_rights_europe_map/ .

Twine, France Winddance (2015) *Outsourcing the womb: Race, class, and gestational surrogacy in a global market. Second Edition.* New York/London: Routledge.

Whittle, Stephen. 2006. "Foreword" In: *The Transgender Studies Reader* Susan Stryker und Stephan Whittle (Hrsg.) New York: Routledge, pp. XI-XVI.

Wierckx K, Van Caenegem E, Pennings G, Elaut E, Dedecker D, Van de Peer F, Weyers S, De Sutter P, T'Sjoen G. 2012 „Reproductive wish in transsexual men." *Human Reproduction* 27/2, 483-7.

Willig, Rasmus. 2012. Recognition and critique: an interview with Judith Butler. *Distinktion: Scandinavian Journal of Social Theory* 13/1, 139-144.

Young, Iris Marion. 2001. "Review of Nussbaum's Sex and Social Justice" *Ethics* 111/4, 819-23.

Young, Iris Marion. 1997. *Intersecting Voices. Dilemmas of Gender, Political Philosophy, and Policy*. Princeton: Princeton University Press.

Zerilli, Linda M.G. 1998. „The Universalism Which is Not One". *Diacritics* 28/2, 3-20.

SUSANNE KLAPPER

INTERSEXUALITÄT IN EINER ZWEIGESCHLECHTLICHEN GESELLSCHAFT

In der westlichen Welt dominiert das Raster der zweifelsfreien Zweigeschlechtlichkeit, in dem intersexuelle Personen marginalisiert, unsichtbar gemacht und diskriminiert werden. Intersexuelle müssen sich einem der beiden Geschlechter zuordnen (lassen). Diese Zuordnung geschieht nicht nur auf dem Papier, sondern ist oft mit so genannten geschlechtsangleichenden Operationen verbunden. Unter diese fallen sowohl genitalverstümmelnde als auch genitalkonstruierende Maßnahmen, die oft mit einer lebenslangen Einnahme von Hormonpräparaten verbunden sind.

Der vorliegende Aufsatz stellt den Versuch einer einführenden Problematisierung des gesellschaftlichen Umgangs mit dem Phänomen Intersexualität dar. Das Ziel meiner Ausführungen liegt darin aufzuzeigen, welche Anforderungen sich an eine vorwiegend zweigeschlechtlich orientierte Gesellschaft richten – Anforderungen des Respekts und des menschenwürdigen Umgangs, eine moralische Basis, die Grundlage auch für Gesetzesnovellierungen bilden sollte.

Im ersten Abschnitt dieses Essays wird die Bandbreite möglicher Erscheinungsformen von Intersexualität dargelegt und eine begriffliche Differenzierung zwischen *Transsexualität* und *Intersexualität* durchgeführt. Ein weiterer Punkt ist eine kurze Skizze des Umgangs mit Intersexuellen in der westlichen Gesellschaft unter geschichtlichem Aspekt. Der nachfolgende Abschnitt erläutert die Rechtslage bezüglich intersexueller Personen, wobei an dieser Stelle gesellschaftliche Reaktionen auf ein neues Gesetz aufgezeigt werden. In einem weiteren Schritt wird die Notwendigkeit einer geschlechtergerechten Sprache thematisiert. Abschließend wird ein Ausblick auf die Entwicklungsmöglichkeiten einer Gesellschaft in Bezug auf den Umgang mit dem Phänomen der Intersexualität gegeben.

Zum Begriff Intersexualität

Das Phänomen Intersexualität umfasst eine Vielzahl möglicher Formen, die einer eindeutigen Trennung zwischen männlichem und weiblichem Geschlecht Widerstand entgegen setzen. Eine strikte Zuordnung stellt sich oftmals als nicht möglich dar, „da auch bei als ‚gesund' geltenden Menschen Varianzen des Chromosomen-, Keimdrüsen- oder Hormongeschlechts vorkommen." (Calvi 2012, 105) Wenn die aus diesen Varianzen resultierenden Körpermerkmale nicht allesamt einem der zwei gesellschaftlich akzeptierten Geschlechter zugeordnet werden können, wird von Intersexualität gesprochen (siehe Richter-Appelt 2010, 111). Diese Entwicklungen kommen prä- und/oder postnatal vor und hinterfragen das getrenntgeschlechtliche Menschenbild. Neben den biologischen Faktoren[1], die das Geschlecht ausmachen, kommen noch soziologische[2] und psychologische[3] Aspekte hinzu. Aufgrund dieser drei Komponenten stellt die soziale Kategorie Geschlecht ein komplexes Feld dar.

Ursachen und Formen von Intersexualität sind sehr vielfältig. Es kann davon ausgegangen werden, dass mindestens eines von 5000 geborenen Kindern weder dem männlichen noch dem weiblichem Geschlecht zugeordnet werden kann (ebenda, 113). Offensivere Schätzungen hingegen beziffern die Häufigkeit Intersexueller mit 1% deutlich höher (siehe Nussberger 2014, 12). Bis zur siebten oder achten Schwangerschaftswoche weist ein ungeborener Mensch noch keine Geschlechtsmerkmale auf, da bis zu diesem Zeitpunkt eine bipotente Gonadenanlage vorhanden ist, aus der sich die Geschlechtsorgane herausbilden (siehe Schweizer 2012 a, 45). 2005 wurden in Chicago drei Hauptgruppen klassifiziert. Diese drei Gruppen, mit denen sämtliche intersexuelle Erscheinungsformen beschrieben werden, tragen in ihrem Namen den Zusatz „DSD", welcher für „Disorders of Sex Development" steht (ebenda, 50). Im Englischen, aber auch im Deutschen, wird das gesamte Phänomen Intersexualität als Störung bezeichnet.[4]

---

[1] Unter diese fallen das genetische, hormonelle und anatomische Geschlecht (siehe Schweizer 2012 b, 21).

[2] Dieser Aspekt beinhaltet gesellschaftliche Rollenerwartungen, denen eine vorherrschende Geschlechtertheorie zugrunde liegt. Verwandt hiermit ist das kulturelle Geschlecht, worunter Inszenierungen des Geschlechts zu verstehen sind (siehe ebenda, 22f.).

[3] Zu diesem Aspekt gehören die Geschlechtsidentität, also das subjektive Geschlechtserleben, die sexuelle Orientierung und, als Schnittpunkt mit dem sozialen Geschlechtsaspekt, die Geschlechtsrolle (ebenda, 24).

[4] Im aktuellen medizinischen Sprachgebrauch setzt sich statt „disorders" zunehmend „differences" durch, was auch im Deutschen mit „Besonderheiten" übersetzt wird

Innerhalb dieser drei Gruppen gibt es weitere biologisch-medizinische Unterscheidungsmöglichkeiten für das Auftreten von Intersexualität. Ich skizziere nun eine kurze erläuternde Aufzählung der häufigsten Formen von Intersexualität, wobei zugunsten der Verständlichkeit fachspezifische Details der biologischen und medizinischen Wissenschaften ausgelassen werden.

Die erste Gruppe umfasst alle Personen mit den Geschlechtschromosomen XX, die sich nicht zu einer Frau entwickelt haben. Das häufigste Beispiel hierfür ist das Adrenogenitale Syndrom. Hierbei tritt während der Schwangerschaft ein Androgenüberschuss[5] auf, der die äußeren Genitalien vergrößert, wobei zugleich innere weibliche Genitalien gebildet werden (ebenda 50f). Die erhöhte Androgenausschüttung ergibt sich aufgrund einer genetisch bedingten stark verminderten Cortisolbildung in der Nebenniere.[6] Dabei kann es bei zusätzlich geringer Bildung des Hormons Aldesteron zu einer Salzverlustkrise kommen, die für Neugeborene lebensbedrohlich ist (ebenda, 55).

Intersexuelle, die nach dem Chicagoer Modell der zweiten Gruppe zugeordnet werden, weisen die Geschlechtschromosomen XY auf. Da sie das körperliche Erscheinungsbild von Frauen haben, nennen sich diese Personen auch XY-Frauen. Für eine derartige Entwicklung gibt es mehrere Ursachen. So entwickeln sich wegen einer gestörten Androgenbiosynthese die inneren Geschlechtsorgane entweder männlich oder nicht ausdifferenziert, während die Genitalien weiblich erscheinen und eine blind endende Vagina umfassen. Ähnliche körperliche Merkmale werden auch durch eine Androgenresistenz bewirkt. In diesem Fall werden Androgene erfolgreich synthetisiert, aber an ihren Zielorten nicht erkannt, so dass sie keine männliche Geschlechtsentwicklung bewirken können. Es gibt außerdem die Form einer partiellen Androgenresistenz, bei der die Androgene nur eingeschränkt wir-

---

(http://www.intersexuelle-menschen.net/aktivitaeten/2015_02_02_didacta_2015.php Stand: Juli 2015).

[5] Androgene sind Sexualhormone, die die Entwicklung und Erhaltung männlicher Geschlechtsorgane und -merkmale stimulieren.

[6] Da an der Cortisolbildung mehrere Enzyme beteiligt sind, kann es aufgrund verschiedener Enzymdefekte zu unterschiedlichen Entwicklungen kommen. So entstehen nicht in allen Fällen intersexuelle Genitalien. Außerdem können die Enzymdefekte bei allen Menschen vorkommen. Bei Ungeborenen mit den Geschlechtschromosomen XY führen allerdings nur vereinzelte Enzymdefekte zu intersexuellen Genitalien (siehe Buselmaier/Tariverdian 2007, 115).

ken können, so dass intersexuelle Genitalien ausgebildet werden (ebenda, 56-58).

Die dritte Gruppe umfasst Personen, die eine numerische Veränderung der Geschlechtschromosomen aufweisen. Hierzu können das Turner- und das Klinefelter-Syndrom gezählt werden (ebenda, 52). Menschen mit dem Turnersyndrom haben nur ein funktionsfähiges X-Chromosom und entwickeln sich wie eine Frau mit einigen Abweichungen (unter anderem geringere Körpergröße, Herzfehler und fehlende Eierstöcke). Das Klinefelter-Syndrom ist weniger eine Form von Intersexualität als eine Form der Chromosomenabweichung, da bei diesen Menschen, die sich zu Männern entwickeln, mit XXY drei Geschlechtschromosomen vorliegen. Das Hauptsymptom sind durch einen sehr geringen Testosteronspiegel verursachte, unterentwickelte Hoden, so dass die Männer unfruchtbar sind. Neben diesen Formen gibt es außerdem so genannte Mosaikformen, dabei hat eine Person Zellen mit XY und Zellen mit X oder, in selteneren Fällen, mit XX. Hierbei handelt es sich um den so genannten „echten Hermaphroditismus"[7], bei welchem verschiedene Formen der Geschlechtsorgane, ihres Entwicklungsstatus' und ihrer Anordnung vorkommen (Buselmaier/Tariverdian 2007, 111).

Dies macht klar, dass es verschiedene Formen von Intersexualität gibt, wobei dies in der Gesellschaft kaum bekannt ist, so dass Intersexuelle oft mit Transsexuellen verwechselt werden. Transsexuelle lassen sich jedoch, anders als Intersexuelle, mühelos in das zweigeschlechtliche System einordnen. Sie zementieren demnach genau genommen das binäre Geschlechtermodell (Calvi 2012, 109). Transsexuelle zeichnen sich dadurch aus, dass sie sich nicht dem Geschlecht, in dem sie geboren wurden, sondern dem gegenteiligen zugehörig fühlen. Ein weiterer großer Unterschied zwischen Transsexuellen und Intersexuellen besteht darin, dass sich erstere meist im Verlauf ihres Lebens für geschlechtsangleichende Operationen entscheiden, während diese an letzteren vorwiegend ungefragt in den ersten Lebensjahren durchgeführt werden.

---

[7] Eine Begriffsunterscheidung zwischen „echtem Hermaphroditismus" und „Pseudohermaphroditismus" gilt als veraltet. Unter dem „Pseudohermaphroditismus" werden sämtliche andere Vorkommnisse zusammengefasst. Der einzige Unterschied besteht lediglich darin, dass beim „echten Hermaphroditismus" sowohl männliches als auch weibliches Keimdrüsengewebe vorliegt (siehe Völling 2010, 245).

Kurze Skizze der Geschichte der Intersexualität

In ihrer Dissertation legt Nussberger eine Übersicht darüber vor, wie sich der Umgang mit Intersexuellen in der westlichen Welt von der Antike bis in die heutige Zeit gewandelt hat. Aufgrund fehlender Quellen gibt es allerdings für das Mittelalter keine Beispiele. Im Laufe der langen Geschichte von der Antike bis zur Gegenwart entstehen, je nach Lage der Forschung, immer neue Klassifikationssysteme, um die verschiedenen intersexuellen Erscheinungsformen zu kategorisieren. Darüber hinaus werden Erklärungsversuche für das Auftreten von Intersexualität entwickelt.

In der Antike werden intersexuell Geborene nicht als Menschen, sondern als Träger unheilvoller Botschaften der Götter wahrgenommen. Beginnende Kriege und Naturereignisse (z. B. Blitzeinschläge) werden mit ihrer Geburt in Zusammenhang gebracht. In der antiken Gesellschaft erzeugen Intersexuelle ein derartiges Unbehagen, dass zur Besänftigung der Götter Zeremonien durchgeführt werden, die meist auf die Tötung der Intersexuellen zielen (siehe Nussberger 2014, 36-39). Andere Berichte aus der Antike erzählen von plötzlichen Geschlechtsumwandlungen, bei denen meist Ärzte anwesend sind und unterstützend eingreifen. Diese Menschen, die sich vor und nach der Umwandlung je einem der etablierten Geschlechter zuordnen lassen, können meist in der Gesellschaft weiterleben, sofern sie die gesellschaftlich vorgesehene Rolle des neuen Geschlechts annehmen (ebenda, 43-48). Erklärungsmodelle der Antike für die Entstehung intersexueller Erscheinungsformen umfassen Theorien über angeborene oder im Mutterleib erworbene Ursachen, aber auch die Negation von Intersexualität überhaupt (ebenda, 54f).

Im 16. und 17. Jahrhundert kommen verschiedene rechtliche Fragen auf, denn Intersexuelle müssen einer Geschlechtskategorie zugeordnet werden, da für Männer und Frauen unterschiedliche Rechte gelten. Für diese Einteilung sind bestimmte Kriterien nötig, anhand derer die Geschlechtszugehörigkeit bestimmt werden kann. Bei der Festlegung dieser Kriterien sind drei verschiedene Fragen ausschlaggebend. Zuerst muss bestimmt werden, wer die Geschlechtszuweisung durchführt. Hinzu kommt die Frage, ob die einmal gefällte Zuweisung wieder rückgängig gemacht werden kann. Drittens liegt das eigentliche Problem jedoch darin, die passenden Kriterien für die Zuweisung zu finden (ebenda, 70). Zu den Diskussionen über die korrekte Geschlechtszuweisung kommen weitere Reglementierungen des Sexuallebens, der Beurteilung der Fähigkeit, in eine Ehe zu treten, der Übernahme kirchlicher Ämter und anderer rechtlicher Angelegenheiten hinzu (ebenda, 62-79). Nebenbei gibt es in dieser Zeit erste Nachweise über Intersexuelle, die ihren Körper zur Schau stellen, wobei unklar bleibt, ob sie dies freiwillig machen (ebenda, 81f). Die Mutmaßungen über die Ursachen für Intersexualität in dieser Zeit werden detaillierter. Neben Erklärungen, die das Verhalten der Eltern beim und nach dem Geschlechtsverkehr ansprechen, gibt es auch solche, die sich auf die Sternenkonstellation zum Zeugungszeitpunkt beziehen (ebenda, 93). Hinzu kommen eine Reihe verschiedener Klassifikationssysteme für Intersexuelle, wobei sich die Autoren dieser Systeme vor allem auf Berichte anderer beziehen und kaum selber intersexuelle Menschen untersucht haben. Nussberger betont hierbei, dass unklar bleibt, ob die Klassifikationssysteme überhaupt Anwendung finden und ob diese irgendwelche Folgen mit sich bringen (ebenda, 97f). Schließlich werden Interscxuclle als Kranke wahrgenommen, und Vorschläge für Interventionen finden Verbreitung. Am häufigsten wird das Entfernen des phallusartigen Gewebes empfohlen, da bei eher weiblichen Intersexuellen die Schamhaftigkeit im Vordergrund steht und durch diese Intervention möglichen neuen Sexualpraktiken entgegengewirkt werden kann. Bei eher männlichen Intersexuellen steht hingegen die korrekte Art des Urinierens im Vordergrund (ebenda, 100).

Die Ursachen für die Entwicklung Intersexueller werden im 19. Jahrhundert nicht mehr in den Umständen zum Zeitpunkt der Zeugung gesehen, vielmehr ist der Fokus auf Entwicklungen des Ungeborenen im Mutterleib gerichtet (ebenda, 118). Dabei entwickelt sich die Vorstellung eines gemeinsamen Ursprungs des männlichen und weiblichen Geschlechts, zugleich bleibt jedoch das unterschiedliche Rollenverständnis der jeweiligen Geschlechter bestehen (ebenda, 123f). Der wichtigste Grund, Intersexuelle zu untersuchen und einem der beiden etablierten Geschlechter zuzuordnen, liegt darin, dass mögliche ungültige Ehen vermieden werden sollen. Bei den Untersuchungen an Intersexuellen werden zunehmend medizinische Instrumente eingesetzt, wodurch diese mit größeren Schmerzen verbunden sind, „was das Ungleichgewicht zwischen Arzt und Patient" (ebenda, 135) festigt.

Neben den schmerzhaften Untersuchungsmethoden werden die schon Jahrzehnte zuvor veröffentlichten Behandlungsmöglichkeiten nun umgesetzt. Bemerkenswert ist hierbei, dass die Entscheidung für Operationen im 19. Jahrhundert meist von Intersexuellen ausgeht, wobei einige Ärzte Eingriffe, aufgrund von Risiken, ablehnen (ebenda, 135-137). Zudem verstärkt sich die Wahrnehmung Intersexueller „als Missbildung, als Abweichung von der Norm ‚Mann' und ‚Frau'" (ebenda 139). Inwiefern diese zunehmend negative Sicht auf Intersexuelle mit den vermehrten Untersuchungs- und Behandlungsmethoden zusammenhängt, ist unklar. Bei den Konzepten für die Ursachen von Intersexualität kommt eine einheitliche Sicht auf, während zuvor mehrere Konzepte parallel existieren. Allerdings erhöht sich das Ungleichgewicht zwischen Ärzten und Intersexuellen, da die Erklärungen oft auf sehr komplexem fachwissenschaftlichem Niveau erfolgen und daher schwieriger zu verstehen sind (ebenda, 172).

Ab dem 19. Jahrhundert geschieht eine weitere Entwicklung, durch die Intersexuelle in einem anderen Licht betrachtet werden. Diese Entwicklung hängt mit der Veröffentlichung eines Tagesbuches einer intersexuellen Person zusammen. Dabei wird der Inhalt als „das grausamste Beispiel für die verhängnisvollen Folgen, die eine irrtümliche Festlegung des Personenstandes bei der Geburt nach sich ziehen könne" (ebenda, 153) bezeichnet. Es rückt durch diese Veröffentlichung erstmals die Gefühlslage von intersexuellen Menschen ins Blickfeld. Bis dahin hat sich das Interesse der Forschung an Intersexuellen hauptsächlich auf ihre sexuellen Neigungen, die geschlechtliche Selbstwahrnehmung und Verhaltensweisen gerichtet. Ab diesem Zeitpunkt jedoch treten psychische Aspekte hinzu (ebenda, 160). Es gibt sogar die Empfehlung, der psychischen Empfindung über die Geschlechtszugehörigkeit gegenüber dem hierzu widersprechenden Ergebnis der damals üblichen, mikroskopischen Untersuchung der Geschlechtsdrüse, Vorrang zu geben (ebenda, 178).

In den letzten Jahrzehnten erarbeitete die Wissenschaft, bedingt durch neu entwickelte Diagnosemöglichkeiten, verschiedene Differenzierungen Intersexueller in Untergruppen, wie sie das Chicagoer Modell beschreibt (ebenda, 211). Die Mitte des 20. Jahrhunderts von Money verbreitete Ansicht, wonach intersexuellen Neugeborenen schnellstmöglich ein Geschlecht zugewiesen werden solle, da die Geschlechterrolle erlernt werde, hat sich als falsch herausgestellt, so dass seither von einer vorgeburtlichen Prägung im Gehirn ausgegangen wird (ebenda, 215 und 228).

1988 wird in England die erste Selbsthilfeorganisation gegründet. Weitere folgen in den westlichen Ländern, wobei sie unterschiedliche Schwerpunkte thematisieren (ebenda, 224-227).

Bis heute werden an den Genitalien intersexueller Menschen Operationen durchgeführt, damit sie einem der beiden etablierten Geschlechter zugeordnet werden können. Begründet werden diese Maßnahmen seit den 50er Jahren des 20. Jahrhunderts mit dem Hinweis auf die Gefahr, dass intersexuelle Kinder „eine nicht-heterosexuelle geschlechtsatypische Entwicklung" (Schönbucher et al. 2012, 209) durchlaufen und dadurch in der Gesellschaft abgelehnt werden. Diese Begründung beruht jedoch wiederum auf einem zweigeschlechtlichen Menschenbild, in dem Heterosexualität als die einzige zulässige sexuelle Orientierung anerkannt wird. Häufig werden Intersexuelle, aufgrund der meist einfacheren Durchführbarkeit, an das weibliche Geschlecht angepasst. Bei diesen Operationen stehen zunächst rein ästhetische Aspekte im Vordergrund und erst später rückt die Komponente der Bedeutung der sexuellen Funktion vermehrt in den Fokus. Dabei zeigen die Ergebnisse der *Hamburger Studie*[8], dass das Ziel der Medizin, nämlich eine möglichst konforme psychosexuelle Entwicklung zu erwirken, nicht umgesetzt wird, da „die sexuelle Lebensqualität von Personen mit Intersexualität beeinträchtigt ist" (ebenda, 216).

Seit den 1990er Jahren wenden sich Intersexuelle mit ihren Geschichten an die Öffentlichkeit. Hierdurch wird bekannt, dass die Genitaloperationen oft traumatisierend und mit körperlichen Leiden verbunden sind (siehe Voß 2012, 67). Zugleich entstehen erste Vereine, in denen die Interessen Intersexueller gebündelt werden (siehe Nussberger, 206). In dieser Zeit wird von Intersexuellen nicht die Intersexualität, sondern der gesellschaftliche Umgang mit ihnen als verletzend wahrgenommen. Durch diese Wahrnehmung stellt sich die generelle Frage, ob „statt der Intersexualität an sich nicht eher die Reaktion auf die Intersexualität als pathologisch betrachtet werden sollte" (ebenda, 233). In einem Fernsehbeitrag beschreibt dies eine intersexuelle Person folgendermaßen: „Das Hauptproblem ist, wie wir zu medizini-

---

[8] Hierbei handelt es sich um die erste deutschlandweit durchgeführte Studie, die die Behandlungserfahrungen von erwachsenen Intersexuellen untersucht (siehe Schweizer/Richter-Appelt, 193).

schen Problemen gemacht werden, dass wir nicht als normale Menschen angesehen werden, sondern als Syndrome und Krankheiten, die geheilt werden müssen." (Raab, W wie Wissen vom 08.11.2014) Es wird die Schaffung einer dritten Geschlechtskategorie diskutiert, eine Überlegung, die mehrheitlich abgelehnt wird. Begründet wird diese ablehnende Haltung mit dem Hinweis auf die Gefahr, dass aufgrund der Zugehörigkeit zu einem neuen Geschlecht eine mögliche Ausgrenzung stattfinden könnte. Ein anderes Argument geht von der Behauptung aus, dass es nur wenige Menschen gebe, die sich keinem der beiden etablierten Geschlechter zugehörig fühlen (Nussberger, 239).

Während in der Antike Intersexuelle als göttliche Botschaften wahrgenommen und meist getötet werden, gibt es später in der Gesellschaft Bestrebungen, sie zunächst formal und anschließend auch mittels Operationen in das zweigeschlechtliche System einzuordnen. Dabei wächst der Einfluss der Mediziner. Gleichzeitig machen vermehrt Einzelne und Vereine auf den Verstoß gegen das Menschenrecht auf körperliche Unversehrtheit aufmerksam.

Die Rechtslage im deutschsprachigen Raum

In der Schweiz wird 2005 der Vorschlag von Büchler und Cottier veröffentlicht, generell auf die personenstandsrechtliche Kategorie Geschlecht zu verzichten. Ihre Begründung hierfür lautet, dass einerseits im schweizerischen Recht die einzig erlaubten Kategorien männlich und weiblich nicht normiert sind und andererseits lehnen sie eine Skala sexueller Identitäten ab wegen der Unklarheit, welche Geschlechter für diese normierende Zuordnung den Maßstab bilden sollen (Nussberger, 233). Dieser Vorschlag wird jedoch bis jetzt nicht realisiert.

Am 1. November 2013 tritt in Deutschland ein neuer Paragraph im Personenstandsgesetz in Kraft. Er besagt: „Kann das Kind weder dem weiblichen noch dem männlichen Geschlecht zugeordnet werden, so ist der Personenstandsfall ohne eine solche Angabe in das Geburtenregister einzutragen." (PStG, Abschn. 2, § 22.3) Es ist dies derzeit das einzige Gesetz im deutschsprachigen Raum, das Intersexualität zumindest anspricht. Dabei handelt es sich nicht um den ersten Gesetzestext, der Intersexualität beinhaltet. 1749 gibt es in Preußen sogar mehrere Paragraphen, die sich mit „Zwittern" befassen, allerdings werden diese Paragraphen mit der Einführung des Bürgerlichen Gesetzbuches 1900 ersatzlos gestrichen. In den preußischen Paragraphen wird der Personenstand ausführlicher behandelt, da zunächst die Eltern ein Geschlecht festlegen müssen und anschließend das Kind, mit der Vollendung des 18. Lebensjahres, wiederum die Möglichkeit hat, sich für ein Geschlecht zu entscheiden (Völling 2010, 205f.). Während es in Preußen eine verpflichtende Geschlechtswahl gibt, kommt im heutigen Deutschland indirekt ein weiteres Geschlecht dazu, wobei dies lediglich durch eine fehlende Angabe gekennzeichnet wird. Da schon zum Zeitpunkt der Geburt eine Entscheidung gefällt werden muss, werden Formen von Intersexualität, die erst in der Pubertät sichtbar werden, weiterhin ausgeschlossen.

Die in Deutschland durchgeführte Gesetzesänderung bezüglich der Geschlechtsangabe im Personenstand löst unterschiedliche Reaktionen aus. So argumentiert Nardi auf einer katholischen Internetseite, dass das neue Gesetz die naturgegebene Wirklichkeit, bezogen auf die Zweiteilung der Geschlechter, verleugne und sogar das Individuum angreife, da schließlich die anthropologische Realität abgestritten werde. Dabei spielt besonders der Verweis auf die pejorativ so bezeichnete „Homo- und Gender-Ideologie" eine Rolle: Diese würde Kinderrechte opfern, wobei ein Zusammenhang zwischen einem Dachverband Homosexueller mit einer Gesetzesänderung zugunsten Intersexueller nicht erklärt wird. Nardi schließt den Artikel mit einem Zitat, in dem die unvermeidlichen psychischen Schäden solcher Intersex-Kinder thematisiert werden (Nardi, Online-Artikel).

Einen differenzierteren Blick wirft die Zeit Online auf das Thema. So werden im Artikel von Meister eine intersexuelle Person, die Sexualforscherin Richter-Appelt und der Vorsitz des Vereins Intersexueller Menschen e.V. zu Wort gelassen und darüber hinaus kurze biologisch-medizinische Erläuterungen zu möglichen Formen gegeben. Kritikpunkte am Gesetz werden ebenfalls genannt. Diese betreffen einerseits die Befürchtung, dass dieses Gesetz erst recht geschlechtsanpassende Operationen verursache, und andererseits die Eintragung selber, da sie den falschen Eindruck erwecke, Intersexuelle hätten kein Geschlecht. Zugleich werden in dem Artikel Fragen angesprochen, die durch das Gesetz offen bleiben. So ist noch unklar, ob erwachsene Intersexuelle im Nachhinein ihre Einträge korrigieren lassen dürfen und ob Menschen ohne Geschlechtseintrag die Heirat erlaubt wird (siehe Meister,

Online-Artikel). Wann und wie derartige Fragen, die sich spätestens dann ergeben, wenn die ersten Menschen ohne Geschlechtseintragung erwachsen sind, geklärt werden, wird sich noch herausstellen.

Eine weitere Meinung zu dieser Gesetzesänderung gibt es auf der Internetseite einer Vereinigung intersexueller Menschen namens *zwischengeschlecht.org*. Auf dieser Seite wird die Änderung sehr kritisch gesehen, da durch die Offenhaltung der Geschlechtsangabe den überforderten Eltern von Seiten der Medizin eher zu einer Operation geraten werde, mit der Begründung der Sorge darüber, dass das Kind sozial ausgeschlossen werde. Hierbei wird besonders hervorgehoben, dass letztlich die Entscheidung über die Geschlechtszugehörigkeit beim medizinischen Personal liegt. Dabei befürchtet zwischengeschlecht.org ebenfalls die soziale Isolation, die aufgrund eines Zwangsoutings durch das Freilassen der Geschlechtsangabe auftritt. Zusätzlich wird mit der vermehrten Durchführung von Abtreibungen intersexueller Ungeborener gerechnet. Der Artikel nimmt die Gesetzesänderung und Kritikpunkte zum Anlass, die eigentlichen Forderungen der Vereinigung zu betonen, welche vor allem auf ein endgültiges Verbot der Genitalverstümmelungen Intersexueller abzielen (siehe *zwischengeschlecht.org* a).

Vor der Aufnahme dieses Paragraphen in das deutsche Recht führt Christiane Völling als erste intersexuelle Person einen Prozess gegen den Arzt, der ihr ohne vorherige oder anschließende Aufklärung die weiblichen Geschlechtsorgane entnommen hat. Völling weist das Adrenogenitale Syndrom auf und wird in ihrer Familie als männlich angesehen und erzogen. In der Biographie beschreibt Völling allerdings ihre Zweifel an der aufgedrängten Geschlechtszugehörigkeit, fügt sich jedoch letztlich der von außen erzwungenen männlichen Geschlechtszuweisung. 1976 wird bei ihr ein weiblicher Chromosomensatz herausgefunden. Völling, zu dem Zeitpunkt 17-jährig, erhält allerdings keine Informationen darüber. Die Entnahme ihrer inneren, weiblichen Geschlechtsorgane erfolgt ein Jahr später, nach der Information darüber, dass möglicherweise karzinogenes Gewebe im Bauchraum vorliege (Völling, 89). Während des Prozesses, den sie 2008 gewinnt, läuft zugleich das Verfahren, das ihren Geschlechtseintrag berichtigen sollte. Aufschlussreich hierbei ist, dass dieser Vorgang in Deutschland bei Intersexuellen *Korrektur* und bei Transsexuellen *Än-*

derung genannt wird und dass nur das Verfahren für Transsexuelle rechtlich festgelegt ist (siehe Völling, 202).

Derzeit läuft in Deutschland der europaweit zweite und weltweit dritte vergleichbare Prozess, wobei diesmal sogar neben dem Chirurgen auch die Universitätsklinik Erlangen angeklagt wird (*zwischengeschlecht.org* b).

Geschlechtergerechte Sprache

In der schriftlichen Sprache haben sich Schreibweisen entwickelt, die das gesamte Spektrum von Geschlechtern, einschließlich der Inter- und Transsexuellen, abdecken sollen, wie beispielweise die Verwendung von Unterstrich oder Sternchen (z. B. Lehrer_innen bzw. Lehrer*innen). Neutrale Wörter zu verwenden, um alle Menschen, egal welchen Geschlechts, anzusprechen, ist eine weitere Möglichkeit (z. B. „Publikum" oder „Auditorium"). Wie aber sieht eine korrekte Anrede und Bezeichnung intersexueller Menschen aus? In Briefen oder bei Ansprachen wird üblicherweise immer von „Frau" oder „Dame" und „Herr" gesprochen. Diese Begriffe implizieren, transportieren und zementieren das tradierte zweigeschlechtliche Menschenbild. Sie sind folglich für die Anrede Intersexueller ungeeignet. Da es in der deutschen Sprache derzeit keine Möglichkeit für die geschlechtsneutrale Ansprache einer einzelnen Person gibt, ist die passende Anredeform am besten über das persönliche Gespräch zu erfragen. Wichtig ist nur, dass möglichst bewusst darauf geachtet wird, alle Menschen miteinzubeziehen und anzusprechen, so dass niemand aufgrund geschlechtlicher Merkmale marginalisiert und diskriminiert wird. Schließlich übt Sprache Macht aus, indem sie Kategorien, Bedeutungen und oftmals Hierarchien erzeugt. Sprache konstituiert Wirklichkeit. Im Extremfall kann dies dazu führen, dass alles, was in der sprachlich-symbolisch konstituierten Ordnung nicht enthalten ist, auch nicht als existent wahrgenommen wird (Calvi 2012, 134f.). Sprache ist also ein zentrales Medium der Sichtbarmachung oder Marginalisierung intersexueller Menschen.

Weitere gebräuchliche Synonyme für Intersexuelle sind – meist pejorativ konnotierte - Begriffe wie „Hermaphroditen" oder „Zwitter". In der Fachliteratur gilt die Verwendung des Terminus *Intersexuelle* als state of the art. Derzeit sind Entwicklungen zu beobachten, dass stattdessen der Begriff „Intergender" favorisiert werden soll, da hierdurch eine Verwechslung mit Begriffen wie Bi- und Homosexualität vermieden wird. Schließlich handelt es sich nicht um eine sexuelle Ausrichtung, sondern um Geschlechtsidentität. Eine derartige Änderung wird ebenfalls für die Bezeichnung Transsexualität empfohlen (siehe Groneberg 2012, 496). Eine Bezeichnung wie „drittes Geschlecht" lässt auf eine numerische Reihung von Geschlechtern schließen, wobei sich hier die Frage stellt, was das erste und zweite Geschlecht sein soll. Nach dem neuen deutschen Recht soll statt männlich oder weiblich gar nichts eingetragen werden. Dieses Auslassen der Geschlechtsangabe wird von Intersexuellen allerdings als diskriminierend empfunden, da sie sehr wohl ein Geschlecht haben und nicht keines (Meister, Online-Artikel). Hierzu gehören auch die Bezeichnungen wie „uneindeutiges" oder „anderes Geschlecht", die beide pejorativ aufgefasst werden können.

Intersexualität und Gesellschaft

Da „eine Begegnung von Mensch zu Mensch immer durch das erste Einordnen in Kategorien gezeichnet ist" (Pulvermüller 2012, 257), werden neue Begegnungen den verschiedenen sozialen Kategorien zugeordnet, wobei in zweigeschlechtlichen Gesellschaften die Kategorie des Geschlechts unvollkommen ist. Dabei gibt es Gesellschaften, in denen Intersexuelle ihren eigenen Platz haben. Historisch können nach der Entdeckung Amerikas auf missionarischen Reisen stark von Europa abweichende Geschlechtersysteme beschrieben werden. Dabei liegen Geschlechterrollenwechsel in verschiedenen Ausprägungen vor (Calvi 2012, 128). In vielen indigenen Völkern werden keine strengen Grenzen zwischen Intersexuellen und Transvestiten gezogen, mit Ausnahme der Navaho. Hier erhalten Intersexuelle eine eigene Bezeichnung und man begegnet ihnen mit Hochachtung (ebenda, 129). Allerdings wird dieser offene Umgang mit Geschlechterbildern durch das aus Europa stammende binäre Geschlechtermodell verdrängt (ebenda, 129f).

Ein komplexes System bewahrt sich hingegen in Indien und Pakistan. Hier gibt es vielfältige Formen von so genannten Hijras. Zu ihnen zählen vor allem Intersexuelle und Männer, die meist impotent sind und sich ihre Genitalien entfernen lassen, um sich durch diese Prozedur der ihnen eigenen Gottheit zu widmen (ebenda, 120-123). Dabei ist zu berücksichtigen, dass der Beitritt zu dieser eigenen Kaste, welche problemlos neben der ebenfalls binären Geschlechtervorstellung Indiens bestehen kann, nicht freiwillig ist. Denn es handelt sich um Personen, die „aufgrund ihrer Genitalien, ihrer Impotenz oder sexuellen Präferenz […] von der Gesellschaft verstoßen werden und hierdurch erst zum Beitritt zu den Hijras motiviert werden." (ebenda, 124) Hier liegt also keine Anerkennung wie bei den indigenen Völkern Nordamerikas zugrunde, sondern der Beitritt ist für die Betroffenen die einzige Möglichkeit, um einen angesehenen Platz in der Gesellschaft zu erhalten. Seit 2009 wird den Personen, die sich zu den Hijras zählen, in Indien und Pakistan ein eigenes Geschlecht zuerkannt, wobei in Pakistan angestrebt wird, Hijras in politische Ämter zu holen. In Indien gelten zumindest homosexuelle Handlungen nicht mehr als strafbar, was deswegen erwähnenswert ist, da diese Handlungen von den Hijras oft praktiziert werden. (ebenda, 126)

Allerdings zeigen diese Beispiele, dass Körperlichkeit das zentrale Element für die Geschlechtszuschreibung bleibt. Da die Körperlichkeit eine derart zentrale Stelle einnimmt, werden bis heute Genitalverstümmelungen an intersexuellen Neugeborenen von medizinischer Seite empfohlen. Die operative Behandlung Intersexueller gilt bisher als medizinische Notwendigkeit. Aufgrund der Schäden, die sich hieraus ergeben, ist allerdings ein anderer medizinischer Umgang mit Intersexualität notwendig (Voß 2012, 69). Bei der Empfehlung zu einer Operation spielt besonders die Unsicherheit der Eltern eine Rolle, so dass diese den Empfehlungen des medizinischen Fachpersonals nachkommen und durch die Operation ihrer elterlichen Verantwortung gerecht werden. Sofern Eltern bereits vorher Informationen zum Thema Intersexualität erhalten, soll ihre Unsicherheit diesbezüglich geringer werden. Damit sich intersexuelle Kinder körperlich und geschlechtlich frei entfalten können, ist es notwendig, dass die Gesellschaft über die Vielzahl der möglichen Geschlechter aufgeklärt wird. Dabei ist die gesamte Breite der Gesellschaft aufzuklären, da schließlich das Kind mit verschiedenen Menschen in Kontakt tritt. Besonders in Kinderkliniken und auf Ämtern sind grundlegende Informationen notwendig, damit einerseits die medizinisch nicht notwendigen Genitaloperationen beendet werden und andererseits Intersexuelle nicht mehr länger mit Transsexuellen verwechselt werden. Es soll schlichtweg die Pathologisierung von Intersexualität aufhören (siehe Calvi 2012, 105).

Ein weiteres Problem stellt die Langsamkeit dar, mit der in der Medizin auf neue humanwissenschaftliche Erkenntnisse und Forschungsergebnisse reagiert wird. So weist zwischengeschlecht.org darauf hin, dass mindestens bis 2013 an der Universitätsklinik Heidelberg genitalkorrigierende Operationen für intersexuelle Kinder angeboten werden (zwischengeschlecht.org c). Daher ist es notwendig, der Unkenntnis und dem Unwillen der Medizin gegenüber einer dem Menschenrecht nach Unverletzlichkeit entsprechenden Behandlung Intersexueller entgegenzuwirken. Hierfür eignet sich das Angebot von Aus- und Weiterbildungsmaßnahmen, dass ärztliche Entscheidungen transparent gemacht werden und dass es Praxis wird, Eltern an spezialisierte Kliniken zu verweisen (siehe Groneberg 2012, 494f). Es ist dringend geboten, die Pathologisierung von Intersexualität im Kontext der Medizin endlich zu verabschieden. Denn sobald Intersexualität als eine natürliche Geschlechtsvariante und nicht mehr als Störung und somit Krankheit wahrgenommen wird, erübrigen sich geschlechtsangleichende Operationen.

Ein weiterer Aspekt ist die Geschlechtsidentität. Darunter wird das Geschlecht verstanden, in dem eine Person lebt. Hierbei ist unklar, inwiefern diese bei Kindern angelegt ist. Die „zwanglose Ausbildung der psychischen Geschlechtsidentität und die Möglichkeit, ihr entsprechend zu leben, sind notwendige Voraussetzungen für das Wohlergehen der Person und sollte Verfassungsschutz genießen." (Groneberg 2012, 487) Um diese Ausbildung zu gewährleisten, sind Eingriffe von außerhalb, vor allem durch Geschlechtszuweisung und Genitaloperationen, zu vermeiden. Für das Kind ist es besser abzuwarten, wie es sich entwickelt und ob es sich für ein Geschlecht entscheidet. Somit erhalten der Umgang der Eltern mit dem Thema Intersexualität und die Erziehung einen hohen Stellenwert. Im Blick auf die Erziehung ist außerdem darauf zu achten, dass die Intersexualität des Kindes nicht verheimlicht und tabuisiert wird. Genau dieses Verheimlichen ist Völling widerfahren. Anschaulich schildert sie, wie hierdurch ihr „Urvertrauen unwiederbringlich zerstört" (Völling 2010, 31) worden ist. Damit Eltern offen mit der Intersexualität ihres Kindes umgehen können, ist es ratsam, dass sie von medizinischer und psychosozialer Betreuung profitieren (siehe Groneberg 2012, 488). Außerdem sollen den

374

Eltern die Grenzen ihrer Entscheidungsgewalt aufgezeigt werden, damit das Wohl des Kindes vor dem Wohl der Eltern beziehungsweise der Familie steht (ebenda, 497f).

Wenn sich Intersexuelle in der westlichen, zweigeschlechtlichen Gesellschaft zu ihrer Intersexualität bekennen, dann verlassen sie das zweigeteilte Geschlechterschema (siehe Calvi 2012, 105). Es ist demnach ein Umdenken in der westlichen Gesellschaft notwendig, damit es Menschen möglich wird, die diversen Geschlechtsidentitäten auch tatsächlich leben zu können (ebenda, 108). Aufgrund aktueller Gleichstellungsbestrebungen wird die Notwendigkeit von Geschlechtergrenzen in Frage gestellt (ebenda, 140). Die dazugehörigen Rollenzuschreibungen für die einzelnen Geschlechter sind auch aus einem anderen Grund in Frage zu stellen.

Herta Nagl-Docekal problematisiert eine Herleitung der Geschlechtsrollen aus der biologischen Ausstattung unserer Leiblichkeit, da gerade derartige Normierungen immer schon contra naturam sind, d. h. unsere körperliche Beschaffenheit ist Aufgabe für unser Handeln (Nagl-Docekal 2000, 26f). Wir sind mit unterschiedlichen körperlichen Merkmalen ausgestattet, mit denen wir handelnd umgehen müssen. Nagl-Docekal arbeitet zwei Argumentationslinien heraus: Es wird entweder behauptet, die Arbeitsteilung zwischen den Geschlechtern sei *naturgegeben* oder *naturgewollt*. (ebenda, 18) Wenn von *naturgegeben* gesprochen wird, wird die soziale Ordnung aus der Natur abgeleitet. Bezüglich des *naturgewollt* bedarf es eines Appells, um die entsprechende soziale Ordnung zu verwirklichen. Die Berufung auf die Naturgegebenheit sozialer Normen führt in einen Biologismus: „Die Ordnung menschlicher Gemeinwesen gilt in dieser Variante als nicht grundsätzlich unterschieden von der Strukturierung des Zusammenlebens von Tieren." (ebenda, 20) Diese Konzeption scheitert jedoch an ihrem Binnenwiderspruch. „Der Begriff ‚Norm' hat nur Sinn im Kontext einer – wie auch immer im einzelnen konzipierten – Freiheitstheorie." (ebenda, 20) Normen „appellieren an Menschen, die sich vor Entscheidungssituationen gestellt sehen. Werden hingegen alle beobachtbaren Tätigkeiten von Menschen als ‚natürliche' Vorgänge betrachtet, so drückt sich darin die Überzeugung aus, dass diese Tätigkeiten restlos durch Instinkte erklärbar sind, auch wenn ein diesbezüglicher empirischer Nachweis zurzeit ‚noch' nicht gelingt." (ebenda, 20) Eine solche Position wird dem alltäglichen Selbstverständnis der

Menschen gar nicht gerecht: Einerseits erleben wir, dass viele leibliche Vorgänge von selbst ablaufen, z. B. der Lidschlussreflex. Andererseits aber stehen Menschen immer wieder in Handlungssituationen, wo sie unter gegebenen Optionen entscheiden und wählen müssen. In jeder Handlungssituation weiß ich, dass ich handeln muss und erwarte die Lösung der Frage ‚Was soll ich tun?‘ nicht von einem unwillkürlich ablaufenden Verhaltensmuster. „Es ist demgemäß nur dann sinnvoll, einen Vorgang als ‚natürlich‘ zu bezeichnen, wenn er sich – aus der Perspektive des Handelns gesprochen – ‚von selbst‘ vollzieht, d. h. nicht aufgrund menschlicher Planung. Damit ist freilich zugleich gesagt, daß es keines normativen Appells bedarf, damit derartige Abläufe zustande kommen. [...] In diesem zweiten Kontext gilt es, unsere eigenen Absichten abzuklären, und ein Hinweis auf eine ‚Absicht der Natur‘ hat keinen zwingenden Charakter. Wer letztere dennoch annimmt, dem droht die Gefahr eines performativen Selbstwiderspruchs: Während sich auf der inhaltlichen Ebene die Natur als ausschlaggebend erweisen soll, bringt die Tatsache, *daß* überhaupt ein Sollen formuliert wird, die Auffassung zum Ausdruck, daß der betreffende Fall gerade nicht einem natürlichen Verlauf anheimgestellt ist." (ebenda, 26)

Eine Überwindung des zweigeschlechtlichen Schemas ist folglich anzustreben, also Geschlecht als etwas Variables und nichts Endgültiges zu betrachten, wie es schon lange von Seiten der queer-Theorie gefordert wird (siehe Calvi 2012, 28). Eine derartige Abschaffung des zweigeschlechtlichen Schemas nimmt überdies der Medizin ihre Legitimationsgrundlage für die operativen Eingriffe, welche schlicht Menschenrechtsverletzungen darstellen (ebenda, 153). Außerdem werden durch ein Durchbrechen der Geschlechtergrenzen soziale Räume für Intersexuelle geschaffen, die bislang fehlen. Diese Räume ermöglichen die Entfaltung und Anerkennung der jeweils individuellen Besonderheiten der Menschen (ebenda, 155).

Schlussüberlegungen

Gezeigt werden sollte, welche Anforderungen sich an eine zweigeschlechtlich orientierte Dominanzkultur richten in Bezug auf den Umgang mit intersexuellen Menschen. Unter Bezugnahme auf medizinische und biologische Forschungsliteratur wurde kurz die Bandbreite der Erscheinungsformen von Intersexualität skizziert und es wurden

376

verschiedene notwendige begriffliche Differenzierungen durchgeführt, die eine spezifischere Herangehensweise an das Thema Intersexualität ermöglichen. Ein kurzer Blick in die Geschichte sollte vor Augen führen, wie in verschiedenen historischen Epochen und in unterschiedlichen Gesellschaftszusammenhängen mit intersexuellen Menschen umgegangen wurde.

Anhand der Geschichte des Umgangs mit Intersexuellen lässt sich der Anstieg des medizinischen Einflusses aufgrund der neuen technischen Diagnosemöglichkeiten aufzeigen. Die Relevanz der Gefühlslage von Intersexuellen tritt erst allmählich in das medizinische Denken ein. Ziel ist, dass das Wohl des Kindes im Zentrum medizinischer Maßnahmen steht. Wenn erreicht ist, dass in der Gesellschaft jedes einzelne Kind, unabhängig von der körperlichen Verfassung, als Person mit Menschenwürde anerkannt wird, wenn also Kinder nicht mehr auf ihre Genitalien reduziert werden, gibt es für Intersexuelle die Chance, dass ihre Lebensrealität ein Stück weit als Normalität anerkannt wird. Eine andere Rolle spielt die Sprache, die keine Stigmatisierung und Verletzung generieren soll. Es bleibt derzeit noch offen, ob sich zuerst die Gesellschaft oder die Sprache oder beides parallel für intersexuelle Menschen öffnet und wie diese Öffnung umgesetzt wird. Stellt man sich selbst die Frage, wie man von anderen behandelt werden möchte, so doch möglichst mit Respekt, zumindest aber mit Akzeptanz. Letztlich können einzelne Menschen die Gesellschaft durch eine derartige Einstellung mit gestalten und verändern.

Bibliographie

Buselmaier, Werner/Tariverdian. *Humangenetik*. Heidelberg: Springer Medizin Verlag 2007.

Calvi, Eva Maria. *Eine Überschreitung der Geschlechtergrenzen? Intersexualität in der ‚westlichen Gesellschaft‘ zwischen konstruierter Nicht-Existenz, Pathologisierung und einem Aufbrechen des binären Geschlechtermodells aus gendertheoretischer Perspektive.* Baden-Baden: Deutscher Wissenschafts-Verlag 2012.

Groneberg, Michael. „Empfehlungen zum Umgang mit Zwischenge-schlechtlichkeit". In Schweizer, Katinka./Richter-Appelt, Hertha (Hrsg.). *Intersexualität kontrovers. Grundlagen, Erfahrungen, Positionen.* Gießen: Psychosozial-Verlag 2012, 485-500.

Nagl-Docekal, Herta. *Feministische Philosophie. Ergebnisse, Probleme, Perspektiven.* Frankfurt am Main: Fischer-Taschenbuch-Verlag 2000.

Nussberger, Erika. *Zwischen Tabu und Skandal. Hermaphroditen von der Antike bis heute.* Wien/Köln/Weimar: Böhlau 2014.

Pulvermüller, J. M. „Gedanken einer Mutter". In Schweizer, Katin-ka./Richter-Appelt, Hertha (Hrsg.). *Intersexualität kontrovers. Grundlagen, Erfahrungen, Positionen.* Gießen: Psychosozial-Verlag 2012, 255-267.

Richter-Appelt, Hertha. „Irritationen des Geschlechts - Varianten der Ge-schlechtsentwicklung". In: Hochleitner, Margarethe (Hrsg.), *Gender Medici-ne. Ringvorlesung an der Medizinischen Universität Innsbruck, Band 3: Se-xualität.* Wien: Facultas.WUV 2010.

Schönbucher, Verena/ Ohms, Julia/Núñez Garcia, David/Schweizer, Katinke/Richter-Appelt, Hertha. „Heterosexuelle Normalität oder sexuelle Lebensqualität? Behandlungsziele im Wandel". In Dies./Richter-Appelt, Hertha (Hrsg.). *Intersexualität kontrovers. Grundlagen, Erfahrungen, Positi-onen.* Gießen: Psychosozial-Verlag 2012, 207-223.

Schweizer, Katinka. „Körperliche Geschlechtsentwicklung und zwischen-geschlechtliche Formenvielfalt". In: Dies./Richter-Appelt, Hertha (Hrsg.). *Intersexualität kontrovers. Grundlagen, Erfahrungen, Positionen.* Gießen: Psychosozial-Verlag 2012, 43-67 (a).

Schweizer, Katinka. „Sprache und Begrifflichkeiten. Intersexualität be-nennen". In: Dies./Richter-Appelt, Hertha (Hrsg.). *Intersexualität kontrovers. Grundlagen, Erfahrungen, Positionen.* Gießen: Psychosozial-Verlag 2012, 19-39 (b).

Schweizer, Katinka/Richter-Appelt, Hertha. „Die Hamburger Studie zur Intersexualität. Ein Überblick". In: Dies./Richter-Appelt, Hertha (Hrsg.). *Intersexualität kontrovers. Grundlagen, Erfahrungen, Positionen.* Gießen: Psychosozial-Verlag 2012, 187-205.

Völling, Christiane. *Ich war Mann und Frau. Mein Leben als Intersexuel-le.* Köln: Fackelträger 2010.

Voß, Hans-Jürgen. *Intersexualität – Intersex. Eine Intervention.* Münster: Unrast-Verlag 2012.

Quellen aus dem Internet

ARD-Beitrag: W wie Wissen, ausgestrahlt am 08.11.2014. Online unter: http://www.daserste.de/information/wissen-kultur/w-wie-wissen/videos/ intersexualitaet-104.html (Stand: Juli 2015).

http://www.intersexuelle-menschen.net/aktivitaeten/2015_02_02_didacta _2015.php (Stand: Juli 2015).

Meister, Christiane. *Gesetzesänderung für Intersexuelle. Junge, Mädchen oder keins von beidem.* Vom 01.11.2013. Online unter: http://www.zeit.de/ wissen/2013-10/intersexualitaet-geschlechtsangabe-personenstandsgesetz-aenderung (Stand: Juli 2015).

Nardi, Guiseppe. *„Intersex": Deutschland führt ab 1. November „drittes" Geschlecht ein – Homo- und Genderideologen jubeln.* Vom 19.08.013. Online unter: http://www.katholisches.info/2013/08/19/intersex-deutschland-fuehrt-ab-1-november-drittes-geschlecht-ein-homo-und-genderideologen-jubeln/ (Stand: Juli 2015).

Personenstandsgesetz der Bundesrepublik Deutschland, Abschnitt 2, §22, Art. 3. Online unter: http://www.gesetze-im-internet.de/bundesrecht/pstg/ gesamt.pdf (Stand: Juli 2015).

http://blog.zwischengeschlecht.info/pages/Bundestag-Staatliches-Zwangsouting-Freipass-fur-Genitalverstummler (a) (Stand: Juli 2015).

http://blog.zwischengeschlecht.info/post/2015/02/19/Nurnberger-Zwitterprozess-gegen-Uni-Klinik-Erlangen (b) (Stand: Juli 2015).

http://blog.zwischengeschlecht.info/post/2013/03/31/Intersex-Genitalverstummler-Markus-Bettendorf (c) (Stand: Juli 2015).

BETTINA ZEHETNER

EMANZIPATION ALS DIENSTLEISTUNG?
FEMINISTISCHE PHILOSOPHIE IN DER PSYCHOSOZIALEN BERATUNG

Ich möchte im folgenden Beitrag feministische Theorie mit meiner Praxis als psychosoziale Beraterin im Verein „Frauen beraten Frauen" verbinden.

> »Ich weiß es nicht!« antworten Frauen in der Beratung auf die Frage, was sie sich wünschen. »Ich kann nicht!« sagen viele, wenn es darum geht, etwas zu verändern. Und immer wieder: »Sagen Sie mir, ob ich normal bin!«

Meine Fragestellung lautet: Was kann feministische Philosophie in der psychosozialen Beratung bewirken?

Meine These: Sie kann der neoliberalen Verwertung von Beratung als „Normalisierung" und „Reparaturwerkstatt" zur noch besseren Anpassung von Frauen entgegenwirken.

Wie kann sie das? Durch Reflexion und Entschleunigung sowie die Methode der genealogischen Kritik, die subversives Potenzial hat.

Ich gliedere meinen Vortrag in 4 Teile: eine kurze Einleitung zur philosophischen Haltung in der Beratung, einige Sätze zur Wirkung von Geschlechternormen, der Hauptteil zur genealogischen Kritik und der Methode der Geschlechterparodie in der Beratung sowie Abschluss und Ausblick.

1. Einleitung: Zur philosophischen Haltung in der psychosozialen Beratung

Für Judith Butler ist eine der wesentlichen philosophischen Fragen, „was eine lebenswerte Welt ausmacht" (Butler 2009, 35). Michel Foucault stellt die Frage nach der „Sorge um sich" (Foucault 1986) ins Zentrum seines Spätwerks und für Ludwig Wittgenstein ist Philosophie die „Arbeit an Einem selbst" (Wittgenstein 1998, 24).

Sie alle bestimmen die philosophische Tätigkeit nicht als Suche nach objektiver Wahrheit, sondern als Arbeit an sich selbst, als Ethos oder „Selbstsorge".

Beratung ist – wie die Philosophie – eine Kultur der Fragen. Ganz unzeitgemäß geht es in der psychsozialen Beratung um Entschleunigung, um die Verlangsamung von Prozessen, um das *Denken vor dem Handeln* als Alternative zu rasch verordneten Lösungen. Psychosoziale Beratung bietet keine Ratschläge an, sondern ganz im Gegenteil problematisiert sie das Selbstverständliche. Sie bietet keine Sicherheit im Sinne „eines richtigen Weges/ einer richtigen Lösung", sondern stellt Fragen und bringt in Bewegung. Eine Art Leitmotiv für Beratung könnte Judith Butlers Frage sein: „Sollten wir uns nicht vor jedem abschließenden oder endgültigen Wissen hüten?" (Butler 2009, 351).

2. Normen als selbstverständliche unmarkierte Positionen in Frage stellen

Zitat einer Ratsuchenden aus einem schriftlichen Beratungsprozess (online):

> „Um als ‚normal' zu gelten, habe ich viel in Kauf genommen. Alles sollte perfekt sein. Das Muttergefühl hat sich gleich eingestellt, das war perfekt. Mit der Vorstellung ‚so muss Ehe sein' hab ich mir die Sicht auf (m)einen eigenen Weg versperrt."

Mit der Haltung „Frauen sind halt fürsorglicher, empathischer, besser im vermitteln, ermutigen, trösten..." („Eine gute Mutter stellt sich selbst zurück") verhinderten die Ratsuchende und ihr Partner eine gerechte Arbeitsteilung und Teilung der Verantwortlichkeit für Sorgetätigkeiten.

Hier kann eine kritische Genealogie ansetzen, eine Spurensuche, um in der Beratung gemeinsam zu entdecken, wie die jeweilige Norm zum Maßstab für die ratsuchende Frau geworden ist. Die individuelle Geschichte ist dabei eng verknüpft mit der gesellschaftlich-kulturellen Ebene, „was in einer Kultur eine Frau/ einen Mann ausmacht". Machtvolle gesellschaftliche Übereinkünfte bilden den impliziten Standard einer Normalisierung. Diese Übereinkünfte explizit zu machen, zur Sprache zu bringen und verhandelbar zu machen ist Aufgabe der Beratung. Das kann zB das Arbeiten an destruktiven inneren Aufträgen (Glaubenssätzen) sein, wie etwa „Eine gute Mutter trennt sich nicht vom Vater ihrer Kinder" (egal wie belastend die Beziehung für sie ist). Hier wird die weiblich konnotierte Qualität des „Ertragens" und

„Durchhaltens" als Stütze patriarchaler Strukturen sichtbar und bearbeitbar (Stichwort „Mittäterschaft").

Normen schreiben sich in Körper ein, Männer und Frauen verkörpern diese Normen: Pierre Bourdieu nennt das die „Somatisierung von Herrschaftsverhältnissen". „In jeder Geste (...) steckt die ganze Gesellschaft." (Kaufmann 1994, 293).

Geschlecht als „Existenzweise" (Maihofer 1995) umfasst eine Vielzahl „weiblicher" und „männlicher" Denk-, Gefühls- und Handlungsweisen, Körperformen, Gesten und Sensibilitäten. Institutionalisierte Verkörperungen sind mehr als individuelles *doing gender*. Durch die performative Struktur von Weiblichkeit und Männlichkeit können wir diese im Wiederholen verschieben und resignifizieren:

Eine Möglichkeit in der Beratung besteht darin, den Fokus auf den Prozess des Verkörperns (embodying) zu legen: Wie sind Verkörperungen von Weiblichkeit und Männlichkeit neu und anders, selbstbestimmter als bisher möglich?

Ein wichtiges Gebiet ist dabei die geschlechtsspezifische Bewertung von Affekten wie Scham und Zorn: Frauen, die von ihrem Partner geschlagen wurden, empfinden häufig „stellvertretend" Scham und Schuld. Frauen wenden Aggression häufig gegen sich selbst, anstatt sie nach außen zu richten. Hier ist es möglich, „Gegenhabitualisierungen" (Landweer 1997) zu entwickeln durch konkrete Arbeit an Haltungen – an inneren Einstellungen ebenso wie an konkreten Körperhaltungen: „androgynes Nachsozialisieren" (Schigl 2012).

In Beziehungskonflikten lähmt die Angst vor Differenzen und Konflikten viele Frauen in ihrer Handlungsfähigkeit: „Anstatt die Zumutung zurückzuweisen erstarre ich" schildern manche. Im Bewusstsein „Ich darf Grenzen setzen" kann dieser Angst vor Konfrontation entgegengewirkt werden. Manchmal ist es sogar möglich, Lust auf Differenzen zu entwickeln, z.B. innerhalb einer Gesprächsgruppe in der Frauenberatung. In meine Gruppe für Frauen in Trennung lade ich immer Frauen ein, die selbst die Trennung von ihrem/r PartnerIn wollen und Frauen, die gegen ihren Willen verlassen wurden – mit dem Ziel, den jeweils anderen Anteil zu erleben.

3. Genealogische Kritik hat subversives Potenzial oder Beratung als emanzipatorischer Prozess GEGEN neoliberale Selbstoptimierung

Beratungen wollen nicht Fürsorgestationen seelischen Elends sein, sondern Aufklärungsräume, Kritik- und Gegenentwürfe (vgl. Thürmer-Rohr 1986).

Der Druck auf Frauen steigt auch durch den neoliberalen Mythos: Glück und Gesundheit sei ein Produkt persönlicher Leistung. Nicht-entsprechen wird als persönliches Versagen erlebt: „Mit mir stimmt etwas nicht, ich schaffe das alles nicht mehr." Die „work-life-balance als scheinbar individuelle Herausforderung.

Die Basis feministischer Beratung ist eine gesellschaftskritische Haltung. Sie setzt der Pathologisierung von Frauen die Politisierung individueller Problemlagen entgegen. Feministische Beratung ist kein Rückzug in die Innerlichkeit, keine Nabelschau. Das Benennen der gesellschaftlichen Bedingungen von Problemen und Erkrankungen entlastet und bietet die Möglichkeit, der Vereinzelung und Selbstbe-schuldigung, dem Gefühl von persönlichem Versagen zu entkommen.

Eine feministische Haltung stellt die Dichotomie Gesundheit - Krankheit in Frage: Krank macht die Anpassung an überfordernde Verhältnisse und widersprüchliche Rollenerwartungen. Krankheit als Verweigerung von Anpassung kann dagegen ein Zeichen psychischer Gesundheit sein.

Feministische Beratung muss sich der Risiken eines backlash be-wusst sein, dem Risiko vereinnahmt zu werden als Reparaturwerkstatt, Instrument der Krisenentschärfung und Maschine permanenter Selbst-optimierung, um dem Markt noch besser zu genügen. – Das alles im Sinne einer Strategie der Vereinzelung als Entpolitisierung. Eine Rat-suchende meinte verzweifelt: „Ich schaff's nicht, meinen Mann dazu zu bringen, seinen Anteil an der Hausarbeit und Kinderbetreuung zu übernehmen." Hier zeigt sich eine paradoxe Verantwortungsübernah-me: Die Frau versteht sich selbst als Feministin und ist darum noch strenger zu sich selbst. Von vielen wird es auch als noch beschämen-der erlebt, „als Feministin" Gewalt durch den Partner zu erleben - und sich nicht gleich trennen zu können. Dabei ist ein Paradox zu beobach-ten: die neoliberale „Pflicht" zur Selbstverwirklichung, Autonomie, Authentizität als Resignifizierung emanzipatorisch gemeinter Begriffe aus der Frauenbewegung, eine Art „Austopfung" aus ihrem emanzipatorischen Verwendungskontext.

Feministische Beratung muss unter allen Umständen ihr gesellschaftskritisches Potenzial und ihre politische Haltung bewahren. Die beraterische Haltung muss kritisch bleiben gegenüber den aktuellen Ansprüchen an Flexibilität, Selbstvermarktung, Geschwindigkeit und Effizienz – auch und gerade dann, wenn viele Frauen in die Beratung kommen mit dem Anspruch, „wieder zu funktionieren".

Feministische Beratung will Raum für Reflexion bieten. Sie will Normen in ihrer Selbstverständlichkeit in Frage stellen und sie verhandelbar machen – einen Raum für eigenwillige Aneignungsmöglichkeiten eröffnen. „Normen nicht als Normalisierungsinstrumente, sondern als gemeinsame Orte kontinuierlicher politischer Arbeit." (Butler 2009, 366)

Die Ambivalenz der bulimischen Strategie beispielsweise manifestiert sich im Schwanken zwischen den Polen Anpassung an die geforderten Weiblichkeitsnormen und dem heimlichen Aufbegehren gegen diese. "Unweibliche" Gier und Aggression werden allein im privaten Raum im Fressanfall ausgelebt – („Ich bin ein gieriges Ungeheuer") – nach außen wird die Fassade kontrollierter, erfolgreicher Weiblichkeit präsentiert (attraktiv, ehrgeizig, erfolgreich, Modell „Powerfrau").

Im Gegensatz dazu stellt die Anorektikerin das weibliche Schlankheitsideal durch ihre Überzeichnung in Frage. Dies zur Verdeutlichung, wie Frauen ihren Körper als Objekt verwenden und dabei Weiblichkeitsnormen verkörpern – zwischen Anpassung und Eigenwilligkeit. Kernthema ist dabei der Kampf um Autonomie: Die Magersüchtige hungert ihren Körper als Projektionsfläche für fremdbestimmte Weiblichkeitsbilder aus; die Bulimikerin zeigt nach außen hin eher genormte Weiblichkeit und würgt die Zumutungen im geheimen hervor.

Das Zur-Sprache-Bringen dieser Konflikte (zB zwischen Autonomie und Anpassung/Fremdbestimmung), und somit das In-die-Beziehung-Bringen kann die Symptome überflüssig machen, indem die Aggression nicht mehr gegen sich selbst gerichtet werden muss, sondern einen anderen Ausdruck als den selbstschädigenden findet.

In Beratungsprozessen wird Geschlecht performativ hergestellt durch Sprech- und Erzählweisen sowie durch Selbstbeschreibungen. Beratung bietet die Möglichkeit, sich anders und neu zu erzählen, etwa die verändernde Wiederholung von Idealen oder (Selbst-) Definitionen: „Frau"/"Weiblichkeit", „Mann"/"Männlichkeit", „Familie", „Partnerschaft", „Ehe", „Muttersein", „Vatersein", ideale Beziehung...

„Lernen, sich zu erzählen, bedeutet auch: lernen, sich anders zu erzählen." (Ricoeur 2006,134), also auch immer wieder Neu-Konstruktionen von Identitäten als Frau in unterschiedlichen Lebensbereichen od. -phasen, etwa die Neuerzählung der „heilen" Zwei-Eltern-Kind-Familie nach einer Trennung oder wenn eine Frau ihre Identität durch einen unerfüllten Kinderwunsch in Frage stellt und sie nach anderen Lebensentwürfen sucht. Wer bestimmt die Norm, wie könnte es anders, lebbarer sein?

Ein Beispiel für eine Resignifizierung: Eine Klientin erkannte, dass ihr Ideal einer konfliktfreien Partnerschaft unerfüllbare Ansprüche an sich selbst beinhaltete.

Sie wollte alles aus- und durchhalten, was an Zumutungen an sie herangetragen wurde, vom entwertenden Verhalten bis zur Alleinzuständigkeit für die Sorgearbeit. Sie wollte die Beziehung um jeden Preis aufrechterhalten. Nach einem längeren Beratungsprozess benannte sie dieses strenge Ideal um in „Realitäts-Killer-Ideal" und konnte damit ihr Ziel in ein weniger überforderndes Modell transformieren. Sie eignete sich die Definitionsmacht für ihre Ideale wieder an, indem sie sich fragte: Was ist mir wichtig in einer Beziehung, was sind meine Wünsche? Ihr Fazit: „Die schöne Fassade brauche ich nicht mehr, ich weiß jetzt, was dahinter stecken kann."

Auch das Gebrauchtwerden als vorrangige Sinnstiftung kann in Frage gestellt werden: klassisches Fallbeispiel „die für andere sorgende Frau":

Eine 45jährige Frau arbeitet im Pflegebereich und fühlt sich nahe am burn-out. Sie unterstützt ihren krebskranken Mann und die erwachsene Tochter. Sie fühlt sich auch für die Betreuung von Mutter und Schwiegermutter verantwortlich. Sie quält sich mit dem Gefühl „Es ist nie genug, was ich leiste". Sie entwickelt im Beratungsprozess die Selbstdiagnose: Erschöpfung an weiblicher „Wohlerzogenheit". Daraufhin entwirft sie eine Strategie der Entschleunigung und Reflexion. Anstatt sofort zu übernehmen, baut sie einen Moment der Verzögerung ein, um sich zu fragen: Wie würde das „wohlerzogene Weibchen" in mir handeln? – und um manchmal genau das Gegenteil davon zu tun. „Was erlaube ich mir stattdessen?" als neue Frage an sich selbst.

Ziel der Beratung ist für sie, sich nicht mehr für die gesamte Sorgearbeit zuständig zu fühlen bzw. zuständig erklären zu lassen. Das entspricht einer Politik der „Entunterwerfung" (sich selbst nicht so, auf diese Weise zu regieren). Daraus ergibt sich die Frage: „Was kann ich angesichts der gegenwärtigen Ordnung des Seins sein?" (Butler 2009a, 237). Insgesamt geht es um ein wiederholtes „Durcharbeiten" von Idealen, Aufträgen und Glaubenssätzen. Das erfordert die Kunst des langsamen Wiederkäuens (vgl. Butler 2009a).

Ein Ziel feministischer Beratung kann folgendes sein: Anstatt möglichst reibungslos zu funktionieren, sich erlauben, Wut zu empfinden über ungerechte Verhältnisse und immer wieder mal NEIN zu Forderungen sagen, die an eine herangetragen werden. Sabine Hark: „Feministische Theorie heute: Die Kunst, ‚Nein' zu sagen" (Hark 2013)

die Verweigerung von Ansprüchen und Weiblichkeitszumutungen. Laurie Penny in ihrem Manifest „Fleischmarkt. Weibliche Körper im Kapitalismus": „Vor allem wollen wir nicht schön und brav sein!" (Penny 2012).

Beratung will – wie die Philosophie - das Selbstverständliche nicht selbstverständlich finden. Dieses Infragestellen eigener Gewissheiten bedarf der Bereitschaft, vertraute Sicherheiten aufzugeben. Die patriarchalen Strukturen der Geschlechterordnung im eigenen Kopf aufzustöbern und aufzulösen – oft ohne neue Sicherheiten – das ist die Herausforderung für die feministische Philosophin ebenso wie für die feministische Beraterin. Da uns diese eigene Gewordenheit aber nicht vorliegt wie ein äußerer Gegenstand neutraler Erkenntnis, bedarf es der Verfremdung und Distanzierung aus der Verstricktheit in unsere eigene Geschichte (Komplizität, Mittäterschaft).

In der Beratung kann das bedeuten, etwas zuspitzen, etwas übertreiben, etwas grell ausleuchten, das bisher im Schatten der Gewohnheit oder der Tradition nicht kritisch betrachtet wurde („Unsere Arbeitsteilung hat sich so ergeben").

Genealogische Kritik arbeitet mit den Mitteln der Dramatisierung und Übertreibung, um die historischen Spuren der Macht im Subjekt (in Normen und Werten, in Institutionen wie der Familie) sichtbar zu machen (vgl. Saar 2009).

Wie entsteht das Subjekt in alltäglichen Praktiken? Wie interpretiert die konkrete Frau Weiblichkeitsnormen und wie eignet sie sich diese an, wie gehen sie „in Fleisch und Blut" über? Zwischen Anpassung und Widerständigkeit, (zwischen sich bestimmen lassen und bestimmt werden) wirkt die Macht produktiv im Innersten des Subjekts: „Ich will ja selbst diese Normen erfüllen, eine „richtige" Frau sein und Anerkennung dafür erlangen".

In der Beratung kann die Parodie von Geschlechternormen befreiend wirken, etwa in Form von Verdichtung und Pointierung: Die Figur des „wohlerzogenen Weibchens" sagt: „Ich bin nur für andere da, brauche selbst nichts, habe keine Bedürfnisse, in mir ist keine Aggression, ich bin niemals wütend, nur traurig..." Die Übertreibung verdeutlicht und ruft Widerspruch hervor – den Einspruch gegen eine Realität, die vor der Infragestellung so übermächtig und unbestreitbar erschienen ist, als könne es keine andere geben. Die Möglichkeit des Anders-Seins taucht auf, wird ent-deckt und ein Stück weit im Beratungsraum (zur Probe) realisiert (der Beratungsraum bildet einen Übergangsraum zwischen Öffentlichkeit und Privatheit).

Kritische Beratung soll das System der Bewertung selbst herausarbeiten: Wie entstehen meine Deutungsgewohnheiten? Die Gewohnheiten des Urteilens zugunsten einer riskanteren Praxis zu brechen kann Neugier entstehen lassen, Neugier auf neue Möglichkeiten, Weiblichkeit und Männlichkeit zu leben, Entdeckungslust und neue Leidenschaften – außerhalb der Beziehungsorientierung des Für-den/die-anderen, mehr Weltoffenheit über die verengte Perspektive „Ich-als-Teil-eines-Paars" hinaus.

4. Abschluss und Ausblick

Ziel feministischer Beratungsarbeit ist nicht die bloße Symptombeseitigung und das Funktionieren im bestehenden System, sondern die Erweiterung von Lebens- und Handlungsmöglichkeiten. Nicht-geschlechterrollenkonformes Verhalten ist gesundheitsfördernd – für Frauen ebenso wie für Männer.

Gefordert ist die Selbstreflexion unserer eigenen normativen Konzepte von Männlichkeit und Weiblichkeit als Berater_innen und Therapeut_innen. Dies mit dem Ziel, nicht die bestehende Geschlechterordnung zu reproduzieren, sondern den Blick jenseits der Entweder-

Oder-Dichotomie zu erweitern. Dazu ist es notwendig, unsere impliziten normativen Vorstellungen davon, was eine Frau oder einen Mann ausmacht, explizit zu machen, zur Sprache zu bringen und damit verhandelbar zu machen. Nicht selten kann dabei das Dazwischen als Mehrwert deutlich werden und die traditionellen „Schrumpfformen" von Weiblichkeit und Männlichkeit können erweitert, lebendiger und vielfältiger gestaltet werden.

Mehr Wissen und Bewusstsein darüber, wie wir „Weiblichkeit" und „Männlichkeit" im Alltag „produzieren", erweitert unsere Handlungsfähigkeit – als Ratsuchende ebenso wie als Berater_innen. Im Bewusstsein: „Ich stelle ‚Weiblichkeit' und ‚Männlichkeit' her" wird diese Herstellung auch anders, selbstbestimmter als bisher, denkbar.

Es geht um die Erschließung des kreativen Potenzials von Philosophie als explorativer Praxis. Es geht darum, Reflexionsräume im Alltagsleben von Frauen zu eröffnen. Für viele ist diese Denk-Zeit und dieser Denk-Raum ein bisher nicht gekannter „Luxus", etwas, das sie sich bisher nicht zugestanden haben. Sie können hier anhand der Frage „Wie will ich leben?" eigenwillige Phantasien entwickeln und das Wünschen wieder lernen. So kann feministische Philosophie in der Beratung als emanzipatorische gesellschaftliche Praxis wirksam werden.

Literatur

Butler, Judith. *Die Macht der Geschlechternormen und die Grenzen des Menschlichen.* Frankfurt/ M.: Suhrkamp, 2009.

Butler, Judith. „Was ist Kritik? Ein Essay über Foucaults Tugend." In: Rahel Jaeggi, Tilo Wesche (Hrsg.): *Was ist Kritik?* Frankfurt/M.: Suhrkamp, 2009a, S. 221-246. (2002 in Dt. Zeitschrift für Philosophie Jg.50, Heft 2, 249-265.)

Foucault, Michel. *Die Sorge um sich.* Sexualität und Wahrheit Bd. 3, Frankfurt/ M.: Suhrkamp, 1986.

Hark, Sabine. „Feministische Theorie heute: Die Kunst, ‚Nein' zu sagen." In: *feministische studien.* „Was ist und wozu heute noch feministische Theorie?" Stuttgart: Lucius. 31. Jg. Nr. 1 Mai 2013, S. 65-71.

Kaufmann, Jean-Claude. *Schmutzige Wäsche. Zur ehelichen Konstruktion von Alltag.* Konstanz: Universitätsverlag, 1994.

Landweer, Hilge. „Fühlen Männer anders? Überlegungen zur Konstruktion von Geschlecht durch Gefühle." In: Silvia Stoller, Helmut Vetter (Hrsg.): *Phänomenologie und Geschlechterdifferenz.* Wien: WUV-Universitätsverlag, 1997, S. 249-273.

Maihofer, Andrea. *Geschlecht als Existenzweise.* Frankfurt/ M.: Ulrike Helmer, 1995.

Penny, Laurie. *Fleischmarkt. Weibliche Körper im Kapitalismus.* Hamburg: Nautilus, 2012.

Ricoeur, Paul. *Wege der Anerkennung: Erkennen, Wiedererkennen, Anerkanntsein.* Frankfurt/M.: Suhrkamp, 2006.

Saar, Martin. „Genealogische Kritik." In: Rahel Jaeggi, Tilo Wesche (Hrsg.): *Was ist Kritik?* Frankfurt/M.: Suhrkamp, 2009, S. 247-265.

Schigl, Brigitte. *Psychotherapie und Gender.* Wiesbaden: Springer. Verlag für Sozialwissenschaften, 2012.

Thürmer-Rohr, Christina. „Die Gewohnheit des falschen Echos." In: *Beiträge zur feministischen Theorie und Praxis* Bd. 17: Neue Heimat Therapie. Köln, 1986, S. 113-120.

Wittgenstein, Ludwig. *Vermischte Bemerkungen.* Oxford: Blackwell Publications, 1988.

Zehetner, Bettina. *Krankheit und Geschlecht. Feministische Philosophie und psychosoziale Beratung.* Wien/Berlin: Turia & Kant, 2012.

ESTHER HUTFLESS

Q : P QUEERING PSYCHOANALYSIS –
RESEARCH GROUP ON BODIES AND SEXUALITIES

Als Psychoanalytiker_innen sind wir von der Wirkkraft der psychoanalytischen Methode als Behandlungstechnik ebenso überzeugt wie von der Bedeutsamkeit und der Radikalität, die der Psychoanalyse und der Freud'schen Theorie noch heute zukommen. Zugleich möchten wir das schwierige Verhältnis zwischen queeren Lebens- und Begehrensweisen und der Psychoanalyse problematisieren und Vorurteile abbauen. Diese Vorurteile führen dazu, dass einerseits die Psychoanalyse in den aktuellen Debatten um Geschlechtsidentität, sexuelle Orientierung, Transidentitäten etc. nicht als adäquater theoretischer wie klinischer Zugang wahrgenommen wird, und andererseits dazu, dass viele potentiell an der Psychoanalyse Interessierte aus Angst vor Diskriminierung und Stigmatisierung den Schritt nicht wagen, eine Psychoanalyse für sich in Betracht zu ziehen oder sich weiter und eingehender mit der Psychoanalyse zu beschäftigen. Diese Angst ist oft nicht unbegründet. Stereotypien über LGBTIQs werden in Vorträgen, Ausbildungsseminaren und Supervisionen weithin unhinterfragt reproduziert. In psychoanalytischen Erstgesprächen müssen sich potentielle nicht eindeutig heterosexuelle Analysand_innen mitunter kritische Bemerkungen zur ihrer Geschlechtsidentität, ihrem Begehren und ihrer Objektwahl gefallen lassen. Umgekehrt scheint dies nicht der Fall: eine heterosexuelle Orientierung wird nicht weiter hinterfragt.

Andererseits hat sich mittlerweile auch schon sehr viel verändert. 1987 wurde Homosexualität, die bis dahin als psychische Erkrankung galt, aus dem Diagnose-Manual (DSM) der American Psychiatric Association und schließlich 1992 aus dem ICD (International Statistical Classification of Diseases and Related Health Problems) der WHO gestrichen, und mittlerweile nehmen auch psychoanalytische Ausbildungsvereine homosexuelle Kandidat_innen auf. Transsexualität, Transidentität bzw. Transgender ist jedoch weiterhin, trotz vielfacher Proteste, als Gender-Dysphoria oder als Störung der Geschlechtsidentität in den psychiatrischen Diagnose-Manualen enthalten und gilt als Persönlichkeits- und Verhaltensstörung. Was transgender und transidente Personen betrifft, so ist der psychoanalytische Diskurs von einer Entpathologisierung noch weit entfernt.

Trotz der Offenheit zumindest gegenüber Schwulen und Lesben ist auch die Psychoanalyse nicht gefeit vor ihrer Geschichte; hegemoniale diskriminierende Diskurse und Vorurteile gegenüber Lesben und Schwulen werden weiterhin unhinterfragt reproduziert. Die Tatsache, dass nun zumindest Lesben und Schwule als Kandidat_innen in psychoanalytische Ausbildungsvereine aufgenommen werden, wirkt sich noch kaum auf die psychoanalytische Theorie und Praxis aus bzw. bleibt unthematisiert. Hinzu kommt, dass viele Analytiker_innen ihre sexuelle Orientierung noch immer verschweigen, aus Angst vor Diskriminierung und Ausschluss innerhalb der psychoanalytischen Vereinigungen.

Historische Kontextualisierung

In der zweiten Hälfte des 19. Jahrhunderts gab es im Wesentlichen zwei entgegengesetzte Ansätze Homosexualität zu verstehen: Karl Heinrich Ulrichs veröffentlichte 1864 die Schrift „Forschungen über das Räthsel der mannmännlichen Liebe", in der er sich u. a. gegen die Verurteilung und Stigmatisierung von gleichgeschlechtlich Liebenden einsetzte und sie als drittes Geschlecht auffasste. 1869 hat der Ungar Karl Maria Kertbeny an Ulrichs angeschlossen und sich gegen die Kriminalisierung und Pathologisierung von Homosexuellen ausgesprochen – der Begriff „Homosexualität" geht übrigens auf Kertbeny zurück. Kertbeny hat wie Ulrichs Homosexualität als normale Variation der menschlichen Sexualität begriffen. Auf der anderen Seite hat Richard von Krafft-Ebing 1886 in seiner „Psychopathia Sexualis" Homosexualität als degenerative neurologische Störung verstanden und sie damit pathologisiert (vgl. Drescher 2008, 445). In Freuds Auffassungen zur Homosexualität sind wohl beide Strömungen – nicht-pathologisierende und pathologisierende – mehr oder weniger präsent.

Sigmund Freud selbst hat Homosexuelle nie von der psychoanalytischen Ausbildung ausgeschlossen und hat sich immer für eine Entpathologisierung der Homosexualität ausgesprochen. In einer 1915 ergänzten Fußnote zu den „Drei Abhandlungen zur Sexualtheorie" schreibt Freud: „Die psychoanalytische Forschung widersetzt sich mit aller Entschiedenheit dem Versuche, die Homosexuellen als eine besonders geartete Gruppe von den anderen Menschen abzutrennen. Indem sie auch andere als die manifest kundgegebenen Sexualerregungen studiert, erfährt sie, daß alle Menschen der gleichgeschlechtlichen Objektwahl fähig sind und dieselbe auch im Unbewußten vollzogen haben" (Freud 1999, 44).

Zwar finden sich im Werk Freuds neben progressiven Aussagen zur Homosexualität auch solche, die problematischen Inhalts sind, auffällig ist jedoch, dass in der Rezeption der psychoanalytischen Theorie weniger die progressiven sondern eher die pathologisierenden Passagen im Werk Freuds zur Norm geworden sind, durch die Stereotypien reproduziert wurden und werden. Vor allem durch die Auffassung, dass Identifizierung und Begehren zwangsläufig entgegengesetzt geschlechtlich codiert sind, wird Heterosexualität essentialisiert und andere Begehrens- und Objektwahl-Konstellationen pathologisiert bzw. als nicht existent aufgefasst. Jemand kann also nicht das Geschlecht haben, das er_/sie_ begehrt (Domenici/Lesser 1995, 3). Die Lesbe etwa begehrt die andere Frau nur, weil sie selbst männlich identifiziert, der Schwule den anderen Mann, weil er weiblich identifiziert sei. Damit stellen alle möglichen Begehrenskonstellationen heterosexuelle Verhältnisse dar, die aufgrund des falschen (hier nämlich des gleichen) biologischen Geschlechts verfehlt werden. Ansätze – auch aus der Psychoanalyse selbst – die Frage der Identifizierung, der Annahme des Geschlechts und der Objektwahl komplexer zu denken, werden vom psychoanalytischen Mainstream kaum auf- oder ernst genommen.

Die Heteronormativität innerhalb der Psychoanalyse macht oftmals auch blind gegenüber den vielfältigen Problemen und Leiden, denen LGBTIQs durch gesellschaftliche und politische Diskriminierung, den Prozess des Outings[1], Homo- und Transphobie, familiäre Konflikte etc. ausgesetzt sind.

---

[1] Die Forschungsgruppe *q : p Queering Psychoanalysis* hat sich hier bewusst für den Begriff „Prozess" entschieden. Ein Outing ist kein singulärer Akt, der mit einem Mal abgeschlossen werden kann. Die heteronormative Verfasstheit unserer Gesellschaft bringt es mit sich, dass LGBTIQs in jeder neuen Situation (z. B. neue Arbeitsstelle, Arztbesuch, Ausbildungsstelle etc.) mit der Frage des Sich-Outens konfrontiert sind und damit auch mit der Frage, ob mögliche Diskriminierung in Kauf genommen oder aber das Privatleben geheim gehalten werden muss. Beides kann zu schwerwiegenden psychischen Konflikten führen.

Es waren vor allem Ernest Jones und Anna Freud, die im Unterschied zu Sigmund Freud, eine stark repressive Haltung gegenüber Homosexuellen einnahmen und den pathologisierenden Diskurs sicherlich wesentlich befeuert haben. Anna Freud hat u.a. 1948 in einem Brief geschrieben: „Aus Erfahrung in der Vergangenheit weiß ich, daß es für kein Seminar und für kein Institut gut ist, Leute mit sexuellen Abnormitäten zuzulassen" (Rauchfleisch 1994, 147). Anna Freud, die selbst mit einer Frau zusammenlebte, wird gegen Ende ihres Lebens zumindest etwas milder und schreibt zur Aufnahme von Schwulen und Lesben in psychoanalytische Vereinigungen: „[d]aß Homosexuelle, charakterliche Eignung und ein entsprechender Leumut vorausgesetzt, zur psychoanalytischen Ausbildung zugelassen werden können – ungeheilt" (ebd.). D. h. jedoch auch, Anna Freud geht weiterhin davon aus, dass es da etwas gäbe, was eigentlich geheilt werden müsse.

Folgeträchtig für das Verhältnis der Psychoanalyse zur Homosexualität war auch der Nationalsozialismus. Die in Deutschland zurück gebliebenen nicht-jüdischen Analytiker wurden 1936 in das *Deutsche Institut für psychologische Forschung und Psychotherapie*, unter der Leitung von Matthias Heinrich Göring („Göring-Institut") eingegliedert. Die psychoanalytische Theorie wurde in Übereinstimmung mit der Nazi-Propaganda gebracht und die Psychoanalyse für die Ziele des NS-Staates nutzbar gemacht. Für die weitere Pathologisierung der Homosexualität spielte Felix Boehm eine tragende Rolle. Boehm leitete eine Forschungsgruppe zur „Homosexualität" und vertrat die Auffassung, dass Homosexualität einen Sittenverfall darstelle und daher geheilt werden müsse. Er war von 1941 bis Kriegsende Gutachter in der Wehrmacht und entschied über Leben und Tod von „‚Simulanten‘, ‚Wehrkraftzersetzenden‘ und ‚Homosexuellen‘".[2]

Wie Robert Friedman zeigt, kam es auch in den 50er Jahren ausgehend von US-amerikanischen Ansätzen zu einer einflussreichen, die Homosexualität pathologisierenden, Theoriebildung (vgl. Friedman 1986, 86f.).

So hat z. B. Edmund Berger, ein einflussreicher Analytiker der *American Academy of Psychoanalysis and Dynamic Psychiatry* 1956

---

[2] Vgl. den Eintrag zu Felix Böhm auf der Seite der Deutschen Psychoanalytischen Gesellschaft http://www.dpg-psa.de/Felix_Boehm.html (4.12.2014). Vgl. auch die Arbeiten von Regine Lockot u.a. Lockot 2013.

in seinem Buch „Homosexuality: Disease or Way of Life" geschrieben:

> „I have no bias against homosexuals; for me they are sick people requiring medical help ... Still, though I have no bias, I would say: Homosexuals are essentially disagreeable people, regardless of their pleasant or unpleasant outward manner ... [their] shell is a mixture of superciliousness, fake aggression, and whimpering. Like all psychic masochists, they are subservient when confronted with a stronger person, merciless when in power, unscrupulous about trampling on a weaker person" (zitiert nach Drescher 2008, 443f.).

Freuds Konzept der psychischen Bisexualität wurde ausgehöhlt, Heterosexualität als Norm gesetzt und Homosexualität als nicht gleichwertiger Ersatz für eine aus Angst abgewehrte Heterosexualität begriffen. Ausgehend davon haben sich Stereotypien über ödipale Konstellationen, die vermeintlich zu Homosexualität bzw. zur „Abwehr" von Heterosexualität führen, verfestigt und damit auch bestimmte stereotype Merkmale, mit denen Menschen mit alternativer sexueller Orientierung bzw. Identität versehen werden. Sicher gab es zu jener Zeit auch andere einflussreiche Theorien, etwa den Kinsey-Report, bei dem eine nicht unbeträchtliche Anzahl an Proband_innen angab über wiederholte homosexuelle Erfahrungen zu verfügen; weiters gab es eine zu Beginn der 70er Jahre von Marcel Saghir und Eli Robins durchgeführte Studie, bei der zwischen homosexuellen und heterosexuellen Personen beiderlei Geschlechts keinerlei signifikante Unterschiede in der von der Psychoanalyse als ausschlaggebend für die sexuelle Orientierung angenommenen Beziehung zum Vater festgestellt werden konnten (vgl. Friedman 1986, 94f.). Daneben versuchte der Analytiker Robert Stoller, der sich sehr intensiv mit Homo-, Inter- und Transsexualität beschäftigt hat, sexualwissenschaftliche Erkenntnisse in die psychoanalytische Theorie zu integrieren und hat wie Richard Friedman in vielen Artikeln die pathologisierende Haltung der Psychoanalyse gegenüber Homosexualität kritisiert (vgl. dazu: Friedman 1986, Stoller 1964, Stoller 1968 a, Stoller 1968 b).[3] Dennoch scheinen sich konservative Ansätze eher verbreitet und die weitere Theoriebildung und Praxis bis heute beeinflusst zu haben. So erklärt die bekannte französische Psychoanalytikerin Janine Chasseguet-Smirgel

---

[3] Nicht unproblematisch ist Stollers Haltung jedoch gegenüber transsexuellen/transgender Personen. Vgl. dazu: Quindeau 2008, 167.

2000 in einem Vortrag: „A homosexual individual shows, through his object choice, that there is something amiss in his identification processes. The building up of a personality mainly depends on identifications. An analyst cannot circumvent such an important problem without rejecting psychoanalysis as a whole" (zitiert nach Hoffman 2000, 301). Darüber hinaus wettert sie in jenem Vortrag gegen die „Political Correctness", von der sie sich nicht den psychoanalytischen Diskurs diktieren lassen will und erweckt so den Eindruck, der psychoanalytische Diskurs sei immer schon per se objektiv und gälte als solcher zu bewahren, insbesondere vor der Lesben- und Schwulen-Bewegung, die der Psychoanalyse eine neue Ausrichtung aufoktroyieren würde.

1991 hat die Amerikanische Psychoanalytische Vereinigung (APA) nach heftigen kontroversen Debatten als erste Vereinigung eine Antidiskriminierungsklausel, die die Ablehnung von Bewerber_innen allein wegen ihrer sexuellen Orientierung untersagte, verabschiedet. Erst 2002 ist die Internationale Psychoanalytische Vereinigung (IPV) mit einer ähnlichen Stellungnahme gefolgt. „Dennoch blieb auch in den Jahren danach die Situation für Lesben und Schwule, die sich für die psychoanalytische Ausbildung interessierten, unübersichtlich: An welchen Instituten würden sie mit welchen Begründungen angenommen oder auch abgelehnt werden, wenn sie ihre Homosexualität offen äußern würden? War die Streichung der pathologisierenden Passagen aus psychoanalytischen Lehrbüchern Ausdruck einer in der Tiefe veränderten Haltung von PsychoanalytikerInnen oder lediglich ein Zugeständnis an einen gesellschaftlichen Paradigmenwechsel und die ihr folgende veränderte Rechtsprechung? War die Pathologisierung nur sang- und klanglos verschwunden, ohne dass falsche Annahmen explizit korrigiert worden und durch neue Konzepte ergänzt worden waren?" (Rudolf-Petersen)

Queering Psychoanalysis

Wie Eve Watson betont, teilen Psychoanalyse und Queer Theory einen gemeinsamen theoretischen Ausgangspunkt: die Auseinandersetzung mit der Frage der Homosexualität. Freud war demnach der Erste, der „normal" unter Anführungszeichen gesetzt und Homosexualität als einen immanenten Aspekt von Sexualität überhaupt begriffen hat (vgl. Watson 2009, 126; De Lauretis 1994, 8). Das Verständnis der

Psychoanalyse von Sexualität im weitesten Sinne unter Einbezug von Begehren, Trieb, Wünschen und Phantasien, von bewussten und unbewussten Anteilen stellt die Grenze von „normal" und „pathologisch" radikal in Frage. So ist es nicht verwunderlich, dass Diego Costa die Psychoanalyse per se als queer versteht: „Its queerness is already there, in its mechanism, its goals, its principles, its language, its flexibility, its history, its ruptures, its multi-valence, and mostly, for its relationship between theory and practice – from the beginning" (Costa 2012, 223). Warum erscheint es uns aber aus heutiger Perspektive wieder notwendig auf diese Queerness und Offenheit der Psychoanalyse hinzuweisen und diese einzufordern?

Die Psychoanalyse war immer eine Theorie und Praxis, die nicht nur das Heilen sondern auch das beständige Forschen in den Vordergrund gestellt und beide Aspekte in produktiver Weise miteinander verbunden hat. Sigmund Freud hat sowohl seine theoretischen Konzepte, als auch seine klinische Praxis immer wieder kritischen Revisionen unterzogen und seine Theorien verändert, umgeworfen und ergänzt. In diesem Sinne möchte ich mich für eine Rückbesinnung auf die Radikalität des offenen und unvoreingenommenen Forschens an den Anfängen der Psychoanalyse aussprechen und für einen produktiven Dialog zwischen Psychoanalyse und Queer Theory. Beide Ansätze können voneinander profitieren. Die Psychoanalyse kann von der Art und Weise profitieren, in der Queer-Theorien die Komplexität, Breite und Offenheit von Geschlecht, sexueller Identität und Orientierung denken, wobei gesellschaftliche Diskurse, die einige Subjekte als normal und andere als pathologisch markieren, mitberücksichtigt werden; zudem ermöglichen queere Ansätze, die binären hierarchischen Kategorien wie männlich/weiblich, homosexuell/heterosexuell, aktiv/passiv zu dekonstruieren und adäquatere Auseinandersetzungen mit Transgender/Transidenitäten in Gang zu setzen; umgekehrt wäre es für queer-theoretische Ansätze fruchtbar sich mit der komplexen Art und Weise zu befassen, in der die Psychoanalyse Subjektwerdung als Phänomen denkt, das über Identität und Identifizierung hinausgeht, in dem unbewusste Prozesse eine Rolle spielen und Verwerfungen und Ausschlüsse nicht nur gesellschaftlich, sondern auch intrapsychisch eine Rolle spielen. Die Forschungsgruppe *q : p Queering Psychoanalysis* will in diesem Sinne die Psychoanalyse nicht umschreiben sondern das, was in ihr immer schon immanent queer und widerständig ist, erneut in den Mittelpunkt stellen und produktiv machen.

Die Forschungsgruppe *q : p – Queering Psychoanalysis. Research Group on Bodies And Sexualities* möchte sich dem Komplex Körper, Sexualitäten und Geschlecht im Besonderen in Zusammenhang mit queeren Perspektiven widmen. Mit dem Begriff „queering Psychoanalysis" möchten wir die Logik und Idee des „Normalen" in der Psychoanalyse kritisch hinterfragen und – ganz im Sinne Freuds – die Hierarchisierung, die sich durch die Entgegensetzung von „normal" und „pathologisch" ergibt, in Frage stellen. Wir möchten *durch* und *mit* der Psychoanalyse produktive theoretische und praktische Zugänge zu Körpern, Sexualität, Geschlecht, Identität, Identifizierung, etc. entwickeln bzw. weiterdenken.

Fragen, die unsere Auseinandersetzung leiten, sind: Wie können Erkenntnisse der Psychoanalyse mit jenen der Queer Theory zusammengedacht werden? Welche Ansätze der Theoretisierung von Geschlecht, Gender, Sexualitäten, Praktiken, Identitäten etc. jenseits von Stereotypisierungen können für die Psychoanalyse wichtige Impulse liefern? Wie tradieren sich gesellschaftliche Vorurteile in Bezug auf Homo- und Transsexualität in der psychoanalytischen Theorie? Auf welche Weise können aktuelle gender- und queer-spezifische Ansätze Eingang in die psychoanalytische Ausbildung finden? Welche Bedeutung hat die sexuelle Orientierung der Analytiker_in für die Arbeit mit queeren oder heterosexuellen Analysand_innen?

Die Gruppe *q : p – Queering Psychoanalysis – Research Group on Bodies and Sexualities* wurde 2014 in Wien gegründet. Nähere Informationen sowie Texte finden Sie auf unserem Blog:
http://queeringpsychoanalysis.wordpress.com/

Literaturangaben

Costa, Diego. „Forget Theory. Praise of Psychoanalysis's Queerness." In: *Trans-cripts 2*, 2012, S. 223-234.

De Lauretis, Theresa. *The Practice of Love: Lesbian Sexuality and Perverse Desire.* Bloomingdale: Indiana University Press, 1994.

Domenici, Thomas; Lesser, Ronnie C. (Hg.). *Disorienting Sexuality. Psychoanalytic Reappraisals of Sexual Identities.* New York: Routledge, 1995.

Drescher, Jack. „A History of Homosexuality and Organized Psychoanalysis." In: *Journal of the American Academy of Psychoanalysis and Dynamic Psychiatry*, 36 (2008): S. 443-446.

Freud, Sigmund. *Drei Abhandlungen zur Sexualtheorie.* In: *Gesammelte Werke*, Band V. Frankfurt am Main: Fischer Verlag, 1999.

Friedman, Robert. „The Psychoanalytic Model of Male Homosexuality: A Historical and Theoretical Critique." In: *The Psychoanalytic Review*, 1986: 73D, S. 79-115.

Hoffman, Leon. „Sexuality as Compromise Formation." In: *Journal of Clinical Psychoanalysis*, 2000: 9, 301-305.

Lockot, Regine. *Die Reinigung der Psychoanalyse, Die Deutsche Psychoanalytische Gesellschaft im Spiegel von Dokumenten und Zeitzeugen (1933-1951).* Gießen: Psychosozial-Verlag, 2013.

Rauchfleisch, Udo. *Schwule, Lesben, Bisexuelle. Lebensweisen – Vorurteile – Einsichten.* Göttingen: Vandenhoeck & Ruprecht, 1994.

Rudolf-Petersen, Almut: Homosexualität und psychoanalytische Ausbildung – Was hat sich verändert? http://www.dpg-institut-hamburg.de/index.php/selbstverstaendnis?id=141, gesichtet am 30. November 2014.

Stoller, Robert. „A Contribution to the Study of Gender Identity." In: *The International Journal of Psychoanalysis*, 1964: 45, S. 220-226.

Stoller, Robert. „A Further Contribution to the Study of Gender Identity." In: *International Journal of Psychoanalysis*, 1968 (a): 49, S. 364-368;

Stoller, Robert. *Sex and Gender.* New York: Science House, 1968 (b).

Watson, Eve. „Queering Psychoanalysis/Psychoanalysing Queer." In: *Annual Review of Critical Psychology*, 2009: 7.

Quindeau, Ilka. *Verführung und Begehren. Die psychoanalytische Sexualtheorie nach Freud.* Stuttgart: Klett-Cotta, 2008.

AUTORINNEN

Brigitte Buchhammer (1961), Philosophin, Lehraufträge an in- und ausländischen Universitäten, Vorträge in Berlin, Paderborn, Washington, Linz. Habilitationsprojekt: Feministische Religionsphilosophie im Anschluss an Hegel. - Gender-Studies, Feministische Philosophie, Sozial-, Rechts-, Moral- und Religionsphilosophie. Forschungsaufenthalt in Washington, Catholic University of America. Publikationen: ‚Religion und Homosexualität'. In: Herta Nagl-Docekal, Wolfgang Kaltenbacher und Ludwig Nagl (Hg), *„ Viele Religionen – eine Vernunft? Ein Disput zu Hegel"*. Wien-Berlin 2008, S. 211 – 233; *Feministische Religionsphilosophie. Philosophisch-systematische Grundlagen.* Philosophie Band 83. LIT-Verlag Wien-Berlin 2011; *‚Was will feministische Religionsphilosophie?'*. In: A. Dunshirn, E. Nemeth, G. Unterthurner (Hg.), *„ Crossing Borders – Grenzen (über)denken – Thinking (across) Boundaries."* S. 747 – 760. http://phaidra.univie.ac.at/o:128384; "Feministische Religionsphilo-sophie – ein innovatives Projekt". In: *Labyrinth* Vol. 16, No. 2, Winter 2014, 66-91. https://brigittebuchhammer.wordpress.com/

Waltraud Ernst, M.A. 1990 Inst. f. Philosophie, Universität Bielefeld, Dr. phil., 1996 Inst. f. Philosophie Universität Wien zum Thema "Möglichkeiten einer feministischen Konzeption der Wissenschaften", 2001-2003 Hertha-Firnberg-Forschungsstelle des FWF am Inst. für Philosophie, Universität Wien zum Thema "Erotische Ökonomien der Wissenschaften", 2004-2010 Leiterin des Zentrums für Interdisziplinäre Frauen- und Geschlechterforschung, Universität Hildesheim, seit 2010 Universitätsassistentin am Institut für Frauen- und Geschlechterforschung, Johannes Kepler Universität Linz, Arbeitsschwerpunkte: Geschlechterkonzeptionen in den Natur- und Technikwissenschaften; Feministische Wissenschafts- und Erkenntnistheorie; Begriffe, Theorien und Methoden der Gender Studies.

Cornelia Eşianu, DDr., Philosophin, Germanistin, Übersetzerin; langjährige Mitarbeiterin und Universitätslektorin am Lehrstuhl für Germanistik an der Alexandru-Ioan-Cuza-Universität in Iaşi/Rumänien; Publikationen: *Poesie – ein Bedürfnis der Philosophie? Der Lösungsversuch eines Problems bei Friedrich Schlegel* (Universität Wien: Dissertation, 2014); *Hypostasen der Identität beim jungen Friedrich Schlegel. Eine Untersuchung von Leben und Werk aus identitätstheo-retischer Sicht,* Bukarest: Verlag Paideia. 2004; Übersetzungen: Manfred Kühn: *Kant. O biografie,* Iaşi, Editura Polirom,

2009; Theodor W. Adorno: *Teorie estetică*. Bukarest: Paralela 45. 2005 (in Zusammenarbeit); Kontakt: *E-Mail: cornelia.esianu@gmx.at*

Dr. Anke Graneß is Elise Richter Fellow at the chair Philosophy in a Global World / Intercultural Philosophy, Department of Philosophy, University of Vienna (Austria). She is the author of Das menschliche Minimum. Globale Gerechtigkeit aus afrikanischer Sicht: Henry Odera Oruka. Frankfurt/New York: Campus 2011. She has also co-edited an anthology on the Kenyan philosopher Henry Odera Oruka: Sagacious Reasoning. H. Odera Oruka in memoriam. Frankfurt/M.: Peter Lang Verlag 1997 (with K. Kresse) and a book on Intercultural Philosophy: Perspektiven interkulturellen Philosophierens. Beiträge zur Geschichte und Methodik von Polylogen. Wien: Facultas/WUV 2012. (with F. Gmainer-Pranzl). Graness has published a number of articles in peer reviewed journals in the area of African philosophy, intercultural philosophy, and global justice. Her research interests include history of philosophy, ethics, political philosophy, and feminist theory. Anke Graness is currently project leader of a FWF funded research project on the History of Philosophy in Africa at the University of Vienna.

Heide Hammer, Philosophin und Mitarbeiterin am Department für medizinische Aus- und Weiterbildung der MedUniWien, übt sich gerne in anti-identitärer Politik im Mantel der Kunst, indem sie Kollektive mitbegründet, die sich nach den jeweiligen Aktionen wieder auflösen, darunter „Statt Wien", „Goldenes Wienerherz", „Neigungsgruppe Donauschwimmen" oder eine übergroße Kollektivromangruppe.

Esther Hutfless ist Philosophin und Psychoanalytikerin. Sie hat jüngst die internationale Forschungsgruppe Queering Psychoanalysis gegründet (siehe http://queeringpsychoanalysis.wordpress.com/). Ihre Forschungsschwerpunkte liegen in den Bereichen Phänomenologie, Psychoanalyse, Dekonstruktion, Poststrukturalismus und Queer-Feministischer Philosophie. Sie arbeitet gegenwärtig zum Thema „Die Zeit der Körper". Publikationen (Auswahl): *In Dir mehr als Dich. Phänomenologien des Begehrens zwischen diskursiver Produktion und leiblichem Zur-Welt-Sein.* Königshausen & Neumann, Würzburg 2011; *Das wilde Sein. Akt – Ereignis – Schöpfung.* In: critica, Zeitschrift für Philosophie und Kunsttheorie, Band I / 2012, 17–29; *Kollaps – Zur politischen Dimension der passage à l'acte.* In: Esther Hutfless, Roman Widholm (Hg.): Reihe Verhältnisse, Band II: Zusammen-bruch, Turia + Kant Verlag, Wien 2012.

Utta Isop ist Philosophin, Geschlechterforscherin und Aktivistin. Ihre Mitherausgeberschaften/ Publikationen sind unter anderen folgende: „When we were gender… Geschlechter erinnern und vergessen. Analysen von Geschlecht und Gedächtnis in den Gender Studies, Queer-Theorien und feministischen Politiken" (2013); „Differenzen leben. Kulturwissenschaftliche und geschlechterkritische Perspektiven auf Inklusion und Exklusion" (2011); „Spielregeln der Gewalt - Kulturwissenschaftliche Beiträge zur Friedens- und Geschlechterforschung" (2009); „Über Geschlechterdemokratie hinaus - Beyond Gender Democracy" (2009). Kontakt: utta.isop@aau.at und utta.isop@gmx.net; Homepage: http://wwwu.uni-klu.ac.at/uisop/wordpress/

Dr. Brigitta Keintzel, Elise-Richter-Stelle: (2014-2018), V-345: Gender: G.W.F. Hegel – Franz Rosenzweig – Jacques Derrida. Forschungsthemen: Europäische Philosophie, Phänomenologie, Ethik und Feministische Theorie, Religiöse, Psychoanalytische und Gender Studien. Publikationen,u.a.: Erstherausgeberin von "Zwischen Hegel und Levinas" Freiburg 2010, Artikel u.a. zu: Illusionen des Gewissens – Melanie Klein und Emmanuel Levinas im Vergleich, 2013, Wissen und Gewissen - Hegel und Levinas, Wien 2012.

Susanne Klapper (1986), aufgewachsen als Älteste von vier Kindern bei Köln; nach neunmonatiger AuPair-Zeit in Finnland Studium von Philosophie und Biologie, später Philosophie und Geschichte an der Universität zu Köln mit dem Ziel Staatsexamen/Lehramt an Gymnasien und Gesamtschulen dafür Graecum und Latinum absolviert, ab 2012 Fortsetzung an der Universität Wien, seit über sieben Jahren geringfügig beschäftigt in der gehobenen Gastronomie.

Birge Krondorfer ist politische Philosophin und feministisch Tätige. Universitätslektorin und Autorin. Moderatorin, Trainerin, Supervisorin. Ehrenamtliches Tun u.a. in der Bildungsstätte Frauenhetz, der Plattform 20000frauen, im Verband feministischer Wissenschafterinnen, der Arge Demokratie braucht Bildung. Temporäre Redakteurin und Herausgeberin. Letzte Co.Hg: Frauen und Politik. Nachrichten aus Demokratien, Wien 2008; Frauen-Fragen. 100 Jahre Bewegung, Reflexion, Vision, Wien 2012; Prekarität und Freiheit? Feministische Wissenschaft, Kulturkritik und Selbstorganisation, Münster 2013; Gerburg Treusch-Dieter Ausgewählte Schriften, Wien/Berlin 2014.

Doris Leibetseder ist seit 2013/14 *Scholar in Residence* in der Beatrice Bain Research Group im Gender and Women's Studies Department an der University of California, Berkeley und seit Oktober 2014 ein *Research Fellow* am

IAS-STS (Institute for Advanced Studies on Science, Technology and Society) in Graz. Auch ist sie Externe Lektorin für die KFU-Graz und die Hauptuniversität Wien. Sie promovierte 2008 am Institut für Philosophie (Uni Wien).

Elisabeth List, geboren 1946,Prof. für Philosophie an der Universität Graz. Lehrtätigkeit international: Norwegen, Schweiz, Deutschland. Arbeitsschwerpunkte: Wissenschaftstheorie, Theorie der Sozial- und Kulturwissenschaften, Gesellschaftstheorie, Feministische Theorie, Theorien des Lebendigen, Biotechnologie und Philosophische Anthropologie. Publikationen: *Denkverhältnisse. Feminismus und Kritik*, Frankfurt am Main 1989, *Die Präsenz des Anderen. Theorie und Geschlechterpolitik*, Frankfurt am Main 1993, *Grenzen der Verfügbarkeit. Die Technik, das Subjekt und das Lebendige*, Wien 2001, *Alfred Schütz, Relevanz und Handeln. Zur Phänomenologie des Alltagswissens*, Konstanz 2004, *Grundlagen der Kulturwissenschaften. Interdisziplinäre Kulturwissenschaften*, Stuttgart 2004, *Vom Darstellen zum Herstellen. Eine Kulturgeschichte der Naturwissenschaften*, Weilers-wist 2007, Ethik des Lebendigen, Weilerswist 2009.

Edit Anna Lukacs, PhD 2008, studierte und forschte in Budapest, Paris, Berlin und Oxford, seit 2011 in Wien, seit April 2014 Elise-Richter-Stelle am Institut für Österreichische Geschichtsforschung, Beschäftigung mit Philosophie des Mittelalters (14.-15. Jh).

Susanne Moser, Mag. Dr.phil, Mag.rer.soc.oec, ist Philosophin, Ökonomin und Mutter dreier Töchter. Sie ist Lektorin an den Universitäten Wien und Graz, an verschiedenen Fachhochschulen und Erwachsenenbildungseinrichtungen sowie wissenschaftliche Mitarbeiterin am Institut für Axiologische Forschungen in Wien. Ihr Forschungsschwerpunkt sind axiologische Fragestellungen im Bereich Feministische Philosophie, Existenzphilosophie, Ethik und Politische Philosophie. Ausgewählte Publikationen: *Freiheit und Anerkennung bei Simone de Beauvoir* (Türingen: edition discord 2002), *Freedom and Recognition in the Work of Simone de Beauvoir* (Frankfurt am Main: Peter Lang 2008), gemeinsam mit Yvanka B. Raynova (Hg.): *Die Feministische Philosophie: Perspektiven und Debatten* (Sofia: OSI & NI, 2000), *Simone de Beauvoir, 50 Jahre nach dem Anderen Geschlecht* (Frankfurt am Main: Peter Lang 2004) und: *Das integrale und das gebrochene Ganze* (Frankfurt am Main: Peter Lang 2005).

402

Alice Pechriggl ist Philosophin und Psychotherapeutin (Gruppenpsychoanalyse, psychoanalytische Psychotherapie) und seit 2003 Professorin am Institut für Philosophie der Universität Klagenfurt. Ihre Forschungsschwerpunkte sind an der Schnittstelle von Philosophie und Gruppen/psychoanalyse sowie im Bereich der Philosophie der Politik und der Geschlechterforschung angesiedelt. http://www.uni-klu.ac.at/philo/inhalt/282.htm

Rodica Pop (born in 1973) has a diploma in History (1997), a master's degree in Anthropology (2005) and a Ph.D. in Philosophy (2010) at "Al. I. Cuza" University from Iasi, Romania, and now she is attending a postdoctoral program at the same university. She is interested in studying the connection between Greek philosophy and Christian theology, in how religion is reflected in the contemporary public space, and, also, in the image of women in literature, philosophy and religion. She has published two books (*The Meaning of Marriage in Plato and the Fathers. From Soma to Sharing the Flesh,* Doxologia publishing house, Iaşi, 2012 and *Two Women Free. About Meanings Search Dostoevsky,* Axis Academic Foundation publishing house, Iaşi, 2012 - both in Romanian) and articles on these topics.

Gertrude Postl, Studium der Philosophie und Germanistik an der Universität Wien. Professorin für Philosophie und Women's and Gender Studies am Suffolk County Community College, Selden, New York, USA. Publikationen u.a.: *Weibliches Sprechen. Feministische Entwürfe zu Sprache und Geschlecht* (Wien: Passagen 1991); „Demokratie als Performativität: zu Irigarays Politik einer sexuellen Differenz" (*texte. psychoanalyse.aesthetik. kulturkritik*, Heft 4, 2012, Wien: Passagen); *Hélène Cixous. Das Lachen der Medusa zusammen mit aktuellen Beiträgen,* (Mitherausgeberin mit Esther Hutfless, Elisabeth Schäfer, Wien: Passagen, 2013). Gegenwärtige Forschungsschwerpunkte: feministische Theorien zu Körper und Sprache, Philosophie und Literatur, Theorien zu Schrift, Text und Textualität.

Esther Redolfi Widmann (geb. 08.09.1972) nach kaufmännischer Ausbildung im Alleinstudium den Reifeabschluss nachgeholt. Es folgte ein berufsbegleitendes Studium der Philosophie an der Universität Trient (Bachelorstudium mit der Abschlussarbeit *Jean-Paul Sartres Die Wege der Freiheit* und Masterstudium mit der Diplomarbeit *Die Darstellung weiblicher Ambiguität im existentialistischen Situationstheater*). Aktuell im Begriff die umfassende Forschungsarbeit *Die Frau als Spannungsverhältnis von Situationsgebundenheit und Freiheit in Simone de Beauvoirs Leben und Werk* an der Universität Innsbruck abzuschließen.

Elisabeth Schäfer ist Philosophin und Externe Lehrbeauftragte am Institut für Philosophie der Universität Wien. Sie arbeitet derzeit als Postdoc-Projektmitarbeiterin im PEEK-Projekt „Artist Philosophers. Philosophy AS Arts-Based-Research" (AR 275-G21) [sponsored by the Austrian Science Funds FWF] an der Universität für Angewandte Kunst Wien. Ihre Forschungsschwerpunkte im Feld der Dekonstruktion, der Queer-Feministischen Philosophie und des Poststrukturalismus sind Fragen der Körperlichkeit, Berührung, Affektivität, Écriture féminine und Ontologie. Von Elisabeth Schäfer ist jüngst im Passagen Verlag gemeinsam mit Esther Hutfless und Gertrude Postl erschienen: *Hélène Cixous. Das Lachen der Medusa. Zusammen mit aktuellen Beiträgen*, Passagen Verlag: Wien 2012. Sie ist Mitbegründerin der Zeitschrift: *Sublin/mes. philosophieren von unten. a queer reviewed journal*: http://sublinesblog.wordpress.com/.

Anne Siegetsleitner studierte in Salzburg Philosophie, Psychologie, Pädagogik sowie Deutsche Philologie. Die Habilitation mit einer Arbeit über Ethik und Moral im Wiener Kreis (Böhlau 2014) erfolgte 2012. Seit Oktober 2013 ist Siegetsleitner Professorin für Praktische Philosophie an der Universität Innsbruck. www.siegetsleitner.net

Mag.a Dr.in Bettina Zehetner Lehrbeauftragte am Institut für Philosophie der Universität Wien und psychosoziale Beraterin im Verein "Frauen beraten Frauen. Institut für frauenspezifische Sozialforschung", Forschungsschwerpunkte: Körper- und Krankheitsdiskurse, Psychosomatik, Verbindung von feministischer Theorie und Praxis, Gewalt und Geschlecht Publikationen: „Krankheit und Geschlecht. Feministische Philosophie und psychosoziale Beratung" Turia + Kant 2012, „Von der Abhängigkeit über die Ambivalenz zur Autonomie. Feministische Beratung bei Trennung und Scheidung." In: In Anerkennung der Differenz. Feministische Beratung und Psychotherapie. Psychosozial-Verlag 2010; http://homepage.univie.ac.at/bettina.zehetner/